Information and Learning in Markets

Information and Learning in Markets

The Impact of Market Microstructure

Xavier Vives

Princeton University Press
Princeton and Oxford

Published by Princeton University Press,
41 William Street, Princeton, New Jersey 08540

In the United Kingdom: Princeton University Press,
6 Oxford Street, Woodstock, Oxfordshire OX20 1TW

ISBN: 978-0-691-12743-9

Library of Congress Control Number: 2008921431

British Library Cataloging-in-Publication Data is available

This book has been composed in Lucida
Typeset by T&T Productions Ltd, London

press.princeton.edu

10 9 8 7 6 5 4 3 2 1

A l'Aurora

A la memòria de la mare i al Martí—que promet continuar la saga

Contents

Preface		**xi**
Introduction and Lecture Guide		**1**
	References	12
1	**Aggregation of Information in Simple Market Mechanisms: Large Markets**	**15**
1.1	Introduction and Overview	15
1.2	Large Cournot Markets	17
1.3	Welfare in Large Cournot Markets with Asymmetric Information	27
1.4	Information Aggregation in Smooth Large Markets	29
1.5	Auctions and Voting	38
1.6	Endogenous Information Acquisition	40
1.7	Summary	45
1.8	Appendix	46
1.9	Exercises	48
	References	51
2	**Aggregation of Information in Simple Market Mechanisms: How Large Is Large?**	**53**
2.1	A General Linear-Normal Cournot Model	54
2.2	Convergence to Price Taking in a Cournot Market	57
2.3	Endogenous Information Acquisition	58
2.4	Convergence to the First-Best: Market Power and Information Aggregation	62
2.5	Convergence in Auctions	67
2.6	Summary	70
2.7	Appendix	71
2.8	Exercises	74
	References	76
3	**Rational Expectations and Supply Function Competition**	**78**
3.1	Rational Expectations Equilibrium: Concepts, Problems, and Welfare	78
3.2	Supply Function Competition and REE in a Continuum Economy	84
3.3	Welfare Analysis of REE	95
3.4	Strategic Supply Function Equilibria and Convergence to a Price-Taking Equilibrium	98
3.5	Double Auctions	100

3.6 Summary 102
3.7 Appendix 102
3.8 Exercises 103
References 105

4 Rational Expectations and Market Microstructure in Financial Markets 107
4.1 Market Microstructure 108
4.2 Competitive Rational Expectations Equilibria 112
4.3 Informed Traders Move First and Face Risk-Neutral Competitive Market Makers 130
4.4 Hedgers and Producers in a Futures Market 135
4.5 Summary 145
4.6 Appendix 147
4.7 Exercises 148
References 152

5 Strategic Traders in Financial Markets 156
5.1 Competition in Demand Schedules 157
5.2 Informed Traders Move First 168
5.3 Market Makers Move First 177
5.4 An Application: Welfare Analysis of Insider Trading 183
5.5 Summary 189
5.6 Exercises 190
References 195

6 Learning from Others and Herding 199
6.1 Herding, Informational Cascades, and Social Learning 200
6.2 Extensions of the Herding Model 204
6.3 A Smooth and Noisy Model of Learning from Others 210
6.4 Applications and Examples 222
6.5 The Information Externality and Welfare 227
6.6 Rational Expectations, Herding, and Information Externalities 236
6.7 Summary 239
6.8 Appendix 240
6.9 Exercises 241
References 244

7 Dynamic Information Aggregation 248
7.1 Rational Expectations, Full-Information Equilibria, and Learning 248
7.2 Learning and Convergence to a Full-Information Equilibrium with Uninformed Firms 253
7.3 Market Dynamics with Asymmetric Information 257
7.4 Slow Learning and Convergence 261
7.5 Summary 266
7.6 Appendix 267
7.7 Exercises 271
References 273

8 Dynamic Rational Expectations Models in Competitive Financial Markets 276
8.1 Dynamic Competitive Rational Expectations 277
8.2 The Impact of Risk-Averse Market Makers 285

8.3 Dynamic Trading with Short-Term Investors 294
8.4 Explaining Crises and Market Crashes 306
8.5 Summary 318
8.6 Appendix 320
8.7 Exercises 324
References 326

9 Price and Information Dynamics in Financial Markets 330
9.1 Sequential Trading, Dynamic Market-Order Markets, and the Speed of Learning from Past Prices 331
9.2 Strategic Trading with Long-Lived Information 339
9.3 Market Manipulation and Price Discovery 347
9.4 Strategic Trading with Short-Lived Information 355
9.5 Strategic Hedging 358
9.6 Summary 360
9.7 Appendix 361
9.8 Exercises 362
References 365

10 Technical Appendix 369
10.1 Information Structures and Bayesian Inference 369
10.2 Normal Distributions and Affine Information Structure 375
10.3 Convergence Concepts and Results 383
10.4 Games and Bayesian Equilibrium 390
References 398

Index 401

Preface

The book analyzes how markets aggregate information and what impact specific market arrangements—the market microstructure—have on the aggregation process and the overall performance of the market. The book builds a bridge between the two main views of markets: informational efficiency and herding. Do prices in the stock market reflect all available information in the hands of traders and fundamental values, or are prices in the hands of short-term speculators, insiders, manipulators, gurus and subject to fads, herding behavior, and bubbles? This is accomplished by bringing together results from the rational expectations literature and recent analysis of herding phenomena in a coherent game-theoretic framework. The strategy of the book is to analyze the different topics considering a basic workhorse asymmetric-information model in a linear-quadratic mean–variance environment. It is found that apparently contending theories, such as market informational efficiency and herding, build in fact on the same principles of Bayesian decision making. The upshot is that we do not need "irrational" agents to explain herding behavior, crises, and crashes. Traders may be rational but learn slowly or even on some occasions disregard private information and end up making persistent errors when acting; or they may be trapped in a coordination failure where everyone loses. However, informational and economic efficiency need not coincide and in general they will not. In any case, the impact of the details of market microstructure on the informational efficiency of the market is crucial.

Target Audience

The target audience for the book is graduate students (or advanced undergraduates with a minimal mathematical background) and researchers at large. The reader will profit most from the book by having knowledge of basic microeconomics and statistics although the techniques used are elementary. The book may prove useful in graduate courses of information economics or market microstructure in finance and as a complement in any course in microeconomics, industrial organization, or macroeconomics to deal with static and dynamic models with asymmetric information. The book aims both to cover some basic material in depth, providing proofs where necessary, and to survey extensions and therefore serve as a guide to the literature. It should prove useful to students and researchers to assimilate quickly the vast literature on information aggregation and get to the frontier of knowledge in the area.

Lecture presentations of the material in the book, coauthored with Giovanni Cespa, are available at http://press.princeton.edu/titles/8655.html. Comments on this book can be uploaded to the website or communicated to me directly. I would be grateful if any errors and omissions are pointed out.

Acknowledgments

This book is the product of my research interest in the topic and graduate teaching in courses in information economics and market microstructure at New York University, Universitat Autònoma de Barcelona, Universitat Pompeu Fabra, and Studienzentrum Gerzensee, as well as lectures delivered, among other places, at Universitat d'Alacant, IESE Business School, INSEAD, and Harvard University. The comments from students on those courses and lectures have contributed to improve the book.

In the long period of gestation of the book, over more than a decade, I have benefited from the research environments at the Institut d'Anàlisi Econòmica (CSIC), Harvard University, New York University, INSEAD, Universitat Pompeu Fabra, and IESE Business School.

The book borrows from the work with coauthors—Lluís Bru, Roberto Burguet, Giovanni Cespa, Byoung Jun, Alex Kovalenkov, Luis Angel Medrano, Simon Messner, Jean-Charles Rochet, and Tim Van Zandt—and has benefited from discussions with and/or the comments of Ramon Caminal, Paolo Colla, Douglas Gale, Antonio Guarino, Carolina Manzano, Andreu Mas-Colell, Meg Meyer, Alessandro Pavan, Asani Sarkar, Peter Norman Sørensen, Jaime Zender, as well as anonymous referees. Sevinc Cukurova, Rodrigo Escudero, and Vahe Sahakyan provided excellent research assistance.

My assistants Angela Hernandez and Coloma Casaus provided excellent secretarial support during different periods of the project.

At Princeton University Press, Richard Baggaley provided encouragement to complete the project. Jon Wainwright at T&T Productions Ltd did a remarkably efficient job at editing the manuscript. Support from the PricewaterhouseCoopers initiative at INSEAD, project SEJ2005-08263 at UPF of the DGI of the Spanish Ministry of Education and Science, and to the Abertis Chair of Regulation, Competition and Public Policy at IESE Business School is gratefully acknowledged.

Information and Learning in Markets

Introduction and Lecture Guide

Information is at the heart of the economy today. Despite this there is still a lively debate over whether markets aggregate the dispersed information of agents in the economy or whether they are at the mercy of herd behavior and fads and in the hands of short-term speculators and insiders. The debate has old roots and goes back at least to the exchange between Hayek and Lange in the 1930s about the economic viability of socialism. While Lange (1936, 1937) argued that socialism was viable because a competitive allocation can be replicated by a central planner, Hayek contended that the superiority of markets was to be found in their ability to aggregate the dispersed information of agents in the economy (Hayek 1945, p. 526):

> The mere fact that there is one price for any commodity—or rather that local prices are connected in a manner determined by the cost of transport, etc.—brings about the solution which (it is just conceptually possible) might have been arrived at by one single mind possessing all the information which is in fact dispersed among all the people involved in the process."

In contrast to Hayek, Keynes in his General Theory pioneered the view of the stock market as a beauty contest where investors try to guess average opinion, instead of fundamentals, and end up chasing the crowd (Keynes 1936, p. 136):

> [P]rofessional investment may be likened to those newspaper competitions in which the competitors have to pick out the six prettiest faces from a hundred photographs, the prize being awarded to the competitor whose choice most nearly corresponds to the average preferences of the competitors as a whole; so that each competitor has to pick, not those faces which he himself finds prettiest, but those which he thinks likeliest to catch the fancy of the other competitors, all of whom are looking at the problem from the same point of view.

This view is consistent with people behaving like a colony of penguins that herd and follow a first individual that jumps of a cliff. Indeed, it has been claimed that markets are in the hands of short-term speculators, insiders, and manipulators who induce bubbles and crashes. To this it may be added that traders are not rational to start with and that market outcomes are heavily influenced by psychological biases, behavioral rules, and persistent mistakes made by decision makers.

The central issue is whether we can trust markets to aggregate information in a world where information is dispersed. Does the stock market reflect the underlying fundamentals of the traded firms? Or, to put the question in more concrete terms, does the price in the futures market for wheat aggregate the relevant information of producers and speculators?

The view of Hayek is optimistic in the sense that we can trust markets to provide the right signals for decision making. Indeed, Hayek thought that the price system is a marvel because of its power in aggregating information.

In this book we will analyze in depth the information aggregation properties of markets and the impact of specific trading arrangements (the market microstructure) on the information aggregation process and the quality or performance of the market.

Hayek's ideas are the basis for the rational expectations models that explain how rational agents make optimal inferences from prices, and other public statistics, about the relevant parameters about which they are uncertain.[1] The statistics that aggregate the dispersed information in the economy are indicators of aggregate activity such as output, employment, investment, or trade volume. The result is that learning from market statistics makes up for the lack of knowledge of traders and producers.

The book will try to disentangle whether the two views of markets, informational efficiency and herding, are compatible. Do prices in the stock market reflect all available information in the hands of traders and fundamental values, or are prices in the hands of short-term speculators, insiders, manipulators, and gurus and subject to fads, herding behavior, and bubbles? We will explain how rational well-informed agents may disregard their private information and make persistent errors when acting. Indeed we will see that we do not need irrational traders with behavioral biases making persistent mistakes to explain, for instance, crises and bubbles, or financial market anomalies like excess volatility. The book therefore does not cover the otherwise very interesting contributions of the behavioral finance literature.[2]

Thinking a little bit more generally, we are asking in what circumstances social learning, that is, learning from the actions of other people, leads to information revelation and efficient outcomes. This cuts across more disciplines than markets and economics and extends to sociology and political science. Indeed, markets are not the only mechanism for the aggregation of information. Deliberation is an old method. Information technology and the Internet have provided a range of instruments to aggregate information, from blogs to wikis to the open source movement, that hint at an information aggregation revolution.[3] Those instruments are based on the desire of people to build a reputation, attain status, or simply driven by altruism and conformation to a social norm. They have proved effective although they are vulnerable to manipulation

---

[1] See Radner (1979) and Grossman (1989).

[2] See Shleifer (2000), Shiller (2005), and Thaler (2005) for accounts of behavioral finance models.

[3] "Wikis" are web pages that can be freely edited by any user with access to them. A leading example is Wikipedia, a free online encyclopedia that can be edited by anyone. In open source projects the source material (e.g., computer code) is available freely for other people to use and improve (typically under the condition that the outcome will also be made freely available). See Sunstein (2006).

and attack. Markets work based on another mechanism: people, each putting their money where their mouth is, prove to be, on average, tremendously effective at aggregating information. Prediction markets, betting on the outcome of an election for example, have recently emerged, combining the features of markets and information technology aggregating procedures.[4] In markets agents learn from other agents with the intermediation of the price system or market aggregates like market shares. For example, a high market share of a brand may provide a signal of the quality of the product similarly to when we buy a best seller because we think that the book must be good. Sometimes people learn directly from the actions of other people. Depositors may run on a bank when they see others doing so, or tourists may decide not to patronize an empty restaurant when visiting a city.

All these information aggregation mechanisms share the Hayekian idea of the power of many minds in collecting information. For example, the "blogosphere" is seen by some analysts as the newest mechanism for society to pool knowledge.[5] It is tempting to think that Hayek's "one single mind possessing all the information which is in fact dispersed among all the people" is represented today by the World Wide Web. The main point, however, is that, very much in line with Hayek's vision, the World Wide Web is not akin to a central planner but to a very decentralized institution with many minds at work. Furthermore, it is yet to be seen whether some of these new information aggregation methods can match the accuracy and economy of knowledge of the price system.

Approach of the Book

This book takes the perspective of explaining aggregation of information and learning in markets with rational agents who understand market conditions and make the most of them. In particular, our agents will be Bayesian and will learn accordingly. We will therefore leave aside bounded rationality and non-Bayesian methods of learning. We concentrate on Bayesian rational models because of the discipline they introduce into the analysis, because they deliver results, including the explanation of market anomalies, and because there is evidence that those models are useful in explaining the behavior of agents. Indeed, a Bayesian model requires making explicit the assumptions of the learning agent

---

[4] See Plott and Sunder (1988) and Forsythe and Lundholm (1990) for experimental evidence on information aggregation by prices, and Wolfers and Zitzewitz (2004) for an introduction to prediction markets. Forsythe et al. (1992) and Berg et al. (2005) show that prices in the Iowa Electronic Market for presidential elections were typically closer to the actual vote shares than opinion polls. According to Chen and Plott (2002) even the price forecasts in the (relatively small) internal market set up by Hewlett-Packard were closer to the actual sales of the company than the official forecast.

[5] From the introduction to the Becker–Posner blog at www.becker-posner-blog.com/archives/2004/12/: "Blogging is a major new social, political, and economic phenomenon. It is a fresh and striking exemplification of Friedrich Hayek's thesis that knowledge is widely distributed among people and that the challenge to society is to create mechanisms for pooling that knowledge. The powerful mechanism that was the focus of Hayek's work, as of economists generally, is the price system (the market). The newest mechanism is the 'blogosphere'."

and the context of learning, and it makes life harder for the researcher when trying to explain a phenomenon. Furthermore, despite the challenges to the Bayesian model coming from the experimental literature emphasizing boundedly rational and error-prone heuristics to explain cognitive judgments under uncertainty, there is recent evidence of the Bayesian optimality of human cognition in realistic scenarios as well as in experimental settings.[6] Market pressure may also imply aggregate behavior consistent with Bayesian prediction even allowing for substantial departures for individual agents.[7]

Our approach will bring together results from the rational expectations literature and recent analysis of herding phenomena in a coherent game-theoretic framework. This framework will be used when considering both competitive and strategic agents. The advantage of such an approach is that the details of the environment are modeled precisely and outcomes are the results of the actions of the agents and the information they have. The approach in the book is game-theoretic but this is not a book of "learning in games"[8]; rather, it emphasizes the consequences of market interaction and social learning for informational and economic efficiency. The book therefore brings together dynamic models of rational expectations with Bayesian learning models, including the herding variety.[9]

The strategy of the book is to analyze the different topics considering a basic workhorse asymmetric-information model in a linear-quadratic mean-variance environment. Most results will be obtained in the context of a model where optimal actions end up being a linear function of the information agents have. The model is developed in two basic versions: a partial equilibrium production market and a financial market. The book examines information aggregation mechanisms, progressing from simple to complex environments: from static to dynamic models, from competitive to strategic agents, from simple market strategies (such as noncontingent orders or quantities) to complex ones (such as price-contingent orders or demand schedules).

This is a book that focuses on theoretical models.[10] A nonexhaustive outline of topics with some of the basic ideas covered in the book follows.

---

[6] See Tversky and Kahneman (1971, 1974), Kahneman et al. (1982), Camerer (1995), and Rabin (1998) for surveys on error-prone heuristics (such as making strong inferences from small samples—"law of small numbers," confirmatory bias—where agents ignore information that contradicts beliefs held, and "representativeness," where agents tend to neglect prior probabilities). Griffiths and Tenenbaum (2006) present recent evidence of the Bayesian optimality of human cognition in realistic scenarios, and Anderson and Holt (1997), Hung and Plott (2001), Cipriani and Guarino (2005), and Drehmann et al. (2005) evidence in experimental settings.

[7] Sandroni (2000, 2005) shows that Bayesian agents drive behavioral non-Bayesian agents out of the market (see the discussion in section 7.1.1). See Jamal and Sunder (1996) and Ackert et al. (1997) for experimental evidence.

[8] See Fudenberg and Levine (1998) for a treatment of this topic.

[9] In the macroeconomics field, see Evans and Honkapohja (2001) for a treatment of adaptive learning models and Ljungqvist and Sargent (2000) for an exhaustive study of recursive methods. See Guesnerie (2001, 2006) for an assessment of rational expectations models.

[10] The reader is referred to Hasbrouck (2007) for a recent survey of empirical market microstructure models.

Outline of Selected Themes and Issues

Herding, Rational Expectations, and the Underlying Information Externality

If the actions of others strongly suggest a certain action, then a rational individual may ignore his own information and follow the crowd or herd. When this happens information is lost and it is not revealed to others. There is no further accumulation of information and an "informational cascade" obtains. The result is that the outcome may be very inefficient. This is an insight derived from the sequential prediction model considered in the herding literature[11] which has been suggested to apply to investors and decision makers in markets. In principle, the results would give support to the pessimistic view of markets and would seem to contradict directly the rational expectations literature with its emphasis, following Hayek's ideas, on the informational properties of markets.

We provide an analytical framework that makes apparent that rational expectations and herding models have in common a basic information externality. Indeed, a trader or agent when acting does not take into account the informational benefits of his action on the other traders or agents. When the trader or agent cannot fine-tune his action to his information (e.g., with discrete actions) and receives signals of bounded strength, then herding on a wrong action occurs with positive probability. This cannot happen with a rich choice set, in which case information will end up being revealed. However, even then with noisy observations revelation will be slow.

Slow Learning from Others and Welfare

Traders learning about the fundamentals of the market will typically learn slowly over time from a noisy public statistic (e.g., the price). A rational (Bayesian) trader will respond to increased price informativeness with decreased weight given to his private information when formulating his trade. This will mean that less of his private information will be incorporated into the public statistic. The result will be that the increase in informativeness in the public statistic will be smaller the larger is his absolute level, slowing down information revelation. Learning from others has a self-correcting property.

What are the welfare consequences? Welfare analysis has typically been neglected in herding models. We introduce an appropriate welfare benchmark with private information. This is team efficiency, where agents use decentralized decision rules but have as a common objective the welfare of a representative agent. The information externality implies that the market outcome is inefficient with respect to this team benchmark, which internalizes the externality. Herd behavior and informational cascades are extreme manifestations of the self-correcting aspect of learning from others. With discrete action spaces and signals of bounded strength, public information may end up overwhelming the private signals of the agents, who may (optimally) choose not to act on

[11] See Banerjee (1992), Bikhchandani et al. (1992), and Chamley (2004) for an assessment.

their information. More generally, "herding" means that agents put too little weight on their private information with respect to the team benchmark and this results in under-accumulation of public information. An interesting possibility is that more public information may hurt. The reason is that a higher amount of public information may reduce the effort to collect private information. A similar analysis can be performed in rational expectations models. The bottom line is that the welfare analysis of "rational expectations" and "herding" models is not qualitatively different.

Information Externalities and Payoff Externalities

With social interaction there is typically both an informational externality and a payoff externality. In a pure prediction model there is only an information externality. How do the informational and the payoff externalities interact? In the first place we show in a static model that informational efficiency is not the same as economic efficiency. We will see that prices in a rational expectations equilibrium of a market with substitute products will tend to convey "too little" information when the informational role of prices prevails over its "index-of-scarcity" role and "too much" in the opposite situation. The market will be team-efficient only in exceptional circumstances (i.e., when the information externality vanishes).

Explaining Market Dynamics

Do prices converge to full-information values as trading periods accumulate? Is the market an effective price-discovery mechanism in the presence of asymmetric information? If so, how fast? How long does the adjustment process takes? How does the payoff externality modify the result of slow learning from others in prediction models?

The results obtained in prediction models generalize to market settings. Traders learn the unknown parameters and prices converge to full-information values with repeated interaction in a stationary market environment. However, learning an unknown parameter and converging to full-information equilibrium is not equivalent. For example, with serial correlation in period shocks it is possible to learn an unknown parameter at a lower speed than converge to a full-information equilibrium. In nonstationary environments learning and convergence are not equivalent.

We find that in market models where traders learn from prices about the information of other traders about a valuation parameter, as in a financial market learning may be fast because of the payoff externality induced by market makers. Market makers induce a deeper market as more information about the fundamental value is revealed by the trading process. With discrete actions, as in the simple prediction models, there is no herding; with a rich choice set and noise in public information, convergence to a full-information equilibrium is fast because risk-averse informed traders respond more intensely to their private signals as market makers induce a deeper market. The role of a competitive market-making sector proves crucial for price discovery. Its presence implies that current prices reflect all public information.

The Impact of Market Microstructure

The information aggregation properties of the market depend on the details of market organization or market microstructure. First of all, information aggregation depends on whether the market mechanism is smooth, like a Cournot market, or has the winner-takes-all feature, like auction or voting mechanisms. The latter aggregate information better than the former both in the sense that they aggregate information in more circumstances and that they do so more economically, that is, without the necessary coming together of a very large number of agents. Second, information aggregation depends on whether agents use noncontingent strategies, like market orders, or price-contingent ones, like limit orders or demand schedules in financial markets. The more complex contingent strategies do better at aggregating information. This also affects the incentives to acquire information. Third, it also matters whether the market is order or quote driven. In order-driven markets informed traders move first while in quote-driven markets uninformed market makers move first.[12]

Can "Market Anomalies" Be Explained?

Market anomalies, seemingly inconsistent with rational expectations models, can in fact be explained without recourse to the irrationality of traders. Excess volatility, where asset prices are more volatile than fundamental values, can be consistent with dynamic trading models where market makers are risk averse and do not fully accommodate shocks. The analysis of patterns of stock prices, or "technical analysis," is valuable if the current price is not a sufficient statistic for public information about the fundamental value. This is typically so except where market makers are risk neutral. However, learning from past prices may be slow. The presence of traders with short horizons may reduce the informational efficiency of the market and explain incentives for investors to herd in information acquisition. For example, short-term traders may care more about the information that other short-term traders have than about the fundamentals, like in Keynes's beauty contest, because of strategic complementarities in information acquisition. Similarly, discrepancies between the average expectations of investors and stock prices, which sometimes may look like a bubble, can be rationalized in the presence of short-term traders who induce multiple market equilibria. More generally, price dynamics in financial markets may have a "Keynesian" or a "Hayekian" flavor depending on parameters such as the degree of persistence of shocks or the amount of residual uncertainty on the liquidation value of the asset.

---

[12] The term *market microstructure* in finance was coined by Garman (1976) in a piece of work about market making. Brunnermeier (2001) provides a nice introduction to market microstructure models in finance.

Crises and Crashes

Sudden and significant drops in asset prices, even in the absence of major news, may be explained with our models, for example, by an abrupt information revelation about the quality of information of investors brought by a small price movement; by a misinterpretation of a price drop due to underestimation of the extent of portfolio trading generating multiple equilibria; or by a liquidity shortage as a result of an underestimation by market timers of the degree of dynamic hedging activity. Crises that arise from a coordination problem of investors, such as exchange rate crises or bank runs, leading to multiple equilibria can be explained with the interaction of private and endogenously generated public information. Policy implications may be derived from the analysis. For example, it need not be true that more transparency is always good since it may coordinate the expectations of investors in a bad equilibrium.

The Impact of Large Traders

Large informed traders are more cautious when responding to their private signals because they are aware of the price impact of their trades. The result is that prices are less informative in their presence. Insiders, when forced to reveal their trades, will engage in dissimulation strategies. Otherwise, they may have incentives to manipulate the market and slow down information revelation. For example, they may do so by using a contrarian strategy to neutralize the potential revelation of information by the trades of competitive informed agents. The effects of insider trading are multiple. Insider trading generates adverse selection, inducing market makers to protect themselves by making the market thinner, and advances the resolution of uncertainty, increasing price informativeness. The first effect tends to be bad for investment and welfare. The impact of the second effect, under risk aversion, depends on what is the alternative to insider trading. If the alternative is that information is disclosed, then insider trading may be good because too much information disclosure destroys insurance opportunities. If the alternative is that no information is collected, then insider trading will typically be bad for welfare.

A relevant issue from the point of view of policy is whether market power or asymmetric information looms larger in accounting for welfare losses in relation to full-information competitive equilibria. The general result is that market power dissipates faster than asymmetric information as a market grows large and supports more traders, and therefore in moderately sized markets asymmetric information is likely to be a larger source of the welfare loss. This is the case in Cournot markets, for example.

Some Conclusions

Apparently contending theories, such as market informational efficiency and herding, in fact build on the same principles of Bayesian decision making. The upshot is that we do not need "irrational" agents to explain herding behavior, crises, and crashes. Traders may be rational but learn slowly or even on some occasions disregard private information and end up making persistent errors when acting; or they may be trapped in a coordination failure. However, informational and economic efficiency need not, and in general will not, coincide. In any case the impact of market microstructure on the informational efficiency of prices is crucial. The stock market conveys information about the fundamentals of firms although the misalignment of stock prices and fundamentals is possible but typically not extremely long-lived.

Outline of Chapters

In chapters 1–3 and 7 we consider mostly "real" partial equilibrium markets, with Cournot competition as the leading example, although we also study auctions, supply function competition, and its relation to rational expectations equilibria (in chapter 3). In chapters 4, 5, 8, and 9 we consider financial markets and spend time explaining how the market microstructure affects trading and the informational efficiency of prices. The equivalent of Cournot competition in a financial setting is when traders submit market orders, while the equivalent of supply function competition is when traders submit demand schedules to a centralized trading mechanism. Chapters 1, 3, 4, and 6 deal with competitive models and chapters 2, 5, and 9 (mostly) deal with models of strategic traders. Chapters 1–5 deal with static models and chapters 6–9 with dynamic models. Chapter 6 builds a bridge between stylized social learning models and dynamic rational expectations models.

Let us review in more detail the content of the chapters and the organization of the book.

Chapters 1 and 2 study market mechanisms, such as auctions or Cournot markets, in which traders do not have the opportunity to condition their actions on prices or other market statistics. This provides a benchmark in which traders can only use their private information to decide how much to trade. In this framework we study under what circumstances the market replicates the outcome of shared-information equilibrium. If it does, we say that the market aggregates information. Chapter 1 studies first in detail large Cournot markets with demand uncertainty and asymmetric information and uncovers when information aggregation obtains, providing a taxonomy and a welfare analysis of the value of information in a general setting. When information aggregation obtains in a "large" market a second issue of interest is how large a market is needed for the result. In any case, as a market grows large strategic behavior vanishes and price-taking obtains.

Chapter 2 analyzes the convergence properties of finite markets to price-taking equilibria as the market gets larger and the number of agents grows. When the limit is first-best efficient, with full-information aggregation, we compare the rates of information aggregation in different market mechanisms and disentangle the sources of the welfare loss at the market solution in terms of market power and private information. Both chapters 1 and 2 compare the information aggregation properties of smooth market mechanisms, like Cournot markets, with auctions.

Chapter 3 introduces the concept of a rational expectations equilibrium (REE), with its different variants—fully revealing REE, partially revealing REE, and noisy REE—in the context of a static partial equilibrium homogeneous product market with demand and cost uncertainty and a continuum of firms. It is shown that not all REE are implementable. That is, not every REE can be seen as the outcome of a well-specified game among market participants. A game form is then considered in which firms compete in supply functions and Bayesian equilibrium in supply functions is studied. The chapter goes on to perform a welfare analysis of REE introducing the appropriate team efficiency benchmark that internalizes information externalities. That is, the chapter checks the alignment of informational efficiency and allocative and productive efficiency. The information externality at the market equilibrium is characterized and related to economic efficiency. The chapter also considers the information aggregation properties of the double auction mechanism.

Chapters 4 and 5 look at the basic static financial market models with asymmetric information and review the impact of different market microstructures with competitive (in chapter 4) and strategic (in chapter 5) players. The standard competitive noisy rational expectations financial market is presented along with variations in which informed traders submit market orders to market makers. A model is presented that has as special cases virtually all the competitive models in the literature. The potential paradox of informationally efficient markets when information is costly to acquire is addressed. Chapter 5 goes on to study strategic behavior in different market structures with simultaneous and sequential order placement, uniform and discriminatory pricing, and distinguishing the cases in which informed traders move first and those in which uninformed traders move first.

Chapter 6 considers social learning models. First it presents the basic sequential decision herding model and variations. It highlights the assumptions that drive the results and develops a basic smooth model of learning from others that serves as a benchmark for the analysis and that is close to rational expectations models. It is found that the basic driving forces in herding and rational expectations models are the same. A self-correcting property of learning from others and its implications in terms of information revelation and its speed are at the center of the chapter. Furthermore, the information externality of social learning is characterized and optimal learning studied. Results are extended to the case where information acquisition is costly and the value of public information studied. Finally, a static version of the model of learning from others with a rational expectations flavor is presented and a welfare analysis is performed.

Chapter 7 deals with dynamic information aggregation models and studies their convergence properties as the number of trading periods grows without bound. The basic model considered is a repeated Cournot model with an uncertain demand parameter and period-specific shocks with firms receiving private signals about the unknown demand. The rate of convergence to full-information equilibrium is characterized in the cases of independent and correlated shocks to demand. Results for the latter case make clear that learning an unknown parameter is not equivalent to converging to full-information equilibrium. A variation of the model with an unknown cost parameter is considered and it is shown that learning and convergence to full-information equilibrium may be slow. The latter is a model of learning from others and extends the results of chapter 6 to an environment with payoff externalities.

Chapters 8 and 9 study dynamic competitive and strategic models of financial markets. They address the difficult issue of solving for and characterizing an equilibrium when risk-averse traders have private information and a long horizon. The resolution of the problem illuminates trading and price temporal patterns and serves as a benchmark to compare with the case in which informed speculators have short horizons. A detailed analysis of the impact of market microstructure on the dynamic properties of market quality parameters, such as price volatility and informativeness, market depth, and volume traded, is performed. These chapters provide explanations for technical analysis, trading with no news, excess volatility, and market crashes, as well as the impact of short-term traders. We also address the interaction between the potential coordination failure of investors, e.g., in an exchange rate crisis, and endogenously determined market signals to generate multiple equilibria. All this is done without introducing any irrationality on the part of traders. The properties of a price-discovery mechanism are studied in both competitive and strategic versions showing the importance of the market microstructure and the presence of strategic traders in the speed of price discovery. The trading strategies of large informed traders are analyzed, including the possibility of dissimulation of trades and market manipulation.

The technical appendix (chapter 10) presents in an accessible way the basic tools needed to follow comfortably the material in the book. These include information structures with particular attention to the Gaussian and related models, convergence properties of random processes, and game-theoretic concepts (such as Bayesian equilibrium). It includes in particular a concise self-contained development of the linear-Gaussian model.

Road Map and Lecture Guide

The book may be read according to different field itineraries:

- Real markets: chapters 1–3, 6, and 7.
- Financial markets (market microstructure): sections 1.1, 1.2, 3.1, chapters 4–6, 8, and 9.

Alternatively, it may be read according to the following model itineraries:

- Static models: chapters 1–5.
- Dynamic models: chapters 6–9.

Or:

- Competitive models: chapters 1, 3, 4, and 6–8, section 9.1.
- Strategic models: chapter 2, section 3.4, chapters 5 and 9.

Readers familiar with Bayesian updating techniques and the basics of rational expectations and interested only in financial markets may jump directly to chapter 4 after reading sections 1.1, 1.2, and 3.1. Readers who are familiar with static models may jump directly to chapter 6.

The level of difficulty of chapters is pretty uniform, with dynamic models being in general more demanding. Chapters 2 and 7 are more demanding and may be skipped in a first reading without major loss of continuity. The same applies to sections which are more advanced (marked with an asterisk ("∗")). Instructors who use the text for advanced undergraduates or masters students with little formal background in economics may want to introduce the major results with the examples which usually follow the major propositions, and present the general results later on. Each chapter is closed by a summary and an appendix with proof of results in the text, and worked-out exercises. The level of difficulty of problems varies from very challenging (marked with a double asterisk ("∗∗")) because of inherent difficulty or the amount of work they require, challenging (marked with an asterisk ("∗")), and easy (with no mark).

References

Ackert, L., B. Church, and M. Shehata. 1997. Market behavior in the presence of costly, imperfect information: experimental evidence. *Journal of Economic Behavior and Organization* 33:61–74.

Anderson, L., and Ch. Holt. 1997. Information cascades in the laboratory. *American Economic Review* 87:847–62.

Banerjee, A. V. 1992. A simple model of herd behavior. *Quarterly Journal of Economics* 107:797–817.

Berg, J., R. Forsythe, T. Nelson, and T. Rietz. 2005. What makes markets predict well? Evidence from the Iowa electronic markets. In *Handbook of Experimental Economic Results* (ed. C. R. Plott and V. Smith). Amsterdam: Elsevier.

Bikhchandani, S., D. Hirshleifer, and I. Welch. 1992. A theory of fads, fashion, custom, and cultural change as informational cascades. *Journal of Political Economy* 100:992–1026.

Brunnermeier, M. 2001. *Asset Pricing under Asymmetric Information.* Oxford University Press.

Camerer, C. 1995. Individual decision-making. In *Handbook of Experimental Economics* (ed. J. Kagel and A. Roth). Princeton University Press.

Chamley, C. 2004. *Rational Herds.* Cambridge University Press.

Chen, K. Y., and C. R. Plott. 2002. Information aggregation mechanisms: concept, design and implementation for a sales forecasting problem. California Institute of Technology, Social Science Working Paper 1131.

Cipriani, M., and A. Guarino. 2005. Herd behavior in a laboratory financial market. *American Economic Review* 95:1427–43.

Drehmann, M., J. Oechssler, and A. Roider. 2005. Herding and contrarian behavior in financial markets: an Internet experiment. *American Economic Review* 95:1403–26.

Evans, G. W., and S. Honkapohja. 2001. *Learning and Expectations in Macroeconomics.* Princeton University Press.

Forsythe, R., and R. Lundholm. 1990. Information aggregation in an experimental market. *Econometrica* 58:309–47.

Forsythe, R., F. Nelson, G. R. Neumann, and J. Wright. 1992. Anatomy of an experimental political stock market. *American Economic Review* 82:1142–61.

Fudenberg, D., and D. Levine. 1998. *The Theory of Learning in Games.* Cambridge, MA: MIT Press.

Garman, M. 1976. Market microstructure. *Journal of Financial Economics* 3:257–75.

Griffiths, T., and J. Tenenbaum. 2006. Optimal predictions in everyday cognition. *Psychological Science* 17:767–73.

Grossman, S. 1989. *The Informational Role of Prices.* Cambridge, MA: MIT Press.

Guesnerie, R. 2001. *Assessing Rational Expectations: Sunspot Multiplicity and Economic Fluctuations.* Cambridge, MA: MIT Press.

——. 2006. *Assessing Expectations,* volume 2: *Eductive Stability in Economics.* Cambridge, MA: MIT Press.

Hasbrouck, J. 2007. *Empirical Market Microstructure.* Oxford University Press.

Hayek, F. 1945. The use of knowledge in society. *American Economic Review* 35:519–30.

Hung, A., and C. R. Plott. 2001. Information cascades: replication and an extension to majority rule and conformity-rewarding institutions. *American Economic Review* 91:1508–20.

Jamal, K., and S. Sunder. 1996. Bayesian equilibrium in double auctions populated by biased heuristic traders. *Journal of Economic Behavior and Organization* 31:273–91.

Kahneman, D., P. Slovic, and A. Tversky. 1982. *Judgment under Uncertainty: Heuristics and Biases.* Cambridge University Press.

Keynes, J. 1936. *The General Theory of Employment, Interest and Money.* Cambridge University Press.

Lange, O. 1936. On the economic theory of socialism. Part One. *Review of Economic Studies* 4(1):53–71.

——. 1937. On the economic theory of socialism. Part Two. *Review of Economic Studies* 4(2):123–42.

Ljungqvist, L., and T. J. Sargent. 2000. *Recursive Macroeconomic Theory.* Cambridge, MA: MIT Press.

Plott, C. R., and S. Sunder. 1988. Rational expectations and the aggregation of diverse information in laboratory security markets. *Econometrica* 56:1085–118.

Rabin, M. 1998. Psychology and economics. *Journal of Economic Literature* 36:11–46.

Radner, R. 1979. Rational expectations equilibrium: generic existence and the information revealed by prices. *Econometrica* 47:655–78.

Sandroni, A. 2000. Do markets favor agents able to make accurate predictions? *Econometrica* 28:1303–41.

——. 2005. Efficient markets and Bayes' rule. *Economic Theory* 26:741–64.

Shiller, R. J. 2005. *Irrational Exuberance.* Princeton University Press.

Shleifer, A. 2000. *Clarendon Lectures: Inefficient Markets.* Oxford University Press.

Sunstein, C. 2006. *Infotopia. How Many Minds Produce Knowledge.* Oxford University Press.

Thaler, R. 2005. *Advances in Behavioral Finance.* Princeton University Press.

Tversky, A., and D. Kahneman. 1971. Belief in the law of small numbers. *Psychology Bulletin* 76:105–10.

——. 1974. Judgement under uncertainty: heuristics and biases. *Science* 185:1124–31.

Wolfers, J., and E. Zitzewitz. 2004. Prediction markets. *Journal of Economic Perspectives* 18:107–26.

Some of the material presented in the book has been adapted from the following:

Bru, L., and X. Vives. 2002. Informational externalities, herding, and incentives. *Journal of Institutional and Theoretical Economics* 158:91–105 (chapter 6).

Burguet, R., and X. Vives. 2000. Social learning and costly information acquisition. *Economic Theory* 15:185–205 (chapter 6).

Jun, B., and X. Vives. 1996. Learning and convergence to a full-information equilibrium are not equivalent. *Review of Economic Studies* 63:653–74 (chapter 7).

Medrano, L., and X. Vives. 2001. Strategic behavior and price discovery. *RAND Journal of Economics* 32:221–48 (chapters 4, 5, and 9).

——. 2004. Regulating insider trading when investment matters. *Review of Finance* 8:199–277 (chapters 4 and 5).

Rochet, J. C., and X. Vives. 2004. Coordination failures and the lender of last resort: was Bagehot right after all? *Journal of the European Economic Association* 2:1116–47 (chapter 8).

Vives, X. 1988. Aggregation of information in large Cournot markets. *Econometrica* 56:851–76 (chapters 1 and 2).

——. 1990. Trade association disclosure rules, incentives to share information and welfare. *RAND Journal of Economics* 21:409–30 (chapter 1).

——. 1993. How fast do rational agents learn? *Review of Economic Studies* 60:329–47 (chapters 6 and 7).

——. 1995. Short term investment and the informational efficiency of the market. *Review of Financial Studies* 8:125–60 (chapters 4 and 8).

——. 1995. The speed of information revelation in a financial market mechanism. *Journal of Economic Theory* 67:178–204 (chapters 4 and 9).

——. 1996. Social learning and rational expectations. *European Economic Review* 40:589–601 (chapter 6).

——. 1997. Learning from others: a welfare analysis. *Games and Economic Behavior* 20:177–200 (chapter 6).

——. 2002. Private information, strategic behavior, and efficiency in Cournot markets. *RAND Journal of Economics* 33:361–76 (chapter 2).

——. 2005. Complementarities and games: new developments. *Journal of Economic Literature* 43:437–79 (chapter 8).

1

Aggregation of Information in Simple Market Mechanisms: Large Markets

The aim of this chapter is to provide an introduction to the most basic models of information aggregation: static simple market mechanisms where traders do not observe any market statistic before making their decisions. Each agent moves only once, simultaneously with other agents, and can condition his action only on his private information. The issue is whether market outcomes replicate or are close to the situation where agents have symmetric information and share the information in the economy. Examples of such market mechanisms are one-shot auctions and quantity (Cournot) and price (Bertrand) competition markets. In chapters 3–5 we will consider market mechanisms in the rational expectations tradition in which agents can use more complex strategies, conditioning their actions on market statistics. For example, a firm may use a supply function as a strategy, conditioning its output on the market price (chapter 3), or a trader may submit a demand schedule to a centralized stock market mechanism (chapters 4 and 5).

The plan of the chapter is as follows. Section 1.1 introduces the topic of information aggregation, some modeling issues, and an overview of results. Section 1.2 analyzes a large Cournot market with demand uncertainty and asymmetric information. It studies a general model and two examples: linear-normal and isoelastic-lognormal. Section 1.3 examines the welfare properties of price-taking equilibria in Cournot markets with private information. Section 1.4 presents a general smooth market model to examine information aggregation and the value of information. Section 1.5 deals with the case of auctions and section 1.6 introduces endogenous information acquisition.

1.1 Introduction and Overview

1.1.1 Do Markets Aggregate Information Efficiently?

As we stated in the Introduction and Lecture Guide, this has been a contentious issue at least since the debate between Hayek and Lange about the economic viability of socialism.

Hayek's basic idea (1945) is that each trader has some information that can be transmitted economically to others only through the price mechanism and trading. A planner cannot do as well without all that information. We say that the market aggregates information if it replicates the outcome that would be obtained if the agents in the economy shared their private information. The Hayekian hypothesis to check is whether a large (competitive) market aggregates information.

In this chapter we study, as a benchmark, market mechanisms that do not allow traders to condition their actions on prices or other market statistics. In this sense we are making things difficult for the market in terms of information aggregation. In chapter 3 we will allow more complex market mechanisms that allow traders to condition on current prices. Market mechanisms such as Cournot or auctions have the property that when a participant submits his or her trade it can condition only on his private information. For example, in a sealed-bid auction a bidder submits his bid with his private knowledge of the auctioned object but without observing the other bids; in a Cournot market firms put forward their outputs with some private estimate of demand conditions but without observing the market-clearing price or the outputs submitted by other producers.

A first question to ask is whether those simple market mechanisms aggregate information, at least when markets have many participants. We must realize, however, that a large market need not be competitive but rather can be monopolistically competitive. Indeed, firms may be small relative to the market but still retain some market power. If a large market is competitive and it aggregates information, then first-best efficiency follows according to the First Welfare Theorem. This means, in particular, that the full-information Walrasian model may be a good approximation to a large market with dispersed private information. In this case informational and economic efficiency go hand in hand. When a large market is not competitive, informational efficiency will not imply in general economic efficiency. We will discuss in detail the relationship between informational and economic efficiency in chapter 3.

Information aggregation does not obtain, in general, in market mechanisms in which outcomes depend continuously (smoothly) on the actions of the players, like quantity (Cournot) or price (Bertrand) competition markets with product differentiation. In fact, why should a market in which each trader conditions only on its private information be able to replicate the shared-information outcome? We will see that a large Cournot market in a homogeneous product world with a common shock to demand in which each producer receives a private signal about the uncertain demand does not aggregate information in general despite firms being approximately price takers. However, in the same context information may be aggregated if there are constant returns or if uncertainty is of the independent-values type, when the types of traders are independently distributed and, in fact, in the aggregate there is no uncertainty.

In contrast, winner-takes-all markets like auctions or voting mechanisms, in which outcomes do not depend continuously on the actions of players, tend to deliver aggregation of information more easily. Winner-takes-all markets force traders to condition effectively on more information when taking their decisions.

1.1.2 Methodological Issues and Welfare

In the following sections we use the continuum model of a large market. We will examine games with a continuum of agents in which no single one of them can affect the market outcomes. This methodology is in line with the literature on large Cournot markets with complete information (Novshek 1980), and with the view that the continuum model is the appropriate formalization of a competitive economy (Aumann 1964). The advantage of working with the continuum model is that it is very easy to understand the statistical reasons why a competitive market with incomplete information does not aggregate information efficiently in general, and to characterize the equilibrium and its second-best properties. One must check that the equilibria in the continuum economy are the limit of equilibria of finite economies and not artifacts of the continuum specification. This will be done in chapter 2.

The analysis of competitive equilibria in asymmetric-information economies is somewhat underdeveloped. To start with, the very notion of competitive equilibrium needs to be defined in an asymmetric-information environment.[1] If the market aggregates information, then the competitive equilibrium corresponds to the standard concept with full information. Otherwise, we may define the concept of Bayesian (price-taking) equilibrium. This is the situation, e.g., in a Cournot market, where firms' strategies depend on their private information but a firm does not perceive to affect the market price. This will be justified if the firm is very small in relation to the market, that is, in a large market.

Whenever the outcome of a large market, in which agents are price takers, is not first-best efficient, the question arises about what welfare property, if any, it has. The answer is that a price-taking Bayesian equilibrium maximizes expected total surplus subject to the restriction that agents use decentralized strategies (that is, strategies which depend only on the private information of the agents). This welfare benchmark for economies with incomplete information is termed *team efficiency* since the allocation would be the outcome of the decision of a team with a common objective (total surplus) but decentralized strategies (Radner 1962). This means that the large market performs as well as possible, subject to the constraint of using decentralized mechanisms. We will see this result in section 1.3.

1.2 Large Cournot Markets

In this section we will consider a large homogeneous product market in which demand is affected by a random shock and each firm has a private estimate of

[1] See Hellwig (1987) for a discussion of the issue. Progress in the study of competitive markets with asymmetric information has been made, among others, by Harris and Townsend (1981), Prescott and Townsend (1984), and Gale (1996).

the shock and sets an output. This is a very simple and standard framework in which to analyze information aggregation. Quantity setting corresponds to the Cournot model of an oligopolistic market. Here we will have many firms and each will be negligible in relation to the size of the market.

There is a continuum of firms indexed by $i \in [0,1]$.[2] Each firm has a convex, twice continuously differentiable, variable cost function $C(\cdot)$ and no fixed costs. Inverse demand is smooth and downward sloping, and given by $p = P(x,\theta)$, where x is average (per capita) output (and also aggregate output since we have normalized the measure of firms to 1) and θ is a random parameter. Firms are quantity setters.

Firm i receives a private signal s_i, a noisy estimate of θ. The signals received by firms are independently and identically distributed (i.i.d.) given θ and, without loss of generality, are unbiased, i.e., $E[s_i \mid \theta] = \theta$.

We make the *convention* that the strong law of large numbers (SLLN) holds for a continuum of independent random variables with uniformly bounded variances. Suppose that $(q_i)_{i\in[0,1]}$ is a process of independent random variables with means $E[q_i]$ and uniformly bounded variances $\text{var}[q_i]$. Then we let $\int_0^1 q_i \, di = \int_0^1 E[q_i] \, di$ almost surely (a.s.). This convention will be used, taking as given the usual linearity property of the integral.[3] In particular, here we have that, given θ, the average signal equals $E[s_i \mid \theta] = \theta$ (a.s.).

Section 1.2.1 characterizes the equilibrium with strictly convex costs, section 1.2.2 its welfare properties, section 1.2.3 deals with the constant marginal cost case, and section 1.2.4 provides some examples.

1.2.1 Bayesian Equilibrium

Suppose that $C(\cdot)$ is strictly convex. A production strategy for firm i is a function $X_i(\cdot)$ which associates an output to the signal received. A market equilibrium is a Bayes–Nash (or Bayesian) equilibrium of the game with a continuum of players where the payoff to player i is given by

$$\pi_i = P(x;\theta)x_i - C(x_i), \quad \text{where } x = \int_0^1 X_i(s_i) \, di,$$

and the information structure is as described above.[4] At equilibrium, $X_i(s_i)$ maximizes

$$E[\pi_i \mid s_i] = x_i E[P(x;\theta) \mid s_i] - C(x_i)$$

and the firm cannot influence the market price $P(x;\theta)$ because it has no influence on average output x. This is, therefore, a price-taking Bayesian equilibrium. Restricting our attention to strategies with bounded means and uniformly bounded variances across players (this would obviously hold, for example, with

---

[2] The interval is endowed with the Lebesgue measure.

[3] See section 10.3.1 for a justification of the convention. Equality of random variables has to be understood to hold almost surely. We will not always insist on this in the text.

[4] See section 10.4.2 for an introduction to Bayesian equilibrium.

a bounded output space), the equilibrium must be symmetric. In particular, with $E[X_i(s_i) \mid \theta] < \infty$ and $\text{var}[X_i(s_i) \mid \theta]$ uniformly bounded across players, the random variables $X_i(s_i)$ are independent (given θ) and, according to our convention on a continuum of independent random variables, we have that

$$\int_0^1 X_i(s_i)\,\mathrm{d}i = \int_0^1 E[X_i(s_i) \mid \theta]\,\mathrm{d}i \equiv \tilde{X}(\theta).$$

It follows that the equilibrium must be symmetric, $X_i(s_i) = X(s_i)$ for all i, since the payoff is symmetric, the cost function is strictly convex and identical for all firms, and signals are i.i.d. (given θ). Indeed, for a given average output $\tilde{X}(\theta)$, the best response of a player is unique and identical for all players: $X_i(s_i) = X(s_i)$. Consequently, in equilibrium the random variables $X(s_i)$ will be i.i.d. (given θ) and their average will equal $\tilde{X}(\theta) = E[X(s_i) \mid \theta]$.

An interior (symmetric) equilibrium $X(\cdot)$, that is, one with positive production for almost all signals, is characterized by the equalization of the expected market price, conditional on receiving signal s_i, and marginal production costs:

$$E[P(x;\theta) \mid s_i] = C'(X(s_i)).$$

This characterizes the price-taking Bayesian equilibrium. Firms condition their output on their estimates of demand but they do not perceive, correctly in our continuum economy, any effect of their action on the (expected) market price. Thus the price-taking Bayesian equilibrium coincides with the Bayesian Cournot equilibrium of our large market.

1.2.2 Welfare and Information Aggregation

If firms were to know θ, then a Walrasian (competitive) equilibrium would be attained and the outcome would be first-best efficient. How does the Bayesian market outcome compare with the full-information first-best outcome, where total surplus (per capita) is maximized contingent on the true value of θ?

Given θ and individual production for firm i at x_i, total surplus (per capita) is

$$\text{TS} = \int_0^x P(z;\theta)\,\mathrm{d}z - \int_0^1 C(x_i)\,\mathrm{d}i, \quad \text{where } x = \int_0^1 x_i\,\mathrm{d}i.$$

If all the firms produce the same quantity, $x_i = x$ for all i, we have

$$\text{TS}(x;\theta) = \int_0^x P(z;\theta)\,\mathrm{d}z - C(x).$$

Given strict convexity of costs, first-best production $X^{\mathrm{o}}(\theta)$ is given by the unique x which solves $P(x;\theta) = C'(x)$. If firms were able to pool their private signals, they could condition their production to the average signal, which equals θ a.s., and attain the first-best by producing $X^{\mathrm{o}}(\theta)$. Will a price-taking Bayesian equilibrium, where each firm can condition its production only on its private information, replicate the first-best outcome?

A necessary condition for any (symmetric) production strategy $X(\cdot)$ to be first-best optimal is that, conditional on θ, identical firms produce at the same marginal cost, namely, $C'(X(s_i)) = C'(X^{\text{o}}(\theta))$ (a.s.). However, with increasing marginal costs this can happen only if $X(s_i) = X^{\text{o}}(\theta)$ (a.s.), which boils down to the perfect-information case. Therefore, we should expect a welfare loss at the price-taking Bayesian equilibrium with noisy signals. Proposition 1.1 states the result and a proof follows.

Proposition 1.1 (Vives 1988). *In a large Cournot market where firms have (symmetric) strictly convex costs and receive private noisy signals about an uncertain demand parameter, there is a welfare loss with respect to the full-information first-best outcome.*

Proof. We show that no symmetric production strategy $X(\cdot)$, and therefore no competitive production strategy, can attain the first-best outcome. Let $\tilde{X}(\theta) = \int_0^1 X(s_i)\,\mathrm{d}i$, then expected total surplus (per capita) contingent on θ is given by

$$E[\mathrm{TS} \mid \theta] = \int_0^{\tilde{X}(\theta)} P(z;\theta)\,\mathrm{d}z - E[C(X(s_i)) \mid \theta].$$

We have that

$$\mathrm{TS}(X^{\text{o}}(\theta);\theta) \geqslant \mathrm{TS}(\tilde{X}(\theta);\theta) > E[\mathrm{TS} \mid \theta].$$

The first inequality is true since $X^{\text{o}}(\theta)$ is the first-best, and the second is true since $\mathrm{TS}(\tilde{X}(\theta);\theta) = \int_0^{\tilde{X}(\theta)} P(z;\theta)\,\mathrm{d}z - C(\tilde{X}(\theta))$, the cost function is strictly convex, $\tilde{X}(\theta) = E[X(s_i) \mid \theta]$, and the signals are noisy (which means that, given θ, $X(s_i)$ is still random). Consequently, $C(\tilde{X}(\theta)) < E[C(X(s_i)) \mid \theta]$ according to a strict version of Jensen's inequality (see, for example, Royden 1968, p. 110). □

1.2.3 Constant Marginal Costs

A necessary condition for the market outcome to be first-best optimal is that marginal costs be constant. Firms will then necessarily produce at the same marginal cost. If the information structure is "regular enough," first-best efficiency is achieved in the price-taking limit (Palfrey 1985; Li 1985). The intuition of the result is as follows. Suppose that marginal costs are zero (without loss of generality) and that inverse demand intersects the quantity axis. Firm i will maximize $E[\pi_i \mid s_i] = x_i E[P(x;\theta) \mid s_i]$, where, as before, x is average output. In this constant-returns-to-scale context a necessary condition for an interior equilibrium to exist is that $E[P(x;\theta) \mid s_i] = 0$ for almost all s_i. Looking at symmetric equilibria, $X_i(s_i) = X(s_i)$ for all i, we know that average production $\tilde{X}(\theta)$ given θ is nonrandom, and therefore $E[P(x;\theta) \mid \theta] = P(\tilde{X}(\theta);\theta)$. We will obtain first-best efficiency if the equilibrium condition, $E[P(\tilde{X}(\theta),\theta) \mid s_i] = 0$ for almost all s_i, implies that price equals marginal cost, $P(\tilde{X}(\theta),\theta) = 0$ for almost all θ.

Palfrey (1985) shows that if the signal and parameter spaces are finite and the likelihood matrix is of full rank (and demand satisfies some mild regularity conditions), then symmetric interior price-taking equilibria are first-best optimal. The result is easily understood with a two-point support example: θ can be either θ_{L} or θ_{H}, $0 < \theta_{\mathrm{L}} \leqslant \theta_{\mathrm{H}}$, with equal prior probability. Firm i may receive a low (s_{L}) or a high (s_{H}) signal about θ with likelihood $\mathrm{P}(s_{\mathrm{H}} \mid \theta_{\mathrm{H}}) = \mathrm{P}(s_{\mathrm{L}} \mid \theta_{\mathrm{L}}) = q$, where $\frac{1}{2} \leqslant q \leqslant 1$. If $q = \frac{1}{2}$, the signal is uninformative; if $q = 1$, it is perfectly informative (see section 10.1.6). Let $\bar{p}$ and $\underline{p}$ be, respectively, the equilibrium prices when demand is high (θ_{H}) and low (θ_{L}). Then

$$\begin{bmatrix} E[p \mid s_{\mathrm{H}}] \\ E[p \mid s_{\mathrm{L}}] \end{bmatrix} = \begin{bmatrix} q & 1-q \\ 1-q & q \end{bmatrix} \begin{bmatrix} \bar{p} \\ \underline{p} \end{bmatrix} = \begin{bmatrix} 0 \\ 0 \end{bmatrix}.$$

If the likelihood matrix is of full rank, i.e., if $q = \frac{1}{2}$, then $\bar{p} = \underline{p} = 0$ and the symmetric interior equilibrium is efficient.

Remark 1.1. For the result to hold, equilibria have to be interior. For example, suppose that $p = \theta - x$ and that $\theta_{\mathrm{L}} = 0$ and $\theta_{\mathrm{H}} = 1$, then at the price-taking Bayesian equilibrium $X(s_{\mathrm{L}}) = 0$ and $X(s_{\mathrm{H}}) = q/(q^2 + (1-q)^2)$. This means that $\tilde{X}(\theta_{\mathrm{H}}) = X(s_{\mathrm{H}})q < X^0(\theta_{\mathrm{H}}) = 1$.

1.2.4 Examples

1.2.4.1 Linear-Gaussian Model

Let $p = \theta - \beta x$ and $C(x_i) = m x_i + \frac{1}{2}\lambda x_i^2$, where m is possibly random and $\lambda \geqslant 0$. In this model only the level of $\theta - m$ matters and therefore without loss of generality let $m = 0$.

The joint distribution of random variables is assumed to yield affine conditional expectations. This, when coupled with the linear-quadratic structure of payoffs, yields a unique (and affine in information) Bayesian equilibrium. A leading example of such an information structure is the assumption of joint normality of all random variables. However, there are other pairs of prior distribution and likelihood which do not require unbounded support for the uncertainty and have the affine conditional expectation property.[5]

The random demand intercept θ is distributed according to a prior density with finite variance σ_θ^2 and mean $\bar{\theta}$. Firm i receives a signal s_i such that $s_i = \theta + \varepsilon_i$, where ε_i is a noise term with zero mean, variance $\sigma_{\varepsilon_i}^2$, and with $\mathrm{cov}[\theta, \varepsilon_i] = 0$. Signals can range from perfect ($\sigma_{\varepsilon_i}^2 = 0$ or infinite precision) to pure noise ($\sigma_{\varepsilon_i}^2 = \infty$ or zero precision). The precision of signal s_i is given by $\tau_{\varepsilon_i} = (\sigma_{\varepsilon_i}^2)^{-1}$. We assume that $E[\theta \mid s_i]$ is affine in s_i. All this implies that (see section 10.1)

$$E[\theta \mid s_i] = (1 - \xi_i)\bar{\theta} + \xi_i s_i, \quad \text{where } \xi_i \equiv \tau_{\varepsilon_i}/(\tau_\theta + \tau_{\varepsilon_i}),$$

and

$$E[s_j \mid s_i] = E[\theta \mid s_i], \quad \mathrm{cov}[s_i, s_j] = \mathrm{cov}[s_i, \theta] = \sigma_\theta^2 \quad \text{for all } j \neq i \text{ and all } i.$$

---

[5] The assumption of normality is very convenient analytically but has the drawback that prices and quantities may take negative values. However, the probability of this phenomenon can be controlled by controlling the parameters of the random variables. Alternatively, we could work with pairs of prior and likelihood functions which admit a bounded support and maintain the crucial property of linear conditional expectations which yields a tractable model. See section 10.2.2.

As τ_{ε_i} ranges from ∞ to 0, ξ_i ranges from 1 to 0. We also assume that the signals received by the firms are identically distributed conditional on θ. Then $\sigma^2_{\varepsilon_i} = \sigma^2_\varepsilon$ and $\xi_i = \xi$ for all i.

In equilibrium $X_i(s_i)$ solves

$$\max_{x_i} E[\pi_i \mid s_i] = E[p \mid s_i]x_i - \tfrac{1}{2}\lambda x_i^2,$$

where $p = \theta - \beta x$ and $x = \int_0^1 X_j(s_j)\,\mathrm{d}j$ and where $X_j(s_j)$ is the strategy used by firm j. Under the assumptions on strategies of section 1.2.1, we have that $\int_0^1 X_j(s_j)\,\mathrm{d}j = \tilde{X}(\theta)$. The optimal response of firm i is identical for all firms provided that $\lambda > 0$, $X(s_i) = E[p \mid s_i]/\lambda$, and equilibria will be symmetric. We are looking for a linear (affine) solution of the type $X(s_i) = as_i + c$, where a and c are coefficients to be determined. It follows that $\tilde{X}(\theta) = \int_0^1 X(s_j)\,\mathrm{d}j = a\int_0^1 s_j\,\mathrm{d}j + c = a\theta + c$ using our convention on the SLLN in our continuum economy: $\int_0^1 s_j\,\mathrm{d}j = \theta + \int_0^1 \varepsilon_j\,\mathrm{d}j = \theta$ since $\int_0^1 \varepsilon_j\,\mathrm{d}j = 0$ (a.s.). The first-order condition (FOC) of the program of firm i yields

$$\lambda X(s_i) = E[\theta \mid s_i] - \beta E[\tilde{X}(\theta) \mid s_i].$$

Therefore, we have that

$$\lambda a s_i + \lambda c = E[\theta \mid s_i] - \beta a E[\theta \mid s_i] - \beta c.$$

Since $E[\theta \mid s_i] = (1-\xi)\bar{\theta} + \xi s_i$, we obtain

$$\lambda a s_i + \lambda c = (1-\beta a)(\xi s_i + (1-\xi)\bar{\theta}) - \beta c.$$

This must hold for (almost) all signals and therefore, solving

$$\lambda a = (1-\beta a)\xi \quad \text{and} \quad \lambda c = (1-\beta a)(1-\xi)\bar{\theta} - \beta c,$$

we obtain

$$a = \frac{\xi}{\lambda + \beta\xi} \quad \text{and} \quad c = \frac{(1-\beta a)(1-\xi)}{\lambda+\beta}\bar{\theta} = \frac{1}{\lambda+\beta}\bar{\theta} - a\bar{\theta}$$

(where in order to obtain the last equality we use the value for a).

In conclusion, we have shown that the unique linear (affine to be precise) function $X(\cdot)$ which satisfies the FOC is given by

$$X(s_i) = a(s_i - \bar{\theta}) + b\bar{\theta}, \quad \text{where } a = \xi/(\lambda + \beta\xi) \text{ and } b = 1/(\lambda + \beta).$$

The linear equilibrium identified can be shown to be in fact the unique equilibrium in the class of strategies with bounded means and uniformly bounded variances (across players). (See remark 1.2 and proposition 7.7 and exercise 7.3 for a proof in a closely related model.)

Average output conditional on θ is given by

$$\int_0^1 X(s_i)\,\mathrm{d}i = \int_0^1 (a(s_i - \bar{\theta}) + b\bar{\theta})\,\mathrm{d}i = a(\theta - \bar{\theta}) + b\bar{\theta}$$

since the average signal conditional on θ equals θ. Note that average output is in fact the same function as the equilibrium strategy $X(\cdot)$ and we may denote it

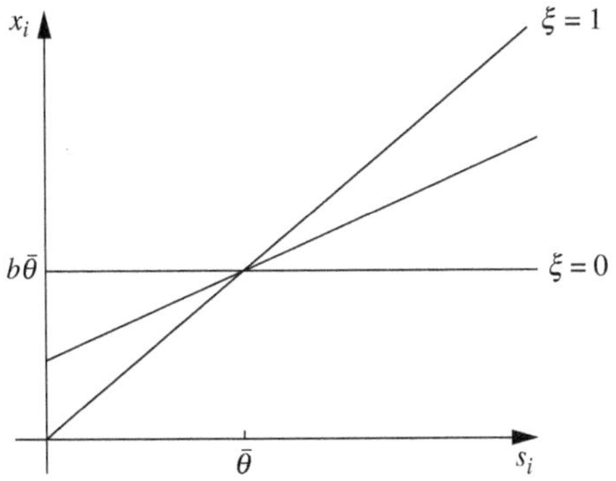

Figure 1.1. Equilibrium strategy of firm i for different values of ξ. The middle line corresponds to $\xi \in (0, 1)$.

by $X(\theta)$. When firms receive no information ($\xi = 0$), then $a = 0$ and production is constant at the level $b\bar{\theta}$; when firms receive perfect information ($\xi = 1$), then $X_i(s_i) = as_i$. As ξ varies from 0 to 1 the slope of the equilibrium strategy, a, increases from 0 to b (see figure 1.1).

When $\lambda = 0$ the equilibrium condition requires that $E[p \mid s_i] = 0$. Restricting our attention to symmetric equilibria, we get that $X(s_i) = s_i/\beta$ provided that $\xi > 0$. Indeed, note that

$$E[p \mid s_i] = E[\theta - \beta x \mid s_i] = E[\theta \mid s_i] - \beta E[X(\theta) \mid s_i] = 0,$$

and therefore

$$E[\theta \mid s_i] - \beta a(E[\theta \mid s_i] - \bar{\theta}) - \beta b\bar{\theta} = (1 - \beta a)E[\theta \mid s_i] + \beta\bar{\theta}(a - b) = 0,$$

which implies that $a = b = 1/\beta$. That is, the above formula is valid on letting $\lambda = 0$, since then $a = b = 1/\beta$. Note that, when the signals are informative ($\xi > 0$), the equilibrium strategies $X(s_i) = s_i/\beta$ do not depend on ξ, the precision of the information. If $\xi = 0$, signals are uninformative and $X(s_i) = \bar{\theta}/\beta$.

In summary, given $\lambda \geqslant 0$ and $\xi \in [0, 1]$ the equilibrium of the continuum economy is given by $X(s_i) = a(s_i - \bar{\theta}) + b\bar{\theta}$ with $a = \xi/(\lambda + \beta\xi)$ ($a = 0$ if $\lambda = \xi = 0$) and $b = 1/(\lambda + \beta)$.

It is worth noting that this equilibrium is the outcome of iterated elimination of strictly dominated strategies if and only if the ratio of the slopes of supply and demand is less than 1 ($\lambda\beta < 1$). This is the familiar cobweb stability condition (see Guesnerie 1992; Heinemann 2004). In this case the equilibrium is the outcome only of the rationality of the players and common knowledge about payoffs and distributions.[6]

Welfare. Assuming that all the firms produce the same quantity $x_i = x$, we have $\text{TS}(x; \theta) = \int_0^x P(z; \theta)\,\mathrm{d}z - C(x)$. Since $P(z; \theta) = \theta - \beta z$ and $C(x) = \frac{1}{2}\lambda x^2$,

[6] See section 10.4.1.1 for the concept of dominated strategy and dominance solvability in games.

we obtain that per capita total surplus with all firms producing output x is given by

$$\mathrm{TS} = \int_0^x (\theta - \beta z)\,\mathrm{d}z - \tfrac{1}{2}\lambda x^2 = \theta x - \left(\frac{\beta + \lambda}{2}\right)x^2.$$

It is immediate then that full-information first-best production is

$$X^{\mathrm{o}}(\theta) = \frac{\theta}{\lambda + \beta} = b\theta,$$

and it equals $X(\theta)$ only if $\xi = 1$ (perfect information) or if $\lambda = 0$ and $\xi > 0$ (constant returns to scale). As ξ goes from 0 to 1, a increases from 0 to b. For $\xi < 1$ and $\lambda > 0$ if θ is high (low) the market underproduces (overproduces) with respect to the full-information first-best. In the constant-returns-to-scale case, average production $X(\theta)$ is independent of the precision of information τ_ε (and of ξ) and the market produces the right amount. Expected total surplus (ETS) at the first-best is

$$\mathrm{ETS}^{\mathrm{o}} = \tfrac{1}{2}bE[\theta^2] = \tfrac{1}{2}b(\sigma_\theta^2 + \bar{\theta}^2).$$

The market ETS can be computed as the sum of per capita consumer surplus $\frac{1}{2}\beta E[(X(\theta))^2]$ and per capita (or firm) profits:

$$E[\pi_i] = \tfrac{1}{2}\lambda E[(X(s_i))^2] = \tfrac{1}{2}\lambda(a^2 \operatorname{var}[s_i] + b^2\bar{\theta}^2).$$

We find that $\mathrm{ETS} = \frac{1}{2}(a\sigma_\theta^2 + b\bar{\theta}^2)$ and therefore the welfare loss $\mathrm{WL} \equiv \mathrm{ETS}^{\mathrm{o}} - \mathrm{ETS}$ equals $\frac{1}{2}(b - a)\sigma_\theta^2$. (See exercise 1.1 for an alternative derivation.)

How does ETS change with variations in the precision of information τ_ε and in the basic uncertainty of demand σ_θ^2?

One would hope that improvements in the precision of information (τ_ε) would increase ETS (reducing the welfare loss). This is indeed the case since ETS increases with a, and a is in turn increasing with τ_ε. Per capita expected consumer surplus (ECS) increases with τ_ε since consumer surplus is a convex function of average output ($\mathrm{CS} = \frac{1}{2}\beta x^2$) and increases in ξ increase the slope of $X(\cdot)$ and make it more variable. It can be checked that expected profits may increase or decrease with τ_ε. Increasing τ_ε increases the sensitivity of output to the signal received by the firm, and this tends to increase expected profits, but it also decreases the variance of the signal, and this tends to depress expected profits. (A fuller explanation of the drivers of the comparative statics of expected profits is given in section 1.4.3.) However, the effect on the welfare of the consumers always dominates the profit effect in the total surplus computation.

With $\lambda > 0$, increasing the basic uncertainty of demand increases ETS (by increasing both ECS and expected profits) but $\mathrm{ETS}^{\mathrm{o}}$ increases by more and the welfare loss increases with[7] σ_θ^2; increasing the precision of information

[7] To show the result notice that

$$\frac{\partial\,\mathrm{WL}}{\partial\sigma_\theta^2} = \frac{1}{2b}(b^2 - a^2).$$

increases ETS and ETS^o stays constant and, therefore the welfare loss decreases with τ_ε. With $\lambda = 0$, WL $= 0$ provided that $\tau_\varepsilon > 0$ (but with $\tau_\varepsilon = 0$, WL increases with σ_θ^2).

Similar results hold when we replace quadratic costs by capacity limits. Indeed, a capacity limit can be interpreted as a very steep marginal cost schedule. This can be formally checked in a model with constant marginal costs and capacity limits with a finite support information structure (see exercise 1.2). The qualitative properties of the capacity model are identical to those of the model analyzed in this section.

1.2.4.2 Isoelastic-Lognormal Model

Let $p = e^\theta x^{-\beta}$, $\beta > 0$, and the information structure be exactly as in section 1.2.4.1, where θ and the error terms of the signals are jointly normally distributed. Firms have constant elasticity cost functions given by

$$C(x_i) = (1+\lambda)^{-1} x_i^{1+\lambda}, \quad \lambda \geqslant 0.$$

We find an equilibrium in log-linear strategies. This specification avoids the unpalatable feature of the linear-normal model where outputs and prices may become negative.

The FOC for profit maximization yields $E[p \mid s_i] = x_i^\lambda$ and, as in the general model, the equilibrium must be symmetric when the cost function is strictly convex (i.e., for $\lambda > 0$). It can be easily checked that there is a unique symmetric equilibrium in which the price is a log-linear function of θ. For this we use the fact that, if z is normally distributed $N(\mu, \sigma^2)$ and r is a constant, then $E[e^{rz}] = e^{r\mu + r^2\sigma^2/2}$ (see section 10.2.4). Postulate an equilibrium of the form $X(s_i) = e^{as_i + b}$. Using our convention about the average of a continuum of independent random variables (which implies that $\int_0^1 e^{\varepsilon_i}\, di = \int_0^1 E[e^{\varepsilon_i}]\, di$) and the properties of lognormal distributions, namely that if $\varepsilon_i \sim N(0, \sigma_\varepsilon^2)$, then $E[e^{\varepsilon_i}] = e^{\sigma_\varepsilon^2/2}$, we obtain

$$\int_0^1 e^{s_i}\, di = \int_0^1 e^{\theta+\varepsilon_i} = e^\theta \int_0^1 e^{\varepsilon_i}\, di = e^\theta e^{\sigma_\varepsilon^2/2} \quad \text{(a.s.)}.$$

This implies that

$$\tilde{X}(\theta) = \int_0^1 X(s_i)\, di = \int_0^1 e^{as_i+b}\, di = e^{a\theta + b + a^2\sigma_\varepsilon^2/2},$$

$$p = e^{(1-\beta a)\theta - \beta(b + a^2\sigma_\varepsilon^2/2)}.$$

From the FOC $E[p \mid s_i] = x^\lambda$ we obtain

$$E[\exp\{(1-\beta a)\theta - \beta(b + \tfrac{1}{2}a^2\sigma_\varepsilon^2)\} \mid s_i] = e^{\lambda a s_i + \lambda b}.$$

Given that $\theta \mid s_i \sim N(\bar{\theta}(1-\xi) + \xi s_i, \sigma_\theta^2(1-\xi))$, we have that the left-hand side

---

Therefore, $\partial\, \mathrm{WL}/\partial\sigma_\theta^2 > 0$ if and only if $b > a$. This is the case if $\lambda > 0$ and $\xi < 1$ or if $\lambda = 0$ and $\xi = 0$ (no information).

equals

$$\exp\{(1-\beta a)(\bar{\theta}(1-\xi)+\xi s_i)+\tfrac{1}{2}(1-\beta a)^2(1-\xi)\sigma_\theta^2-\beta(b+\tfrac{1}{2}a^2\sigma_\varepsilon^2)\}.$$

By identifying coefficients on s_i we obtain $a = \xi/(\lambda+\beta\xi)$. Doing the same with the constant term, substituting for the value of a, and using the fact that $\xi = \tau_\varepsilon/(\tau_\varepsilon+\tau_\theta) = \sigma_\theta^2/(\sigma_\theta^2+\sigma_\varepsilon^2)$ and therefore $\sigma_\varepsilon^2 = ((1-\xi)/\xi)\sigma_\theta^2$, and simplifying, we obtain

$$b = \frac{1-\xi}{\lambda+\beta}\left[\left(\frac{\lambda}{\lambda+\beta\xi}\right)\bar{\theta}+\left(\frac{\sigma_\theta^2}{2(\lambda+\beta\xi)^2}\right)[\lambda^2-\beta\xi]\right].$$

In conclusion, the equilibrium is given by

$$X(s_i) = \mathrm{e}^{as_i+b},$$

where

$$a = \frac{\xi}{\lambda+\beta\xi} \quad \text{and} \quad b = \frac{1-\xi}{\lambda+\beta}\left(\frac{\lambda}{\lambda+\beta\xi}\bar{\theta}+\frac{\lambda^2-\beta\xi}{(\lambda+\beta\xi)^2}\frac{\sigma_\theta^2}{2}\right).$$

Note that the full-information output (corresponding to the case $\xi = 1$ and $\sigma_\varepsilon^2 = 0$) is $X^{\mathrm{o}}(\theta) = \mathrm{e}^{\theta/(\lambda+\beta)}$.

The output of a firm is more sensitive to its signal the better the information is (a increases and b decreases with ξ) and $E[\pi_i]$ increase or decrease with ξ depending on whether demand is elastic or inelastic (β smaller or larger than 1). The same forces as in the linear-normal model are present here. Profits are a convex function of output; increasing ξ increases the responsiveness of output to the signal, this induces more output variation and is good for expected profits. However, as in section 1.2.3, the decreased variance of the signal works in the opposite direction, decreasing expected profits. With constant returns to scale the (full-information) competitive outcome is obtained and then $E[\pi_i]$ are independent of ξ.

1.2.5 Summary

The main learning points of the section are the following.

- A large market, even inducing price-taking behavior, may fail to be first-best efficient because of a lack of information aggregation.
- This is the case for a large Cournot market with common-value uncertainty and decreasing returns because firms with different demand assessments will not produce at the same marginal cost.
- With constant returns to scale a large Cournot market will aggregate information under regularity conditions. In this case the market attains the first-best aggregate output and this is all that matters for welfare purposes.

1.3 Welfare in Large Cournot Markets with Asymmetric Information

The first-best full-information outcome is too stringent a benchmark of comparison for the market outcome. The reason goes back to the idea of Hayek that the private information of agents may not be easily communicable and therefore that there is no omniscient center that knows the realization of the uncertainty θ. The welfare benchmark must therefore be a decentralized one where agents use strategies which are measurable in their information. This is the approach pioneered in Vives (1988). In our market we will say that an allocation is *team-efficient* if it maximizes expected total surplus with decentralized strategies. A team is a group of people with a common objective. Team allocations with private information have been studied by Radner (1962). This will be equivalent to the solution to the problem of a planner who wants to maximize expected total surplus and can control the action (strategy) of an agent but can make it contingent only on the private information of the agent and not on the information of other agents.

We show below that the allocation of a price-taking equilibrium in a Cournot market is team-efficient, where each firm follows a production rule, contingent on its private information, with the common objective of maximizing expected total surplus. That is, the price-taking market solves the team problem with expected total surplus as an objective function. This provides a general welfare characterization of price-taking equilibrium in a Cournot market with private information allowing for a general information structure. A price-taking equilibrium obtains in the case of a continuum of firms as in section 1.2.

Consider an n-firm Cournot market. Firm i, $i = 1, \dots, n$, has smooth convex costs, $C(x_i; \theta_i)$, where x_i is its output. Inverse demand is given by $P(x; \theta_0)$, a smooth and downward-sloping function of total output $x = \sum_{j=1}^{n} x_j$. Suppose that firm i receives a private signal vector s_i about the (potentially) random parameters (θ_0, θ_i). At a price-taking Bayesian equilibrium, firm i maximizes its expected profits (conditional on receiving signal s_i):

$$E[\pi_i \mid s_i] = E[P(x; \theta_0) \mid s_i]x_i - E[C(x_i; \theta_i) \mid s_i],$$

without taking into account the influence of its output on the market price $P(x; \theta_0)$. That is, for an interior equilibrium we find that (for almost all s_i) the expected price equals the expected marginal cost:

$$E[P(x; \theta_0) \mid s_i] = E[\mathrm{MC}(x_i; \theta_i) \mid s_i].$$

The following result provides an analogue to the First Welfare Theorem for price-taking Bayesian equilibria. We say that firms use decentralized strategies if each firm can choose its output as a function only of its own signal.

Proposition 1.2 (Vives 1988). *In a smooth Cournot private-information environment, price-taking Bayesian equilibria maximize expected total surplus (ETS) subject to the use of decentralized production strategies.*

Proof. The maximization of ETS subject to decentralized production strategies is the problem of a team whose members have as common objective

$$\mathrm{ETS} = E\left[\int_0^x P(z;\theta_0)\,\mathrm{d}z - \sum_{j=1}^{n} C(X_j(s_j);\theta_j)\right],$$

with strategies $X_j(s_j)$, $j = 1,\dots,n$, where $x = \sum_{j=1}^{n} X_j(s_j)$. Under our assumptions the optimal decision rules are determined (for interior solutions) by the set of FOCs $E[\partial TS/\partial x_i \mid s_i] = 0$ or, equivalently, $E[P(x;\theta_0) \mid s_i] = E[\mathrm{MC}(x_i;\theta_i) \mid s_i]$. Indeed, a set of decision rules are optimal if and only if they are person-by-person optimal given that the team function is concave and differentiable (Radner 1962, theorem 1). The conditions are fulfilled in our case. Now, price-taking firm i will maximize

$$E[\pi_i \mid s_i] = E[P(x;\theta_0) \mid s_i]x_i - E[C(x_i;\theta_i) \mid s_i],$$

yielding an FOC,

$$E[P(x;\theta_0) \mid s_i] = E[\mathrm{MC}(x_i;\theta_i) \mid s_i].$$

These conditions are sufficient given our assumptions and therefore the solutions to both problems coincide. □

The result also applies to our continuum economy. Consider the payoff for player $i \in [0,1]$, $\pi_i = P(x;\theta)x_i - C_i(x_i)$, where $P(\,\cdot\,;\theta)$ is smooth and downward sloping and $C_i(\,\cdot\,)$ is smooth and strictly convex. We have that $\mathrm{TS} = \int_0^x P(z;\theta)\,\mathrm{d}z - \int_0^1 C_i(x_i)\,\mathrm{d}i$, where $x = \int_0^1 x_i\,\mathrm{d}i$. The team problem is to find strategies $(X_i(\,\cdot\,))_{i\in[0,1]}$, with bounded means $E[X_i(s_i) \mid \theta] < \infty$ and uniformly bounded variances $\mathrm{var}[X_i(s_i) \mid \theta]$ across players, that maximize ETS. We have that

$$\int_0^1 X_i(s_i)\,\mathrm{d}i = \int_0^1 E[X_i(s_i) \mid \theta]\,\mathrm{d}i \equiv \tilde{X}(\theta)$$

and

$$\mathrm{ETS} = E\left[\int_0^{\tilde{X}(\theta)} P(z;\theta)\,\mathrm{d}z - \int_0^1 C_i(X_i(s_i))\,\mathrm{d}i\right].$$

The Bayesian equilibrium implements the team-efficient solution.

Remark 1.2. The fact that equilibria can also be obtained as the outcome of the optimization of a strictly concave welfare function can be used to show uniqueness of the equilibrium. For example, if the welfare function is quadratic and strictly concave, as is TS in the linear-normal model of section 1.2.4.1, the team solution is unique and therefore the Bayesian equilibrium is also unique (in the class of strategies with bounded means and uniformly bounded variances across players). The insight is more general and applies whenever the outcome of a game can be replicated optimizing an appropriate potential function. We will use it to show uniqueness of a Bayesian equilibrium in a game with a finite number of players in chapter 2 (see proposition 2.1 and its proof).

Remark 1.3. Price-taking Bayesian equilibria will differ from Bayesian Cournot equilibria in a market with a finite number of firms. This is so because at a Bayesian Cournot equilibrium a firms takes into account the impact of its output on the market price. However, as the economy increases in size (increasing at the same time the number of firms and consumers, perhaps because of lowering of entry costs) Bayesian Cournot equilibria converge to price-taking Bayesian equilibria, as we will see in section 2.2. At the limit economy with a continuum of firms they coincide. Proposition 1.2 applies similarly to the Bayesian equilibrium of the limit continuum economy. A price-taking Bayesian equilibrium is efficient as long as only decentralized strategies can be used.

Remark 1.4. According to proposition 1.2, in a Cournot environment there is no room for a planner to improve on market performance taking as given decentralized decision making. This contrasts with environments where agents can condition on prices and therefore there are potential informational externalities with prices as a public signal. Chapter 3 will deal with the welfare analysis of such models in the rational expectations tradition.

In summary, we have claimed that an appropriate welfare benchmark for our incomplete-information economy is team efficiency, where expected total surplus is maximized subject to the use of decentralized strategies, and we have shown that a price-taking equilibrium is team-efficient. This means in particular that a *large* Cournot market, where firms are effectively price takers, is team-efficient.

1.4 Information Aggregation in Smooth Large Markets

A large market need not aggregate information, that is, it need not replicate the shared-information outcome, as we have seen in the Cournot case in section 1.2. In fact, we will see in this section that a large market aggregates information only in very particular circumstances other than the independent-values case. Furthermore, large markets may be competitive (price-taking) or monopolistically competitive. In the latter case, each firm produces a differentiated commodity, is negligible in the sense that its actions alone do not influence the profits of any other firm, and has some monopoly power (this is the Chamberlinian large group case).[8] The monopolistically competitive market is not efficient even with complete information. That is, even if the market were to aggregate information, there would be a welfare loss in relation to the full-information first-best allocation. A question arises about the value of information in this situation.

In this section we present a quadratic payoff game for which monopolistic competition is a leading example. The monopolistically competitive market

[8] See Vives (1990 and chapter 6 in 1999).

will be a large market linear-quadratic model with normally distributed random variables that encompasses Cournot or Bertrand competition with product differentiation and uncertainty of common- or private-value type.

More generally, consider a game among a continuum of players where each player has a (symmetric) smooth payoff function $\pi(y_i, \tilde{y}; \theta_i)$ with y_i the action of player i, $\tilde{y}$ a vector of statistics (e.g., mean and variance) that characterizes the distribution of the actions of players, and θ_i a possibly idiosyncratic payoff-relevant random parameter. Suppose that player i receives a signal s_i about the parameter θ_i. As before a strategy for player i is a measurable function $Y_i(\cdot)$ from the signal space to the action space of the player. A set of strategies $(Y_i(\cdot))_{i\in[0,1]}$ forms a Bayesian equilibrium if for any player (almost surely)

$$Y_i(s_i) \in \arg\max_{z_i} E[\pi(z_i, \tilde{y}; \theta_i) \mid s_i],$$

where $\tilde{y}$ is the vector of statistics that characterizes the equilibrium distribution of the actions of players. As in section 1.2 player i when optimizing takes as given the equilibrium statistics since his action cannot influence them. A linear-quadratic-Gaussian specification of the game is presented in the following section. We in turn analyze information aggregation and perform a welfare analysis.

1.4.1 A Linear-Quadratic-Gaussian Model

Consider a quadratic profit function model with a continuum of players. The payoff to player i is

$$\pi(y_i, y; \theta_i) = \theta_i y_i - \tfrac{1}{2}\omega_1 y_i^2 - \omega_2 y y_i,$$

where $(-\partial^2\pi/(\partial y_i)^2) = \omega_1 > 0$ ensures strict concavity of π with respect to the firm's action y_i (in the real line), and where $y = \int_0^1 y_j \, \mathrm{d}j$ denotes the average action. Actions are strategic complements (substitutes) if $\partial^2\pi/\partial y_i \partial y = -\omega_2 > (<) \; 0$.[9] Under complete information the best response of a player to the aggregate action y is

$$y_i = \frac{\theta_i - \omega_2 y}{\omega_1}.$$

Since the slope of the best response is

$$\kappa \equiv \frac{\partial^2\pi/\partial y_i \partial y}{-\partial^2\pi/(\partial y_i)^2} = -\frac{\omega_2}{\omega_1},$$

this quotient provides a natural measure of the degree of strategic complementarity or substitutability. A game is of strategic complementarities if the best response for each player increases with the actions of rivals. We assume that the slope $\kappa < 1$ and therefore $\omega_1 + \omega_2 > 0$ always. This allows for games of strategic substitutability and of strategic complementarities with a bounded degree of complementarity. An example of a strategic complementarity ($\omega_2 < 0$) game is

[9] Section 10.4.1.2 provides a brief introduction to games of strategic complementarities.

provided by an adoption externalities or investment complementarities game in which y_i is the adoption or investment effort with return $(\theta_i - \omega_2 y)y_i$ and cost $\frac{1}{2}\omega_1 y_i^2$.[10] The return to adoption or investment increases with the aggregate effort y.

We can obtain Bertrand and Cournot competition, with linear demands and constant unit costs (equal to zero without loss of generality), by choosing parameters appropriately. The case of Cournot competition with quadratic production costs can also be accommodated. The payoffs are in line with the following demand system with random intercepts (x and p are, respectively, average quantity and price):

$$p_i = \alpha_i - (1-\delta)x_i - \delta x \quad \text{with } \delta \in [0,1],$$
$$x_i = \beta_i - (1+\gamma)p_i + \gamma p \quad \text{with } \gamma \geqslant 0,$$

where (p_i, x_i) is the price–output pair of firm i. We can obtain the second equation by inverting the first and letting $\beta_i = (\alpha_i - \delta\tilde{\alpha})/(1-\delta)$ and $\gamma = \delta/(1-\delta)$ with $\tilde{\alpha} = \int_0^1 \alpha_i \, di$. When $\delta = 0$, the firms are isolated monopolies, and when $\delta = 1$, they are perfect competitors because then the product is homogeneous and firms are price takers. The parameter δ represents the degree of product differentiation and when $0 < \delta < 1$ the market is monopolistically competitive. In the quantity competition (Cournot) case, let $\theta_i = \alpha_i$, $\frac{1}{2}\omega_1 = 1 - \delta$, and $\omega_2 = \delta$. In the price competition (Bertrand) case, let $\theta_i = \beta_i$, $\frac{1}{2}\omega_1 = 1 + \gamma$, and $\omega_2 = -\gamma$. In the Cournot case with homogeneous product and increasing marginal costs (as in section 1.2) we set $\omega_1 = \lambda$, $\omega_2 = \beta$, and $\theta_i = \theta$ to obtain $\pi_i = (\theta - \beta x)x_i - \frac{1}{2}\lambda x_i^2$. Note that in the Cournot (Bertrand) $\omega_2 > 0$ ($\omega_2 < 0$) case actions are strategic substitutes (complements).

Assume that the information structure is symmetric and given as follows.[11] Each pair of parameters (θ_i, θ_j) is jointly normally distributed with $E[\theta_i] = \bar{\theta}$, $\operatorname{var}[\theta_i] = \sigma_\theta^2$, and $\operatorname{cov}[\theta_i, \theta_j] = \varsigma\sigma_\theta^2$ for $j \neq i$, $0 \leqslant \varsigma \leqslant 1$. Agent i receives a signal $s_i = \theta_i + \varepsilon_i$, where $\theta_i \sim N(\bar{\theta}, \sigma_\theta^2)$, $\varepsilon_i \sim N(0, \sigma_\varepsilon^2)$, and $\operatorname{cov}[\varepsilon_i, \varepsilon_j] = 0$ for $j \neq i$. The error terms of the signals are also independent of the θ parameter. The precision of signal s_i is given by $\tau_{\varepsilon_i} = (\sigma_\varepsilon^2)^{-1}$. As before we let $\xi = \tau_\varepsilon/(\tau_\theta + \tau_\varepsilon)$.

Our information structure encompasses the cases of "common value" and of "private values." For $\varsigma = 1$ the θ parameters are perfectly correlated and we are in a *common-values* model. When signals are perfect, $\sigma_{\varepsilon_i}^2 = 0$ for all i, and $0 < \varsigma < 1$, we will say we are in a *private-values* model. Agents receive idiosyncratic shocks, which are imperfectly correlated, and each agent observes his shock with no measurement error. When $\varsigma = 0$, the parameters are independent, and we are in an *independent-values* model.

It is not difficult to see (see section 10.2.3) that

$$E[\theta_i \mid s_i] = \xi s_i + (1-\xi)\bar{\theta} \quad \text{and} \quad E[s_j \mid s_i] = E[\theta_j \mid s_i] = \xi\varsigma s_i + (1 - \xi\varsigma)\bar{\theta}.$$

---

[10] Models in this vein have been presented by, among many others, Diamond (1982), Bryant (1983), Dybvig and Spatt (1983), and Matsuyama (1995).

[11] See section 10.2.3 for results on the family of information structures to which the one presented here belongs.

When signals are perfect, $\xi = 1$, $E[\theta_i \mid s_i] = s_i$, and $E[\theta_j \mid s_i] = \varsigma s_i + (1-\varsigma)\bar{\theta}$. When they are not informative, $\xi = 0$ and $E[\theta_i \mid s_i] = E[\theta_j \mid s_i] = \bar{\theta}$.

We can also derive the relationship between θ_i, s_i, and the average parameter $\tilde{\theta} = \int_0^1 \theta_j \, dj$. The average parameter $\tilde{\theta}$ is normally distributed with mean $\bar{\theta}$ and variance equal to $\varsigma\sigma_\theta^2$. This is in accordance with the finite-dimensional analogue for the average of a collection of symmetrically correlated random variables (see section 10.2.3). We have that $E[\theta_i \mid \tilde{\theta}] = \tilde{\theta}$, $E[\tilde{\theta} \mid \theta_i] = E[\theta_j \mid \theta_i] = \varsigma\theta_i + (1-\varsigma)\bar{\theta}$, $E[\tilde{\theta} \mid s_i] = E[\theta_j \mid s_i]$, and

$$E[\theta_i \mid \tilde{\theta}, s_i] = (1-d)\tilde{\theta} + ds_i,$$

where $d = (\sigma_\theta^2(1-\varsigma))/(\sigma_\theta^2(1-\varsigma) + \sigma_\varepsilon^2) = (\tau_\varepsilon(1-\varsigma))/(\tau_\varepsilon(1-\varsigma) + \tau_\theta) = (1-\varsigma)/(\xi^{-1}-\varsigma)$. If signals are perfect, then $d = 1$ and $E[\theta_i \mid \tilde{\theta}, s_i] = s_i$. If signals are useless or correlation is perfect ($\varsigma = 1$), then $d = 0$ and $E[\theta_i \mid \tilde{\theta}, s_i] = \tilde{\theta}$. If both signals and correlation are perfect, then $E[\theta_i \mid \tilde{\theta}, s_i] = \tilde{\theta} = s_i$ (a.s.).

There is a unique symmetric Bayesian equilibrium in linear strategies in the incomplete-information game. This is also the case if agents share information. Observe that $\tilde{s} = \int_0^1 \theta_i \, di + \int_0^1 \varepsilon_i \, di = \tilde{\theta}$, since $\int_0^1 \varepsilon_i \, di = 0$ according to our convention on the average of i.i.d. random variables as the error terms ε_i are uncorrelated and have mean zero. Agents who share information need only know the average signal $\tilde{s}$ (on top of their signal). Indeed, given the information structure and linear equilibrium, $(s_i, \tilde{s})$ is a sufficient statistic[12] in the estimation of θ_i by agent i, that is, to estimate θ_i with the pooled information available, firm i need only look at $(s_i, \tilde{s})$. Furthermore, with $\tilde{s}$ ($= \tilde{\theta}$) the firm can predict with certainty the aggregate action y since y depends only on $\tilde{\theta}$ in a linear equilibrium. The following proposition characterizes the equilibrium. The proof is in the appendix.

Proposition 1.3 (Vives 1990). *There is a unique symmetric linear Bayesian equilibrium in the case of both private and shared information. The equilibrium strategy of agent i in the private-information case is given by $Y(s_i) = a(s_i - \bar{\theta}) + b\bar{\theta}$, where $a = \xi/(\omega_1 + \omega_2\varsigma\xi)$, $\xi = \tau_\varepsilon/(\tau_\varepsilon + \tau_\theta)$, and $b = 1/(\omega_1 + \omega_2)$. In the shared-information case, it is given by $Z(s_i, \tilde{\theta}) = \hat{a}(s_i - \tilde{\theta}) + b\tilde{\theta}$, where $\hat{a} = d/\omega_1$ and $d = (1-\varsigma)/(\xi^{-1} - \varsigma)$.*

Note that $\omega_1 + \omega_2\varsigma\xi > 0$ since $\omega_1 > 0$, $\omega_1 + \omega_2 > 0$, and $0 < \varsigma\xi < 1$. Therefore, a and $\hat{a}$ are nonnegative and b is positive.

Remark 1.5. As in sections 1.2.1 and 1.3 there cannot be asymmetric equilibria as long as we restrict our attention to equilibria with bounded means and uniformly bounded variances (across players). It can be checked that the equilibrium can be obtained by optimizing a strictly concave potential (or team) function which delivers a unique solution.

---

[12] See section 10.1.4 for the statistical concept of sufficiency. Intuitively, an aggregate signal about a parameter is a sufficient statistic for the information available if the posterior distribution given the aggregate signal is the same as the one given all the individual signals.

1.4.2 When Does a Large Market Aggregate Information?

The linear-quadratic model has a certainty-equivalence property. The expected value of an individual (as well as average) action, with either pooling or not pooling of information, equals $b\bar{\theta}$, which is the action agents would choose if they did not have any information. However, equilibria are not independent of pooling arrangements except in particular circumstances. The exceptions are if $a = \hat{a}$ and $\tilde{\theta} = \bar{\theta}$ (a.s.) or if $b = a = \hat{a}$. The first case obtains if there is no correlation between parameters, $\varsigma = 0$ (independent values) and the second obtains if $\omega_1(1-\xi) = \omega_2\xi(1-\varsigma)$. This latter equality obviously holds in the perfect-information case, $\varsigma = \xi = 1$. It cannot hold if $\omega_2 < 0$ (strategic complements), or for ω_1 and ω_2 different from zero, in the common-value case ($\varsigma = 1$, $\xi \in (0,1)$), or in the private values case ($\xi = 1$, $\varsigma \in (0,1)$).

In summary, the large market aggregates information if and only if $\varsigma(\omega_1(1-\xi) - \omega_2\xi(1-\varsigma)) = 0$.

In line with our previous analysis in the common-value case (section 1.2.1), the equality holds with constant marginal costs, $\omega_1 = \lambda = 0$ (Palfrey 1985), but it does not hold with strictly convex costs, $\lambda > 0$, provided signals are not perfect, $\xi < 1$ (Vives 1988). With independent values the information aggregation result should not be surprising because in the limit there is no aggregate uncertainty. In equilibrium a firm can predict with certainty the average action in the market. In fact, what seems surprising is that there are *any* circumstances under which information aggregation obtains when aggregate uncertainty (coupled with imperfect signals) remains in the limit.

The knife-edge information aggregation result of the common-value case with constant marginal costs extends to other parameter configurations along the curve $\omega_1(1-\xi) - \omega_2\xi(1-\varsigma) = 0$. In general, in our linear-normal model the equilibrium strategy of firm i in the shared-information regime depends both on its private signal s_i and on the average signal, which in the limit equals the average parameter: $\tilde{s} = \tilde{\theta}$. Parameter configurations along the line $\omega_1(1-\xi) - \omega_2\xi(1-\varsigma) = 0$ have the property that the equilibrium strategy does not depend on $\tilde{\theta}$ in the limit. This may seem surprising, since when $\varsigma > 0$ the average market output $\tilde{y}$ is random and firms can predict it exactly knowing the average parameter $\tilde{\theta}$. How can an agent not respond to the information contained in $\tilde{\theta}$? Notice first that $\tilde{\theta}$ gives information about the average action $Y(\tilde{\theta})$ and about θ_i, since the θ_i parameters are correlated. In the Cournot model (with actions being strategic substitutes) a high $\tilde{\theta}$ is good news for agent i since this means that θ_i is likely to be high but it is bad news for agent i at the same time since it means that $Y(\tilde{\theta})$ is also likely to be high, which tends to lower the payoff of the agent. For the specific parameter configurations $\omega_1(1-\xi) - \omega_2\xi(1-\varsigma) = 0$ it so happens that the two forces exactly balance out and it is optimal not to respond to changes in $\tilde{\theta}$. It is worth noting, however, that this could not happen if the actions of the firms were strategic complements $\omega_2 < 0$ (say, prices in a differentiated product market with constant marginal costs) since then a low

$\tilde{\theta}$ is bad news on two counts: it means that the demand intercept β_i and the average price are likely to be low and then the agent wants to set a low price. In this situation it is never optimal not to respond to $\tilde{\theta}$.

In summary, a large smooth market aggregates information only in particular circumstances. An important example is when types are independent because then there is no aggregate uncertainty. Another relevant case is when there is Cournot competition, common-value uncertainty, and constant returns. In general, however, we should not expect to have information aggregation when there is aggregate uncertainty in a smooth market.

1.4.3 Welfare Analysis and the Value of Information

Suppose that we are in the (usual) case that the market does not aggregate information. Will more precise private information for all players always be to the benefit of each one of them? The answer turns out to depend on whether competition is of the strategic substitutes or complements type. Let us consider the common-value case.

In the common-value case expected profits increase with a uniform increase in the precision of the signal τ_ε with strategic complements (Bertrand case) and may increase or decrease with τ_ε with strategic substitutes (Cournot case). In any case expected profits increase with prior uncertainty σ_θ^2 (Vives (1990) and exercise 1.4). However, expected profits always increase with a uniform increase in the precision of the signals for a given signal correlation ($\mathrm{cov}[s_i, s_j]/\mathrm{var}[s_i]$), and for given signal precisions, expected profits increase (decrease) with increased correlation of signals with strategic complements (substitutes) (see section 8.3.1 in Vives 1999). With strategic complements (substitutes) an increased (decreased) signal correlation is good for expected profits. The reason is that with strategic complements (substitutes) best responses are upward (downward) sloping. Once the correlation of the signals received by players is controlled for, increasing the precision of signals is always good.

The consequences for welfare in the monopolistic competition model are as follows. Expected consumer and total surplus increase (decrease) with the precision of private information in the Cournot (Bertrand) case. The intuition for these results is derived from the form of the consumer surplus function. Expected consumer surplus as a function of quantities is a convex combination of the variance of individual and average output, and expected consumer surplus as a function of prices increases with the variance of individual prices and decreases with the variance of the average price and with the covariance of the demand shock and the individual price. (See exercise 1.4.)

It is worth noting again that, in contrast to the competitive economy in section 1.2, even if firms were to have complete information there would be a welfare loss in the market due to monopolistic behavior. Furthermore, under incomplete information, the monopolistically competitive market is not team-efficient. That is, the market allocation does not maximize expected total surplus subject to decentralized strategies since the team-efficient allocation would imply that expected prices are equal to marginal costs.

Angeletos and Pavan (2007a) provide a characterization of the equilibrium and efficient use of information as well as the social value of information in a closely related model that generalizes the quadratic payoff structure in the common-value case including the dispersion (standard deviation) of the actions of the players. This allows encompassing other applications such as beauty contest games where the payoff to a player depends also on the distance between the action of the player and the actions of other players (Morris and Shin 2002). Angeletos and Pavan find that stronger complementarity increases the sensitivity of equilibrium actions to public information, raising aggregate volatility while stronger substitutability increases the sensitivity to private information, raising the cross-sectional dispersion of actions.

Consider a symmetric game with a continuum of players in which the payoff to player i is $\pi(y_i, y, \sigma_y; \theta)$ with y_i his action, $y = \int_0^1 y_i \, di$ the average action, $\sigma_y = (\int_0^1 (y_i - y)^2 \, di)^{1/2}$ the standard deviation of the action distribution, and θ a common payoff-relevant random parameter. Assume that $\pi(y_i, y, \sigma_y; \theta) = u(y_i, y; \theta) + \frac{1}{2}\nu\sigma_y^2$ with u quadratic and

$$\frac{\partial^2 u}{(\partial y_i)^2} < 0, \qquad \frac{\partial^2 u}{(\partial y_i)^2} + 2\frac{\partial^2 u}{\partial y_i \partial y} + \frac{\partial^2 u}{(\partial y)^2} < 0, \qquad \frac{\partial^2 u}{(\partial y_i)^2} + \nu < 0$$

to ensure global concavity (note that $\nu = \partial^2\pi/(\partial\sigma_y)^2$). It is also assumed that the slope of the best response of a player is less than 1:

$$\kappa \equiv \frac{\partial^2\pi/\partial y_i \partial y}{-\partial^2\pi/(\partial y_i)^2} < 1.$$

Each player receives a private and a public signal about θ and all variables are jointly normally distributed.

Angeletos and Pavan characterize the linear equilibrium of the game. The equilibrium can be shown to be unique as in proposition 1.3 and remark 1.5.[13] They show that the equilibrium strategy is a convex combination of the expectation of the full-information equilibrium allocation and the expectation of aggregate activity (both conditional on the information set of a player) where the weight given to the latter is precisely κ. This is called the "equilibrium degree of coordination" by Angeletos and Pavan but we will call it the degree of complementarity. When $\kappa = 0$ the equilibrium strategy is just the best predictor of the full-information equilibrium allocation. This means that the weights, respectively, to public and private information, in the equilibrium strategy are just the Bayesian weights. When $\kappa > 0$ there is strategic complementarity and players then weigh more public information, and when $\kappa < 0$ there is strategic substitutability and players then weigh less public information. The reason is that, with strategic complementarity, when a player wants to align his action with the average action, to predict the average action it is better to weigh more

[13] In the paper it is claimed to be the unique one, at least if $\kappa \in (-1, 1)$.

public information, while, with strategic substitutability, when a player wants to differentiate his action from the average action, it is better to weigh more private information. An increase in κ decreases the dispersion of equilibrium activity ($\mathrm{d}\,\mathrm{var}[y_i - y]/\mathrm{d}\kappa < 0$) and increases the nonfundamental volatility as measured by $\mathrm{d}\,\mathrm{var}[y - y^{\mathrm{f}}]/\mathrm{d}\kappa > 0$, where y^{f} is the full-information equilibrium allocation.

Angeletos and Pavan also perform a welfare analysis using team efficiency as a benchmark. This is defined in relation to the aggregate welfare of the players in the game. An allocation is then team-efficient if it maximizes the expected utility of a representative player using a (symmetric) decentralized strategy. We introduced this benchmark in section 1.3 using as team function total surplus in a partial equilibrium market. Both definitions are closely connected. Indeed, with the present definition this would imply, in the context of the competitive linear-normal economy of section 1.2.4.1, for example, to take consumers with quasilinear quadratic preferences as players who at the same time own the firms. We would then see that the price-taking Bayesian allocation is also team-efficient under the present definition. At the team-efficient solution both payoff externalities and the efficient use of information, with no communication, are taken into account. A team-efficient allocation is then uniquely characterized by a convex combination of the expectation of the (full-information) first-best allocation and the expectation of aggregate activity (both conditional on the information set of a player) where the weight given to the latter is

$$\kappa^{\mathrm{e}} \equiv 1 - \frac{\partial^2\pi/(\partial y_i)^2 + 2(\partial^2\pi/\partial y_i\partial y) + \partial^2\pi/(\partial y)^2}{\partial^2\pi/(\partial y_i)^2 + \partial^2\pi/(\partial\sigma_y)^2}.$$

In the quadratic environment it then follows that the efficient allocation for the original game can be replicated by the equilibrium of a fictitious game with the same information structure, in which the full-information equilibrium equals the first-best allocation of the original economy and where the degree of complementarity is precisely κ^{e}. This is the fictitious degree of complementarity that guarantees efficiency under incomplete information once we have efficiency under complete information. Some interesting results follow.

In an efficient economy (that is, one which is efficient under complete information and for which $\kappa = \kappa^{\mathrm{e}}$), the social value of public versus private information increases with κ (we have that $(\partial E[\pi]/\partial\tau_\eta)/(\partial E[\pi]/\partial\tau_\varepsilon) = \tau_\varepsilon/(1-\kappa)\tau_\eta$, where τ_ε (τ_η) is the precision of the private (public) information).

If we take an economy which is efficient under complete information, then when $\kappa > \kappa^{\mathrm{e}}$ ($\kappa < \kappa^{\mathrm{e}}$) there is overreaction (underreaction) to public information and excessive nonfundamental volatility (cross-sectional dispersion).

An example is provided by the beauty contest model of Morris and Shin (2002). The idea of the beauty contest goes back to Keynes and views the financial market as a contest where investors try to guess what other investors will do instead of trying to assess the fundamentals (see the Introduction and Lecture

Guide and section 8.3). In this example,

$$\pi(y_i, y, \sigma_y; \theta) = -(1-r)(y_i - \theta)^2 - r\left(L_i - \int_0^1 L_i \, \mathrm{d}i\right)$$

with $r \in (0,1)$ and $L_i = \int_0^1 (y_i - y_j)^2 \, \mathrm{d}j = (y_i - y)^2 + \sigma_y^2$. Note that $\int_0^1 L_i \, \mathrm{d}i = 2\sigma_y^2$.

Players try to get close to θ but derive a private value from taking an action close to others. However, socially the latter attempt is a waste since $\int_0^1 \pi_i \, \mathrm{d}i = -(1-r)\int_0^1 (y_i - \theta)^2 \, \mathrm{d}i$. This economy is efficient under complete information,

$$\kappa = \frac{\partial^2 \pi / \partial y_i \partial y}{-\partial^2 \pi / (\partial y_i)^2} = \frac{2r}{2} = r \quad \text{and} \quad \kappa^{\mathrm{e}} = 0$$

(since $\partial^2 \pi / (\partial y)^2 = -2r$ and $\partial^2 \pi / (\partial \sigma_y)^2 = 2r$). Therefore, there is overreaction to public information and excessive nonfundamental volatility. In fact, Morris and Shin (2002) show that welfare may decrease with the precision of public information. This fact has prompted a debate on the desirability of transparency of central bank policy. The point is that the disclosures of a central bank may reduce welfare whenever the beauty contest analogy applies to financial markets (see Morris and Shin 2005; Hellwig 2005; Svensson 2006; Woodford 2005). We will come back to this issue in chapter 3 and in the models of pure informational externalities in chapter 6.[14]

Another example is provided by new Keynesian business cycle models (e.g., Woodford 2002; Hellwig 2005), where the economy is efficient under complete information. However, in this case welfare increases with public information (Hellwig 2005). The reason is that in those models the externality with the dispersion in relative prices is negative ($\partial^2 \pi / (\partial \sigma_y)^2 < 0$), due to imperfect substitutability across goods in a monopolistic competition model, and this leads to a higher κ^{e} with $\kappa < \kappa^{\mathrm{e}}$.

Angeletos and Pavan (2007a) also look at the monopolistic competition model developed in this section, which is not efficient under complete information, and derive some comparative statics results with respect to information parameters. For example, expected profits increase with the precision of public information when competition is of the strategic complements variety. In this case (as in the quadratic model of section 1.4.1) we have that $\kappa^{\mathrm{e}} = 2\kappa$.[15]

Angeletos and Pavan (2007b) look at Pigouvian corrective tax policy in a similar environment and show that if the government can set marginal tax rates contingent on aggregate activity the (decentralized) efficient allocation can be

---

[14] Calvó-Armengol and de Martí (2007) consider a game with n players with payoffs similar to the beauty contest example and model the signals received as the outcome of communication in a network.

[15] There is in fact an apparent contradiction of their corollary 10 (Cournot competition), in which they claim that expected profits increase with the precision of private information, with the comparative statics result presented above that expected profits may increase or decrease with this precision (see exercise 1.4). This is due to the fact that corollary 10 only holds under the parameter restriction $\kappa > -1$ and this fact is not stated in the corollary.

implemented. The basic idea is to introduce taxes that control payoff externalities, so that the complete information equilibrium coincides with the first best allocation, and make agents perceive the fictitious degree of complementarity κ^e instead of the true κ, so that there is a socially efficient use of information. Tax progressivity is a crucial instrument for the first objective and the sensitivity of marginal taxes to aggregate activity to the second. It is found, for example, that in economies which are inefficient only under incomplete information and for which $\kappa > \kappa^e$, marginal optimal taxes are increasing in aggregate activity. In this way the perceived degree of complementarity is reduced.

1.5 Auctions and Voting

In this section we examine information aggregation properties of auction and voting mechanisms. We will see how auctions aggregate information under less restrictive conditions than smooth market mechanisms, such as a Cournot market. The better information aggregation properties of auction and voting mechanisms are explained by their winner-takes-all feature. This property implies that a bidder, while submitting his bid, or a voter, while casting his vote, has to think, respectively, of the implications that winning or being pivotal for the election outcome have in terms of the signals that other players may have received. That is, the bidder, effectively, has to condition on the information that winning conveys. In section 1.5.1 we examine common-value auctions and in section 1.5.2 we draw some connections with voting mechanisms.

1.5.1 Information Aggregation in Common-Value Auctions

Do auction markets aggregate information efficiently? This question got an affirmative answer in the studies of Wilson (1977) and Milgrom (1979, 1981). Wilson (1977) considers a first-price auction (the bidder with the highest bid wins the object and pays his bid) where buyers have some private information about the common value θ of the good to be sold and shows that, under certain regularity conditions, as the number of bidders tends to ∞ the maximum bid is almost surely equal to the true value. Milgrom (1979) obtains a necessary and sufficient condition on the information structure so that convergence to the true value is in probability.[16] The (second price) Vickrey auction has the same type of limiting properties (Milgrom 1981).

The conditions required for obtaining aggregation of information are relatively strong. In equilibrium, winning the object means that the other $n - 1$ bidders have received worse signals about the value of the object (the "winner's curse" since this means that the winner may have overestimated the value of the object). Consider the following illustration of the winner's curse in a common-value auction. An oil tract is auctioned and bidders have private estimates (signals) of its value. If bidders were to bid naively, each one just on the basis of

[16] See section 10.3.1 for an account of the different convergence concepts for random variables.

his private estimate, the winner would have overbid. The reason is that winning means that you have bid above the other bidders. To avoid the winner's curse, each bidder has to condition his bid not only on his private signal but also on the information that winning the auction conveys (Milgrom and Weber 1982). Now, for a high bid to be optimal, when $n - 1$ is large, the signal of the bidder must be quite strong. In particular, it must be the case that for any value θ there is a signal for which, conditional on winning, the bidder puts very small probability on a value lower than θ.[17]

Pesendorfer and Swinkels (1997) show that information aggregation is obtained under less stringent information conditions provided that supply also becomes large as the number of bidders grows (see also Kremer 2002). Pesendorfer and Swinkels consider an auction of k identical objects of unknown value. The k highest bidders obtain an object and pay the $(k + 1)$th bid. Each bidder receives a signal of bounded precision (more precisely, the posterior of a bidder after receiving a signal has full support, with density bounded away from zero and infinity) before submitting his bid. This contrasts with the setup in Wilson and Milgrom. Pesendorfer and Swinkels characterize the unique symmetric Bayesian equilibrium. They show that a necessary and sufficient condition for the equilibrium price to converge in probability to the true value is that both the number of objects sold k and the number of bidders who do not receive an object $n - k$ go to ∞. The driving force behind the convergence result is that a loser's curse is added (losing means that at most $n - k$ of the other buyers bid below your own bid) to the usual winner's curse (winning means that at most k of the other buyers bid above your own bid). When both k and $n - k$ tend to ∞, then signals need not be very strong for the equilibrium price to converge to the value. The reason is that a bid on the brink of winning or losing conveys precise information on the true value. Furthermore, for the result to hold supply need not grow in proportion to demand (it may grow less quickly) and only a vanishing fraction of bidders may be informed.

1.5.2 Voting

Voting aggregates information in ways similar to auctions. Consider a two-candidate election in which voters have private information about a common-value characteristic θ of the alternatives. For example, the common unknown value may be the quality of a public good about which voters have different assessments. The connection between auctions and elections is that a voter must condition his beliefs about θ on the event that his vote is pivotal (that is, that his vote can change the outcome of the election) in the same way that a bidder must condition his bid on the event that he wins the auction (with the highest bid).

---

[17] Milgrom's (1981) necessary and sufficient condition for information aggregation with a finite set of values is that for any $\theta < \theta'$ and any constant K there is a signal s' which yields a likelihood ratio on θ' versus θ of at least K. (See section 10.1.5 for an explanation of the likelihood ratio.)

Feddersen and Pesendorfer (1997) analyze an election with two alternatives A and Q in which the payoff to a voter depends on his type, the (one-dimensional) state of nature, and the winning alternative. Voting is costless. Each voter knows his type (types are i.i.d.) and receives a private signal about the uncertain state of nature. The alternative Q wins the election if it gets at least a fraction of votes q. Feddersen and Pesendorfer characterize symmetric Bayes–Nash equilibria of the voting game in which no voter uses a weakly dominated strategy. In equilibrium there are types who always vote for A, types who always vote for Q, and the rest cast their vote depending on the signal received (i.e., they take an "informative action").

Feddersen and Pesendorfer show that elections aggregate information. That is, the alternative chosen under shared information obtains with probability close to 1 in a large election with private information. We say that an election is close if in equilibrium the winning candidate obtains a fraction of votes very close to the winning percentage. Feddersen and Pesendorfer show that although the fraction of voters who take an informative action tends to 0 as the number of voters grows unboundedly, large elections are almost always very close. As a consequence, elections are decided by those who take an informative action. However, information aggregation is not obtained in general if the distribution from which preference types are drawn is uncertain. An interesting related insight is that uninformed voters may prefer to abstain rather than vote because of the analogue to the winner's curse in the context of the election (Feddersen and Pesendorfer 1996). This is so because uninformed voters may abstain to maximize the probability that informed voters are pivotal and decide the outcome of the election.

In summary, when the market mechanism has the winner-takes-all feature, as in auctions or voting mechanisms, information aggregation seems to be facilitated. The reason is that these mechanisms force agents to take into consideration the informational implications of their winning the auction or being pivotal in the election.

1.6 Endogenous Information Acquisition

In this section we examine the implications of costly information acquisition for information aggregation in the context of the Cournot market of section 1.2.[18] We confirm that with endogenous information acquisition a large Cournot market with decreasing returns does not aggregate information and does not attain first-best efficiency. Furthermore, the welfare loss increases with the cost of information acquisition. The market, however, is still second-best optimal when firms can only use decentralized production strategies. The case of constant returns to scale is more subtle.

[18] Milgrom (1981) and Milgrom and Weber (1982) consider information acquisition in auctions.

After setting up the model we deal first with the decreasing-returns-to-scale case (section 1.6.1) and then with the constant-returns-to-scale case (section 1.6.2).

Consider the model with a continuum of firms, uncertain demand, and linear-normal specification of the example in section 1.2.4.1: $p = \theta - \beta x$ and $C(x_i) = \frac{1}{2}\lambda x_i^2$. The timing of events is as follows. In the first stage firms contract information (a sample) of a certain precision about the unknown parameter θ. At the second stage firms receive their private signals and compete in quantities. The precision of information of firm i, τ_{ε_i}, is proportional to the sample size the firm obtains.[19] The cost of obtaining information with precision τ_{ε_i} is $c\tau_{\varepsilon_i}$, where $c > 0$. It will be more convenient to work with ξ_i ($\xi_i \equiv \tau_{\varepsilon_i}/(\tau_\theta + \tau_{\varepsilon_i})$) and, with some abuse of language, we will speak of ξ_i as the precision of information of firm i. The cost of obtaining information ξ_i will then be given by $\varphi(\xi_i) = (c/\sigma_\theta^2)(\xi_i/(1 - \xi_i))$. Purchase of zero precision ($\xi_i = 0$) is costless and to purchase perfect information ($\xi_i = 1$) is infinitely costly. The parameters ξ_i are common knowledge at the second stage (in a competitive market, though, a firm needs to know only the average precision).

An alternative would be to consider the case where firms purchase precision simultaneously with their output choice or, equivalently, that the precision acquisition by a firm is not observable by the rivals. In this case a strategy for firm i is a pair $(\xi_i, X_i(\cdot))$ determining the precision purchased and the output strategy. In our continuum economy it does not matter whether the precisions purchased are observable or not. Note first that if $(\xi_i, X_i(\cdot))_{i\in[0,1]}$ is a Nash equilibrium of the one-shot game, then necessarily $(X_i(\cdot))_{i\in[0,1]}$ is a (Bayes) Nash equilibrium of the market game for given $(\xi_i)_{i\in[0,1]}$. Let ξ denote the average information precision in the market. Then equilibrium strategies and expected profits of firm i at the market stage are easily seen to depend only on ξ_i and ξ. This means that there is no strategic effect derived from the information purchases at the first stage. The reason is that a single firm must take the average ξ as given. It follows that equilibrium precisions, both at the one-shot and two-stage games, will solve

$$\operatorname*{Max}_{\xi_i} \Pi_i(\xi_i, \xi) = E[\pi_i] - \varphi(\xi_i).$$

1.6.1 Decreasing Returns to Scale

Assuming that $\lambda > 0$ (increasing marginal costs), we can find a price-taking Bayesian equilibrium of this (continuum) economy as in section 1.2 for given $(\xi_i)_{i\in[0,1]}$. Let us postulate $X_i(s_i) = a_i(s_i - \bar{\theta}) + b\bar{\theta}$ as a candidate linear equilibrium strategy for firm i.

---

[19] The model is taken from Vives (1988). Li et al. (1987) model information acquisition similarly.

We then have that

$$\int_0^1 X_i(s_i)\,\mathrm{d}i = \int_0^1 (a_i(s_i - \bar{\theta}) + b\bar{\theta})\,\mathrm{d}i$$
$$= a(\theta - \bar{\theta}) + \int_0^1 a_i\varepsilon_i\,\mathrm{d}i + b\bar{\theta} = a(\theta - \bar{\theta}) + b\bar{\theta},$$

where $a = \int_0^1 a_j\,\mathrm{d}j$, and, assuming that $\operatorname{var}[a_i\varepsilon_i]$ is uniformly bounded across firms and given that $E[a_i\varepsilon_i] = 0$, we have $\int_0^1 a_i\varepsilon_i\,\mathrm{d}i = 0$ according to our convention on the integral.

We can use the FOC $E[p \mid s_i] = \lambda X_i(s_i)$, where $E[p \mid s_i] = E[\theta \mid s_i] - \beta E[\tilde{X}(\theta) \mid s_i]$ and $E[\tilde{X}(\theta) \mid s_i] = a(E[\theta \mid s_i] - \bar{\theta}) + b\bar{\theta}$ to solve for the parameters a_i and obtain $a_i = \xi_i/(\lambda + \beta\xi)$ and $b = 1/(\lambda + \beta)$. Note that $\operatorname{var}[a_i\varepsilon_i] = \xi_i(\lambda + \beta\xi)^{-2}(\tau_{\varepsilon_i} + \tau_\theta)^{-1}$, which is bounded between 0 and 1. Using the FOC it is immediate that

$$E[\pi_i] = \tfrac{1}{2}\lambda E[(X_i(s_i))^2] = \frac{\lambda}{2}\left(b^2\bar{\theta}^2 + \frac{\xi_i\sigma_\theta^2}{(\lambda + \beta\xi)^2}\right).$$

Expected profits for firm i increase with ξ_i and decrease with ξ. The total payoff for firm i is

$$\Pi_i(\xi_i, \xi) = \frac{\lambda}{2}\left(\frac{\xi_i}{(\lambda + \beta\xi)^2}\sigma_\theta^2 + \frac{1}{(\lambda + \beta)^2}\bar{\theta}^2\right) - \frac{c}{\sigma_\theta^2}\frac{\xi_i}{1 - \xi_i}.$$

The marginal benefit to a firm to acquire information decreases with the average amount of information purchased by the other firms ξ. This means that ξ_i and ξ are strategic substitutes in the payoff of firm i. More information in the market reduces the incentive for any firm to do research. A firm wants information to estimate the market price $p = \theta - \beta x$. When firms have better information (ξ is high) the market price varies less since producers match better production decisions with the changing demand. Consequently, for high ξ an individual firm has less incentive to acquire information.

The FOC (which is sufficient) is given by

$$\frac{\partial \Pi_i}{\partial \xi_i} = \frac{\lambda\sigma_\theta^2}{(\lambda + \beta\xi)^2} - \frac{c}{\sigma_\theta^2}\frac{1}{(1 - \xi_i)^2} \leqslant 0.$$

It will hold with equality if $\xi_i > 0$. Since the equilibrium will be symmetric, we let $\xi_i = \xi$ and solve for ξ. We obtain

$$\xi^* = \max\left\{0, \frac{\sigma_\theta^2 - \sqrt{2c\lambda}}{\beta\sqrt{2c/\lambda} + \sigma_\theta^2}\right\},$$

which can be written in terms of the precision of the signal as

$$\tau_\varepsilon^* = \max\left\{0, \frac{1 - \tau_\theta\sqrt{2c\lambda}}{\lambda + \beta}\sqrt{\frac{\lambda}{2c}}\right\}.$$

It is immediate that the precision purchased is monotone in cost c. If $c = 0$, firms obtain perfect information ($\tau_\varepsilon^* = \infty$); as c increases, τ_ε^* decreases monotonically until c is so high that no information is purchased. Furthermore, τ_ε^*

increases with σ_θ^2. More uncertainty (or less prior public knowledge τ_θ) induces the firms to acquire more information. The relationship between the slope of marginal costs (λ) and τ_ε^* is not monotonic: for both small and large λ, expected profits at the market stage are low and consequently there is low expenditure on research, and τ_ε^* peaks at intermediate values of λ. It increases with λ for low values of λ and decreases for high values.

Differentiated products. The results generalize to differentiated products. This is easily seen by noting that the model examined is formally equivalent to a linear demand differentiated product market with constant marginal costs (equal to zero for simplicity) as studied in section 1.4. The results obtained apply, therefore, to the case of Cournot competition with payoff for firm i given by $\pi_i = (\theta - \frac{1}{2}\lambda x_i - \beta x)x_i$, and to the case of Bertrand competition with payoff $\pi_i = (\theta - \frac{1}{2}\lambda p_i - \beta p)p_i$. An interesting difference is that with price competition and differentiated products, ξ_i and ξ are strategic complements in the payoff of firm i. The reason is that, as other firms are now better informed, the intercept of the residual demand of firm i, $\theta - \beta\tilde{p}(\theta)$, is more variable because $\beta < 0$ and the average price $\tilde{p}(\theta)$ is more responsive to θ.[20]

Welfare. The first-best outcome with costly acquisition of information is just the full-information first-best. This can best be understood by considering finite-economy approximations to the large market. It is verified in section 2.3 that, as finite economies grow large, in the sense that the numbers of consumers and firms grow as the market is replicated, the optimal expenditure on information converges to zero in per capita terms and the precision of the aggregate signal tends to ∞. That is, when a centralized planner determines the purchase of an aggregate signal and sets output to maximize expected total surplus, then as the market grows large less and less information is purchased per firm but at the same time the aggregate precision grows unboundedly.

From section 1.2.4.1 we know that in the continuum economy the first-best per capita expected total surplus with no cost of information acquisition is given by $\mathrm{ETS}^0 = (\frac{1}{2}b)E[\theta^2]$, where $b = 1/(\lambda + \beta)$. With decreasing returns to scale, a competitive market always falls short of this first-best level unless the cost of information is zero. If the competitive market spends a positive per capita amount on information, it cannot attain first-best efficiency, which involves zero average expenditure on information acquisition. If the market does not buy any information, then the precision of signals is zero and again an inefficient outcome obtains. The welfare loss is given by $\frac{1}{2}(b - a)\sigma_\theta^2 + c\tau_\varepsilon^*$, where $a = \xi^*/(\lambda + \beta\xi^*)$. This is immediate from section 1.2.4.1 adding the cost of information. It is always positive unless $c = 0$, in which case $b = a$.

Nevertheless, with decreasing returns the market is team-efficient: expected total surplus is maximized given that firms can base their decisions only on their private information. We know from proposition 1.2 that, contingent on ξ, the market works like a team which maximizes expected gross surplus (gross of

[20] See exercise 8.15 in Vives (1999) for the duopoly case.

the cost of information) and attains $\mathrm{EGS}(\xi) = \frac{1}{2}(a\sigma_\theta^2 + b\bar{\theta}^2)$, where $a = \xi/(\lambda + \beta\xi)$. The team maximizes $\mathrm{EGS}(\xi) - \varphi(\xi)$. The FOC of the optimization problem, which is also sufficient for a maximum to obtain, is exactly as in the market solution. The reason is that at the first stage there is no private information and with negligible single players each firm has the right (second-best) incentives to purchase information.

Proposition 1.4. *With endogenous information acquisition a competitive market with increasing marginal costs works like a team which chooses expenditures on information acquisition and decentralized production rules to maximize total expected surplus.*

As a corollary to the proposition we obtain that the welfare loss with respect to the first-best increases with the cost of information. This is easily seen since with increasing marginal costs, the competitive market acts as if it were solving the team program

$$\operatorname*{Max}_{\tau_\varepsilon} \phi(\tau_\varepsilon, c) = \mathrm{EGS}(\tau_\varepsilon) - c\tau_\varepsilon.$$

Therefore, using the envelope condition,

$$\frac{\mathrm{d}\phi(\tau_\varepsilon^*, c)}{\mathrm{d}c} = \frac{\partial\phi}{\partial c}(\tau_\varepsilon^*, c) = -\tau_\varepsilon^*,$$

and the net expected total surplus of the market decreases with the cost of information (as long as $\tau_\varepsilon^* > 0$). The following proposition summarizes the market performance with respect to the first-best with increasing marginal costs.

Proposition 1.5. *With endogenous and costly information acquisition a competitive market with decreasing returns always falls short of first-best efficiency. Furthermore, the welfare loss increases with the cost of information as long as the market expenditure on information acquisition is positive.*

1.6.2 Constant Returns to Scale

In the constant-returns-to-scale case ($\lambda = 0$), no equilibrium exists if information acquisition is costly. The argument is as follows. Notice first that in equilibrium it must be the case that no firm makes any profit at the market stage when prices and quantities are set. With constant returns to scale, equilibrium at the second stage implies that the expected value of the market price conditional on the signal received by any firm is nonpositive. Otherwise the firm would expand indefinitely. Therefore, firms cannot purchase any information in equilibrium since this would imply negative profits. Furthermore, zero expenditures on information acquisition are not consistent with equilibrium either. If no firm purchases information, there are enormous incentives for any firm to get some information and make unbounded profits under constant returns to scale. With no firm acquiring information the average output in the market is nonrandom and any firm with some information could make unbounded profits by shutting down operations if the expected value of the market price conditional on the received signal is nonpositive and producing an unbounded amount otherwise.

The nonexistence of equilibrium argument does not depend on the linear-normal specification and we will encounter it later when we deal with the Grossman–Stiglitz paradox in section 4.2.2. The nonexistence result is also reminiscent of Wilson's analysis of informational economies of scale (Wilson 1974). He finds that the compounding of constant returns in physical production with information acquisition yields unbounded returns in models where the choice of the decision variable applies in the same way to the production of all units of output. Obviously, this implies nonexistence of a competitive equilibrium. The fact that no equilibrium exists with endogenous information acquisition under constant returns is particular to the continuum model. With a finite number of firms an equilibrium exists in the two-stage model and it approaches the first-best efficient outcome when the market grows large. The analysis is deferred to section 2.3.

1.6.3 Summary

In a large Cournot market with uncertain demand where firms acquire information, we can draw the following conclusions.

- With decreasing returns there is a welfare loss with respect to the first-best outcome and it increases with the cost of information. Yet the market is team-efficient and maximizes expected total surplus subject to the use of decentralized production strategies.
- With constant returns there is no welfare loss and the market acquires the right amount of information.
- Information acquisition decisions by firms are strategic substitutes (if competition were to be à la Bertrand in a differentiated product environment, then they would be strategic complements).

1.7 Summary

In this chapter we have examined how simple market mechanisms—such as Cournot or auctions, in which agents do not have the opportunity to condition on market statistics—aggregate information. The market aggregates information if it replicates the outcome of competition when all agents pool their information in the economy. The chapter has introduced information aggregation in standard partial equilibrium models and some of the basic tools for the analysis:

- The idealization of a large market as a continuum of players.
- Price-taking (Bayesian) equilibria in markets with incomplete information.

- The linear-normal model and the computation and characterization of linear equilibria.
- The concept of team efficiency as a welfare benchmark for an incomplete-information economy.

The main results are as follows.

- Except in the independent-values case or in particular circumstances, smooth market mechanisms, such as Cournot with homogeneous product or Bertrand with differentiated products, do not aggregate information as the market grows large.
- Auctions, like voting mechanisms, tend to aggregate information under less restrictive conditions. This is because of their winner-takes-all feature which forces bidders to condition effectively on the information that winning conveys.
- A large homogeneous product Cournot market under private information will not be first-best efficient, except possibly under constant returns to scale. However, it is team-efficient, that is, it maximizes total expected surplus under the constraint of using of decentralized strategies. The property also holds with costly information acquisition.
- The strategies of agents in incomplete-information economies, and the relative weights to private and public information in particular, depend on the degree of strategic complementarity or substitutability of payoffs. This may explain, for example, patterns of under- or overreaction to public information with respect to the team-efficient benchmark.

1.8 Appendix

Proof of proposition 1.3 (see p. 32). We first derive the linear equilibrium in the case of private information, where each player conditions on his signal only. Player i maximizes over y_i:

$$E[\pi(y_i, y; \theta_i) \mid s_i] = E[\theta_i \mid s_i]y_i - \tfrac{1}{2}\omega_1 y_i^2 - \omega_2 E[y \mid s_i]y_i,$$

where y is the random equilibrium average action y. We obtain the following FOC,

$$E[\theta_i \mid s_i] - \omega_1 y_i - \omega_2 E[y \mid s_i] = 0,$$

and, since $\omega_1 > 0$, the best response of player i is

$$y_i = \frac{E[\theta_i \mid s_i] - \omega_2 E[y \mid s_i]}{\omega_1}.$$

We are looking for a linear symmetric equilibrium of the form $Y(s_i) = as_i + \hat{b}$, where the parameters a and $\hat{b}$ need to be determined. It follows that

$$y = \int_0^1 Y(s_j)\,\mathrm{d}j = a\int_0^1 \theta_j\,\mathrm{d}j + a\int_0^1 \varepsilon_j\,\mathrm{d}j + \hat{b} = a\tilde{\theta} + \hat{b}$$

since according to our convention $\int_0^1 \varepsilon_j \, dj = 0$ (a.s.). We know that $E[\theta_i \mid s_i] = \xi s_i + (1-\xi)\bar{\theta}$ and $E[\tilde{\theta} \mid s_i] = E[\theta_j \mid s_i] = \xi\varsigma s_i + (1-\xi\varsigma)\bar{\theta}$.

It must therefore hold that

$$as_i + \hat{b} = \frac{\xi s_i + (1-\xi)\bar{\theta} - \omega_2(a(\xi\varsigma s_i + (1-\xi\varsigma)\bar{\theta}) + \hat{b})}{\omega_1}.$$

Identifying coefficients we obtain

$$\omega_1 a = \xi - \omega_2 \xi\varsigma a \quad \text{and} \quad \omega_1 \hat{b} = (1-\xi)\bar{\theta} - \omega_2(1-\xi\varsigma)\bar{\theta}a - \omega_2 \hat{b}$$

and, since $\omega_1 + \omega_2 > 0$,

$$a = \frac{\xi}{\omega_1 + \omega_2\xi\varsigma} \quad \text{and} \quad \hat{b} = \left(\frac{1}{\omega_1+\omega_2} - a\right)\bar{\theta}.$$

It follows that linear symmetric Bayesian equilibrium strategies in the private-information case are given by

$$Y(s_i) = as_i + \left(\frac{1}{\omega_1+\omega_2} - a\right)\bar{\theta} = a(s_i - \bar{\theta}) + b\bar{\theta},$$

where a and b are given as in the proposition. We have that $E[y(s_i)] = b\bar{\theta}$ since $E[s_i - \bar{\theta}] = 0$.

Next we derive the symmetric linear Bayesian equilibrium strategies in the shared-information case, where each firm conditions both on its signal and the average parameter $\tilde{\theta}$ (since $\tilde{s} = \tilde{\theta}$). The FOC is given by

$$E[\theta_i \mid s_i, \tilde{\theta}] - \omega_1 y_i - \omega_2 E[y \mid s_i, \tilde{\theta}] = 0,$$

which, since $\omega_1 > 0$, implies that

$$y_i = \frac{E[\theta_i \mid s_i, \tilde{\theta}] - \omega_2 E[y \mid s_i, \tilde{\theta}]}{\omega_1}.$$

We are looking for a linear symmetric equilibrium of the form $Z(s_i, \tilde{\theta}) = \hat{a}s_i + \hat{b}\tilde{\theta} + \hat{c}$, where the parameters $\hat{a}$, $\hat{b}$, and $\hat{c}$ need to be determined. With hindsight we let $\hat{c} = 0$. We therefore have that $z = \int_0^1 Z(s_i, \tilde{\theta}) \, di = \hat{a}\tilde{\theta} + \hat{b}\tilde{\theta} = (\hat{a} + \hat{b})\tilde{\theta}$ since $\tilde{s} = \int_0^1 s_i \, di = \tilde{\theta}$.

It must therefore hold that

$$\hat{a}s_i + \hat{b}\tilde{\theta} = \frac{E[\theta_i \mid s_i, \tilde{\theta}] - \omega_2 z}{\omega_1}.$$

From the properties of conditional expectations with normal distributions we have that

$$E[\theta_i \mid s_i, \tilde{\theta}] = (1-d)\tilde{\theta} + ds_i,$$

where $d = (1-\varsigma)/(\xi^{-1} - \varsigma)$. Then

$$\hat{a}s_i + \hat{b}\tilde{\theta} = \frac{(1-d)\tilde{\theta} + ds_i - \omega_2(\hat{a}+\hat{b})\tilde{\theta}}{\omega_1},$$

from which $\hat{a} = d/\omega_1$ and $\omega_1 \hat{b} = (1-d) - \omega_2(\hat{a}+\hat{b})$, and therefore, since $\omega_1 + \omega_2 > 0$,

$$\hat{b} = \frac{(1-d) - \omega_2 \hat{a}}{\omega_1 + \omega_2} = \frac{1}{\omega_1 + \omega_2} - \hat{a} = b - \hat{a}.$$

In conclusion, linear symmetric Bayesian equilibrium strategies in the shared-information case are given by

$$Z(s_i, \tilde{\theta}) = \hat{a}(s_i - \tilde{\theta}) + b\tilde{\theta},$$

where $\hat{a}$ and b are as in the proposition. We also have that $E[Z(s_i, \tilde{\theta})] = b\bar{\theta}$ since $E[s_i - \tilde{\theta}] = 0$. □

1.9 Exercises

1.1 (*expected surplus in the linear-normal model*). Consider the linear model of section 1.2.4.1. Show that expected gross surplus (per capita) at the market solution is given by $E[\int_0^{\tilde{X}(\theta)} P(z;\theta)\,\mathrm{d}z] = a\sigma_\theta^2 + b\bar{\theta}^2 - \frac{1}{2}\beta(a^2\sigma_\theta^2 + b^2\bar{\theta}^2)$ and expected cost by $E[C(X_i(s_i))] = \frac{1}{2}\lambda[a^2\sigma_\theta^2/\xi + b^2\bar{\theta}^2]$. Conclude that ETS $= \frac{1}{2}(a\sigma_\theta^2 + b\bar{\theta}^2)$. Show also that per capita expected consumer surplus

$$E\left[\int_0^{\tilde{X}(\theta)} P(z;\theta)\,\mathrm{d}z\right] - P(\tilde{X}(\theta),\theta)\tilde{X}(\theta)$$

is given by $\frac{1}{2}\beta E[(\tilde{X}(\theta))^2]$.

Hint. The first part is a straight computation using the equilibrium expressions. For the second you do not need to know the form of $\tilde{X}(\theta)$.

** **1.2** (*information aggregation in a Cournot market with capacity constraints and a finite support information structure*). Consider a market with inverse demand $p = \theta - \beta x$, with firms receiving private signals about the uncertain θ and competing in quantities. Firm i has a capacity of production k_i. This enables the firm to produce at zero cost up to the capacity limit. We will assume here a finite support information structure where θ can take two values, θ_{H} and θ_{L}, $\theta_{\mathrm{H}} \geqslant \theta_{\mathrm{L}} > 0$ with equal prior probability. Let $\mu = \frac{1}{2}(\theta_{\mathrm{H}} + \theta_{\mathrm{L}})$. Firm i may receive a low (s_{L}) or high (s_{H}) signal about θ with a likelihood $\mathrm{P}(s_{\mathrm{H}} \mid \theta_{\mathrm{H}}) = \mathrm{P}(s_{\mathrm{L}} \mid s_{\mathrm{L}}) = \ell$, where $\frac{1}{2} \leqslant \ell \leqslant 1$. If $\ell = \frac{1}{2}$, the signal is uninformative; if $\ell = 1$, it is perfectly informative. Signals received by firms are i.i.d. conditional on θ. With these assumptions:

(i) Check that $E[\theta \mid s_{\mathrm{H}}] = \ell\theta_{\mathrm{H}} + (1-\ell)\theta_{\mathrm{L}}$, $E[\theta \mid s_{\mathrm{L}}] = (1-\ell)\theta_{\mathrm{H}} + \ell\theta_{\mathrm{L}}$, $\mathrm{P}(s_{\mathrm{H},j} \mid s_{\mathrm{H},i}) = \ell^2 + (1-\ell)^2$, and $\mathrm{P}(s_{\mathrm{H},j} \mid s_{\mathrm{L},i}) = 2\ell^2(1-\ell)$ with $j \neq i$.

(ii) Let $\varsigma \equiv \ell^2 + (1-\ell)^2$, $\Delta = \theta_{\mathrm{H}} - \theta_{\mathrm{L}}$, $\ell \in [\frac{1}{2}, 1]$, and assume that $\ell\theta_{\mathrm{L}} > (1-\ell)\theta_{\mathrm{H}}$. Show that when all firms have a common capacity k there is a unique symmetric Bayesian equilibrium in which each firm produces according to $X(s_{\mathrm{H}}) = \bar{y} \equiv \omega\theta_{\mathrm{H}} - (\omega-1)\theta_{\mathrm{L}}$ and $X(s_{\mathrm{L}}) = \underline{y} \equiv \omega\theta_{\mathrm{L}} - (\omega-1)\theta_{\mathrm{H}}$ if $k \geqslant \bar{y}$, where $\omega = \ell/(2\ell - 1)$ if $\ell > \frac{1}{2}$ and $\omega = \frac{1}{2}$ if $\ell = \frac{1}{2}$; $X(s_H) = k$ and $X(s_L) = \underline{z} \equiv (E[\theta \mid s] - (1 - \varsigma)k)/\varsigma$ if $\bar{y} > k > E[\theta \mid s]$ and $X(s_H) = X(s_L) = k$ otherwise.

(iii) Show that in equilibrium the average output $\tilde{X}(\theta)$ equals θ if $k \geqslant \bar{y}$, $q(\theta)$ if $\bar{y} > k > E[\theta \mid s]$ (where $q(\theta_H) = (k(\varsigma + \ell - 1) + E[\theta \mid s_L](1 - \ell))/\varsigma$ and $q(\theta_L) = (\ell E[\theta \mid s_L] - (\ell - \varsigma)k)/\varsigma)$, and k otherwise, provided the signals are informative ($\ell > \frac{1}{2}$). When does the market aggregate information?

Solution. Follow similar steps as in section 1.2.4.1. See Vives (1986).

****1.3** (*investment in flexibility under uncertainty and private information*). Consider the same market as in exercise 1.2 but now each firm has an opportunity in a first stage to invest in capacity. Firm i may purchase a capacity k_i at the cost ck_i ($c > 0$). Assume that $\ell\theta_L > (1 - \ell)\theta_H$.

(i) Show that there is a unique symmetric subgame-perfect equilibrium of the two-stage investment-quantity setting game.[21] The equilibrium capacity k^* is given by

$$k^* = \max\left\{0, \bar{\theta} - c, \bar{\theta} - c + \frac{\Delta(\ell - \frac{1}{2}) - c}{2\varsigma - 1}\right\}.$$

(ii) Show that if $c < \bar{c} \equiv \Delta(\ell - \frac{1}{2})$ the equilibrium investment in k^* increases with a mean-preserving spread of demand (i.e., with Δ) and increases or decreases with the precision of the information (i.e., ℓ) according to whether c is larger or smaller than $\tilde{c} \equiv (1 - 4\ell(1 - \ell))\Delta/(4(2\ell - 1))$. If $c > \bar{c}$, then k^* is independent of Δ and ℓ. Interpret the results in terms of the effect of uncertainty in investment in flexibility. Distinguish between increases in prior uncertainty Δ and increases in the variability of beliefs ℓ.

(iii) *Welfare.* Show that $k^* = \arg\max\{\mathrm{EGS}(k) - ck\}$, where $\mathrm{EGS}(k)$ is the expected gross total surplus with capacity k.

(iv) Show that there is a welfare loss with respect to the full-information first-best unless the cost of capacity c is zero or high enough ($c \geqslant \frac{1}{2}\Delta$). The welfare loss is decreasing with the precision of information if $\Delta(\ell - \frac{1}{2}) > c > 0$ and independent of the latter if $\frac{1}{2}\Delta > c > \Delta(\ell - \frac{1}{2})$. Interpret the results.

Solution. See Vives (1986).

1.4 (*welfare in the monopolistic competition model with a common value*). The linear demand system for differentiated products of section 1.4.1 can be obtained from the optimizing behavior of a representative consumer who maximizes the quadratic utility

$$U = \int_0^1 \alpha_i x_i \, \mathrm{d}i - \frac{1}{2}\left(\delta x^2 + (1 - \delta)\int_0^1 x_i^2 \, \mathrm{d}i\right)$$

[21] A subgame-perfect equilibrium requires that for any investment decision at the first stage, a Nash equilibrium in outputs obtains at the second stage. This rules out incredible threats. Nash equilibria only require optimizing behavior along the equilibrium path.

minus expenditure $\int_0^1 p_i x_i \, di$, where $x = \int_0^1 x_i \, di$. Consumer surplus (CS) in terms of quantities is given by $\frac{1}{2}(\delta x^2 + (1-\delta)\int_0^1 x_i^2 \, di)$ and in terms of prices by

$$\frac{1}{2}\left((1-\delta)\int_0^1 \beta_i^2 \, di + \delta\tilde{\beta}^2 + (1+\gamma)\int_0^1 p_i^2 \, di - \gamma p^2 - 2\int_0^1 \beta_i p_i \, di\right),$$

where $\tilde{\beta} = \int_0^1 \beta_i \, di$ and, as before, $\beta_i = (\alpha_i - \delta\tilde{\alpha})/(1-\delta)$ and $\gamma = \delta/(1-\delta)$. Note that $\tilde{\beta} = \tilde{\alpha}$.

Since costs are assumed to be zero, U represents total surplus (TS). Consider the common-value case ($\varsigma = 1$) and show that

(i) expected consumer surplus in the Cournot case $\mathrm{ECS_C}$ increases and in the Bertrand case $\mathrm{ECS_B}$ decreases with the precision of information τ_ε;

(ii) expected profits increase with τ_ε in the Bertrand case ($E[\pi_{\mathrm{B}}]$) and may increase or decrease with τ_ε in the Cournot case ($E[\pi_{\mathrm{C}}]$); expected profits in both cases increase with prior uncertainty σ_θ^2;

(iii) expected total surplus in the Cournot case $\mathrm{ETS_C}$ increases and in the Bertrand case $\mathrm{ETS_B}$ decreases with the precision of information τ_ε.

Interpret the results in terms of the impact on the variability of individual and aggregate strategies and potential covariance of the uncertain parameters with strategies. What would be the impact on welfare if firms were to share information?

Solution. Let $\xi = \tau_\varepsilon/(\tau_\theta + \tau_\varepsilon)$. From the equilibrium strategies in proposition 1.3 and the expressions for CS obtain that

$$\frac{\partial\,\mathrm{ECS_C}}{\partial\xi} = \frac{2 - 4\delta + 2\delta^2 + 3\delta(1-\delta)\xi}{(2 - 2\delta + \delta\xi)^3}\frac{\sigma_\theta^2}{2} > 0$$

and

$$\frac{\partial\,\mathrm{ECS_B}}{\partial\xi} = -\frac{(12-\xi)\gamma + (6+\xi)\gamma^2 + 6}{(2 + 2\gamma - \gamma\xi)^3}\frac{\sigma_\theta^2}{2} < 0.$$

Note that in equilibrium $E[\pi_{\mathrm{C}}] = (1-\delta)E[x_i^2]$ and $E[\pi_{\mathrm{B}}] = (1+\gamma)E[p_i^2]$ and derive the results for profits from the equilibrium strategies in proposition 1.3. Furthermore, obtain that

$$\frac{\partial\,\mathrm{ETS_C}}{\partial\xi} = \frac{6 - 12\delta + 6\delta^2 + \delta(1-\delta)\xi}{(2 - 2\delta + \delta\xi)^3}\frac{\sigma_\theta^2}{2} > 0$$

and

$$\frac{\partial\,\mathrm{ETS_B}}{\partial\xi} = \frac{(4-3\xi)\gamma + (2-\xi)\gamma^2 + 2}{(2 - 2\gamma - \gamma\xi)^3}\frac{\sigma_\theta^2}{2} < 0.$$

For the effect of information sharing note that it is equivalent to letting $\xi = 1$. (See Vives (1990) for more details.)

References

Angeletos, G. M., and A. Pavan. 2007a. Efficient use of information and social value of information. *Econometrica* 75:1103–42.

——. 2007b. Policy with dispersed information. Mimeo.

Aumann, R. 1964. Markets with a continuum of traders. *Econometrica* 32:39–50.

Bryant, J. 1983. A simple rational expectations Keynes-type model. *Quarterly Journal of Economics* 98:525–28.

Calvó-Armengol, A., and J. de Martí. 2007. On optimal communication networks. Mimeo.

Diamond, P. 1982. Aggregate demand management in search equilibrium. *Journal of Political Economy* 90:881–94.

Dybvig, P. H., and C. S. Spatt. 1983. Adoption externalities as public goods. *Journal of Public Economics* 20:231–47.

Feddersen, T., and W. Pesendorfer. 1996. The swing voter's curse. *American Economic Review* 86:408–24.

——. 1997. Voting behavior and information aggregation in elections with private information. *Econometrica* 65:1029–58.

Gale, D. 1996. Equilibria and Pareto optima of markets with adverse selection. *Economic Theory* 7:207–35.

Guesnerie, R. 1992. An exploration of the eductive justifications of the rational-expectations hypothesis. *American Economic Review* 82:1254–78.

Harris, M., and R. Townsend. 1981. Resource allocation under asymmetric information. *Econometrica* 49:33–64.

Hayek, F. 1945. The use of knowledge in society. *American Economic Review* 35:519–30.

Heinemann, M. 2004. Are rational expectations equilibria with private information eductively stable? *Journal of Economics* 82:169–94.

Hellwig, C. 2005. Heterogeneous information and the welfare effects of public information disclosures. UCLA mimeo.

Hellwig, M. F. 1987. Some recent developments in the theory of competition in markets with adverse selection. *European Economic Review* 31:319–25.

Kremer, I. 2002. Information aggregation in common value auctions. *Econometrica* 70:1675–82.

Li, L. 1985. Cournot oligopoly with information sharing. *RAND Journal of Economics* 16:521–36.

Li, L., R. McKelvey, and T. Page. 1987. Optimal research for Cournot oligopolists. *Journal of Economic Theory* 42:140–66.

Matsuyama, K. 1995. Complementarities and cumulative processes in models of monopolistic competition. *Journal of Economic Literature* 33:701–29.

Milgrom, P. R. 1979. A convergence theorem for competitive bidding and differential information. *Econometrica* 47:679–88.

——. 1981. Rational expectations, information acquisition, and competitive bidding. *Econometrica* 49:921–43.

Milgrom, P. R., and R. Weber. 1982. A theory of auctions and competitive bidding. *Econometrica* 50:1089–122.

Morris, S., and H. Shin. 2002. The social value of public information. *American Economic Review* 92:1521–34.

——. 2005. Central bank transparency and the signal value of prices. *Brookings Papers on Economic Activity* 2:1–66.

Novshek, W. 1980. Cournot equilibrium with free entry. *Review of Economic Studies* 47:473–86.

Palfrey, T. 1985. Uncertainty resolution private information aggregation, and the Cournot competitive limit. *Review of Economic Studies* 52:69–83.

Pesendorfer, W., and J. Swinkels. 1997. The loser's curse and information aggregation in common value auctions. *Econometrica* 65:1247–81.

Prescott, E., and R. Townsend. 1984. Pareto optima and competitive equilibria with adverse selection and moral hazard. *Econometrica* 52:21–45.

Radner, R. 1962. Team decision problems. *Annals of Mathematical Statistics* 33:857–81.

Royden, H. L. 1968. *Real Analysis.* New York: Macmillan.

Svensson, L. 2006. Social value of public information. Comment: Morris and Shin (2002), Is actually pro-transparency, not con. *American Economic Review* 96:448–52.

Vives, X. 1986. Investment in flexibility in a competitive market with incomplete information. CARESS Working Paper 86-08, University of Pennsylvania.

——. 1988. Aggregation of information in large Cournot markets. *Econometrica* 56:851–76.

——. 1990. Trade associations, disclosure rules, incentives to share information and welfare. *RAND Journal of Economics* 21:409–30.

——. 1999. *Oligopoly Pricing: Old Ideas and New Tools.* Boston, MA: MIT Press.

Wilson, R. 1975. Informational economies of scale. *Bell Journal of Economics* 6:184–95.

——. 1977. A bidding model of perfect competition. *Review of Economic Studies* 44:511–18.

Woodford, M. 2002. Imperfect common knowledge and the effects of monetary policy. In *Knowledge, Information, and Expectations in Modern Macroeconomics: In Honor of Edmund S. Phelps* (ed. P. Aghion, R. Frydman, J. Stiglitz, and M. Woodford). Princeton University Press.

——. 2005. Central bank communication and policy effectiveness. *Proceedings,* Federal Reserve Bank of Kansas City, August, pp. 399–474.

2

Aggregation of Information in Simple Market Mechanisms: How Large Is Large?

This chapter continues the study of simple market mechanisms in the context of markets with a finite number of participants. In chapter 1 we assumed that market participants were so small that they could not influence prices. What if this is not true and strategic behavior is possible? How large does a market need to be for price-taking behavior to be a reasonable approximation? If a large market aggregates information, how fast does it happen? Which is the more important obstacle to efficiency: market power or lack of information aggregation? Do the answers to the questions depend on the type of market mechanism, say Cournot or auction? Do they depend on the type of uncertainty and information?

The theme of the chapter is to analyze the finite-economy approximations to large markets, convergence to price-taking behavior and information aggregation, as well as its speed, as the economy grows large. In order to do this, the chapter introduces the tools needed for the study of strategic behavior with incomplete information. There are at least two reasons to undertake the convergence analysis as a market grows large.

The first reason is to check consistency with the analysis in a continuum economy (as performed in chapter 1). The equilibria in the continuum economy should be the limit of equilibria of finite economies and not an artifact of the continuum specification. For example, one method to analyze the convergence properties of the Cournot mechanism under incomplete information is to consider replica markets, where demand is replicated as the number of firms increases, and obtain in this manner a well-defined competitive limit market. With increasing marginal costs of production this can be understood as treating the size of the market (say, the number of consumers) as an exogenous parameter and then making it grow. It can then be seen that the number of firms that would enter (and pay a fixed cost of entry) in a free-entry equilibrium grows at the same rate as the market.

The second reason is practical and is to understand how large a market should be so that the results obtained in the large (continuum) market context are applicable to finite economies, and to see how quickly price-taking behavior, and information aggregation if this is the case, emerges as the economy grows large. Indeed, even if a large market aggregates information and first-best efficiency is obtained in the limit, we may still wonder how large a market should be to approach efficiency. That is, if as the market grows large the full-information competitive outcome is approached, how fast is this happening? What is the rate of convergence to efficiency? The issue is important; if convergence is obtained and yet its speed is very slow, it means that a very large market is needed for the competitive approximation to work.

Here is a preview of the results we obtain in the chapter for the case of uncertainty of the independent-values type, where as the market grows large a first-best efficient outcome is obtained. We find that convergence is fast in auctions, in contrast to a Cournot market. Furthermore, we will see that the reason for the slow convergence in the Cournot market is the rate at which information is aggregated and not the rate at which market power is dissipated. In contrast, winner-takes-all markets like auctions tend to deliver aggregation of information more easily and faster, in the sense that with a smaller number of participants we are closer to the shared-information outcome. As we have seen in chapter 1, winner-takes-all markets force traders to condition effectively on more information when taking their decisions.

Section 2.1 presents a general n-firm Cournot model in the linear-normal setup. Section 2.2 analyzes convergence to price-taking behavior as the market grows large, providing in addition a foundation for the use of the continuum model. Section 2.3 studies convergence properties with costly information acquisition. Section 2.4 studies the case where convergence to the full-information first-best is obtained, and disentangles market power from information aggregation as different determinants of the convergence rate. Section 2.5 analyzes the convergence properties of the auction mechanism. The appendix (section 2.7) collects some proofs.

2.1 A General Linear-Normal Cournot Model

In this section we consider a linear-quadratic Cournot model in a homogeneous product market with n firms, each having random production costs.[1] As in section 1.4 the information structure allows, as extremes, for private values (correlated types or cost parameters with perfect signals) and for a common value (with noisy signals). This model provides the finite-economy counterpart of the linear-normal continuum models discussed in sections 1.2–1.4.

Consider thus a market for a homogeneous product with m consumers, each with quasilinear preferences and having the net benefit function

$$U(x) - px \quad \text{with } U(x) = \alpha x - \tfrac{1}{2}\beta x^2,$$

where α and β are positive parameters and x is the consumption level. Suppose that there are n firms in the market with firm i producing x_i and a total output of $\sum_{i=1}^n x_i$. This gives rise to the inverse demand $P_m(\sum_{i=1}^n x_i) = \alpha - \beta x_m$, where $x_m = (\sum_{i=1}^n x_i)/m$. The size of the market is parameterized by the number of

[1] Sections 2.1 and 2.2 are based on Vives (2007).

consumers m. We will consider here an n-replica market where $n = m$ and x_n is the average or per capita output. Firm i produces according to a quadratic cost function

$$C(x_i, \theta_i) = \theta_i x_i + \tfrac{1}{2}\lambda x_i^2,$$

where θ_i is a random parameter and $\lambda > 0$. Total surplus is therefore given by $\text{TS} = nU(x_n) - \sum_{i=1}^n C(x_i, \theta_i)$ and per capita surplus by $\text{TS}/n = U(x_n) - (\sum_{i=1}^n C(x_i, \theta_i))/n$.

As we will see below this replica market can also be interpreted as a market parameterized by the number of consumers and where firms can enter by paying a positive fixed entry cost. Then the free-entry number of firms is of the order of the number of consumers. A large market is then a market with a large number of consumers.

The information structure is the finite-number-of-firms version of the one considered in section 1.4 (see also section 10.2.3). *Ex ante*, before uncertainty is realized, all firms face the same prospects. The vector of random variables $(\theta_1, \dots, \theta_n)$ is jointly normally distributed with $E[\theta_i] = \bar{\theta}$, $\text{var}[\theta_i] = \sigma_\theta^2$, and $\text{cov}[\theta_i, \theta_j] = \varsigma\sigma_\theta^2$, for $j \neq i$, $0 \leqslant \varsigma \leqslant 1$. It follows that the average parameter $\tilde{\theta}_n \equiv (\sum_{i=1}^n \theta_i)/n$ is normally distributed with mean $\bar{\theta}$, $\text{var}[\tilde{\theta}_n] = (1 + (n-1) \times \varsigma)\sigma_\theta^2/n$, and $\text{cov}[\tilde{\theta}_n, \theta_i] = \text{var}[\tilde{\theta}_n]$.

Firm i receives a signal $s_i = \theta_i + \varepsilon_i$, where $\varepsilon_i \sim N(0, \sigma_\varepsilon^2)$, $\text{cov}[\varepsilon_i, \varepsilon_j] = 0$ for $j \neq i$, and $\text{cov}[\theta_i, \varepsilon_j] = 0$ for all i and j. Under the normality assumption (as well as with the generalized affine information structure; see section 10.2.2), conditional expectations are affine. As before we let $\xi \equiv \tau_\varepsilon/(\tau_\theta + \tau_\varepsilon)$.

There is common knowledge about payoff functions and distributions of random variables. The only (potential) private information of firm i is its private signal s_i.

Remark 2.1. This model can also be interpreted as the finite-economy counterpart of the continuum model of section 1.4. Indeed, the profits of firm i can be rewritten as

$$\pi_i = \left(\alpha - \theta_i - \left(\frac{\beta}{n} + \frac{\lambda}{2}\right)x_i - \frac{\beta}{n}\sum_{j\neq i} x_j\right)x_i = \left(\alpha - \theta_i - \frac{\lambda}{2}x_i - \frac{\beta}{n}\sum_{j=1}^{n} x_j\right)x_i,$$

which in the limit as $n \to \infty$ yields

$$\pi_i = (\alpha - \theta_i - \tfrac{1}{2}\lambda x_i - \beta x)x_i,$$

where x is the average output. In this interpretation with Cournot or Bertrand competition with product differentiation (with $\omega_1 = \frac{1}{2}\lambda$ and $\omega_2 = \beta$ in section 1.4), the limit market is monopolistically competitive.

Equilibrium. The following proposition characterizes the Bayesian Cournot equilibrium and the price-taking Bayesian Cournot equilibrium (denoted by a superscript "c" for "competitive"). The proof is standard (but a good exercise for the reader) and is presented in the appendix (section 2.7).

Proposition 2.1 (Vives 2007). *There is a unique Bayesian Cournot equilibrium and a unique price-taking Bayesian Cournot equilibrium. They are symmetric, and affine in the signals. The strategies of the firms are given (respectively) by*

$$X_n(s_i) = b_n(\alpha - \bar{\theta}) - a_n(s_i - \bar{\theta}) \quad \textit{and} \quad X_n^c(s_i) = b_n^c(\alpha - \bar{\theta}) - a_n^c(s_i - \bar{\theta}),$$

where

$$a_n = \frac{\xi}{2\beta/n + \lambda + \beta\varsigma\xi((n-1)/n)}, \qquad b_n = \frac{1}{\lambda + \beta((1+n)/n)},$$

$$a_n^c = \frac{\xi}{\beta/n + \lambda + \beta\varsigma\xi((n-1)/n)}, \qquad b_n^c = \frac{1}{\lambda + \beta}.$$

Remark 2.2. From the FOC of profit maximization it is immediate that in equilibrium expected profits for firm i are given by

$$E[\pi_n] = \left(\frac{\lambda}{2} + \frac{\beta}{n}\right) E[(X_n(s_i))^2].$$

Remark 2.3. In the case of independent values (i.e., $\varsigma = 0$ and $\tau_\varepsilon = \infty$), the formulas are valid for a general distribution of the uncertainty.

Remark 2.4. The replica market considered can, in fact, be the outcome of free entry into a market parameterized by its size. Consider a market with m consumers (the size of the market), n firms producing a total output of $\sum_{i=1}^n x_i$ and inverse demand $P_m(\sum_{i=1}^n x_i) = \alpha - \beta(\sum_{i=1}^n x_i)/m$. Suppose now that at a first stage firms decide whether to enter the market or not. If a firm decides to enter, it pays a fixed cost $F > 0$. At a second stage each active firm i, upon observing its signal s_i, sets an output level. Given that n firms have entered, a Bayesian Cournot equilibrium is realized. Suppose that parameters are in a range that for any cost realization a firm wants to produce. Given our assumptions, for any n there is a unique, and symmetric, equilibrium yielding expected profits $E[\pi_n]$ for each firm (as in proposition 2.1). A free-entry equilibrium is a subgame-perfect equilibrium of the two-stage game. A subgame-perfect equilibrium requires that, for any entry decisions at the first stage, a Bayes–Nash equilibrium in outputs obtains at the second stage. Given a market of size m, the free-entry number of firms $n^*(m)$ is approximated by the solution to $E[\pi_n] = F$ (provided F is not so large to prevent any entry). It can be checked that $n^*(m)$ is of the same order as m (Vives 2002). This means that the ratio of consumers to firms is bounded away from zero and infinity for any market size. We can therefore reinterpret the replica market as a free-entry market parameterized by market size.

Measures of speed of convergence. Next we examine the convergence properties of this finite Cournot market as the economy grows. Before stating the convergence results we will recall measures of speed of convergence. (See section 10.3.2 for a fuller development and related definitions and measures.) Whenever $n^{-\upsilon} b_n \xrightarrow[n]{} k$ for some nonzero constant k the sequence (of real numbers) b_n is of the *order* n^υ, with υ a real number. We say that the sequence of random variables $\{y_n\}$ converges in *mean square* to zero at the rate $1/\sqrt{n^r}$ (or that y_n is of the order $1/\sqrt{n^r}$) if $E[y_n^2]$ converges to zero at the rate $1/n^r$ (i.e., $E[y_n^2]$ is of the order $1/n^r$). Given that $E[y_n^2] = (E[y_n])^2 + \text{var}[y_n]$, a sequence $\{y_n\}$ such that $E[y_n] = 0$ and $\text{var}[y_n]$ is of order $1/n$ converges to zero at the rate $1/\sqrt{n}$. For example, if the random parameters $(\theta_1, \dots, \theta_n)$ are i.i.d. with finite variance, then $\tilde{\theta}_n - \bar{\theta}$ converges (in mean square) to 0 at the rate of $1/\sqrt{n}$ because $E[\tilde{\theta}_n - \bar{\theta}] = 0$ and $\text{var}[\tilde{\theta}_n] = \sigma_\theta^2/n$.

A more refined measure of convergence speed for a given convergence rate is provided by the *asymptotic variance*. Suppose that $\{y_n\}$ is such that $E[y_n] = 0$ and $E[y_n^2] = \text{var}[y_n]$ converges to 0 at the rate $1/n^r$ for some $r > 0$. Then the asymptotic variance is given by the constant $\text{AV} = \lim_{n\to\infty} n^r \text{var}[y_n]$. A higher asymptotic variance means that the speed of convergence is slower. It is worth noting that if the sequence $\{y_n\}$ is normally distributed, then $\sqrt{n^r}(y_n)$ converges in distribution to $N(0, \text{AV})$. Indeed, a normal random variable is characterized by mean and variance and we have that $\text{var}[\sqrt{n^r}(y_n)] = n^r \text{var}[y_n]$ tends to AV as $n \to \infty$.

2.2 Convergence to Price Taking in a Cournot Market

In this section we show that Bayesian Cournot equilibria converge to (Bayesian) price-taking equilibria as $n \to \infty$. This justifies the use of the continuum model as an approximation to the large Cournot market. We also characterize the speed at which this convergence occurs.

We consider, in turn, convergence to price taking and convergence to the continuum model as the economy is replicated. The following proposition characterizes the convergence of the Bayesian Cournot equilibrium to a price-taking equilibrium. The proof is in the appendix (section 2.7).

Proposition 2.2 (Vives 2007). *As the market grows large, the market price p_n (at the Bayesian Cournot equilibrium) converges in mean square to the price-taking Bayesian Cournot price p_n^c at the rate of $1/n$. (That is, $E[(p_n - p_n^c)^2] \to 0$ at the rate of $1/n^2$.) The difference between (per capita) expected total surplus at the market outcome and at the price-taking Bayesian Cournot equilibrium $(\text{ETS}_n^c - \text{ETS}_n)/n$ is of order $1/n^2$.*

As the market grows large, market power (in terms of the margin over marginal cost) dissipates at the rate of $1/n$ and the welfare loss with respect to the price-taking equilibrium at the rate of $1/n^2$. As we will see in section 2.3.2, these are the same rates of convergence as in the Cournot oligopoly with no uncertainty. Price-taking Bayesian Cournot equilibria provide the right benchmark of comparison because they maximize ETS subject to the use of decentralized strategies (proposition 1.2).

The following proposition characterizes convergence of the Bayesian Cournot equilibria to the price-taking equilibrium of the continuum economy as the market grows large. The proof is in the appendix (section 2.7).

Proposition 2.3 (Vives 2007). *As the economy is replicated, the Bayesian Cournot equilibrium converges to the equilibrium in the continuum limit economy:* $X(s_i) = b(\alpha - \bar{\theta}) - a(s_i - \bar{\theta})$, *where* $a = \xi/(\lambda + \beta\varsigma\xi)$ *and* $b = 1/(\lambda + \beta)$. *The Bayesian Cournot price* p_n *converges (in mean square) to* $p = \alpha - \beta(b(\alpha - \bar{\theta}) - a(\tilde{\theta} - \bar{\theta}))$ *at the rate of* $1/\sqrt{n}$ *and* $\sqrt{n}(p_n - p)$ *converges in distribution to*

$$N(0, \beta^2 a^2((1 - \varsigma)\sigma_\theta^2 + \sigma_\varepsilon^2)).$$

Convergence to the equilibrium of the continuum economy happens at the rate $1/\sqrt{n}$ at which the average error in the signals of the agents $(1/n)\sum_{i=1}^n \varepsilon_i \to 0$. Convergence is slower, according to the asymptotic variance $\beta^2 a^2((1-\varsigma)\sigma_\theta^2 + \sigma_\varepsilon^2)$, with larger σ_θ^2 or β, and faster with larger ς or λ. A larger ρ means that we are closer to a common-value environment. The effect of an increase in σ_ε^2 is ambiguous: the direct effect is to slow down convergence but the indirect effect is to lower the response to information, which has the opposite effect.

In summary, in the context of a general Cournot model, which allows for private or common values, we have checked that the equilibria obtained in the continuum Cournot markets in chapter 1 are not an artifact but the limit of equilibria in finite economies. Furthermore, the convergence rate to the limit equilibrium is $1/\sqrt{n}$ for prices, where n is the "size" of the market, and convergence is slower for higher prior uncertainty and faster when closer to a common-value environment. Finally, convergence to price taking is faster, at the rate of $1/n$ for prices and $1/n^2$ for the welfare loss (i.e., the deadweight loss with respect to price taking).

2.3 Endogenous Information Acquisition

The convergence result can be extended to the case of costly information acquisition. Consider the finite-economy counterpart of the continuum model in section 1.6. That is, a sequence of replica markets with the n-replica consisting of n symmetric firms (each with cost $C(x_i) = \frac{1}{2}\lambda x_i^2$, $\lambda \geqslant 0$) and n consumers giving rise to an inverse demand $p = \theta - \beta(\sum_{i=1}^n x_i)/n$, where $\sum_{i=1}^n x_i$ is the total output in the market. This model is a slight variation of the one presented in section 2.1 with a common-value information structure.

Competition proceeds in two stages. At the first stage firm i contracts the precision of its signal τ_{ε_i} at constant per unit cost $c \geqslant 0$ for a total cost $c\tau_{\varepsilon_i}$. For convenience and given that $\xi_i \equiv \tau_{\varepsilon_i}/(\tau_\theta + \tau_{\varepsilon_i})$, we will consider the purchase of "precision" ξ_i for a given $\tau_\theta = (\sigma_\theta^2)^{-1}$ at cost for firm i:

$$\varphi(\xi_i) = \frac{c}{\sigma_\theta^2}\frac{\xi_i}{1 - \xi_i}.$$

The purchased precisions are observable and at the second stage firms compete in quantities once each firm has received its private signal. Let us consider in turn the cases of decreasing returns ($\lambda > 0$), constant returns ($\lambda = 0$), and discuss the effects of the observability of the purchases of information precision.

2.3.1 Decreasing Returns

Consider the second stage where firm i has a signal of precision ξ_i. It is possible to show, similarly to the proof of proposition 2.1, that there is a unique Bayesian Cournot equilibrium and that is given by

$$X_{in}(s_i) = a_{in}(s_i - \bar{\theta}) + b_n\bar{\theta} \quad \text{for } i = 1, \dots, n,$$

where

$$a_{in} = \frac{n}{\beta}\left(\frac{\gamma_{in}}{1 + \sum_{j=1}^{n} \gamma_{jn}}\right),$$
$$b_n = \frac{\lambda + \beta/n}{(\lambda + \beta)(\lambda + 2\beta/n)},$$
$$\gamma_{in} = \frac{\xi_i\beta/n}{(\lambda + 2\beta/n) - \xi_i\beta/n}.$$

The expected profits of firm i are given by

$$E[\pi_{in}] = \left(\frac{\lambda}{2} + \frac{\beta}{n}\right)E[(X_{in}(s_i))^2]$$

and the first-stage payoff for given precisions is $\Pi_{in}(\xi_1, \dots, \xi_n) = E[\pi_{in}] - \varphi(\xi_i)$. Suppose that the purchases of information precision are observable. A Nash equilibrium of the game with payoffs $\Pi_{in}(\xi_1, \dots, \xi_n)$ will constitute a subgame-perfect equilibrium of the two-stage game. Indeed, a subgame-perfect equilibrium requires that, for any profile of precision purchases at the first stage, a Bayes–Nash equilibrium in outputs obtains at the second stage. It can be checked that Π_{in} is strictly quasiconcave in ξ_i (i.e., $\partial^2\Pi_{in}/\partial\xi_i^2 < 0$ for $\partial\Pi_{in}/\partial\xi_i = 0$) and that competition is of the strategic substitutes type ($\partial^2\Pi_{in}/\partial\xi_i\partial\xi_j < 0$ for $j \neq i$). It then follows that there is a unique symmetric equilibrium $\xi_{in}^* = \xi_n^*$, $i = 1, \dots, n$.[2] Let $\phi_n(\xi) \equiv (\partial\Pi_{in}/\partial\xi_i)|_{\xi_j=\xi,\, j=1,\dots,n}$. The unique symmetric subgame-perfect equilibrium of the two-stage game ξ_n^* solves in ξ, $\phi_n(\xi) = 0$ provided the solution is positive and equals zero otherwise. Some computations show that

$$\phi_n(\xi) = \frac{(\lambda + 2\beta/n)(1 + (n-1)\gamma_n) + (n-1)\gamma_n\xi\beta/n}{((\lambda + 2\beta/n)(1 + (n-1)\gamma_n) - (n-1)\gamma_n\xi\beta/n)^3}\left(\frac{\lambda}{2} + \frac{\beta}{n}\right)\left(\frac{\beta}{n}\right)^4\sigma_\theta^2 - \frac{c}{\sigma_\theta^2}\frac{1}{(1-\xi)^2},$$

where

$$\gamma_n = \frac{\beta\xi/n}{(\lambda + 2\beta/n) - \beta\xi/n}.$$

The solution ξ_n^* will be positive if $\sigma_\theta^2 > 2\sqrt{c(\frac{1}{2}\lambda + \beta/n)}$. It is easily checked that ξ_n^* tends to

$$\xi^* = \max\left\{0, \frac{\sigma_\theta^2 - \sqrt{2c\lambda}}{\beta\sqrt{2c/\lambda} + \sigma_\theta^2}\right\}$$

[2] See Vives (1988 and sections 2.3.2 and 5 in 1999).

as $n \to \infty$. This is exactly the solution obtained in the continuum economy in section 1.6 when $\lambda > 0$.

In order to perform the welfare analysis, consider the problem of a planner that has to purchase an aggregate signal, with the same cost structure as above and that sets output to maximize expected total surplus. At the first-best solution the result is that as $n \to \infty$ the first-best optimal expenditure on information converges to zero in per capita terms and the precision of the aggregate signal goes to ∞. The argument is as follows. Consider the n-replica market and suppose there is a center which purchases an aggregate signal $\tilde{s}_n$ with precision $1/w_n$. Given the pooled signal $\tilde{s}_n = (\sum_{i=1}^n s_i)/n$, expected per capita total surplus (gross of information costs), conditional on $\tilde{s}_n$, is $E[\theta \mid \tilde{s}_n]x - \frac{1}{2}(\beta + \lambda)x^2$, where x is average production. Optimal production is given by $X^{\mathrm{o}}(\tilde{s}_n) = E[\theta \mid \tilde{s}_n]/(\beta + \lambda)$. Expected total surplus as a function of the precision of the signal $1/w_n$ is then

$$\frac{n}{2(\beta + \lambda)} E[(E[\theta \mid \tilde{s}_n])^2] - \frac{c}{w_n} = \frac{n}{2(\beta + \lambda)} \left(\frac{\sigma_\theta^2}{\sigma_\theta^2 + w_n} \sigma_\theta^2 + \bar{\theta}^2 \right) - \frac{c}{w_n}.$$

It then follows that the optimal purchase of information precision is

$$\frac{1}{w_n^{\mathrm{o}}} = \max\left\{ \left(\frac{\sqrt{n}}{\sqrt{2(\beta + \lambda)c}} - \frac{1}{\sigma_\theta^2} \right), 0 \right\},$$

which tends to ∞ as n goes to ∞. Nevertheless, the expenditure on information in per capita terms converges to zero as $n \to \infty$ since $(c/nw_n^{\mathrm{o}}) \underset{n}{\to} 0$. In the limit, per capita expenditure on information is zero and the full-information first-best is achieved.

2.3.2 Constant Returns

With constant returns to scale firms will purchase information ($\xi_n^* > 0$) if n is large enough; ξ_n^* will decrease with n for large n and will eventually converge to 0.[3] Recall that no equilibrium exists with costly research in the continuum economy (section 1.6). The key observation is that with a finite number of firms expected profits are positive at the market equilibrium and incentives to acquire information are not destroyed. With a large number of firms, given that a firm's rivals are purchasing some information, the optimal response of the firm is also to acquire some information. With many firms and constant returns, all firms purchase a vanishing amount of information. The average precision in the market converges to zero as n goes to ∞. No equilibrium exists with costly information acquisition in the continuum economy but zero average expenditure on information ($\xi^* = 0$) is the limit of a unique sequence of subgame-perfect equilibria of the finite approximating economies.

With constant returns to scale the analysis of market optimality is more delicate. We have found that in the continuum limit no equilibrium exists but

[3] This follows from $\sigma_\theta^2 > 2\sqrt{c\beta/n}$ for n large enough and from the expression of $\phi_n(\xi)$ when $\lambda = 0$.

for any finite n the equilibrium does exist and involves a vanishing but positive average expenditure on information. What is the limit of per capita total expected surplus as the market grows? It can be checked (exercise 2.1) that the total precision of information in the market tends to ∞ as we replicate the economy (it is of order $\sqrt{n}$) while the average expenditure on research tends to 0 (it is of order $1/\sqrt{n}$). This implies that in the limit first-best efficiency is obtained! The explanation is as follows. Fix a large n. We then know that every firm buys a small amount of information. If firms were price takers, an almost efficient outcome would obtain: with constant returns (and the affine information structure) the market aggregates information and average expenditure on information is small. By increasing n, firms eventually become price takers; they always buy some information, and the average expenditure on research tends to 0. The limit is thus the first-best outcome.

Li et al. (1987) also consider information acquisition with constant-returns-to-scale technology but they do not replicate demand when the number of firms increases. They find that the aggregate purchase of information may be positive in the competitive limit even though the purchase of an individual firm is zero. The welfare analysis indicates that the total expenditure on information acquisition undertaken by the market can be either too much, if the cost of research is low, or too little, if the cost of research is high. It is worth noting that, when examining the convergence properties of equilibria without replicating demand, the "limit" market is not well-defined. Consider the Cournot model without uncertainty and with constant marginal costs: if demand is not replicated when increasing the number of firms, individual outputs are zero in the limit while aggregate output equals the competitive output.

2.3.3 Strategic Aspects

In the continuum model of section 1.6, whether or not information precision purchases were observable did not matter. In a finite economy with n firms, it is no longer true that secret and overt information acquisition have the same consequences. Indeed, if precisions are observable, there is a strategic effect with a finite number of players. It is possible to show that equilibrium precisions will be larger in the two-stage game with observable precisions. This is in fact true, irrespective of whether market competition is of the strategic substitutes or complements variety. The reason is that in both cases there is an incentive to overinvest strategically in information acquisition. By acquiring more information in the Cournot (Bertrand) case the rivals respond less (more) to their information. This makes the residual demand faced by the firm more variable, and it is good for expected profits provided that the firm has some information.

The consequences for equilibrium expected profits (including costs of information acquisition), however, are different in Bertrand and Cournot. Consider firms with symmetric cost functions. Then with price competition, expected profits increase in the strategic two-stage game, in contrast with the case where information acquisition is secret, because a firm likes the rival to be better informed. Competition for the acquisition of information is then of the strategic complements variety. With quantity rivalry, competition for the acquisition of information is of the strategic substitutes type. It turns out that equilibrium expected profits decrease in the strategic two-stage game (Hauk and Hurkens 2001). This is not immediate because all firms have acquired more information.[4]

As the number of firms grows the outcome of any of the two games (one shot or simultaneous move and two-stage) in the Cournot market converges to the outcome we have obtained in the continuum economy. The reason is that, as should be expected, the strategic effect disappears.

2.3.4 Summary

With costly information acquisition in the Cournot market:

- The equilibrium of the limit continuum economy can be rationalized as the limit of equilibria of finite economies provided returns are decreasing.
- With constant returns the limit economy is not well-behaved and there is no equilibrium despite the fact that finite economies are close to efficiency when large.
- When there are a finite number of firms and information acquisition is observable, firms tend to overinvest strategically (and the same would be true if competition were to be à la Bertrand in a product differentiation environment).

2.4 Convergence to the First-Best: Market Power and Information Aggregation

Next we study the case in which the limit is first-best efficient (with i.i.d. uncertainty) and the market aggregates information, and we decompose the speed of convergence in terms of information aggregation and market power effects.

2.4.1 An Independent-Values Cournot Model[5]

Assume now in the model of section 2.1 that the random cost parameters (θ_i) are drawn independently from a distribution with bounded support (independent-values model). In this case convergence to the first-best will be obtained. In order to disentangle market power and information aggregation effects we also consider the two full-information regimes (Cournot and competitive) on top of the private-information Bayesian equilibria. Variables in the nonstrategic regimes are denoted by the superscript "c" ("competitive"); variables in the full-information regimes are denoted by the superscript "f" ("full information").

---

[4] See Vives (1999, chapter 8) for a full analysis of the incentives for firms to acquire and share information in oligopoly.

[5] This section follows Vives (2002).

Table 2.1. Regimes and strategies.

Information	Strategic	Price taking
Private	Bayesian Cournot $X_n(\theta_i)$	Price-taking Bayesian Cournot $X_n^{\mathrm{c}}(\theta_i)$
Full	Cournot $X_n^{\mathrm{f}}(\theta_i, \tilde{\theta}_n)$	Competitive $X_n^{\mathrm{fc}}(\theta_i, \tilde{\theta}_n)$

Table 2.1 presents the different regimes and the corresponding notation for strategies.

At private-information equilibria the strategy of firm i depends only on its type θ_i. At full-information equilibria it will depend on the realization of all types, which given the structure of the model can be summarized in $(\theta_i, \tilde{\theta}_n)$, where $\tilde{\theta}_n = (1/n)\sum_{j=1}^{n}\theta_j$. A unique (and linear) equilibrium for each regime is easily derived (similar to the proof of proposition 2.1).

Assuming that the underlying parameters are such that for any cost realization each firm wants to produce a positive quantity in any of the regimes[6] and letting $\beta = 1$ we find the following:

$$\begin{aligned}
X_n(\theta_i) &= b_n(\alpha - \bar{\theta}) - a_n(\theta_i - \bar{\theta}); & a_n &= \frac{1}{\lambda + 2/n}, & b_n &= \frac{1}{\lambda + (1+n)/n}, \\
X_n^{\mathrm{c}}(\theta_i) &= b_n^{\mathrm{c}}(\alpha - \bar{\theta}) - a_n^{\mathrm{c}}(\theta_i - \bar{\theta}); & a_n^{\mathrm{c}} &= \frac{1}{\lambda + 1/n}, & b_n^{\mathrm{c}} &= \frac{1}{\lambda + 1}, \\
X_n^{\mathrm{f}}(\theta_i, \tilde{\theta}_n) &= b_n^{\mathrm{f}}(\alpha - \bar{\theta}) - a_n^{\mathrm{f}}(\theta_i - \tilde{\theta}_n); & a_n^{\mathrm{f}} &= a_n^{\mathrm{c}}, & b_n^{\mathrm{f}} &= b_n, \\
X_n^{\mathrm{fc}}(\theta_i, \tilde{\theta}_n) &= b_n^{\mathrm{fc}}(\alpha - \tilde{\theta}_n) - a_n^{\mathrm{fc}}(\theta_i - \tilde{\theta}_n); & a_n^{\mathrm{fc}} &= \lambda^{-1}, & b_n^{\mathrm{fc}} &= b_n^{\mathrm{c}}.
\end{aligned}$$

Average outputs in each case are easily obtained: $x_n^{\mathrm{c}} = b_n^{\mathrm{c}}(\alpha - \bar{\theta}) - a_n^{\mathrm{c}}(\tilde{\theta}_n - \bar{\theta})$, $x_n = b_n(\alpha - \bar{\theta}) - a_n(\tilde{\theta}_n - \bar{\theta})$, $x_n^{\mathrm{f}} = b_n(\alpha - \tilde{\theta}_n)$, and $x_n^{\mathrm{fc}} = b_n^{\mathrm{c}}(\alpha - \tilde{\theta}_n)$. In the price-taking markets (i.e., when there is no market power difference), expected outputs (and prices) are the same with full and private information. Market power lowers expected output from $b_n^{\mathrm{c}}(\alpha - \bar{\theta})$ in the price-taking regimes to $b_n(\alpha - \bar{\theta})$ in the regimes with market power ($b_n < b_n^{\mathrm{c}}$). Furthermore, the Bayesian Cournot equilibrium outputs are the least sensitive and the full-information price-taking outputs are the most sensitive to own costs; both intermediate regimes have an equal intermediate sensitivity ($a_n < a_n^{\mathrm{f}} = a_n^{\mathrm{c}} < a_n^{\mathrm{fc}}$). Observe that keeping market power constant a firm reacts more to its cost realization with full information.

2.4.2 Convergence Rates

The following proposition characterizes the convergence of the Bayesian Cournot equilibrium to the full-information competitive equilibrium as the market grows large and decomposes its rate into market power and information aggregation effects. The proof is similar to the proof of proposition 2.2 and is left as an exercise.

[6] This means that the relative inefficiency of firms is never so large as to imply the shutdown of inefficient producers. A small λ constrains the support of θ_i in order for outputs to be positive.

Proposition 2.4 (Vives 2002). *As the market grows large the Bayesian Cournot equilibrium price p_n converges (in mean square) to the full-information competitive price p_n^{fc} at the rate of $1/\sqrt{n}$. The (per capita) expected deadweight loss at the market outcome $(\text{ETS}_n^{\text{fc}} - \text{ETS}_n)/n$ is of order $1/n$. The orders of magnitude are driven by information aggregation and not by market power:*

(i) *Information is aggregated at the rate $1/\sqrt{n}$ while market power is dissipated faster, at the rate $1/n$: $p_n^{\text{c}} - p_n^{\text{fc}}$ and $p_n^{\text{c}} - p_n^{\text{f}}$ are both of order $1/\sqrt{n}$, and $p_n^{\text{f}} - p_n^{\text{fc}}$ and $p_n - p_n^{\text{c}}$ are both of order $1/n$.*

(ii) *The terms $(\text{ETS}_n^{\text{fc}} - \text{ETS}_n^{\text{c}})/n$ and $(\text{ETS}_n^{\text{f}} - \text{ETS}_n)/n$ are of order $1/n$, while $(\text{ETS}_n^{\text{c}} - \text{ETS}_n)/n$ and $(\text{ETS}_n^{\text{fc}} - \text{ETS}_n^{\text{f}})/n$ are of order $1/n^2$.*

To explain (i) note that the change over the dimension of market power (while keeping information private) $p_n - p_n^{\text{c}}$ inherits the order of the expected price difference $E[p_n - p_n^{\text{c}}]$, which is $1/n$. The change over the dimension of information (while fixing price-taking behavior) $p_n^{\text{c}} - p_n^{\text{fc}}$ is of order $\tilde{\theta}_n - \bar{\theta}$, which is $1/\sqrt{n}$.[7] The interaction between both effects is easily seen to be of the same order as the market power term. This means that the difference $p_n - p_n^{\text{fc}}$ will inherit the order of $p_n^{\text{c}} - p_n^{\text{fc}}$ (information aggregation), $1/\sqrt{n}$, which is higher than the order of $p_n - p_n^{\text{c}}$ (market power), $1/n$. A similar analysis establishes the same result for the alternative decomposition $p_n - p_n^{\text{fc}} = p_n - p_n^{\text{f}} + p_n^{\text{f}} - p_n^{\text{fc}}$. Now $p_n - p_n^{\text{f}}$ is of the order $1/\sqrt{n}$ (information aggregation) and $p_n^{\text{f}} - p_n^{\text{fc}}$ is of the order $1/n$ (market power).

The difference in expected prices between a strategic and a price-taking regime (be it with private information, $p_n - p_n^{\text{c}}$, or with full information, $p_n^{\text{f}} - p_n^{\text{fc}}$) is of order $1/n$, which is the same as in markets with no uncertainty, and is explained by the rate at which market power vanishes. Indeed, in a full-information Cournot equilibrium

$$\frac{p_n^{\text{f}} - (\sum_{i=1}^{n} \text{MC}(x_{in}^{\text{f}}, \theta_i))/n}{p_n^{\text{f}}} = \frac{1/n}{\eta}$$

and the order of magnitude of the margin over the average marginal cost is $1/n$ provided the elasticity of demand η is bounded away from zero and infinity.

The variance of the price difference keeping market power constant, $p_n^{\text{c}} - p_n^{\text{fc}}$ or $p_n - p_n^{\text{f}}$, is driven by information aggregation, that is, by the discrepancy between the sample mean and the population mean of the cost parameters, $\tilde{\theta}_n - \bar{\theta}$, which is of order $1/\sqrt{n}$. A firm in a private-information regime has to estimate the market price (price-taking case) or residual demand (Cournot case), which depends on the average realization of the cost parameter, and his strategy will depend only on his cost realization (and the known population mean).

---

[7] We have that $p_n - p_n^{\text{c}} = E[p_n - p_n^{\text{c}}] + (a_n - a_n^{\text{c}})(\tilde{\theta}_n - \bar{\theta})$ and the second term is easily seen to be of lower order than $1/n$; $p_n^{\text{c}} - p_n^{\text{fc}} = (a_n^{\text{c}} - b_n^{\text{c}})(\tilde{\theta}_n - \bar{\theta})$ and $(a_n^{\text{c}} - b_n^{\text{c}})$ is of the order of a constant.

To explain result (ii) in the proposition consider the decomposition:

$$\text{Deadweight loss} = \text{Information aggregation loss} + \text{Market power loss},$$
$$(\mathrm{ETS}_n^{\mathrm{fc}} - \mathrm{ETS}_n)/n = (\mathrm{ETS}_n^{\mathrm{fc}} - \mathrm{ETS}_n^{\mathrm{c}})/n + (\mathrm{ETS}_n^{\mathrm{c}} - \mathrm{ETS}_n)/n,$$

or, alternatively,

$$(\mathrm{ETS}_n^{\mathrm{fc}} - \mathrm{ETS}_n)/n = (\mathrm{ETS}_n^{\mathrm{f}} - \mathrm{ETS}_n)/n + (\mathrm{ETS}_n^{\mathrm{fc}} - \mathrm{ETS}_n^{\mathrm{f}})/n,$$

which in terms of orders of magnitude yields

$$1/n \approx 1/n + 1/n^2.$$

Market power dissipates according to the rate of the market without uncertainty. This yields an expected deadweight loss of order $1/n^2$, be it in the full information or in the private-information case. In the full-information case (where the deadweight loss is $(\mathrm{ETS}_n^{\mathrm{fc}} - \mathrm{ETS}_n^{\mathrm{f}})/n$) this is a well-known result. The full-information competitive equilibrium is determined by the intersection of aggregate (average) demand $D(p) = \alpha - p$ with aggregate (average) supply $S(p) = \lambda^{-1}(p - \tilde{\theta}_n)$, yielding an average output of $(\alpha - \tilde{\theta}_n)/(\lambda + 1)$. Instead, the full-information Cournot outcome yields an average output of

$$\frac{\alpha - \tilde{\theta}_n}{\lambda + (1 + n)/n}.$$

The difference is of order $1/n$ (see, for example, section 4.4 in Vives 1999) and consequently the deadweight loss due to allocative inefficiency

$$\tfrac{1}{2}(1 + \lambda)E[(x_n^{\mathrm{f}} - x_n^{\mathrm{fc}})^2]$$

(the area of the "Harberger triangle") is of order $1/n^2$. (See figure 2.1.) To this we should add the productive inefficiency

$$\tfrac{1}{2}\lambda \operatorname{var}[(x_{in}^{\mathrm{fc}} - x_n^{\mathrm{f}}) - (x_{in}^{\mathrm{fc}} - x_n^{\mathrm{fc}})]$$

associated with not producing the Cournot output vector in a cost-minimizing way (again inducing a deadweight loss of the same order $1/n^2$).[8]

Similarly, in the private-information case the order of both allocative and productive inefficiencies with respect to the price-taking Bayesian equilibrium (or decentralized team solution) is $1/n^2$. In both the full- and private-information cases, market power affects the deadweight loss (DWL) not only by decreasing expected output (since $b_n = b_n^{\mathrm{f}} < b_n^{\mathrm{c}} = b_n^{\mathrm{fc}}$) but also by making firms less sensitive to their costs (respectively, $a_n^{\mathrm{f}} < a_n^{\mathrm{fc}}$ and $a_n < a_n^{\mathrm{c}}$). Both allocative and productive inefficiency are impaired by the same order of magnitude.

When information aggregation is at stake, while keeping market power constant, the DWL is driven by the variance terms because expected output does not change when switching from one regime to another. In a parallel fashion to

[8] See the appendix (section 2.7) for an explanation of the decomposition of the deadweight loss in allocative and productive inefficiency.

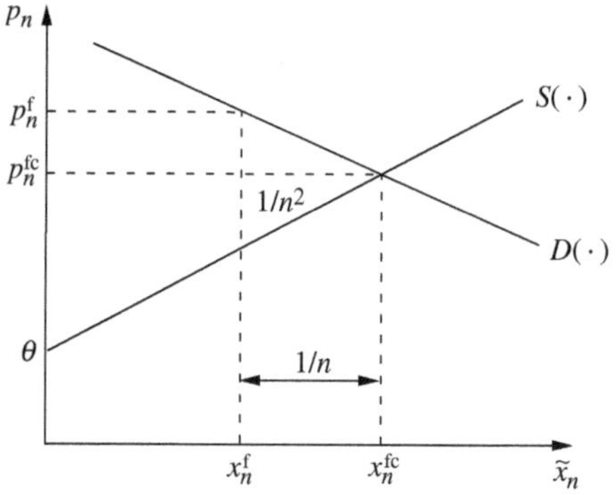

Figure 2.1. Deadweight loss due to market power with full information.

Table 2.2. Deadweight loss.

	Deadweight loss due to: Market power	Private information
Positive:		
Bayes-Cournot (ETS_n)	$\Delta W^{\mathrm{c}}_n = (\mathrm{ETS}^{\mathrm{c}}_n - \mathrm{ETS}_n)/n$	$\Delta W^{\mathrm{f}}_n = (\mathrm{ETS}^{\mathrm{f}}_n - \mathrm{ETS}_n)/n$
Normative:		
competitive ($\mathrm{ETS}^{\mathrm{fc}}_n$)	$\Delta \underline{W}^{\mathrm{c}}_n = (\mathrm{ETS}^{\mathrm{fc}}_n - \mathrm{ETS}^{\mathrm{f}}_n)/n$	$\Delta \underline{W}^{\mathrm{f}}_n = (\mathrm{ETS}^{\mathrm{fc}}_n - \mathrm{ETS}^{\mathrm{c}}_n)/n$
	Order $1/n^2$	Order $1/n$

figure 2.1, we have, for example, that the discrepancy between x^{c}_n and x^{fc}_n is of order $1/\sqrt{n}$ and, correspondingly, the allocative DWL is of order $1/n$.[9]

Table 2.2 summarizes the order of magnitude of the welfare effects of price distortions.

2.4.3 How Large Is Large: Simulations

A natural question is how large a market should be so that the asymptotic (rate) results apply. Simulations with the model show that n need not be very large.[10] In the decomposition of $\mathrm{DWL}_n = \mathrm{ETS}^{\mathrm{fc}}_n - \mathrm{ETS}_n$ in terms of $\Delta \underline{W}^{\mathrm{f}}_n = (\mathrm{ETS}^{\mathrm{fc}}_n - \mathrm{ETS}^{\mathrm{c}}_n)$ and $\Delta W^{\mathrm{c}}_n = (\mathrm{ETS}^{\mathrm{c}}_n - \mathrm{ETS}_n)$, there is a critical $\bar{n}$ beyond which $\Delta \underline{W}^{\mathrm{f}}_n > \Delta W^{\mathrm{c}}_n$. The

[9] We have that $(\mathrm{ETS}^{\mathrm{fc}}_n - \mathrm{ETS}^{\mathrm{c}}_n)/n = \frac{1}{2}((\beta + \lambda)\operatorname{var}[x^{\mathrm{c}}_n - x^{\mathrm{fc}}_n] + \lambda \operatorname{var}[(x^{\mathrm{c}}_{in} - x^{\mathrm{c}}_n) - (x^{\mathrm{fc}}_{in} - x^{\mathrm{fc}}_n)])$. We know that $x^{\mathrm{c}}_n - x^{\mathrm{fc}}_n = (b^{\mathrm{c}}_n - a^{\mathrm{c}}_n)(\tilde{\theta}_n - \bar{\theta})$, $(b^{\mathrm{c}}_n - a^{\mathrm{c}}_n)$ is of the order of a constant and $\operatorname{var}[\tilde{\theta}_n - \bar{\theta}]$ is of the order $1/n$. Furthermore, $(x^{\mathrm{c}}_{in} - x^{\mathrm{c}}_n) - (x^{\mathrm{fc}}_{in} - x^{\mathrm{fc}}_n) = a^{\mathrm{fc}}_n(\theta_i - \tilde{\theta}_n) - a^{\mathrm{c}}_n(\theta_i - \tilde{\theta})$, which again yields a productive efficiency loss of order $1/n$ because of the leading term $\tilde{\theta}_n$.

[10] Simulations have been performed in the following parameter range: $\beta = 1$, $\alpha - \bar{\theta}$ in $\{2, 6.5\}$, and λ and σ^2_θ in $\{\frac{1}{10}, \frac{1}{2}, 1, 2, 10\}$. Only $\alpha - \bar{\theta}$ matters for the comparisons we perform. We get $\alpha - \bar{\theta} = 2$ with, for example, $\alpha = 3$, $\bar{\theta} = 1$ and $\alpha - \bar{\theta} = 6.5$ with, for example, $\alpha = 10$, $\bar{\theta} = 3.5$. (Some of the parameter combinations in the simulations violate the sufficient conditions for positive outputs.)

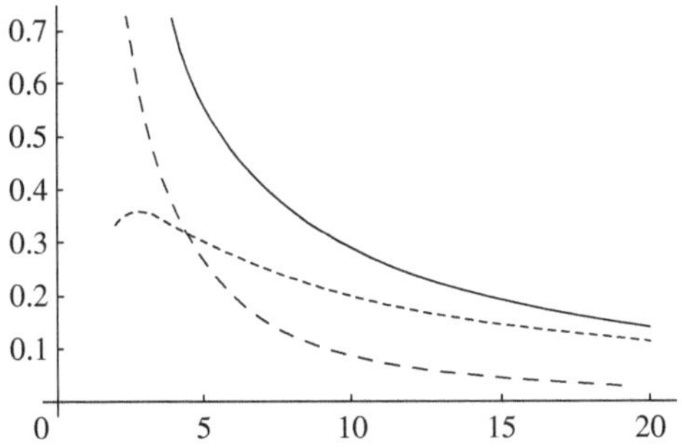

Figure 2.2. Parameter values: $\alpha - \bar{\theta} = 6.5$, $\lambda = \frac{1}{2}$, $\sigma_\theta^2 = 2$; $\mathrm{DWL}_n = \Delta W_n^{\mathrm{c}} + \Delta \underline{W}_n^{\mathrm{f}}$ (DWL_n is the continuous line, the market power effect ΔW_n^{c} is the long-dashed line, and the information effect $\Delta \underline{W}_n^{\mathrm{f}}$ is the short-dashed line).

critical $\bar{n}$ decreases with σ_θ^2 and increases with λ. When uncertainty is significant and marginal costs are not very steep, $\bar{n}$ is below 10 firms. It may also happen that $\bar{n}$ is below 2. The market power term ΔW_n^{c} is typically always decreasing with n, while the information term $\Delta \underline{W}_n^{\mathrm{f}}$ first increases and then decreases with n. This yields a total deadweight loss DWL_n which is, typically, always decreasing with n. Figure 2.2 displays the case with $\alpha - \bar{\theta} = 6.5$, $\lambda = \frac{1}{2}$, and $\sigma_\theta^2 = 2$, which yields $\bar{n} = 4.4$.[11]

2.4.4 Summary

In an independent-values Cournot market, convergence to first-best efficiency, as the market grows large, is attained at a slow rate because information aggregation is slow (at the rate $1/\sqrt{n}$) and despite the fact that market power vanishes quickly (at the rate $1/n$). Even for moderately sized markets we have that the lack of information aggregation looms larger than market power in the welfare loss with respect to the first-best outcome.

2.5 Convergence in Auctions

We saw in section 1.5 how auctions would aggregate information. In this section we will see that in auctions with independent valuations convergence to efficiency is faster than in the smooth Cournot market mechanism. That is, in an auction a smaller market is sufficient to get close to the full-information outcome.

In section 2.5.1 we survey results on the convergence to efficiency and price-taking behavior as the auction market grows large. Section 2.5.2 presents a procurement example where firms with random and independent costs bid for the right to face a downward-sloping demand curve.

---

[11] Similar results, with the possible exception of the comparative statics with respect to λ, are obtained with the decomposition of DWL_n in terms of $\Delta \underline{W}_n^{\mathrm{c}} = \mathrm{ETS}_n^{\mathrm{fc}} - \mathrm{ETS}_n^{\mathrm{f}}$ and $\Delta W_n^{\mathrm{f}} = \mathrm{ETS}_n^{\mathrm{f}} - \mathrm{ETS}_n$.

2.5.1 Convergence to Efficiency and Price-Taking Behavior

With independent valuations across bidders we may expect auction prices to converge to efficient prices as the number of bidders grows large. In particular, Swinkels (1999) shows that this is the case in a generalized first-price auction. This is a discriminatory auction of several identical units of an object, where each bidder submits one or more bids, and each of the m highest bidders wins an object. The winners pay what they have bid. Asymptotic efficiency holds without any symmetry assumption among the bidders.

It would be interesting to know, however, the rate at which convergence to efficiency occurs. If convergence is fast, then with a moderately sized market the standard (full-information) competitive model provides a good approximation and the market outcome is approximately efficient. This is the case of the k-double auction with traders having independent valuations. At a k-double auction the bids of buyers and sellers are aggregated (respectively) into a demand and a supply schedule. Their intersection defines an interval of potential market-clearing prices $[\underline{p}, \bar{p}]$ from which $(1-k)\underline{p} + k\bar{p}$ is selected with $k \in [0,1]$.

Rustichini et al. (1994) show that, in this auction with n buyers and n sellers, each with unit demands and supplies, respectively, and independent reservation values, trader misrepresentation at symmetric, increasing, differentiable equilibria (and the discrepancy between the market price and the full-information competitive price) is of order $1/n$ and the corresponding inefficiency of order $1/n^2$. Rustichini et al. do not establish the existence of equilibrium in the double auction. This is done by Jackson and Swinkels (2005) in a private-value environment. Satterthwaite and Williams (2002) establish that this rate of convergence is the fastest among all mechanisms in the i.i.d. environment.[12] Cripps and Swinkels (2006) extend the results to a generalized private-value setting where bidders can be asymmetric and can demand or supply multiple units. Under some regularity conditions and a weak requirement of "a little independence" (amounting to each player having a small idiosyncratic component in his valuation), Cripps and Swinkels find that as the number of players n grows all nontrivial equilibria of the double auction converge to the competitive outcome and inefficiency vanishes at the rate of $1/n^{2-\alpha}$ for any $\alpha > 0$. In short, with few traders the outcome of the k-double auction is close to the competitive one. This contrasts with the slower rate of convergence of the Cournot market mechanism with independent costs.

Gong and McAfee (1996) extend the work on double auctions by Rustichini et al. (1994) to general information structures. Gong and McAfee show that either with private values (where agents receive perfect signals about their types and

[12] In the symmetric k-double auction, the efficiency issue is whether the number of objects being sold is the right one, while in the asymmetric auctions considered by Swinkels (1999) the efficiency question is whether the objects go to the bidders with the highest valuations. See also Satterthwaite and Williams (1989) and Williams (1991).

the types are allowed to be correlated) or when buyers and sellers are symmetric (in terms of utility functions and distributions) the price-taking equilibrium maximizes expected total surplus under the constraint of using decentralized strategies. Then the discrepancy between the strategic equilibrium (Bayesian bidding equilibrium at the double auction) and the nonstrategic (price-taking) equilibrium bid is of order $1/n$ and the associated expected inefficiency of order $1/n^2$.[13] These results are consistent with those obtained in the Cournot setting with a general information structure (see proposition 2.2).

An interesting application to an Internet auction environment similar to eBay is presented by Peters and Severinov (2006). They consider a decentralized trading mechanism where sellers with a unit of a homogeneous good who set reserve prices for their independently run second-price auctions. Each buyer has a unit demand, has a private value for the good, and can bid and move between auctions. A perfect Bayesian equilibrium, with a simple strategy, is characterized. It is found that in a large finite market, and under the assumption that the valuation of a trader takes each positive value with positive probability, sellers post reserve prices equal to their costs.

2.5.2 Price Competition with Independent Constant Marginal Costs

Consider now price competition in a homogeneous product market with constant marginal costs, which are identically and independently distributed on a compact interval with positive continuous density. In this case sellers bid for the right to supply the market, that is, to face the downward-sloping demand curve.[14] (With constant marginal costs the replication of demand only introduces a scale factor, which we will ignore here.) The Bayesian Bertrand equilibrium of this price competition model has been considered by Hansen (1988) and Spulber (1995). The firm that quotes the lowest price gets all the market (if more than one firm quotes the lowest price, they share the market). It is well-known that with complete information the equilibrium price equals the cost of the second, more efficient firm and there is no productive inefficiency because the lowest-cost firm supplies the market.

With incomplete information it can be shown (see Spulber 1995) that there is a unique and symmetric Bayesian Bertrand equilibrium $p_n(\theta)$, which is increasing and differentiable. The equilibrium strategy is given by the solution to the following differential equation, with an appropriate boundary condition,

$$p_n(\theta) - \theta = \frac{p_n'(\theta)D(p_n(\theta))}{(n-1)h(\theta)D(p_n(\theta)) - p_n'(\theta)D'(p_n(\theta))},$$

[13] The result may not hold if buyers and sellers are asymmetric. Then the social planner takes into account externalities between buyers and sellers which individual nonstrategic agents do not care about. The situation is akin to a noisy rational expectations model, in which the trade of an agent creates an information externality for others (see chapter 3).

[14] With increasing marginal costs we should worry about rationing schemes for unsatisfied demand where firms refuse to serve customers at the quoted price and things get complicated.

where $h(\theta)$ is the hazard rate of the distribution (the probability that the cost of a rival equals θ given that it is not less than θ). Under standard boundedness conditions, $p_n(\theta) - \theta$ will be of order $1/n$ and, therefore, so will the margin of the winning firm $p_n(\theta_{\min}) - \theta_{\min}$.

Given that $p_n(\theta)$ is increasing there is no productive inefficiency, and the lowest-cost firm supplies the market. Furthermore, the deadweight loss due to allocative inefficiency is of order $1/n^2$. The winner-takes-all nature of the competition implies that the equilibrium strategy depends on $(n-1)h(\theta)$, that is, on the probability that, conditional on having the lowest cost, a rival also has the lowest cost. The higher the probability the lower the margin, ceteris paribus. The firm conditions on its cost realization and on the event of winning the contest. The consequence is that in the Bertrand game a firm is effectively conditioning on more information than in the Cournot game. In the latter case a firm has to estimate the average cost of (active) rivals and relies only on its cost realization. The auction/Bertrand mechanism aggregates information better than the Cournot mechanism and this explains the different rates at which prices converge to marginal cost in the presence of incomplete information. In chapter 3 we will study the information aggregation properties of supply function competition where firms can condition on the market price.

2.5.3 Summary

Equilibrium prices in auctions with independent values converge quickly to the full-information competitive price (at the rate of $1/n$, where n is the size of the market, be it the common number of buyers and sellers in a k-double auction or the number of bidders in a first-price auction). Correspondingly, the deadweight loss is of order $1/n^2$. This contrasts with Cournot markets, where the rates are, respectively, $1/\sqrt{n}$ and $1/n$.

2.6 Summary

In this chapter we have introduced strategic behavior and looked at large Cournot and auction markets, which induce behavior close to competitive. We have checked whether the continuum model of chapter 1 is a good approximation in a large market and how large a market needs to be for the approximation to be good. In other words, we have looked at the convergence properties as markets grow large and potentially price-taking behavior and information aggregation are obtained. The results are as follows.

In a general Cournot market:

- Equilibria of the continuum economy (derived in chapter 1) are found to be the limits of equilibria of finite economies and the convergence rate is characterized. Moreover, convergence is faster with common values.

- Convergence to price-taking behavior is fast (at the rate of $1/n$, where n is the "size" of the market) and the associated deadweight loss vanishes quickly (at the rate of $1/n^2$).

With independent values:

- Both Cournot and auction markets aggregate information, and as the market grows large an efficient outcome is obtained.
- However, convergence is faster in the auction market because a Cournot market aggregates information slowly (at the rate of $1/\sqrt{n}$ and this slow convergence dominates, even in moderately sized markets, the faster dissipation of market power).
- The deadweight loss in the Cournot market is of order $1/n$ while in an auction it is of order $1/n^2$.

2.7 Appendix

Proof of proposition 2.1 (see p. 56). Drop the subscript "n" labeling the replica market and let $\beta = 1$ to ease notation. We consider first the Bayesian Cournot equilibrium. We check that the candidate strategies form an equilibrium. The expected profits of firm i conditional on receiving signal s_i, and assuming that firm j, $j \neq i$, uses strategy $X_j(\cdot)$, are

$$E[\pi_i \mid s_i] = x_i\left(\alpha - E[\theta_i \mid s_i] - \frac{1}{n}\sum_{j\neq i} E[X_j(s_j) \mid s_i] - \left(\frac{1}{n} + \frac{\lambda}{2}\right)x_i\right).$$

Then FOCs yield

$$2\left(\frac{1}{n} + \frac{\lambda}{2}\right)x_i(s_i) = \alpha - E[\theta_i \mid s_i] - \frac{1}{n}\sum_{j\neq i} E[X_j(s_j) \mid s_i] \quad \text{for } i = 1, \dots, n.$$

Plugging in the candidate equilibrium strategy and using the formulas for the conditional expectations for $E[\theta_i \mid s_i]$ and $E[s_j \mid s_i]$ (see section 10.2),

$$E[\theta_i \mid s_i] = \xi s_i + (1 - \xi)\bar{\theta} \quad \text{and} \quad E[s_j \mid s_i] = E[\theta_j \mid s_i] = \xi\varsigma s_i + (1 - \xi\varsigma)\bar{\theta},$$

it is easily checked that the candidate equilibrium strategies satisfy the FOC (which are also sufficient in our model). To prove uniqueness (1) we show that the Bayesian Cournot equilibria of our game are in one-to-one correspondence with person-by-person optimization of an appropriately defined concave quadratic team function; (2) we note that person-by-person optimization is equivalent in our context to the global optimization of the team function (since the random term does not affect the coefficients of the quadratic terms and the team function is concave in actions (Radner 1962, theorem 4)); and (3) we invoke the result by Radner, which implies that in our linear-quadratic model with the type of uncertainty considered and jointly normal random variables, the components of the unique Bayesian team decision function of the equivalent team problem are affine (Radner 1962, theorem 5). Based on the above three observations we conclude that the affine Bayesian Cournot equilibrium is the unique equilibrium.[15]

Let us show (1) by displaying an appropriate team function G. A team decision rule $(X_1(s_1),\dots,X_n(s_n))$ is person-by-person optimal if it cannot be improved by changing only one component $X_i(\cdot)$. (This just means that each agent maximizes the team objective conditional on his information and taking as given the strategies of the other agents.) Let $G(x) = \pi_i(x) + f_i(x_{-i})$, where

$$f_i(x_{-i}) = \sum_{j\neq i}(\alpha - \theta_j)x_j - \left(\frac{1}{n} + \frac{\lambda}{2}\right)\sum_{j\neq i} x_j^2 - \frac{1}{2n}\sum_{\substack{k\neq j,\\ k,j\neq i}} x_k x_j.$$

This yields

$$G(x) = \sum_j(\alpha - \theta_j)x_j - \left(\frac{1}{n} + \frac{\lambda}{2}\right)\sum_j x_j^2 - \frac{1}{2n}\sum_{i\neq j} x_i x_j.$$

We obtain the same outcome by solving either $\max_{x_i} E[\pi_i \mid s_i]$ or $\max_{x_i} E[G \mid s_i]$ since $f_i(x_{-i})$ does not involve x_i.

A similar argument establishes the result for the price-taking equilibrium. Then the FOC for firm i is given by

$$\lambda x_i(s_i) = \alpha - E[\theta_i \mid s_i] - \frac{1}{n}\sum_j E[X_j(s_j) \mid s_i],$$

and the solution is a (person-by-person) maximum of a team problem with an objective function which is precisely the ETS as shown in proposition 1.2. □

In order to perform welfare comparisons and prove propositions 2.2 and 2.4 we will need the following lemma.

Lemma 2.1. *The difference in (per capita) ETS between a price-taking regime R and another regime with strategies based on less information (that is, on a weakly coarser information partition) is given by*

$$\frac{\mathrm{ETS}^R - \mathrm{ETS}}{n} = \frac{1}{2}\left(\beta E[(x_n - x_n^R)^2] + \lambda\left(\sum_{i=1}^{n}\frac{E[(x_{in} - x_{in}^R)^2]}{n}\right)\right).$$

The result follows by considering a Taylor series expansion of TS (stopping at the second term due to the quadratic nature of the payoff) around price-taking equilibria. The key to simplifying the computations is to notice that at price-taking equilibria total surplus is maximized. Note that, if the strategies and the information structure are symmetric, then $E[(x_{in} - x_{in}^R)^2]$ is independent of i and therefore $\sum_{i=1}^n E[(x_{in} - x_{in}^R)^2]/n = E[(x_{in} - x_{in}^R)^2]$.

[15] This method of showing uniqueness of Bayesian Cournot equilibria in linear-quadratic models with normal distributions (or, more generally, with affine information structures) has been used by Basar and Ho (1974) and Vives (1988).

Allocative and productive inefficiency. We can decompose the total inefficiency with respect to price-taking regime R in allocative and productive inefficiency. The latter is associated with the production of an average output in a non-cost-minimizing way. The former is associated with the loss in surplus when producing, in a cost-minimizing way, an average output different from the benchmark. Consider a symmetric-information structure and strategies. When average outputs x_n and x_n^R are produced in a cost-minimizing way, then for all i, $x_{in} - x_{in}^R = x_n - x_n^R$.[16] This implies that pure allocative inefficiency is given by $\frac{1}{2}(\beta + \lambda)E[(x_n - x_n^R)^2]$. The residual is due to productive inefficiency and can be expressed as $\frac{1}{2}\lambda E[(u_i - v_i)^2]$, where $u_i = x_{in} - x_n$ and $v_i = x_{in}^R - x_n^R$. We can thus write $(\text{ETS}^R - \text{ETS})/n = \frac{1}{2}((\beta + \lambda)E[(x_n - x_n^R)^2] + \lambda E[(u_i - v_i)^2])$. Note that $E[(u_i - v_i)^2] = \text{var}[u_i - v_i]$ because $E[u_i] = E[v_i] = 0$.

Proof of proposition 2.2 (see p. 57). Consider without loss of generality the case $\beta = 1$. Let

$$y_n = p_n - p_n^c = x_n^c - x_n = (b_n^c - b_n)(\alpha - \bar{\theta}) + (a_n - a_n^c)(\tilde{s}_n - \bar{\theta}).$$

Recall that $E[y_n^2] = (E[y_n])^2 + \text{var}[y_n]$. We have that $E[y_n] = (b_n^c - b_n) \times (\alpha - \bar{\theta})$ because $E[\tilde{s}_n] = \bar{\theta}$. It is easily seen that $(b_n^c - b_n)$ is of order $1/n$ (indeed, $n(b_n^c - b_n) \to 1/(1 + \lambda)^2$ as $n \to \infty$). Therefore, $(E[y_n])^2$ is of order $1/n^2$. Furthermore, $\text{var}[y_n] = (a_n - a_n^c)^2 \text{var}[\tilde{s}_n]$. We have that $\text{var}[\tilde{s}_n] = ((1 + (n-1)\varsigma)\sigma_\theta^2 + \sigma_\varepsilon^2)/n$, which is of the order of a constant for $\varsigma > 0$ (or $1/n$ for $\varsigma = 0$), and that $(a_n - a_n^c)$ is of order $1/n$ (because $n(a_n - a_n^c) \to -\xi(\varsigma\xi + \lambda)^{-2}$ as $n \to \infty$). Therefore, the order of $\text{var}[y_n]$ is $1/n^2$ for $\varsigma > 0$ (or $1/n^3$ for $\varsigma = 0$). We conclude that in any case the order of $y_n = p_n - p_n^c$ is $1/n$. Now consider $(\text{ETS}_n^c - \text{ETS}_n)/n$. According to the above lemma and given that equilibria are symmetric we have that $(\text{ETS}_n^c - \text{ETS}_n)/n = \frac{1}{2}(\beta E[(x_n - x_n^c)^2] + \lambda E[(x_{in} - x_{in}^c)^2])$. We have just shown that $E[(x_n - x_n^c)^2]$ is of order $1/n^2$. We have that

$$E[(x_{in} - x_{in}^c)^2] = (E[x_{in} - x_{in}^c])^2 + \text{var}[x_{in} - x_{in}^c].$$

Now, $E[x_{in} - x_{in}^c]$ is of the same order as $E[x_n - x_n^c]$, $1/n$, and $\text{var}[x_{in} - x_{in}^c] = (a_n - a_n^c)^2(\sigma_\theta^2 + \sigma_\varepsilon^2)$ is of order $1/n^2$ because $(a_n - a_n^c)$ is of order $1/n$. Therefore, $E[(x_{in} - x_{in}^c)^2]$ is of order $1/n^2$. We conclude that $(\text{ETS}_n^c - \text{ETS}_n)/n$ is of order $1/n^2$. □

Proof of proposition 2.3 (see p. 58). For the first part, from proposition 2.1 we have that

$$\lim_{n\to\infty} a_n = \lim_{n\to\infty} \frac{\xi}{2\beta/n + \lambda + \beta\varsigma\xi((n-1)/n)} = \frac{\xi}{\lambda + \beta\varsigma\xi} = a$$

and

$$\lim_{n\to\infty} b_n = \lim_{n\to\infty} \frac{1}{\lambda + \beta((1+n)/n)} = \frac{1}{\lambda + \beta} = b.$$

[16] An immediate implication of cost minimization when producing average output x is that $x_i = x + (\tilde{\theta}_n - \theta_i)/\lambda$.

Hence,

$$\lim_{n\to\infty} X_n(s_i) = \lim_{n\to\infty}(b_n(\alpha - \bar{\theta}) - a_n(s_i - \bar{\theta})) = b(\alpha - \bar{\theta}) - a(s_i - \bar{\theta}) = X(s_i).$$

For the second part of the proposition note that $x_n = b_n(\alpha - \bar{\theta}) - a_n(\tilde{s}_n - \bar{\theta})$. We have that

$$p_n = \alpha - \beta(b_n(\alpha - \bar{\theta}) - a_n(\tilde{s}_n - \bar{\theta})) \quad \text{and} \quad p = \alpha - \beta(b(\alpha - \bar{\theta}) - a(\tilde{\theta} - \bar{\theta}))$$

and $E[p_n - p] = \beta(b - b_n)(\alpha - \bar{\theta})$ since $E[\tilde{s}_n] = E[\tilde{\theta}] = \bar{\theta}$. Note that $(b - b_n)$, and therefore $E[p_n - p]$, tends to 0 as $n \to \infty$. Since $\operatorname{var}[p_n - p] = E[(p_n - p)^2] - (E[p_n - p])^2$, in order to conclude that $\lim_{n\to\infty} E[(p_n - p)^2] = 0$ it is sufficient to show that

$$\lim_{n\to\infty} \operatorname{var}[\sqrt{n}(p_n - p)] = \beta^2 a^2((1 - \varsigma)\sigma_\theta^2 + \sigma_\varepsilon^2).$$

From which it follows that $\sqrt{n}(p_n - p)$ converges in distribution to

$$N(0, \beta^2 a^2((1 - \varsigma)\sigma_\theta^2 + \sigma_\varepsilon^2))$$

because $p_n - p$ is normally distributed. We have that

$$\begin{aligned}\operatorname{var}[\sqrt{n}(p_n - p)] &= n\beta^2 \operatorname{var}[a_n\tilde{s}_n - a\tilde{\theta}] \\ &= \beta^2 \frac{a_n^2 n^{-1}(\sigma_\theta^2(1 + \varsigma(n-1)) + \sigma_\varepsilon^2) + a\varsigma\sigma_\theta^2(a - 2a_n)}{n^{-1}}.\end{aligned}$$

Using L'Hôpital's rule and the fact that $\partial a_n/\partial n$ is of the order of $1/n^2$ we obtain

$$\begin{aligned}&\lim_{n\to\infty} \operatorname{var}[\sqrt{n}(p_n - p)] \\ &\quad = \beta^2 \lim_{n\to\infty} \bigg\{2a_n \frac{\partial a_n}{\partial n}\bigg(\frac{(1 + \varsigma(n-1))\sigma_\theta^2}{n} + \frac{\sigma_\varepsilon^2}{n}\bigg) \\ &\qquad\qquad + a_n^2\bigg(-\frac{(1 - \varsigma)\sigma_\theta^2}{n^2} - \frac{\sigma_\varepsilon^2}{n^2}\bigg) - 2\frac{\partial a_n}{\partial n} a\varsigma\sigma_\theta^2\bigg\}\bigg/\bigg(-\frac{1}{n^2}\bigg) \\ &\quad = \beta^2 a^2((1 - \varsigma)\sigma_\theta^2 + \sigma_\varepsilon^2).\end{aligned}$$

□

2.8 Exercises

2.1 (*optimality of information acquisition under constant returns*). Show in the endogenous information acquisition model of section 2.3 that if returns are constant then as $n \to \infty$ the subgame-perfect equilibrium outcome of the two-stage game attains the first-best.

Solution. With constant returns to scale, the equilibrium output strategies given a common precision ξ are given by $X_n(s_i) = a_n(s_i - \bar{\theta}) + b\bar{\theta}$ with $a_n = n\xi/\beta(2 + (n-1)\xi)$ and $b = 1/2\beta$. Substituting in the expression for per capita total gross surplus and taking expectations, we obtain

$$\mathrm{EGS}_n = \frac{n(2 + n)}{2(1 + n)^2\beta}\bar{\theta}^2 + \frac{n\xi((n-1)\xi + 3)}{((n-1)\xi + 2)^2}\frac{\sigma_\theta^2}{2\beta}.$$

Therefore, per capita expected total surplus at the market equilibrium ξ_n^* is

$$\mathrm{ETS}_n = \mathrm{EGS}_n - \frac{c}{\sigma_\theta^2} \frac{\xi_n^*}{1 - \xi_n^*}.$$

As $n \to \infty$ ξ_n^* converges to zero and $n\xi_n^*$ to ∞. This implies that $\mathrm{ETS}_n \xrightarrow[n]{} (\bar{\theta}^2 + \sigma_\theta^2)/2\beta$, which is the first-best level.

2.2 (*measuring the Harberger triangle*). A typical empirical assessment of the deadweight loss due to market power uses an approximation at the industry level with data on profit returns and sales positing a certain value for the elasticity of demand (under constant returns the deadweight loss is approximated by $R\eta d^2/2$, where R is revenue, η the demand elasticity, and d the relative price distortion from the competitive level). Harberger and others have obtained low estimates for the welfare loss (Scherer and Ross 1990, chapter 18). Consider a Cournot market with uncertain costs which are private information to the firms as in section 2.4. What are the implications of the analysis in the section for the estimation of the Harberger triangle?

Solution. Harberger's small estimates should not be surprising from the perspective of the results in section 2.4 because in moderately sized markets the effect of market power may be relatively small. However, accounting for incomplete information would increase the deadweight loss estimate. According to our model the true deadweight loss due to allocative inefficiency is given by $\frac{1}{2}(\beta + \lambda)((E[x_n - x_n^{\mathrm{fc}}])^2 + \mathrm{var}[x_n - x_n^{\mathrm{fc}}])$. The Harberger approach would approximate it by the first term in the sum, which is of order $1/n^2$, while the second is of order $1/n$. Under full information the approximation is fine (because then $\mathrm{var}[x_n^{\mathrm{f}} - x_n^{\mathrm{fc}}]$ is of order $1/n^3$) but not so with private information. Furthermore, to the allocative inefficiency measure the loss due to productive inefficiency $(\frac{1}{2}\lambda\,\mathrm{var}[(x_{in} - x_n) - (x_{in}^{\mathrm{fc}} - x_n^{\mathrm{fc}})])$ should be added. The deadweight loss would be higher by an order of magnitude. For example, with a market concentration equivalent of ten firms ($n = 10$), while the true relative deadweight loss is of the order of 10%, the estimated deadweight loss ignoring private information would be of the order of only 1%.

2.3 (*welfare with price competition and private information*). Examine the welfare properties of the procurement auction model of section 2.5.2. Compare in particular expected total surplus with full information and with private information.

Solution. The deadweight loss is larger under full than under incomplete information. Contrary to the Cournot case, we have that $\mathrm{ETS}_n^{\mathrm{f}} < \mathrm{ETS}_n$. The reason is that with incomplete information a firm tends to be more aggressive and sets a price below the expected price with complete information. Denote by θ_{next} the cost of the second-most efficient firm. The result is that $p(\theta_{\min}) < E[\theta_{\mathrm{next}} \mid \theta_{\min}]$. Indeed, with inelastic demand the revenue equivalence theorem would apply (think of Bertrand competition with complete information as an open descending auction) and we would have that $p(\theta_{\min}) = E[\theta_{\text{next}} \mid \theta_{\min}]$. This balances exactly the fact that in the first-price auction raising the bid a little bit increases profit when winning but reduces the probability of winning. If demand is elastic, then the profit increase when winning is strictly smaller and therefore the optimum bid must be smaller than before. The fact that incomplete information may improve welfare should not be surprising; because we are in a second-best world, there is no guarantee that welfare increases by moving toward full information while maintaining market power. The Cournot model is more "regular" and lifting one distortion at a time improves welfare (see Hansen 1988; Vives 2002).

2.4 (*competition policy implications*). What policy implications can you draw from the relative weights of market power and private information as sources of welfare loss? Does your answer depend on the type of competition in the market?

Hint. Speculate on the basis of the results in the chapter.

References

Basar, T., and V. C. Ho. 1974. Informational properties of the Nash solutions to two stochastic nonzero-sum games. *Journal of Economic Theory* 7:370–87.

Cripps, M., and J. Swinkels. 2006. Efficiency of large double auctions. *Econometrica* 74:47–92.

Gong, J., and P. McAfee. 1996. The general double auction mechanism. In *Advances in Applied Microeconomics* (ed. M. Baye), volume 6, pp. 63–96. JAI Press.

Hansen, R. 1988. Auctions with endogenous quantity. *RAND Journal of Economics* 19:44–58.

Hauk, E., and S. Hurkens. 2001. Secret information acquisition in Cournot markets. *Economic Theory* 18:661–81.

Jackson, M., and J. Swinkels. 2005. Existence of equilibrium in single and double private value auctions. *Econometrica* 73:93–139.

Li, L., R. McKelvey, and T. Page. 1987. Optimal research for Cournot oligopolists. *Journal of Economic Theory* 42:140–66.

Peters, M., and S. Severinov. 2006. Internet auctions with many traders. *Journal of Economic Theory* 130:220–45.

Radner, R. 1962. Team decision problems. *Annals of Mathematical Statistics* 33:857–81.

Rustichini, A., M. A. Satterthwaite, and S. R. Williams. 1994. Convergence to efficiency in a simple market with incomplete information. *Econometrica* 62:1041–63.

Satterthwaite, M. A., and S. R. Williams. 1989. The rate of convergence to efficiency in the buyer's bid double auction as the market becomes large. *Review of Economic Studies* 56:477–98.

Scherer, F. M., and D. Ross. 1990. *Industrial Market Structure and Economic Performance*, 3rd edn. Boston, MA: Houghton Mifflin.

Spulber, D. 1995. Bertrand competition when rivals' costs are unknown. *Journal of Industrial Economics* 43:1–11.

Swinkels, J. 1999. Asymptotic efficiency for discriminatory private value auctions. *Review of Economic Studies* 66:509–28.

Vives, X. 1988. Aggregation of information in large Cournot markets. *Econometrica* 56:851–76.

——. 1999. *Oligopoly Pricing: Old Ideas and New Tools.* Boston, MA: MIT Press.

——. 2002. Private information, strategic behavior, and efficiency in Cournot markets. *RAND Journal of Economics* 33:361–76.

——. 2007. Strategic supply function competition with private information. Mimeo.

Williams, S. R. 1991. Existence and convergence of equilibria in the buyer's bid double auction. *Review of Economic Studies* 58:351–74.

3

Rational Expectations and Supply Function Competition

In the first two chapters we examined whether simple market mechanisms would aggregate information. In those mechanisms each agent can condition his action only on his private information and, somewhat strikingly, in some cases such as auctions the market would aggregate information. In this chapter we will consider more complex market mechanisms where traders can also condition on a market statistic like the price. The concept of rational expectations equilibrium (REE) considers the role of prices as aggregators of information. Prices therefore serve a dual role as index of scarcity and conveyor of information. In other words, they clear the markets and aggregate information. In this chapter we will analyze REE with asymmetric information in the partial equilibrium market introduced in chapters 1 and 2. Chapters 4 and 5 will analyze REE in financial markets. The chapter will make clear the potential misalignment between informational and economic efficiency.

The chapter is organized as follows. Section 3.1 presents the concept of REE, its variations, problems associated with some formulations, and welfare aspects. Section 3.2 provides a foundation for REE in a competitive market where firms compete in supply functions. The section also provides illustrations of the different types of REE according to the amount of information they reveal (fully or partially revealing and with and without noise). Section 3.3 offers an introduction to the welfare analysis of REE. Section 3.4 makes some remarks on strategic aspects when agents have market power and examines the convergence to price-taking behavior as the market grows. Section 3.5 considers double auctions, presents an example of a fully revealing REE which is implementable as a double auction, and provides a strategic foundation for the equilibrium.

3.1 Rational Expectations Equilibrium: Concepts, Problems, and Welfare

3.1.1 What Are Rational Expectations?

Traders have rational expectations when they know the correct model of the functioning of the market (i.e., the link between prices and state of the economy) and make optimal inferences from prices and other public statistics about uncertain and relevant market parameters of the economy. According to the rational expectations hypothesis, agents anticipate the future according to the true probability distribution of future events. Agents are endowed with their private information and a correct model of the relationship between equilibrium prices and other agents' information. The beliefs of agents influence their actions, which in turn affect the true probability distributions or correct beliefs. A rational expectations equilibrium is then a fixed point of a map from beliefs to correct beliefs mediated by the actions of agents. Agents form expectations using optimally the information they have in the context of an equilibrium. Rational expectations are, therefore, just equilibrium expectations.

An early formulation of the formation of equilibrium expectations by a cloth manufacturer is contained in Marshall's *Principles*:

> In estimating the wages required to call forth an adequate supply of labour to work a certain class of looms he might take the current wages...or he might argue...that looking forward over several years so as to allow for immigration he might take the normal rate of wages at a rather lower rate than that prevailing at the time...or [the cloth manufacturer] might think that wages of weavers...were abnormally low...in consequence of a too sanguine view having been taken of the prospects of the trade a generation ago.[1]

The cloth manufacturer is entertaining different possibilities to form expectations: stationary or static (taking the current wages) or "rational" using a model of wage formation which depends on immigration (supply). In rational expectations a producer has a model that relates the endogenous variables to forecast (the wages) to their exogenous determinants (labor supply as conditioned by immigration in this case).

The seminal idea on the role of prices in aggregating and efficiently transmitting information, as we have claimed before, is due to Hayek (1945, p. 526):

> We must look at the price system as such a mechanism for communicating information if we want to understand its real function—a function which, of course, it fulfills less perfectly as prices grow more rigid. (Even when quoted prices have become quite rigid, however, the forces which would operate through changes in price still operate to a considerable extent through changes in the other terms of the contract.) The most significant fact about this system is the economy of knowledge with which it operates, or how little the individual participants need to know in order to be able to take the right action.

Hayek in this paragraph emphasizes the efficiency of the price system as information aggregator. This was a criticism of the planning idea, pushed by Oskar Lange and others, that a center could set competitive prices using a general equilibrium model inducing an efficient allocation of resources. Hayek's point is that the central planner may be much better informed than any individual

[1] Book V, chapter V, section 1, as quoted in Grossman (1981).

agent in the economy but he will not have the aggregate or collective information of agents in the economy, each one of them with his little piece of knowledge of local conditions. In contrast, the market can aggregate the dispersed information in the economy with prices. The local information of traders is hardly transmittable to a center according to Hayek (1945, pp. 519–20):

> The peculiar character of the problem of a rational economic order is determined precisely by the fact that the knowledge of the circumstances of which we must make use never exists in concentrated or integrated form, but solely as the dispersed bits of incomplete and frequently contradictory knowledge which all the separate individuals possess. The economic problem of society is thus not merely a problem of how to allocate "given" resources—if "given" is taken to mean given to a single mind which deliberately solves the problem set by these "data." It is rather a problem of how to secure the best use of resources known to any of the members of society, for ends whose relative importance only these individuals know. Or, to put it briefly, it is a problem of the utilization of knowledge not given to anyone in its totality.

3.1.2 Rational Expectations Equilibrium

The idea of equilibrium expectations together with Hayek's insight of viewing the price system as a way to transmit information yield the building blocks of the rational expectations model. The concept of rational expectations for competitive economies was first proposed by Muth (1960, 1961) and later developed by Lucas (1972) (and Green 1973). Asymmetric information was also introduced soon after (see Radner (1979) and Grossman (1981) for surveys). A competitive REE is a competitive equilibrium in which agents understand the relationship between prices and the state of the world and optimize according to their updated beliefs.

The issue still remains of how the interaction of people produces the desired aggregation of information and how agents come to form rational expectations. This is basically a dynamic issue (see the discussion in section 7.1). We will distinguish there between learning within and learning about rational expectations. Hayek himself seems to also entertain an evolutionary approach to such expectation formation (see, for example, p. 18 in Hayek 1973).

Rational expectations models have been widely used in many applications. REE can be of different types depending on the amount of information they reveal, namely they can be fully revealing or partially revealing. An REE is fully revealing if prices reveal all the information of agents. In the finance literature it is said that the REE is (strongly) informationally efficient if the price is a sufficient statistic for the information dispersed in the market (Fama 1970; Grossman 1978), that is, if by looking at the price agents can recover a sufficient statistic for the private information in the economy. This implies that observing the price leads to the same equilibrium as if all agents pooled their information.[2] If an REE is not fully revealing, then it is partially revealing. This may be

---

[2] See section 10.1.4 for the concept of sufficient statistic.

because of noise or because there are not enough prices in relation to sources of uncertainty. In the empirical finance literature the price is termed semi-strong informationally efficient if it reflects only public information (see, for example, Fama 1970, 1976). A taxonomy of REE will be provided in section 3.2.

The concept of competitive fully revealing REE (FRREE) is not without problems. At an FRREE, agents, by looking at the market price, know all they need to know about the uncertain state of the world to take action. This means that they will disregard their private signals. How is it then possible that the price reflects all the information agents have? That is, what are the game and the market microstructure that yield such a result?[3] This points to the potential problem: FRREE may not be "implementable."[4] This is the situation where we cannot find a trading mechanism (in a well-specified game) that delivers an equilibrium which is an FRREE. Indeed, in an REE it is implicitly assumed that the equilibrium is obtained with a Walrasian auctioneer who clears the market. When this equilibrium exists, the question is whether there is a specific mechanism of trade (i.e., a specific game) that has that equilibrium. However, FRREE are implementable if each agent is informationally "small" or irrelevant in the sense that his private information can be predicted by the joint information of the other agents (Postlewaite and Schmeidler 1986; Palfrey and Srivastava 1986; Blume and Easley 1990; see Gul and Postlewaite (1992) and Mas-Colell and Vives (1992) for results on the implementation of efficient allocations in large economies).

There are other associated problems with the competitive REE concept. If information is costly to acquire, then at an FRREE agents will have no incentive to purchase information. (Why should they if the market price is a sufficient statistic for the information needed to take action?) The outcome is that the equilibrium breaks down (this is the Grossman and Stiglitz (1980) paradox of informationally efficient markets, which we will introduce in section 4.2.2). Furthermore, if a competitive REE is defined in a finite economy, then traders realize that prices convey information but do not realize the impact of their actions on the price (this is the "schizophrenia" problem of Hellwig (1980)). The solution to the latter problem is either to consider a large economy (as in this chapter) or to explicitly model strategic behavior (considered in chapter 5 and in Kyle (1989)).

The present chapter will employ a setup of supply function competition, with a continuum of traders, which implements REE. In this setup traders will be informationally small and will have incentives to be price takers. In addition, we are interested in the welfare properties of REE.

3.1.3 Welfare Analysis

The welfare analysis of rational expectations equilibria is not trivial since asymmetric information presents methodological issues that have to be considered.

---

[3] Technically speaking, if we were to insist that prices be measurable in excess demand functions, then FRREE (when the price is a sufficient statistic for the decision problem of the agents) would not exist (see Beja 1977; Anderson and Sonnenschein 1982).

[4] See section 10.4.3 for a brief introduction to implementation and mechanism design.

First of all, we have to decide upon which perspective we take for the analysis: *ex ante*, interim, or *ex post*. *Ex ante* the state of nature is drawn but not observed; at the interim stage agents receive private signals (and an agent only observes his private information); and *ex post* the state of nature is revealed. An allocation is Pareto optimal if there is no other allocation that increases the expected utility of one agent without lowering the expected utility of another. *Ex ante* Pareto optimality refers to the unconditional expected utilities of agents; interim Pareto optimality refers to the expected utilities of each agent conditional on his private signal, and for any possible signal; and *ex post* Pareto optimality refers to the expected utilities of agents after all information or the state of the world has been revealed. It is easy to see that *ex ante* Pareto optimality implies interim Pareto optimality, which in turn implies *ex post* Pareto optimality. Indeed, suppose that an allocation is interim inefficient. This means that we can find an *ex ante* improvement. Similarly, if an allocation is *ex post* inefficient, we can find an interim improvement. It should also be clear that *ex ante* efficiency is more demanding than *ex post* efficiency because the former requires not only efficiency for every state of the world but also insurance across states. In a quasilinear utility world, like the models considered in this chapter, where insurance is not at stake, *ex ante* and *ex post* optimality coincide (see Laffont 1985, 1989).

Second, we should define the appropriate benchmark to compare REE outcomes with asymmetric information. A benchmark in the spirit of Hayek is to consider allocations which are feasible and maximize *ex ante* expected utility of agents subject to using decentralized allocations, that is, those which are measurable with respect to the information of agents. This is equivalent to a team problem where agents share a common objective, a weighted average of the utilities of agents, and only allocations measurable with respect to the private information of agents can be used. In our quasilinear world the common team objective will be expected total surplus. This is the same welfare benchmark as in section 1.3 when analyzing a Cournot model with a continuum of firms and private information. The team-efficient solution internalizes payoff and information externalities. All this is in the spirit of Hayek since the idea is that the private information of agents is not transmittable to a center.

Finally, another issue with welfare analysis is to consider that agents must be given incentives to reveal their private information or, in other words, respect incentive compatibility constraints.[5] We would then be interested in allocations, which are implementable in a game of incomplete information. The characterization of incentive-compatible constrained allocations is facilitated by the revelation principle. According to this principle we can restrict our attention to so-called direct mechanisms where the strategy space of an agent is just his type space (the space of private signals).[6] We can then discuss *ex ante* and interim incentive-efficient allocations (they are, respectively, Pareto optimal *ex*

[5] This is the same approach as in Harris and Townsend (1981) and Gale (1996).
[6] See section 10.4.3.

ante and interim in the class of *ex ante* and interim incentive-compatible allocations (see Holmström and Myerson 1983)). *Ex post* there is no need to consider incentive constraints because information has already been revealed. We will not pursue this avenue here (see Laffont 1985; Messner and Vives 2001).

Competitive REE may be inefficient from the welfare point of view precisely because they reveal too much information. An FRREE must be *ex post* Pareto optimal (Grossman 1981) but may be interim (and therefore *ex ante*) Pareto inefficient (Laffont 1985). An FRREE is *ex post* Pareto optimal since it can be viewed as the competitive equilibrium of an economy with fully informed agents and therefore, according to the first welfare theorem, it cannot be improved upon by a social planner with access to the pooled information of agents. The reason for the potential inefficiency of an FRREE at the interim (and therefore *ex ante*) stage is that by revealing (too much) information the FRREE may eliminate valuable insurance opportunities. This insight goes back to Hirshleifer (1971). Suppose that there are two risk-averse consumers with the same strictly concave utility function, two goods, and two equiprobable states. The consumers cannot distinguish the states. Consumer 1 gets one unit of the good in state 1 and consumer 2 one unit in state 2 and in each state there is only one unit in total. If there is no information in the spot market equilibrium, each consumer gets half of each good and obtains insurance. Suppose now that the market price is fully revealing, then in each state the consumers know that one good is worthless and there cannot be trade.[7]

The situation is different when a complete set of markets can be organized *ex ante* because then insurance opportunities are seized and an *ex ante* Pareto-optimal allocation is obtained at the REE. Interestingly, a no-trade theorem then holds: opening markets at the interim stage does not change the equilibrium allocation provided traders are (strictly) risk averse and the prior distributions of traders are concordant (Milgrom and Stokey 1982).[8] That is, if an allocation is already Pareto optimal and new information arrives, then agents will not trade on the basis of this new information to move to another allocation. In fact, interim efficiency of the initial allocation is sufficient for the no-trade result because the allocation is then also *ex post* efficient (Holmström and Myerson 1983). There are no incentives then to move from this allocation even with new asymmetric information. The idea is that whenever the only motive for trade is for a trader to find an advantageous bet, because the initial allocation is efficient, if any other trader accepts the bet proposed, then someone must be losing (strictly with strict risk aversion). This no-trade result will be explored in section 8.2.2 in the context of a financial market.

An FRREE is always *ex post* Pareto optimal but a partially revealing one need not be so. Laffont (1985) presents an example in a quasilinear utility linear-normal model of a partially revealing linear REE which is *ex post* inefficient.

---

[7] See example 19.H.1 in Mas-Colell et al. (1995).

[8] Beliefs are concordant if traders agree on the conditional likelihood of any given realization of the signal considered (the price in this case).

In sections 3.2 and 3.4 we consider a quasilinear model which generalizes the case considered by Laffont (1985), in the form of supply function competition, and show that even restricting feasible allocations to be linear and facing the same communications constraints than the market, linear REE are not, in general, team-efficient. We characterize precisely why this is so and examine the potential misalignment of informational and economic efficiency.

3.2 Supply Function Competition and REE in a Continuum Economy

This section presents the supply function competition model (as in Messner and Vives 2001), for which demand and costs are a variation of the partial equilibrium example presented in section 1.2.4.1. It characterizes equilibrium and provides a taxonomy of REE.

A continuum of firms, indexed in the unit interval $i \in [0,1]$, compete in a homogeneous product market facing a linear downward sloping inverse demand: $P(x) = \alpha + u - \beta x$, where $x = \int_0^1 x_i \, di$ is the aggregate output, with x_i the individual output, and also per capita output in our continuum economy (since we have normalized the measure of firms to 1) and α and β positive parameters. We will drop the subscript of a variable or parameter when averaging it over the population of firms. The demand intercept u is random and normally distributed with zero mean and finite variance σ_u^2 (we write $u \sim N(0, \sigma_u^2)$). Firm i produces according to a strictly convex cost function:

$$C_i(x_i) = [\gamma s_i^1 + \theta^1 + \upsilon_i(\gamma s_i^2 + \theta^2)]x_i + \tfrac{1}{2}\lambda(x_i)^2,$$

where x_i is the output of the firm, $\lambda > 0$, and $\gamma \geqslant 0$. Firms may also differ in their costs by the known constants υ_i distributed over the interval $(0,2)$ with $\int_0^1 \upsilon_i \, di = 1$ and $\int_0^1 (\upsilon_i - 1)^2 \, di = \sigma_\upsilon^2$. Costs are affected by the unobservable random parameters θ^1 and θ^2 as well as by the signals that the firm receives about them, s_i^1 and s_i^2, respectively. Signals are of the type $s_i^k = \theta^k + \varepsilon_i^k$, where $\theta^k \sim N(\bar{\theta}^k, \sigma_{\theta k}^2)$ and $\varepsilon_i^k \sim N(0, \sigma_{\varepsilon k}^2)$, $k = 1, 2$, for all i. The random variables θ^k, ε_i^k are mutually independent for any i and k. This means in particular that error terms are uncorrelated across firms. The parameter $\gamma \geqslant 0$ determines the sensitivity of firms' costs to their private signals.[9]

To ease notation and without loss of generality we set the means of the cost parameters equal to zero: $\bar{\theta}^1 = \bar{\theta}^2 = 0$.[10]

We can think of the random variables θ^1 and θ^2 as industry-specific cost parameters and therefore common to all firms, while s_i^1 and s_i^2 are firm-specific components of the costs which depends on the private signals received.

[9] As noted in section 1.2.4.1 the normality assumption implies that quantities and prices may take negative values. It also implies that, for some realizations of the random parameters and signals, costs may be decreasing with output. Again, the probability of these phenomena can be controlled with appropriate choices of the parameters of the information structure.

[10] In the analysis that follows we work mostly with precisions and let as usual $\tau_y = (\sigma_y^2)^{-1}$ denote the precision of the normal random variable y.

For example, s_i^1 and s_i^2 may be related to firm-specific contracts for input procurement while (θ^1, θ^2) are related to spot market prices for the inputs.

Firms' costs are differentially affected by the term $(\gamma s_i^2 + \theta^2)$. For example, firms with a lower v_i might be more efficient in using type 2 input.

A potential example of the model is electricity generation. Electricity producers often face uncertainty about generating conditions and this creates asymmetric information among firms. The random parameters θ^k, $k = 1, 2$, could relate to prices of inputs like fuel, coal, or gas. The signals could correspond to contracts signed and θ^k to the price in the spot market that will prevail at the production stage. For instance, s_i^1 is the contract price for gas for firm i, while θ^1 is the spot price for gas, with all firms using the same gas technology (let us say combined cycle turbines); s_i^2 is the contract price for a bundle of coal and fuel for firm i, while θ^2 is the spot price for this bundle, with different firms using different bundles and/or plants of different efficiencies.

As in chapter 1 we make the convention that error terms cancel in the aggregate: $\int_0^1 \varepsilon_i^1 \, di = \int_0^1 \varepsilon_i^2 \, di = 0$ (a.s.). The aggregation of all individual signals will reveal the underlying uncertainty: $\int_0^1 s_i^k \, di = \theta^k + \int_0^1 \varepsilon_i^k \, di = \theta^k$. The profit of firm i is given by $\pi_i = P(x)x_i - C_i(x_i)$.

3.2.1 Rational Expectations Equilibria

A (competitive) rational expectations equilibrium is a (measurable) price functional mapping the state of the world (θ^1, θ^2, u) into prices $P(\theta^1, \theta^2, u)$ and a set of outputs x_i, $i \in [0, 1]$, such that:

1. Every firm i maximizes its expected profit $E[\pi_i \mid G_i]$ conditional on its information $G_i = \{s_i^1, s_i^2, p\}$ knowing the functional relationship $P(\theta^1, \theta^2, u)$ as well as the underlying distributions of the random variables.
2. Markets clear: $\int_0^1 x_i \, di = \beta^{-1}(\alpha + u - p)$.

That is, each firm optimizes taking prices as given, as in the usual competitive equilibrium, but inferring from prices whatever information can be retrieved.

Our model provides examples of the different types of REE. We now display a fully revealing REE which is not implementable. Suppose that demand is nonrandom ($\sigma_u^2 = 0$ and $u \equiv 0$), firms have *ex ante* symmetric cost functions ($v_i = 1$ for all i), and signals do not affect cost ($\gamma = 0$). Then only $\theta^1 + \theta^2$ matters since marginal cost for firm i is given by $\theta^1 + \theta^2 + \lambda x_i$. Consider the competitive equilibrium of a full-information market in which the firms know $\theta^1 + \theta^2$. At this equilibrium, price equals marginal cost, $p = \theta^1 + \theta^2 + \lambda x_i$, and therefore individual supply is $x_i = \lambda^{-1}(p - (\theta^1 + \theta^2))$. The equilibrium price is given by the market-clearing condition $\int_0^1 x_i \, di = \beta^{-1}(\alpha - p)$ and is equal to

$$p = \frac{\lambda\alpha + \beta(\theta^1 + \theta^2)}{\lambda + \beta}.$$

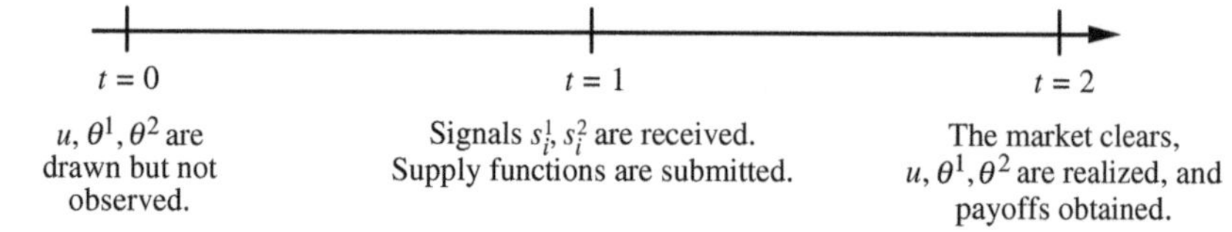
$t = 0$
$t = 1$
$t = 2$
u, θ^1, θ^2 are drawn but not observed.
Signals s_i^1, s_i^2 are received. Supply functions are submitted.
The market clears, u, θ^1, θ^2 are realized, and payoffs obtained.

Figure 3.1.

We claim that this allocation is also a fully revealing REE (FRREE) of our economy. Indeed, by looking at the price each firm learns $\theta^1 + \theta^2$, which is the only relevant uncertainty, and the allocation is an REE because firms optimize and markets clear. In fact, this is a typical way to construct an FRREE.[11]

However, this REE has a strange property because the price is fully revealing but the supply of a firm is independent of the signals received. How has the information been incorporated into the price? That is, what is the game and the market microstructure that yields such a result? In this case we cannot find a game that delivers as equilibrium the FRREE and the displayed FRREE is not implementable.

Let us go back to our general specification. We will restrict our attention to REE which are the outcome of a well-specified game. That is, REE which are implementable. The natural way to implement competitive REE is to consider competition in supply functions in a market where each trader is negligible (as in R. Wilson (1979) or Kyle (1989), in which traders choose demand functions; see also chapters 4 and 5).

The timing of the game is the following. At $t = 0$ random variables θ^1, θ^2, and u are drawn but not observed. At $t = 1$ firms observe their own private signals, s_i^1 and s_i^2, and submit supply functions $X_i(s_i^1, s_i^2, \cdot)$ with $x_i = X_i(s_i^1, s_i^2, p)$, where p is the market price. The strategy of a firm is therefore a map from the signal space to the space of supply functions. Finally, the market clears—supplies are aggregated and crossed with demand to obtain an equilibrium price[12]—and payoffs are collected at $t = 2$. (See figure 3.1.) An implementable REE is associated with a Bayes–Nash equilibrium of the game in supply functions. We will restrict our attention to linear Bayesian supply function equilibria (LBSFE).[13]

In the electricity example firms bid supply functions to the pool.[14] When a firm submits its supply schedule it has some information on its cost conditions but is uncertain about the signals received by rivals. Obviously, our modeling would correspond to a competitive pool.

The procedure to solve for an LBSFE is standard:

---

[11] See the technical note in the appendix (section 3.7) for the existence of REE.

[12] We can assume that the market closes if there is no market-clearing price and that if there are many the one that maximizes volume is chosen.

[13] Section 10.4.2 provides an introduction to Bayesian equilibrium and examples with the linear-normal specification.

[14] In many electricity markets firms bid supply schedules to a pool (for example, in the United Kingdom, California, Spain, and the Nordic countries). See Green and Newbery (1992). Green (1996) characterizes and calibrates a linear supply model for the U.K. market.

(1) Posit linear strategies (with undetermined coefficients) for each firm i in terms of the information $G_i = \{s_i^1, s_i^2, p\}$ and using the market-clearing condition and the conjectured strategies, derive a linear relationship $P(\theta^1, \theta^2, u)$ between prices and the state of the world.

(2) Derive the posterior beliefs for each firm about (θ^1, θ^2) (in the linear-normal specification the posterior beliefs for firm i are summarized by the linear conditional expectations $E[\theta^k \mid G_i]$, $k = 1, 2$, which depend on the undetermined coefficients of the price function).

(3) Work through the optimization of the firms to obtain revised linear optimal strategies (this is feasible because payoffs are quadratic and conditional expectations are linear).

(4) Identify coefficients of the initial and revised linear strategies and obtain a set of equations for the parameters of the strategies. The solution to the system of equations is an equilibrium. With the present setup it can be shown that the solution is unique unless $\sigma_u^2 = 0$ and $\gamma = 0$, in which case there is no LBSFE.

In general, the solution to an REE is a fixed point problem (from conjectured strategies to actual strategies, or from conjectured price function to actual price function; or from initial beliefs to correct beliefs).

In order to characterize an LBSFE we first conjecture that firms use strategies of the following form:

$$x_i = \hat{b}_i + \hat{c}_i p - a_i^1 s_i^1 - a_i^2 s_i^2.$$

Aggregate output is given by

$$\begin{aligned} x &= \int_0^1 x_i \,\mathrm{d}i = \hat{b} + \hat{c}p - a^1\theta^1 - \int_0^1 a_i^1 \varepsilon_i^1 \,\mathrm{d}i - a^2\theta^2 - \int_0^1 a_i^2 \varepsilon_i^2 \,\mathrm{d}i \\ &= \hat{b} + \hat{c}p - a^1\theta^1 - a^2\theta^2, \end{aligned}$$

where $\hat{b} = \int_0^1 \hat{b}_i \,\mathrm{d}i$, $\hat{c} = \int_0^1 \hat{c}_i \,\mathrm{d}i$, $a^k = \int_0^1 a_i^k \,\mathrm{d}i$, $k = 1, 2$, all assumed to be well-defined, and since, according to our convention on the average error terms of the signals, $\int_0^1 a_i^k \varepsilon_i^k \,\mathrm{d}i = 0$ (a.s.) provided that $\mathrm{var}[a_i^k \varepsilon_i^k]$ is uniformly bounded across agents. Given that $\mathrm{var}[\varepsilon_i^k] = \sigma_{\varepsilon^k}^2$ it is sufficient that a_i^k, $k = 1, 2$ be uniformly bounded (see section 10.3.1). In equilibrium this will be the case. Therefore, we are restricting our attention to candidate linear equilibria with parameters a_i^k, $k = 1, 2$, uniformly bounded in i and with well-defined average parameters $\hat{b}$ and $\hat{c}$. These are the linear equilibria for which the price will be a linear function of (θ^1, θ^2, u), $P(\theta^1, \theta^2, u)$.

Using the inverse demand function $p = \alpha + u - \beta x$ we obtain that, provided $\hat{c} > -1/\beta$,

$$p = (1 + \beta\hat{c})^{-1}(\alpha - \beta\hat{b} + z),$$

where the random variable $z = u + \beta(a^1\theta^1 + a^2\theta^2)$ is informationally equivalent to the price. The variable z proves very useful in characterizing REE. Note that z (and the price) will provide in general a noisy signal of the unknown parameters

(θ^1, θ^2) because u is random. We can write the information available to firm i as $G_i = \{s_i^1, s_i^2, z\}$.

Let us posit strategies of the form

$$x_i = b_i - a_i^1 s_i^1 - a_i^2 s_i^2 + c_i z.$$

Aggregate output and price are then given by

$$x = b - a^1\theta^1 - a^2\theta^2 + cz \quad \text{and} \quad p = \alpha + u - \beta x = \alpha - \beta b + (1 - \beta c)z,$$

respectively (where $b = \int_0^1 b_i \, di$ and $c = \int_0^1 c_i \, di$). In equilibrium we will have that $1 - \beta c > 0$ and $1 + \beta \hat{c} > 0$ and p and z will move together.

Firm i solves the problem $\max_{x_i} E[px_i - C_i(x_i) \mid s_i^1, s_i^2, p]$. In particular, firms condition on their private signals s_i^1 and s_i^2, which in turn implies that the market-clearing price will be a function of the aggregation of private signals or, equivalently, according to our convention on the average error terms of the signals, of (θ^1, θ^2). Since the distribution of random variables and the underlying model are common knowledge, firms can infer how aggregate private information enters the pricing function and use this information in the estimation of the underlying cost uncertainty.

The optimal (interior) production of firm i is determined by the FOC

$$\frac{\partial E[\pi_i \mid s_i^1, s_i^2, p]}{\partial x_i} = p - E[\mathrm{MC}_i(x_i) \mid s_i^1, s_i^2, p] = 0,$$

where the marginal cost for firm i is given by

$$\mathrm{MC}_i(x_i) = [\gamma s_i^1 + \theta^1 + \upsilon_i(\gamma s_i^2 + \theta^2)] + \lambda x_i.$$

The optimization problem is strictly concave given strict convexity of the cost function. The supply function for firm i is given by

$$X_i(s_i^1, s_i^2, p) = \lambda^{-1}[p - \gamma(s_i^1 + \upsilon_i s_i^2) - E[\theta^1 + \upsilon_i\theta^2 \mid s_i^1, s_i^2, p]]$$

or, with some abuse of notation,

$$X_i(s_i^1, s_i^2, z) = \lambda^{-1}[\alpha - \beta b + (1 - \beta c)z - \gamma(s_i^1 + \upsilon_i s_i^2) - E[\theta^1 + \upsilon_i\theta^2 \mid s_i^1, s_i^2, z]].$$

Using properties of the normal distribution we can calculate conditional expectations and solve for the linear equilibrium by identifying coefficients with the candidate linear strategies $x_i = b_i - a_i^1 s_i^1 - a_i^2 s_i^2 + c_i z$.

First we present a characterization in a simplified, and classical, version of the model with noisy demand and unidimensional uncertainty. This will deliver a noisy REE. We characterize the linear equilibrium in the general case and turn afterwards to a version with certain demand and multidimensional uncertainty which will deliver a rich class of REE (fully revealing and partially revealing).

3.2.2 Noisy Demand and One-Dimensional Uncertainty

Consider a particular case where signals do not affect costs ($y = 0$); costs are symmetric, i.e., $v_i = 1$ for all i; only θ^1 is uncertain, $\tau_{\theta^2} = \infty$ (assume also that $\theta^2 = 0$); and demand is noisy, $\sigma_u^2 > 0$.[15] The uncertain cost parameter is denoted by θ and firm i receives a signal $s_i = \theta + \varepsilon_i$. The cost function of firm i is therefore given by

$$C(x_i) = \theta x_i + \tfrac{1}{2}\lambda x_i^2.$$

In order to characterize an LBSFE note first that in this case we can restrict our attention without loss of generality to symmetric strategies since we restrict our attention to equilibria with linear price functionals of the form $P(\theta, u)$. Indeed, the solution to the problem of firm i

$$\max_{x_i} E[px_i - C(x_i) \mid s_i, p]$$

is unique (given strict concavity of profits) and symmetric across firms (since the cost function and signal structure is symmetric across firms). Specializing the argument in section 3.2.1 and positing strategies of the form

$$x_i = b - as_i + cz,$$

where the random variable $z = u + \beta a\theta$ is informationally equivalent to the price (with $\beta c < 1$), we can write the information available to firm i as $G_i = \{s_i, z\}$ or $G_i = \{s_i, p\}$ and the supply function of firm i as

$$X(s_i, z) = \lambda^{-1}(\alpha - \beta b + (1 - \beta c)z - E[\theta \mid s_i, z]).$$

Using the four-step procedure stated above (see exercise 3.1) we can solve for the linear equilibrium by identifying coefficients with the candidate linear strategy $x_i = b - as_i + cz$ by calculating $E[\theta \mid s_i, z]$.

An alternative way of characterizing the LBSFE is the following. Note that the FOC for firm i, $E[p - \mathrm{MC}(x_i) \mid s_i, z] = 0$, has to hold on average given the private signal of the firm. That is,

$$E[E[p - \mathrm{MC}(X(s_i, p)) \mid s_i, p] \mid s_i] = E[p - \mathrm{MC}(X(s_i, p)) \mid s_i] = 0.$$

Given normality, we immediately obtain (see section 10.2 and recall that $E[s_i] = 0$ by assumption):

$$E[p - \mathrm{MC}(x_i) \mid s_i] = E[p - \mathrm{MC}(x_i)] + \frac{\mathrm{cov}[p - \mathrm{MC}(x_i), s_i]}{\mathrm{var}[s_i]} s_i = 0.$$

Since the equation has to hold for all possible signals s_i and $\mathrm{var}[s_i] > 0$ we must have

$$E[p - \mathrm{MC}(x_i)] = 0 \quad \text{and} \quad \mathrm{cov}[p - \mathrm{MC}(x_i), s_i] = 0.$$

Some algebra yields that the first equality is equivalent to $b = \alpha/(\beta + \lambda)$ and the second to $c = (a(\lambda(\tau_\varepsilon + \tau_\theta) + \beta\tau_\varepsilon) - \tau_\varepsilon)/(a\beta\tau_\varepsilon(\lambda + \beta))$. At an LBSFE firms make

[15] This is considered in Vives (2007a).

efficient private use of the signals and this yields in particular the elimination of the covariation between signals and the margin $E[(p - \mathrm{MC}(x_i))s_i] = 0$.

Furthermore, using a similar reasoning (i.e., the properties of normal distributions), we would obtain that at an LBSFE agents also make efficient use of public information, eliminating the covariation between the margin and public information:

$$E[(p - \mathrm{MC}(x_i))z] = 0.$$

This equality can be seen to be equivalent to

$$c = \frac{1}{\lambda + \beta} - \frac{\beta a \tau_u (1 - \lambda a)}{\tau(\lambda + \beta)},$$

where $\tau \equiv (\mathrm{var}[\theta \mid p])^{-1} = \tau_\theta + \beta^2 a^2 \tau_u$ is the precision of the price (public information) about θ. In the relevant range this equation yields c as a decreasing function of a. In equilibrium the parameters a and c are determined by the intersection of the (privately) efficient use of private information and the efficient use of public information. The efficient use of private information yields c as an increasing function of a. From the two curves in (a, c) space (see figure 3.2) it follows that

$$a = \frac{\tau_\varepsilon}{\lambda(\tau_\varepsilon + \tau)} \quad \text{and} \quad c = \frac{1}{\beta + \lambda} - \frac{\beta a \tau_u}{(\beta + \lambda)(\tau_\varepsilon + \tau)}.$$

From the second equality it is immediate that $c < 1/(\beta + \lambda)$ provided that $a \geqslant 0$. The equilibrium parameter a is determined as the unique (real) solution of the cubic equation

$$a = \frac{\tau_\varepsilon}{\lambda(\tau_\varepsilon + \tau_\theta + \tau_u \beta^2 a^2)}.$$

At the LBSFE, a decreases from $\tau_\varepsilon / \lambda(\tau_\theta + \tau_\varepsilon)$ to 0, and c from $(\beta + \lambda)^{-1}$ to $-\infty$ as τ_u ranges from 0 to ∞ (the latter follows since in equilibrium

$$c = \frac{1}{\beta + \lambda} - \frac{\beta a \tau_u}{(\beta + \lambda)(\tau_\varepsilon + \tau)} = \frac{1}{\beta + \lambda} - \frac{\beta \lambda \tau_u a^2}{(\beta + \lambda)\tau_\varepsilon} \quad \text{and} \quad \tau_u a^2 \to \infty$$

as $\tau_u \to \infty$). This can also be seen from figure 3.2 by looking at how the curve of efficient use of public information moves with τ_u since the curve of the private efficient use of private information does not depend on τ_u.

The less noise in demand the less firms rely on private and the more on public information to estimate costs. As $\tau_u \to \infty$ the precision of prices τ also tends to ∞.

The strategy of firm i is of the form $x_i = \alpha(\beta + \lambda)^{-1} - a s_i + c z$ or, recalling that $p = \alpha - \beta b + (1 - \beta c) z$, $\beta c < 1$, the supply function is given by

$$X(s_i, p) = \hat{b} - a s_i + \hat{c} p,$$

where it is easily checked that $\hat{b} = b(1 - \lambda \hat{c})$, where

$$b = \frac{\alpha}{\lambda + \beta} \quad \text{and} \quad \hat{c} = \frac{c}{1 - \beta c}.$$

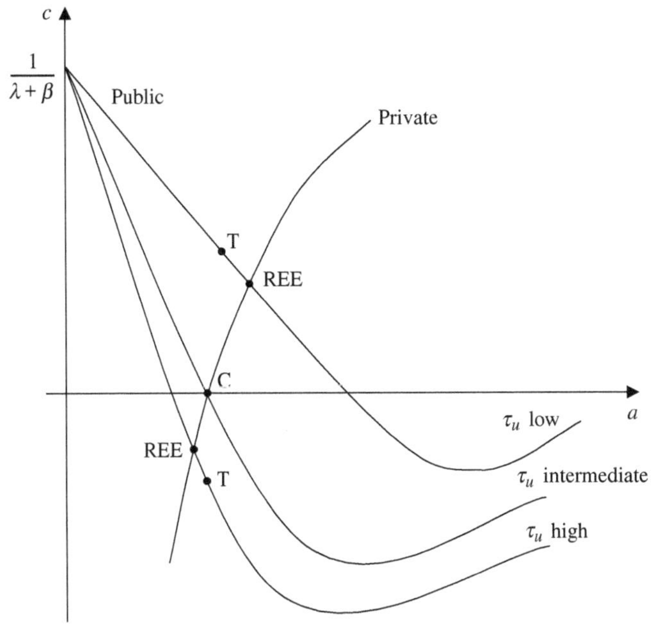

Figure 3.2. Determination of the LBSFE (labeled REE) parameters (a, c) as the intersection of the efficient use of private information ("Private") and the efficient use of public information ("Public"), illustrated for τ_u high, intermediate, and low. "T" stands for the team solution, "REE" for the rational expectations equilibrium, and "C" for the Cournot solution.

It is worth noting that the slope $\hat{c}$ of the supply function may be negative. We have that $c > (<)\ 0$ if and only if $a > (<)\ \tau_\varepsilon/(\lambda(\tau_\varepsilon + \tau_\theta) + \beta\tau_\varepsilon)$ and $c = 0$ if and only if $a = \tau_\varepsilon/(\lambda(\tau_\varepsilon + \tau_\theta) + \beta\tau_\varepsilon)$. (See figure 3.2.) Given that a is strictly decreasing with τ_u, we have that $\hat{c} > 0$ and supply functions are increasing for τ_u small, and that $\hat{c} < 0$ and supply functions are decreasing for τ_u large.

The price serves a dual role as an index of scarcity and as a conveyor of information. Indeed, a high price has a direct effect, increasing the competitive supply of a firm, but also conveys news that costs are high. If $\tau_u = 0$, then demand is so noisy that the price conveys no information on costs and $\hat{c} = 1/\lambda$ from the supply function $X(s_i, p) = \lambda^{-1}(p - E[\theta \mid s_i])$. As τ_u increases, then the slope $\hat{c} = (1 - \tau_u\beta a/(\tau_\varepsilon + \tau))/(\lambda + \tau_u\beta^2 a/(\tau_\varepsilon + \tau))$ decreases because of the informational component of price, becomes negative at some point, and, as $\tau_u \to \infty$, tends to $-1/\beta$ (since $\tau_u a/(\tau_\varepsilon + \tau_\theta + \beta\tau_u a^2) \to \infty$ from the fact that as $\tau_u \to \infty$ both $a \to 0$ and $\tau_u a^2 \to \infty$ and therefore $\tau_u a \to \infty$). In the particular case where the scarcity and informational effects balance, firms set a zero weight ($c = 0$) on public information. In this case firms do not condition on the price and the model reduces to the Cournot model where firms compete in quantities and $\hat{c} = 0$ (as in chapter 1). However, in this particular case, when supply functions are allowed, not reacting to the price (public information) is optimal. We may think that for reasonable parameter values supply will be upward sloping, the scarcity effect dominating the information effect, but this need not always be the case.[16]

The equilibrium is partially revealing (with $0 < \tau_u < \infty$ and $0 < \tau_\varepsilon < \infty$) and therefore expected total surplus is strictly greater under first-best production (full information) than in the REE. The reason is that firms produce under uncertainty and rely on estimation, which is costly because of errors, and costs are strictly convex.

Firms take public information z, or p, as given and use it to form probabilistic beliefs about the underlying uncertain cost parameter θ. This in turn determines coefficients a and c for private and public information, respectively. At the same time, the informativeness of public information z depends on the sensitivity of strategies to private information a. In the LBSFE firms behave as information takers and thus, from the viewpoint of an individual firm, public information is perceived as exogenous. This lies at the root of the informational externality present at the LBSFE. Firms do not take into account their impact on public information and therefore on other firms.

In three particular cases the information externality vanishes.

The first is when signals are perfectly informative ($\tau_\varepsilon = \infty$). Then we are back to a full-information competitive equilibrium. As we know, this is Pareto optimal. We then have that $c = 1/(\beta + \lambda)$, $a = \hat{c} = 1/\lambda$, $\hat{b} = 0$, and $X(s_i, p) = \lambda^{-1}(p - \theta)$. In this case firms do not have anything to learn from the price.

The second is when signals are uninformative about the common cost parameter θ ($\tau_\varepsilon = 0$). Then $a = 0$, $c = 1/(\beta + \lambda)$, $\hat{c} = 1/\lambda$, and $X(s_i, p) = \lambda^{-1}(p - \bar{\theta}) = \lambda^{-1}p$ (since by assumption $\bar{\theta} = 0$). In this case the price has no information to convey.

The third is when demand is extremely noisy ($\tau_u = 0$). Then $c = 1/(\beta + \lambda)$, $\hat{c} = 1/\lambda$, and $a = \tau_\varepsilon/(\lambda(\tau_\varepsilon + \tau_\theta))$, with $X(s_i, p) = \lambda^{-1}(p - E[\theta \mid s_i])$. In this case public information (the price) is pure noise.

3.2.3 Characterizing the Linear Supply Function Equilibrium in the General Case

An LBSFE of the general model of section 3.2.1 can be characterized using the described four-step procedure. Another way to obtain the result is to observe that at an LBSFE firm i will solve

$$\max_{c_i} E[px_i - C_i(x_i)]$$

subject to

$$\begin{aligned} x_i &= b_i - a_i^1 s_i^1 - a_i^2 s_i^2 + c_i z, \\ z &= u + a^1\theta^1 + a^2\theta^2, \end{aligned}$$

[16] C. Wilson (1979, 1980) finds an upward-sloping demand schedule in a market with asymmetric information with quality known only to the sellers.

and

$$E[p - \mathrm{MC}_i(x_i)] = E[(p - \mathrm{MC}_i(x_i))s_i^1] = E[(p - \mathrm{MC}_i(x_i))s_i^2] = 0.$$

The last constraints are the multidimensional equivalents of those derived in section 3.2.2. The last two equations determine the coefficients in the strategy as a function of c_i and its average c, $a_i^1 = f_1(c_i, c)$, $a_i^2 = f_2(\upsilon_i, c_i, c)$, and $E[p - \mathrm{MC}_i(x_i)] = 0$ yields $b_i = 1/(1+\lambda)$. (See exercise 3.2 for the expressions of the functions f_1 and f_2.) The FOCs of the problem (which are sufficient because profits are strictly quasiconcave in c_i: $(\partial^2 E[\pi_i]/\partial c_i^2) < 0$, when $\partial E[\pi_i]/\partial c_i = 0$) are, for each i,

$$\frac{\partial E[\pi_i]}{\partial c_i} = E\left[(p - \mathrm{MC}_i(x_i))\left(-\frac{\partial a_i^1}{\partial c_i}s_i^1 - \frac{\partial a_i^2}{\partial c_i}s_i^2 + z\right)\right] = E[(p - \mathrm{MC}_i(x_i))z] = 0.$$

This is so since $E[(p - \mathrm{MC}_i(x_i))s_i^1] = E[(p - \mathrm{MC}_i(x_i))s_i^2] = 0$. Then, averaging over agents $E[(p - \mathrm{MC}_i(x_i))z] = 0$ and using the averages of $a_i^1 = f_1(c_i, c)$, $a_i^2 = f_2(\upsilon_i, c_i, c)$, which depend on c, we obtain an equation in the average coefficient c, which has a unique solution. This pins down a unique LBSFE whenever (i) $\sigma_u^2 > 0$ or (ii) $\sigma_u^2 = 0$ and $\gamma > 0$ (see exercise 3.2).

If $\gamma = 0$ and $\sigma_u^2 = 0$, then the equilibrium equations are inconsistent and no linear equilibrium exists.

3.2.4 Nonnoisy Demand and Multidimensional Uncertainty

Suppose now that demand is not noisy ($\sigma_u^2 = 0$), that cost uncertainty is multidimensional (θ^1, θ^2), and that signals directly affect costs $\gamma > 0$. Then solving through the equilibrium equations, and letting $\alpha = \beta = 1$ to ease notation, we obtain the unique solution (Messner and Vives 2001):

$$\begin{aligned}
a_i^1 &= \frac{\gamma}{\lambda} + \frac{\tau_{\varepsilon^1}(1 - \upsilon_i)}{\lambda(\tau_{\theta^1} + \tau_{\varepsilon^1} + \tau_{\theta^2} + \tau_{\varepsilon^2})},\\
a_i^2 &= \upsilon_i\frac{\gamma}{\lambda} + \frac{\tau_{\varepsilon^2}(\upsilon_i - 1)}{\lambda(\tau_{\theta^1} + \tau_{\varepsilon^1} + \tau_{\theta^2} + \tau_{\varepsilon^2})},\\
c_i &= c + c_2(\upsilon_i - 1),\\
b_i &= \frac{1}{\lambda + 1},\\
c &= \frac{1}{\lambda + 1}\frac{\gamma - \lambda}{\gamma},\\
c_2 &= -\frac{\tau_{\theta^1} + \tau_{\varepsilon^1}}{\gamma(\tau_{\theta^1} + \tau_{\varepsilon^1} + \tau_{\theta^2} + \tau_{\varepsilon^2})},
\end{aligned}$$

and $a^1 = a^2 = \gamma/\lambda$.

Since $a^1 = a^2 = \gamma/\lambda > 0$, $z = (\gamma/\lambda)(\theta^1 + \theta^2)$, and the price $p = 1 - b + (1 - c)z$ reveals $\theta^1 + \theta^2$. This means that price equals average marginal cost, $p = \mathrm{MC}$ $(= \int_0^1 \mathrm{MC}_i \, di)$ and therefore average production is at the full-information first-best level. Then if costs are symmetric ($\upsilon_i = 1$), public information together with $s_i^1 + s_i^2$ is fully revealing for the cost of firm i. This may

Table 3.1. REE cases with nonrandom demand.

$\sigma_u^2 = 0$	$\gamma = 0$	$\gamma > 0$
$\upsilon_i = 1$ for all i	FRREE (not implementable)	FRREE (privately revealing)
$\upsilon_i \in (0, 2)$ $(\sigma_\upsilon^2 > 0)$	Nonexistence of linear REE	Partially revealing REE

be termed a "privately revealing" REE, where the price plus the private signals of a trader are a sufficient statistic for the pooled information of the traders (Allen 1981). This provides an instance of an FRREE which is implementable. The equilibrium will be *ex post* Pareto optimal. If $\sigma_\upsilon^2 > 0$, then $G_i = \{s_i^1, s_i^2, z\}$ is partially revealing for the cost of firm i. This provides an instance of nonnoisy partially revealing REE.

When firms have *ex ante* symmetric cost functions ($\upsilon_i = 1$ for all i) and signals do not affect cost ($\gamma = 0$), only $\theta^1 + \theta^2$ matters and we can define a fully revealing REE (FRREE). However, this equilibrium is not implementable. The nonexistence of an LBSFE, when signals do not affect cost directly ($\gamma = 0$), is easy to understand in the above setting. In this case equilibrium would call for $a^1 = a^2 = 0$ but then prices cannot reveal any information. Furthermore, if prices do not reveal any information, then firms have an incentive to rely on their signals and this makes the price informative.

The model is parsimonious in displaying a full variety of types of REE as well as highlighting the potential problems with the concept. If demand is nonrandom ($\sigma_u^2 = 0$ with $u = 0$), the model encompasses the following cases (table 3.1 summarizes them):

(i) an FRREE which is not implementable, when firms have *ex ante* symmetric cost functions ($\upsilon_i = 1$ for all i) and signals do not affect costs ($\gamma = 0$);

(ii) an FRREE which is implementable as an LBSFE under symmetry, if signals do affect costs ($\gamma > 0$);

(iii) a (nonnoisy) partially revealing REE with asymmetric cost functions which is implementable as an LBSFE, if $\gamma > 0$; and

(iv) no (linear) REE, if $\gamma = 0$.

If demand is random ($\sigma_u^2 > 0$), then there is a noisy REE which is implementable as an LBSFE for any $\gamma \geqslant 0$.

Below we also summarize the cases in which there is no information externality through prices:

(i) when public information is pure noise ($\tau_u = 0$);

(ii) when signals are uninformative ($\tau_{\varepsilon^1} = \tau_{\varepsilon^2} = 0$);

(iii) in the full-information case ($\tau_{\varepsilon^1} = \tau_{\varepsilon^2} = \infty$); and

(iv) when the equilibrium is fully revealing ($\tau_u = \infty$, $\gamma > 0$, and $\upsilon_i = 1$ for all i).

In the first three cases there is nothing to learn from prices, and in case (iv) everything is revealed. In cases (iii) and (iv) there is no welfare loss at the LBSFE with respect to the first-best because the market outcome replicates the full-information competitive equilibrium. Otherwise, there is a welfare loss.

3.2.5 Summary

In our continuum economy:

- Partially revealing REE are implementable as Bayesian supply function equilibria.
- At an LBSFE supply may be downward sloping if the informational role of prices dominates their role as index of scarcity. Indeed, high prices may indicate high costs to a firm.
- At the LBSFE, except in very particular circumstances, there is an informational externality since a firm, when reacting to its private information, does not take into account the impact of its action on the informativeness of the price, which affects all firms.
- Unless REE are fully revealing (privately revealing), there is a welfare loss with respect to the full-information competitive outcome.
- Fully revealing REE are implementable in supply functions only if private signals are payoff relevant since otherwise a firm does not have incentives to condition on its private information.

3.3 Welfare Analysis of REE

We consider here the case of section 3.2.2 and perform a welfare analysis (Vives 2007a). The benchmark we will use is the same as in chapter 1: the team solution that maximizes expected total surplus subject to the use of linear decentralized strategies. This is in the spirit of Hayek where the private signals of agents cannot be communicated to a center. The team-efficient solution internalizes the information externalities of the actions of agents and is restricted to use the same type of strategies as the market (decentralized and linear). Indeed, an agent when reacting to his information does not take into account the contribution he makes to public information by influencing public statistics with his action.

At the team-efficient solution, expected total surplus (ETS) is maximized under the constraint that firms use decentralized linear production strategies. That is,

$$\max_{a,b,c} \mathrm{ETS} = \max_{a,b,c} E\left[(\alpha + u - \tfrac{1}{2}\beta x)x - \int_0^1 C(x_i)\,\mathrm{d}i\right]$$

subject to $x_i = b - as_i + cz$, with $x = b - a\theta + cz$ and $z = u + a\beta\theta$.

Given that $\partial x_i/\partial a = -s_i + c\beta\theta$, $\partial x_i/\partial b = 1$, $\partial x_i/\partial c = z$, the team solution is characterized by the following FOC:

$$\begin{aligned}\frac{\partial \text{ETS}}{\partial a} &= E\left[\int_0^1 (p - \text{MC}(x_i))(-s_i + c\beta\theta)\,\text{d}i\right]\\ &= E[(p - \text{MC}(x_i))(-s_i + c\beta\theta)] = 0,\\ \frac{\partial \text{ETS}}{\partial b} &= E\left[\int_0^1 (p - \text{MC}(x_i))\,\text{d}i\right] = E[(p - \text{MC}(x_i))] = 0,\\ \frac{\partial \text{ETS}}{\partial c} &= E\left[\int_0^1 (p - \text{MC}(x_i))z\,\text{d}i\right] = E[(p - \text{MC}(x_i))z] = 0.\end{aligned}$$

We know from section 3.2.2 that the constraint $E[p - \text{MC}(x_i)] = 0$ is equivalent to $b = \alpha/(\beta + \lambda)$, and $E[(p - \text{MC}(x_i))z] = 0$ to $c(a) = 1/(\beta + \lambda) - \beta a\tau_u(1 - \lambda a)/\tau(\beta + \lambda)$, where $\tau = \tau_\theta + \beta^2 a^2 \tau_u$. Replacing c by $c(a)$ in the expression for ETS it can be shown that ETS is strictly concave in a (at least when $c(\cdot)$ is strictly decreasing). Evaluating $\partial \text{ETS}/\partial a$ at the LBSFE, where $E[(p - \text{MC}(x_i))s_i] = 0$, we obtain that $\partial \text{ETS}/\partial a = c\beta E[(p - \text{MC}(x_i))\theta]$ and note that at the LBSFE we have that $c(\cdot)$ is strictly decreasing (see figure 3.2). We know that

$$E[(p - \text{MC}(x_i))s_i] = E[(p - \text{MC}(x_i))\theta] + E[(p - \text{MC}(x_i))\varepsilon_i] = 0$$

and therefore that

$$\begin{aligned}E[(p - \text{MC}(x_i))\theta] &= -E[(p - \text{MC}(x_i))\varepsilon_i] = E[\text{MC}(x_i)\varepsilon_i]\\ &= E[(\theta + \lambda x_i)\varepsilon_i] = -\lambda a \sigma_\varepsilon^2 < 0\end{aligned}$$

since ε_i is independent of all other random variables of the model. We conclude that at the LBSFE

$$\text{sgn}\left(\frac{\partial \text{ETS}}{\partial a}\right) = \text{sgn}(-\beta c^{\text{REE}}).$$

Therefore, for $\tau_\varepsilon > 0$ and $\tau_u > 0$, the solutions coincide only if $c^{\text{REE}} = 0$. This is the case if at the LBSFE $c = (a(\lambda(\tau_\varepsilon + \tau_\theta) + \beta\tau_\varepsilon) - \tau_\varepsilon)/\tau_\varepsilon(\beta + \lambda)a\beta = 0$ or when $a = \tau_\varepsilon/(\lambda(\tau_\varepsilon + \tau_\theta) + \beta\tau_\varepsilon)$ (the intermediate case in figure 3.2). When firms do not respond to the price ($c = 0$) the model reduces to a Cournot model with private information. Recall that in chapter 1 we showed that a Cournot market with private information and a continuum of firms solves a team problem with ETS as objective function. For $c^{\text{REE}} < 0$ the distortion is positive and a should be increased while the contrary is true for $c^{\text{REE}} > 0$. The team optimal solution uses public information efficiently but is not bound by the privately efficient use of information. At the REE there is excessive (insufficient) weight given to private information whenever τ_u is small (large) and supply functions are increasing (decreasing). (See figure 3.2.)

There is no information externality when firms have perfect information ($\tau_\varepsilon = \infty$) and the full-information first-best is obtained (and price equals marginal cost); when the price contains no information ($\tau_u = 0$) and when signals are uninformative ($\tau_\varepsilon = 0$). In the latter two cases the team and the market solutions coincide. For both the team and the market solutions, when $\tau_u = 0$, $E[(p - \mathrm{MC}_i)z] = 0$ implies that $c = 1/(\beta + \lambda)$ and $a = \tau_\varepsilon/\lambda(\tau_\varepsilon + \tau_\theta)$, and when $\tau_\varepsilon = 0$ we have that $a = 0$ and $c = 1/(\beta + \lambda)$.

The conclusion is that when costs are *ex ante* symmetric team efficiency requires an increase (decrease) in c when c^{REE} is negative (positive). For $c^{\mathrm{REE}} < 0$ the informational role of the price dominates and the price reveals too little information. In this case more weight should be given to private signals so that public information becomes more revealing. On the contrary, when the price is mainly an index of scarcity, $c^{\mathrm{REE}} > 0$, then the price reveals too much information and a should be decreased. Only in the knife-edge (Cournot) case, where $c^{\mathrm{REE}} = 0$, is the REE team-efficient.

Remarks on incentive efficiency. Let us now restrict the reference class of allocations to those which are implementable: that is, feasible and incentive compatible, where agents are given incentives to reveal their types, and having the same communication constraints as the LBSFE—that is, which use the same pieces of aggregate information as the market—as we have imposed in the team solution. This would define a class of linear Bayesian incentive-compatible mechanisms (LBICMs), in which the allocations would be bound by the privately efficient use of private information. Obviously, the REE will belong to this class as long as it is a linear Bayesian supply function equilibrium. This is the approach taken in Laffont (1985).

The team outcome, however, will not belong to such a class because at this solution the agents are assumed to share the common team objective and therefore they are not bound by the privately efficient use of private information but by the efficient use of public information. Then it is possible to show that the incentive-efficient weight given to private information, which maximizes ETS in the class of LBICMs, is midway between the team and the market REE outcomes. This means in particular that the direction of the distortions at the REE in relation to the efficient incentive solution is the same as if we compare the REE with the team solution.

The case considered by Laffont (1985) corresponds to multidimensional uncertainty with $\gamma > 0$, $\sigma^2_{\theta 1} = \sigma^2_{\theta 2}$, $\sigma^2_{\varepsilon 1} = \sigma^2_{\varepsilon 2}$, and nonnoisy demand $\tau_u = \infty$. This is the symmetric-information structure version of the model in section 3.2.4. Laffont finds that the partially revealing linear REE is restricted efficient in the class of LBICMs which face the same communication constraints as the market. This class of mechanisms is as close as possible to a linear REE and therefore it can be considered to be the best possible case for the market to attain efficiency. However, whenever firms are asymmetric ($\sigma^2_\upsilon > 0$) the incentive-efficient solution and the REE coincide if and only if $\tau_{\varepsilon_2}\tau_{\theta_1} - \tau_{\varepsilon_1}\tau_{\theta_2} = 0$. When this is not the case partially revealing REE prices will tend to have the wrong informational mix. Even if aggregate production is at its first-best level at the REE, because there is no noise in demand, it may pay to distort allocative efficiency to improve productive efficiency to raise welfare in an incentive-compatible way (see Messner and Vives 2001).

3.3.1 Summary

- The welfare benchmark to compare a linear REE, in the spirit of Hayek where the private signals of agents cannot be communicated to a center, is the team solution that maximizes expected total surplus subject to the use of linear decentralized strategies.
- REE will not be team-efficient even in the most favorable case when the allowed allocations share similar properties as the market equilibrium (like being linear in information and facing the same communication constraints). The reason is that the market in general does not internalize the informational externality when prices convey information. REE will be team-efficient only in exceptional circumstances when the information externality vanishes.
- REE prices will tend to convey "too little" information when the informational role of prices prevails over its "index-of-scarcity" role and "too much" in the opposite situation.

3.4 Strategic Supply Function Equilibria and Convergence to a Price-Taking Equilibrium

Up to now we have considered a large market where each firm was negligible. In a finite market firms are strategic and at a Bayesian equilibrium in supply functions firms are aware of their market power and the potential information leakage from their actions via prices.[17] This will tend to make them more cautious, a theme that we will develop in chapter 5 in the context of a financial market. This provides a natural extension of REE to imperfect competition. We can examine the information aggregation properties and convergence to price-taking behavior of supply function equilibria (SFE) as the market grows large. This exercise offers a strategic foundation for the continuum models of the previous sections. Exercise 3.4 asks the reader to check that the equilibrium in versions of the continuum market in section 3.2 provides a good approximation of a large finite market, where firms have some monopoly power (much as we have checked in chapter 2 in relation to the continuum economy models of chapter 1).

Vives (2007b) shows the convergence of the supply function equilibrium of finite economies to the limit equilibrium of a continuum market in the model of section 2.1 but now with n firms competing in supply functions instead of quantities. Inverse demand in the n-replica market, where consumers and firms are replicated at the same rate, is given by

$$P_n(X) = \alpha - \frac{\beta}{n}X$$

[17] Klemperer and Meyer (1989) study supply function competition under uncertainty but with symmetric information.

and the costs of firm i by

$$C(x_i) = \theta_i x_i + \tfrac{1}{2}\lambda x_i^2,$$

where α is nonrandom and θ_i is normally distributed. The θ_i parameters are correlated with correlation coefficient $\varsigma \in [0,1]$. Firm i receives a signal s_i about θ_i and signals are of the same precision. The characterization of linear equilibria with supply function competition when there is market power and private information needs some careful analysis in order to model the capacity of a firm to influence the market price at the same time that the firm learns from the price. The procedure to deal with this issue is explained in section 5.1 in the context of demand schedule competition in a financial market.

It can be shown that for a given n there is a unique linear Bayesian supply function equilibrium provided that $\varsigma < 1$. At this equilibrium the price p_n reveals the aggregate information $\tilde{s}_n = (\sum_{i=1}^n s_i)/n$. The equilibrium is privately revealing, i.e., $(s_i, \tilde{s}_n)$ is a sufficient statistic for firm i of the joint information in the market. The incentives to collect information are preserved because for firm i the signal s_i still helps in estimating θ_i even though p_n reveals $\tilde{s}_n$. The equilibrium already aggregates information for any size of the market and therefore there is no issue of information aggregation. This is in sharp contrast to the analogous Cournot model considered in section 2.1. If $\varsigma = 1$ and $0 < \sigma_\varepsilon^2 < \infty$, we are in the model of section 3.2.2 when signals do not affect costs and demand is not noisy. In this case there is a fully revealing REE but it is not implementable.

At the equilibrium there is no welfare loss due to private information, only due to market power. It is also found that firms are more cautious reacting to their private signals and use steeper supply functions when they have market power. It is interesting to also note that, again in contrast to the Cournot model, increasing the noise in the private signal σ_ε^2 or the correlation of the random cost parameters ς makes the slope of supply steeper and tends to increase margins. The reason is that when σ_ε^2 or ς increase firms learn more from the price and a high price may convey the bad news that costs are high (since the price reveals the average cost signal $\tilde{s}_n$). Indeed, it may also happen that supply is downward sloping for this motive. The phenomenon is akin to the winner's curse in common-value auctions (see section 1.5.1): a bidder refrains from bidding aggressively because winning conveys the news that the signal the bidder has received was too optimistic (i.e., the highest signal in the pool of bidders). In our supply function model a firm refrains from competing aggressively because a high price conveys the bad news that costs are high. The results are also reminiscent of asymmetric-information models where traders submit steeper schedules to protect themselves against adverse selection, as we will see in chapter 5.

As the market grows, market power vanishes and convergence to price-taking behavior is obtained. In the limit market the price is a linear function of $\tilde{\theta} = \int_0^1 \theta_i \, di$. As in the Cournot case of proposition 2.3 on p. 58, convergence to price-taking equilibria is faster when we are closer to a common-value environment or with less prior uncertainty.

3.5 Double Auctions

In the model considered so far consumers are passive. Reny and Perry (2006) analyze a double auction with a unit mass of agents, a proportion μ of buyers, and $1 - \mu$ of sellers. Each agent desires at most one unit of the good. The value of the good is given by a random variable θ taking values in the unit interval. Each agent receives a conditionally independent signal about θ also distributed in the unit interval. The state of the good and the vector of signals of the agents are assumed to be strictly affiliated (and the densities of the random variables are smooth and positive).[18] It is also assumed that the valuation of an agent is strictly increasing with his signal and weakly increasing with θ. The valuation of a trader receiving a signal s is $v(s, \theta)$.

According to the double auction rules, once traders have received their signals they submit bids to the auctioneer. A buyer (seller) indicates the maximum (minimum) price he is willing to pay for (sell) the desired unit. The auctioneer then forms supply and demand schedules with the bids and finds a market-clearing price. Buyers with bids above the market-clearing price obtain one unit and those with bids below the market-clearing price part with nothing. In contrast to the supply function equilibrium of section 3.2.2, and as in the models of chapter 1, traders cannot condition on the market price because they submit a single bid contingent only on private information. Obviously, each trader understands the strategies that others use in equilibrium and takes this into account when formulating his bid.

Let $F(\cdot \mid \theta)$ be the distribution function of a signal conditional on θ and denote by $s_\mu(\theta)$ the μth percentile of $F(\cdot \mid \theta)$ (that is, the signal s satisfying $F(s \mid \theta) = \mu$). Let $\theta_\mu(s)$ be the "inverse" of $s_\mu(\theta)$; that is, the state θ in which $s_\mu(\theta)$ is closest to s. We have $\theta_\mu(s_\mu(\theta)) = \theta$ for all $\theta \in [0, 1]$; $\theta_\mu(s) = 0$ if $s < s_\mu(0)$ and $\theta_\mu(s) = 1$ if $s > s_\mu(1)$. For a given μ there is a unique FRREE $p(\theta) = v(s_\mu(\theta), \theta)$, which is implementable as a Bayesian equilibrium of the double auction in symmetric increasing bidding strategies, where a buyer or seller bids $v(s, \theta_\mu(s))$.[19] It is worth remarking that the result also holds in the common-value case where the valuation v is independent of s. Exercise 3.5 provides an example and a proof of the statement.

It is worth noting that the equilibrium is efficient, that is, the units are allocated to the traders with the highest signals and therefore valuations. This should not be surprising since the FRREE is just the competitive equilibrium when the state θ is known. Efficiency depends on symmetry. However, most likely asymmetries could be accommodated if bidders were allowed to bid schedules instead of being forced to submit single bids. Indeed, in the supply

[18] See section 10.1.5 for the concept of affiliation.

[19] The strategies are uniquely determined only in the range $[s_\mu(0), s_\mu(1)]$. All the increasing functions that agree with $v(s, \theta_\mu(s))$ on this range also constitute a Bayesian equilibrium (and lead to the same allocation). Reny and Perry argue that the salient equilibrium, when considering finite approximations to the limit continuum market, is to bid $v(s, 0)$ for $s < s_\mu(0)$ and $v(s, 1)$ for $s > s_\mu(1)$.

function model of section 3.2 it is easy to see that with one-dimensional aggregate uncertainty (θ^1 nonrandom or $\tau_{\theta^1} = \infty$), a strict private-value component in payoffs ($\gamma > 0$) and asymmetric traders ($\sigma_{\upsilon}^2 > 0$), the equilibrium is fully revealing of the aggregate uncertainty θ^2, implementable in supply functions, and also efficient.

In short, the market with a continuum of bidders has a unique FRREE which is, indeed, price taking and efficient. This FRREE is also a Bayesian equilibrium of the double auction, one with symmetric strictly increasing bidding strategies. The FRREE may be implementable as a double auction even in a pure common-value case. This is so because of the nature of the double auction mechanism with bids for a single unit. At the FRREE, buyers and sellers are indifferent about whether to use their private signal and they may as well use it.

Reny and Perry also provide a strategic foundation for the FRREE in a finite market counterpart of the double auction continuum model. In the limit market continuum model, it has been claimed that there is a unique FRREE which is price taking and efficient. This FRREE is also a Bayesian equilibrium of the double auction, one with symmetric strictly increasing bidding functions. In the double auction with a finite number of buyers and sellers, a rationing rule has to be established for traders who bid exactly the market-clearing price. Reny and Perry show, with the maintained assumptions of the continuum market and using a symmetry-preserving rationing rule, that with enough buyers and sellers and with a sufficiently fine grid of prices then, generically in the valuation functions of the traders and the fineness of the grid, there is a Bayesian equilibrium in monotone increasing bid functions which is very close to the unique FRREE of the continuum economy. The strategy of the (involved) proof is to show an appropriate continuity property for the equilibrium in the limit market. The main obstacle in the proof is that with a finite number of traders the strategies of buyers and sellers are not symmetric. Indeed, buyers want to underbid while sellers want to overbid in order to affect the price according to their respective conflicting interests. The consequence is that it need not be true that the signal of each agent is affiliated with the order statistics of the bids of other agents. This fact—failure of "single crossing"—implies that standard proofs from auction theory that rely on relationships between affiliation and order statistics with symmetric strategies do not apply. However, the importance of asymmetries vanishes in large markets because in the limit price-taking behavior obtains. With a finite number of traders, buyers have incentives to underbid and sellers to overbid to influence the market price in their favor. Such incentives disappear as the market grows large.

Serrano-Padial (2007) studies the pure common-value double auction with a continuum of traders where a fraction of them are naive (in the sense that they use a fixed bidding strategy independent of what other traders do). Naive traders can be thought to be noise or liquidity traders. He finds that nonnegligible amounts of naive trade are compatible with fully revealing prices. The results can be applied to prediction markets.

3.6 Summary

In this chapter we have learned how to compute and characterize linear REE. In the context of a classical partial equilibrium production market we have provided a classification of REE and studied them as Bayesian supply function equilibria. The main results are as follows.

- Partially revealing REE are implementable as Bayesian supply function equilibria. Fully revealing REE will be implementable in supply functions only if private signals are payoff relevant since otherwise a firm will not have incentives to condition on its private information. However, an FRREE may be implementable as a double auction even in a pure common-value case.
- At the REE, except in very particular circumstances, there is an informational externality since a firm when reacting to its private information does not take into account the impact of its action on the informativeness of the price, which affects all firms and consumers.
- Unless an REE is fully revealing, there will be a welfare loss with respect to the full-information competitive outcome.
- Under risk aversion REE may be *ex ante* inefficient by revealing too much information and eliminating valuable insurance opportunities (this is known as the Hirshleifer effect).
- The benchmark to compare the REE, in the spirit of Hayek where the private signals of agents cannot be communicated to a center, is the team solution that maximizes expected total surplus subject to the use of linear decentralized strategies.
- REE will not be team-efficient even in the most favorable case when agents are risk neutral and the allowed allocations share similar properties to the market equilibrium (like facing the same communication constraints). The reason is that the market in general cannot internalize the informational externality when prices convey information.
- REE prices will tend to convey "too little" information when the informational role of prices prevails over its index of scarcity role and "too much" in the opposite situation.
- Partially or privately revealing REE in competitive markets can be provided a strategic foundation in finite economies where traders have market power.

3.7 Appendix

Note on the existence of REE. In an asymmetric-information environment with complete markets the existence of a fully revealing REE (FRREE) is guaranteed under the standard conditions for existence of a competitive equilibrium of the full-information economy. With complete markets there is a market, and a price, for every contingency or state of the world. In other words, each state of the world is insurable. Consider the Arrow–Debreu equilibrium of an artificial economy in which agents pool their information. The price functional at this equilibrium (i.e., the map from signals to prices) is fully revealing (invertible), because there is a price for each state, and it must be an REE, indeed an FRREE (Grossman 1981). With incomplete markets a potential problem is the discontinuity in the mapping, which goes from beliefs to correct beliefs given the actions induced by the beliefs. Radner (1979) showed that an FRREE exists generically with a finite set of possible signals. That is, the map from signals to prices is, most likely, invertible. In general the dimensionality of the signal space ($\dim S$) relative to the dimensionality of the price space ($\dim P$ or the number of relative prices) plays a crucial role. When $\dim S < \dim P$, then again an FRREE exists generically (Allen 1981). When $\dim S > \dim P$, then generically REE exist but are not fully revealing (Jordan 1983). When $\dim S = \dim P$, then there are robust examples of nonexistence of REE (Jordan and Radner 1982). See chapter 19 in Mas-Colell et al. (1995) for an introduction to REE models in general equilibrium.

3.8 Exercises

3.1 (*derivation of an LBSFE*). Consider the model in section 3.2.2 (with $\gamma = 0$, $\sigma_u^2 > 0$, $\upsilon_i = 1$ for all i, $\tau_{\theta^2} = \infty$ and $\theta^2 \equiv 0$). Denote the only uncertain cost parameter by θ. Show that there is a unique LBSFE and that it is symmetric using the standard four-step procedure.

Solution. From

$$X(s_i, z) = \lambda^{-1}[\alpha - \beta b + (1 - \beta c)z - E(\theta \mid s_i, z)] = b - as_i + cz$$

and

$$E[\theta \mid s_i, z] = \frac{\tau_\varepsilon}{\tau_\varepsilon + \tau} s_i + \frac{\beta \tau_u a}{\tau_\varepsilon + \tau} z + \frac{\tau_\theta}{\tau_\varepsilon + \tau} \bar{\theta},$$

where $\tau = \tau_\theta + \tau_u \beta^2 a^2$ (and recall that $\bar{\theta} = 0$ by assumption), obtain the coefficients in the linear strategy by identification:

$$a = \frac{\tau_\varepsilon}{\lambda(\tau_\varepsilon + \tau)}, \quad c = \frac{1}{\beta + \lambda} - \frac{\beta \tau_u a}{(\tau_\varepsilon + \tau)(\beta + \lambda)}, \quad \text{and} \quad b = \frac{\alpha}{\beta + \lambda}.$$

3.2 (*uniqueness of the linear REE*). Show that the linear REE of the model in section 3.2 is unique whenever (i) $\sigma_u^2 > 0$ or (ii) $\sigma_u^2 = 0$ and $\gamma > 0$. To ease notation let $\alpha = \beta = 1$.

Hint. From $E[p - \mathrm{MC}_i(x_i)] = \mathrm{cov}[p - \mathrm{MC}(x_i), s_i^1] = \mathrm{cov}[p - \mathrm{MC}_i(x_i), s_i^2] = 0$, conclude that

$$a_i^1 = f_1(c_i, c) \equiv a^1(1 + \xi^1(c_i - c)),$$
$$a_i^2 = f_2(v_i, c_i, c) \equiv a^2(v_i + \xi^2 \lambda^{-1}((1 - c(1 + \lambda))(v_i - 1) + \lambda(c_i - c))),$$
$$b_i = \frac{1}{1 + \lambda},$$

where

$$a^k = h_k(c) \equiv \frac{\gamma + \xi^k}{\xi^k(1 - c(1 + \lambda) + \lambda)} \quad \text{and} \quad \xi^k \equiv \frac{\tau_{\varepsilon^k}}{\tau_{\varepsilon^k} + \tau_{\theta^k}}, \quad k = 1, 2.$$

Consider the condition $E[(p - \mathrm{MC}_i(x_i))z] = 0$, take the average over agents and use the equations $a^k = h_k(c)$, $k = 1, 2$, to derive an equilibrium equation for c, i.e., $f(c) = 0$, and show that it has a unique solution. See Messner and Vives (2001) for more details.

****3.3** (*strategic foundation of the continuum large market*). Consider the same market and information structure as in section 3.2, but now with n firms competing in supply functions. Inverse demand in the n-replica market is given by $P_n(X) = 1 + u - X/n$, where X is total output. (i) Consider the version of the model of section 3.2.2, characterize the linear Bayesian supply function equilibrium for a given n, and show that the limit as $n \to \infty$ is given by the linear equilibrium in the continuum market (prices converge in mean square to the limit price similarly to proposition 2.3). (ii) Do the same as in (i) for the version of the model of section 3.2.3 but suppose that θ^1 is nonrandom ($\tau_{\theta^1} = \infty$ and let $\theta^1 \equiv 0$). Is the equilibrium in the finite economy in case (ii) fully revealing? What about case (i)? Interpret the exercises, respectively, as providing a strategic foundation for (i) noisy REE and (ii) FRREE.

Hint. Get inspiration from the methods of chapter 2 (leading to proposition 2.3) for Cournot markets and from the characterization of demand function equilibria in the financial market of section 5.1. See also Messner and Vives (2001) and Vives (2007b) for related models and results.

3.4 (*FRREE in a double auction*). Consider a double auction for a good with a continuum of traders, half of them buyers and half of them sellers. Each agent desires at most one unit of the good. The valuation for a trader is $v = \theta + s$, where θ is the state and s the signal received by the trader. The state θ is uniformly distributed on $[0, 1]$, and given θ each signal is independently drawn uniformly from $[0, \theta]$. Show that $p(\theta) = \frac{3}{2}\theta$ is the only FRREE price. Show also that it is an equilibrium of the double auction for any trader, receiving a signal s, to use the bidding strategy $3s$. Show that the double auction price coincides with the FRREE price. Check that in the pure common-value case $v = \theta$ the equilibrium is $p(\theta) = \theta$ and the bidding strategy is $2s$.

Solution. From the fact that each signal is uniformly and independently drawn from $[0, \theta]$, it follows that half the traders have a signal above $\frac{1}{2}\theta$. For the trader $s = \frac{1}{2}\theta$ to be indifferent we must have $p(\theta) - \theta = \frac{1}{2}\theta$ and the result follows. For the common-value case one needs to proceed in a similar way. See Reny and Perry (2006).

References

Allen, B. 1981. Generic existence of completely revealing equilibria for economies with uncertainty when prices convey information. *Econometrica* 49:1173–99.

Anderson, R., and H. Sonnenschein. 1982. On the existence of rational expectations equilibrium. *Journal of Economic Theory* 26:261–78.

Beja, A. 1977. The limits of price information in Market processes. Institute of Business and Economic Research, University of California Working Paper 61.

Blume, L., and D. Easley. 1990. Implementation of Walrasian expectations equilibria. *Journal of Economic Theory* 51:207–27.

Fama, E. F. 1970. Efficient capital markets: a review of theory and empirical work. *Journal of Finance* 25:383–417.

——. 1976. *Foundations of Finance.* New York: Basic Books.

Gale, D. 1996. Equilibria and Pareto optima of markets with adverse selection. *Economic Theory* 7:207–35.

Green, J. R. 1973. Information, efficiency and equilibrium. Harvard Institute of Economic Research, Harvard University Discussion Paper 284.

Green, R. J. 1996. Increasing competition in the British electricity spot market. *Journal of Industrial Economics* 44:205–16.

Green, R. J., and D. Newbery. 1992. Competition in the British electricity spot market. *Journal of Political Economy* 100:929–53.

Grossman, S. J. 1978. Further results on the informational efficiency of competitive stock markets. *Journal of Economic Theory* 18:81–101.

——. 1981. An introduction to the theory of rational expectations under asymmetric information. *Review of Economic Studies* 48:541–59.

Grossman, S. J., and J. Stiglitz. 1980. On the impossibility of informationally efficient markets. *American Economic Review* 70:393–408.

Gul, F., and A. Postlewaite. 1992. Asymptotic efficiency in large exchange economies with asymmetric information. *Econometrica* 60:1273–92.

Harris, M., and R. M. Townsend. 1981. Resource allocation under asymmetric information. *Econometrica* 49:33–64.

Hayek, F. A. 1945. The use of knowledge in society. *American Economic Review* 35:519–30.

——. 1973. *Law, Legislation and Liberty*, volume I: *Rules and Order.* University of Chicago Press.

Hellwig, M. F. 1980. On the aggregation of information in competitive markets. *Journal of Economic Theory* 22:477–98.

Hirshleifer, J. 1971. The private and social value of information and the reward to incentive activity. *American Economic Review* 61:561–74.

Holmström, B., and R. Myerson. 1983. Efficient and durable decision rules with incomplete information. *Econometrica* 51:1799–819.

Jordan, J. 1983. On the efficient markets hypothesis. *Econometrica* 51:1325–43.

Jordan, J., and R. Radner. 1982. Rational expectations in microeconomic models: an overview. *Journal of Economic Theory* 26:201–23.

Klemperer, P., and M. Meyer. 1989. Supply function equilibria in oligopoly under uncertainty. *Econometrica* 57:1243–77.

Kyle, A. S. 1989. Informed speculation with imperfect competition. *Review of Economic Studies* 56:317–55.

Laffont, J. J. 1985. On the welfare analysis of rational expectations equilibria with asymmetric information. *Econometrica* 53:1–29.

——. 1989. *Economics of Uncertainty and Information.* Cambridge, MA: MIT Press.

Lucas, R. E. 1972. Expectations and the neutrality of money. *Journal of Economic Theory* 4:103–24.

Mas-Colell, A., and X. Vives. 1993. Implementation in economies with a continuum of agents. *Review of Economic Studies* 60:613–29.

Mas-Colell, A., M. D. Whinston, and J. R. Green. 1995. *Microeconomic Theory.* Oxford University Press.

Messner, S., and X. Vives. 2001. Informational and economic efficiency in REE with asymmetric information. Center for Economic Policy Research, Discussion Paper 2678. (Previous title: "Allocative and productive efficiency in REE with asymmetric information.")

Milgrom, P. R., and N. L. Stokey. 1982. Information, trade and common knowledge. *Journal of Economic Theory* 27:288–312.

Muth, J. F. 1960. Optimal properties of exponentially weighted forecasts. *Journal of the American Statistical Association* 290:299–306.

——. 1961. Rational expectations and the theory of price movements. *Econometrica* 29:315–35.

Palfrey, T. R., and S. Srivastava. 1986. Private information in large economies. *Journal of Economic Theory* 39:34–58.

Postlewaite, A., and D. Schmeidler. 1986. Implementation in differential information economies. *Journal of Economic Theory* 39:14–33.

Radner, R. 1979. Rational expectations equilibrium: generic existence and the information revealed by prices. *Econometrica* 49:655–78.

Reny, P., and M. Perry. 2006. Toward a strategic foundation for rational expectations equilibrium. *Econometrica* 74:1231–69.

Serrano-Padial, R. 2007. Strategic foundations of prediction markets and the efficient markets hypothesis. Mimeo.

Vives, X. 2007a. Endogenous public information and welfare. Mimeo.

——. 2007b. Strategic supply function competition with private information. Mimeo.

Wilson, C. 1979. Equilibrium and adverse selection. *American Economic Review* 69:313–17.

——. 1980. The nature of equilibrium in markets with adverse selection. *Bell Journal of Economics* 11:108–30.

Wilson, R. 1979. Auction of shares. *Quarterly Journal of Economics* 93:675–89.

4

Rational Expectations and Market Microstructure in Financial Markets

In this chapter we review the basic static (or quasistatic) models of financial markets with asymmetric information in a competitive environment. Strategic traders are introduced in chapter 5. The dynamic trading counterpart of the models in chapters 4 and 5 is to be found in chapters 8 and 9. We study both rational expectations models, where traders have the opportunity to condition on prices as in chapter 3, and models where traders use less complex strategies and cannot condition on prices as in the simple market mechanisms of chapter 1. We also consider mixed markets where some traders use complex strategies such as demand schedules or limit orders and other traders use simple strategies such as market orders.

We are mainly concerned with studying the determinants of market quality parameters, such as trading intensity, volatility, liquidity, informativeness of prices, and volume, when the information about the fundamentals is dispersed among the traders in the market. The general theme of this chapter, as well as of chapter 5, is that private information and the market microstructure, i.e., the details of how transactions are organized or the specifics of trading mechanisms, matter a lot for market quality parameters. The chapter will present the basic noisy rational expectations model of a financial market with asymmetric information and study the main variants. We will try to answer questions such as:

- How are prices determined? Does it make a difference if informed or uninformed traders move first?
- Do prices reflect noise or information about the fundamentals?
- What determines the liquidity of a market?
- What drives the traded volume?
- What are the incentives to acquire information in an informationally efficient market?
- Does it make a difference if market makers are risk averse?
- What determines the volatility of prices?
- What are the incentives of traders to use different types of orders?

Section 4.1 reviews the diversity of market microstructures in financial markets and outlines the material covered in the chapter.

4.1 Market Microstructure

The market microstructure of financial markets is very rich. Many different types of agents intervene in a trading system; for example, market makers, specialists, dealers, scalpers, and floor traders. Market making refers in general to the activity of setting prices to equilibrate demand and supply for securities at the potential risk of holding or releasing inventory to buttress market imbalances. *Specialists* in the New York Stock Exchange (NYSE) have the obligation to keep markets "deep, continuous in price, and liquid." They do this by handling orders and trading on their own account to smooth imbalances. The defining characteristic of a *dealer* is his obligation to accommodate trades at the set prices. A *scalper* is a type of broker who, dealing on his own account, tries to obtain a quick profit from small fluctuations of the market. A *floor trader* is generally a stock exchange member trading for his own account or for an account he controls. Traders can place many different types of orders; price formation and market rules differ in different markets and the sequence of moves by the agents involved is market specific. Trading rules and the institutional structure define an extensive form according to which the game between market participants is played.[1]

4.1.1 Types of Orders

The main *types of orders* that traders can place are market orders, limit orders, and stop (loss) orders. A *market order* specifies a quantity to be bought or sold at whatever price the market determines. There is no execution risk therefore but there is price risk. A market order is akin to the quantity strategy of a firm in a Cournot market (chapter 1).

A *limit order* specifies a quantity to be bought (sold) and a limit price below (above) which to carry the transaction. A buy limit order can only be executed at the limit price or lower, and a sell order can only be executed at the limit price or higher. This reduces the price risk but exposes the trader to execution risk because the order will not be filled if the price goes above (below) the limit price. A *stop order* is like a limit order but the limits are inverted, specifying a quantity to be sold (bought) and a limit price below (above) which to carry the transaction. The idea is that if the price goes below (above) a certain point the asset is sold (bought) to "stop" losses (to profit from raising prices). Markets

[1] For further references, see Harris (2003), who provides an excellent survey of the institutional details of the microstructure of financial markets. O'Hara (1994) provides an early introduction to market microstructure models. Madhavan (2000), Brunnermeier (2001), and Biais et al. (2005) provide more recent and advanced surveys, and Hasbrouck (2007) deals with the empirical research. Lyons (2001) provides a comprehensive treatment of the market microstructure of foreign exchange markets.

typically impose price and time priority rules on the execution of the limit order: older orders and/or orders that offer better terms of trade are executed first.

A *demand schedule* can be formed by combining appropriately a series of limit and stop orders. A demand schedule specifies a quantity to be bought (sold if negative) for any possible price level. The demand schedule is akin to the supply function of a firm (chapter 3). The advantage of the demand schedule is that (in the limit) it eliminates both the price and the execution risk. The drawback is that it is more complex and therefore more costly to implement.

4.1.2 Trading Systems

Trading systems can be classified as order or quote driven. In an *order-driven* system, traders place orders before prices are set either by market makers or by a centralized mechanism or auction. Typically the orders of investors are matched with no intermediaries (except the broker who does not take a position himself) and provide liquidity to the market. Trading in an order-driven system is usually organized as an auction which can be continuous or in batches at discrete intervals. A batch auction can be an open-outcry (like in the futures market organized by the Chicago Board of Trade) or electronic. Recently, crossing networks using prices derived from other markets have emerged. In many continuous systems there is order submission against an electronic limit-order book where orders have accumulated. If a limit order does not find a matching order and execution is not possible, it is placed in the limit-order book.

In most of these systems a batch auction is used to open continuous trading (as in Euronext, the successor in Paris of the Paris Bourse, which merged with the NYSE in 2007, Deutsche Börse, or Tokyo Stock Exchange). For example, in the Deutsche Börse with the Xetra system there is an opening auction that begins with a call phase in which traders can enter and/or modify or delete existing orders before the price determination phase. The indicative auction price is displayed when orders are executable.[2] Furthermore, volatility interruptions may occur during auctions or continuous trading when prices lay outside certain predetermined price ranges. A volatility interruption is followed by an extended call phase. Intraday auctions interrupt continuous trading. There is also a closing batch auction.[3]

In a *quote-driven* system (such as NASDAQ or SEAQ at the London Stock Exchange), market makers set bid and ask prices or, more generally, a supply schedule, and then traders submit their orders. The latter mechanism is also called a continuous dealer market because a trader need not wait to get his order executed, taking a market maker as the counterpart.[4] However, the term

---

[2] Otherwise the best bid/ask limit is displayed. See Xetra Market Model Release 3 at www.exchange.de. We will deal with the preopening auction in chapter 9.

[3] All these auctions have three phases: call, in which orders can be entered or preexisting orders modified or canceled, price determination, and order book balancing (which takes place only if there is a surplus).

[4] Other markets organized as dealerships are the foreign exchange market, U.S. Treasury bills secondary market, and the bond market.

dealer market is probably best kept for use when dealers quote uniform bid and ask prices rather than when market makers post schedules which build a limit-order book. In a quote-driven system dealers provide liquidity.

Many trading mechanisms are *hybrid* and mix features of both systems. The NYSE starts with a batch auction and then continues as a dealer market where there is a specialist for each stock who manages the order book and provides liquidity. There is now competition at the NYSE between marker makers and the electronic limit-order book to provide liquidity. The 2006 Hybrid NYSE Market Initiative aims at enhancing off-floor competition to the specialist. The London Stock Exchange (LSE) now uses an electronic limit-order book for small orders while keeping the dealer mechanism for large orders. SETS at the LSE is an order-driven system for the most liquid stocks. In general, markets have evolved toward a pure electronic limit-order market or at least toward allowing for customer limit orders competing with the exchange market makers (e.g., Euronext Paris or the evolution in the NYSE, including the acquisition of the limit-order market Archipelago).

In both order-driven and quote-driven systems, market makers potentially face an adverse selection problem because traders may possess private information about the returns of the asset and may exploit the market makers.[5] The order-driven system has a signaling flavor, because the potentially informed party moves first, while the quote-driven system has a screening flavor, because the uninformed party moves first by proposing a schedule of transaction to which potentially informed traders respond. Signaling models tend to have multiple equilibria, while nonexistence of equilibrium is a possible feature of screening models.[6] In this book we concentrate on asymmetric information as friction in the price formation of assets in the spirit of Bagehot (1971). Other frictions like order-handling costs (see, for example, Roll 1984) and inventory effects (see, for example, Ho and Stoll 1983) are not the focus of attention, although we do study models with risk-averse market makers where inventory effects are prominent. Asymmetric-information models have a parallel in auctions models with a common-value component, while the inventory models have a parallel in private-value auctions.

A further dimension along which trading mechanisms may differ is the pricing rules: every unit sold at the same price (*uniform pricing*) or different units sold at different prices (*discriminatory pricing*). Batch auctions typically involve uniform prices, while a trader submitting to the limit-order book a large enough order will get different prices corresponding to different limit prices. This is because several limit orders are needed to fill his order. Transactions occur at

---

[5] Adverse selection in an insurance context arises when the person or firm insured knows more than the insurance company about the probability of the loss happening (i.e., about the risk characteristics). In general, an adverse selection problem relates to the unfavorable consequences for uninformed parties of the actions of privately informed ones. This is akin to the lemons' problem studied by Akerlof (1970) and the adverse selection problem in insurance markets of Rothschild and Stiglitz (1976).

[6] See chapter 13 in Mas-Colell et al. (1995).

multiple prices as the trader "walks up" the book getting worse terms. In many dealer markets the order of the customer is filled by a single dealer (who may retrade with other dealers) at a uniform price.

Trading mechanisms also differ in other dimensions like anonymity, *ex ante* and *ex post* transparency, or retrading opportunities. Transparency refers to information on quotes, quantities, and identity of traders. *Ex post* transparency refers to the disclosure rules after trading and *ex ante* transparency refers to information available in the trading process. In an open book all limit orders are observable for all investors, while in a closed book traders do not see the book. The intermediate situation is when only some limit orders are observable. For example, often only members of the stock exchange observe the whole order book while investors observe only the best or some of the best quotes (e.g., in Xetra). The information disclosed about the identities of the traders varies across exchanges although there is a tendency to anonymity. In a fragmented dealer market a trader does not observe the quotations of dealers other than the one he is dealing with, while in a centralized limit-order-book market price quotations are observable.[7] Fragmented markets may impair liquidity but enhance competition.[8]

A canonical model of trade is the Walrasian auction, where all traders are in a symmetric position and simultaneously submit demand schedules to a central market mechanism that finds a (uniform) market-clearing price. In fact, in the nineteenth century Walras (1889) was inspired to build his market model by the batch auctions of the Paris Bourse.

It is worth recalling some terminology about the informational efficiency of prices from chapter 3. Prices are said to be *strongly informationally efficient* if the price is a sufficient statistic for the private information dispersed in the market. Prices are said to be *semi-strong informationally efficient* if they incorporate all available public information.

4.1.3 Outline

We deal in this chapter with a competitive environment and in chapter 5 with strategic traders. We look at competitive and strategic behavior in models of simultaneous submission of orders, be it demand schedules in the rational expectations tradition or market orders, and of sequential order submission considering the cases where informed traders or uninformed traders move first. As we have seen the former is typical of order-driven systems while the latter is typical of quote-driven systems. In the models considered uninformed traders who submit limit orders (or generalized demand schedules), and provide liquidity to the market, are identified with market makers. The basic benchmark dynamic models of price formation with adverse selection of Kyle (1985) and Glosten and Milgrom (1985) are dealt with in chapter 9. In chapters 4 and 5 we

[7] Under some circumstances the two systems are equivalent (see exercise 5.9 in chapter 5).

[8] See Pagano (1989), Battalio et al. (1997), and Biais et al. (2005).

only deal with static models. The models considered are highly stylized. The complexities of trading with limit orders are finessed.[9] In this chapter we only consider models of uniform pricing and defer models of discriminatory pricing to chapter 5 (section 5.3). The standard competitive noisy rational expectations financial market, with a model that has as special cases virtually all the competitive models in the literature, is presented in section 4.2.1. The potential paradox of the existence of informationally efficient markets when information is costly to acquire is addressed in section 4.2.2. Section 4.3 considers the case when informed traders move first and prices are set by competitive risk-neutral market markers. Informed traders may submit demand schedules or market orders. Section 4.4 introduces producers that want to hedge in a futures market and examines the impact of private information on the possibilities of insurance and real decisions. This section does away with the presence of noise traders in the market. In all models considered in the chapter we will assume constant absolute risk aversion (CARA) utility functions and normally distributed random variables. The CARA-normal model is the workhorse model in the study of financial markets with asymmetric information.

4.2 Competitive Rational Expectations Equilibria

In this section we study the standard competitive rational expectations model with asymmetric information in a setup that encompasses several variations developed by Hellwig (1980), Grossman and Stiglitz (1980), Diamond and Verrecchia (1981), Admati (1985), who considers a multiasset market, and Vives (1995a). We start with the canonical framework in which traders compete in demand schedules (section 4.2.1) and examine Grossman and Stiglitz's paradox about the impossibility of an informationally efficient market when information is costly to acquire (section 4.2.2).

4.2.1 The CARA-Gaussian Model

Consider a market with a single risky asset, with random fundamental value θ, and a riskless asset (with unitary return) which are traded by risk-averse agents, indexed in the interval $[0,1]$ endowed with the Lebesgue measure, and noise traders. The utility derived by trader i from the return

$$\pi_i = (\theta - p)x_i$$

of buying x_i units of the risky asset at price p is of the CARA type and is given by

$$U_i(\pi_i) = -\mathrm{e}^{-\rho_i \pi_i},$$

where ρ_i is the CARA coefficient. The nonrandom initial wealth of traders is normalized to zero (this is without loss of generality with CARA preferences).

[9] See the survey on limit-order markets by Parlour and Seppi (forthcoming) for a state-of-the-art account of research in the area taking into account dynamic strategies.

Trader i may be informed, i.e., endowed with a piece of information about the *ex post* liquidation value θ, or uninformed, i.e., inferring information only from the price. Noise traders are assumed to trade in the aggregate according to a random variable u. This is typically justified by exogenous liquidity motives. We could also think that from the perspective of investors in a stock the number of shares that float is a random variable. In section 4.4 we do away with the assumption of exogenous noise and introduce traders who have a hedging motive.

We specify the model assuming that there is a proportion μ of traders who are informed (and receive a private signal s_i about θ) and a proportion $(1-\mu)$ who are uninformed (and can be considered market makers). Both types of traders can condition their trade on the price but only informed trader i observes the signal s_i. We thus have that the information set of informed trader i is $\{s_i, p\}$ while for an uninformed trader it is $\{p\}$. For informed traders $\rho_i = \rho_{\mathrm{I}} > 0$ and for uninformed traders $\rho_i = \rho_{\mathrm{U}} \geqslant 0$.

It is assumed that all random variables are normally distributed: θ with mean $\bar{\theta}$ and variance σ_θ^2; $s_i = \theta + \varepsilon_i$, where θ and ε_i are uncorrelated, errors have mean zero, variance σ_ε^2, and are also uncorrelated across agents; u has zero mean and variance σ_u^2 and is uncorrelated with the rest of random variables. The expected volume of noise trading $E[|u|]$ is proportional to its standard deviation σ_u.[10] Note also that we therefore assume that all informed traders receive signals of the same precision. As in the previous chapters the convention is made that, given θ, the average signal of a positive mass μ of informed agents with $\sigma_\varepsilon^2 < \infty$, $(\int_0^\mu s_i \, \mathrm{d}i)/\mu$ equals almost surely (a.s.) θ (i.e., $\int_0^\mu \varepsilon_i \, \mathrm{d}i = 0$).[11] The distributional assumptions made are common knowledge among the agents in the economy. Recall that we denote the precision of random variable x (that is, $(\sigma_x^2)^{-1}$) by τ_x.

The present formulation is a particular case of the more general model in which the degree of risk aversion and the precision of the private signal of traders are allowed to be different and are given by (measurable) functions: $\rho : [0,1] \to \mathbb{R}_+$ and $\tau_\varepsilon : [0,1] \to \mathbb{R}_+ \cup \{\infty\}$ with values, respectively, ρ_i and τ_{ε_i} for $i \in [0,1]$. The parameter ρ_i^{-1} is the *risk tolerance* of trader i. An important parameter is the *risk-adjusted information advantage* of trader i, $\rho_i^{-1}\tau_{\varepsilon_i}$, and its population average. The results presented in this section are easily extended to the general case provided that ρ_i^{-1} and τ_{ε_i} are uniformly bounded across traders (Admati (1985) considers the general multiasset model). This boundedness assumption ensures that traders with very low risk aversion or very precise information do not loom large in the market outcome.[12]

Under our symmetry assumptions we will be interested in symmetric equilibria with traders of the same type using the same trading strategy. Denote

---

[10]The natural measure of volume is $E[|u|]$ because otherwise buys and sells would cancel ($E[u] = 0$). Recall that for z normal with $E[|u|] = 0$ and variance σ_u^2 we have that $E[|u|] = (2/\pi)^{1/2}\sigma_u$.

[11]See section 10.3.1 for more details.

[12]The assumption would also be needed to apply our conventions about the law of large numbers to the continuum economy.

by $X_{\mathrm{I}}(s_i, p)$ the trade of informed trader $i \in [0, \mu]$, and by $X_{\mathrm{U}}(p)$ the trade of uninformed trader $i \in (\mu, 1]$. A symmetric rational expectations equilibrium (REE) is a set of trades, contingent on the information that traders have, $\{X_{\mathrm{I}}(s_i, p)$ for $i \in [0, \mu]$; $X_{\mathrm{U}}(p)$ for $i \in (\mu, 1]\}$, and a (measurable) price functional $P(\theta, u)$ (i.e., prices measurable in (θ, u)) such that:

(i) Markets clear:

$$\int_0^{\mu} X_{\mathrm{I}}(s_i, p)\,\mathrm{d}i + \int_{\mu}^{1} X_{\mathrm{U}}(p)\,\mathrm{d}i + u = 0 \quad \text{(a.s.)}.$$

(ii) Traders in $[0, 1]$ optimize[13]:

$$X_{\mathrm{I}}(s_i, p) \in \arg\max_z E[U_i((\theta - p)z) \mid s_i, p] \text{ for } i \in [0, \mu],$$

$$X_{\mathrm{U}}(p) \in \arg\max_z E[U_i((\theta - p)z) \mid p] \text{ for } i \in (\mu, 1].$$

Traders understand the relationship between prices and the underlying uncertainty (θ, u). That is, they conjecture correctly the function $P(\cdot, \cdot)$, and update their beliefs accordingly. Typically, the equilibrium will not be fully revealing due to the presence of noise (u). We will then have an example of noisy REE. Without noise the REE may have paradoxical features.

Grossman (1976) analyzed the market with a finite number of informed traders, no uninformed traders, and no noise (say $u < 0$ represents the nonrandom supply of shares). The REE is defined similarly as above and a fully revealing equilibrium (FRREE) is shown to exist.[14] The market is strongly informationally efficient. To show that this FRREE exists the competitive equilibrium of an artificial full-information economy (in which all private signals are public) is computed and then it is checked that this equilibrium is also a (linear) REE of the private-information economy (as in chapter 3). The equilibrium has a puzzling property: demands are independent of private signals and prices! Demands are independent of private signals because the price is fully revealing, that is, the price is a sufficient statistic for θ. Demands are also independent of prices because a higher price, apart from changing the terms of trade (classical substitution effect), also raises the perceived value of the risky asset (information effect). In the model the two effects exactly offset each other (see Admati 1989). However, this equilibrium is not implementable: the equilibrium cannot be derived from the equilibrium of a well-defined trading game. For example, given that demands are independent of private signals, how is it that prices are sufficient statistics for the private information in the economy? This cannot arise from a market-clearing process of price formation. Indeed, in the Grossman economy each trader is not informationally small: his signal is not irrelevant when compared with the pooled information of other traders. (See exercise 4.1 for the details of the Grossman example.)

[13] Almost all traders in $[0, 1]$ optimize. As usual we will not insist on this qualification.

[14] DeMarzo and Skiadas (1999) show that this FRREE is unique (in the CARA-normal context).

There is a natural game in demand schedules which implements partially revealing REE in the presence of noise as a Bayesian equilibrium in the continuum economy. Note that with a continuum of traders each agent is informationally "small" (see section 3.1). In the continuum economy there is always a trivial FRREE in which $p = \theta$, traders are indifferent about the amounts traded and end up taking the counterpart in the aggregate of noise traders. This FRREE is not implementable and would not be an equilibrium if we were to insist that prices be measurable in excess demand functions as in Anderson and Sonnenschein (1982); see section 3.1.

Let traders therefore use demand schedules as strategies. This is the parallel to firms using supply functions as strategies in the partial equilibrium market of chapter 3. At the interim stage, once each trader has received his private signal, traders submit demand schedules contingent on their private information (if any), noise traders place their orders, and then an auctioneer finds a market-clearing price (as in (i) of the above definition of an REE). We will study the linear Bayesian equilibria of the demand schedule game.

In general we can allow traders to use general demand schedules which allow for market, limit, and stop orders.[15] Market-clearing rules should be defined given the strategies of traders. We can assume that if there is more than one market-clearing price, then the one with the minimum absolute value (and the positive one if there is also a negative price with the same absolute value) is chosen. If there is no market-clearing price, then the market shuts down (and traders get infinitely negative utility, for example, with the auctioneer setting a price equal to $\pm\infty$).

When traders optimize they take into account the (equilibrium) functional relationship between prices and the random variables in the environment (θ and u). Trader i's strategy is a mapping from his private information to the space of demand functions (correspondences, more generally). Let $X_{\mathrm{I}}(s_i, \cdot)$ be the demand schedule chosen by an informed trader when he has received signal s_i. When the signal of the trader is s_i and the price realization is p, the desired position of the agent in the risky asset is then $X_{\mathrm{I}}(s_i, p)$. Similarly, for an uninformed trader the chosen demand schedule is represented by $X_{\mathrm{U}}(p)$. Noise traders' demands aggregate to the random variable u.

Using standard methods we can characterize linear Bayesian equilibria of the demand function game. The CARA-normal model admits linear equilibria because optimization of the CARA expected utility under normality reduces, as we shall see, to the optimization of a mean–variance objective, and normality, as we know, yields linear conditional expectations.

We restrict our attention to linear equilibria with price functionals of the form $P(\theta, u)$. Linear Bayesian equilibria in demand functions will be necessarily

[15] The schedules should have some continuity and convexity properties. A series of limit (stop) orders would be represented by a downward-sloping (upward-sloping) schedule of step functions. "All-or-nothing" orders, in which a partial execution is not accepted, violate the assumption that the demand schedule is convex valued (see Kyle 1989).

noisy (i.e., $\partial P/\partial u \neq 0$) since, as we have argued, a fully revealing equilibrium is not implementable. If traders receive no private signals, then the price will not depend on the fundamental value θ (see example 4.1).

The profits of trader i with a position x_i are $\pi_i = (\theta - p)x_i$, yielding a utility $U_i(\pi_i) = -e^{-\rho_i \pi_i}$. Recall that if z is normally distributed $N(\mu, \sigma^2)$ and r is a constant, then $E[e^{rz}] = e^{r\mu + r^2\sigma^2/2}$. Given x_i, and when the price p is in the information set G of the trader, $\pi_i \mid G$ is normally distributed (given that p is linear in θ and u and all random variables have a joint normal distribution). Maximization of the CARA utility function conditional on the information set G,

$$E[U(\pi_i) \mid G] = -E[e^{-\rho_i \pi_i} \mid G] = -\exp\{-\rho_i(E[\pi_i \mid G] - \tfrac{1}{2}\rho_i \operatorname{var}[\pi_i \mid G])\},$$

is equivalent to the maximization of[16]

$$E[\pi_i \mid G] - \tfrac{1}{2}\rho_i \operatorname{var}[\pi_i \mid G] = E[\theta - p \mid G]x_i - \tfrac{1}{2}\rho_i \operatorname{var}[\theta - p \mid G]x_i^2.$$

This is a strictly (for $\rho_i > 0$) concave problem which yields

$$x_i = \frac{E[\theta - p \mid G]}{\rho_i \operatorname{var}[\theta - p \mid G]} = \frac{E[\theta \mid G] - p}{\rho_i \operatorname{var}[\theta \mid G]},$$

where $G = \{s_i, p\}$ for an informed trader and $G = \{p\}$ for an uninformed trader.

Because of the assumed symmetric *ex ante* signal structure and risk aversion ($\rho_i = \rho_{\mathrm{I}}$) for informed traders, demand functions for the informed will be identical in equilibrium, and the same is true for the uninformed. It follows that

$$E[\pi_i \mid G] - \tfrac{1}{2}\rho_i \operatorname{var}[\pi_i \mid G] = \frac{(E[\theta - p \mid G])^2}{2\rho_i \operatorname{var}[\theta - p \mid G]}$$

and so the expected utility for a trader with information set $G(-E[\exp\{-\rho_i \pi_i\} \mid G])$ is given by

$$-\exp\{-\rho_i(E[\pi_i \mid G] - \tfrac{1}{2}\rho_i \operatorname{var}[\pi_i \mid G])\} = -\exp\left\{-\frac{(E[\theta - p \mid G])^2}{2 \operatorname{var}[\theta - p \mid G]}\right\}.$$

This expression will be handy when we are interested in calculating expected utilities.

To solve for a linear REE a standard approach is the following. First, a linear price conjecture $p = P(\theta, u)$ common for all agents is proposed. Second, using this conjecture, beliefs about θ are updated; that is, expressions for $E[\theta - p \mid G]$ and $\operatorname{var}[\theta - p \mid G]$ for informed and uninformed traders are derived. Third, asset demands are computed as above. Then market clearing yields the actual relation between p and (θ, u). Finally, the price conjecture must be self-fulfilling. This pins down the undetermined coefficients in the linear price functional. To this we should add the requirement that prices be measurable in excess demand functions.

To solve for a linear Bayesian equilibrium in demand schedules, we follow similar steps. First, positing linear strategies for the traders we find, using the

[16] The parallel to the marginal production cost in the Cournot model (with exogenous slope λ; see chapter 1) is the term $\rho_i \operatorname{var}[\theta - p \mid G]$, which is determined endogenously in equilibrium.

market-clearing condition, an expression for p in terms of θ and u. Second, using this expression we update beliefs about θ. Third, we compute the asset demands for informed and uninformed types. Finally, we identify the coefficients of the linear demands imposing consistency between the conjectured and the actual strategies. If in the first step we want to consider potentially asymmetric strategies, we must (as in section 3.2.1) restrict our attention to uniformly bounded signal sensitivities of the strategies across traders (as well as bounded average parameters in the linear strategies) in order to use our convention on the law of large numbers in the continuum economy and obtain a linear price functional of the form $P(\theta, u)$. This restriction is equivalent to considering equilibria with linear price functionals of the form $P(\theta, u)$.

The following proposition characterizes the linear Bayesian equilibrium.

Proposition 4.1. *Let $\rho_{\mathrm{I}} > 0$ and $\rho_{\mathrm{U}} > 0$. There is a unique Bayesian linear equilibrium in demand functions with a linear price functional of the form $P(\theta, u)$. It is given by*

$$X_{\mathrm{I}}(s_i, p) = a(s_i - p) - b_{\mathrm{I}}(p - \bar{\theta}) \quad \text{and} \quad X_{\mathrm{U}}(p) = -b_{\mathrm{U}}(p - \bar{\theta}),$$

where $a = \rho_{\mathrm{I}}^{-1}\tau_{\varepsilon}$,

$$b_{\mathrm{I}} = \frac{\tau_{\theta}}{\rho_{\mathrm{I}} + \mu\tau_{\varepsilon}\tau_u(\mu\rho_{\mathrm{I}}^{-1} + (1-\mu)\rho_{\mathrm{U}}^{-1})}, \quad \text{and} \quad b_{\mathrm{U}} = \rho_{\mathrm{I}}\rho_{\mathrm{U}}^{-1}b_{\mathrm{I}}.$$

In addition,

$$P(\theta, u) = \lambda z + \bar{\theta},$$

where $z = \mu a(\theta - \bar{\theta}) + u$ and $\lambda = (\mu(a + b_{\mathrm{I}}) + (1-\mu)b_{\mathrm{U}})^{-1}$.

Proof. Given the *ex ante* symmetric-information structure and risk aversion for the informed and uninformed, who face a strictly concave optimization problem at a linear price equilibrium of the form $P(\theta, u)$, we know that the demand functions of the informed and of the uninformed will be identical in each class:

$$X_{\mathrm{I}}(s_i, p) = as_i - c_{\mathrm{I}}p + \hat{b}_{\mathrm{I}} \quad \text{and} \quad X_{\mathrm{U}}(p) = -c_{\mathrm{U}}p + \hat{b}_{\mathrm{U}}.$$

From the market-clearing condition

$$\int_0^{\mu} X_{\mathrm{I}}(s_i, p)\,\mathrm{d}i + (1-\mu)X_{\mathrm{U}}(p) + u = 0$$

and letting $\tilde{b} = \mu\hat{b}_{\mathrm{I}} + (1-\mu)\hat{b}_{\mathrm{U}}$ and $\lambda = (\mu c_{\mathrm{I}} + (1-\mu)c_{\mathrm{U}})^{-1}$, provided $\mu c_{\mathrm{I}} + (1-\mu)c_{\mathrm{U}} > 0$, we obtain

$$p = \lambda(\mu a\theta + u + \tilde{b}).$$

Let $\mu a > 0$, then the random variable $\hat{z} \equiv \theta + (1/\mu a)u$ is informationally equivalent to the price and $\hat{z} = (p - \lambda\tilde{b})/(\lambda\mu a)$. Prices will be normally distributed because they are a linear transformation of normal random variables. We have that $\mathrm{var}[\theta \mid p] = \mathrm{var}[\theta \mid \hat{z}]$ and it is immediate from the properties of normal distributions (see sections 10.1 and 10.2) that the precision incorporated in prices in the estimation of θ, $\tau \equiv (\mathrm{var}[\theta \mid p])^{-1}$, is given by $\tau = \tau_{\theta} + \tau_u(\mu a)^2$

(indeed, see section 10.2, τ is the sum of the precision of the prior τ_θ and the precision of the public signal, conditional on θ, $\hat{z} \equiv \theta + (1/\mu a)u$). It follows that

$$E[\theta \mid p] = E[\theta \mid \hat{z}] = \frac{\tau_\theta \bar{\theta} + (\mu a)^2 \tau_u \hat{z}}{\tau} = \frac{\tau_\theta \bar{\theta} + \mu a \tau_u \lambda^{-1}(p - \lambda \tilde{b})}{\tau}.$$

From the optimization of the CARA utility of an uninformed trader, we obtain

$$X_{\mathrm{U}}(p) = \frac{E[\theta \mid p] - p}{\rho_{\mathrm{U}} \operatorname{var}[\theta \mid p]} = -c_{\mathrm{U}} p + \hat{b}_{\mathrm{U}},$$

and identifying coefficients it is immediate that

$$c_{\mathrm{U}} = \frac{1}{\rho_{\mathrm{U}}}\left(\tau - \frac{\mu a \tau_u}{\lambda}\right) \quad \text{and} \quad \hat{b}_{\mathrm{U}} = \frac{\tau_\theta \bar{\theta} - \mu a \tau_u \tilde{b}}{\rho_{\mathrm{U}}}.$$

From the optimization of the CARA utility of an informed trader, we obtain

$$X_{\mathrm{I}}(s_i, p) = \frac{E[\theta \mid s_i, p] - p}{\rho_{\mathrm{I}} \operatorname{var}[\theta \mid s_i, p]} = a s_i - c_{\mathrm{I}} p + \hat{b}_{\mathrm{I}},$$

where from the properties of normal distributions $(\operatorname{var}[\theta \mid s_i, p])^{-1} = \tau_\varepsilon + \tau$. Furthermore, proceeding in a similar way as before,

$$\begin{aligned} E[\theta \mid s_i, p] = E[\theta \mid s_i, \hat{z}] &= \frac{\tau_\varepsilon s_i + \tau_\theta \bar{\theta} + (\mu a)^2 \tau_u \hat{z}}{\tau_\varepsilon + \tau} \\ &= \frac{\tau_\varepsilon s_i + \tau_\theta \bar{\theta} + \mu a \tau_u \lambda^{-1}(p - \lambda \tilde{b})}{\tau_\varepsilon + \tau}. \end{aligned}$$

Identifying coefficients it is immediate that $a = \rho_{\mathrm{I}}^{-1} \tau_\varepsilon$, $c_{\mathrm{I}} = \rho_{\mathrm{I}}^{-1}(\tau_\varepsilon + \tau - \mu a \tau_u/\lambda)$, and $\hat{b}_{\mathrm{I}} = \rho_{\mathrm{I}}^{-1}(\tau_\theta \bar{\theta} - \mu a \tau_u \tilde{b})$. It follows that

$$\lambda = \frac{1 + \mu a(\mu \rho_{\mathrm{I}}^{-1} + (1 - \mu)\rho_{\mathrm{U}}^{-1})\tau_u}{\mu a + (\mu \rho_{\mathrm{I}}^{-1} + (1 - \mu)\rho_{\mathrm{U}}^{-1})\tau} > 0$$

and

$$\tilde{b} = \frac{(\mu \rho_{\mathrm{I}}^{-1} + (1 - \mu)\rho_{\mathrm{U}}^{-1})\tau_\theta \bar{\theta}}{1 + (\mu \rho_{\mathrm{I}}^{-1} + (1 - \mu)\rho_{\mathrm{U}}^{-1})\mu a \tau_u} = (\lambda^{-1} - \mu a)\bar{\theta}.$$

From these expressions we immediately obtain $\hat{b}_{\mathrm{I}} = b_{\mathrm{I}} \bar{\theta}$, where $b_{\mathrm{I}} = \tau_\theta / (\rho_{\mathrm{I}} + \mu \tau_\varepsilon \tau_u (\mu \rho_{\mathrm{I}}^{-1} + (1 - \mu)\rho_{\mathrm{U}}^{-1}))$, $c_{\mathrm{I}} = a + b_{\mathrm{I}}$, and $\hat{b}_{\mathrm{U}} = b_{\mathrm{U}} \bar{\theta}$, where $b_{\mathrm{U}} = c_{\mathrm{U}} = \rho_{\mathrm{I}} \rho_{\mathrm{U}}^{-1} b_{\mathrm{I}}$, and the expressions for $X_{\mathrm{I}}(s_i, p) = a(s_i - p) - b_{\mathrm{I}}(p - \bar{\theta})$ and $X_{\mathrm{U}}(p) = -b_{\mathrm{U}}(p - \bar{\theta})$ follow. The expression for the price $p = \lambda z + \bar{\theta}$, where $z = \mu a(\theta - \bar{\theta}) + u$, follows from $p = \lambda(\mu a \theta + u + \tilde{b})$ and the expressions for λ and $\tilde{b}$. This proves the proposition. It is worth noting that the computations can be shortened, with hindsight, if we postulate from the beginning the linear forms $X_{\mathrm{I}}(s_i, p) = a(s_i - p) - b_{\mathrm{I}}(p - \bar{\theta})$ and $X_{\mathrm{U}}(p) = -b_{\mathrm{U}}(p - \bar{\theta})$. □

Since $b_{\mathrm{U}} > 0$, uninformed traders sell (buy) when the price is above (below) the prior expectation of the asset value, i.e., they lean against the wind. This is the typical behavior of market makers. Uninformed traders face an adverse selection problem because they do not know if trade is mainly motivated by informed or by noise traders. For example, when $\rho_{\text{I}} = \rho_{\text{U}}$ it is immediate that the trading intensity of the uninformed (b_{U}) decreases with the proportion of informed traders μ.

Informed agents trade for two reasons. First, they speculate on their private information, buying or selling depending on whether the price is larger or smaller than their signal according to a trading intensity directly related to their risk tolerance ρ_{I}^{-1} and precision of information τ_ε. The responsiveness to private information a is independent of the amount of noise trading and the (prior) variance of θ. This is so since an increase in noise trading τ_{U}^{-1} or prior variance τ_θ^{-1} increases risk (by increasing $\operatorname{var}[\theta \mid s_i, p]$) but also increases the conditional expected return $(E[\theta \mid s_i, p] - p)$, because it makes private information more valuable. The two effects exactly offset each other in the present framework. (This independence of a with respect to τ_{U}^{-1} will not hold if traders have market power; see exercise 5.1.) The second component of the trade of informed agents is related to their market-making capacity, similar to the uninformed traders, with associated trading intensity b_{I}. The parameter b_{I} depends positively on the amount of noise trading τ_{U}^{-1}, and negatively on the average risk tolerance in the market $\mu\rho_{\text{I}}^{-1} + (1-\mu)\rho_{\text{U}}^{-1}$. If uninformed traders are risk neutral (i.e., $\rho_{\text{U}} \to 0$), then $b_{\text{I}} = 0$ and informed agents do not trade for market-making purposes. If the prior on the fundamental value is uniform (improper with $\tau_\theta = 0$), then $b_{\text{I}} = b_{\text{U}} = 0$ and there is no market-making trade.

Prices equal the weighted average of the expectations of investors about the fundamental value plus a noise component reflecting the risk premium required for risk-averse traders to absorb noise traders' demands. The weights are according to the risk-adjusted information of the different traders. Indeed, from the fact that the demand of informed and uninformed traders can also be expressed, respectively, as

$$X_{\text{I}}(s_i, p) = \rho_{\text{I}}^{-1}(\tau_\varepsilon + \tau)[E[\theta \mid s_i, p] - p] \quad \text{and} \quad X_{\text{U}}(p) = \rho_{\text{U}}^{-1}\tau[E[\theta \mid p] - p],$$

and from the market-clearing condition, it is immediate that

$$p = \frac{\rho_{\text{I}}^{-1}(\tau_\varepsilon + \tau)\int_0^\mu E[\theta \mid s_i, p]\,\mathrm{d}i + (1-\mu)\rho_{\text{U}}^{-1}\tau E[\theta \mid p] + u}{\mu\rho_{\text{I}}^{-1}(\tau_\varepsilon + \tau) + (1-\mu)\rho_{\text{U}}^{-1}\tau}.$$

If the uninformed traders become risk neutral ($\rho_{\text{U}} \to 0$), then $p \to E[\theta \mid p]$ and prices are semi-strong efficient (that is, they reflect all publicly available information). The average expectation of informed traders is $\mu^{-1}\int_0^\mu E[\theta \mid s_i, p]\,\mathrm{d}i$. With no informed traders ($\mu = 0$) prices are the average of the expectations of the uninformed traders plus a risk-bearing term,

$$p = E[\theta \mid p] + \rho_{\text{U}}\tau^{-1}u = \bar{\theta} + \rho_{\text{U}}\tau_\theta^{-1}u,$$

and with no uninformed traders ($\mu = 1$) prices are the average of the expectations of informed investors $\int_0^1 E[\theta \mid s_i, p]\,\mathrm{d}i$ plus a risk-bearing term,

$$p = \int_0^1 E[\theta \mid s_i, p]\,\mathrm{d}i + \rho_{\text{I}}(\tau_\varepsilon + \tau)^{-1}u.$$

We now examine the following market quality parameters: depth, price informativeness, volatility, and expected volume traded by the informed.

Market depth. The depth of the market is given by the parameter λ^{-1}. A change of noise trading by one unit moves prices by λ. A market is deep if a noise trader shock is absorbed without moving prices much, and this happens when λ is low. Market depth is equal to the average responsiveness of traders to the market price $\lambda^{-1} = \mu(a + b_{\mathrm{I}}) + (1 - \mu)b_{\mathrm{U}}$. Traders provide liquidity to the market by submitting demand schedules and stand willing to trade conditionally on the market price. It is easily checked that the depth of the market λ^{-1} increases with τ_θ and decreases with τ_u and ρ_{U}. All this accords to intuition: higher volatility of fundamentals (or, equivalently, a lower precision of prior information) and a higher degree of risk aversion of uninformed traders (market makers) decrease the depth of the market. Market makers protect themselves from the adverse selection problem by reducing market liquidity when they are more risk averse and/or there is less precise public information. At the same time more noise trading increases market depth as the market makers feel more confident that they are not trading against informed investors. In fact, as we will see, without noise traders the market collapses. The effect of the other parameters on λ^{-1} is ambiguous. In particular, an increase in the proportion of informed traders μ has an ambiguous impact on λ^{-1}. For example, when $\rho_{\mathrm{U}} = \rho_{\mathrm{I}}$ it is immediate that $b_{\mathrm{U}} = b_{\mathrm{I}} = b$ and $\lambda^{-1} = \mu a + b$. Increasing μ raises μa (the informativeness of price) and decreases b (the price sensitivity of traders). The increase in the informativeness of price tends to increase market depth (since it diminishes the inventory risk for risk-averse traders) but this is counterbalanced by a decreased price sensitivity of traders because of increased adverse selection.

There is evidence that market makers do face an adverse selection problem and that spreads reflect asymmetric information (see Glosten and Harris (1988) for evidence in the NYSE; Lee et al. (1993) find that depth decreases around earning announcements, when asymmetric information may be more important). Furthermore, there is evidence that trades have a permanent impact on prices, pointing toward the effects of private (or public) information (see Hasbrouck 2007).

Price informativeness and volatility. The random variable $z = \mu a(\theta - \bar{\theta}) + u$ can be understood as the informational content of the price since $p = \lambda z + \bar{\theta}$. It follows immediately that $E[p] = \bar{\theta}$. This is so because we assume on average a zero supply of shares, $E[u] = 0$. With a positive expected supply $E[u] < 0$ there is a positive risk premium, $E[p] - \bar{\theta} = \lambda E[u] < 0$, because agents are risk averse and need a premium to absorb a positive supply of shares. The comparative statics of the risk premium therefore follow those of the liquidity parameter λ. (See section 4.4 for results on risk premia in a more complex model.)

Prices are biased in the sense that $E[\theta \mid p]$ is smaller or larger than p if and only if p is above or below $\bar{\theta}$. Indeed (see the proof of proposition 4.1), from

$$X_{\mathrm{U}}(p) = \frac{E[\theta \mid p] - p}{\rho_{\mathrm{U}} \operatorname{var}[\theta \mid p]} = -\rho_{\mathrm{I}}\rho_{\mathrm{U}}^{-1} b_{\mathrm{I}}(p - \bar{\theta}),$$

it follows that

$$E[\theta \mid p] - p = \rho_{\mathrm{I}} b_{\mathrm{I}} \tau^{-1}(\bar{\theta} - p)$$

since $\tau^{-1} = \operatorname{var}[\theta \mid p]$. We can also write the demand of an informed trader as

$$X_{\mathrm{I}}(s_i, p) = \rho_{\mathrm{I}}^{-1}\tau_{\varepsilon}(s_i - p) + \rho_{\mathrm{I}}^{-1}\tau(E(\theta \mid p) - p).$$

This highlights the fact that an informed agent trades exploiting his private information (with intensity according to the risk-tolerance-weighted precision of private information $\rho_{\mathrm{I}}^{-1}\tau_{\varepsilon}$) and exploiting price discrepancies with public information on the fundamental value, i.e., market making (with intensity according to the risk-tolerance-weighted precision of public information $\rho_{\mathrm{I}}^{-1}\tau$).

In their market-making activity risk-averse traders buy when $E[\theta \mid p] > p$, and this happens when $p < \bar{\theta}$. Prices with risk-averse market makers exhibit *reversal* (*negative drift*) since $\operatorname{sgn}(E[\theta - p \mid p - \bar{\theta}]) = \operatorname{sgn}(-(p - \bar{\theta}))$ (the price variation $(\theta - p)$ goes in the opposite direction to the initial variation $(p - \bar{\theta})$).

Price *precision* in the estimation of θ is given by $\tau = \tau_{\theta} + \tau_u(\mu a)^2$. When prices are fully revealing, $p = \theta$ and τ is infinite; when they are pure noise, $\tau = \tau_{\theta}$. This can be easily seen if we recall that $\tau \equiv (\operatorname{var}[\theta \mid p])^{-1}$. If $p = \theta$, then $\operatorname{var}[\theta \mid p] = 0$ and if p is pure noise, $\operatorname{var}[\theta \mid p] = \operatorname{var}[\theta]$. Price precision increases with $\rho_{\mathrm{I}}^{-1}\tau_{\varepsilon}$ (the risk-tolerance-adjusted informational advantage of informed traders), τ_{θ}, μ, and τ_u, and is independent of ρ_{U}. All these effects accord with intuition. Lower volatility of fundamentals, a higher proportion of informed traders, more precise signals, lower noise trading, and less risk aversion of the informed contribute to a higher informativeness of prices. The fact that with more informed traders prices become more informative means that there is strategic substitutability in information acquisition since, when public information is more precise, there is less incentive to acquire a private signal.

The *volatility* of prices $\operatorname{var}[p] = \lambda^2((\mu a)^2\sigma_{\theta}^2 + \sigma_u^2) = \lambda^2\tau(\tau_{\theta}\tau_u)^{-1}$ depends, ceteris paribus, negatively on market depth λ^{-1}, and positively on price precision, prior volatility, and noise trading. Price precision depends on the aggregate trading intensity of informed agents and market depth depends on the price responsiveness of both informed and uninformed agents. Volatility increases with ρ_{U} and σ_{θ}^2. In both instances market depth λ^{-1} decreases, and with increases in σ_{θ}^2 there is a further direct impact. It can be checked that the effect of changes in the other parameters on $\operatorname{var}[p]$ is ambiguous (because of their indirect impact via market depth).

Expected traded volume. The expected (aggregate) volume traded by informed agents is given by $E[|\int_0^{\mu} X_{\mathrm{I}}(s_i, p)\,\mathrm{d}i|]$. Given that if $x \sim N(0, \sigma^2)$, then $E[|x|] =$

$\sigma\sqrt{2/\pi}$, we have

$$E\left[\left|\int_0^\mu X_{\rm I}(s_i,p)\,\mathrm{d}i\right|\right] = E[|\mu(a(\theta-p)-b_{\rm I}(p-\bar\theta))|]$$
$$= \mu(\mathrm{var}[a(\theta-p)-b_{\rm I}(p-\bar\theta)])^{1/2}\sqrt{2/\pi}$$

since $E[a(\theta-p)-b_{\rm I}(p-\bar\theta)] = 0$. Substituting the expression for $\mathrm{var}[a(\theta-p)-b_{\rm I}(p-\bar\theta)]$, we obtain that

$$E\left[\left|\int_0^\mu X_{\rm I}(s_i,p)\,\mathrm{d}i\right|\right] = \mu(\sigma_\theta^2 a^2(1-(a+b_{\rm I})\lambda\mu)^2+\sigma_u^2(a+b_{\rm I})^2\lambda^2)^{1/2}\sqrt{2/\pi}.$$

When noise trading vanishes ($\sigma_u \to 0$), then $b_{\rm I} \to 0$ and $\lambda \to 1/\mu a$ and the expected trade of informed speculators tends to 0. This is so because the precision incorporated into prices tends to ∞ and therefore the information advantage of informed traders disappears. In fact, trade collapses as $\sigma_u \to 0$ ($b_{\rm U}$ and $b_{\rm I}$ also tend to 0 and there is no market-making-based trade). There is trade because of the presence of noise traders. Without noise traders the no-trade theorem applies since the initial endowments are a Pareto-optimal allocation for the risk-averse traders (see sections 10.3.1 and 10.4).

When the precision of information τ_ε of informed agents tends to ∞ so does their trade intensity a, market depth λ^{-1}, and price precision τ, with the result that the expected trade of informed agents tends to $\sqrt{2/\pi}\sigma_u$ and market making vanishes ($b_{\rm U}$ and $b_{\rm I}$ tend to 0).

4.2.1.1 Examples

The following examples show that the above model encompasses several of the models presented in the literature.

Example 4.1 (no informed traders ($\mu = 0$)). This corresponds to an REE with no asymmetric information. In this case traders condition only on the price, from which they learn the amount of noise trading: $p = \lambda u + \bar\theta$, where $\lambda = b_{\rm U}^{-1}$ and $b_{\rm U} = \tau_\theta/\rho_{\rm U}$. The price does not depend on the fundamental value θ since demands do not depend on informative signals.[17] It is worth noting that if $\mu > 0$, then $b_{\rm U} < \tau_\theta/\rho_{\rm U}$. That is, in the presence of informed agents, uninformed traders react less to the price, decreasing market depth because of the adverse selection problem they face. Indeed, when an uninformed trader knows that informed traders are present in the market he will be more cautious responding to price movements because he does not know whether the price moves because of noise traders or because of the trades of informed.

Example 4.2 (no uninformed traders ($\mu = 1$)). This case corresponds to the limit equilibrium of Hellwig (1980).[18] Then there are only informed and noise

[17] Similarly, when the precision of information of informed traders (τ_ε) tends to 0 so does their informational trade intensity a. In the limit we then have $b_{\rm U} = \tau_\theta/\rho_{\rm U}$ and $b_{\rm I} = \tau_\theta/\rho_{\rm I}$ (the only potential difference between an informed (I) and an uninformed (U) trader is in the degree of risk aversion).

[18] The model in Diamond and Verrecchia (1981) is closely related.

traders. Informed traders have to "make the market." We then have $a = \rho_{\mathrm{I}}^{-1}\tau_{\varepsilon}$, $b_{\mathrm{I}} = \tau_{\theta}/(\rho_{\mathrm{I}}+a\tau_u)$, $\lambda = (a+b_{\mathrm{I}})^{-1} = ((\tau_{\varepsilon}+\tau)/(\rho_{\mathrm{I}}+a\tau_u))^{-1}$, and $\tau = \tau_{\theta}+\tau_u a^2$.

Example 4.3 (competitive risk-neutral market makers ($\rho_{\mathrm{U}} \to 0$)). This corresponds to the static model in Vives (1995a). Then $E[\theta \mid p] = p$ in the limit as $\rho_{\mathrm{U}} \to 0$. This follows immediately from $X_{\mathrm{U}}(p) = (E[\theta \mid p]-p)/(\rho_{\mathrm{U}}\operatorname{var}[\theta \mid p])$. When $\rho_{\mathrm{U}} \to 0$ it must be that $E[\theta \mid p] = p$, otherwise uninformed traders would take unbounded positions. When $E[\theta \mid p] = p$ then informed traders withhold from market making and only speculate.[19] Taking the limit of equilibrium parameters as $\rho_{\mathrm{U}} \to 0$ we obtain $a = \rho_{\mathrm{I}}^{-1}\tau_{\varepsilon}$, $b_{\mathrm{I}} = 0$, $b_{\mathrm{U}} = \tau_{\theta}/(\mu a(1-\mu)\tau_u)$, $\lambda = (\mu a/\tau)\tau_u$, and $\tau = \tau_{\theta}+\tau_u(\mu a)^2$. Prices exhibit no drift since $E[\theta - p \mid p - \bar{\theta}] = 0$. This case is examined in more detail in section 4.3.

4.2.2 Information Acquisition and the Grossman–Stiglitz Paradox

Let us consider a slightly different version of the model where all informed traders observe the same signal s and where $\theta = s+\varepsilon$ with s and ε independent and $E[\varepsilon] = 0$ (Grossman and Stiglitz 1980). The liquidation value is now the sum of two components, one of which (s) is observable at a cost k. The random variables (s, ε, u) are jointly normally distributed. Suppose also that $\rho_{\mathrm{I}} = \rho_{\mathrm{U}} = \rho$ and that noise trading has mean $E[u] = -1$. That is, there is a normalized mean exogenous supply of shares of 1. Apart from the above modifications the market microstructure is as in the previous section.

With these assumptions the derivation of the demand of the informed is simplified because s is a sufficient statistic for (s, p). Indeed, the price cannot contain more information than the joint information of traders s. We have that $E[\theta \mid s,p] = E[\theta \mid s] = s$, $\operatorname{var}[\theta \mid s,p] = \operatorname{var}[\theta \mid s] = \sigma_{\varepsilon}^2$, and

$$X_{\mathrm{I}}(s,p) = \frac{E[\theta \mid s,p]-p}{\rho\operatorname{var}[(\theta-p) \mid s,p]} = a(s-p), \quad \text{with } a = (\rho\sigma_{\varepsilon}^2)^{-1}.$$

For a given proportion of informed traders μ, market clearing implies that

$$\mu X_{\mathrm{I}}(s,p) + (1-\mu)X_{\mathrm{U}}(p) + u = 0,$$

and therefore at the (unique) linear equilibrium the price will be informationally equivalent to $(\mu a)s + u$ or $w = s + (\mu a)^{-1}u$. The price will be of the form

$$P(s,u) = \alpha_1 + \alpha_2 w, \quad \text{where } w = s + (\mu a)^{-1}u,$$

for some appropriate constants α_1 and $\alpha_2 > 0$. Once again, the price functional depends on s and not on θ because s is the joint information of traders. The more informative the price about s, the less the incentive to acquire information. The price will be more informative the higher the precision of the noise

[19] Similarly, in Kyle (1989, theorem 6.1) it is shown that as the aggregate risk-bearing capacity of uninformed speculators or "market makers" grows without bound, in the limit prices are unbiased in the sense that $E[\theta \mid p] = p$.

term $(\mu a)^{-1}u$, which equals $(\mu a)^2\tau_u$. The precision of p or w in the estimation of s is $(\text{var}[s \mid w])^{-1} = \tau_s + (\mu a)^2\tau_u$. If $\mu = 0$, then there is no information available on θ and in equilibrium $p = \bar{\theta} + \rho\sigma_\theta^2 u$ (this follows immediately from the demand of an uninformed trader $X_{\mathrm{U}}(p) = (\bar{\theta} - p)/\rho\sigma_\theta^2$ and the market-clearing condition).

When there is no noise ($\sigma_u^2 = 0$) there is a fully revealing equilibrium (in which $p = s - a^{-1}$ and p reveals s) and both informed and uninformed traders have the same demands. It is worth noting that this is an FRREE which is implementable as a Bayesian equilibrium in demand functions. This is due to the residual uncertainty ε left in the liquidation value given s. At the price $p = s - a^{-1}$ all traders demand one unit and absorb the exogenous nonrandom unit supply of shares. With $E[u] = 0$ we would have $p = s$ and no trade.

Consider now a two-stage game in which first traders decide whether to purchase the signal s at cost k or remain uninformed. At the second stage we have a market equilibrium contingent on the proportion μ of traders who have decided to become informed. From section 4.2 we know that the conditional expected utility of an informed trader is given by

$$-\exp\left\{-\frac{(E[(\theta - p) \mid s, p])^2}{2\,\text{var}[(\theta - p) \mid s, p]}\right\} = -\exp\left\{-\frac{(E[\theta \mid s] - p)^2}{2\,\text{var}[\theta \mid s]}\right\}$$
$$= -\exp\left\{-\frac{(s - p)^2}{2\sigma_\varepsilon^2}\right\},$$

and for an uninformed trader

$$E[U(\pi_{\mathrm{U}}) \mid p] = -\exp\left\{-\frac{(E[(\theta - p) \mid p])^2}{2\,\text{var}[(\theta - p) \mid p]}\right\} = -\exp\left\{-\frac{(E[\theta \mid p] - p)^2}{2\,\text{var}[\theta \mid p]}\right\}.$$

We claim (see the appendix to the chapter for a proof) that the expected utility of the informed trader conditional on public information (the price) and taking into account the cost k of getting the signal is given by

$$E[U(\pi_{\mathrm{I}}) \mid p] = e^{\rho k} E\left[-\exp\left\{-\frac{(s - p)^2}{2\sigma_\varepsilon^2}\right\} \;\middle|\; p\right]$$
$$= e^{\rho k}\sqrt{\frac{\text{var}[\theta \mid s]}{\text{var}[\theta \mid p]}}\,(E[U(\pi_{\mathrm{U}}) \mid p]).$$

Taking expectations on both sides and denoting by $\mathrm{EU_I}(\mu)$ and $\mathrm{EU_U}(\mu)$, respectively, the expected utility of an informed and an uninformed trader, it follows that

$$\frac{\mathrm{EU_I}(\mu)}{\mathrm{EU_U}(\mu)} = \phi(\mu) \equiv e^{\rho k}\sqrt{\frac{\text{var}[\theta \mid s]}{\text{var}[\theta \mid w]}} = e^{\rho k}\sqrt{\frac{\sigma_\varepsilon^2}{(\tau_s + (\mu a)^2\tau_u)^{-1} + \sigma_\varepsilon^2}}$$

given that $\text{var}[\theta \mid p] = \text{var}[\theta \mid w] = \text{var}[s \mid p] + \sigma_\varepsilon^2$.

The right-hand side $\phi(\mu)$ increases with μ. Given that utilities are negative this means that as μ increases $\mathrm{EU_I}$ goes down relative to $\mathrm{EU_U}$. Indeed, we have that as the proportion of informed traders increases the informativeness of

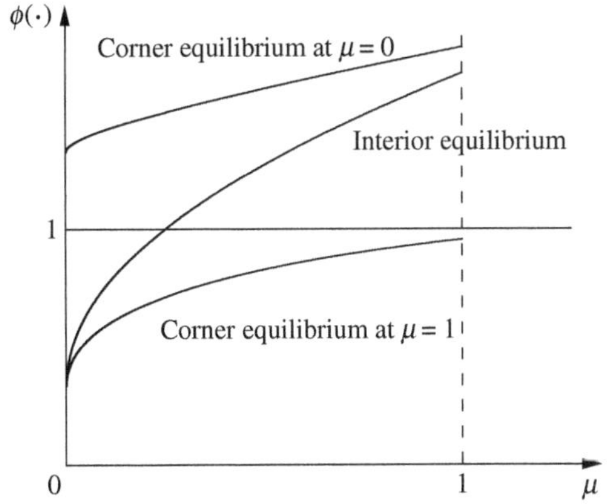

Figure 4.1. Interior or corner equilibria depending on the position of $\phi(\cdot)$, the relative expected utilities of the informed and uninformed.

prices increases and the informational advantage of the informed decreases. This implies that there is strategic substitutability in information acquisition. Given that $\phi(\mu)$ is increasing we have a unique equilibrium in the two-stage game (see figure 4.1). Any $\mu \in [0, 1]$ for which $\mathrm{EU_I}(\mu) = \mathrm{EU_U}(\mu)$ (or $\phi(\mu) = 1$) will be an equilibrium. Indeed, at an interior equilibrium the expected utility of both types of traders must be equalized. If $\phi(1) < 1$ ($\phi(0) > 1$), then $\mu = 1$ ($\mu = 0$) is an equilibrium. For k large (small) no one (everyone) is informed, and for intermediate k there is an interior solution. Note that in this case as noise trading vanishes ($\tau_u \to \infty$) the mass of informed traders must tend to zero ($\mu \to 0$) since the informativeness of the price system $\tau_s + (\mu a)^2\tau_u$ is to be kept constant so that $\mathrm{EU_I}(\mu) = \mathrm{EU_U}(\mu)$ (or $\phi(\mu) = 1$).

An interesting case (the Grossman–Stiglitz paradox) arises when there is no noise trading. Then, unless k is large, in which case the equilibrium is $\mu = 0$, there is no equilibrium (in pure strategies). Indeed, consider an equilibrium candidate with $\mu > 0$. Then we know that the price must be fully revealing and the expected utility of both informed and uninformed should be the same. However, the informed must pay k and the expected utilities derived from trade must be equal. Therefore, $\mu > 0$ is not possible in equilibrium. Suppose that k is not so large so that it pays for a trader to become informed if everyone else is uninformed; that is, $\phi(0) < 1$ or $e^{\rho k} < ((\sigma_s^2 + \sigma_\varepsilon^2)/\sigma_\varepsilon^2)^{1/2}$. Then $\mu = 0$ cannot be an equilibrium either. This is the Grossman–Stiglitz paradox about the impossibility of informationally efficient markets. If the price is fully revealing, then it does not pay to acquire information and therefore the price cannot contain any information. If no trader acquires information, and the cost of information is moderate, then there are incentives for a single trader to purchase information.

The paradox is resolved, obviously, if there is noise trading because the price is then not fully revealing and it pays, in equilibrium, to obtain information provided it is not excessively costly. For an interior equilibrium the informativeness of prices τ decreases with k (as k increases the equilibrium μ falls) and ρ, and is independent of σ_u. An increase in noise trading induces two effects that exactly balance each other: it increases the equilibrium proportion of informed traders and for a given μ reduces price informativeness. It is possible to check that as noise trading $\sigma_u \to 0$ the proportion of informed traders μ as well as expected trade tend to zero.

Muendler (2007) revises the paradox to find existence of a fully revealing equilibrium with information acquisition when there are a finite number of traders. Recall that in the context of a competitive market with a continuum of agents and constant returns to scale (section 1.6.2) we already saw that no equilibrium with costly information acquisition would exist. However, the existence of equilibrium is restored with a finite number of agents (section 2.3.2).

Other work has characterized information acquisition in the presence of noise in trading. Diamond and Verrecchia (1981) consider a CARA-normal model where each trader receives an idiosyncratic endowment shock of the risky asset and information about the fundamental value is dispersed among the traders (i.e., each trader receives a private signal about θ of the type $s_i = \theta + \varepsilon_i$). The simplifying assumption is made that the correlation between the aggregate endowment shock u and the idiosyncratic one u_i is zero.[20] This makes the model basically equivalent to the noise trader model. Diamond and Verrecchia show that there is a unique linear partially revealing equilibrium. Verrecchia (1982) extends the model to a population of traders who may differ in their levels of risk aversion and adds an information acquisition stage to the model (similarly as we did in section 1.6 for the Cournot model), where to acquire precision τ_ε a trader incurs a cost $C(\tau_\varepsilon)$, where $C(\cdot)$ is a strictly increasing convex function. Verrecchia finds that less risk-averse traders purchase more precision of information. This is so since a trader with low risk aversion will trade more aggressively in the risky asset and will therefore be willing to spend more to protect his position. From this it follows that the informativeness of prices is decreasing with increases in risk aversion (measured by a first-order stochastic dominance shift in the distribution of risk aversion coefficients in the economy).[21]

Strategic complementarity and multiplicity of equilibria. There are several attempts in the literature to introduce strategic complementarity in information acquisition in variants of the Grossman and Stiglitz model. In a model with risk-neutral traders who face a borrowing constraint, with noise traders, and where the fundamentals follow a binomial distribution, Barlevy and Veronesi (2000) claimed that as more traders acquire information prices need not become more informative and, in consequence, traders may want to acquire more information. This has been proved incorrect by Chamley (2007) because of a mistake in

[20] Diamond and Verrecchia (1981) assume that each trader receives an (independent) endowment shock with variance $K\sigma_u^2$, where K is the number of traders. As $K \to \infty$ the average per capita supply u has variance σ_u^2 (and is uncorrelated with individual supplies).

[21] See section 10.1.5 for the definition of first-order stochastic dominance shift in a distribution.

the expression for the value of information. The strategic complementarity in information acquisition and the existence of multiple equilibria may be restored if the fundamentals and noise trading are correlated (Barlevy and Veronesi 2007).

Multiplicity of linear REE is also obtained by Lundholm (1988) in a variation of the model by Diamond and Verrecchia (1981) where traders, on top of their private conditionally independent signals, also have available a public signal with an error term which is correlated with the error terms in the private signals. In this case a sufficiently high correlation in the errors will imply that more favorable (public or private) news may lead to lower prices. This happens because correlated signals provide both direct and indirect information on θ. Indeed, a higher value of one signal indicates a higher θ but, with positive correlation in the errors, it also indicates larger errors in the other signals. The latter indirect effect may come to dominate the first direct effect for large enough error correlation.[22]

Ganguli and Yang (2007) consider another variation of the model of Diamond and Verrecchia (1981) with a positive correlation between the aggregate endowment shock u and the idiosyncratic endowment shock of a trader $u_i = u + \eta_i$ (with $\int \eta_i \, di = 0$) and with endogenous information acquisition. They obtain that either there is no linear partially revealing equilibrium or there are two linear partially revealing equilibria.[23] In one equilibrium prices become more informative about θ as the proportion of informed μ increases and in the other the opposite happens. The price in the second equilibrium has a higher informativeness about θ than in the first equilibrium. The first equilibrium shares the features of the equilibrium in Grossman and Stiglitz (1980) and information acquisition decisions about the fundamental value are strategic substitutes. In the second equilibrium they are strategic complements. As the correlation between the aggregate endowment shock and the idiosyncratic one tends to 0, the first equilibrium converges to the (unique) partially revealing equilibrium in Diamond and Verrecchia (1981).

Multiplicity arises in the Ganguli and Yang model because the individual endowment shock of a trader helps the reading of information about θ in the price (which depends on the aggregate endowment shock) even if the trader receives a private (noisy) signal about θ. A high level of price informativeness is self-fulfilling since it implies that an informed trader puts less weight on his endowment shock when trying to estimate θ and this translates into a smaller weight given to the aggregate endowment shock in the price, making it in turn less noisy. An analogous argument can be made for a low level of price informativeness.[24] The implications for the cost of capital (i.e., the required return to hold the stock of the firm $E[\theta - p]$ or negative of the risk premium) depend

---

[22] With imperfect competition the effect disappears and we obtain a unique equilibrium (Manzano 1999).

[23] Linear equilibria exist if and only if $4\mu\rho^{-2}\tau_\varepsilon\tau_\eta \leqslant 1$ (using the usual notation).

[24] In section 4.4 we present a model where there is also positive correlation between the individual and the aggregate endowment shocks of traders but where, as in the original Grossman and

on which equilibrium obtains. For a positive expected supply of shares, the expected stock price is increasing (decreasing) in μ in the first (second) equilibrium. This means that the cost of capital for a firm will decrease with μ in the first equilibrium and increase with μ in the second.[25] Strategic complementarity in information acquisition may lead to multiple equilibria in the information market. The model can be extended to allow traders to receive (or purchase) information on both the payoff and supply/noise trading u (instead of each trader receiving a random endowment shock). With conditionally independent signals, information about u allows traders to extract more information about θ from prices. In this model there are also two linear equilibria and in either one of them information acquisition decisions may be strategic complements or substitutes depending on information parameters.[26] Strategic complementarity occurs because with more informed traders the identification problem for the uninformed may become worse.

As we will see in section 8.4 models with nonmonotone demand schedules and, more generally, with multiple equilibria (both in the financial and in the information markets) prove useful when trying to explain frenzies in asset prices and market crashes. In the Barlevy and Veronesi (2000) model, and contrary to the models in this chapter, the demand of the informed may be upward sloping. The reason is that a low price may be bad news and indicate to the uninformed that the asset value is very low (much as in section 3.2.2 a high price may be bad news as an indicator of high costs and may yield a downward-sloping supply curve for firms). Admati (1985) also obtains upward-sloping demands in a standard CARA-normal noisy rational expectations model with multiple assets.

Veldkamp (2006) finds that a market for information in a multimarket extension of the Grossman–Stiglitz model also introduces a strategic complementarity that works through the price of information. It is claimed that when many investors buy a piece of information its price is lower in a competitive market (because information has a high fixed cost and low variable cost of production) and this entices other investors to purchase the same information, even though it may be less valuable. The result is that investors only buy information about a subset of the assets and asset prices comove because news about one asset will affect the prices of the other assets. High covariance of asset prices in relation to the covariance of fundamentals has remained a puzzle (e.g., Barberis

---

Stiglitz formulation, all the informed receive the same signal (and they do not learn anything new about θ from the price). In this case there is always a unique linear partially revealing equilibrium.

[25] Easley and O'Hara (2004) analyze the effects of public and private information on the cost of capital and conclude (analyzing an equilibrium similar to Grossman and Stiglitz) that shifting information from public to private increases the cost of capital to a firm. (Note that this is a different comparative statics exercise than increasing the proportion of informed traders where the total amount of information increases.)

[26] Palomino (2001) also allows traders to have private information about aggregate supply/noise trading and obtains a unique equilibrium but in his model there is no common component in the endowments of traders and therefore with price-taking behavior it is akin to the Diamond and Verrecchia (1981) model.

et al. 2005). Veldkamp claims that the model can explain observed patterns of price comovements in asset prices since asset price correlations are above what a model with a constant price of information or a model where traders would purchase information about all the assets would predict.[27] An important tenet of the model, obtained by assuming a perfectly contestable market for information, is that the price of information equals the average cost of producing the news.[28]

4.2.3 Summary

The main results to retain from the standard model with noise trading are the following:

- Informed agents trade to profit both from their private information and from deviations of prices from expected fundamental values given public information (i.e., for market-making purposes).
- Uninformed traders act as market makers providing liquidity to the market and trade less aggressively in the presence of privately informed traders because of adverse selection.
- Prices equal a weighted average, according to the risk-tolerance-adjusted information of traders, of the expectations of investors about the fundamental value plus a noise component.
- Market makers protect themselves from the adverse selection problem by reducing market liquidity (the depth of the market) when they are more risk averse and/or there is less precise public information. The opposite happens when there is more noise trading.
- The informativeness of prices increases with the risk-tolerance-adjusted informational advantage of informed traders, with the proportion of informed traders, and decreases with the volatility of fundamentals and the amount of noise trading. There is strategic substitutability in information acquisition.
- The volatility of prices depends, ceteris paribus, negatively on market depth, and positively on price precision, prior volatility, and noise trading. In any case, volatility increases with the degree of risk aversion of uninformed traders and with prior volatility.

Departures from the standard model introducing correlation between idiosyncratic and common endowment shocks, between fundamentals and noise trading, between the error terms of private and public signals, or with traders receiving private signals on the amount of noise trading yield multiple (linear)

---

[27] Kodres and Pritsker (2002) explain comovement and contagion with portfolio rebalancing effects and Kyle and Xiong (2001) and Yuan (2005) with financial constraints.

[28] See section 5.1 in Vives (1999) for an overview of contestable markets.

equilibria in the financial market and, potentially, strategic complementarity in information acquisition. Another way to obtain strategic complementarity in information acquisition is with economies of scale in information production.

4.3 Informed Traders Move First and Face Risk-Neutral Competitive Market Makers

In this section we consider a trading game in which informed traders move first, with a proportion of them using demand schedules and the complementary proportion market orders, and risk-neutral market makers set prices. We will derive the pricing implications of the presence of risk-neutral market makers and the differential impact of traders using market orders and demand schedules.

Let us go back to the model in section 4.2.1 but now consider a situation where informed traders and noise traders move first.[29] Informed traders can submit demand schedules or market orders (we will explain later why this may be so). Their orders are accumulated in a limit-order book. The limit-order book is observed by a competitive risk-neutral market-making sector which sets prices. This competitive sector can be formed of scalpers, floor traders, and different types of market makers. The competitive market-making sector observes the book $L(\cdot)$, which is a function of p, and sets price (informationally) efficiently:

$$p = E[\theta \mid L(\cdot)].$$

The efficient pricing (zero expected profit) condition can be justified with Bertrand competition among risk-neutral market makers who have the same information, and each one of them observes the limit-order book. Introducing risk-neutral market makers means that a risk-averse agent will be willing to trade and hold the risky asset only if he has an informational advantage. This market microstructure involves sequential moves; however, as we will see below, it can be seen to be equivalent to simultaneous submission of orders by all traders.

There is a continuum of informed traders, indexed in the interval $[0, 1]$, with common constant coefficient of absolute risk aversion ρ. The information structure is as in section 4.2.1 but now a proportion ν of traders submit demand schedules while a proportion $1 - \nu$ place market orders. We restrict our attention to linear equilibria with price equilibrium of the form $P(\theta, u)$. Given the symmetric-information structure and preferences of traders without loss of generality we concentrate attention on symmetric linear Bayesian equilibria where the same type of trader uses the same strategy. Demands will have the form derived from the CARA representation and will be identical within each class of informed traders: $X(s_i, p)$, $i \in [0, \nu]$, and $Y(s_i)$, $i \in (\nu, 1]$.

---

[29] See Medrano (1996). Vives (1995b, section 2) considers the model where informed traders submit market orders.

Suppose that the strategies of informed traders are given as follows:

$$X(s_i, p) = a(s_i - \bar{\theta}) + \zeta(p) \quad \text{and} \quad Y(s_i) = c(s_i - \bar{\theta}),$$

where a and c are trading intensities and $\zeta(\cdot)$ is a linear function.[30] The noisy limit-order book schedule is given by (using the convention that the average signal equals θ a.s.)

$$L(p) = \int_0^{\nu} X(s_i, p)\,\mathrm{d}i + \int_{\nu}^{1} Y(s_i)\,\mathrm{d}i + u = z + \nu\zeta(p),$$

where $z = A(\theta - \bar{\theta}) + u$ and $A = \nu a + (1 - \nu)c$. The competitive market-making sector observes $L(\cdot)$, a linear function of p, and sets $p = E[\theta \mid L(\cdot)] = E[\theta \mid z]$. Notice that the random intercept z of the limit-order schedule $L(\cdot)$ is what is informative about θ. As before, the random variable z is observationally equivalent to the market price and can be thought as representing the new information contained in the market price. From standard normal theory and $p = E[\theta \mid z]$, it follows that $p = \lambda z + \bar{\theta}$, where $\lambda = \tau_u A/\tau$ and $\tau = \tau_\theta + \tau_u A^2$.

Since p is a linear function of z and is normally distributed, we have that $p = E[\theta \mid z] = E[\theta \mid p]$. This implies that the set of Bayesian linear equilibria of the sequential game and the one with simultaneous placement of orders to an auctioneer (as in section 4.2) will be equivalent if there is a positive mass of competitive risk-neutral market makers. Indeed, in this case in equilibrium we have necessarily that $E[\theta \mid p] = p$ because otherwise the competitive risk-neutral market makers would like to take unbounded positions.

Market makers take the counterpart of the limit-order book and clear the market. An important effect of the existence of a risk-neutral competitive market-making sector is that *total volatility*, the sum of the volatility of price increments $\text{var}[p - \bar{\theta}] + \text{var}[\theta - p]$, is constant and equal to prior volatility of θ, σ_θ^2. In fact, since $\text{var}[\theta \mid p] = \text{var}[\theta - p]$ total volatility can also be expressed as the sum of conditional volatilities $\text{var}[p \mid \bar{\theta}] + \text{var}[\theta \mid p]$. This is a direct consequence of semi-strong efficient pricing: $p = E[\theta \mid p]$. Note that $\text{var}[\theta - p] = \text{var}[\theta] - 2\,\text{cov}[\theta, p] + \text{var}[p]$ but $\text{cov}[\theta, p] = \text{var}[p]$. (The latter follows since $p = E[\theta \mid p]$, $E[\theta p] = E[E[\theta p \mid p]] = E[pE[\theta \mid p]] = E[p^2]$, and $E[p] = E[\theta]$.) We conclude that $\text{var}[\theta - p] = \text{var}[\theta] - \text{var}[p]$. Now, it is well-known (see DeGroot 1970, p. 69) that if $\text{var}[\theta]$ is finite, then $\text{var}[\theta] = E[\text{var}[\theta \mid p]] + \text{var}[E[\theta \mid p]]$. Therefore, if $p = E[\theta \mid p]$, then $\text{var}[\theta] = \text{var}[\theta \mid p] + \text{var}[p]$ (recall that (θ, p) are jointly normally distributed and consequently $\text{var}[\theta \mid p]$ is nonrandom). Therefore, *ex ante* price volatility is given by

$$\text{var}[p] = \text{var}[\theta] - \text{var}[\theta \mid p] = \tau_\theta^{-1} - \tau^{-1}$$

and increases with the precision incorporated in prices τ. Prices are more volatile if they are more informative. We therefore have that

$$\text{var}[p - \bar{\theta}] + \text{var}[\theta - p] = \text{var}[p \mid \bar{\theta}] + \text{var}[\theta \mid p] = \text{var}[\theta].$$

---

[30] Without loss of generality (with hindsight) in the linear symmetric class for each class of traders.

An increase in the informativeness of prices only brings forward the resolution of uncertainty, increasing $\operatorname{var}[p]$ and decreasing $\operatorname{var}[\theta \mid p]$, leaving the sum constant. This is the result of risk-neutral competitive market making.

When market makers are risk averse, as in section 4.2, then the direct link between price informativeness and volatility is broken. Then, as we have seen, $\operatorname{var}[p] = \lambda^2\tau(\tau_\theta\tau_u)^{-1}$ and prices may be more volatile because there is more noise trading or because the market is shallower, for a given level of price precision.

The demands of informed traders are easily derived (see exercise 4.2). The following proposition states the results.

Proposition 4.2. *There is a unique linear Bayesian equilibrium. It is given by*

$$X(s_i,p) = a(s_i - p), \quad Y(s_i) = c(s_i - \bar{\theta}), \quad \textit{and} \quad p = \lambda z + \bar{\theta},$$

where $a = \rho^{-1}\tau_\varepsilon$, $c = (\rho(\sigma_\varepsilon^2 + \operatorname{var}[p]))^{-1}$, $z = A(\theta - \bar{\theta}) + u$, $\lambda = \tau_u A/\tau$, $\tau = \tau_\theta + \tau_u A^2$, $\operatorname{var}[p] = \tau_\theta^{-1} - \tau^{-1}$, *and* $A = \nu a + (1-\nu)c$. *The parameter* c *is the unique solution to the cubic equation*

$$c\left(\tau_\theta + \frac{\tau_\varepsilon\tau_u(\nu\rho^{-1}\tau_\varepsilon + (1-\nu)c)^2}{\tau_\theta + \tau_u(\nu\rho^{-1}\tau_\varepsilon + (1-\nu)c)^2}\right) = \rho^{-1}\tau_\varepsilon\tau_\theta.$$

Market orders versus limit orders. The strategies of traders using demand schedules are as before in its private-information speculative component. Those of traders using market orders depend on the discrepancy between the private signal realization and the prior mean, weighted by a trading intensity c which is inversely related to risk aversion ρ, noisiness in the signal σ_ε^2, and the volatility of prices, $\operatorname{var}[p]$. Indeed, risk-averse traders using market orders dislike price volatility. It is precisely because market order traders have to bear price risk that their trading intensity is smaller than that of a limit-order trader: $c < a$.

The precision incorporated into prices now depends on the average responsiveness of traders to private information A. As the proportion ν of traders using demand schedules increases A increases. As a result price precision τ as well as volatility $\operatorname{var}[p]$ also increases. The direct effect of traders increasing their trading intensity as they switch from using market orders to demand schedules is larger than the indirect effect reducing the trading intensity of those using market orders due to the increased price volatility. The effect of ν on market depth λ^{-1} is ambiguous. An increase in δ tends to provide more liquidity to the market and make prices more informative but at the same time worsens the adverse selection problem faced by market makers because the order book is more likely to contain information-based orders.[31]

It should be clear that if the cost of placing a market order or a demand schedule were to be the same, all traders would prefer to place the schedule. However, we need a series of limit and stop orders to construct a demand schedule.

[31] Note that $\partial(\lambda^{-1})/\partial\nu = (1 - \tau_\theta(\tau_u A^2)^{-1})(a - c)$. Since $a - c > 0$, we have that λ^{-1} increases with ν when the incremental precision incorporated in the price due to trade $\tau_u A^2$ is larger than the prior precision τ_θ.

Placing a demand schedule is bound to be more costly. Suppose that placing a demand schedule involves a (differential) fixed cost and that traders can choose whether to place a schedule and incur the cost or to place a market order at no cost. It is possible to show (Medrano 1996) that, provided the differential fixed cost is neither too high nor too low, there will be at least one interior equilibrium, in which traders partition themselves according to the type of orders they place. Informed traders with a high risk-tolerance-adjusted informational advantage (that is, with high $\rho_i^{-1}\tau_{\varepsilon_i}$) place demand schedules while the remaining traders place market orders. Traders with a high $\rho_i^{-1}\tau_{\varepsilon_i}$ are willing to pay more to obtain the information contained in the price (that is, they benefit more from observing the price). This is akin to the result in the endogenous information model of Verrecchia (1982), where traders with high $\rho_i^{-1}\tau_{\varepsilon_i}$ are willing to spend more to improve their information. The reason is that traders with high $\rho_i^{-1}\tau_{\varepsilon_i}$ trade more aggressively and therefore benefit more from extra information.

We analyze next the comparative statics of the equilibria for two extreme cases: $\nu = 1$ and $\nu = 0$.

When all informed traders use demand schedules ($\nu = 1$) an increase in noise trading reduces directly the precision of prices τ (and price volatility) even though the trading intensity of informed agents is not affected. An increase in risk aversion or in the noisiness of private information induces a decrease in τ via a decreased trading intensity of informed agents. The depth of the market λ^{-1} increases with noise trading τ_u^{-1} and is nonmonotonic in ρ and τ_ε. In equilibrium, and depending on parameter values, the depth of the market may be increasing with the risk tolerance and the precision of information of informed agents. The explanation is that these changes increase the trading intensity of informed agents, which tends to decrease market depth, but this may be more than compensated for by the induced increase in the precision of prices.[32] The result is that we have that λ^{-1} increases with $a = \rho^{-1}\tau_\varepsilon$ if and only if $\tau_\theta - \tau_u a^2 < 0$. An increase in the precision of private information, leading to an increase in a, will imply a larger λ^{-1} if noise trading is small (τ_u large) and the levels of risk tolerance and precision of private information large (which imply that a is large).

The expected (aggregate) volume traded by informed agents is

$$E\left[\left|\int_0^1 X(s_i, p)\,\mathrm{d}i\right|\right] = (2/\pi)^{1/2} a\sqrt{\tau^{-1}}$$

(see exercise 4.3). Expected trading volume of the informed is increasing with noise trading τ_u^{-1}. When $\tau_\varepsilon \to 0$ so does the expected trade of the informed. The market makers then offer the counterpart to noise traders, $\lambda = 0$ and $p = \bar{\theta}$.

When all informed traders use market orders ($\nu = 0$) we have a model which is a financial market counterpart of the Cournot model of chapter 1 (while

[32] This explanation is therefore different from the one in Subrahmanyam (1991), where the phenomenon is attributed to an increase in the degree of competition among a finite number of insiders.

the rational expectations model in section 3.1 or the case $\nu = 1$ is a financial market counterpart of the supply function competition model of chapter 3). Exercise 4.4 provides the comparative statics of the model.

There are several studies of the choice between market and limit orders in the literature. Brown and Zhang (1997) show, consistently with the model in this section, that a market with traders using limit orders induces more informational price efficiency than one with traders using market orders since in the former execution price risk is moderated. Chakravaty and Holden (1995) analyze this choice by an informed trader in a quote-driven system. In this case the informed trader may exploit limit orders by submitting a market order. Foucault (1999) analyzes the choice in a dynamic model and concludes that it is better to place a limit (market) order when the spread is large (tight). This analysis is extended by Goettler et al. (2005). Harris and Hasbrouck (1996) and Biais et al. (1995) provide evidence consistent with the last two theoretical pieces. Wald and Horrigan (2005) analyze the choice of a risk-averse investor between a limit and a market order and estimate the parameters of the model with NYSE data.

4.3.1 Summary

The main learning points of the section are:

- The presence of a competitive risk-neutral market-making sector induces prices to reflect all publicly available information.[33] That is, the market is semi-strong informationally efficient and prices are volatile because they are informative.
- As a consequence, total volatility is constant and equal to the volatility of fundamentals. An increase in informativeness of prices only brings forward the resolution of uncertainty.
- Sequential and simultaneous order placement need not yield different outcomes. This is so in the presence of competitive risk-neutral market makers.
- Risk-averse traders using market orders are more cautious when responding to their information than limit-order (demand-schedule) traders because they are subject to price volatility.
- As a result, when the proportion of traders using demand schedules increases, so does price precision and volatility (and the impact on market depth is ambiguous).
- Whenever there is a differential fixed cost to submit a demand schedule instead of a market order, traders with a large risk-tolerance-adjusted informational advantage place demand schedules while the others place market orders.

[33] However, the precision of prices (i.e., their informational content) is the same as in a model where market makers are privately informed and risk averse. In other words, if we let $\mu = 1$ in the model of section 4.2.1 and $\nu = 1$ in the model of section 4.2.3, the informational content of the equilibrium price is the same in the two models: $\tau = \tau_\theta + \tau_u a^2$ with $a = \rho^{-1}\tau_\varepsilon$.

*4.4 Hedgers and Producers in a Futures Market

Up to now we have considered markets where some exogenous noise traders are present and drive the trade. Their presence is motivated by unspecified liquidity reasons and allows for REE not to be fully revealing as well as trade in the presence of asymmetric information. This is unsatisfactory because the decisions of noise traders are not modeled, it is not explained why these traders are willing to lose money in the market, and consequently a proper welfare analysis cannot be performed. In this section we endogenize the presence of noise traders with risk-averse hedgers. We present a variation of the model of section 4.2 replacing noise traders by risk-averse competitive hedgers and assuming that all informed traders receive the same signal (as in Grossman and Stiglitz (1980), see section 4.2.2; we follow Medrano and Vives (2007)).

We want to examine the relationships between information and insurance in a financial market populated by risk-averse traders and the derived incentives for real investment. The model will allow us to study the welfare consequences of improvements in private information and of public-information release. Several papers in the literature emphasize the allocational role of financial prices guiding production and investment decisions (e.g., Leland 1992; Dow and Gorton 1997; Subrahmanyam and Titman 1999). Chen et al. (2007) display empirical evidence on how managers learn from the (private) information in the stock price and incorporate it in their corporate investment decisions. In the model of the present section the informativeness of prices in the financial market will affect production incentives only indirectly since real decisions are taken before the financial market opens.

The risky asset is a futures contract for a good (say, agricultural product or raw material) with future random spot price θ. The futures contract trades at price p. Producers want to hedge their production in the futures market at $t = 2$ and obtain private information at $t = 1$ about the future value of the product once the production process has been set (say, the seeds have been planted) at $t = 0$ (as in Bray (1981, 1985), see the timeline below).

We first set up the model and the demands for the different traders, then analyze the market equilibrium and study the effect of information on production. A preview of the results follows. The private information of producers cannot help production decisions, because it comes too late, but allows them to speculate in the futures market. This creates adverse selection in the futures market where uninformed speculators (market makers) and other hedgers operate. This will tend to diminish the hedging effectiveness of the futures market and consequently diminish the output of risk-averse producers (since they will be able to hedge less of their production). The adverse selection is aggravated with more precise private information. Adverse selection is eliminated if the signal received by producers is made public. However, more public information may decrease production (and the expected utility of all traders) because it destroys insurance opportunities (this is the "Hirshleifer effect," see section 3.1 and also section 5.4). The model also shows under what circumstances hedgers have demands of the "noise trader" form.

4.4.1 A Futures Market with Hedgers

We have a single risky asset (the futures contract), with random liquidation value θ (the future spot price), and a riskless asset, with unitary return, traded among a continuum of risk-averse competitive uninformed speculators (market makers), a continuum of risk-averse competitive hedgers, and a continuum of risk-averse competitive informed speculators. The risky asset is traded at a price p and thus generates a return $\theta - p$.

Informed traders. There is a continuum of informed traders with mass one. They are producers of a good with random future spot price θ. The representative informed trader:

- Receives a private signal $s = \theta + \varepsilon$, where θ and ε are independent, and $E[\varepsilon] = 0$.
- Has a level of production q with cost function $C(q) = c_1 q + \frac{1}{2}c_2 q^2$, where $c_1 \geqslant 0$ and $c_2 \geqslant 0$.
- Is risk averse with CARA utility: $U_{\mathrm{I}}(W_{\mathrm{I}}) = -\mathrm{e}^{-\rho_{\mathrm{I}} W_{\mathrm{I}}}$, $\rho_{\mathrm{I}} > 0$, where $W_{\mathrm{I}} = \theta q - C(q) + (\theta - p)x_{\mathrm{I}}$ is his final wealth when buying x_{I} futures contracts. His position in the futures market is then $q + x_{\mathrm{I}}$.
- Submits a demand schedule contingent on the private information s he observes. If $x_{\mathrm{I}} > 0$, he is a net buyer of futures, while he is a net supplier if $x_{\mathrm{I}} < 0$. In equilibrium we will see that $E[x_{\mathrm{I}}] < 0$ and informed traders will sell on average.

An informed trader has three motives to trade in the market for futures. First, he is interested in trading in order to hedge part of the risk coming from his production q ($\theta q - C(q)$ is the random value of the producer's endowment before trading in the securities' market that needs to be hedged). Second, he may trade for speculative reasons in order to exploit his private information about θ. Finally, he will also speculate on the differences between prices and the expected value of θ (i.e., for market-making purposes).

Market makers. There is a continuum of competitive uninformed speculators (or market makers) also with unitary mass. The final wealth of a representative market maker buying x_{U} shares at price p is given by $W_{\mathrm{U}} = (\theta - p)x_{\mathrm{U}}$, where his initial nonrandom wealth is normalized to zero.[34] Market makers trade in order to obtain profits by absorbing some of the risks that the informed traders and hedgers try to hedge (their trades are not motivated by any informational advantage or any need for hedging). A representative market maker is risk averse

[34] Recall that with constant absolute risk aversion, a trader's demand for a risky asset does not depend on his initial nonrandom wealth, and we can assume (without loss of generality) that speculators have zero initial wealth.

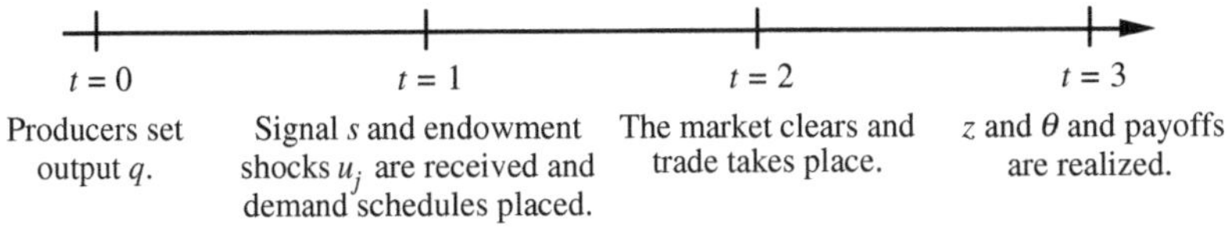

Figure 4.2.

with CARA utility $U_{\mathrm{U}}(W_{\mathrm{U}}) = -\mathrm{e}^{-\rho_{\mathrm{U}} W_{\mathrm{U}}}$, $\rho_{\mathrm{U}} > 0$, and submits a demand schedule. Since they have rational expectations, they use their observation of the price to update their beliefs about θ.

Hedgers. There is a continuum of competitive hedgers with unitary mass, indexed in the interval $[0, 1]$. Hedger j:

- Has an initial endowment u_j of an asset with future (random) value z correlated with θ. This could be the random production of a related good which is not traded in a futures market.
- Has final wealth $W_j = u_j z + (\theta - p)x_j$ when buying x_j shares at price p.
- Is risk averse with CARA utility $U_{\mathrm{H}}(W_j) = -\mathrm{e}^{-\rho_{\mathrm{H}} W_j}$, $\rho_{\mathrm{H}} > 0$.
- Privately observes u_j and places a demand schedule contingent on his private information u_j.

We assume that u_j may be written as $u_j = u + \eta_j$, where u and η_j are independent (and η_j is independent of η_i for all $j \neq i$). The usual convention that errors cancel out in the aggregate, $\int_0^1 \eta_j \,\mathrm{d}j = 0$ a.s., will be used. As a result, $\int_0^1 u_j \,\mathrm{d}j = \int_0^1 (u + \eta_j)\,\mathrm{d}j = u + \int_0^1 \eta_j \,\mathrm{d}j = u$ a.s., so that u is the aggregate risky endowment of the hedgers. A hedger uses the observation of the price to update his beliefs about θ. Hedgers' main motive to trade is to reduce risks. However, the endowment shock to hedger j is his private information and therefore their demand also has a speculative component.

Timing. At $t = 0$, producers choose the level of production q. The level of production q is public information. At $t = 1$, each producer receives a private signal s about θ and hedger j an endowment shock u_j, and the demand schedules of all traders placed. At $t = 2$, the market-clearing price is set and trade occurs. Finally, at $t = 3$, the terminal values z and θ are realized and agents consume (see figure 4.2).

Distributional assumptions. All random variables are assumed to be normally distributed: $\theta \sim N(\bar{\theta}, \sigma_\theta^2)$, $z \sim N(\bar{z}, \sigma_z^2)$, $u \sim N(0, \sigma_u^2)$, $\varepsilon \sim N(0, \sigma_\varepsilon^2)$, and $\eta_j \sim N(0, \sigma_\eta^2)$ for all j. Without loss of generality, we assume that z may be written as $z = \sigma_z[(r_{\theta z}/\sigma_\theta)\theta + \sqrt{1 - r_{\theta z}^2}\, y]$, where $r_{\theta z}$ is the correlation coefficient between z and θ, and $y \sim N(0, 1)$ is independent of any other variable in the model. Moreover, we assume that $\mathrm{cov}[\theta, u] = \mathrm{cov}[s, u] = \mathrm{cov}[\theta, u_j] = \mathrm{cov}[s, u_j] = \mathrm{cov}[\theta, \varepsilon] = \mathrm{cov}[\theta, \eta_j] = \mathrm{cov}[u, \eta_j] = \mathrm{cov}[s, \eta_j] = \mathrm{cov}[\varepsilon, u] = \mathrm{cov}[\varepsilon, \eta_j] = 0$ for all j and $\mathrm{cov}[\eta_j, \eta_l] = 0$ for all $j \neq l$.

Let ξ denote the square of the correlation coefficient between s and θ, $\xi \equiv \sigma_\theta^2/(\sigma_\theta^2+\sigma_\varepsilon^2)$, and let ξ_u denote the square of the correlation coefficient between u and u_j, $\xi_u \equiv \sigma_u^2/(\sigma_u^2+\sigma_\eta^2)$. Throughout the section, the subscript "I" will refer to the informed traders, the subscript "U" will refer to the uninformed speculators, and the subscript "H" will refer to the hedgers.

4.4.2 Equilibrium in the Futures Market

We will restrict our attention to Bayesian linear equilibria with price functional of the form $P(s,u)$. In order to find the linear equilibrium we follow the standard procedure. We posit candidate linear strategies, derive the linear relationship between prices and the underlying random variables, work through the optimization problems of traders to derive their demands, and finally determine the coefficients of the linear strategies. Given the information structure and preferences of the different types of traders, and as in section 4.2.1, the equilibrium will be symmetric (i.e., the same strategy for each class of traders).

The strategies may be written (with hindsight and without loss of generality) as follows. For an informed trader,

$$X_{\mathrm{I}}(s,p) = a(s-\bar{\theta}) + b_{\mathrm{I}}(\bar{\theta}-p) - \gamma_{\mathrm{I}} q,$$

where a, b_{I}, and γ_{I} are endogenous nonrandom parameters.[35]

For a market maker,

$$X_{\mathrm{U}}(p) = b_{\mathrm{U}}(\bar{\theta}-p) - \gamma_{\mathrm{U}} q,$$

where b_{U} and γ_{U} are endogenous nonrandom parameters.

For hedger j,

$$X_{\mathrm{H}}(p,u_j) = b_{\mathrm{H}}(\bar{\theta}-p) - \delta u_j - \gamma_{\mathrm{H}} q,$$

where b_{H}, γ_{H}, and δ are endogenous nonrandom parameters.

The market-clearing condition is

$$X_{\mathrm{U}}(p) + X_{\mathrm{H}}(p,u) + X_{\mathrm{I}}(p,s) = 0,$$

where $X_{\mathrm{H}}(p,u) = \int_0^1 X_{\mathrm{H}}(p,u_j)\,\mathrm{d}j = b_{\mathrm{H}}(\bar{\theta}-p) - \delta u - \gamma_{\mathrm{H}} q$ (since $\int_0^1 u_j\,\mathrm{d}j = u$) is the hedgers' aggregate demand. Given the linear strategies posited above, the equilibrium price is a linear function of the private information s, the hedgers' random aggregate endowment u (errors η_j cancel in the aggregate), and production q:

$$p = \bar{\theta} - \Gamma q + \frac{a(s-\bar{\theta}) - \delta u}{\Lambda},$$

where $\Gamma = (\gamma_{\mathrm{I}} + \gamma_{\mathrm{U}} + \gamma_{\mathrm{H}})/\Lambda$ and $\Lambda = b_{\mathrm{I}} + b_{\mathrm{U}} + b_{\mathrm{H}}$.

Hedger j will choose x_j to maximize $E[U_{\mathrm{H}}(W_j) \mid p, u_j]$, where $W_j = u_j z + (\theta - p)x_j$, or (since all random variables, including the price, are normally distributed)

$$-\exp\{-\rho_{\mathrm{H}}(E[W_j \mid p,u_j] - \tfrac{1}{2}\rho_{\mathrm{H}} \operatorname{var}[W_j \mid p,u_j])\}.$$

---

[35] That is, we should write $X_{\mathrm{I}}(s,p) = as - b_{\mathrm{I}}p + \varphi_{\mathrm{I}}$ but in equilibrium we will have $\varphi_{\mathrm{I}} = (-a+b_{\mathrm{I}})\bar{\theta} - \gamma_{\mathrm{I}} q$ (and similarly for the other types of traders).

We have that $E[W_j \mid p, u_j] = u_j E[z \mid p, u_j] + (E[\theta \mid p, u_j] - p)x_j$ and $\operatorname{var}[W_j \mid p, u_j] = u_j^2 \operatorname{var}[z \mid p, u_j] + x_j^2 \operatorname{var}[\theta - p \mid p, u_j] + 2u_j x_j \operatorname{cov}[z, \theta - p \mid p, u_j]$. From the FOC, hedger j's optimal demand for shares is given by

$$X_{\mathrm{H}}(p, u_j) = \frac{E[\theta - p \mid p, u_j] - \rho_{\mathrm{H}} u_j \operatorname{cov}[z, \theta - p \mid p, u_j]}{\rho_{\mathrm{H}} \operatorname{var}[\theta - p \mid p, u_j]}.$$

Hedger j's demand may be decomposed into two terms:

- Speculative demand: $E[\theta - p \mid p, u_j]/\rho_{\mathrm{H}} \operatorname{var}[\theta - p \mid p, u_j]$, which will depend on q (because this helps reading the information about s in the price) and on u_j provided that $\xi_u > 0$ (because then u_j contains information on u which in turn helps to recover information about s in the price).
- Hedge supply: $(-\operatorname{cov}[z, \theta - p \mid p, u_j]/\operatorname{var}[\theta - p \mid p, u_j])u_j$, which can be seen to be equal to $-(\sigma_{\theta z}/\sigma_\theta^2)u_j$.[36] The amount of the hedger's initial endowment (u_j) that is hedged in the market is proportional to the correlation between the value of the hedger's asset z and the return of the risky security $\theta - p$ conditional on the hedger's information $\{p, u_j\}$.

Similarly (just looking at the speculative component), optimization of the CARA utility for an uninformed yields

$$X_{\mathrm{U}}(p) = \frac{E[\theta - p \mid p]}{\rho_{\mathrm{U}} \operatorname{var}[\theta - p \mid p]},$$

which is linear in p since $\operatorname{var}[\theta - p \mid p]$ is constant and $E[\theta - p \mid p]$ is linear in p due to the normality assumption. All the speculators will place the same demand schedule (since all of them have the same information), so that the speculators' aggregate demand $X_{\mathrm{U}}(p)$ will be given by the same expression. The demand will depend on q because the knowledge of q is needed to infer information about s from the price.

The representative informed trader's maximization problem is the following:

$$\max_{x_{\mathrm{I}}} E[-\mathrm{e}^{-\rho_{\mathrm{I}} W_{\mathrm{I}}} \mid s, p],$$

where $W_{\mathrm{I}} = \theta q - C(q) + (\theta - p)x_{\mathrm{I}}$. Given normality this is equivalent to maximizing

$$\begin{aligned} E[W_{\mathrm{I}} \mid s, p] &- (\tfrac{1}{2}\rho_{\mathrm{I}}) \operatorname{var}[W_{\mathrm{I}} \mid s, p] \\ &= qE[\theta \mid s] + x_{\mathrm{I}}\{E[\theta \mid s] - p\} - (\tfrac{1}{2}\rho_{\mathrm{I}})(x_{\mathrm{I}} + q)^2 \operatorname{var}[\theta \mid s]. \end{aligned}$$

Note that the price does not provide an informed trader with any further information about θ over and above the signal s and therefore $E[\theta \mid s, p] =$

---

[36] Since $z = \sigma_z[(r_{\theta z}/\sigma_\theta)\theta + \sqrt{1 - r_{\theta z}^2}\, y]$ and y is independent of any other random variable we have that

$$\frac{\operatorname{cov}[z, \theta - p \mid p, u_j]}{\operatorname{var}[\theta - p \mid p, u_j]} = \sigma_z \left(\frac{r_{\theta z}}{\sigma_0}\right) \frac{\operatorname{cov}[\theta, \theta - p \mid p, u_j]}{\operatorname{var}[\theta - p \mid p, u_j]},$$

which gives the result since $\operatorname{cov}[\theta, \theta - p \mid p, u_j] = \operatorname{var}[\theta \mid p, u_j]$, $\operatorname{var}[\theta - p \mid p, u_j] = \operatorname{var}[\theta \mid p, u_j]$, and $r_{\theta z} = \sigma_{\theta z}/\sigma_\theta \sigma_z$.

$E[\theta \mid s]$ and $\operatorname{var}[\theta \mid s, p] = \operatorname{var}[\theta \mid s]$. However, although the price has no information to aggregate, it is still useful from the informed trader's point of view since it allows him to infer the exact amount of noise trading (and thus eliminate the price risk it creates). If $\rho_{\mathrm{I}} \operatorname{var}[\theta \mid s] > 0$, then

$$X_{\mathrm{I}}(s, p) = \frac{E[\theta \mid s] - p}{\rho_{\mathrm{I}} \operatorname{var}[\theta \mid s]} - q,$$

where $E[\theta \mid s] = \bar{\theta} + \xi(s - \bar{\theta})$ and $\operatorname{var}[\theta \mid s] = (1 - \xi)\sigma_\theta^2$. We may write the demand as

$$X_{\mathrm{I}}(s, p) = \frac{1}{\rho_{\mathrm{I}}\sigma_\varepsilon^2}(s - p) + \frac{1}{\rho_{\mathrm{I}}\sigma_\theta^2}(\bar{\theta} - p) - q = a(s - \bar{\theta}) + b_{\mathrm{I}}(\bar{\theta} - p) - q,$$

where $a = 1/(\rho_{\mathrm{I}}\sigma_\varepsilon^2)$ and $b_{\mathrm{I}} = 1/(\rho_{\mathrm{I}}(1 - \xi)\sigma_\theta^2)$.

An informed trader's asset position can be decomposed into two terms:

- Speculative demand: $(E[\theta \mid s] - p)/(\rho_{\mathrm{I}} \operatorname{var}[\theta \mid s])$, according to which the informed trader buys (sells) if his estimate of the asset liquidation value is greater (lower) than the price.
- Hedge supply, q: since the representative informed agent is strictly risk averse and a price taker, he hedges all the endowment risk, $\gamma_{\mathrm{I}} = 1$ (provided that he is imperfectly informed, i.e., $\sigma_\varepsilon^2 > 0$ or $\xi < 1$).

In order to characterize a linear equilibrium, using the expression for the price, the expressions for $E[\theta \mid p, u_j]$, $\operatorname{var}[\theta \mid p, u_j]$, $E[\theta \mid p]$, and $\operatorname{var}[\theta \mid p]$ are plugged back into $X_{\mathrm{H}}(p, u_j)$ and $X_{\mathrm{U}}(p)$ and a solution is found for the undetermined coefficients of the linear strategies. The result is presented in the following proposition (see Medrano and Vives (2007) for a proof).

Proposition 4.3. *If $\xi < 1$, there is a unique linear Bayesian equilibrium. It is characterized by*

$$\begin{aligned}
X_{\mathrm{U}}(p) &= b_{\mathrm{U}}(\bar{\theta} - p) - \gamma_{\mathrm{U}} q,\\
X_{\mathrm{H}}(u, p) &= b_{\mathrm{H}}(\bar{\theta} - p) - \delta u - \gamma_{\mathrm{H}} q,\\
X_{\mathrm{I}}(s, p) &= a(s - \bar{\theta}) + b_{\mathrm{I}}(\bar{\theta} - p) - q,\\
p &= \bar{\theta} - \Gamma q + \frac{a(s - \bar{\theta}) - \delta u}{\Lambda},
\end{aligned}$$

where

$$\Lambda = b_{\mathrm{I}} + b_{\mathrm{U}} + b_{\mathrm{H}}, \quad \Gamma = \frac{1 + \gamma_{\mathrm{U}} + \gamma_{\mathrm{H}}}{\Lambda}, \quad a = \frac{1}{\rho_{\mathrm{I}}\sigma_\varepsilon^2}, \quad b_{\mathrm{I}} = \frac{1}{\rho_{\mathrm{I}}(1 - \xi)\sigma_\theta^2},$$

$$b_{\mathrm{U}} = \frac{\delta^2\sigma_u^2\sigma_\theta^{-2}(\rho_{\mathrm{H}}((1 - \xi_u)\delta^2\sigma_u^2 + a^2\sigma_\varepsilon^2) + a\xi_u)}{(\rho_{\mathrm{U}}(\delta^2\sigma_u^2 + a^2\sigma_\varepsilon^2) + a)(\rho_{\mathrm{H}}((1 - \xi_u)\delta^2\sigma_u^2 + a^2\sigma_\varepsilon^2) + a) - a^2},$$

$$b_{\mathrm{H}} = \frac{\delta^2\sigma_u^2\sigma_\theta^{-2}((1 - \xi_u)\rho_{\mathrm{U}}(\delta^2\sigma_u^2 + a^2\sigma_\varepsilon^2) - a\xi_u)}{(\rho_{\mathrm{U}}(\delta^2\sigma_u^2 + a^2\sigma_\varepsilon^2) + a)(\rho_{\mathrm{H}}((1 - \xi_u)\delta^2\sigma_u^2 + a^2\sigma_\varepsilon^2) + a) - a^2},$$

$$\gamma_{\mathrm{H}} = \frac{-a}{\rho_{\mathrm{H}}((1 - \xi_u)\delta^2\sigma_u^2 + a^2\sigma_\varepsilon^2)(1 + aE)},$$

with $E = (1/\rho_{\mathrm{U}})(\delta^2\sigma_u^2 + a^2\sigma_\varepsilon^2)^{-1} + (1/\rho_{\mathrm{H}})((1-\xi_u)\delta^2\sigma_u^2 + a^2\sigma_\varepsilon^2)^{-1}$*. The parameter* δ *is the unique solution of the (implicit) cubic equation*

$$\delta = \left(\frac{\sigma_{\theta z}}{\sigma_\theta^2}\right)\left\{1 + \frac{\xi_u}{\rho_{\mathrm{H}}(\rho_{\mathrm{I}}\sigma_\varepsilon^2(1-\xi_u)\delta^2\sigma_u^2 + \rho_{\mathrm{I}}^{-1})}\right\}^{-1}.$$

From the solution to the cubic equation for δ *we obtain the rest of the equilibrium parameters.*

The expected price is equal to the prior expected liquidation value minus a *risk premium*, $\bar{p} = \bar{\theta} - \Gamma q$. The risk premium is positive and is directly proportional to the level of the endowment of informed traders (production), where $\Gamma = (1 + \gamma_{\mathrm{U}} + \gamma_{\mathrm{H}})/\Lambda$. The equilibrium parameter $\Lambda = b_{\mathrm{I}} + b_{\mathrm{U}} + b_{\mathrm{H}}$ is related to market depth. In terms of our previous λ we have that $\lambda \equiv |\partial p/\partial u| = \delta/\Lambda$. The market is deeper the more traders respond to price movements and the less hedgers react to their endowment shock (where $0 < \delta < \sigma_{\theta z}/\sigma_\theta^2$).

The price is informationally equivalent to $\{a(s - \bar{\theta}) - \delta u\}$ and therefore information (s) and the aggregate endowment shock (u) are the sources of price volatility. As before the *price precision* is $\tau \equiv (\mathrm{var}[\theta \mid p])^{-1}$, where, since the price is also informationally equivalent to $\{\theta + \varepsilon - (\delta/a)u\}$ given that $a > 0$,

$$\tau = \tau_\theta + \frac{1}{\tau_\varepsilon^{-1} + \delta^2(a^2\tau_u)^{-1}}.$$

The price contains information about θ if and only if traders with information on fundamentals trade on the basis of that information (i.e., $a > 0$). Thus, it is natural to expect that the higher the traders' sensitivity to information on fundamentals, the more informative the price. This is true in equilibrium.

Producers, on average, are net suppliers of the risky asset. That is, $E[x_i] = q((a + b_{\mathrm{I}})\Gamma - 1) < 0$. Since the risk premium is positive, the *ex ante* expected value of the speculative demand is positive but the hedge supply $-q$ is larger in equilibrium.

The following patterns can be shown (see Medrano and Vives 2007): increasing ξ increases the trading signal sensitivity of informed traders (a) and this drives price precision τ upward (the latter follows from the expression for τ and the easily checked fact that δ decreases with τ_ε or ξ). Simulations (see footnote 38 for the parameter grid) show that increases in ξ decrease the price responsiveness of market makers (b_{U}) and hedgers (b_{H}). Uninformed traders protect themselves by attempting to reduce market depth (increasing Λ^{-1}) when the informed have a signal of better quality. This effect together with the increase in a dominates (in the simulations) the other effects (such as the decrease in δ) and drives price volatility $\mathrm{var}[p] = \Lambda^{-1}(a^2(\sigma_\theta^2 + \sigma_\varepsilon^2) + \delta^2\sigma_u^2)$ up. We have that δ/Λ is hump-shaped as a function of ξ. Note that $\Lambda = b_{\mathrm{I}} + b_{\mathrm{U}} + b_{\mathrm{H}}$, where b_{U} and b_{H} are strictly decreasing with ξ and $b_{\mathrm{I}} = 1/\rho_{\mathrm{I}}(1-\xi)\sigma_\theta^2$ is strictly increasing with ξ. For ξ low, the first effect dominates and δ/Λ increases with ξ, while the opposite occurs for ξ high. (As $\xi \to 1$ we have that b_{I} and Λ both tend to ∞, and b_{U} and b_{H} tend to 0.) Consequently, market depth $(\delta/\Lambda)^{-1}$ is U-shaped as a function of information precision ξ.

If $\xi = 1$ (perfect information) or $\rho_{\mathrm{I}} = 0$ (risk neutrality for the informed), the only possible equilibrium would be characterized by $p = E[\theta \mid s]$. The informed are indifferent about what to trade since $p = E[\theta \mid s]$. The market makers are also indifferent if $\xi = 1$ (since then $p = E[\theta \mid s] = E[\theta \mid p] = \theta$ and they face no risk $\mathrm{var}[\theta \mid p] = 0$), and they do not trade if $\rho_{\mathrm{I}} = 0$ (since then $p = E[\theta \mid s] = E[\theta \mid p]$ but they face risk). This would constitute a fully revealing REE but it is not implementable in demand functions.

4.4.3 Hedgers and Noise Traders

The market microstructure models we have studied assume the existence of noise traders: agents that trade randomly for unspecified liquidity reasons. Are there circumstances in which rational expected utility maximizing agents give rise to demands for assets of the "noise trader" form? Are expected losses an appropriate measure of their welfare? The answer is that the order flow will contain an exogenous supply u (independent of any deep parameter of the model) whenever z is perfectly correlated with θ and the risk-tolerance-adjusted informational advantage of a hedger is vanishingly small (ξ_u/ρ_{H} tending to 0). This happens if hedgers are infinitely risk averse ($\rho_{\mathrm{H}} \to \infty$) or if there is no correlation between each individual endowment shock u_j and the average u ($\xi_u \to 0$).[37] In the first case hedgers just get rid of all the risk associated with their endowment and supply u in the aggregate. In the second, hedgers are exactly like market makers because they have no informational advantage. In the aggregate they again supply u but now they take a speculative position also. In both cases we can evaluate their expected utility. Indeed, according to the above proposition, as ξ_u/ρ_{H} or ξ/ρ_{I} tends to 0, $\delta \to \sigma_{\theta z}/\sigma_{\theta}^2$, and if in addition $\sigma_{\theta z} = \sigma_{\theta}^2$, the equilibrium demand of the hedgers tends to $X_{\mathrm{H}}(u) = b_{\mathrm{H}}(\bar{\theta} - p) - u - \gamma_{\mathrm{H}} q$, with $b_{\mathrm{H}} \geqslant 0$ and $\gamma_{\mathrm{H}} < 0$. (Furthermore, as $\xi/\rho_{\mathrm{I}} \to 0$ we have that $\gamma_{\mathrm{H}} \to 0$.) If $\rho_{\mathrm{H}} \to \infty$, then $b_{\mathrm{H}}, \gamma_{\mathrm{H}} \to 0$ and $X_{\mathrm{H}}(u) \to -u$.

In summary, "noise trader" type demands arise when hedgers are very risk averse (or when their personal shock is almost uncorrelated with the aggregate one). This will have important implications for the welfare analysis of the impact of parameter changes on the utility of hedgers. Their utility is typically evaluated in noise trader models in terms of the losses they make, i.e., as if they were risk neutral. In the usual CARA-normal models the expected losses of noise traders (trading u) are $\lambda\sigma_u^2$, where λ^{-1} is market depth.

4.4.4 Production, Insurance, and Private Information

For a given q, a producer's *ex ante* expected utility, after long and tedious manipulation (see exercise 4.5), can be seen to be given by the product of three terms:

---

[37] Sarkar (1994) presents results in related models. As stated in section 4.2.2 the case of no correlation between the individual and aggregate endowment shocks is considered in Diamond and Verrecchia (1981) and Verrecchia (1982).

the utility derived from the speculative demand $|SG_I|$, the utility derived from the insurance achieved via the hedge supply $|IG_I|$, and the utility coming from production $\exp\{-\rho_I(q\bar{\theta} - C(q) - \frac{1}{2}\rho_I q^2 \sigma_\theta^2)\}$. That is,

$$J_I(q) \equiv E[-\exp\{-\rho_I W_I\}] = -|SG_I||IG_I| \exp\{-\rho_I(q\bar{\theta} - C(q) - \tfrac{1}{2}\rho_I q^2 \sigma_\theta^2)\},$$

where

$$|SG_I| = \left\{1 + \frac{\rho_I^2(1-\xi)\sigma_\theta^2(\xi\sigma_\theta^2 + \delta^2(b_U + b_H)^{-2}\sigma_u^2)}{(\rho_I(1-\xi)\sigma_\theta^2 + (b_U + b_H)^{-1})^2}\right\}^{-1/2}$$

and

$$|IG_I| = \exp\{-\tfrac{1}{2}\rho_I^2 \sigma_\theta^2 d q^2\}.$$

The key endogenous parameter d represents the hedging effectiveness of the market. It is a complicated expression of the deep parameters of the model (see exercise 4.5). The speculative term has two components. The term $\xi\sigma_\theta^2$ is associated with gains from private information and the term $\delta^2(b_U + b_H)^{-2}\sigma_u^2$ with gains from market making. The private information gains disappear, obviously, when there is no private information ($\xi = 0$).

The optimal production level solves $\max_q J_I(q)$ or, equivalently,

$$\max_q \{q\bar{\theta} - C(q) - \tfrac{1}{2}\rho_I \sigma_\theta^2 q^2 (1-d)\}.$$

The optimal level of production is obtained by equating (expected) marginal value $\bar{\theta}$ to marginal cost $C'(q) + \rho_I\sigma_\theta^2(1-d)q$, which is the sum of the marginal production costs $C'(q) = c_1 + c_2 q$ and the (opportunity) cost related to the riskiness of real investment $\rho_I\sigma_\theta^2(1-d)q$. The optimal level of real investment increases with d, which is a measure of hedging effectiveness of the asset market from a producer's point of view (see figure 4.3):

$$q^* = \frac{\bar{\theta} - c_1}{c_2 + \rho_I\sigma_\theta^2(1-d)}.$$

To perform comparative statics with the model is complicated because of the complexity of the equations determining the endogenous equilibrium parameters. However, using simulations we can obtain results.[38]

The direct impact of an increase in risk aversion ρ_I or underlying risk σ_θ^2 is to decrease q^*. There are other indirect effects operating through d but the simulations performed with the model indicate that the direct effects prevail. An increase in the cost parameters c_1, c_2 unambiguously decreases production.

[38] We postulate as a central case that $\rho_H \geqslant \rho_I > \rho_U$ and that volatilities are not too far from market values (similar to those in, for example, Leland (1992)). The ranking of coefficients of risk aversion seems reasonable: hedgers are the most risk averse and market makers the least. The base case has $\rho_H = 3$, $\rho_I = 2$, and $\rho_U = 1$; volatilities are given by $\sigma_\theta = 0.2$, $\sigma_u = 0.1$, $\sigma_z = 0.2$, and covariances by $\sqrt{\xi_u} = 0.1$, $r_{\theta z} = \sigma_{\theta z}/\sigma_\theta\sigma_z = 0.91$; and $\bar{\theta} = 1$, ξ ranges from 0 to 1. We consider a case with positive production costs, $c_1 = 0.9$, $c_2 = 0.02$, and another with no costs $c_1 = c_2 = 0$. We also consider variations in ρ_H, ρ_I, $\sqrt{\xi_u}$, σ_u, and σ_θ: a volatility of the fundamental value of $\sigma_\theta = 0.6$, which is of the NASDAQ type in contrast with the base case of $\sigma_\theta = 0.2$, which is of the NYSE type; $\rho_H = 6$, $\rho_I \in \{0.1, 0.2, 0.5, 1.5\}$, high noise scenarios with $\sigma_u \in \{0.5, 0.6, 0.7\}$ and $\sqrt{\xi_u} \in \{0.4, 0.5\}$.

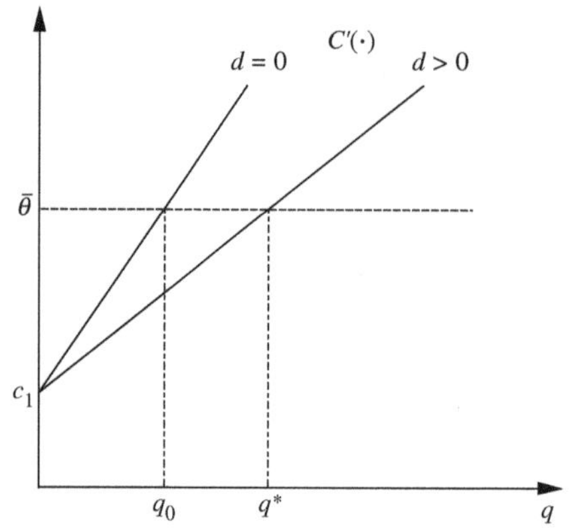

Figure 4.3. Investment (q) and hedging effectiveness of the market (d).

When the market is totally ineffective in hedging, or there is no futures market, $d = 0$ and $q^* = q_0 \equiv (\bar{\theta} - c_1)/(c_2 + \rho_{\mathrm{I}}\sigma_\theta^2)$ (see figure 4.3). This happens as $\xi \to 1$ (see exercise 4.5). The parameter d decreases with ξ according to the simulation of the model. The better the private information of producers the more the futures market faces an adverse selection problem and its hedging effectiveness is reduced.

A producer's *ex ante* expected utility may be written as the product of the speculative component with production and insurance gains

$$J_{\mathrm{I}}(q^*) = -|\mathrm{SG_I}| \exp\{-\tfrac{1}{2}\rho_{\mathrm{I}}(\bar{\theta} - c_1)q^*\}.$$

The speculative component of utility is hump-shaped in ξ. For low ξ an increase in signal precision improves speculative benefits but for high ξ the opposite happens because information revelation is "too strong." Production and insurance gains decrease with ξ because q^* decreases with ξ. The result is that $J_{\mathrm{I}}(q^*)$ decreases with ξ for "normal" values of parameters or is hump-shaped with ξ for more extreme parameter configurations (high noise scenarios).

The uninformed speculators' *ex ante* expected utility $\mathrm{EU_U}$ can be seen (see exercise 4.5) to increase, for given $\mathrm{var}[E[\theta \mid p] - p]$ and $\mathrm{var}[\theta \mid p]$, with the risk premium Γq, which is just the expected margin $E[\theta - p] = \bar{\theta} - \bar{p} = \Gamma q$. The risk premium decreases as ξ increases and this leads to a decrease in $\mathrm{EU_U}$. In all cases considered in the simulations we find that $\mathrm{EU_U}$ decreases with ξ.

The expressions for the expected utility of a hedger $\mathrm{EU_H}$ are complicated (and we need to assume that ξ_u/ρ_{H} is small since otherwise $\mathrm{EU_H}$ diverges to $-\infty$) but an increase in ξ typically decreases $\mathrm{EU_H}$ because q decreases with ξ. This happens for all simulations performed. Note that $\mathrm{EU_H}$ tends to also increase with the risk premium or, equivalently, decrease with $\bar{p} = \bar{\theta} - \Gamma q$. Indeed, when a hedger hedges his endowment the return is precisely p and a higher expected level of p increases the risk borne by the agent.[39]

[39] If $\theta = z$, so that $\sigma_{\theta z} = \sigma_\theta^2$, and the endowment is completely hedged $x_j = -u_j$, then $W_j = u_j z + (\theta - p)x_j = u_j p$.

Interestingly, when the precision of information is high, market depth increases with ξ but EU_H decreases. This means that looking at the usual cost of trading in noise trading models is misleading and this happens precisely when the demands of hedgers are close to the noise trader form, that is, when ξ_u/ρ_H is small.

In short, for a very wide range of parameter values we have that more private information is Pareto inferior because it aggravates the adverse selection problem and reduces the hedging effectiveness of the futures market and production. This means that all market participants would prefer that there is no private information in the market. The question arises whether this is true also with public disclosure of information. With public disclosure adverse selection is eliminated and this should increase market depth but the impact on production is ambiguous *ex ante*. The reason is that a public signal also reduces insurance opportunities (this is nothing else but the "Hirshleifer effect," see section 3.1). Again there are scenarios where all market participants end up losing with more public information. (See exercise 4.6.)[40]

4.4.5 Summary

The typical (and unmodeled) noise trader behavior corresponds to risk-averse rational hedgers with a high degree of risk aversion and/or when correlation between individual and aggregate endowment shocks is very low. This implies that the usual welfare analysis of noise trader models based on the losses that those traders make, and which depends on market depth, may be misleading. Indeed, market depth may increase but the expected utility of hedgers may still decrease. Private information creates adverse selection and may decrease the welfare of all market participants because it reduces the hedging effectiveness of the market. The same may happen with public information because of the destruction of insurance opportunities. The consequence is that having more information may yield Pareto inferior outcomes.

4.5 Summary

In this chapter we have examined static financial market models in the frame of rational expectations with asymmetric information. A general theme of the chapter is that market microstructure matters when it comes to the informational properties of prices in financial markets and how uninformed traders protect themselves from informed trading by making the market less liquid. A recurrent result is how risk aversion for competitive traders makes agents cautious when trading and responding to their private signals. In chapter 5 we will

[40] Interestingly, the welfare effects of public information depend on whether information is dispersed or not. Diamond (1985), in a variation of the models of Diamond and Verrecchia (1981) and Verrecchia (1982) with endogenous dispersed information, finds that releasing public information improves welfare because it reduces costly private-information acquisition by traders and makes traders's beliefs more homogeneous.

see how market power for strategic traders plays a similar role to risk aversion for competitive traders.

The main insights from the standard model with a unique linear REE are as follows.

- Prices reflect private information about the returns of the asset through the trades of investors but typically not perfectly. Indeed, prices reflect the fundamentals and noise or shocks to preferences of investors.
- A perfect informationally efficient market is impossible whenever information is costly to acquire.
- In the presence of traders with private information, market makers and other uninformed agents face an adverse selection problem and protect themselves by increasing the bid–ask spread and reducing market depth. If market makers are risk averse, then price volatility increases with their degree of risk aversion.
- The informativeness of prices increases with the risk-tolerance-adjusted informational advantage of informed traders, with the proportion of informed, and decreases with the volatility of fundamentals and the amount of noise trading.
- Information acquisition displays strategic substitutability.
- The presence of a risk-neutral competitive fringe of market makers with no privileged information makes prices reflect all public available information. That is, it makes the market a semi-strong informationally efficient market and the price of the risky asset equals the expected fundamental value given publicly available information.
- In a semi-strong efficient market:
    - Prices are volatile because they are informative about fundamentals.
    - Total volatility is constant and a more informative price just advances the resolution of uncertainty.
- Risk-averse traders using market orders are more cautious than limit-order traders because the former bear price risk. As a consequence, if the proportion of traders using limit orders or demand schedules (instead of market orders) increases, prices are more informative and more volatile (and the impact on market depth is ambiguous).
- Whenever there is a differential fixed cost to submit a demand schedule instead of a market order, traders with a large risk-tolerance-adjusted informational advantage place demand schedules while the others place market orders.
- Noise trader demands are close to demands by rational utility maximizing hedgers with a large degree of risk aversion. It is then possible that market depth increases coexist with decreases in the expected utility of hedgers.

- An increase in either private or public information may be Pareto inferior because the hedging effectiveness of the market is impaired. With private information this happens because of adverse selection and with public information because of the Hirshleifer effect.

Departures from the standard model (such as having private signals on noise trading, or correlation between individual and aggregate endowment shocks, fundamentals and noise trading, or error terms of private and public signals) introduce multiple (linear) equilibria in the financial market and, potentially, strategic complementarity in information acquisition. Another way to obtain strategic complementarity in information acquisition is with economies of scale in information production. The end result may be multiple equilibria in both the financial market and the market for information acquisition. This allows for a rich pattern of explanations of different phenomena in financial markets.

4.6 Appendix

Claim (section 4.2.2). The expected utility of an informed trader conditional on public information (the price) and taking into account the cost k of getting the signal is given by

$$E[U(\pi_{\mathrm{I}}) \mid p] = \mathrm{e}^{\rho k}\sqrt{\frac{\mathrm{var}[\theta \mid s]}{\mathrm{var}[\theta \mid p]}}(E[U(\pi_{\mathrm{U}}) \mid p]).$$

Proof. We know from section 4.2.2 that

$$E[U(\pi_{\mathrm{I}}) \mid p] = \mathrm{e}^{\rho k}E\left[-\exp\left\{-\frac{(s-p)^2}{2\sigma_\varepsilon^2}\right\} \Bigm| p\right].$$

Let $y = (s-p)/\sqrt{2\sigma_\varepsilon^2}$. It follows that

$$E[y \mid p] = \frac{1}{\sqrt{2\sigma_\varepsilon^2}}(E[s \mid p] - p) = \frac{1}{\sqrt{2\sigma_\varepsilon^2}}(E[\theta \mid p] - p)$$

($E[s \mid p] = E[E[\theta \mid s] \mid p] = E[\theta \mid p]$ because $s = E[\theta \mid s]$ and p is a noisy version of s) and

$$\mathrm{var}[y \mid p] = \frac{1}{2\sigma_\varepsilon^2}\mathrm{var}[s \mid p] = \frac{1}{2\sigma_\varepsilon^2}(\mathrm{var}[\theta \mid p] - \sigma_\varepsilon^2)$$

since from $\theta = s + \varepsilon$ and the independence of s and ε we have that $\mathrm{var}[\theta \mid p] = \mathrm{var}[s \mid p] + \sigma_\varepsilon^2 = \mathrm{var}[s \mid p] + \mathrm{var}[\theta \mid s]$.

Recall that (see section 10.2.4) if y conditional on p is normally distributed with mean $E[y \mid p]$ and $\mathrm{var}[y \mid p]$, then

$$E[\mathrm{e}^{-y^2} \mid p] = \frac{1}{\sqrt{1 + 2\,\mathrm{var}[y \mid p]}}\exp\left\{-\frac{(E[y \mid p])^2}{1 + 2\,\mathrm{var}[y \mid p]}\right\}$$

and it follows that

$$E\left[\exp\left\{-\frac{(s-p)^2}{2\sigma_\varepsilon^2}\right\} \Bigm| p\right] = \sqrt{\frac{\mathrm{var}[\theta \mid s]}{\mathrm{var}[\theta \mid p]}}\exp\left\{-\frac{(E[\theta \mid p] - p)^2}{2\,\mathrm{var}[\theta \mid p]}\right\}.$$

The result follows since

$$E[U(\pi_U) \mid p] = -\exp\left\{-\frac{(E[\theta \mid p] - p)^2}{2\operatorname{var}[\theta \mid p]}\right\}.$$

□

4.7 Exercises

4.1 (*a paradoxical fully revealing equilibrium*). Consider a variation of the CARA-normal model of section 4.2.1 with n informed traders, no uninformed traders, and no noise (with $u = \bar{u} < 0$ with probability 1). Find a linear fully revealing REE using Grossman's method (using the competitive equilibrium of an artificial shared-information economy). Check the result with the usual procedure of positing a linear REE price function and work through the optimization and updating rules of traders. Check that in equilibrium the demands of traders are independent of private signals and the price. How can prices be a sufficient statistic for the information of traders and the demand of traders be independent of the signals of traders?

Solution. In a shared-information economy the CARA demand of a trader is $(E[\theta \mid \tilde{s}_n] - p)/\rho_I \operatorname{var}[\theta \mid \tilde{s}_n]$, where $\tilde{s}_n \equiv (1/n)\sum_{i=1}^n s_i$ is a sufficient statistic for the signals of traders. Market clearing then implies that $p = E[\theta \mid \tilde{s}_n] + \rho_I \operatorname{var}[\theta \mid \tilde{s}_n]\bar{u}/n$, which again is a sufficient statistic for the signals of traders (because $E[\theta \mid \tilde{s}_n]$ is). It is immediate that this price is an FRREE price for the asymmetric-information economy. The properties of the demands follow by simple manipulation. (See Grossman 1976.)

4.2 (*derivation of CARA demands*). Consider the competitive market in section 4.3 and derive the demands for both classes of informed traders.

Solution. At a linear equilibrium both θ and p are normally distributed. The demand of a trader with information set G, with $G = \{s_i, p\}$ if the trader places a demand schedule and $G = \{s_i\}$ if he places a market order, is then $E[(\theta - p) \mid G]/\rho \operatorname{var}[(\theta - p) \mid G]$. Given that $E[\theta \mid p] = p$ we have that $E[\theta \mid s_i, p] = (\tau_\varepsilon s_i + \tau p)/(\tau_\varepsilon + \tau)$ and $(\operatorname{var}[\theta \mid s_i, p])^{-1} = \tau_\varepsilon + \tau$. It then follows that $E[\theta \mid s_i, p] - p = \tau_\varepsilon(\tau_\varepsilon + \tau)^{-1}(s_i - p)$, and therefore $X(s_i, p) = \rho^{-1}\tau_\varepsilon(s_i - p)$ for a trader placing a demand schedule. For traders placing market orders we find that $E[\theta - p \mid s_i] = (1 - \lambda A)\tau_\varepsilon(\tau_\varepsilon + \tau_\theta)^{-1}(s_i - \bar{\theta})$ and $\operatorname{var}[\theta - p \mid s_i] = (1 - \lambda A)^2 \operatorname{var}[\theta \mid s_i] + \lambda^2\sigma_u^2$ with $\operatorname{var}[\theta \mid s_i] = (\tau_\varepsilon + \tau_\theta)^{-1}$. It then follows that $Y(s_i) = E[\theta - p \mid s_i]/(\rho \operatorname{var}[\theta - p \mid s_i]) = (\rho(\sigma_\varepsilon^2 + \operatorname{var}[p]))^{-1}(s_i - \bar{\theta})$ and therefore c is given implicitly by $c = (\rho(\sigma_\varepsilon^2 + \operatorname{var}[p]))^{-1}$. This is a cubic equation $c = a\tau_\theta/(\tau_\theta + \tau_\varepsilon\tau_u A^2/\tau)$, with $A = \nu a + (1 - \nu)c$ and $a = \rho^{-1}\tau_\varepsilon$, with a unique solution in c.

4.3 (*trading volume in a competitive market*). In the same market as in exercise 4.2, show that when all informed traders use demand schedules ($\nu = 1$) the expected (aggregate) volume traded by informed agents is $E[|\int_0^1 X(s_i, p)\,di|] = (2/\pi)^{1/2} a\sqrt{\tau^{-1}}$.

Solution. For z normal with mean 0 and standard deviation σ_z we know that $E[|z|] = (2/\pi)^{1/2}\sigma_z$. We then have $\text{var}[\int_0^1 X(s_i, p)\,\mathrm{d}i] = a^2\,\text{var}[\theta - p]$ and it is easily checked that when $p = E[\theta \mid p]$, $\text{var}[\theta - p] = \sigma_\theta^2 - \text{var}[p] = \text{var}[\theta \mid p]$. Indeed, the first equality follows from $\text{var}[\theta - p] = \text{var}[\theta] + \text{var}[p] - 2\,\text{cov}[\theta, p]$ and the projection theorem for normal random variables: $\text{cov}[\theta - E[\theta \mid p], E[\theta \mid p]] = 0$ because with $E[\theta \mid p] = p$ we have that $\text{cov}[\theta, p] = \text{cov}[E[\theta \mid p], p] = \text{var}[p]$. For the second equality we know that $\text{var}[p] = \sigma_\theta^2 - \text{var}[\theta \mid p]$.

4.4 (*comparative statics of basic market parameters*). In the same market as in exercise 4.2, perform a comparative statics analysis of the relevant market parameters when all informed traders use market orders ($\nu = 0$) and interpret the results.

Solution (see Vives 1995b, proposition 2.2).

(i) The responsiveness of informed agents to private signals (c) decreases with ρ, σ_ε^2, and σ_θ^2 and increases with σ_u^2.

(ii) The informativeness of the price (τ) decreases with ρ, σ_ε^2, σ_θ^2, and σ_u^2.

(iii) The *ex ante* volatility of prices ($\text{var}[p]$) decreases with ρ, σ_ε^2, and σ_u^2 and increases with σ_θ^2.

(iv) The (expected) volume traded by informed agents ($E[|\int_0^1 X(s_i)\,\mathrm{d}i|] = (2/\pi)^{1/2} c\sigma_\theta$) decreases with ρ and σ_ε^2 and increases with σ_u^2.

Interpretation. The effects with respect to ρ and σ_ε^2 accord with intuition. Increases in σ_θ^2 decrease the price precision for a fixed c and induce market makers to raise λ. Informed agents respond by trading less intensely accentuating the decrease in τ. The *ex ante* volatility of prices is positively related to their informativeness: $\text{var}[p] = \tau_\theta^{-1} - \tau^{-1}$. Therefore, all factors (except σ_θ^2) which increase τ will also increase $\text{var}[p]$. A higher σ_θ^2 has a double impact on $\text{var}[p]$: a negative indirect effect, since it decreases τ, and a positive direct effect which dominates. Increases in noise (σ_u^2) increase c since in equilibrium they induce a lower volatility of prices. Noise has a negative direct effect on the informativeness of prices (that is, for a constant parameter a) and a positive indirect effect through c. The direct effect dominates. This is due to the presence of risk aversion.

****4.5** (*expected utilities in the futures market model*). Consider the model in section 4.4 and first derive the expressions for the expected utility of the informed $J_{\text{I}}(q)$ as stated in section 4.4.4 with

$$d = (1-\xi)\frac{(-E[X_{\text{I}}(s,p)]/q + \rho_{\text{I}}(\xi/\sigma_\theta^2)\,\text{cov}[E[\theta \mid s], X_{\text{I}}(s,p)])^2}{1 + \text{var}[X_{\text{I}}(s,p)]}$$

$$= (1-\xi)\frac{\left(1 - \dfrac{\Gamma}{\rho_{\text{I}}(1-\xi)\sigma_\theta^2} + \dfrac{\xi}{(1-\xi)\sigma_\theta^2}\left(\xi - \dfrac{a}{\Lambda}\right)\right)^2}{1 + \dfrac{(\xi\Lambda - a)^2\sigma_\theta^2/\xi + \delta^2\sigma_u^2}{\Lambda^2(1-\xi)\sigma_\theta^2}},$$

where the endogenous parameters a, Λ, and Γ are as in proposition 4.3. Show that $d \to 0$ as $\xi \to 1$. Why is this so?

Show next that the expected utility of an uninformed trader is given by

$$\mathrm{EU_U} \equiv E[-\mathrm{e}^{-\rho_\mathrm{U} W_\mathrm{U}}] = -|\mathrm{SG_U}| \exp\left\{-\frac{1}{2}\frac{(\Gamma q)^2}{\mathrm{var}[E[\theta \mid p] - p] + \mathrm{var}[\theta \mid p]}\right\},$$

where

$$|\mathrm{SG_U}| = \left\{1 + \frac{\mathrm{var}[E[\theta \mid p] - p]}{\mathrm{var}[\theta \mid p]}\right\}^{-1/2},$$

$$\mathrm{var}[E[\theta \mid p] - p] = \frac{[\delta^2\sigma_u^2 + a^2(\sigma_\theta^2 + \sigma_\varepsilon^2) - a\Lambda\sigma_\theta^2]^2}{\Lambda^2[\delta^2\sigma_u^2 + a^2(\sigma_\theta^2 + \sigma_\varepsilon^2)]}.$$

Finally, derive the following expression for the *ex ante* expected utility of a hedger with endowment shock u_j when he does not trade in the futures market and his wealth is $u_j z$:

$$-\left[1 - \rho_\mathrm{H}^2\sigma_z^2\frac{\sigma_u^2}{\xi_u}\right]^{-1/2} \exp\left\{\frac{\rho_\mathrm{H}^2\bar{z}^2\sigma_u^2}{2(\xi_u - \rho_\mathrm{H}^2\sigma_z^2\sigma_u^2)}\right\},$$

provided that $\rho_\mathrm{H}^2\sigma_z^2\sigma_{u_j}^2 = \rho_\mathrm{H}^2\sigma_z^2\sigma_u^2/\xi_u < 1$. Otherwise, the expected utility diverges to $-\infty$.

Hint. Use the following result (see section 10.2.4) and follow a similar procedure as in the proof of the claim in section 4.2.2. If $x \sim N(\bar{x}, \sigma_x^2)$ and $y \sim N(\bar{y}, \sigma_y^2)$, then

$$E[\mathrm{e}^{x-y^2}] = \frac{1}{\sqrt{1 + 2\sigma_y^2}} \exp\left\{\bar{x} + \frac{\sigma_x^2}{2} - \frac{(\bar{y} + \mathrm{cov}[x, y])^2}{1 + 2\sigma_y^2}\right\}.$$

For example, from $X_\mathrm{U}(p) = (E[\theta \mid p] - p)/(\rho_\mathrm{U}\,\mathrm{var}[\theta \mid p])$ obtain

$$E[-\mathrm{e}^{\rho_\mathrm{U} W_\mathrm{U}} \mid p] = -\exp\left\{-\frac{(E[\theta \mid p] - p)^2}{2\,\mathrm{var}[\theta \mid p]}\right\}.$$

To obtain the unconditional expected utility it suffices to apply the result taking $z = 0$ and $y = (E[\theta \mid p] - p)/\sqrt{2\,\mathrm{var}[\theta \mid p]}$, so that

$$\begin{aligned} &E[-\mathrm{e}^{-\rho_\mathrm{U} W_\mathrm{U}}] \\ &\quad = E[E[-\mathrm{e}^{-\rho_\mathrm{U} W_\mathrm{U}} \mid p]] \\ &\quad = E\left\{-\exp\left\{-\frac{(E[\theta \mid p] - p)^2}{2\,\mathrm{var}[\theta \mid p]}\right\}\right\} \\ &\quad = -\left\{1 + \frac{\mathrm{var}[E[\theta \mid p] - p]}{\mathrm{var}[\theta \mid p]}\right\}^{-1/2} \exp\left\{-\frac{1}{2}\frac{(E[E(\theta \mid p) - p])^2}{\mathrm{var}[\theta \mid p] + \mathrm{var}[E[\theta \mid p] - p]}\right\} \end{aligned}$$

and the result follows since $E[E(\theta \mid p) - p] = \bar{\theta} - \bar{p} = \Gamma q$. (See Medrano and Vives (2007) for details on the computation of other expected utilities.)

****4.6** (*public disclosure and the Hirshleifer effect*). Consider the model in section 4.4 and assume now that the signal received by producers becomes public information at $t = 1$.

(i) Show that if $\xi < 1$ then there is a unique linear REE in the futures market characterized by

$$X_{\mathrm{U}}(s,p) = a_{\mathrm{U}}(s-\bar{\theta}) + b_{\mathrm{U}}(\bar{\theta}-p),$$
$$X_{\mathrm{H}}(u) = a_{\mathrm{H}}(s-\bar{\theta}) + b_{\mathrm{H}}(\bar{\theta}-p) - \delta u,$$
$$X_{\mathrm{I}}(s,p) = a_{\mathrm{I}}(s-\bar{\theta}) + b_{\mathrm{I}}(\bar{\theta}-p) - q,$$
$$p = E[\theta \mid s] - \frac{q}{\Lambda} - \frac{\delta u}{\Lambda},$$

where

$$a_{\mathrm{I}} = \frac{\xi}{\rho_{\mathrm{I}}(1-\xi)\sigma_\theta^2}, \quad b_{\mathrm{I}} = \frac{1}{\rho_{\mathrm{I}}(1-\xi)\sigma_\theta^2}, \quad a_{\mathrm{U}} = \frac{\xi}{\rho_{\mathrm{U}}(1-\xi)\sigma_\theta^2},$$
$$b_{\mathrm{U}} = \frac{1}{\rho_{\mathrm{U}}(1-\xi)\sigma_\theta^2}, \quad a_{\mathrm{H}} = \frac{\xi}{\rho_{\mathrm{H}}(1-\xi)\sigma_\theta^2}, \quad b_{\mathrm{H}} = \frac{1}{\rho_{\mathrm{H}}(1-\xi)\sigma_\theta^2},$$
$$\delta = \frac{\sigma_{\theta z}}{\sigma_\theta^2}, \quad \text{and} \quad \Lambda = \frac{1}{(1-\xi)\sigma_\theta^2}\left(\frac{1}{\rho_{\mathrm{I}}} + \frac{1}{\rho_{\mathrm{U}}} + \frac{1}{\rho_{\mathrm{H}}}\right).$$

The equilibrium level of production chosen is

$$q = \frac{\bar{\theta} - c_1}{c_2 + \rho_{\mathrm{I}}\sigma_\theta^2(1-d)},$$

where

$$d = (1-\xi)\left(\frac{1/\rho_{\mathrm{U}} + 1/\rho_{\mathrm{H}}}{1/\rho_{\mathrm{I}} + 1/\rho_{\mathrm{U}} + 1/\rho_{\mathrm{H}}}\right)^2 \times \frac{1}{1 + (1-\xi)\sigma_\theta^2(1/\rho_{\mathrm{I}} + 1/\rho_{\mathrm{U}} + 1/\rho_{\mathrm{H}})^{-2}\delta^2\sigma_u^2}.$$

(ii) What happens when $\xi = 1$?

(iii) Show that if ξ increases, then:

(a) Trading intensities increase.
(b) The market becomes deeper (Λ increases).
(c) The level of production decreases.
(d) The futures price becomes more informative.
(e) The risk premium (q/Λ) is lower.
(f) The expected utilities of both producers and market makers decrease.

(iv) Conjecture the comparative statics properties of price volatility and the expected utility of hedgers with respect to ξ.

(v) How do you interpret the results? What happens to the hedging effectiveness of the market as ξ tends to 1? Is it possible that, by providing more public information, all traders lose? Is it possible that in a deeper market hedgers see their expected utility diminished?

(vi) Let $\sigma_{\theta z}/\sigma_\theta^2 = 1$ and $\rho_H \to \infty$ so that we are in the noise trader case, and $\rho_U \to \infty$. Then the depth of the market is $\rho_I^{-1}/((1-\xi)\sigma_\theta^2) = \rho_I^{-1}(\tau_\theta + \tau_z)$. Show that this is larger than when there is dispersed information (i.e., than λ^{-1} in proposition 4.1 when $\mu = 1$).

Solution. See Medrano and Vives (2007). The relationship between the expected utility of hedgers and ξ is ambiguous.

4.7 (*the effects of overconfidence*). Speculate about the consequences for price informativeness, market depth, and traded volume of the presence of overconfident informed traders (this is, the situation where an informed trader believes that the precision of his private signal is larger than it actually is). Do the exercise assuming first that the information endowments are given and second allowing for endogenous information acquisition.

Hints. Kyle and Wang (1997), Odean (1998), and Benos (1998), in (strategic) models where informed traders submit market orders, find a positive effect of overconfidence on the above-mentioned market parameters because of the positive externality overconfident traders have on other investors. García et al. (2007) find in a competitive model à la Grossman–Stiglitz an irrelevance result of overconfidence on informational efficiency when endogenous information acquisition is allowed. The reason is that when information acquisition decisions are strategic substitutes rational traders purchase less information in the presence of overconfident traders (and exactly compensate for the increase in price precision because of the presence of overconfident traders). Other applications with overconfident traders are Caballé and Sàkovics (2003) and Daniel et al. (1998, 2001).

References

Admati, A. 1985. A noisy rational expectations equilibrium for multi-asset securities markets. *Econometrica* 53:629–57.

——. 1989. Information in financial markets: the rational expectations approach. In *Financial Markets and Incomplete Information* (ed. S. Bhattacharya and G. M. Constantinides), pp. 139–52. Totowa, NJ: Rowman and Littlefield.

Akerlof, G. 1970. The market for "lemons": quality uncertainty and the market mechanism. *Quarterly Journal of Economics* 84:488–500.

Anderson, R., and H. Sonnenschein. 1982. On the existence of rational expectations equilibrium. *Journal of Economic Theory* 26:261–78.

Bagehot, W. 1971. The only game in town. *Financial Analysts Journal* 22:12–14.

Barberis, N., A. Shleifer, and J. Wurgler. 2005. Comovement. *Journal of Financial Economics* 75:283–318.

Barlevy, G., and P. Veronesi. 2000. Information acquisition in financial markets. *Review of Economic Studies* 67:79–90.

——. 2007. Information acquisition in financial markets: a correction. Chicago Fed Working Paper 2007-06.

Battalio, R., J. Green, and R. Jennings. 1997. Do competing specialists and preferencing dealers affect market quality? *Review of Financial Studies* 10:969–93.

Benos, A. 1998. Aggressiveness and survival of overconfident traders. *Journal of Financial Markets* 1:353–83.

Biais, B., P. Hillion, and C. Spatt. 1995. An empirical analysis of the limit order book and the order flow in the Paris Bourse. *Journal of Finance* 50:1655–89.

Biais, B., L. Glosten, and C. Spatt. 2005. Market microstructure: a survey of microfoundations, empirical results, and policy implications. *Journal of Financial Markets* 8:217–64.

Bray, M. 1981. Futures trading, rational expectations, and the efficient market hypothesis. *Econometrica* 49:575–96.

——. 1985. Rational expectations, information and asset markets: an introduction. *Oxford Economic Papers* 37:161–95.

Brown, D. P., and Z. M. Zhang. 1997. Market orders and market efficiency. *Journal of Finance* 52:277–308.

Brunnermeier, M. 2001. *Asset Pricing under Asymmetric Information.* Oxford University Press.

Caballé, J., and J. Sàkovics. 2003. Speculating against an overconfident market. *Journal of Financial Markets* 6:199–225.

Chakravaty, S., and C. Holden. 1995. An integrated model of market and limit orders. *Journal of Financial Intermediation* 4:213–41.

Chamley, C. 2007. Strategic substitutability in "Information acquisition in financial markets" by Barlevy and Veronesi (2000). Mimeo.

Chen, Q., I. Goldstein, and W. Jiang. 2007. Price informativeness and investment sensitivity to stock price. *Review of Financial Studies* 20:619–50.

Daniel, K., D. Hirshleifer, and A. Subrahmanyam. 1998. A theory of overconfidence, self attribution, and security market under- and over-reaction. *Journal of Finance* 53:1839–85.

——. 2001. Overconfidence, arbitrage, and equilibrium asset pricing. *Journal of Finance* 56:921–65.

DeGroot, M. 1970. *Optimal Statistical Decisions.* New York: McGraw-Hill.

DeMarzo, P., and C. Skiadas. 1999. Aggregation, determinacy, and informational efficiency for a class of economies with asymmetric information. *Journal of Economic Theory* 80:123–52.

Diamond, D. W. 1985. Optimal release of information by firms. *Journal of Finance* 60: 1071–94.

Diamond, D. W., and R. E. Verrecchia. 1981. Information aggregation in a noisy rational expectations economy. *Journal of Financial Economics* 9:221–35.

Dow, J., and G. Gorton. 1997. Stock market efficiency and economic efficiency: is there a connection? *Journal of Finance* 52:1087–129.

Easley, D., and M. O'Hara. 2004. Information and the cost of capital. *Journal of Finance* 59:1553–83.

Foucault, T. 1999. Order flow composition and trading costs in a dynamic limit order market. *Journal of Financial Markets* 2:99–134.

Ganguli, J., and L. Yang. 2006. Complementarities and multiplicity with a common endowment shock. Mimeo.

García, D., B. Urosevic, and F. Sangiorgi. 2007. Overconfidence and market efficiency with heterogeneous agents. *Economic Theory* 30:313–36.

Glosten, L., and L. Harris. 1988. Estimating the components of the bid-ask spread. *Journal of Financial Economics* 21:123–42.

Glosten, L., and P. R. Milgrom. 1985. Bid, ask and transaction prices in a specialist market with heterogeneously informed traders. *Journal of Financial Economics* 17:71–100.

Goettler, R., C. Parlour, and U. Rajan. 2005. Equilibrium in a dynamic limit order market. *Journal of Finance* 60:2149–92.

Grossman, S. 1976. On the efficiency of competitive stock markets where traders have diverse information. *Journal of Finance* 31:573–85.

Grossman, S., and J. Stiglitz. 1980. On the impossibility of informationally efficient markets. *American Economic Review* 70:393–408.

Harris, L. 2003. *Trading and Exchanges. Market Microstructure for Practitioners.* Oxford University Press.

Harris, L., and J. Hasbrouck. 1996. Market vs. limit orders: the SuperDOT evidence on order submission strategy. *Journal of Financial and Quantitative Analysis* 31:213–31.

Hasbrouck, J. 2007. *Empirical Market Microstructure.* Oxford University Press.

Hellwig, M. F. 1980. On the aggregation of information in competitive markets. *Journal of Economic Theory* 22:477–98.

Ho, T., and H. Stoll. 1983. The dynamics of dealer markets under competition. *Journal of Finance* 38:1053–74.

Kodres, L., and M. Pritsker. 2002. A rational expectation model of financial contagion. *Journal of Finance* 57:769–99.

Kyle, A. S. 1985. Continuous auctions and insider trading. *Econometrica* 53:1315–35.

——. 1989. Informed speculation with imperfect competition. *Review of Economic Studies* 56:317–56.

Kyle, A. S., and F. A. Wang. 1997. Speculation duopoly with agreement to disagree. *Journal of Finance* 52:2073–90.

Kyle, A. S., and W. Xiong. 2001. Contagion as a wealth effect. *Journal of Finance* 56:1401–39.

Lee, C., B. Mucklow, and M. J. Ready. 1993. Spreads, depths, and the impact of earnings information: an intraday analysis. *Review of Financial Studies* 6:345–74.

Leland, H. E. 1992. Insider trading: should it be prohibited? *Journal of Political Economy* 100:859–87.

Lundholm, R.. 1988. Price-signal relations in the presence of correlated public and private information. *Journal of Accounting Research* 26:107–18.

Lyons, R. K. 2001. *The Microstructure Approach to Exchange Rates.* Cambridge, MA: MIT Press.

Madhavan, A. 2000. Market microstructure: a survey. *Journal of Financial Markets* 3: 205–58.

Manzano, C. 1999. Price-signal relations in an imperfectly competitive financial market with public and private information. *Journal of Accounting Research* 37:451–63.

Mas-Colell, A., M. D. Whinston, and J. R. Green. 1995. *Microeconomic Theory.* Oxford University Press.

Medrano, L. A. 1996. Market versus limit orders in an imperfectly competitive security. UPF Working Paper 165.

Medrano, L. A., and X. Vives. 2007. Information, hedging, and welfare. Mimeo.

Muendler, M. 2007. The possibility of informationally efficient markets. *Journal of Economic Theory* 133:467–83.

Odean, T. 1998. Volume, volatility, price and profit when all traders are above average. *Journal of Finance* 53:1887–934.

O'Hara, M. 1994. *Market Microstructure Theory*. Cambridge: Blackwell.

Pagano, M. 1989. Endogenous market thinness and stock market liquidity. *Review of Economic Studies* 56:269–88.

Palomino, F. 2001. Informational efficiency: ranking markets. *Economic Theory* 18:683–700.

Parlour, C., and D. Seppi. Forthcoming. Limit order markets: a survey. In *Handbook of Financial Intermediation and Banking* (ed. A. W. A. Boot and A. V. Thakor). New York: Elsevier Science.

Roll, R.. 1984. A simple implicit measure of the effective bid–ask spread in an efficient market. *Journal of Finance* 39:1127–39.

Rothschild, M., and J. Stiglitz. 1976. Equilibrium in competitive insurance markets: an essay on the economics of imperfect information. *Quarterly Journal of Economics* 90:629–49.

Sarkar, A. 1994. On the equivalence of noise trader and hedger models in market microstructure. *Journal of Financial Intermediation* 3:204–12.

Subrahmanyam, A. 1991. Risk aversion, market liquidity, and price efficiency. *Review of Financial Studies* 4:417–41.

Subrahmanyam, A., and S. Titman. 1999. The going-public decision and the development of financial markets. *Journal of Finance* 54:1045–82.

Veldkamp, L. 2006. Information markets and the comovement of asset prices. *Review of Economic Studies* 73:823–45.

Verrecchia, R. 1982. Information acquisition in a noisy rational expectations economy. *Econometrica* 50:1415–30.

Vives, X. 1995a. Short-term investment and the informational efficiency of the market. *Review of Financial Studies* 8:125–60.

——. 1995b. The speed of information revelation in a financial market mechanism. *Journal of Economic Theory* 67:1, 178–204.

——. 1999. *Oligopoly Pricing: Old Ideas and New Tools*. Cambridge, MA: MIT Press.

Wald, J. K., and H. T. Horrigan. 2005. Optimal limit order choice. *Journal of Business* 78:597–619.

Walras, L. 1889. *Eléments d'Économie Politique Pure, ou Théorie de la Richesse Sociale* (1st edn, 1874, Lausanne: Corbaz), 2nd rev. edn. Lausanne: Rouge.

Yuan, K. 2005. Asymmetric price movements and borrowing constraints: a rational expectations equilibrium model of crises, contagion, and confusion. *Journal of Finance* 60:379–411.

5
Strategic Traders in Financial Markets

In this chapter we review basic static models of financial markets with asymmetric information in the presence of strategic traders. We are interested in finding out the impact of large traders on the informational properties of prices and other main market quality parameters. We will do so in a variety of market microstructures where traders compete simultaneously in demand schedules, as well as those in which informed traders move first and those in which market makers move first. We will also look at the consequences of traders using market orders and of discriminatory pricing.

Hellwig (1980) pointed at the "schizophrenia" problem of price-taking behavior in a competitive rational expectations equilibrium (REE) with a finite number of traders. Traders, when submitting their demands, would take into account the information content of the price but not the price impact of their trade. The problem disappears in a large market as we have seen in chapters 3 and 4. Another solution is proposed in Kyle (1989) modeling directly the strategic equilibrium where traders are aware of the price impact of their trades and compete in demand schedules (in an REE with imperfect competition). The advantage of modeling strategic behavior is that it allows for the consideration of large traders. This is indeed realistic in circumstances such as some commodity futures markets, government security auctions, or when insiders in a firm have information about a merger prospect. Furthermore, some of the paradoxes of strongly informationally efficient markets (see chapter 3) are avoided. In a market with strategic traders, in contrast to a competitive market, even under risk neutrality large traders will have incentives to acquire costly information because they will refrain from trading too aggressively. The modeling of strategic traders with risk aversion is more complex, however, and therefore a relevant question is when we can use the shortcut of a competitive approximation to the strategic equilibrium.

In this chapter we will check that as the market grows large the strategic equilibria of finite economies converge to the competitive REE of an idealized limit continuum economy (as described, for example, by Admati (1985) or Vives (1995b)). Furthermore, we will find out when we can safely use competitive REE as an approximation of the "true" strategic equilibria. That is, when a competitive REE is close to the strategic equilibrium. The general result is that the competitive approximation works, even in a moderately sized market, basically when competitive traders have incentives to be restrained in their trading (e.g., when they are risk averse or have poor information).

A general theme of the chapter is to examine the trading incentives of agents with market power and the consequences for market quality parameters. A large informed trader may refrain from trading aggressively to avoid an adverse price and information leakage impact, and the market microstructure may affect his incentive. Market makers with market power may induce large spreads.

The plan of the chapter is as follows. We introduce strategic considerations by analyzing competition in demand schedules (Kyle 1989) and the speed of convergence to price-taking equilibria as the market grows large in section 5.1. We consider in section 5.2 the case where informed traders move first, distinguishing between the cases where they use market orders and demand schedules, and studying the potential multiplicity of equilibria. In section 5.3 we deal with the case where (uninformed) market makers move first and also consider discriminatory pricing schemes. As stated in chapter 4 when informed traders move first we have a signaling flavor in an order-driven market while when uninformed traders move first we have a screening flavor in a quote-driven market. Section 5.4 contains an application to the welfare analysis of insider trading.

5.1 Competition in Demand Schedules

In this section we examine the strategic counterpart of the competitive REE model studied in section 4.2.1 and how the strategic and competitive equilibria get closer as the size of the market increases and supports more informed traders. We are also interested in finding out whether competitive equilibria provide a good approximation to the strategic equilibrium in markets with a finite number of traders.

We start by discussing the potential multiplicity of equilibria in markets with strategic traders who compete in demand schedules. Think of a uniform price auction of a nonrandom amount of shares (or, equivalently, nonrandom liquidity trading $-\bar{u} > 0$, recall that u is the net demand of noise traders in our models in chapter 4) where a finite number of bidders compete in demand schedules. Wilson (1979) shows that the set of equilibria is very large because all that matters for a trader is to choose a demand schedule that goes through the optimal point in the residual supply curve it faces. Then some of the equilibria are very collusive even though the game is noncooperative and one-shot. The basic mechanism to sustain low prices is that bidders by submitting very steep demands schedules increase the effective marginal cost of other traders and induce them to compete more softly. A similar point is made in Grossman (1981) in the context of an oligopoly model. Klemperer and Mayer (1989) show that adding uncertainty in the Grossman model one can obtain a unique equilibrium in schedules provided the support of the uncertainty is unbounded. If uncertainty has bounded support, then the range of equilibria is reduced but still some may be quite collusive (see Vives 1999, section 7.2).

Back and Zender (1993), motivated by Treasury auctions, analyze a uniform-price auction where a finite number of bidders submit demand schedules which are nonincreasing left-continuous functions and there is a maximum quantity of the asset to be sold. The stop-out price for the auction is the highest price at which the aggregate excess demand is nonnegative (or is the reserve price in the auction if there is excess supply at all prices). The asset value may be random and bidders may receive signals about the value. Back and Zender find that there is a continuum of symmetric nonlinear equilibria, which are independent of the signals received by bidders, many of them very unfavorable for the seller. There is also a class of symmetric linear equilibria and many other equilibria (see Kremer and Nyborg (2004), who analyze the case of risk-neutral bidders when the value of the asset is known, and who also show that underpricing can be controlled by manipulating tick size and the quantity grid when both prices and quantities are discrete). If the supply of the asset is random, then the range of equilibria is reduced, but a continuum of equilibria remains since supply is bounded above, and the expected revenue of the seller increased. Many of the collusive equilibria in the uniform-price auction can be eliminated if the seller may withdraw part of the supply after observing the bids (Back and Zender 2001) and the seller can also enhance expected revenue by precommitting to an increasing supply curve that makes the amount on offer endogenous with the price (LiCalzi and Pavan 2005). In section 5.3.1 we provide some further comments on the implications of the potential multiplicity of equilibria when comparing uniform versus discriminatory auctions.

Kyle (1989) considers demand schedule competition when the uncertainty (noise trading) has unbounded support (and also introduces private information) and characterizes the unique symmetric linear equilibrium. We look at his model and variations in the rest of this section.

5.1.1 REE with Imperfect Competition

Kyle (1989) considers a strategic version of the competitive REE model studied in section 4.2.1. There are n informed and m uninformed traders or "market makers." All other assumptions in the model are the same as in section 4.2.1 (in particular, traders have CARA preferences and all random variables in the model are normally distributed). Traders submit simultaneously demand schedules to an auctioneer, who clears the market.

Kyle characterizes the symmetric linear Bayesian equilibria (SLBE) of the game. Consider the candidate SLBE

$$X_{\mathrm{I}}(s_i, p) = as_i - c_{\mathrm{I}}p + b_{\mathrm{I}} \quad \text{and} \quad X_{\mathrm{U}}(p) = b_{\mathrm{U}} - c_{\mathrm{U}}p.$$

From the market-clearing condition,

$$\sum_{i=1}^{n} X_{\mathrm{I}}(s_i, p) + mX_{\mathrm{U}}(p) + u = 0,$$

we obtain that

$$p = \lambda\Big(nb_{\mathrm{I}} + mb_{\mathrm{U}} + u + a\sum_{i=1}^{n} s_i\Big), \quad \text{where } \lambda = (nc_{\mathrm{I}} + mc_{\mathrm{U}})^{-1}.$$

As in chapter 4 we can take as an index of the depth of the market λ^{-1}. The price is informationally equivalent to $\hat{z} = (na)^{-1}(\lambda^{-1}p - nb_{\mathrm{I}} - mb_{\mathrm{U}}) = \theta + n^{-1}\sum_{i=1}^{n}\varepsilon_i + (an)^{-1}u$ and therefore (see section 10.2) the price precision $(\mathrm{var}[\theta \mid p])^{-1}$ is given by

$$\tau = \tau_\theta + \frac{1}{(n\tau_\varepsilon)^{-1} + (n^2a^2\tau_u)^{-1}} = \tau_\theta + \phi_{\mathrm{U}} n\tau_\varepsilon,$$

where $\phi_{\mathrm{U}} = na^2\tau_u/(\tau_\varepsilon + na^2\tau_u)$ represents the fraction of the precision of the informed traders revealed to the uninformed by the price. Similarly, letting

$$\hat{z}_i = \frac{\lambda^{-1}p - as_i - nb_{\mathrm{I}} - mb_{\mathrm{U}}}{(n-1)a} = \theta + \frac{1}{n-1}\sum_{k\neq i}\varepsilon_k + \frac{u}{(n-1)a},$$

we have that $\{s_i, p\}$ and $\{s_i, \hat{z}_i\}$ are informationally equivalent, and letting $\tau_{\mathrm{I}} = (\mathrm{var}[\theta \mid s_i, p])^{-1}$, we obtain that

$$\tau_{\mathrm{I}} = \tau_\theta + \tau_\varepsilon + \phi_{\mathrm{I}}(n-1)\tau_\varepsilon,$$

where $\phi_{\mathrm{I}} = (n-1)a^2\tau_u/(\tau_\varepsilon + (n-1)a^2\tau_u)$ represents the fraction of the precision of the other $n-1$ informed traders revealed to one informed trader by the price. When $\phi_{\mathrm{I}} = \phi_{\mathrm{U}} = 1$ prices are fully revealing.

It then follows from the informational equivalence of p and $\hat{z}$ that $E[\theta \mid p] = E[\theta \mid \hat{z}]$ and

$$E[\theta \mid p] = \frac{\tau_\theta}{\tau}\bar{\theta} + \frac{\phi_{\mathrm{U}}\tau_\varepsilon}{a\tau}(\lambda^{-1}p - nb_{\mathrm{I}} - mb_{\mathrm{U}}),$$

and from the informational equivalence of $\{s_i, p\}$ and $\{s_i, \hat{z}_i\}$ that $E[\theta \mid s_i, p] = E[\theta \mid s_i, \hat{z}_i]$ and

$$E[\theta \mid s_i, p] = \frac{\tau_\theta}{\tau_{\mathrm{I}}}\bar{\theta} + \frac{(1-\phi_{\mathrm{I}})\tau_\varepsilon}{\tau_{\mathrm{I}}}s_i + \frac{\phi_{\mathrm{I}}\tau_\varepsilon}{a\tau_{\mathrm{I}}}(\lambda^{-1}p - nb_{\mathrm{I}} - mb_{\mathrm{U}}).$$

In equilibrium each trader faces (and optimizes against) a linear residual supply curve. Consider informed trader i. Given the linear strategies of the rest of the traders, he faces the residual supply, $p = p_{\mathrm{I}i} + \lambda_{\mathrm{I}}x_i$, where $\lambda_{\mathrm{I}} = ((n-1)c_{\mathrm{I}} + mc_{\mathrm{U}})^{-1}$ and $p_{\mathrm{I}i}$ is a linear function of the signals of the other informed traders as well as u. This means, in particular, that conditioning on the price is the same as conditioning on the intercept of the residual supply. In this way informed trader i takes into account the influence of his action on the market price. Profits of speculator i are given by $\pi_i = (\theta - p_{\mathrm{I}i} - \lambda_{\mathrm{I}}x_i)x_i$ and are normally distributed conditional on $\{s_i, p_{\mathrm{I}i}\}$. We then have that CARA expected utility maximization is equivalent to choosing x_i to maximize

$$(E[\theta \mid p_{\mathrm{I}i}, s_i] - p_{\mathrm{I}i})x_i - (\lambda_{\mathrm{I}} + \tfrac{1}{2}\rho_{\mathrm{I}}\mathrm{var}[\theta \mid p_{\mathrm{I}i}, s_i])x_i^2.$$

The optimal solution (subject to the second-order condition $2\lambda_{\mathrm{I}} + \rho_{\mathrm{I}} \operatorname{var}[\theta \mid p_{\mathrm{I}i}, s_i] > 0$) yields

$$x_i = \frac{E[\theta \mid p_{\mathrm{I}i}, s_i] - p_{\mathrm{I}i}}{2\lambda_{\mathrm{I}} + \rho_{\mathrm{I}} \operatorname{var}[\theta \mid p_{\mathrm{I}i}, s_i]}. \qquad (*)$$

Given that $E[\theta \mid p_{\mathrm{I}i}, s_i] = E[\theta \mid p, s_i]$ (and $\operatorname{var}[\theta \mid p_{\mathrm{I}i}, s_i] = \operatorname{var}[\theta \mid p, s_i]$) and $p_{\mathrm{I}i} = p - \lambda_{\mathrm{I}} x_i$, we can solve for x_i in $(*)$ to obtain

$$X_{\mathrm{I}}(s_i, p) = \frac{E[\theta \mid s_i, p] - p}{\lambda_{\mathrm{I}} + \rho_{\mathrm{I}} \operatorname{var}[\theta \mid s_i, p]} \quad \text{with } \lambda_{\mathrm{I}} = ((n-1)c_{\mathrm{I}} + mc_{\mathrm{U}})^{-1}.$$

Similarly, for an uninformed trader we obtain (subject to the second-order condition $2\lambda_{\mathrm{U}} + \rho_{\mathrm{U}} \operatorname{var}[\theta \mid p] > 0$)

$$X_{\mathrm{U}}(p) = \frac{E[\theta \mid p] - p}{\lambda_{\mathrm{U}} + \rho_{\mathrm{U}} \operatorname{var}[\theta \mid p]} \quad \text{with } \lambda_{\mathrm{U}} = (nc_{\mathrm{I}} + (m-1)c_{\mathrm{U}})^{-1}.$$

Remark 5.1. There are two reasons why a trader restricts his trade: market power (λ_{I} or $\lambda_{\mathrm{U}} > 0$) and risk aversion (ρ_{I} or $\rho_{\mathrm{U}} > 0$). When $\lambda_{\mathrm{I}} = \lambda_{\mathrm{U}} = 0$ we are in a competitive (price-taking) model. A large trader restricts his trade because he takes into account the (adverse) price impact of his trade and the information leakage through the price that a larger responsiveness to private information entails.

The linear equilibrium can be characterized as usual from the expressions for the conditional expectations $E[\theta \mid p]$ and $E[\theta \mid s_i, p]$ and variances $\operatorname{var}[\theta \mid p]$ and $\operatorname{var}[\theta \mid s_i, p]$, obtaining a linear expression for each demand and identifying coefficients with the candidate equilibrium demands. In equilibrium we obtain, indeed, that the responsiveness to private information is positive, $a > 0$.

Kyle (1989, theorem 5.1) finds that a unique symmetric linear equilibrium exists if $n \geqslant 2$ and $m \geqslant 1$, or $n \geqslant 3$ and $m = 0$, or $n = 0$ and $m \geqslant 3$. If $n = 1$, an SLBE exists if m is large enough (however, it does not exist if, for a given $m \geqslant 2$, ρ_{U} is large enough). If $n + m \leqslant 2$, then an SLBE does not exist. Given that noise traders have inelastic demands, for a linear equilibrium to exist there must be enough competition among informed and/or uninformed agents. For example, with one speculator (informed or uninformed) expected profits blow up by effectively setting an infinite positive price when $u > 0$ and infinite negative price when $u < 0$.

The informational incidence parameter $\zeta \equiv \lambda a \tau_{\mathrm{I}} / \tau_{\varepsilon}$ is of interest. It represents the increase in the price when the informed trader's valuation of the asset goes up by one dollar as a result of a higher signal realization s_i (for the private estimate of trader i to go up by one dollar, the signal s_i must go up by $(\tau_{\varepsilon}/\tau_{\mathrm{I}})^{-1}$ and from $p = \lambda(nb_{\mathrm{I}} + mb_{\mathrm{U}} + u + a\sum_{i=1}^{n} s_i)$ prices increase by λa for every unit increase in s_i). In equilibrium it can be shown that $\zeta \leqslant \frac{1}{2}$ and prices never transmit more than half the pooled private information of traders. Indeed, we have that $\tau_{\mathrm{I}} = \tau_{\theta} + \tau_{\varepsilon} + \phi_{\mathrm{I}}(n-1)\tau_{\varepsilon}$ and $\tau = \tau_{\theta} + \phi_{\mathrm{U}} n \tau_{\varepsilon}$ with $0 \leqslant \phi_{\mathrm{I}} \leqslant \zeta \leqslant \frac{1}{2}$ and $\phi_{\mathrm{I}} < \phi_{\mathrm{U}}$.

The expected trading losses of noise traders are given by $\lambda\sigma_u^2$ (this is immediate from the price function and $E[(\theta - p)u] = -E[pu] = -\lambda E[u^2]$). As in chapter 4 noise traders lose money proportionally to their amount of trade and the market liquidity parameter λ.

The equilibrium with imperfect competition should be contrasted with the competitive (price-taking) one. At a price-taking Bayesian equilibrium, as in chapter 2, traders use strategies contingent on their information but do not perceive any influence of their actions on prices. At a price-taking Bayesian equilibrium an informed (uninformed) trader behaves as if $\lambda_{\mathrm{I}} = 0$ ($\lambda_{\mathrm{U}} = 0$). It is worth noting that the informational requirements for a competitive REE are less stringent than the ones for a demand schedule equilibrium. In the price-taking case each trader needs to know only, apart from his own preferences and the structure of the market, the statistical properties of prices (that is, the relationship between signals, noise trading, and prices). In the strategic case each trader needs to also know the strategies of other traders including the number of informed and uninformed in order to optimize against his residual supply schedule.

A price-taking Bayesian equilibrium (with a finite number of traders) exists whenever $\sigma_u^2 > 0$ and $\rho_{\mathrm{I}} > 0$. The informational parameter in the competitive market ($\phi_{\mathrm{I}}^{\mathrm{c}}$) is larger than with imperfect competition (ϕ_{I}): $\phi_{\mathrm{I}}^{\mathrm{c}} > \phi_{\mathrm{I}}$. Furthermore, as $(\rho_{\mathrm{I}}^2 \sigma_u^2)/\tau_\varepsilon(n-1) \to 0$ (that is, as the risk-bearing capacity of informed traders becomes large with respect to the amount of noise trading or the pooled information of informed traders grows), $\phi_{\mathrm{I}}^{\mathrm{c}}$ tends to 1 and prices becomes fully revealing at the price-taking outcome.

The following results for the imperfectly competitive market are also derived in Kyle (1989):

- With imperfect competition as $(\rho_{\mathrm{I}}^2 \sigma_u^2)/\tau_\varepsilon(n-1) \to 0$, $\zeta \to \frac{1}{2}$ (and ϕ_{I} remains below and bounded away from $\frac{1}{2}$). Prices are less informative with imperfect competition because in this case traders are aware that by trading more intensely on their private information more of it is leaked into the price. In fact, with imperfect competition as noise trading vanishes prices do not become fully revealing because informed traders refrain from trading. When there is no noise trading there is no trade because an *ex ante* Pareto-optimal allocation is already achieved with risk-averse traders and the no-trade theorem applies (see section 3.1).
- The fact that the informational efficiency parameters ϕ_{I} and ϕ_{U} are bounded above by $\frac{1}{2}$ does not prevent prices from becoming fully revealing in some circumstances. For example, as the informed speculators become perfectly informed ($\tau_\varepsilon \to \infty$) their trading intensity tends to ∞, price becomes fully revealing and the informed displace the uninformed in market trading (and all these conditions are equivalent). Furthermore, market depth λ^{-1} becomes infinite and the profits of the informed vanish.
- An increase in m (or a decrease in ρ_{U}) increases the parameters ϕ_{I} and ϕ_{U} because it flattens the residual supply schedule faced by an informed trader, enticing the trader to trade more intensely by responding to his

private signal. (This is in contrast to the price-taking case where m plays no role in the precision of prices.)

- For a finite number m of market makers, prices "overreact" in the sense that $E[\theta - \bar{\theta} \mid p] = \beta(p - \bar{\theta})$ for some $\beta \in (0, 1)$ (and, in contrast with the competitive case (see p. 121), this happens even for $\rho_U = 0$ because for finite m uninformed traders have market power). Indeed, in this model a sufficient condition to have that $E[\theta \mid p] = p$ in equilibrium is that uninformed traders have no market power and are risk neutral. This follows from the demand of uninformed traders because if semi-strong efficient pricing does not hold then an uninformed trader would take unbounded positions. In fact, as $m \to \infty$ then $E[\theta \mid p] - p \to 0$ even if the uninformed are risk averse. This is so because the amount of noise trading is fixed and, therefore, the risk-bearing capacity of the uninformed $m\rho_U^{-1}$ is large in relation to the amount of noise trading σ_u.[1]

Closed-form solutions can be obtained when traders are risk neutral ($\rho_I = 0$). For example, let $n = 1$, then for $m \to \infty$ we get $\zeta = \frac{1}{2}$ and $\phi_U = \tau_\theta(2\tau_\theta + \tau_\varepsilon)^{-1}$, and when the risk-neutral speculator becomes perfectly informed ($\tau_\varepsilon \to \infty$) we have that $\tau \to 2\tau_\theta$. With $m = 0$ and n risk-neutral informed traders it can be checked that at the SLBE the responsiveness to private information a increases with the private precision of signals τ_ε and with the volume of noise trading σ_u^2 and is independent of τ_θ; market depth $\lambda^{-1} = nc_I$ increases with the precision of public information τ_θ and with σ_u^2; price precision increases with τ_θ and τ_ε (and is independent of σ_u^2 because of risk neutrality). More noise trading entices informed traders to trade more aggressively, more information is impounded in the price, demand schedules become more elastic, and market depth increases. Better public information mitigates the adverse selection problem and induces traders to submit more elastic schedules and a deeper market. This is similar to the competitive case. With risk aversion (Wang and Zender 2002) similar results hold except that now price precision does depend on noise trading σ_u^2. Also, as in the competitive case, increasing ρ reduces $\lambda^{-1} = nc_I$. (See exercise 5.1.) Note, however, that in the competitive case (see section 4.2.1) trading intensity a is independent not only of τ_θ but also of τ_u. The reader is invited to think why market power makes a difference.

5.1.2 Free Entry and Large Markets

Consider the following scenario in which we endogenize the number of informed speculators. There are two stages and a countable infinity of potential traders with CARA coefficient ρ. In a first stage any trader (except noise traders) can become informed (that is, can receive a signal of fixed precision about the value of the asset) by paying a fixed amount $F > 0$. In a second stage the speculators who have decided to enter compete as in the previous section to

[1] See theorem 7.4 in Kyle (1989).

make money out of the noise traders. Free entry of uninformed speculators, even if they are risk averse, implies that the market at the second stage is semi-strong efficient. Since they have no entry cost the uninformed will enter until $E[\theta \mid p] = p$.[2]

The equilibrium number of informed traders is determined as follows. Let $\pi_i(n)$ denote the equilibrium random profits of informed trader i when n have entered and denote by $\Pi(n)$ the certainty equivalent of profits that makes a trader indifferent between making this payment to be one of the informed speculators or remain uninformed. We have that, because of exponential utility, $\Pi(n)$ is independent of initial wealth and

$$-e^{-\rho\Pi(n)} = E[-e^{-\rho\pi_i(n)}].$$

Let $n^*(\sigma_u)$ denote the equilibrium number of informed speculators in the imperfect competition model when noise trading has standard deviation σ_u. A natural measure of the size of the market is precisely noise trading volume σ_u. $n^*(\sigma_u)$ is given by the largest n such that

$$\Pi(n) \geqslant F.$$

As shown in Kyle (1989, theorem 10.2), there is a unique free-entry equilibrium of the two-stage game.

As the market grows large we should expect more informed traders to enter and a price-taking equilibrium to obtain. We are interested in whether the competitive REE considered in section 4.2.1 is the limit of the strategic equilibria of the growing markets. More precisely, the limit should be the equilibrium corresponding to example 4.1 of section 4.2.1 since this is the case with a competitive risk-neutral market-making sector (see exercise 5.5 for the general case). The following proposition (due to Kovalenkov and Vives 2007) states when the limit result is obtained.

Proposition 5.1. *Let $\rho > 0$ and $F^* \equiv (1/2\rho)\log(1 + \tau_\varepsilon/\tau_\theta)$. In a large market, as $\sigma_u \to \infty$, three cases appear in a free-entry equilibrium:*

1. *If $F \geqslant F^*$, then no trader chooses to become informed and prices contain no information.*

2. *If $0 < F < F^*$, then the endogenous number of informed speculators $n^*(\sigma_u)$ grows proportionally to σ_u. Prices are noisy indicators of the fundamental value in the limit market.*

3. *If $F = 0$, then all traders choose to become informed and prices are fully revealing.*

---

[2] Alternatively, we may assume that at the second stage there is a competitive risk-neutral market-making sector and then no risk-averse trader will choose to enter if he does not purchase information.

Let us now present a sketch of the argument. Consider first the case of a given number of informed speculators n. It can be shown (Kyle 1989, theorem 10.1) that

$$\Pi(n) = \frac{1}{2\rho}\log\left(1 + \frac{(1-\phi_{\mathrm{I}})(1-\phi_{\mathrm{U}})\tau_\varepsilon}{\tau}\frac{1-2\zeta}{(1-\zeta)^2}\right).$$

Furthermore, it can be checked (see exercise 5.2) that

$$0 \leqslant \Pi(n) \leqslant F^* \equiv \frac{1}{2\rho}\log\left(1 + \frac{\tau_\varepsilon}{\tau_\theta}\right)$$

for any n and σ_u, and that if n grows faster than σ_u, then $\Pi(n) \to 0$ since

$$\frac{(1-\phi_{\mathrm{I}})(1-\phi_{\mathrm{U}})\tau_\varepsilon}{\tau}\frac{1-2\zeta}{(1-\zeta)^2} \to 0,$$

and if n grows more slowly than σ_u, then $\Pi(n) \to F^* \equiv (1/2\rho)\log(1 + \tau_\varepsilon/\tau_\theta)$. Now allow for an endogenous number of speculators n. If $F = 0$, then all traders become informed and prices become fully revealing. If $F \geqslant F^*$, then it does not pay to become informed and prices are unrelated to the fundamental value. If n grows unboundedly as $\sigma_u \to \infty$, it should be that $\Pi(n) \to F$. Indeed, for fixed σ_u speculators will enter until $\Pi(n)$ is just above F. As n grows unboundedly $\Pi(n)$ gets closer and closer to F. If $0 < F < F^*$, then n must grow unboundedly as $\sigma_u \to \infty$ (otherwise $\Pi(n) \to F^*$ and there would be more entry since $F < F^*$). Therefore, if $0 < F < F^*$, then $n^*(\sigma_u)$ must grow at the same rate as σ_u (since if n grows faster than σ_u then $\Pi(n) \to 0$ and if it grows more slowly $\Pi(n) \to F^*$). In fact, we have that $\sigma_u/n^*(\sigma_u) \to \sigma_{u_0}$ as $\sigma_u \to \infty$ for some appropriate constant σ_{u_0} related to F. In this case the limit market corresponds to the market with a continuum of traders of example 4.1 in section 4.2.1 with noise trade given by σ_{u_0}, and prices and trades converge in mean square to the noisy price-taking equilibrium of the limit market. (An argument will be provided in the next section.)

Hence, for the whole range of intermediate values of F we obtain that the endogenous number of informed speculators is proportional to the standard deviation of the noise trade and this is the case that has as limit the usual continuum model. Thus, it is natural to consider sequences of markets where the numbers of informed speculators are proportional to σ_u. Consider thus a sequence of markets where at the nth market there are n informed agents and noise trade is given by $u(n) = nu_0$ with $\operatorname{var}[u_0] = \sigma_{u_0}^2$. That is, the standard deviation of the noise trade σ_u grows at the rate n. This provides a natural replica economy with a well-defined competitive limit analogous to the Cournot replica markets considered in chapter 2.

The question also arises of whether the competitive REE of the idealized limit economy or the one of the finite economy provides a better approximation to the true strategic equilibrium of a market with a given number of informed traders. To this end it is worth remarking that the results of proposition 5.1 hold when we replace strategic behavior by price-taking behavior. We can define for the price-taking equilibrium model, as in the strategic model, the certainty equivalent of profits $\Pi^{c}(n)$ and the equilibrium number of informed speculators $n_c^*(\sigma_u)$ (see exercise 5.2). The latter is defined as the largest n such that $\Pi^{c}(n) \geqslant F$. Again, there is a unique free-entry equilibrium of the two-stage game in the price-taking case.

In the next section we will see that as the number of informed traders n grows the strategic and competitive equilibria converge[3] and that they both tend to the competitive equilibrium of the limit continuum economy (as in Hellwig (1980), Admati (1985), or Vives (1995a)). We will characterize the rate at which strategic and competitive equilibria converge and the rate at which they tend to the competitive equilibrium of the limit economy.

* 5.1.3 Convergence to Price Taking

Taking as given the strategic equilibrium as the "true" description of market interaction, do price-taking equilibria provide a reasonable approximation? We will see that provided that informed traders are risk averse the price-taking REE of the finite economy will be close to the strategic REE; this is not the case for the equilibrium of the limit continuum economy.

Consider sequences of markets where the numbers of informed speculators are proportional to σ_u. At the nth market there are n informed agents. Let $u(n) = nu_0$ with $\mathrm{var}[u_0] = \sigma_{u_0}^2$. In order to compare convergence rates for prices, consider the following decomposition:

$$p_n - p_\infty = (p_n - p_n^{c}) + (p_n^{c} - p_\infty).$$

The term $(p_n - p_n^{c})$ captures the difference between equilibrium prices for the price-taking p_n^{c} and strategic equilibria p_n in the same finite market. The term $(p_n^{c} - p_\infty)$ captures the change in the competitive price from the finite market p_n^{c} to the limit market p_∞.

As in chapter 2, to compare orders of magnitude of random variables we use the mean square (see section 10.3.1). It is easy to see that $E[(p_n - p_\infty)^2]$ will inherit the order of the higher-order term of $E[(p_n - p_n^{c})^2]$ or $E[(p_n^{c} - p_\infty)^2]$.[4] The term $E[(p_n - p_n^{c})^2]$ corresponds to the strategic effect and the term $E[(p_n^{c} - p_\infty)^2]$ to the limit effect. We will see that $E[(p_n - p_n^{c})^2]$ converges to zero faster than $E[(p_n^{c} - p_\infty)^2]$ and therefore $E[(p_n - p_\infty)^2]$ inherits the order of $E[(p_n^{c} - p_\infty)^2]$ (they both converge to zero at exactly the same speed).

Given competitive market making, the expectation of the differences in equilibrium prices vanish and we need to compare only the rates of convergence of variances. It is possible to show (see Kovalenkov and Vives 2007) that

$$\sqrt{E[(p_n - p_n^{c})^2]} = \sqrt{\mathrm{var}[p_n - p_n^{c}]}$$

[3] As in theorem 9.2 of Kyle (1989), the limits of the imperfectly competitive and price-taking equilibria coincide whenever n as well as $\rho_{\mathrm{I}}^2\sigma_u^2/\tau_\varepsilon n$ tend to ∞. Then ζ, ϕ_{I}, and ϕ_{U} tend to 0.

[4] We have that $E[(p_n - p_\infty)^2] = E[(p_n - p_n^{c})^2] + E[(p_n^{c} - p_\infty)^2] + 2\,\mathrm{cov}[p_n - p_n^{c}, p_n^{c} - p_\infty]$. Using Hölder's inequality (see, for example, Royden 1968, p. 113) we obtain that $\mathrm{cov}[p_n - p_n^{c}, p_n^{c} - p_\infty] \leqslant (E[(p_n - p_n^{c})^2])^{1/2}(E[(p_n^{c} - p_\infty)^2])^{1/2}$, and therefore the covariance term will be of smaller order than the higher-order term of $E[(p_n - p_n^{c})^2]$ and $E[(p_n^{c} - p_\infty)^2]$.

is of order $1/n$, and

$$\sqrt{E[(p_n^{\mathrm{c}} - p_\infty)^2]} = \sqrt{\mathrm{var}[p_n^{\mathrm{c}} - p_\infty]}$$

is of order $1/\sqrt{n}$. Therefore,

$$\sqrt{E[(p_n - p_\infty)^2]} = \sqrt{\mathrm{var}[p_n - p_\infty]}$$

inherits the higher order, i.e., $1/\sqrt{n}$.

An informal explanation of the result follows. Recall that the demand of an informed trader in a strategic equilibrium is given by

$$X_{\mathrm{I}}(p, s_i) = \frac{E[\theta \mid p, s_i] - p}{\lambda_{\mathrm{I}} + \rho\,\mathrm{var}[\theta \mid p, s_i]},$$

where λ_{I} is the slope of inverse supply schedule facing the individual informed trader. In the competitive case $\lambda_{\mathrm{I}} = 0$. It can be checked that λ_{I} is of order $1/n$ and this explains why market power vanishes at the rate $1/n$.[5]

In a symmetric linear equilibrium, prices in a finite economy with n informed traders, either p_n^{c} or p_n, are a linear function of the fundamental value θ, its expectation $\bar{\theta}$, the base noise trading u_0, and the average error in the signals of the traders $(1/n)\sum_{i=1}^{n}\varepsilon_i$. The dependence of prices on this average error term obtains from the market-clearing condition when aggregating the demands of informed traders. Prices in the limit economy depend on the same variables except $(1/n)\sum_{i=1}^{n}\varepsilon_i$. Indeed, in the limit economy the term that includes the errors in the signals of the traders washes out because of the strong law of large numbers ($(1/n)\sum_{i=1}^{n}\varepsilon_i \xrightarrow[n]{} 0$ a.s.). The distance between p_n^{c} (or p_n) and the limit price p_∞ depends on $(1/n)\sum_{i=1}^{n}\varepsilon_i$ and this average error term converges to 0 at a rate of $1/\sqrt{n}$ as $n \to \infty$.

A similar result can be shown to hold for utilities:

$$\sqrt{E\bigg[\bigg(\frac{U(\pi_n^{\mathrm{c}})}{U(\pi_n)} - 1\bigg)^2\bigg]}$$

is of order $1/n$, while

$$\sqrt{E\bigg[\bigg(\frac{U(\pi_n^{\mathrm{c}})}{U(\pi_\infty)} - 1\bigg)^2\bigg]} \quad \text{and} \quad \sqrt{E\bigg[\bigg(\frac{U(\pi_n)}{U(\pi_\infty)} - 1\bigg)^2\bigg]}$$

are of order $1/\sqrt{n}$.

The asymptotic variances of convergence for the limit and strategic effects provide a refined measure of the speed of convergence for a given convergence rate. Their characterization (see Kovalenkov and Vives 2007) confirms the idea that the competitive approximation works even in a moderately sized market when the informationally adjusted risk-bearing capacity of the informed traders is not very large (i.e., basically when competitive traders have incentives to be restrained in their trading).

[5] This follows from conditions (B.8) and (B.9) in Kyle (1989).

As traders become risk neutral, the contrast between the competitive and the strategic cases is stark when they have to acquire the information at cost $F > 0$. While in the strategic case $\lim_{\rho \to 0} n^*(\sigma_u)$ is of order $\sigma_u^{2/3}$ for σ_u large, in the price-taking case $\lim_{\rho \to 0} n_c^*(\sigma_u) = 0$. No traders choose to become informed in the price-taking case because of their closeness to risk neutrality. If they chose to become informed, they would trade so aggressively that they would (almost) reveal their private information and would make (close to) zero profits. This is an example of the Grossman and Stiglitz (1980) informational efficiency paradox described in section 4.2.2. In the strategic case the informed traders take into account the effect of their actions on the price and therefore can restrict their trade. So the incentives to acquire information do not disappear as more traders decide to become informed. It is worth noting that in the limit as $\rho \to 0$, unlike the risk-averse case, the number of informed traders grows less than proportionally with the size of the market σ_u. The reason is that risk neutrality implies fiercer competition among informed traders (see exercise 5.3).

An interesting case arises when the total precision is bounded and does not change with n, i.e., $n\tau_\varepsilon = \tau_E$, where τ_E is a given constant. As n increases, there is monopolistically competitive behavior in the limit (see exercise 5.4). García and Sangiorgi (2007) consider the case of free entry of uninformed speculators and endogenize the information of traders by purchase from a monopolistic seller of information. They find that when $\rho\sigma_u$ is large then the information provider sells information to all traders, and with a large number of traders the monopolistically competitive limit is approached. When $\rho\sigma_u$ is small then the information monopolist sells only to one trader.

5.1.4 Summary

The main learning points of this section are related to the modeling of REE with imperfect competition with competition in demand schedules and private information. Competition in demand schedules generates a vast multiplicity of equilibria whenever supply or demand uncertainty is nonrandom or has bounded support. The result is that collusive outcomes can arise in a one-shot game. In the CARA-normal model a unique symmetric linear equilibrium exists and we obtain the following results:

- A large trader has potentially two reasons to restrict his trade: risk aversion and market power.
- Large traders are more cautious than small ones when reacting to their private information because they are aware of the price impact and the information leakage of their trades.
- The result is that prices tend to be less informative in the presence of large traders.
- With free entry and costly information acquisition the number of informed traders grows in proportion to the volume of noise trading (size of the market).

- When the informationally adjusted risk-bearing capacity of the informed traders is not very large, a price-taking rational expectations equilibrium is not far from its strategic counterpart as long as a moderate number of traders are present in the market. This rationalizes the use of competitive rational expectations equilibria. However, when traders are risk neutral competitive and strategic equilibria are very far apart.

5.2 Informed Traders Move First

In this section we take another look at the sequential trade model with large informed traders. Noise and informed traders move first and competitive market makers set prices upon observing the order flow (the aggregate net orders from investors to market makers). We analyze the nature of the game between competitive and strategic traders and market makers, examine the incentives of large informed traders to confuse market makers and their effect on market parameters such as depth, price informativeness, and volatility, and the differential impact of informed traders using market orders or demand schedules. We will deal first with a generalized version of the market order static model in Kyle (1985), with a large informed trader and a competitive informed fringe facing risk-neutral competitive market makers, discuss the conditions for uniqueness of equilibrium in this signaling environment (Rochet and Vila 1994), and finally examine a demand schedule game in which the informed can also infer the amount of noise trading.

5.2.1 The Market Order Game

A single risky asset, with random (*ex post*) liquidation value θ, and a riskless asset, with unitary return, are traded among noise traders, a fringe of risk-averse competitive informed agents of mass $(1-\mu)$, and a large risk-neutral informed trader (the "insider") of mass μ with the intermediation of competitive risk-neutral market makers.[6] We can think in terms of the model in section 4.3 where a mass μ of the competitive informed form a coalition. The coalition obtains the value of θ by pooling the information of their members, who trade in a correlated way (and it is further assumed that this large trader is risk neutral). The rest of informed traders $(1-\mu)$ remain competitive. All traders, except market makers, use market orders. If $\mu = 1$, we have the one-shot auction in Kyle (1985). If $\mu = 0$, we have the model in section 4.3 with $\nu = 0$ (that is, all informed traders submitting market orders as in the static model in Vives (1995b)). The insider acts strategically, that is, takes into account the effect his demand has on prices. For simplicity, we assume that the large trader is risk neutral and observes the liquidation value θ in advance. The profits of the insider buying μy units of the asset at price p are given by $\pi = (\theta - p)\mu y$. His

[6] In section 5.4 we will define a precise meaning of being an "insider" from the legal point of view.

initial wealth is normalized to zero. The insider submits a market order $\mu Y(\theta)$, contingent on the private information θ he observes.

There is a fringe of competitive informed agents indexed in the interval $[\mu, 1]$. Each competitive informed agent receives a (private) signal of the same precision about the unknown θ, is risk averse, and $\rho > 0$ is the (common) constant coefficient of absolute risk aversion. The initial wealth of informed agents is also normalized to zero. Noise traders (in the aggregate) submit an order u. The distributional assumptions on random variables are as in section 4.2.3. In our context (and as in chapter 4) there is no loss of generality in restricting our attention to symmetric strategies for the competitive traders. An informed trader submits a market order $X(s_i)$, contingent on the private signal s_i he receives.

Market makers are risk neutral and set prices efficiently conditional on the observation of the order flow:

$$\omega = \int_{\mu}^{1} X(s_i)\,\mathrm{d}i + \mu y + u.$$

Consequently, $E[\theta \mid \omega] = p$.

We will look for a linear (symmetric) perfect Bayesian equilibrium (PBE) of the game.[7] A PBE is a set of functions (strategies) for the insider $\theta \mapsto y = Y(\theta)$, each competitive informed trader $s_i \mapsto x_i = X(s_i)$, and a price function $\omega \mapsto p = P(\omega)$, such that each informed trader maximizes expected utility taking as given the (correctly anticipated) price functional and the strategies of the other traders, and market makers set prices with a fixed (and correct) conjecture about the strategies of the informed traders, $Y(\cdot)$ and $X(\cdot)$: $P(\omega) = E[\theta \mid \omega]$. We can assume that any observed order flow is compatible with the conjectured strategies of the informed traders (this is the case with random variables that have unbounded support in our normal model).[8]

The characterization of linear PBE proceeds as follows.

Market makers, given conjectured strategies (without loss of generality)

$$X(s_i) = a(s_i - \bar{\theta}) \quad \text{and} \quad Y(\theta) = \alpha(\theta - \bar{\theta}),$$

know that $(1-\mu)^{-1}\int_{\mu}^{1} X(s_i)\,\mathrm{d}i = a(\theta - \bar{\theta}) \equiv X(\theta)$, and therefore

$$\omega = (1-\mu)X(\theta) + \mu Y(\theta) + u = A(\theta - \bar{\theta}) + u,$$

where $A = \mu\alpha + (1-\mu)a$. Given the properties of normal distributions, it is immediate that $P(\omega) = E(\theta \mid \omega) = \lambda\omega + \bar{\theta}$, where $\lambda = \tau_u A/\tau$ and $\tau = \tau_\theta + \tau_u A^2$.

Given a conjectured price functional of the form $P(\omega) = \lambda\omega + \bar{\theta}$, informed traders optimize. The insider must choose y to maximize $E[\pi \mid \theta] = \mu y(\theta - E[p \mid \theta])$. Anticipating (correctly) the average strategy for the competitive

[7] See section 10.4.4 for a definition of perfect Bayesian equilibrium.

[8] The set of linear PBE of the above game is the same as the set of linear Bayesian equilibria of the game in which all traders place orders simultaneously with the competitive risk-neutral market makers placing demand schedules and the auctioneer setting a market-clearing price. In this latter case necessarily $p = E[\theta \mid p]$, and with linear equilibria p will be linear in ω and, therefore, with normal random variables, $E[\theta \mid p] = E[\theta \mid \omega]$.

fringe of $X(\theta) = a(\theta - \bar{\theta})$, he obtains $E[p \mid \theta] = \lambda((1-\mu)X(\theta) + \mu y) + \bar{\theta}$, which yields an optimal strategy

$$Y(\theta) = \alpha(\theta - \bar{\theta}) \quad \text{with } \alpha = [\lambda^{-1} - (1-\mu)a]/2\mu$$

(if the second-order condition $\lambda > 0$ holds).

Competitive informed trader i chooses x_i to maximize $E[\pi_i \mid s_i] - \frac{1}{2}\rho \operatorname{var}[\pi_i \mid s_i]$, where $\pi_i = (\theta - p)x_i$, because of CARA utility and joint normality of $\theta - p$ and s_i. The optimal demand will be the same function for any competitive trader and is given by

$$X(s_i) = \frac{E[\theta - p \mid s_i]}{\rho \operatorname{var}[\theta - p \mid s_i]}.$$

Knowing that $p = \lambda\omega + \bar{\theta}$, with $\lambda = \tau_u A/\tau$, the computation of $E[\theta - p \mid s_i]$ and $\operatorname{var}[\theta - p \mid s_i]$ follows as in exercise 4.2 (using the fact that $\tau = \tau_\theta/(1-\lambda A)$) and

$$\frac{E[\theta - p \mid s_i]}{\rho \operatorname{var}[\theta - p \mid s_i]} = a(s_i - \bar{\theta}),$$

where $a = (\rho[\sigma_\varepsilon^2 + \operatorname{var}[p]])^{-1} = (\rho[\tau_\varepsilon^{-1} + \tau_\theta^{-1} - \tau^{-1}])^{-1}$. (Recall that we have $\operatorname{var}[p] = \tau_\theta^{-1} - \tau^{-1}$ since $p = E[\theta \mid p]$.)

Restricting our attention to (Bayesian) equilibria in linear strategies, it follows that there is a unique equilibrium. The next proposition presents the result. (The reader is asked to provide a proof. *Hint:* obtain an equation in A and show that it has a unique solution.)

Proposition 5.2. *There is a unique linear equilibrium. For $\mu > 0$, it is given by*

$$Y(\theta) = \alpha(\theta - \bar{\theta}), \quad X(s_i) = a(s_i - \bar{\theta}), \quad \text{and} \quad p = \lambda\omega + \bar{\theta},$$

where $\omega = A(\theta - \bar{\theta}) + u$. The parameters a and α are the unique positive solution of the two-equation system:

$$a = (\rho[\tau_\varepsilon^{-1} + \tau_\theta^{-1} - \tau^{-1}])^{-1} \quad \text{and} \quad \alpha = [\lambda^{-1} - (1-\mu)a]/2\mu,$$

with $\lambda = \tau_u A/\tau$, $\tau = \tau_\theta + \tau_u A^2$, and $A = \mu\alpha + (1-\mu)a$.

If $\mu = 1$, we obtain the static equilibrium described by Kyle (1985, p. 1319). We then have that $\tau = 2\tau_\theta$ and from this it follows that $\alpha = \sigma_u/\sigma_\theta$ and $\lambda = \sigma_\theta/2\sigma_u$. The expected profits of the insider equal the losses of noise traders: $\lambda\sigma_u^2 = \frac{1}{2}\sigma_u\sigma_\theta$. They are proportional to prior uncertainty (as measured by σ_θ) and to the amount of noise trading (proportional to σ_u). With more noise trading the insider can hide his orders and trade more aggressively because then the market makers when observing a high-order flow do not know whether this is because θ or u is high. The insider is aware of the impact of his trading on the informativeness of prices and trades so that only half his information is impounded in the prices ($\tau = 2\tau_\theta$). It is worth noting that the amount of noise trading does not influence the precision of prices. This happens because the insider is risk neutral and increases in noise trading are met by more aggressive trading on a one-to-one basis (i.e., α is proportional to σ_u).

We turn now to the general case $\mu \in (0,1)$. In equilibrium the trading intensities of the competitive informed agents and the insider are positive. It is obvious that $a > 0$, and α has to be positive also since it is easily seen that the expected profit of the insider equals $\mu\alpha/\tau$. Furthermore, for a given market depth, λ^{-1}, α is decreasing in the responsiveness of competitive informed agents to private signals a. The more competitive informed agents trade, the less the insider is willing to trade. Examining the equation in A that determines the equilibrium, it is easily seen that the informativeness of prices (τ) and the average responsiveness to private information (A) decrease with the coefficient of risk aversion ρ, with the noise in the signals τ_ε^{-1}, and with the prior variance of the value of the asset τ_θ^{-1}. A increases with the amount of noise trading. Furthermore, A, and therefore τ, decrease with the size of the insider μ. Since volatility $\mathrm{var}[p] = \tau_\theta^{-1} - \tau^{-1}$ is positively associated with τ, a increases with μ. The trading intensity of the insider α is decreasing with its weight μ provided that $\mu < \frac{1}{2}$ although it may have overall a U-shaped pattern since α will be increasing with μ when μ is close enough to 1 and ρ is small. A typical pattern is for α to be decreasing with μ.

Simulations with the model[9] indicate that α is increasing in ρ and τ_ε^{-1}. If ρ and/or τ_ε^{-1} decrease, competitive agents will trade more aggressively and, as a consequence, the price will be more informative and the expected asset return $(\theta - p)$ conditional on the insider's information will be lower. The insider will respond by reducing α. Furthermore, α and a decrease with τ_θ^{-1}, and increase with noise trading τ_u^{-1}. Market depth decreases with μ and increases with τ_u^{-1}. The precision of the price τ decreases with τ_u^{-1} (note that an increase in τ_u^{-1} decreases A but the direct impact on $\tau = \tau_\theta + \tau_u A^2$ dominates in the simulations and τ decreases). We have that $\mathrm{var}[p] = \tau_\theta^{-1} - \tau^{-1}$. Therefore, all factors (except τ_θ) which increase τ will also increase $\mathrm{var}[p]$. A higher τ_θ^{-1} has a double impact on $\mathrm{var}[p]$: a negative indirect effect, since it decreases τ, and a positive direct effect which dominates.

Volume traded. Total volume traded, denoted by TV, is given by the sum of the absolute values of the demands coming from the different agents in the model divided by 2. The expectation of the total volume traded is given by

$$E[\mathrm{TV}] = \frac{1}{2}\left(E\left[\int_\mu^1 |x_i|\,\mathrm{d}i\right] + \mu E[|y|] + E[|\omega|] + E[|u|]\right),$$

where $\int_\mu^1 |x_i|\,\mathrm{d}i$, $x_i = X(s_i)$, is the volume traded by the fringe of informed agents; $\mu|y|$, $y = Y(\theta)$, is the volume traded by the insider; $|\omega|$ is the volume traded by the market makers, the counterpart of the order flow

$$\omega = \int_\mu^1 x_i\,\mathrm{d}i + \mu y + u;$$

[9] Nonexhaustive simulations have been performed in the following grid of basic parameter values: $\rho \in \{0.5, 1, 2, 4, 5\}$, τ_θ, τ_ε, τ_u in $\{0.5, 1, 2, 5\}$, and $\mu \in \{0.2, 0.5, 0.8\}$.

and $|u|$ is the trading volume coming from the noise traders. We divide by 2 to avoid double counting of buys and sells. Note that, because of symmetry, the expected aggregate volume traded by informed agents is

$$E\left[\int_{\mu}^{1} |x_i|\, di\right] = (1-\mu)E[|x_i|].$$

The behavior of the total trading volume is driven by the behavior of the volume traded by informed (competitive plus insider) agents.

The simulations show that the effect of noise trading on the (expected) trading volume is positive (if σ_u increases, the insider, the market makers, and the competitive informed agents all trade more). Increases in the coefficient of risk aversion and/or the noise in the signals induce competitive agents to trade less and induce the insider to trade more. The order flow becomes more likely to reflect the order coming from the insider and, as a result, the market makers are less willing to trade and the total trading volume is reduced. The same thing happens when the weight of the insider increases since then his aggregate traded volume increases. (See exercise 5.7 for the equilibrium expressions of trading volume.)

A noisy strategy for the insider? A question may arise about whether the insider may have incentives to introduce noise in his demand for the risky asset in order to hide his information. It turns out that (as in Kyle 1985) it does not pay for the insider to place a noisy market order. The reason is that the insider is optimizing against a fixed conjecture on the behavior of market makers (a fixed λ). Given any λ it is then optimal not to introduce noise in the order since the only effect of placing a noisy order is just to distort trade from its optimal level given θ.

A simple argument establishes the result. Suppose that the insider after observing the realization of θ chooses a demand $Y(\theta)$ to which he can add normally distributed noise η, uncorrelated with θ and u, with mean zero and variance σ_η^2. The insider observes θ, chooses the quantity y and σ_η^2. Then he draws a realization of η and places the market order $\mu(Y(\theta)+\eta)$. The other agents do not observe σ_η^2 (or $Y(\theta)$) but have a conjecture (in equilibrium correct) about the insider's choice of σ_η^2. The market makers observe the order flow $\omega = x + \mu[y+\eta] + u$ and set the price $p = E[\theta \mid \omega]$. Restricting our attention to linear equilibria, the price may be written as

$$p = \lambda\omega + \bar{\theta} \quad \text{or} \quad p = \bar{\theta} + \lambda\{(1-\mu)X(\theta) + \mu Y(\theta)\} + \lambda\{\mu\eta + u\}.$$

The precision of the price is now given by

$$\tau = \tau_\theta + \frac{A^2}{\mu^2\tau_\eta^{-1} + \tau_u^{-1}}.$$

The insider will choose y and σ_η^2 to maximize

$$E[(y+\eta)(\theta - p) \mid \theta] = \mu(yE[\theta - p \mid \theta] - \lambda\mu\sigma_\eta^2)$$

since η, θ, and u are mutually independent.[10] Given that $E[\theta - p \mid \theta]$ does not depend on the variance of η it is then optimal to set $\sigma_\eta^2 = 0$ (and $Y(\theta) = \alpha(\theta - \bar{\theta})$, where α is given in proposition 5.2). In other words, suppose there is an equilibrium with positive noise added to the insider's market order. This equilibrium entails a certain λ. Then it pays the insider to reduce the noise to zero (and this deviation is unobservable) and trade according to his information θ.

If the insider were to be able to commit publicly to add noise of a certain variance σ_η^2 before receiving his information θ, then he will have incentives to do so. Suppose that no noise is added, then adding a little bit of noise will have no first-order impact on trading profits for a given λ but it will influence λ in a favorable way for the insider. In summary, when σ_η^2 is observable the insider introducing noise faces a trade-off between hiding his order at the same time that market depth is increased and absorbing losses because of the random trading. We will see in section 9.1 how the insider will have an incentive to add noise in a dynamic setting where he has to disclose his trades *ex post*.

Multiasset markets and contagion. The static model in Kyle (1985) is generalized by Caballé and Krishnan (1994) to multiple assets and multiple strategic informed traders (similarly to the multimarket competitive analysis of Admati (1985)). Caballé and Krishnan characterize a linear equilibrium as a function of appropriate covariance matrices and show that the relationship between the price and order flow vectors is governed by a symmetric positive definite matrix.

Pasquariello (2007) builds on Kyle (1985) and Caballé and Krishnan (1994) and shows that financial contagion can be an equilibrium outcome even though the three main channels of contagion through financial linkages studied in the literature—correlated information (e.g., King and Wadhwani 1990), correlated liquidity (e.g., Kyle and Xiong 2001; Yuan 2005), and portfolio rebalancing (e.g., Kodres and Pritsker 2002)—are ruled out by construction. In the model investors receive separate signals about local and common factors affecting terminal payoffs (i.e., there is no correlated information); noise trading is independent across assets and there are no short-selling constraints (i.e., liquidity is not correlated); and investors are risk neutral (i.e., there is no portfolio rebalancing channel of contagion). Imperfect competition among investors and heterogeneous information yield contagion in the sense that there is excess comovement of asset prices (beyond what is justified by fundamentals). This comes about because strategic risk-neutral investors trade across different assets to camouflage their information advantage about one asset trying to minimize the information impact of their trades and jam the cross-inference process of market makers. The model suggests that the process of generation and disclosure of information in emerging markets may explain their vulnerability to financial contagion.

---

[10] We have $E[(y+\eta)(\theta - p) \mid \theta] = yE[\theta - p \mid \theta] + E[\eta(\theta - p) \mid \theta]$ but $E[\eta\theta \mid \theta] = E[\eta u \mid \theta] = 0$, and therefore $E[\eta(\theta - p) \mid \theta] = -\lambda\mu\sigma_\eta^2$. Note also that $E[\theta - p \mid \theta] = \theta - \bar{\theta} - \lambda\{(1-\mu)X(\theta) + \mu Y(\theta)\}$.

* 5.2.2 Multiple or Unique Equilibrium?

We have shown that a unique linear equilibrium exists. However, potentially many other equilibria may exist. For example, Biais and Rochet (1997) find a continuum of equilibria in a version of the model with $\mu = 1$, noise trading u with a discrete distribution with support -1 and $+1$ with equal probability, and θ also with a discrete distribution with support -2, -1, 1, and 2, all with equal probability. Multiplicity of equilibria are typical in signaling games because the concept of PBE does not put any restriction on out-of-equilibrium beliefs. Those are the beliefs that traders must form when they observe something that should not have happened in equilibrium (see section 10.4.4). For example, what should market makers infer if they see an order flow which, given the conjectured strategy for the insider, is not possible? By choosing appropriately out-of-equilibrium beliefs, affecting the corresponding λ chosen by market makers, typically many equilibria can be sustained. In the model we have considered with noise distributed continuously over an unbounded support (normally distributed) any order flow is compatible with equilibrium behavior by the insider and therefore we do not have to worry about out-of-equilibrium beliefs. This means, in particular, that the insider optimizes against a fixed (conjectured) λ set by the market makers.

However, with $\mu = 1$, a variation of the model admits a unique equilibrium. Rochet and Vila (1994), using techniques from mechanism design (see section 10.4.3 for a summary introduction), show that the equilibrium is unique globally (that is, not only in the class of linear equilibria) in a modified market order game in which (u, θ) have a joint distribution on a compact support and where the insider observes the amount of noise trading before placing his order. In this case the insider therefore has both fundamental (θ) and nonfundamental (u) information.

The mechanism design approach in this case tries to find the optimal organization of the market from the point of view of noise traders. The problem is finding a menu of contracts offered to the insider specifying for each order flow ω the price $P(\omega)$ and potential transfer $T(\omega)$ to the insider that minimize its profit (which is the cost of trading for the noise traders). The trading game we consider is included as a possibility: $T(\omega) = 0$ and $P(\omega) = E(\theta \mid \omega)$. Let

$$\Pi(u, \theta) \equiv \max_{\omega}\{(\theta - P(\omega))(\omega - u) + T(\omega)\}.$$

Contracts have to be incentive compatible and individually rational. It is possible to show that the incentive compatibility constraints, which ensure truthful revelation by the insider, boil down to the requirement that $\Pi(u, \theta) + u\theta$ be convex. The individual rationality or participation constraint is just that the profits of the insider cannot be negative, $\Pi(u, \theta) \geqslant 0$. The result is that the equilibrium of the modified market order game minimizes, as unique solution, the expected profits of the insider subject to the incentive compatibility and individual rationality constraints. The uniqueness property in this case follows because of the zero-sum feature of the game played by the informed agent and market makers, derived from the inelastic demand of noise traders.

As we will see in the next section, the modified market order game is equivalent to a demand schedule game and with normal distributions its linear equilibrium has very similar properties to the linear equilibrium of the market order game.

5.2.3 The Demand Schedule Game

We now study a version of the general model in which the insider and the informed traders submit demand schedules instead of market orders. Informed trader i submits a demand schedule $X(s_i, p)$, contingent on the private signal s_i (as before, we assume without loss of generality that competitive informed traders use a symmetric strategy). Similarly, the insider's strategy is a demand function contingent on his private information (θ), $Y(\theta, p)$. Noise traders are assumed to submit the aggregate order u and market makers quote prices efficiently on the basis of public information and the aggregate limit-order book, which is just a noisy version of the aggregate orders of informed agents,

$$L(p) = \int_{\mu}^{1} X(s_i, p)\,\mathrm{d}i + \mu Y(\theta, p) + u.$$

The competitive market-making sector observes the linear function of p, $L(\cdot)$, and sets prices efficiently: $p = E[\theta \mid L(\cdot)]$. As before this sequential trading procedure is easily seen to be equivalent to the Walrasian simultaneous placement of demand schedules with competitive risk-neutral market makers. The following proposition characterizes the equilibrium. (Exercise 5.8 asks the reader for a proof.)

Proposition 5.3. *Under the assumptions, in the demand schedule game there exists a unique linear equilibrium:*

$$X(s_i, p) = a(s_i - p), \quad Y(\theta, p) = \alpha(\theta - p), \quad p = \lambda z + \bar{\theta}, \quad \textit{and} \quad z = A(\theta - \bar{\theta}) + u,$$

where $a = \tau_\varepsilon/\rho$, $\alpha = (2\mu\lambda)^{-1}$, $A = \mu\alpha + (1-\mu)a$, $\lambda = \tau_u A/\tau$, $\tau = \tau_\theta + \tau_u A^2$. *In equilibrium we have that*

$$\lambda = \tfrac{1}{2}[(\tau_\theta/\tau_u) + (1-\mu)^2 a^2]^{-1/2}.$$

When $\mu = 1$, the equilibrium can be obtained as the limit of the Kyle (1989) model when $n = 1$ and $\rho_{\mathrm{I}} = 0$ as $m \to \infty$ (see section 5.1). The equilibrium is the same as in the modified market order game in which the insider observes the amount of noise trading before placing his order (Rochet and Vila 1994). In the linear equilibrium as derived in the proposition above the insider can infer u from the price because he knows θ. The insider, therefore, not only has knowledge of fundamentals but also market knowledge inferred from the price.

Comparing the market order game (section 5.2.1, denoted by superscript "MO") with the demand schedule game when $\mu = 1$, we have that $\alpha^{\mathrm{MO}} = \alpha =$

σ_u/σ_θ, $\tau^{\text{MO}} = \tau = 2\tau_\theta$, and $\lambda^{\text{MO}} = \lambda = \sigma_\theta/2\sigma_u$, with the result that the insider makes the same expected profits in both games. However, for $\mu < 1$, informed traders react more to their private information in the demand schedule game, $a^{\text{MO}} < \tau_\varepsilon/\rho$ and $\alpha^{\text{MO}} < \alpha$. Risk-averse competitive speculators when using market orders restrict their trading because they dislike the variance of the price. The risk-neutral "insider," provided that there is a positive mass of competitive informed speculators, also restricts his trading when using a market order.

Total volume traded follows easily as in the market order model. The expectation of the total volume traded is given by

$$E[\text{TV}] = \frac{1}{2}\left(\frac{2}{\pi}\right)^{1/2}\left(\mu\left(\frac{\alpha^2}{\tau}\right)^{1/2} + (1-\mu)a\left(\frac{1}{\tau_\varepsilon}+\frac{1}{\tau}\right)^{1/2} + \left(\sigma_u^2 + \frac{A^2}{\tau}\right)^{1/2} + \sigma_u\right),$$

where the first summand corresponds to trading by the insider, the second by the competitive informed fringe, the third by the market makers, and the fourth by noise traders. Comparative static results are easily derived. For example, when the relative size of the insider increases—or when competitive traders are more risk averse or less well informed—market depth diminishes, the insider is more cautious and price informativeness declines. When noise trading increases market depth increases, the insider is less cautious, and it can be checked that price informativeness diminishes. In this case all types of traders increase their trading and total expected trading volume increases with more noise trading. (The reader is invited to conjecture and check other comparative statics results for total trading volume.)

5.2.4 Summary

The main learning points when informed traders move first are the following:

- A large informed trader (insider) will try to hide behind liquidity traders in order to preserve his informational advantage. However, the insider does not have an incentive to add noise to his order to confuse market makers.
- Market depth and price precision decrease with the relative weight of the insider in the market.
- Increases in noise trading lead to increased market depth, more insider activity, and diminished price informativeness, with all types of traders increasing their trading volume.
- A multimarket extension of the model can explain contagion in financial markets.
- Informed traders, strategic or competitive, react more to their private signals if they use demand schedules instead of market orders.
- Despite the signaling nature of the game between informed and uninformed there are market microstructures for which there is a unique equilibrium.

5.3 Market Makers Move First

We now examine markets which are quote driven. That is, where market makers move first, post schedules, and then the potentially informed traders submit orders. This extensive form is akin to a screening problem where uninformed agents move first. We analyze the adverse selection problem that those market makers face and the implications for the bid–ask spread in a discriminatory pricing context. So far we have only considered uniform pricing schemes, in which all the units are transacted at the same price. However, in a limit-order book (as in the electronic book of Euronext, for example) there is price discrimination. When a trader faces the book typically his order will be executed at different prices because the trader will pick orders at different limit prices. To highlight the differences between uniform and discriminatory pricing we will concentrate first on the case where market makers do not face informed traders.

5.3.1 Uniform versus Discriminatory Pricing

We compare uniform versus discriminatory pricing when market makers face no adverse selection and study the benchmark case where they are uninformed.

Consider a situation where m market makers (uninformed speculators) compete for the orders of noise traders as in the model of section 5.1.1 where there are no informed traders ($n = 0$). Suppose, however, that now market maker i posts a trading schedule $P_i(z)$, indicating the marginal price at which the market maker trades the zth unit that builds up a limit-order book. The total payment to the market maker for x_i units of the stock will be $T_i(x_i) = \int_0^{x_i} P_i(z)\,dz$. Different units are transacted at different prices. With *discriminatory pricing*, if a marker maker posts a demand schedule $X_{\mathrm{U}}(p)$, then (assuming that $X_{\mathrm{U}}(\cdot)$ is invertible) each marginal unit z is transacted at a price $P(z) = X_{\mathrm{U}}^{-1}(z)$. Strategic incentives are obviously altered in relation to the uniform pricing case. Now market makers can bid more aggressively because when bidding for a marginal unit they do not have to worry about inframarginal losses.

In the Kyle (1989) model (section 5.1.1) there is uniform pricing and we know that for $n = 0$ and $m \geqslant 3$ there is a unique symmetric linear equilibrium (with u normally distributed). Given that the price conveys no information on θ we have that the schedule posted by a market maker is

$$X_{\mathrm{U}}(p) = \frac{E[\theta \mid p] - p}{\lambda_{\mathrm{U}} + \rho_{\mathrm{U}} \operatorname{var}[\theta \mid p]} = \frac{\bar{\theta} - p}{((m-1)c_{\mathrm{U}})^{-1} + \rho_{\mathrm{U}}\sigma_\theta^2}.$$

This can be written in terms of the inverse demand as

$$p = \bar{\theta} - \rho_{\mathrm{U}}\sigma_\theta^2 y - ((m-1)c_{\mathrm{U}})^{-1} y,$$

where y is the quantity traded. The term $\bar{\theta} - \rho_{\mathrm{U}}\sigma_\theta^2 y$ represents the trader's marginal valuation of the risky asset (which decreases with y when $\rho_{\mathrm{U}}\sigma_\theta^2 > 0$). The strategic effect is given by $-((m-1)c_{\mathrm{U}})^{-1} y$, where $c_{\mathrm{U}} = -X_{\mathrm{U}}'(p) > 0$. It is the amount that the trader shades his bid because he is aware of his market power. In a linear equilibrium it is easily seen that $X_{\mathrm{U}}(p) = c_{\mathrm{U}}(\bar{\theta} - p)$, where $c_{\mathrm{U}} = (m-2)/((m-1)\rho_{\mathrm{U}}\sigma_\theta^2)$ and therefore $p(y) = \bar{\theta} - (\rho_{\mathrm{U}}\sigma_\theta^2((m-1)y)/(m-2))$. For a general distribution of u the equilibrium is the unique one in the linear class but there is, in fact, a continuum of nonlinear equilibria when u has compact support (see Wang and Zender (2002, proposition 3.4), who assume that u has support in $[0,1]$, with linear hazard rate, and that bidders submit nonincreasing piecewise continuously differentiable demand schedules).[11] An interesting aspect of the nonlinear equilibria is that even if traders are risk neutral we have that there is price shading and in equilibrium $p < \bar{\theta}$. Some of the equilibria are quite "collusive" indeed. Only in the linear equilibrium we have that $p = \bar{\theta}$ when $\rho_{\mathrm{U}} = 0$. With discriminatory auctions the scope of collusion is reduced. In fact, Wang and Zender (2002) show that when bidders have mean-variance preferences, are risk averse, and with an inverted Pareto distribution for u (the hazard rate of u is linear over $[0,1]$), in the discriminatory auction there is a unique equilibrium and it is linear (as long as there is a zero reserve price and attention is restricted to weakly downward sloping bid schedules). (The expression of the equilibrium is given in exercise 5.6.) In the discriminatory case if bidders are risk neutral, we have that $p = \bar{\theta}$ in equilibrium. Risk aversion is needed for the presence of market power in a discriminatory auction. An analogy would be Bertrand competition with homogeneous product where with constant and equal marginal costs there is no market power while there may be with increasing marginal costs (see Vives 1999, section 5.1). Risk aversion implies that the marginal valuation of the asset decreases with the quantity demanded (in parallel to increasing marginal costs in an oligopoly model). In contrast, in the uniform-price auction bidders may enjoy market power even if they are risk neutral (as it would happen in a Cournot oligopoly model with constant marginal costs). (It should be noted that mean-variance preferences yield the same outcome as the CARA-normal model in a uniform auction but not in the discriminatory auction.)

Viswanathan and Wang (2002) compare the linear uniform-pricing solution above with the outcome of discriminatory pricing. In the latter case (and under the maintained assumptions of CARA utilities and normally distributed asset values) they find that, in a symmetric equilibrium in demand schedules (which are piecewise continuously differentiable),

$$p = \bar{\theta} - \rho_{\mathrm{U}}\sigma_\theta^2 y + ((m-1)X_{\mathrm{U}}'(p))^{-1}H(u),$$

where $H(u) = \Lambda(u)/g(u)$, $g(u)$ is the density function of noise trading (or exogenous random supply) u and $\Lambda(u)$ solves

$$\Lambda'(u) = \rho_{\mathrm{U}}\Lambda(u)((\bar{\theta} - p(u) - m^{-1}\rho_{\mathrm{U}}\sigma_\theta^2)m^{-1} - p(u)) - g(u).$$

In this setup the strategic term is therefore $((m-1)X_{\mathrm{U}}'(p))^{-1}H(u)$. In the uniform-pricing case the strategic term affects the slope of the demand function

[11] The nonlinear equilibria are indexed by a parameter and when this parameter tends to ∞ we recover the linear equilibrium.

(it is proportional to y) while in the discriminatory case it affects the intercept of the demand function. Note that for $y = 0$ with uniform pricing $p = \bar{\theta}$, while with discriminatory pricing $p < \bar{\theta}$ (with downward-sloping demand schedules). The zero-quantity discount with discriminatory pricing arises because market makers are risk averse and do not know whether noise traders will want to buy or sell more than the marginal unit.

When market makers have mean–variance preferences and the hazard rate of u is linear, Viswanathan and Wang (2002) compare the linear uniform-pricing solution with the discriminatory one and they find that in equilibrium discriminatory pricing[12] entails a flatter demand schedule but also a zero-quantity discount of size proportional to the maximum size of the orders of customers, i.e., noise traders (see exercise 5.6). Discriminatory pricing intensifies competition among market makers. However, when the number of market makers m increases demand curves become flatter with uniform pricing but steeper under discriminatory pricing (although the price discount is reduced). Therefore, uniform pricing tends to be more attractive for the customer for m large enough.[13]

Wang and Zender (2002) introduce asymmetric information about θ among bidders (market makers) in a generalized auction (that has as particular cases uniform and discriminatory pricing) and characterize symmetric equilibria in the mean–variance framework restricting our attention to equilibria where bid schedules are additively separable in the private signal of the bidder and price. They find that only when bidders are risk neutral is there an equilibrium in which they submit flat schedules. This means that except in this case equilibria involve bid shading or demand reduction, be it in the uniform or in the discriminatory auction context.

There is evidence that market makers have market power. This is documented by Christie and Schultz (1994) and Christie et al. (1994) for NASDAQ dealers before the 1997 reform. Large spreads were sustained using a wide pricing grid. Barclay et al. (1999) find that the effect of the 1997 reform was to decrease spreads substantially. Entry also has a negative impact on spreads (see Wahal 1997; Ellis et al. 2002).

5.3.2 Market Makers Facing Adverse Selection

In this section we will study how market makers may protect themselves against adverse selection when they post trading schedules in advance of the orders of informed traders and how competition among market makers affects the outcome.

Copeland and Galai (1983) in an early contribution presented a simple model in which an uninformed monopolistic market maker sets a bid and ask price and faces with some probability a trader perfectly informed about the liquidation

[12] Recall that, with discriminatory pricing, equilibria under mean–variance preferences are different from equilibria under CARA preferences.

[13] See Viswanathan and Wang (2004) for dynamic models of interdealer trading.

value of the risky asset and with the complementary probability a liquidity trader. The market maker gains with the latter but loses with the former. The market maker tries to protect himself from the adverse selection problem by widening the spread, which in turn reduces the probability that the liquidity trader shows up. A higher probability of facing an informed trader (a more severe adverse selection problem) widens the spread.

Let us consider the model of Biais et al. (2000), who extend Bernhardt and Hughson (1997), to study the effect of competition on spreads and welfare in a limit-order-book market. There are m risk-neutral market makers and a single risk-averse informed trader (with CARA utility with coefficient ρ) who receives a shock u to his endowment of the risky asset, which has liquidation value θ, and a signal s about θ. The information structure is similar to the Grossman–Stiglitz model (section 4.2.2). It is assumed that $\theta = s + \varepsilon$, where s and ε are independent. The distributions of u and s have bounded supports. Recall that this structure means in particular, with no need of the normality assumption, that $E[\theta \mid s] = s$ and $\operatorname{var}[\theta \mid s] = \operatorname{var}[\varepsilon]$. It is also assumed that ε is normally distributed.

The structure and timing of the trading game is as follows:

(1) Market makers simultaneously post trading schedules $P_i(z)$ that build up a limit-order book: $P_i(z)$ is the marginal price at which market maker i trades the zth unit. The transfer payment to market maker i for x_i units of the stock is then $T_i(x_i) = \int_0^{x_i} P_i(z)\,dz$. With an increasing schedule $P_i(\cdot)$, a sequence of marginal prices $P_i(z)$ can be interpreted as a sequence of limit orders yielding a convex transfer $T_i(\cdot)$. Note that market maker i offers a schedule contingent only on his own trades x_i and not on total volume $x = \sum_{i=1}^{m} x_i$.

(2) The informed trader, contingent on the realization of endowment shock u and signal s, determines the vector of trades (market orders) with market makers x_i, $i = 1, \dots, m$.

(3) Finally, ε, and therefore $\theta = s + \varepsilon$, are realized and consumption occurs. There is discriminatory pricing as different units trade at different prices. Each additional unit is more expensive if $P_i(\cdot)$ is increasing.[14]

The final wealth of the informed trader is $W = (u + x)\theta - T(x)$, where $x = \sum_{i=1}^{m} x_i$ and $T(x) = \sum_{i=1}^{m} T_i(x_i)$; W is normally distributed conditional on $\{u, s\}$. The informed trader will maximize

$$E[W \mid u, s] - \tfrac{1}{2}\rho \operatorname{var}[W \mid u, s] = (u + x)s - \tfrac{1}{2}\rho(u + x)^2\sigma_\varepsilon^2 - T(x),$$

which equals $[us - \frac{1}{2}\rho u^2\sigma_\varepsilon^2] + [vx - \frac{1}{2}\rho x^2\sigma_\varepsilon^2 - T(x)]$, where $v \equiv s - \rho\sigma_\varepsilon^2 u$. The first term is independent of x and represents the reservation utility of the

[14] From the perspective of mechanism design, this can be seen as competition among mechanisms. Each market maker is a principal offering a trading mechanism $T_i(x_i)$ with the interpretation that he is willing to trade x_i against a transfer $T_i(x_i)$. A convex transfer schedule can be implemented by menus of limit orders.

trader. The second term represents the gains from trade (or the informational rent in the mechanism design interpretation). The parameter v is the marginal valuation for the risky asset, increasing with s and decreasing with the inventory u. This parameter reduces a potentially two-dimensional screening problem into a one-dimensional one. The informed agent has two motives for trade: a liquidity reason after the endowment shock (to rebalance the portfolio) and an informational reason because of the private signal.

The maximization of *ex ante* social welfare would lead to setting $x^{o}(v) = E[-u \mid v]$. This optimizes an *ex ante* risk-sharing subject to the *ex ante* participation constraint of market makers. Biais et al. (2000) examine the PBE of the game under some regularity conditions on the distribution for v.

The monopolistic market-making case ($m = 1$) was analyzed by Glosten (1989) under somewhat different assumptions. He concluded that there exists a strictly positive bid–ask spread for infinitesimally small trades. In other words, the supply schedule is discontinuous for orders around zero. This is confirmed in the present formulation where it is also established that monopolistic market making lowers trading volume $|x(v)|$. The monopolist market maker optimizes the gains from trade minus the informational rent which needs to be given to the informed trader. This results in a trading volume and total welfare which are lower than optimal. Trading schedules can be convex or concave (in the latter case it implies quantity discounts).

In the oligopolistic case ($m > 1$) each market maker behaves as a monopolist facing a residual demand curve determined by the supply schedules chosen by the other market makers and the optimal demand of the informed trader. It can be shown that there is a unique equilibrium in convex supply schedules. The equilibrium is symmetric and market makers charge positive markups and make positive expected profits. Trading volume is larger than in the monopolistic case but lower than optimal. Because of adverse selection some traders are excluded from the market (those with lower willingness to trade) and there is also a strictly positive bid–ask spread for infinitesimally small trades. The outcome is one of imperfect competition. On the one hand, a single market maker would have an incentive to deviate from the collusive (monopolistic) outcome and increase trade with the informed agent. On the other hand, market makers retain market power. Indeed, marginal prices are increasing with the size of trade because market makers protect themselves against informed trading. The latter combined with the optimal response of the informed agent determines a residual demand curve with finite elasticity for every market maker.

This imperfect competition result disappears in a (pure) private-value environment. Indeed, if there is no asymmetric information about θ and adverse selection arises only out of the idiosyncratic endowment shock to the trader then, as long as $m \geqslant 2$, trading volume is optimal. The reason is that now marginal prices need no longer be increasing with the amount traded to reflect the informational content of trade. (This is akin to Bertrand competition with homogeneous products and constant and equal marginal costs for the firms.)

With common values, adverse selection reduces the aggressiveness of competition in supply schedules. Each market maker faces a residual demand with finite elasticity. (This is akin to Bertrand competition with differentiated products and constant and equal marginal costs for the firms.) The phenomenon is related to the winner's curse in common-value auctions (see section 1.5.1): a bidder refrains from bidding aggressively because winning conveys the news that the signal the bidder has received was too optimistic (the highest signal in the pool).

Increasing the number of market makers reduces market power. As m grows expected profits decline and tend to 0, and trading volume increases for all v, while a strictly positive small bid–ask spread is still observed in the limit. The informational rent for the informed trader increases with m. The limit market has features of a monopolistically competitive equilibrium in which market makers charge a positive markup but make zero profits because they trade an infinitesimal amount. This is as in Glosten (1994), who considered the competitive case and showed that the limit price for the marginal buy order y is the upper tail of the conditional expectation $P(y) = E[\theta \mid x \geqslant y]$ (and analogously for a sell order: $P(y) = E[\theta \mid x \leqslant y]$). Indeed, market makers cannot condition on the total size of the trade x when setting the bid–ask spread. For example, when facing a buy order for y market makers know that the limit order at a certain price is hit when the total size of the trade x is *at least* no smaller than the cumulated depth of the book up to that price. It then follows from risk-neutral competitive market making that $P(y) = E[\theta \mid x \geqslant y]$. It is worth noting that there is a spread even for small trades. The reason is that, under discriminatory pricing, market makers do not know whether the informed trader will want to buy more than the marginal unit. An infinitesimal order has a discrete impact on the price because it conveys a noninfinitesimal amount of information. This is why the bid–ask spread subsists even for very small orders.

Under uniform pricing and perfect competition among market makers we would have that for an order of any size x expected profits are zero: $P(x) = E[\theta \mid x]$. This is akin to the order-driven system studied by Kyle (1985) (see section 5.2.1) where Bertrand competition among market makers drives their expected profits down to zero (because they move second and observe the same order flow). Glosten (1989) compares perfect competition and the specialist system under uniform pricing. He finds that the specialist system stays open for larger market sizes than with perfect competition among market makers. In a competitive system market makers reduce liquidity and make the price schedule steeper to protect themselves against the adverse selection problem of large orders. This may induce a market breakdown (understood as no trade being the unique equilibrium outcome) for very large orders.[15] Instead, the

[15] Market breakdown due to adverse selection was established by Akerlof (1970). The work by Glosten (1989) in financial markets has been extended by Bhattacharya and Spiegel (1991), Spiegel and Subrahmanyam (1992), Bhattacharya et al. (1995), and, more recently, by Mailath and Nöldeke (2007).

specialist (a monopolist) can cross-subsidize trades with different order sizes and is able to keep the market open for larger trades. Discriminatory pricing with the limit-order book, by favoring larger orders, can accomplish the same objective even with perfect competition.[16]

5.3.3 Summary

In this section we have examined equilibria when uninformed traders move first and we have considered uniform (dealership market) and discriminatory pricing (limit-order-book market). While under uniform pricing there is typically a vast multiplicity of equilibria in demand schedules, under discriminatory pricing, and mild restrictions, we obtain a unique equilibrium. Comparison of the two trading mechanisms is complicated by this fact. We have obtained the following results for the discriminatory pricing case:

- Risk aversion is needed for the existence of market power of market makers. This is in contrast with the uniform-pricing case where market power may exist even with risk neutrality.
- Discriminatory pricing tends to intensify competition among market makers because they do not have to worry about inframarginal losses when bidding for orders.
- Market makers may face a basic adverse selection problem as they set bid and ask prices not knowing whether forthcoming trade is informed or not.
- There is a strictly positive bid–ask spread even for infinitesimal trades independent of the market structure if market makers are risk averse and/or face adverse selection. This is so because with discriminatory pricing market makers do not know whether (informed or noise) traders will want to trade more than the marginal trade.
- Market makers facing adverse selection charge positive markups and make positive expected profits even if they are risk neutral and compete in supply schedules. Traders with lower willingness to trade are excluded from the market. The market power of market makers declines as their number increases. In the limit they charge a positive bid–ask spread but make zero profits.

*5.4 An Application: Welfare Analysis of Insider Trading

The aim of this section is to suggest a general environment for conducting a welfare analysis of insider trading that supersedes the shortcomings of the received literature and identifies the trade-offs involved in forcing insiders to disclose their information before trading.

[16] Dennert (1993) presents a model where an increase in competition may hurt liquidity traders. In his model market makers make zero expected profits in equilibrium but increasing the number of market makers hurts liquidity traders because it increases the risk exposure of an individual market maker and worsens the adverse selection problem.

Insider trading is a particular case of informed trading involving a breach of fiduciary duty toward those on the other side of the trades or where the trader—the "insider"—uses information over which he has no property rights. For example, in the case of the biotechnology company ImClone, Samuel Waksal (former CEO of the firm) was charged with insider trading. According to the accusation, he attempted to sell shares of the company two days before it became public that the cancer drug Erbitux developed by the company would not pass the U.S. Federal Drug Administration test. Furthermore, he allegedly tipped family members (who sold about $10 million of the stock over the following two days) and his friend Martha Stewart, who also sold shares the day before the announcement (*Financial Times*, June 13, 2002). There is also evidence that insiders do trade in advance of information release and earn excess returns (see Seyhun 1992, 1986; Damodaran and Liu 1993; Aboody and Lev 2000).

Many countries regulate insider trading. Leading regulations include an "abstain-or-disclose" rule in the United States (SEC rule 10b-5 of the 1934 Act) and a prohibition against trading on inside information in the EU (Directive 2003/6/EC on insider dealing and market manipulation (market abuse)). Recently, tougher disclosure requirements have been imposed in the United States and in some European countries in order to avoid early selective disclosure of material information (to large investors, for example). Despite the general concern and the fact that there is evidence that enforcement of insider trading laws reduces the cost of equity in a country (Bhattacharya and Daouk 2002), the welfare consequences of the regulation of insider trading are less well understood.

We review briefly the received literature and propose a framework for the analysis of insider trading based on the analysis in Medrano and Vives (2004).

5.4.1 Received Literature

The received literature has highlighted three main related effects of insider trading in terms of creating adverse selection, accelerating the resolution of uncertainty, and modifying insurance and hedging opportunities. However, further progress in the analysis of the effects of insider trading has been hampered by methodological problems.

The first effect is due to adverse selection. Insider trading is seen as a tax which increases the bid–ask spread and reduces market depth (King and Roell 1988). A potential effect is then the reduction of *ex ante* investment before trading in the stock market occurs (Manove 1989; Ausubel 1990; Bhattacharya and Nicodano 2001). For example, Ausubel (1990) considers an exchange economy, with rational traders and a unique rational expectations equilibrium, in which private information is received after investment by both the (competitive) insider and outsiders. Preventing insider trading increases the expected return of outsiders, this induces them to invest more and this may benefit insiders. The outcome is that a ban on insider trading may be Pareto superior. However, in his model inside information has no productive value (and is unrelated to investment).

The second effect is the advance resolution of uncertainty. The presence of insiders will tend to make prices more informative.[17] Leland (1992) shows that the average investment level may be higher with insider trading because risk-averse outsiders increase the demand for the risky asset associated with investment. Expected stock prices will tend to increase, decreasing the risk premium (decreasing the conditional volatility of returns and increasing the *ex ante* volatility of prices). Leland also performs a welfare analysis that is subject to the usual problems in noise-trader models and concludes that liquidity traders and outside investors are hurt and that insiders and owners of firms issuing shares benefit (because of a higher issuing price). The net effect of insider trading is ambiguous (positive if investment is very sensitive to the current price, risk aversion of investors is low, and liquidity trading has low volatility). Repullo (1999) shows that some of Leland's results are not robust to the introduction of noise in the information of the insider and analyzes some variations of the model with investment prior to trading. For example, the insider has no effect when modeled as having a positive mass instead of zero mass as in Leland. Furthermore, in Leland (1992) the insider is external to the firm and risk averse but perfectly informed, and he takes into account the effect of his trade on the price. The entrepreneur is risk neutral and price taking and, in fact, is forced to float the firm because (in the model) the expected fundamental value is larger than the expected price. Finally, in Leland's model the firm does not learn anything from the stock price.

The third is the impact of insider trading on risk sharing and hedging in particular. It is well-known from the work of Hirshleifer (1971) that early revelation of information (before traders are able to take a hedging position) may destroy insurance possibilities. Insider trading will then tend to hurt uninformed hedgers. However, early revelation of information may also help insurance possibilities. If uncertainty about risk factors not correlated with the endowment of the hedger is resolved early, then the stock is more correlated with the hedgers' endowment and hedging opportunities may improve (Dow and Rahi 2003).

In summary, despite the accumulation of work on the effects of insider trading, the analysis has been hampered by one or more of the following:

- Assumption of exogenous noise traders.
- Assumption of competitive behavior by agents (such as the insider) with potential market power.
- Ill-defined incentives to float the firm or project (e.g., risk-neutral entrepreneur selling the firm when the expected price is lower than its fundamental value).

---

[17] However, Fishman and Hagerty (1992) show that the presence of insiders may discourage information collection by outside investors/analysts, possibly leading to less informative prices. In their model, stock prices guide the entry decisions of potential entrants.

- Information emanating from outside the firm or with no productive value being considered "inside" information.

5.4.2 A Framework for the Analysis

We now sketch how to model the impact of insider trading on the investment and welfare of market participants when all agents are rational and aware of their position in the market.

Consider the following situation. A risk-averse entrepreneur (or a coalition of insiders, who can be the initial owners of the firm) has a project requiring investment and wants to hedge it partially by selling shares of the firm in the stock market. The market is as in section 4.4 but now instead of a competitive sector of producers there is a single entrepreneur and we have, as before, competitive risk-averse market makers and hedgers, who have a random endowment of an asset correlated with the project of the firm. The entrepreneur invests and sets the number of shares to be issued at $t = 0$. He obtains information about the value of the project in the course of production at $t = 1$. The stock market opens at $t = 2$ and the entrepreneur trades together with market makers and hedgers. Neither the stock price nor private information have a chance to affect investment.

In section 4.4 we have considered producers who wanted to hedge part of their production in the futures market at $t = 2$. Here we can think that at $t = 2$ a secondary market for the stock opens. The firm remains under the control of a coalition of insiders (the initial owners have sold only a small fraction of the firm). For example, a coalition of insiders in a high-tech company learn valuable information about the effectiveness of a new drug being developed by the firm that will shortly be released to the market.[18] Still, a second scenario would be a venture capitalist starting a new project and deciding to go public at $t = 0$ and the firm being floated with an IPO (Initial Public Offering) auction at $t = 2$. The model would then be about trading in the primary market.[19]

Under the maintained assumptions of section 4.4, replacing the competitive sector of informed traders by the monopolistic informed trader or insider, it is possible to characterize linear equilibria at the market stage with and without insider trading (Medrano and Vives 2004). It is found that, much as in section 4.1, the combination of market power and adverse selection in the presence of hedgers may prevent the existence of a linear equilibrium. It is worth recalling that Bhattacharya and Spiegel (1991), for example, have already shown how the market may break down because of asymmetric information when there are

---

[18] Or perhaps the manager provides information or an early warning to the major shareholders in exchange for a promise of nonintervention (Maug 2002). The project cannot be floated at the investment stage because of agency problems; the manager, say, must keep shares in order to lessen a moral hazard problem. Alternatively, information disclosure associated with the flotation would tip competitors who could move and copy the product. This may be particularly relevant in high-tech industries (see Campbell 1979; Yosha 1995).

[19] At $t = 0$ the firm would file a preliminary prospectus (which must be approved by the SEC if in the United States).

informational and hedging motives for trade.[20] However, a linear equilibrium always exists when the combined risk-tolerance-weighted informational advantage of the insider (ξ/ρ_{I}) and the hedgers (ξ_u/ρ_{H}) is not very high. This happens in particular when the main trading motive for hedgers and the entrepreneur is insurance. It is worth noting that hedgers also have an informational advantage over market makers since they can use their endowment shock to filter better information about the fundamental value in the price. When the insider has no information there is no adverse selection problem; when he has private information then hedgers also have an informational advantage with respect to uninformed speculators. For example, if the squared correlation coefficient ξ_u between u and u_j is close to unity, then hedger j can recover from the price basically the information of the insider because he observes u_j and this is very close to u.

Despite the complexity of the analysis in which market power is combined with the presence of hedgers, it is possible to obtain analytical results for the case when the risk-tolerance-adjusted informational advantage of the hedgers ξ_u/ρ_{H} is small, and extend these results with simulations to a broad region of the parameter space. It is found that the level of investment increases with the hedging effectiveness of the asset market from the point of view of the entrepreneur. This hedging effectiveness (in general) decreases with the precision of the information of the entrepreneur/insider. An insider with better information will be able to speculate more profitably but to hedge less of his investment. The expression for investment is as in section 4.4 for q^* (but with an endogenous parameter d for the hedging effectiveness of the market a still more complicated function of the deep parameters of the model).

If the signal received by the entrepreneur is public knowledge (and not perfect), then an equilibrium always exists. As the precision of the signal increases, there is an increase in market depth, price volatility, and the average stock price along with a decrease in investment and in the expected utility of the insider, market makers, and (for reasonable parameter values) hedgers. Public-information revelation leads to less uncertainty about the payoff of the project and to a deeper market, as market makers do not ask for a large discount to trade on the risky asset. However, the hedging capacity of the market decreases from the entrepreneur's point of view as the public signal is more precise. This is because early revelation of information destroys insurance opportunities (the Hirshleifer (1971) effect), which dominates the potentially beneficial effect of an increased market depth. The dark side of information revelation looms larger. Despite the increase in market depth hedgers are hurt by the increase in volatility and decrease in the risk premium.

---

[20] In their model, if a linear equilibrium fails to exist, then nonlinear equilibria in some feasible class do not exist either, with the exception of a degenerate no-trade equilibrium.

5.4.3 Regulating Insider Trading

Suppose now that we want to evaluate the possibility of regulating insider trading. The question is whether the entrepreneur/insider should be allowed to trade on his private information. What is the alternative to not trading on the basis of private information: a regime of public disclosure (PD) of the signal or a regime where no private information (NI) is used? In fact, the regimes NI and PD arise where an "abstain-or-disclose" rule is applied to corporate insiders. In our context, the entrepreneur or coalition of insiders, when trading on the basis of their acquired private information, would be subject to the U.S. "abstain-or-disclose" rule or the EU prohibition on insider dealing. In the case of an IPO, if there is new material information after the filing at $t = 0$, the firm must file again the prospectus. This is equivalent to disclosure. Under the EU Directive on insider dealing, issuers have the obligation to disclose inside information.

The effects of an "abstain-or-disclose" rule depend on whether information is acquired for free or at a cost. If the entrepreneur learns the signal for free in the course of his activity, then when faced with the choice of disclosing the information and trading or not disclosing and not being able to trade, he will choose to disclose because otherwise he cannot hedge the investment risk. In this case the relevant benchmark for welfare comparison is the PD regime. If learning the signal has a cost, then the entrepreneur has no motive to acquire it since the information must be disclosed before being used. The relevant benchmark for welfare comparison is then a regime in which the entrepreneur has no private information (NI).

Using a combination of analytic and simulation methods it is possible to obtain the following results (Medrano and Vives 2004). When compared with the NI regime (with costly information acquisition), insider trading increases the informativeness of prices and, for reasonable parameter values, price volatility. It also reduces market depth and investment, inducing an increase in the expected price and so reducing the risk premium. The result is that the expected utility of all traders decreases. Hedgers are hurt because market depth is reduced and price volatility is increased. In general, insider trading is Pareto inferior because of adverse selection. The possibility remains that for an entrepreneur who is close to risk neutral or in high-noise scenarios, where the aggregate endowment shock of hedgers is very volatile, the insider gains with insider trading. This is so because of the speculative gains he can make with his private information.

When compared with the PD regime (with costless information acquisition), insider trading reduces market depth but, unlike before, also reduces price precision and price volatility. The result is that, except for a very large risk-tolerance-adjusted informational advantage of the insider, insider trading reduces real investment and risk premia, as well as the expected utility of the insider and the speculators. Two negative forces impinge upon the hedging effectiveness of the stock market and therefore investment: adverse selection and public-information revelation (Hirshleifer effect). With insider trading there is adverse selection but public-information disclosure is minimized. The PD regime eliminates adverse selection but maximizes public-information disclosure. For reasonable parameter values, adverse selection weighs more and investment is smaller with insider trading than in the PD regime. The effect on hedgers is ambiguous and depends on the precision of information of the insider. For a low precision of the insider's information, the reduction in price volatility is small and hedgers are hurt by insider trading and the opposite happens when the precision of the insider's information is high. For a large risk-tolerance-adjusted informational advantage of the insider, investment increases with insider trading because with public disclosure of the signal the Hirshleifer effect is severe and insider trading is Pareto superior.

In summary, if the insider has information and no obligation to disclose it, then some of his information is leaked into prices and becomes public. This revelation of information has weaker effects than public disclosure because there is only partial revelation. However, because of adverse selection, market makers will now demand a larger premium to accommodate orders. The net effect on welfare and investment depends on the benchmark of comparison.

Our framework can shed light on several public policy issues in relation to insider trading: (1) an abstain-or-disclose rule; (2) a laissez-faire policy; (3) the rationale for the EU Directive on insider dealing considering information of a "precise nature"; and (4) regulations concerning the early selective release of material information. (Exercise 5.11 asks the reader to derive some policy conclusions along those lines from the analysis.)

The issues raised by our approach have a parallel in the literature on security design (Demange and Laroque 1995, 2002; Rahi 1996). Demange and Laroque (2002) consider a setting similar to this section, but in a competitive stock market with risk-neutral market makers. The authors study how the entrepreneur might design the securities to be offered in the market, depending on different informational assumptions about the signals received by outsiders. An insight from their analysis is that the entrepreneur may want to favor projects for which the asymmetry of information is less pronounced.

5.5 Summary

In this chapter we have examined static financial market models in the framework of rational expectations with strategic traders. A general theme of the chapter is that large traders, even if they are risk neutral, refrain from trading aggressively because they are aware of their price and information impact. The effect of strategic trading on market quality parameters depends on specific features of the market microstructure. Other main results are as follows.

- Prices tend to be less informative and the market more shallow in the presence of large informed traders.

- The presence of strategic traders resolves paradoxes arising in the competitive REE paradigm. For example, large traders, even if they are risk neutral, trade cautiously and prevent prices from becoming fully revealing. The result is that incentives to acquire costly information are preserved even under risk neutrality.
- When the informationally adjusted risk-bearing capacity of the informed traders is not very large, a price-taking REE is not far from its strategic counterpart as long as a moderate number of traders are present in the market. This rationalizes the use of competitive rational expectations equilibria when traders are not close to risk neutrality.
- A large informed trader (insider) will try to hide behind liquidity traders in order to preserve his informational advantage but he does not have an incentive to add noise to his order. Market depth and price precision decrease with the relative weight of the insider in the market.
- Informed traders react more to their private signals if they use demand schedules instead of market orders.
- Despite the signaling nature of the game between informed and uninformed traders, when the former move first there are market microstructures for which there is a unique equilibrium.
- While uniform-price auctions have typically multiple equilibria in demand schedules, under discriminatory pricing, and mild restrictions, there is a unique equilibrium.
- Discriminatory pricing tends to intensify competition among market makers but it implies a strictly positive bid–ask spread even for infinitesimal trades independent of the market structure provided market makers are risk averse and/or face adverse selection.
- Market makers that move first and face adverse selection charge positive markups and make positive expected profits even though they are risk neutral and compete by posting supply schedules. The market power of market makers declines as their number increases. In the limit they charge a positive bid–ask spread but make zero profits.
- Insider trading induces adverse selection and advances the resolution of uncertainty. Its welfare impact depends on the trade-off between the two effects, in particular on the hedging effectiveness of the market, and the relevant benchmark of comparison depending on whether or not information is costly to acquire.

5.6 Exercises

5.1 (*strategic competition with informed traders*). Consider the model of strategic competition in demand schedules (section 5.1.1) with no uninformed speculators and $n > 2$ informed traders. Compute the linear Bayesian equilibrium in demand schedules when the traders are risk averse (with CARA coefficient

$\rho > 0$) and when they are risk neutral (with $\rho = 0$). Perform a comparative statics analysis of the responsiveness to private information, market depth, and the precision of prices. Interpret the results.

Solution. Follow the steps to compute an SLBE of section 5.1.1 to obtain the following system of equations for the unknown parameters $(a, b_{\mathrm{I}}, c_{\mathrm{I}})$:

$$a = \frac{\tau_\varepsilon}{\lambda_{\mathrm{I}}\tau_{\mathrm{I}} + \rho + \phi_{\mathrm{I}}\tau_\varepsilon/a},$$

$$c_{\mathrm{I}} = \frac{\tau_{\mathrm{I}} - \phi_{\mathrm{I}}\tau_\varepsilon(n-1)c_{\mathrm{I}}/a}{\lambda_{\mathrm{I}}\tau_{\mathrm{I}} + \rho + \phi_{\mathrm{I}}\tau_\varepsilon/a},$$

$$b_{\mathrm{I}} = \frac{\tau_\theta\bar{\theta} + \phi_{\mathrm{I}}\tau_\varepsilon(1-(n-1)b_{\mathrm{I}})/a}{\lambda_{\mathrm{I}}\tau_{\mathrm{I}} + \rho + \phi_{\mathrm{I}}\tau_\varepsilon/a},$$

with $\phi_{\mathrm{I}} = (n-1)a^2\tau_u/(\tau_\varepsilon + (n-1)a^2\tau_u)$ and $\tau_{\mathrm{I}} = \tau_\theta + \tau_\varepsilon + \phi_{\mathrm{I}}(n-1)\tau_\varepsilon$. From this system obtain a cubic equation in a which has as a unique positive solution

$$\rho\tau_\varepsilon^{-1}a^3 + \frac{n}{n-1}a^2 + \frac{\rho\tau_u^{-1}}{n-1}a - \frac{(n-2)\tau_\varepsilon\tau_u^{-1}}{(n-1)^2} = 0$$

and derive

$$c_{\mathrm{I}} = a\left(1 + \frac{\tau_\theta}{\tau_\varepsilon(1+(n-1)\phi_{\mathrm{I}})}\right) \quad \text{and} \quad b_{\mathrm{I}} = (c_{\mathrm{I}} - a)\bar{\theta} + \frac{\phi_{\mathrm{I}}}{1+(n-1)\phi_{\mathrm{I}}}.$$

In the risk-neutral case a closed-form solution is obtained and the equilibrium parameters are given by

$$a = \left(\frac{(n-2)\tau_\varepsilon}{n(n-1)\tau_u}\right)^{1/2},$$

$$c_{\mathrm{I}} = \frac{2\tau_\theta + n\tau_\varepsilon}{n^2}\left(\frac{n(n-2)}{(n-1)\tau_u\tau_\varepsilon}\right)^{1/2},$$

$$b_{\mathrm{I}} = \frac{2\bar{\theta}\tau_\theta}{n^2}\left(\frac{n(n-2)}{(n-1)\tau_u\tau_\varepsilon}\right)^{1/2}.$$

Market depth $\lambda^{-1} = nc_{\mathrm{I}}$ increases with τ_θ and in σ_u^2, and with τ_ε if and only if $n\tau_\varepsilon \geqslant 2\tau_\theta$. We have that $\tau = \tau_\theta + (n(n-2)/(2n-3))\tau_\varepsilon$ (τ is independent of τ_u because of risk neutrality). (See Wang and Zender (2002) for the case $\rho > 0$.)

***5.2** (*information acquisition and free entry*). Derive the following expressions for the certainty equivalents of profits for the (respectively) competitive and strategic models of section 5.1.2:

$$\Pi^{\mathrm{c}}(n) = \frac{1}{2\rho}\log\left[1 + \frac{(1-\phi_{\mathrm{I}}^{\mathrm{c}})(1-\phi_{\mathrm{U}}^{\mathrm{c}})\tau_\varepsilon}{\tau^{\mathrm{c}}}\right],$$

$$\Pi(n) = \frac{1}{2\rho}\log\left[1 + \frac{(1-\phi_{\mathrm{I}})(1-\phi_{\mathrm{U}})\tau_\varepsilon}{\tau}\frac{(1-2\zeta)}{(1-\zeta)^2}\right],$$

where the endogenous parameters are as defined in the text. Show that $\Pi(n)$ and $\Pi^{\mathrm{c}}(n)$ are in the interval $[0, F^*]$, where $F^* \equiv (1/2\rho)\log[1 + \tau_\varepsilon/\tau_\theta]$ for any

n. Show also that both

$$\frac{(1-\phi_{\mathrm{I}}^{\mathrm{c}})(1-\phi_{\mathrm{U}}^{\mathrm{c}})\tau_\varepsilon}{\tau^{\mathrm{c}}} \quad \text{and} \quad \frac{(1-\phi_{\mathrm{I}})(1-\phi_{\mathrm{U}})\tau_\varepsilon}{\tau}\frac{(1-2\zeta)}{(1-\zeta)^2}$$

converge to

(i) $\tau_\varepsilon/(\tau_\theta+\tau_\varepsilon^2/\rho^2\sigma_{u_0}^2) < \tau_\varepsilon/\tau_\theta$ if n grows at the same rate as σ_u and $\sigma_u/n \to \sigma_{u_0}$;

(ii) $\tau_\varepsilon/\tau_\theta$ if n grows more slowly than σ_u; and

(iii) 0 if n grows faster than σ_u.

Solution. Use the property (see section 10.2.4) that if $x \sim N(0,\sigma_x^2)$, $y \sim N(0,\sigma_y^2)$, and $\operatorname{cov}[x,y] = \sigma_{xy}$, then, for any $\rho \geqslant 0$ and if $\rho\sigma_x\sigma_y < 1+\rho\sigma_{xy}$, we have that $E[\mathrm{e}^{-\rho xy}] = [(1+\rho\sigma_{xy})^2 - \rho^2\sigma_x^2\sigma_y^2]^{-1/2}$ to calculate $E[-\mathrm{e}^{-\rho\pi_i(n)}]$, where $\pi_i(n) = (\theta - p)x_i$ (note that $E[\theta - p] = E[\theta - E[\theta \mid p]] = 0$ and $E[x_i] = E[X_{\mathrm{I}}(s_i,p)] = 0$ since $E[E[\theta \mid s_i,p]-p] = 0$). (See the proof of theorem 10.1 in Kyle (1989).) For the rest use the characterization, respectively, of the competitive $\phi_{\mathrm{I}}^{\mathrm{c}}$ and strategic ϕ_{I} equilibrium parameters (Kyle 1989, lemma 7.1):

$$\frac{\sigma_u^2\rho^2}{(n-1)\tau_\varepsilon} = \frac{(1-\phi_{\mathrm{I}}^{\mathrm{c}})^3}{\phi_{\mathrm{I}}^{\mathrm{c}}} \quad \text{and} \quad \frac{\sigma_u^2\rho^2}{(n-1)\tau_\varepsilon} = \frac{(1-\phi_{\mathrm{I}})^3}{\phi_{\mathrm{I}}}\frac{(1-2\zeta)^2}{(1-\zeta)^2}$$

and note that the limits of the imperfectly competitive and price-taking equilibria coincide whenever n as well as $\rho^2\sigma_u^2/\tau_\varepsilon n$ tend to ∞, then ζ, ϕ_{I}, and ϕ_{U} tend to 0 (theorem 9.2 in Kyle 1989). See Kovalenkov and Vives (2007) for more details.

5.3 (*information acquisition at the strategic and price-taking equilibria under risk neutrality*). Consider the market in exercise 5.2 with n risk-neutral informed traders. Find the expected profits for an informed trader in the strategic case and show that they are of order $\sigma_u n^{-3/2}$. Conclude that the order of magnitude of the free-entry number of informed traders is $\sigma_u^{2/3}$. What would be the expected profits and the free-entry number of traders with price-taking behavior?

Solution. $E[\pi(n)] = \lambda\sigma_u^2/n$, where

$$\lambda = \left(\tau_\varepsilon + \frac{2\tau_\theta}{n}\right)^{-1}\left(\frac{(n-1)\tau_\varepsilon}{n(n-2)\sigma_u^2}\right)^{1/2}.$$

We see that λ is of order $(\sigma_u n^{1/2})^{-1}$ and therefore $E[\pi(n)]$ is of order $\sigma_u n^{-3/2}$. The result follows since at a free-entry equilibrium $E[\pi(n)]$ equals approximately F.

5.4 (*monopolistic competition*). Consider the market in exercise 5.1 but now the total amount of information of informed traders is constant, $n\tau_\varepsilon = \tau_E$. Show that, as $n \to \infty$, $\tau = \tau_\theta + \phi_{\mathrm{I}}\tau_E \to \frac{1}{2}\tau_E$ and that the slope of residual supply that an informed trader faces as $n \to \infty$ is $\lambda_{\mathrm{I}} = (\tau_E\tau_u)^{1/2}/(2\tau_\theta + \tau_E) > 0$. What do you conclude from that? Suppose now that traders have to pay a cost $F > 0$ to become informed. Find the number of entrants and show that it tends to ∞ as $F \to 0$.

Solution. See Kyle (1989). The limit equilibrium is monopolistically competitive because informed traders face an upward-sloping supply curve despite being small relative to the market.

***5.5** (*convergence to the competitive REE*). Consider the Kyle (1989) model of section 5.1 and replica markets defined by the number of informed n, uninformed $m_n = n(\mu^{-1} - 1)$, $\mu > 0$, and noise trading u_n with the standard deviation of noise trading growing proportionately to n. Index the replica by the number of informed traders and keep a fixed proportion of them $\mu = (n/(m_n + n))$ in the market. Obtain the linear competitive REE of section 4.1 (proposition 4.1) as the limit of the linear equilibria of replica markets as $n \to \infty$. Do we obtain $E[\theta \mid p] = p$?

Solution. The convergence result is obtained as in Kovalenkov and Vives (2007). In the limit it is not true that $E[\theta \mid p] = p$ because the number of uninformed m_n grows at the same rate as the standard deviation of noise trading and the risk-bearing capacity of the uninformed is not large in relation to noise trading.

***5.6** (*uniform and discriminatory pricing*). Consider again strategic competition in demand schedules (section 5.3.1) with m uninformed traders (and no informed traders, $n = 0$) with mean–variance preferences and with linear hazard rate for u, $(1-G(z))/g(z) = \vartheta(1-u)$, with u distributed on $[0,1]$ with density g and distribution function G, and ϑ a positive parameter. Find the unique symmetric linear equilibrium in demand functions for uniform and discriminatory pricing. Compare them and show that the equilibrium demand curve is flatter in the discriminatory case (limit-order-book market) but that there is a zero-quantity discount.

Solution. With uniform pricing the equilibrium is given by

$$p(y) = \bar{\theta} - \frac{\rho_{\mathrm{U}}\sigma_\theta^2(m-1)y}{m-2};$$

with discrimination it is given by

$$p(y) = \bar{\theta} - \frac{\rho_{\mathrm{U}}\sigma_\theta^2(\vartheta + (m-1)y)}{m(1+\vartheta) - 1}.$$

See Viswanathan and Wang (2002).

5.7 (*trading volume with market orders and a large trader*). In the market order game of section 5.2.1 show that in equilibrium, $E[|x_i|] = (2/\pi)^{1/2}a(\sigma_\varepsilon^2 + \sigma_\theta^2)^{1/2}$, $E[|y|] = (2/\pi)^{1/2}\alpha\sigma_\theta$, $E[|\omega|] = (2/\pi)^{1/2}(\sigma_u^2 + A^2\sigma_\theta^2)^{1/2}$, $E[|u|] = (2/\pi)^{1/2}\sigma_u$, and $E[\mathrm{TV}] = (2\pi)^{-1/2}((1-\mu)a(\sigma_\varepsilon^2 + \sigma_\theta^2)^{1/2} + \mu\alpha\sigma_\theta + (\sigma_u^2 + A^2\sigma_\theta^2)^{1/2} + \sigma_u)$. Try to verify the comparative statics statements in the text.

Solution. The results are immediate from the fact that if z is normally distributed with $E[z] = 0$, then $E[|z|] = (2/\pi)^{1/2}(\text{var}[z])^{1/2}$. We have that $x_i = a(s_i - \bar{\theta})$ and therefore $E[x_i] = 0$ ($E[s_i] = \bar{\theta}$). Furthermore, $\text{var}[x_i] = a^2 \text{var}[s_i - \bar{\theta}]$ and $\text{var}[s_i] = \tau_\varepsilon^{-1} + \tau_\theta^{-1}$. We then have that $E[|x_i|] = (2/\pi)^{1/2} a(\tau_\varepsilon^{-1} + \tau_\theta^{-1})^{1/2}$, given that $a \geqslant 0$, and, similarly, $E[|y_n|] = (2/\pi)^{1/2}(\alpha^2/\tau_\theta)^{1/2}$. Finally, $E[|\omega|] = E[|\int_\mu^1 x_i \, di + \mu y + u|] = E[|A(\theta - \bar{\theta}) + u|]$. Since u is independent of $(\theta - \bar{\theta})$ and $E(\omega) = 0$, we have that $E[|\omega|] = (2/\pi)^{1/2}(\text{var}[\omega])^{1/2} = (2/\pi)^{1/2}(\text{var}[u] + A^2 \text{var}[\theta - \bar{\theta}])^{1/2} = (2/\pi)^{1/2}(\sigma_u^2 + A^2\sigma_\theta^2)^{1/2}$. The expression for $E[\text{TV}]$ follows. For the comparative statics statements the dependence of a and α on the parameters of interest needs to be taken into account.

5.8 (*derivation of demand schedule equilibrium*). Prove proposition 5.3.

Sketch of proof. At a linear equilibrium the intercept of the limit-order book will be informative about θ (as in the competitive model of section 4.3). The properties of prices can be derived. Then find the parameters in the linear demand functions of traders by the usual method and obtain $a = \tau_\varepsilon/\rho$ and $\alpha = (2\mu\lambda)^{-1}$. Note that price precision can be seen to be given by $\tau = \tau_\theta/(1 - \lambda A)$. Using this expression and $\lambda = \tau_u A/\tau$, where A is a function of λ given that $a = \tau_\varepsilon/\rho$ and $\alpha = (2\mu\lambda)^{-1}$, obtain a quadratic equation in λ, $4(\tau_\theta/\tau_u)\lambda^2 + [1 + 2(1-\mu)a\lambda]^2 = 2[1 + 2(1 - \mu)a\lambda]$, which has a unique positive solution (fulfilling the SOC for the insider $\lambda > 0$). The result is that $\lambda = \frac{1}{2}[(\tau_\theta/\tau_u) + (1 - \mu)^2 a^2]^{-1/2}$.

5.9 (*fragmentation versus transparency*). Consider two different quote-driven systems in which risk-averse market makers compete for a market order of a customer. In a centralized market each market maker observes the quotes of the rivals, in a fragmented market he does not. Draw an analogy with auction theory and use the revenue equivalence theorem to show that the expected spread should be equal in both types of markets.

Solution. See Biais (1993).

***5.10** (*information sales*). Suppose that in the competitive market of section 4.3 with all informed traders submitting a demand schedule ($\nu = 1$) (and with a risk-neutral market-making sector) the private signal observed by an informed trader is sold by a monopolistic analyst who knows θ and may add independent noise to each reported signal. It is assumed that the signals are reported truthfully by the analyst.

(i) Find out how much a trader would be willing to pay for a private signal of precision τ_ε.

(ii) Find the optimal precision of the signal from the point of view of the seller. Note that it minimizes market depth. Explain why.

(iii) Show that the solution in (ii) gives exactly the same outcome of a market with a single risk-neutral insider submitting a market order (equilibrium in proposition 5.2 with $\mu = 1$ as in Kyle (1985)). Explain why this is so.

Solution. (i) Using the properties of CARA utilities (see the technical appendix and similarly to the analysis in section 4.2.2) the payment that makes indifferent a trader between observing a signal with precision τ_ε and no signal (only the price) when the other traders are observing a signal of precision τ_ε is $\phi(\tau_\varepsilon) = (2\rho)^{-1}\ln(1+\tau_\varepsilon\tau^{-1}) = (2\rho)^{-1}\ln(1+\rho\tau_u^{-1}\lambda)$ with τ the precision of prices at the competitive equilibrium: $\tau = \tau_\theta + \tau_u(\rho^{-1}\tau_\varepsilon)^2$. (ii) The optimization of $\phi(\tau_\varepsilon)$ yields $\rho^{-1}\sqrt{\tau_\theta/\tau_u}$. It minimizes market depth λ^{-1} because $\phi(\tau_\varepsilon) = (2\rho)^{-1}\ln(1+\rho\tau_u^{-1}\lambda)$. (iii) Immediate from proposition 5.2. (See Admati and Pfleiderer (1986) and Cespa (forthcoming).)

5.11 (*regulation of insider trading*). On the basis of the analysis in section 5.4, speculate about

(i) the consequences of imposing an abstain-or-disclose rule;

(ii) the effect of a laissez-faire policy;

(iii) the rationale for the EU Directive on insider dealing which considers regulating the use of information of a "precise nature"; and

(iv) proposed regulations concerning the early selective release of material information.[21]

Hint. See Medrano and Vives (2004).

5.12 (*a uniform-price auction with private information*). Reinterpret the Kyle (1989) model when there are no uninformed traders (exercise 5.1) as a uniform-price auction for a divisible asset (say, a Treasury auction) with private information. Suppose that total supply is $1+\alpha$, where $\alpha > 0$ and that noncompetitive demand is $\alpha + u$, where u is as in the Kyle model (think that σ_u is much smaller than α to minimize the probability that noncompetitive bidders sell to the Treasury). Find the expected revenue of the seller $(1+\alpha)E[p]$ (where p is the equilibrium price) and $E[p] = \bar{\theta} - \lambda(1-\phi_{\mathrm{I}})/(n\zeta)$ and show that it increases with the precision of public information τ_θ. Interpret the result in terms of mitigating the winner's curse.

Solution. See exercise 5.1 and Wang and Zender (2002).

References

Aboody, D., and B. Lev. 2000. Information asymmetry, R&D and insider gains. *Journal of Finance* 55:2747–66.

Admati, A. 1985. A noisy rational expectations equilibrium for multi-asset securities markets. *Econometrica* 53:629–57.

[21] The fair disclosure rule of the U.S. Securities and Exchange Commission (SEC) states that "when an issuer, or person on its behalf, discloses material nonpublic information to certain enumerated persons (in general, securities market professionals and holders of the issuer's securities who may well trade on the basis of the information), it must make public disclosure of that information." (see the SEC's home page at www.sec.gov/rules/final/33-7881.htm).

Admati, A., and P. Pfleiderer. 1986. A monopolistic market for information. *Journal of Economic Theory* 39:400–38.

Akerlof, G. 1970. The market for "lemons": quality uncertainty and the market mechanism. *Quarterly Journal of Economics* 84:488–500.

Ausubel, L. M. 1990. Insider trading in a rational expectations economy. *American Economic Review* 80:1022–41.

Back, K., and J. F. Zender. 1993. Auctions of divisible goods: on the rationale for the Treasury experiment. *Review of Financial Studies* 6:733–64.

——. 2001. Auctions of divisible goods with endogenous supply. *Economics Letters* 73:29–34.

Barclay, M., W. Christie, J. Harris, E. Kandel, and P. Schultz. 1999. Effects of market reform on the trading costs and depths of NASDAQ stocks. *Journal of Finance* 54:1–34.

Bernhardt, D., and E. Hughson. 1997. Splitting orders. *Review of Financial Studies* 10:69–101.

Bhattacharya, S., and G. Nicodano. 2001. Insider trading, investment, and liquidity: a welfare analysis. *Journal of Finance* 56:1141–56.

Bhattacharya, U., and H. Daouk. 2002. The world price of insider trading. *Journal of Finance* 57:75–108.

Bhattacharya, U., and M. Spiegel. 1991. Insiders, outsiders, and market breakdown. *Review of Financial Studies* 4:255–82.

Bhattacharya, U., P. Reny, and M. Spiegel. 1995. Destructive interference in an imperfectly competitive multi-security market. *Journal of Economic Theory* 65:136–70.

Biais, B. 1993. Price formation and equilibrium liquidity in fragmented and centralized markets. *Journal of Finance* 48:157–85.

Biais, B., and J.-C. Rochet. 1997. Risk sharing, adverse selection and market structure. In *Financial Mathematics* (ed. B. Biais, T. Bjórk, J. Cvitanié, N. El Karoui, and M. C. Quenez), pp. 1–51. Springer.

Biais, B., D. Martimort, and J.-C. Rochet. 2000. Competing mechanisms in a common value environment. *Econometrica* 68:799–837.

Caballé, J., and M. Krishnan. 1994. Imperfect competition in a multi-security market with risk neutrality. *Econometrica* 62:695–704.

Campbell, T. 1979. Optimal investment financing decisions and the value of confidentiality. *Journal of Financial Quantitative Analysis* 14:913–24.

Cespa, G. Forthcoming. Information sales and insider trading with long-lived information. *Journal of Finance.*

Christie, W., and P. Schultz. 1994. Why do NASDAQ market makers avoid odd-eighth quotes? *Journal of Finance* 49:1813–40.

Christie, W., J. Harris, and P. Schultz. 1994. Why did NASDAQ market makers stop avoiding odd-eighth quotes? *Journal of Finance* 49:1841–60.

Copeland, T. E., and D. Galai. 1983. Information effects on the bid–ask spread. *Journal of Finance* 38:1457–69.

Damodaran, A., and C. Liu. 1993. Insider trading as a signal of private information. *Review of Financial Studies* 6:79–120.

Demange, G., and G. Laroque. 1995. Private information and the design of securities. *Journal of Economic Theory* 65:233–57.

——. 2002. Investment, security design and information. In *Banking, Capital Markets and Corporate Governance* (ed. H. Osano and T. Tachibanaki). Palgrave.

Dennert, J. 1993. Price competition between market makers. *Review of Economic Studies* 60:735–51.

Dow, J., and R. Rahi. 2003. Informed trading, investment and economic welfare. *Journal of Business* 76:430–54.

Ellis, K., R. Michaely, and M. O'Hara. 2002. The making of a dealer market: from entry to equilibrium in the trading of NASDAQ stocks. *Journal of Finance* 57:2289–316.

Fishman, M., and K. Hagerty. 1992. Insider trading and the efficiency of stock prices. *RAND Journal of Economics* 23:106–22.

García, D., and F. Sangiorgi. 2007. Information sales and strategic trading. Mimeo.

Glosten, L. R. 1989. Insider trading, liquidity, and the role of monopolist specialist. *Journal of Business* 49:211–35.

——. 1994. Is the electronic open limit-order book inevitable? *Journal of Finance* 49:1127–61.

Grossman, S. 1981. An introduction to the theory of rational expectations under asymmetric information. *Review of Economic Studies* 48:541–59.

Grossman, S., and J. Stiglitz. 1980. On the impossibility of informationally efficient markets. *American Economic Review* 70:393–408.

Hellwig, M. F. 1980. On the aggregation of information in competitive markets. *Journal of Economic Theory* 22:477–98.

Hirshleifer, J. 1971. The private and social value of information and the reward to inventive activity. *American Economic Review* 61:561–74.

King, M., and A. Roell. 1988. Insider trading. *Economic Policy* 6:163–93.

King, M., and S. Wadhwani. 1990. Transmission of volatility between stock markets. *Review of Financial Studies* 3:5–33.

Klemperer, P., and M. Mayer. 1989. Supply function equilibria in oligopoly under uncertainty. *Econometrica* 57:1243–77.

Kodres, L., and M. Pritsker. 2002. A rational expectations model of financial contagion. *Journal of Finance* 57:2, 769–99.

Kremer, I., and K. Nyborg. 2004. Underpricing and market power in uniform price auctions. *Review of Financial Studies* 17:849–77.

Kovalenkov, A., and X. Vives. 2007. Competitive rational expectations equilibria without apology. Mimeo.

Kyle, A. S. 1985. Continuous auctions and insider trading. *Econometrica* 53:1315–35.

——. 1989. Informed speculation with imperfect competition. *Review of Economic Studies* 56:317–56.

Kyle, A. S., and W. Xiong. 2001. Contagion as a wealth effect. *Journal of Finance* 56:1401–40.

Leland, H. E. 1992. Insider trading: should it be prohibited? *Journal of Political Economy* 100:859–87.

LiCalzi, M., and A. Pavan. 2005. Tilting the supply schedule to enhance competition in uniform-price auctions. *European Economic Review* 49:227–50.

Mailath, G., and G. Nöldeke. 2007. Does competitive pricing cause market breakdown under extreme adverse selection? PIER Working Paper Archive 07-022, Penn Institute for Economic Research, University of Pennsylvania.

Manove, M. 1989. The harm from insider trading and informed speculation. *Quarterly Journal of Economics* 104:823–84.

Maug, E. 2002. Insider trading legislation and corporate governance. *European Economic Review* 46:1569–97.

Medrano, L., and X. Vives. 2004. Regulating insider trading when investment matters. *Review of Finance* 2:199–277.

Pasquariello, P. 2007. Imperfect competition, information heterogeneity, and financial contagion. *Review of Financial Studies* 20:391–426.

Rahi, R. 1996. Adverse selection and security design. *Review of Economic Studies* 63: 287–300.

Repullo, R. 1999. Some remarks on Leland's model of insider trading. *Economica* 66: 359–74.

Rochet, J.-C., and J. L. Vila. 1994. Insider trading without normality. *Review of Economic Studies* 61:131–52.

Royden, H. L. 1968. *Real Analysis.* New York: Macmillan.

Seyhun, N. 1986. Insiders' profits, costs of trading and market efficiency. *Journal of Financial Economics* 16:189–212.

——. 1992. The effectiveness of the insider trading sanctions. *Journal of Law and Economics* 149:172–75.

Spiegel, M., and A. Subrahmanyam. 1992. Informed speculation and hedging in a noncompetitive securities market. *Review of Financial Studies* 5:307–29.

Viswanathan, S., and J. J. D. Wang. 2002. Market architecture: limit-order books versus dealership markets. *Journal of Financial Markets* 5:127–67.

——. 2004. Inter-dealer trading in financial markets. *Journal of Business* 77:987–1040.

Vives, X. 1995a. Short-term investment and the informational efficiency of the market. *Review of Financial Studies* 8:125–60.

——. 1995b. The speed of information revelation in a financial market mechanism. *Journal of Economic Theory* 67:178–204.

——. 1999. *Oligopoly Pricing: Old Ideas and New Tools.* Boston, MA: MIT Press.

Wahal, S. 1997. Entry, exit, market makers, and the bid-ask spread. *Review of Financial Studies* 10:871–901.

Wang, J. J. D., and J. Zender. 2002. Auctioning divisible goods. *Economic Theory* 19:673–705.

Wilson, R. 1979. Auctions of shares. *Quarterly Journal of Economics* 93:675–98.

Yosha, O. 1995. Information disclosure and the choice of financing source. *Journal of Financial Intermediation* 4:3–20.

Yuan, K. 2005. Asymmetric price movements and borrowing constraints: a rational expectations equilibrium model of crises, contagion, and confusion. *Journal of Finance* 60:379–411.

6
Learning from Others and Herding

In the preceding chapters we have considered static models of market interaction in which agents would learn from prices and their private signals. This is not the only way for agents to learn about the parameters they are uncertain about. To start with, learning is a dynamic process. Furthermore, agents can also learn from other agents and, in particular, from the actions of other agents. Actions speak louder than words, the saying goes. Examples abound: consumers purchase the most popular brands, tourists patronize well-attended restaurants, and readers buy best-sellers. Learning from others can use informal routes like word-of-mouth. There has been a surge of interest in social learning, the process by which certain nonprice mechanisms in society aggregate the information of individuals. In this chapter we introduce dynamic models of social learning as a stepping stone to addressing the dynamics of information in full-fledged market environments, which will be the object of study in chapters 7–9. The present chapter builds a bridge between social learning and dynamic rational expectations models.

The social learning literature has emphasized the possibility of inefficient outcomes in contexts with fully rational agents. For example, agents may "herd" on a wrong action, disregarding valuable private information (see Banerjee (1992), Bikhchandani et al. (1992), and the monograph by Chamley (2004a)). This literature stresses market failure as an outcome of rational decisions taken by Bayesian agents. The market failure theme has a parallel in the study of excess volatility and crashes in financial markets, fads, and coordination failures (see, for example, Shiller (1981, 1984, 1989) and De Long et al. (1990), who, however, emphasize behavioral explanations). The literature on rational expectations and market efficiency provides a striking contrast with its emphasis on the market mechanism as an aggregator of the dispersed information of agents as we have seen in previous chapters. In this chapter, in the tradition of the social learning literature, we restrict our attention mostly to pure prediction/information externality models. That is, for the most part we obviate payoff externalities among agents to concentrate on interactions arising from information. It is well-known that in games of strategic complementarities, in which the marginal payoff of one agent increases with the actions of the other players, players tend to act alike or "herd." The most notable example are coordination games where multiple equilibria are the norm.[1] We introduce payoff externalities in chapters 7–9. The present chapter builds connections between social learning and rational expectations models. The common ground of both models is an information externality problem. The difference between the herding and the rational expectations model lies more in the "discrete" versus the "smooth" nature of each model than in a difference in underlying driving forces.

The chapter introduces the dynamics of Bayesian updating and learning and central results like the self-correcting property of learning from others by Bayesian agents. It characterizes the learning process and its speed, the basic information externality present in dynamic learning environments and provides a welfare benchmark for dynamic incomplete-information economies (extending the analysis in chapters 1–3 based on team efficiency to a dynamic environment). The chapter studies questions such as the dynamics of beliefs and volatility, the effects of endogenous information acquisition, and whether more public information may hurt welfare. The latter may have important policy implications since in many instances public agencies, like a central bank, have to ponder whether to release information. The plan of the chapter is as follows. The herding/informational cascades model as well as several extensions are presented in section 6.1. A benchmark smooth and noisy version model of learning from others is examined in section 6.2. Section 6.3 explores applications to market environments and some links with dynamic rational expectations equilibria. Section 6.4 characterizes the information externality present in models of learning from others from the point of view of welfare analysis. Section 6.5 performs a welfare analysis in a static version of the model with a rational expectations flavor.

6.1 Herding, Informational Cascades, and Social Learning

Consider the following stylized example reported in Banerjee (1992). Suppose that there is a population of 100 people, each person having to choose between two unknown restaurants A and B. It is known that restaurant A is slightly better than restaurant B. More concretely, there is a common prior probability of 0.51 that restaurant A is better than restaurant B. People arrive in sequence at the restaurants and each person has a private assessment of the quality of each restaurant (a noisy private signal of the same precision for everyone) and observes the choices of the predecessors. The signal provides good or bad news about restaurant A. A signal favorable to A combined with the prior knowledge would make a single person choose this restaurant. Each person, therefore, has to decide whether to go to restaurant A or B on the basis of his signal and the previous choices of other restaurant patrons.

Suppose that 99 people have received bad news about A and the remaining person good news about A. However, it so happens that the patron with good

[1] See section 10.4 for a brief introduction to the theory of games of strategic complementarities and Vives (chapter 2 in 1999, 2005) for more complete treatments. See section 8.4.2 for an application to the modeling of crises.

news about A is first in line. He will decide to go to A. Then the second person in line infers that the news about B of the first in line is bad and also goes to A because this restaurant is a priori better with a slightly higher probability. Indeed, his good signal cancels with the bad draw of the first in line and he goes with the prior. The second person in line "herds" and does not follow his private information. The actions of the second person conform to those of the first one. *Herding* is typically understood as conformity of actions. When there is herding an agent may imitate the predecessor against the information contained in his own signal.

The second person in line chooses A irrespective of his signal. This means that his choice conveys no information about his signal to the third person in line. His problem is exactly the same as the second person in line and therefore he will go to restaurant A. This will also happen for the rest of the line and everyone ends up going to A, although with high probability B is better. We say that the second person in line starts an informational cascade, where no further information accumulates.

In this context with a sequence of decision makers, who are imperfectly informed and each of whom observes the actions of predecessors, we say that an *informational cascade* arises when an agent, as well as all successors, makes a decision independently of the private information received. Then the actions of predecessors do not provide any information to successors and therefore any learning stops. After the informational cascade starts, the beliefs of the successor do not depend on the action of the predecessor. A cascade implies herding but a herd can arise even with no cascade (and in a herd there may be learning).[2] As we will see later (section 6.5), we could also take a more general view and define *herding* as the situation where agents put too little weight on their private signals with respect to an appropriately defined welfare benchmark.

Putting together all the private signals would indicate that B is better with probability close to 1. This sequential decision-making process does not aggregate information and leads to an inefficient outcome.

The insight of the example extends to a model with two states of the world, two signals, and two actions ($2 \times 2 \times 2$ model). Suppose that agents have to decide in sequence whether they adopt or reject a project with unknown value $\theta \in \{0, 1\}$, each with equal probability (without loss of generality). The cost of adoption is $c = \frac{1}{2}$. Each agent $i = 1, \dots, t$ (t can be infinite) decides to adopt or reject ($x_i \in \{\text{adopt}, \text{reject}\}$) on the basis of a private, binary, conditionally independent signal $s_i \in \{s_{\text{L}}, s_{\text{H}}\}$ with $\text{P}(s_{\text{H}} \mid \theta = 1) = \text{P}(s_{\text{L}} \mid \theta = 0) = \ell > \frac{1}{2}$, and the history of past actions $x^i \equiv \{x_1, \dots, x_{i-1}\}$. Denote by θ_i the posterior probability that the state is high given public information $x^i : \theta_i = \text{P}(\theta = 1 \mid x^i)$. We can call θ_i the public belief. Note that $E[\theta \mid x^i] = 1 \times \theta_i + 0 \times (1 - \theta_i) = \theta_i$. It then follows that there is an interval of public beliefs $(1 - \ell, \ell)$ such that for beliefs above the upper threshold ℓ everyone adopts, independently of the realized signal, and for beliefs below the lower threshold $1 - \ell$ everyone rejects,

[2] Çelen and Kariv (2004a) distinguish experimentally between herds and cascades.

independently of the realized signal. The reason is that when the public belief θ_i is strictly above ℓ, even after receiving a bad signal, according to Bayes's formula the private belief of the agent is strictly larger than $\frac{1}{2}$. The case of $\theta_i < 1 - \ell$ is similar (see exercise 6.1). This means that learning takes place only when beliefs are in the interval $(1 - \ell, \ell)$, in which case an agent adopts only if he receives good news. Otherwise, the agent will herd (follow the public belief independently of his private signal) and an informational cascade will ensue. Once the cascade has started all agents choose the same action from this period on.

It can be shown that the probability that a cascade has not started when it is the turn of i to move converges to zero exponentially as i increases, and there is a positive probability that agents herd on the wrong action.[3] The results extend to a sequential decision model where each agent moves at a given time, choosing among a finite number of options, having observed the actions of the predecessors and receiving an exogenous discrete signal (not necessarily binary) about the uncertain relative value of the options (Bikhchandani, Hirshleifer, and Welch (1992) or BHW for short).[4]

In the models in this family the payoff to an agent depends on the actions of others only through the information they reveal. That is, these are models of pure information externalities. In those models informational cascades occur, with agents eventually disregarding their private information and relying only on public information. Furthermore, it is possible that all agents "herd" on a wrong choice despite the fact that the pooled information of agents reveals the correct choice.

What is at the root of the extreme potential inefficiency of incorrect herds? It is a combination of an information externality, an agent when acting does not take into account the informational effects of his actions on successors, and two assumptions of the BHW model: discrete actions and signals of bounded strength.

With continuous action spaces (containing potentially optimal actions) and agents being rewarded according to the proximity of their action to the full-information optimal action convergence to the latter obtains (see Lee (1993) and section 6.2.1). In this case the actions of agents are always sufficient statistics for their information, all information of agents is aggregated efficiently, and the correct choice eventually identified. With a discrete action space (and discrete signals) there is always a positive probability of herding in a nonoptimal action since agents cannot fine-tune their actions to their information and actions cannot be sufficient statistics for agents' posteriors. As the set of possible actions becomes richer, cascades on average take longer to form and aggregate more information.

---

[3] The reader is referred to Bikhchandani et al. (1998) for a complete introduction to the model and its applications.

[4] Banerjee (1992) presents a similar model with a continuous action space and degenerate payoffs according to which only by hitting the right choice do agents obtain a positive payoff.

The second assumption is that signals are imperfect, identically distributed, and discrete and this implies that they are of bounded strength, which is necessary for a cascade to occur. Smith and Sørensen (2000) show, in the context of the BHW model, that if signals are of unbounded strength, then (almost surely) eventually all agents learn the truth and take the right action.[5] That is, eventually a herd on the right action occurs. With signals of unbounded strength, incorrect herds are overturned by the action of an agent with a sufficiently informative contrary signal (and this individual eventually appears). With signals of (uniformly) bounded strength, herding occurs (almost surely) and it may be on the wrong action. An example of signals of unbounded strength is provided by the model with two states of the world $\theta \in \{0, 1\}$, two actions, and normally distributed signals $s_i = \theta + \varepsilon_i$, with error terms independently distributed across agents $\varepsilon_i \sim N(0, \sigma_\varepsilon^2)$. Then if an agent receives a very high signal, he may believe that the state is high ($\theta = 1$) despite a strong public belief to the contrary.[6]

In fact, except when signals are discrete, informational cascades need not arise. Chamley (2003) argues that for reasonable distributions for the signals cascades will not occur. Convergence to the correct action, however, will be slow. He shows that in the two-states-of-the-world–two-actions model with unbounded beliefs, the public belief converges (in probability) to the truth no faster than $1/t$, while if signals were observable convergence would be exponentially faster. The reason for the slow convergence is the self-correcting property of learning from others (due to Vives (1993) and examined in detail in section 6.3). Suppose that the state of the world is high. Then the public belief converges to $\theta = 1$. However, as the public belief tends to 1, and most agents adopt, it is increasingly unlikely that an agent appears with a sufficiently low signal that it induces this agent to reject adoption. Since there is some probability that this agent appears, the herd is informative and the public belief tends to 1. Nonetheless, because the probability of such an agent appearing tends to 0, the informativeness of the herd and the rate of learning diminish.

In summary, either with continuous action spaces and regular payoffs, or with discrete action spaces and signals of potentially unbounded strength, incorrect herds cannot arise and convergence to the optimal action obtains. In this sense incorrect herds are not a robust phenomenon. What is robust is the self-correcting property of learning from others and the fact that learning from others is slow when there are frictions, be it in the form of discrete actions (with a dramatic effect) or because of noise. In section 6.3 we will see how noise slows down learning when agents can choose from a continuum of actions. Common to all models is the presence of the information externality and the associated inefficiencies it generates.

---

[5] See section 10.1.6 for a formal definition of signals or beliefs of bounded strength.

[6] See Chamley (2003) for a simulation of this example.

6.2 Extensions of the Herding Model

Several extensions of the basic model have been considered in the literature. We will consider in turn partial informational cascades, endogenous order of moves, learning from neighbors and/or reports of predecessors, and payoff externalities and reputational herding.

6.2.1 Partial Informational Cascade

Gale (1996) presents a simple model with the property that, although a full-informational cascade can never occur, outcomes may be inefficient. Suppose that each of n agents, $i = 1, \dots, n$, has to make a binary choice, to invest or not to invest in a project, and receives an independent signal s_i uniformly distributed on $[-1, 1]$. The payoff to investing is given by $\theta = \sum_{i=1}^{n} s_i$. The optimal investment is achieved if all agents invest if and only if $\sum_{i=1}^{n} s_i > 0$.

If agents decide in sequence (exogenously given by $i = 1, \dots, n$), then $i = 1$ invests if and only if $s_1 > 0$, $i = 2$ invests if and only if $s_2 + E[s_1 \mid \text{action of } i = 1] > 0$, and so on. If $i = 1$ has invested, then $i = 2$ invests if and only if $s_2 + E[s_1 \mid s_1 > 0] = s_2 + \frac{1}{2} > 0$. If $i = 1, 2$ have invested, then $i = 3$ invests if and only if $s_3 + \frac{3}{4} > 0$. The result is that the more agents have invested the more extreme must a signal be to overturn the "partial" informational cascade (similarly as when we discussed the role of signal strength above). Obviously, the outcome need not be efficient. For example, for $n = 2$, we may have both agents investing with $s_1 + s_2 < 0$. This model highlights the difference between cascades and herds. A herd may occur even if there is no cascade.

6.2.2 Endogenous Order of Moves

In the basic model the order in which individuals act is exogenously given. If the order of moves is endogenous, then agents learn both from the actions and the delay (no-action) of other agents. There is a trade-off between the urgency of acting (impatience) and the benefit of waiting and acting with superior information.

According to Gul and Lundholm (1995) this trade-off creates clustering (similarity of agents' actions) by allowing first movers to infer some of the information of later movers and by allowing agents with more extreme signals to act first. Gul and Lundholm consider a continuous-time model where agent i, $i = 1, 2$, receives an independent signal s_i uniformly distributed on $[0, 1]$. Agents need to predict $\theta = s_1 + s_2$. The utility of agent i making prediction q_i at time t_i is given by $-(\theta - q_i)^2 - \alpha\theta t_i$, where $\alpha > 0$. A strategy for player i can be described in this context by a function $t_i(s_i)$ which gives the (latest) time at which the player will move given that other players have not moved and that the player has received s_i. It can be shown that at the unique symmetric equilibrium $t(s_i)$ is (strictly) decreasing and continuous and $t(1) = 0$. This means that when the first player moves it reveals his signal. Then the second agent moves immediately since there is no longer any benefit of waiting.

Clustering is explained by two factors: "anticipation" and "ordering." An agent now learns not only from predecessors but also from successors. The reason is anticipation: an agent learns something from the lack of action of another agent about the signal this agent has and this makes the prediction of the first agent similar to the successor's prediction. Furthermore, agents with extreme signals have a higher cost of waiting and will act first, revealing their signals. The forecasts of agents then tend to cluster together because of the higher impact of extreme signals on the forecasted variable. The basic results of the model still hold with n agents. Despite the fact that information is used "efficiently" in Gul and Lundholm's context the informational externalities present are not internalized and there is room for Pareto improvements.

Chamley and Gale (1994) explore the forms of market failure involved in delaying action in an investment model and how they depend on the speed of reaction of agents. Gale (1996) presents a simpler model, of which we have already seen the exogenous sequencing case. Consider now a discrete time two-agent version of the Gale (1996) model with endogenous sequencing and discount factor δ. An agent can invest in any period and his decision is irreversible. The agent with a higher signal will be more impatient to invest. The reason is that the expected value of investing in the first period equals s_i and the cost of delay is $(1 - \delta)s_i$. It is possible to show that there is a unique equilibrium in which agent i invests in the first period if and only if his signal is above a certain threshold $s_i > \bar{s}$. If agent i waits, he will invest in the second period if and only if someone invested in the first period (that is, $s_j > \bar{s}$, $j \neq i$). The equilibrium $\bar{s}$ must balance the cost $(1 - \delta)\bar{s}$ and the option value of delaying. The latter is computed as follows. If agent i does not delay and agent j does not invest in the first period, agent i will regret his decision if $s_i + E[s_j \mid s_j < \bar{s}] < 0$. This happens with probability $\mathrm{P}(s_j < \bar{s})$. The equilibrium $\bar{s}$ is then the unique solution to $(1-\delta)\bar{s} = -\delta\mathrm{P}(s_j < \bar{s})(\bar{s} + E[s_j \mid s_j < \bar{s}])$. In this equilibrium there is no full-information aggregation and agents may ignore their own information. The result may be that an inefficient outcome obtains (for example, it may be that $s_1, s_2 > 0$ but there is no investment because $s_i < \bar{s}$, $i = 1, 2$). It is worth noting that the game ends in two periods even if potentially there are many. If there has been no investment by the end of the second period this is the end of the story: investment collapses. In fact, if there is no investment in the first period this means there will never be investment because no new information will be revealed. The results generalize to more than two agents and then the game finishes in finite time.

In Chamley and Gale (1994) time is also discrete, there is discounting with factor δ, and each agent, $i = 1, \dots, n$, receives a binary signal that provides ($s_i = 1$) or does not provide ($s_i = 0$) an investment opportunity. The payoff to the investment $\pi(\tilde{n})$ increases with the realized number of investment opportunities $\tilde{n} = \sum_{i=1}^{n} s_i$. A player that invests at date t gets a payoff $\delta^{t-1}\pi(\tilde{n})$. A player that does not invest gets a zero payoff. An agent has to decide whether to invest or wait. By investing early the agent reveals that he had an investment opportunity. For any history of actions three things may happen in a symmetric PBE (in behavioral strategies).[7] If the beliefs about $\tilde{n}$ are pessimistic enough no one invests and the game ends (in the next period the situation will not change). If the beliefs about $\tilde{n}$ are optimistic enough, everyone invests and the game also ends. If beliefs about $\tilde{n}$ are intermediate, then an agent randomizes between investing now and waiting. This balances the incentives to invest if no one else does (because then by not investing nothing is learned and in the next period the agent faces the same situation) and the option value of waiting (if other people with an option to invest do so, then it is better to wait and learn from them). Market failure tends to lead to too little information revelation and it may involve "collapse" in the sense that no information is revealed at all and there is no investment.

The model of social learning, extended by Chamley (2004b), considers a general social learning model with irreversible investment of a fixed size for each of a finite number of agents, endogenous timing, and any distribution of private information. The payoff of exercising the option in period t is given by $\delta^{t-1}(\theta - c)$, where δ is the discount factor, θ is a productivity parameter fixed by nature, not observable, and which can take a high or a low value, and $c > 0$ is the cost of investment. If the agent never invests, he gets a payoff of zero. In any period agents still in the market have available the history of the number of investments in each past period. Chamley finds that generically there may be multiple equilibria which generate very different amounts of information. In one equilibrium information revealed by aggregate activity is large and most agents delay investment (only the most optimistic invest), and in the other information revealed by aggregate activity is small and most agents rush to invest (only the most pessimistic delay). Equilibrium strategies are of the cutoff type, where an agent will invest if only if his private belief about the good state is larger than some value. The presence of multiple equilibria is linked to the presence of strategic complementarities in certain regions (where larger cutoffs for the strategies of rivals imply as a best response a large cutoff for the strategy of the player).[8] This is a model where strategic complementarities may arise solely out of informational externalities. Chamley also considers the model with a continuum of agents and noisy observation of the aggregate activity along the lines of Vives (1993). The previous results are shown to be robust in this case.

Zhang (1997) also introduces heterogeneity in the precision of the signals received by agents. This precision is also private information to the agents. There are two types of investment projects (two states) and each agent receives a two-point support signal with random precision. Time is continuous, there is discounting, and when an agent moves the choice is observed. At the unique

[7] A behavioral strategy involves randomization over possible actions at each information set of a player (see Fudenberg and Tirole 1991).

[8] See Vives (2005). Section 8.4.2 spells out a model with strategic complementarities.

equilibrium in pure strategies of the game there is an initial delay and then the agent with the highest precision moves first and everyone else follows immediately. A delayed investment cascade always occurs. The agent with the highest precision moves first because he has the highest expected return from investing as well as the cost of waiting. The second agent will do as the first irrespective of his information because he has a signal of lower quality (given the binary signal). The rest of the agents will follow because the action of the second agent is not informative and waiting is costly. The result is inefficient for two reasons. First because of strategic delay, which is costly. Second, because of incomplete-information aggregation (herding) as investment depends only on the signal of highest precision.

6.2.3 Learning from Neighbors and/or Reports from Predecessors

In the basic model it is assumed that each agent observes the entire sequence of the actions of his predecessors. Smith and Sørensen (1995) assume that agents observe imperfect signals ("reports") of some of their predecessors' posterior beliefs and consider two cases: learning from aggregates (the aggregate number of agents taking each action, for example) and learning from samples of individuals. The latter encompasses word-of-mouth learning and bounded memory. They find in both cases that complete learning obtains eventually with unbounded informativeness of private signals. The analysis is complicated because public beliefs need not be martingales. Smith and Sørensen find systematic biases in the forecasts agents make of future beliefs held by successors, with "mean reversion" in the sampling case and the converse "momentum" in the aggregate statistic case.

Banerjee and Fudenberg (2004) have studied word-of-mouth learning in a model of successive generations making choices between two options. They find that convergence to the efficient outcome obtains if each agent samples at least two other agents, each person in the population is equally likely to be sampled, and signals are sufficiently informative. Convergence is obtained without agents observing the popularity or "market shares" of each choice.

Caminal and Vives (1996, 1999) consider a model of consumer learning about quality and firm competition where consumers learn both from word-of-mouth and market shares. (A stylized version of the consumer side of the model is presented in section 6.4.)

Ellison and Fudenberg (1993, 1995) depart from rational learning by examining the consequences of agents using exogenously specified decision rules to learn from neighbors and with word-of-mouth communication. In Ellison and Fudenberg (1993) agents use a weighted average of past experience and popularity of choice. An early model of social memory with popularity weighting is provided in Smallwood and Conlisk (1979).

Gale and Kariv (2003) extend the social learning model to consider learning in a network and agents are allowed to choose a different action in each date. Convergence of actions is studied as well as the impact of network architecture.

Çelen and Kariv (2004b) build on the model of Gale (1996) to study the case where each of a sequence of agents observes only the (binary) action of the predecessor. With imperfect information it is found that beliefs and actions cycle forever: long periods of herding can be observed but switches to the other action do occur. As time passes the herding periods become longer and longer and the switches increasingly rare.

Callander and Hörner (2006) consider a variant of the BHW model where agents are differentially informed and they do not observe the entire sequence of decisions but only the number of agents having chosen each option. Now it is not known what earlier agents knew when making their choices. This has important implications. Majorities may be wrong as in BHW, and in fact they are more likely to be wrong than right when there is enough heterogeneity in information accuracy. Take the restaurant example (section 6.1) but suppose that in the town there are tourists and locals. Locals have better information than tourists about the quality of the restaurant but otherwise they are indistinguishable from tourists. People arrive at the restaurant one at a time but in random order. An agent has to then decide based on the number of patrons seated at the restaurant (but, unlike in Banerjee (1992), not knowing in which order they arrived) and his private signal. The inference from the observation of a lone dissenter would vary if he were to be the first (a tourist who arrived at random?) or the last (a local who knows better?). Callander and Hörner show that the lone dissenter is more likely to be right if there are more tourists than locals and if their information is sufficiently more accurate. Then the wisdom of the minority holds. This is a finding of antiherding that is purely informational (instead of reputational, as we will see in the next section).

6.2.4 Payoff Externalities and Reputational Herding

Payoff externalities can lead easily to agents taking similar actions. This is the case, for example, in coordination games or, more generally, games of strategic complementarities where the incremental benefit of the action of a player increases with the actions of other players. A typical example would be an adoption game with network externalities.

It is well-known that payoff externalities can be an obstacle to communication. In a cheap talk game an informed sender sends a message to a receiver who chooses an action that affects the payoff of the sender. Although information is not verifiable there can be communication provided that the preferences of sender and receiver have some degree of congruency. However, if preferences are completely opposed, no communication is possible (see Crawford and Sobel 1982; Vives 1999, section 8.3.4).

Reputational herding models introduce informational externality considerations in principal–agent models. Typically, the action of an agent affects the beliefs of a principal as well as his payoff. The payoff to the agent depends on the beliefs of the principal. Suppose that agents are of low or high ability and they want to impress the principal (but neither knows the type of an agent). Scharfstein and Stein (1990) and Graham (1999) find that if the signals of the high ability agents are positively correlated, then they tend to choose the same investment projects and therefore there is an incentive for second movers to imitate first movers. This happens in a context where agents do not learn about their type when receiving their signals. Herding may occur even if signals are conditionally independent if agents learn about their type (Ottaviani and Sørensen 2000). The same occurs if agents receive an additional signal about their type (Trueman 1994; Avery and Chevalier 1999). Other models in which the agents know their type and herding arises are Zwiebel (1995) and Prendergast and Stole (1996). Effinger and Polborn (2001) find that antiherding occurs (that is, the second expert always opposes the report of the first expert) if the value of being the *only* high ability agent is sufficiently large.[9] Morris (2001) presents a model of political correctness where an informed advisor wants to convey his information to an uninformed decision maker who has the same preferences. He finds that an advisor who is sufficiently concerned about his reputation will suppress information in order to avoid an adverse inference about his type.

6.2.5 Evidence

There are several papers that have tried to find evidence for or against herding behavior. Evidence of herding-type phenomena in analysts' forecasts, as well as some antiherding evidence, can be found in Graham (1999), Hong et al. (2000), Welch (2000), Zitzewitz (2001), Lamont (2002), Bernhardt et al. (2006), and Chen and Jiang (2006). For evidence in mutual fund performance, see Hendricks et al. (1993), Grinblatt et al. (1995), Wermers (1999), and Chevalier and Ellison (1999). See also Foster and Rosenzweig (1995) for evidence of learning from others in agriculture.

However, a main problem of empirical work is that there are typically no data on the private information of agents and that the estimation of herding is not structural (and therefore not linked to the theory).[10] This difficulty is overcome in experimental designs. Anderson and Holt (1997) and Hung and Plott (2001) find experimental evidence in favor of the herding and informational cascades as predicted by the Bayesian theoretical model. Some of this evidence is disputed by Huck and Oechssler (2000), Nöth and Weber (2003), Kübler and Weizsäcker (2004), and Çelen and Kariv (2004a), although the latter find that over time agents tend to Bayesian updating. The papers that dispute

[9] Effinger and Polborn (2001, pp. 386–87) offer the following illustration in the economics profession: "A real-life example of antiherding can be found in the economic research industry, and in particular in the empirical branch. After the publication of an applied econometric paper, the next paper concerned with the same topic seems much more likely to find different results than the same results; moreover, the effect seems to be too great as to be explained purely by chance, even if econometric results were completely independent of the available data. A possible explanation for the phenomenon is the same as for antiherding in our model. The payoff for the second econometrician (in terms of expected reputation, publication possibilities and so on) is much higher if he finds a different result than if he finds the same result as his predecessor."

[10] An exception is Cipriani et al. (2005), who propose a structural estimation of herd behavior with transaction data of the NYSE.

the predictions of the theoretical model present explanations of the experimental results based on the bounded rationality of participants. In particular, Kübler and Weizsäcker (2004) look at the case where signals in the basic herding model are costly to acquire. The theoretical prediction then is that only the first player buys a signal and makes a decision based on his information. The others herd behind the first agent. However, in the experimental results too many signals are bought. This is interpreted in terms of the limited depth of the reasoning process of players. Goeree et al. (2007) find that observed behavior with long sequences of decision makers does not conform to the theoretical predictions in an environment theoretically prone to information cascades. Goeree et al. develop a quantal response equilibrium model with implications that find support in the experimental data.

Guarino et al. (2007) study a BHW-type model in which only one of two possible actions is observable to others. Agents decide in some random order that they do not know. When called upon, agents are only informed about the total number of other agents who have chosen the observable action before them. The result then is that only the aggregate cascade on the observable action arises in equilibrium. A cascade on the unobservable action never arises. Guarino et al. test the model experimentally and find support in the data.

6.2.6 Conclusion

The basic model and the extensions considered are still very rough approximations to the phenomenon of social learning. Indeed, the interaction of agents is constrained to a rigid sequential procedure in which individuals take decisions in turn having observed past decisions. Although many examples have been given to apply the basic model—ranging from choice of investments, stores, technologies, candidates for office, number of children, drugs, medical decisions, and religion, to all kinds of fads—it is not immediately obvious that the model actually fits any of those situations well. A fortiori, the model is still far from capturing the functioning of markets in which there is an explicit price formation mechanism, agents have a large flexibility in terms of actions (quantities and/or prices, for example), interact both simultaneously and sequentially, observe aggregate statistics of the behavior of others, and the system is subject to shocks. In the next section we consider a stylized statistical prediction model which seems closer to these stylized features of markets and helps to understand some robust principles of learning from others. At center stage there is the inefficiency of equilibrium in the presence of informational externalities. Furthermore, the model is a step in the direction of bridging the gap with dynamic rational expectations models (to be dealt with in chapters 7–9).

6.3 A Smooth and Noisy Model of Learning from Others

In this section, which follows Vives (1993) and sections 2 and 3 of Vives (1997), the basic model of learning from others with noisy observation is presented, a particular case of which is the sequential decision model with smooth objective and continuous action sets. The model is extended to allow for endogenous information acquisition, and short-lived or long-lived agents.

6.3.1 Slow Learning with Noisy Public Information

Consider a model where in each period $t = 0, 1, \dots$ there is a generation (a continuum) of short-lived agents, each trying to predict a random variable θ, unobservable to them. The expected loss to agent i in period t when choosing an action/prediction q_{it} is the mean squared error: $L_{it} = E[(\theta - q_{it})^2]$.

Agent i in period t has available a *private signal* $s_{it} = \theta + \varepsilon_{it}$, where $\varepsilon_{it} \sim N(0, \sigma_\varepsilon^2)$, $\operatorname{cov}[\varepsilon_{it}, \varepsilon_{jt}] = \varsigma\sigma_\varepsilon^2$, $i \neq j$, $\varsigma \in [0, 1]$. Similarly as in section 1.4, the convention is made that the average $\varepsilon_t = \int_0^1 \varepsilon_{it}\, di$ is a normal random variable with zero mean, and variance and covariance with ε_{it} both equal to $\varsigma\sigma_\varepsilon^2$.[11] All random variables are jointly normally distributed. Let $\bar{\theta} = 0$. When $\varsigma = 0$ there is no correlation between the error terms of the signals and, again by convention, $\varepsilon_t = 0$ (a.s.). The agent also has available a public-information vector $p^{t-1} = \{p_0, \dots, p_{t-1}\}$, where p_t is the average action of agents in period t plus noise, $p_t = \int_0^1 q_{it}\, di + u_t$, and $\{u_t\}_{t=0}^{\infty}$ is a white noise process. In short, agent i in period t has available the information vector $I_{it} = \{s_{it}, p^{t-1}\}$.

Agent i in period t then solves

$$\operatorname*{Min}_{q} E[(\theta - q)^2 \mid I_{it}]$$

and sets $q_{it} = E[\theta \mid I_{it}]$. It follows that the period expected loss L_{it} is given by $L_{it} = E[E[(\theta - E[\theta \mid I_{it}])^2 \mid I_{it}]] = E[\operatorname{var}[\theta \mid I_{it}]]$. (Given the information structure L_{it} will be symmetric across players and, because of linearity and normality, $\operatorname{var}[\theta \mid I_{it}]$ will be nonrandom.)

Remark 6.1. It is worth noting that the formal analysis of the model would be unchanged if agent i in period t had an *idiosyncratic* expected loss function $L_{it} = E[(\theta + \eta_{it} - q_{it})^2]$ with η_{it} being a random variable with zero mean and finite variance σ_η^2, independently distributed with respect to the other random variables of the model. In this case $L_{it} = E[(\theta - q_{it})^2] + \sigma_\eta^2$ and the agent faces the same minimization problem as before. With idiosyncratic loss functions private signals can be thought to be *endogenous* and represent *word-of-mouth* communication. When agent i in period t obtains his payoff we may suppose he learns $\theta + \eta_{it}$ and communicates it to a friend of the next generation. That is, the signal received by i in period $t + 1$ is $\theta + \eta_{it}$. This corresponds to the model provided η_{it} has the same properties as the error terms ε_{it}. In this case the realized payoffs in period t generate information for other agents in period $t + 1$.

If the signals of agents of the same generation are perfectly correlated ($\varsigma = 1$), then we have sequential decision making as in the basic herding model with

[11] This convention is in accord with the finite-dimensional version of the stochastic process of the error terms. See section 10.2.3.

minor variations but with transmission noise. In this case there is a *representative agent* in each period and the model is purely *sequential*, with agents taking actions in turn.

Agents act simultaneously in every period and noise ensures that their average action does not fully reveal θ. The dynamics of public information are easily characterized. Let us posit that the strategies of agents in period t are linear (and symmetric given the symmetric-information structure): $q_{it} = a_t s_{it} + \varphi_t(p^{t-1})$, with a_t the weight given to private information and φ_t a linear function of p^{t-1}. Now, the current public statistic is given by

$$p_t = \int_0^1 q_{it}\, \mathrm{d}i + u_t = a_t(\theta + \varepsilon_t) + u_t + \varphi_t(p^{t-1}),$$

where $\varepsilon_t = \int_0^1 \varepsilon_{it}\, \mathrm{d}i$ is normally distributed. The public signal in period t, p_t, is a linear function of $z_t = a_t(\theta + \varepsilon_t) + u_t$ and past public signals p^{t-1} and is normally distributed since it is a linear combination of normal random variables. Consequently, $q_{it+1} = E[\theta \mid s_{it+1}, p^t]$ is again a linear function of s_{it+1} and p^t. Further, it is clear that for $t = 0$ the induction process to claim linearity of the solution can be started since $E[\theta \mid s_{i0}]$ is linear in s_{i0} because of normality.

Letting $z_t = a_t(\theta + \varepsilon_t) + u_t$, we have that $p_t = z_t + \varphi_t(p^{t-1})$ and that the vector of public information p^t can be inferred from the vector z^t and vice versa. The variable z_t is the new information about θ in p_t. From normality of the random variables it is immediate that the conditional expectation $\theta_t \equiv E[\theta \mid p^t] = E[\theta \mid z^t]$ is a sufficient statistic for public information p^t in the estimation of θ. It follows that the sequence of public beliefs $\{\theta_t\}$ follows a martingale (with $\theta_{-1} \equiv \bar{\theta}$ and relative to the history of public information z^t)

$$E[\theta_t \mid \theta_{t-1}] = E[E[\theta \mid z^t] \mid z^{t-1}] = E[\theta \mid z^{t-1}] = \theta_{t-1},$$

since, when conditioning, the coarser information set (i.e., the one with less information) dominates.[12] Since the conditional expectation is a sufficient statistic for normal random variables, it also follows that $\theta_t = E[\theta \mid \theta_t]$ and therefore $\mathrm{var}[\theta] = \mathrm{var}[\theta \mid \theta_t] + \mathrm{var}[E[\theta \mid \theta_t]] = \mathrm{var}[\theta \mid \theta_t] + \mathrm{var}[\theta_t]$.

Let $\tau_t \equiv (\mathrm{var}[\theta \mid \theta_t])^{-1}$ denote the informativeness (precision) of public information $\theta_t \equiv E[\theta \mid z^t]$, with $z_k = a_k(\theta + \varepsilon_k) + u_k$, $k = 0, \dots, t$, in the estimation of θ. Noting that we can condition equivalently on the variables $\hat{z}_k = \theta + \varepsilon_k + (a_t)^{-1} u_k$, and recalling that $\mathrm{var}[\varepsilon_t] = \varsigma\sigma_\varepsilon^2$ and $\mathrm{var}[a_t^{-1} u_k] = a_t^{-2}\sigma_u^2$, we obtain (see section 10.2.1) that

$$\tau_t = \tau_{t-1} + (\varsigma\tau_\varepsilon^{-1} + (a_t^2\tau_u)^{-1})^{-1} = \tau_\theta + \sum_{k=0}^{t} (\varsigma\tau_\varepsilon^{-1} + (a_k^2\tau_u)^{-1})^{-1}.$$

The result is that the random vector (s_{it}, θ_{t-1}) is sufficient in the estimation of θ based on $I_{it} = \{s_{it}, z^{t-1}\}$ (that is, $E[\theta \mid s_{it}, z^{t-1}] = E[\theta \mid s_{it}, \theta_{t-1}]$). The posterior mean of θ with information $I_{it} = \{s_{it}, \theta_{t-1}\}$ is a weighted average

12 See section 10.3. It is in fact a general result that posterior (Bayesian) beliefs have the martingale property.

of the signals received with weights according to their precisions (the private signal with precision τ_ε and the public with precision τ_{t-1}):

$$E[\theta \mid s_{it}, \theta_{t-1}] = a_t s_{it} + (1 - a_t)\theta_{t-1}, \quad \text{with } a_t = \tau_\varepsilon/(\tau_\varepsilon + \tau_{t-1}).$$

From the martingale property of $\{\theta_t\}$ we have that (i) $\mathrm{cov}[\Delta\theta_t, \Delta\theta_{t-1}] = 0$, where $\Delta\theta_t = \theta_t - \theta_{t-1}$, and (ii) $\mathrm{var}[\Delta\theta_t] = \mathrm{var}[\theta_t] - \mathrm{var}[\theta_{t-1}]$. Furthermore, because of normality, $\mathrm{var}[\theta_t] - \mathrm{var}[\theta_{t-1}] = \mathrm{var}[\theta_t \mid \theta_{t-1}]$. (See section 10.3.3.)

We then have that the total volatility of public information up to period t, $\sum_{k=0}^{t}\mathrm{var}[\Delta\theta_k]$, equals $\sum_{k=0}^{t}\mathrm{var}[\theta_k \mid \theta_{k-1}]$ and adds up to current volatility $\mathrm{var}[\theta_t]$:

$$\sum_{k=0}^{t}\mathrm{var}[\Delta\theta_k] = \sum_{k=0}^{t}\mathrm{var}[\theta_k \mid \theta_{k-1}] = \mathrm{var}\left[\sum_{k=0}^{t}\Delta\theta_k\right] = \mathrm{var}[\theta_t],$$

since $\sum_{k=0}^{t}\Delta\theta_k = \theta_t - \bar{\theta}$ and from the martingale properties (i) and (ii). Furthermore, since $\mathrm{var}[\theta] = \mathrm{var}[\theta \mid \theta_t] + \mathrm{var}[\theta_t]$, we obtain that $\mathrm{var}[\theta_t] = \tau_\theta^{-1} - \tau_t^{-1}$, and therefore $\mathrm{var}[\theta_t \mid \theta_{t-1}] = \mathrm{var}[\theta_t] - \mathrm{var}[\theta_{t-1}] = \tau_{t-1}^{-1} - \tau_t^{-1}$.

As a benchmark let us take the case where there is no noise in the public statistic ($\tau_u = \infty$). Then the order of magnitude of $\tau_t = \tau_\theta + (t+1)\tau_\varepsilon\varsigma^{-1}$ is t for $\varsigma > 0$. In this case the new information in p_t, $a_t(\theta + \varepsilon_t)$, reveals the relevant information of agents. Indeed, even though $a_t \xrightarrow[t]{} 0$ as $t \to \infty$, $a_t > 0$, and therefore the sequence of noisy signals $\{\theta + \varepsilon_t\}$ can be inferred from the sequence of new information $\{a_t(\theta + \varepsilon_t)\}$. Therefore, there is learning about θ as t grows and learning is at the standard rate $1/\sqrt{t}$ (as in the usual case of i.i.d. noisy observations of θ) since the order of magnitude of τ_t is t. When $\tau_u = \infty$ there is no information externality since public information is a sufficient statistic for the information of agents.

However, when there is noise in public information a notable property of the information dynamics of the system is that public precision is accumulated unboundedly but at a slow rate. The result is a manifestation of a *self-correcting property* of learning from others whenever agents are imperfectly informed and public information is not a sufficient statistic of the information agents have (Vives 1993, 1997). Indeed, the weight given to private information a_t decreases with the precision of public information τ_{t-1}, and the lower a_t is, the less information is incorporated in the public statistic p_t because $\tau_t = \tau_{t-1} + (\varsigma\tau_\varepsilon^{-1} + (a_t^2\tau_u)^{-1})^{-1}$. A higher inherited precision of public information τ_{t-1} induces a low current response to private information a_t, which in turn yields a lower increase in public precision $\tau_t - \tau_{t-1}$. In this sense learning from others is self-defeating. Conversely, a lower inherited precision of public information τ_{t-1} induces a high current response to private information a_t, which in turn yields a higher increase in public precision. In this sense learning from others is self-enhancing.

The self-enhancing aspect means that public precision τ_t will be accumulated unboundedly. If this were not the case, the weight given to private precision $a_t = \tau_\varepsilon/(\tau_\varepsilon + \tau_{t-1})$ would be bounded away from zero, necessarily implying that

$\tau_t = \tau_{t-1} + (\varsigma\tau_\varepsilon^{-1} + (a_t^2\tau_u)^{-1})^{-1}$ grows unboundedly, which is a contradiction.[13] As $\tau_t \to \infty$, $a_t = \tau_\varepsilon/(\tau_\varepsilon + \tau_{t-1}) \to 0$.

The self-defeating aspect means that accumulation is slow. Note that $a_t\tau_t \xrightarrow[t]{} \tau_\varepsilon$. Indeed, $\lim_{t\to\infty} a_t\tau_t = \lim_{t\to\infty} a_t\tau_{t-1} = \lim_{t\to\infty}(\tau_\varepsilon^{-1} + \tau_{t-1}^{-1})^{-1} = \tau_\varepsilon$ since $a_t \xrightarrow[t]{} 0$ and $\tau_t \xrightarrow[t]{} \infty$. It is possible to show (Vives 1993, 1997) that

$$t^{-1/3}\tau_t \xrightarrow[t\to\infty]{} (3\tau_u\tau_\varepsilon^2)^{1/3}.$$

The result implies that τ_t grows at the rate of $t^{1/3}$. This slow learning result is quite remarkable since it means that for a large number of observations, if, to attain a certain level of public precision, (approximately) 10 rounds more are needed when there is no noise in the public statistic ($\tau_u = \infty$), we need (approximately) 1000 additional rounds to obtain the same precision in the presence of noise ($\tau_u < \infty$). This is the difference between the usual linear rate of learning t and the cubic concave rate of $t^{1/3}$. The result also demonstrates that the social learning model with perfect observation of the actions of others is not robust.

The rate of learning (accumulation of public precision) is independent of the level of noise. However, the asymptotic precision (or constant of convergence) $(3\tau_u\tau_\varepsilon^2)^{1/3}$ increases with less noise (higher τ_u) and more precise signals (higher τ_ε). This asymptotic precision influences the "slope" of convergence. (See the $\delta = 0$ case in figure 6.2 for the shape of τ_t when $\tau_u < \infty$; when $\tau_u = \infty$, τ_t would grow linearly with t.) More noise in the public statistic or in the signals slows down learning of θ by decreasing the asymptotic precision but it does not alter the convergence rate. Indeed, the asymptotic precision (or the inverse of the asymptotic variance) is a refined measure of the speed of convergence for a given convergence rate.[14]

The proof of the result is somewhat involved.[15] A heuristic argument to show that τ_t is of order $t^{1/3}$, $\tau_t \approx t^{1/3}$ for short, that $a_t \approx t^{-1/3}$, and that $t^{-1/3}\tau_t \xrightarrow[t]{} (3\tau_u\tau_\varepsilon^2)^{1/3}$ runs as follows. Let $\tau_t \approx Kt^{\upsilon}$ for some $K > 0$ and $\upsilon > 0$. Then $a_t \approx \tau_\varepsilon K^{-1}t^{-\upsilon}$ (because $a_t \approx \tau_\varepsilon\tau_t^{-1}$ from $a_t = \tau_\varepsilon/(\tau_\varepsilon + \tau_{t-1})$) and therefore $\tau_t = \tau_\theta + \sum_{k=0}^{t}(\varsigma\tau_\varepsilon^{-1} + (a_k^2\tau_u)^{-1})^{-1} \approx \tau_u\tau_\varepsilon^2K^{-2}\sum_{k=0}^{t}k^{-2\upsilon}$. The term $\sum_{k=0}^{t}k^{-2\upsilon}$ can be seen to be of order $t^{1-2\upsilon}/(1-2\upsilon)$.[16] Now the equality $\upsilon = 1 - 2\upsilon$ implies that $\upsilon = \frac{1}{3}$. Furthermore, $K = \tau_u\tau_\varepsilon^2K^{-2}$ and therefore $K = (3\tau_u\tau_\varepsilon^2)^{1/3}$. The result obtains because as t grows unboundedly, $a_t \to 0$ and so does the amount of new information incorporated into p_t, which is represented by $z_t = a_t(\theta + \varepsilon_t) + u_t$.

---

[13] Similarly, in Banerjee and Fudenberg (2004) convergence to efficiency is obtained when people use samples larger than one because this allows the possibility of "mixed" samples which are relatively uninformative and consequently induces agents to rely on their private information and enhance the information flow into the system. This is again the self-enhancing aspect of learning from others.

[14] See section 10.3.2 for a discussion of measures of speed of convergence.

[15] It follows from an extension of lemma 7.2 in chapter 7 (from Vives 1993) to the case $\varsigma > 0$ and the fact that $a_t\tau_t \xrightarrow[t]{} \tau_\varepsilon$. A version of the proof of the result (adapted from Chamley (2004a)) is provided in the appendix (section 6.8).

[16] See lemma 7.4 in section 7.6.

The fact that $\tau_t \to \infty$ as t grows implies that $\theta_t \to \theta$ with probability 1 (almost surely) and in mean square. The latter is easily checked because, given that $E[\theta_t] = E[\theta]$, $E[(\theta - \theta_t)^2] = \text{var}[\theta - \theta_t]$ and, given that $\theta_t = E[\theta \mid \theta_t]$, $\text{var}[\theta - \theta_t] = \text{var}[\theta \mid \theta_t] = \tau_t^{-1}$, and $\tau_t^{-1} \xrightarrow[t]{} 0$. In fact, convergence (a.s. and in mean square) of the sequence of public beliefs to a limit random variable follows directly from the martingale convergence theorem because $\{\theta_t\}$ is a bounded martingale (since $\text{var}[\theta_t] \leqslant \text{var}[\theta] < \infty$, see section 10.3.3). Furthermore, the speed of learning is slow, at the rate of $1/\sqrt{t^{1/3}}$: $\sqrt{t^{1/3}}(\theta_t - \theta)$ tends in distribution to a normal random variable with zero mean and variance $(3\tau_u\tau_\varepsilon^2)^{-1/3}$. This is immediate because $t^{1/3}\,\text{var}[\theta - \theta_t] = t^{1/3}\tau_t^{-1} \xrightarrow[t]{} (3\tau_u\tau_\varepsilon^2)^{-1/3}$ as $t \to \infty$. Proposition 6.1 summarizes the slow learning results. Denote by $\xrightarrow{\text{L}}$ convergence in law (distribution).

Proposition 6.1 (slow learning (Vives 1993, 1997)). *As $t \to \infty$:*

(i) $a_t \to 0$ *and* $\tau_t \to \infty$;

(ii) $\theta_t \to \theta$ *almost surely and in mean square;*

(iii) $t^{-1/3}\tau_t \to (3\tau_u\tau_\varepsilon^2)^{1/3}$; *and*

(iv) $\sqrt{t^{1/3}}(\theta_t - \theta) \xrightarrow{\text{L}} N(0, (3\tau_u\tau_\varepsilon^2)^{-1/3})$.

It is interesting to analyze the implications of the results for the evolution of the *cross section of beliefs* in the population. Identify the belief of agent i with his prediction

$$q_{it} = E[\theta \mid s_{it}, \theta_{t-1}] = a_t s_{it} + (1 - a_t)\theta_{t-1}, \quad \text{with } a_t = \tau_\varepsilon/(\tau_\varepsilon + \tau_{t-1}).$$

The distribution of beliefs will be normal and characterized by its average $q_t = \int_0^1 q_{it}\,\mathrm{d}i$ and dispersion $\int_0^1 (q_{it} - q_t)^2\,\mathrm{d}i$. Let $\varsigma = 0$ to illustrate. Noting that $q_t = a_t\theta + (1 - a_t)\theta_{t-1}$, using our convention $\int_0^1 s_{it}\,\mathrm{d}i = \theta$ (a.s.), $\theta_t = E[\theta \mid z^t] = (\tau_u \sum_{k=1}^t a_k z_k)/\tau_t$ and therefore $E[\theta_t \mid \theta] = (1 - \tau_\theta/\tau_t)\theta$ (see section 10.2.1), we easily obtain that

$$E[q_t \mid \theta] = (1 - \tau_\theta/(\tau_\varepsilon + \tau_{t-1}))\theta$$

and

$$E\left[\int_0^1 (q_{it} - q_t)^2\,\mathrm{d}i\right] = E[(q_{it} - q_t)^2] = \frac{\tau_\varepsilon}{(\tau_\varepsilon + \tau_{t-1})^2}.$$

Given that τ_t grows as $t^{1/3}$ we obtain that $E[q_t \mid \theta]$ increases monotonically in a concave way to θ (since the function $\varphi(\tau) = -\tau_\theta/(\tau_\varepsilon + \tau)$ is concave) and $E[(q_{it} - q_t)^2]$ decreases monotonically in a convex way to 0 (since the function $\phi(\tau) = \tau_\varepsilon/(\tau_\varepsilon + \tau)^2$ is convex).

With perfect correlation of the signals of agents ($\varsigma = 1$), we have a representative agent each period and we are in the context of the herding models of the last section with the representative agent of each generation taking actions in sequence. With no noise in public information, actions are then fully revealing of the information of agents and public precision τ_t grows at the rate of n. With noisy observation of the actions the self-correcting property of learning from others implies that τ_t grows much more slowly, at the rate of $t^{1/3}$, despite the continuous action space.

With an agent at every period we may also think that observational noise comes from the very action that an agent takes because of an idiosyncratic element. Denote the agent in period t, agent t, then with the idiosyncratic expected loss function $E[(\theta + u_t - q_t)^2]$ if agent t observes the random shock u_t then his action will be $q_t = E[\theta \mid s_t, \theta_{t-1}] + u_t$ and successors of t by observing the history of actions have only noisy observations of signals of the predecessors.

Herd behavior and informational cascades are extreme manifestations of the self-defeating aspect of learning from others. With discrete action spaces and signals of bounded informativeness public information may end up overwhelming the private signals of the agents, who may (optimally) choose not to act on their information.

At the other extreme, an instance where convergence obtains at the standard rate $1/\sqrt{t}$ is when at every period there is a positive mass of perfectly informed agents. The reason is that perfectly informed agents cannot learn from public information and therefore put constant weight on their (perfect) signals. The consequence is that at every round the amount of information incorporated into the public statistic is bounded away from zero ($a_t \xrightarrow[t]{} a_\infty > 0$) and learning is not self-defeating. We will examine this situation in section 7.4. Exercise 7.4 generalizes proposition 6.1 to the case of a general distribution of private precisions in the population (including the case that a positive mass has infinite precision).

Larson (2006) analyzes the representative agent version of the model ($\varsigma = 1$) but where in each period some agents may die and the representative agent observes the average action of all agents still alive with no noise. It is found that if the population size is stable (with agents departing at the same rate they arrive), then public precision accumulates at the fast rate of t (as in the representative agent version of the model with no noise). However, if the population grows, then the rate of accumulation of public precision slows down to $\log(t)$. The combination of population growth and the fact that agents cannot perfectly observe the order in which predecessors acted explains the result. The reason is that by observing the average action the error terms in early private signals persist for a long time since early, less informed decisions cannot be distinguished from later, better informed ones.

6.3.2 Endogenous Information Acquisition[17]

Suppose now that the error terms in the signals are uncorrelated ($\varsigma = 0$) and that private signals have to be purchased at a cost, increasing with and convex in the precision τ_ε of the signal, according to a smooth function $C(\cdot)$ that satisfies $C(0) = 0$, $C' > 0$ for $\tau_\varepsilon > 0$ and $C'' \geqslant 0$. Thus, there are nonincreasing returns to information acquisition. The model is otherwise as before, in

[17] The analysis follows Burguet and Vives (2000).

particular, there are $t = 0, 1, 2, \dots$ generations of short-lived agents and the information structure is the same. Each agent is interested in minimizing the sum of the prediction loss and the information costs

$$\operatorname*{Min}_{(q,\tau_\varepsilon)} (E[(\theta - q)^2 \mid I] + C(\tau_\varepsilon)),$$

where I is the information set of the agent with a private signal of precision τ_ε, the choice variable, and a public signal which summarizes public-information history. The linear-normal structure means that, as in section 6.3.1, public information also follows a normal distribution. Denote the precision of the public signal by τ. Notice that the solution to the problem is $q = E[\theta \mid I]$ and, given τ_ε and τ, the prediction loss is just the inverse of the total precision of the information of the agent: $L(\tau_\varepsilon, \tau) = \operatorname{var}[\theta \mid I] = (\tau_\varepsilon + \tau)^{-1}$. Thus, for given inherited precision of public information τ, the representative agent will minimize over τ_ε

$$\Lambda(\tau_\varepsilon, \tau) = L(\tau_\varepsilon, \tau) + C(\tau_\varepsilon).$$

The expected loss $\Lambda(\tau_\varepsilon, \tau)$ is strictly convex in τ_ε and there will be a unique solution to the minimization problem $y^{\mathrm{m}}(\tau)$ as a function of τ. Let $g^{\mathrm{m}}(\cdot)$ be the market policy function that yields the dynamics of public precision τ. Given τ and private precision purchase $y^{\mathrm{m}}(\tau)$, the weight given to private information is $a = y^{\mathrm{m}}(\tau)/(y^{\mathrm{m}}(\tau)+\tau)$, and therefore public precision in the following period is given by $g^{\mathrm{m}}(\tau) = \tau + \tau_u[y^{\mathrm{m}}(\tau)/(y^{\mathrm{m}}(\tau) + \tau)]^2$. The following proposition characterizes $y^{\mathrm{m}}(\cdot)$ and $g^{\mathrm{m}}(\cdot)$.

Proposition 6.2 (Burguet and Vives 2000). *If $\tau \geqslant [C'(0)]^{-1/2}$, then $y^{\mathrm{m}}(\tau) = 0$. Otherwise, $y^{\mathrm{m}}(\tau) > 0$ and $y^{\mathrm{m}}(\cdot)$ is a (strictly) decreasing, differentiable function of τ. If $C'(0) = 0$, then $y^{\mathrm{m}}(\cdot) \to 0$ as $\tau \to \infty$. The market policy function g^{m} is increasing for τ large enough (for τ close enough to $[C'(0)]^{-1/2}$ if $C'(0) > 0$).*

Proof. From $(\partial\Lambda/\partial\tau_\varepsilon)|_{\tau_\varepsilon=0} = C'(0) - \tau^{-2}$ we have that $y^{\mathrm{m}} = 0$ whenever $\tau \geqslant [C'(0)]^{-1/2}$. Otherwise, the solution is interior, $y^{\mathrm{m}}(\tau) > 0$, and the FOC of the minimization problem yields $y - [C'(y)]^{-1/2} = -\tau$. The left-hand side is strictly increasing and ranges from $-\infty$ to $+\infty$. Therefore this FOC defines implicitly y^{m}. From the implicit function theorem,

$$\frac{\mathrm{d}y^{\mathrm{m}}}{\mathrm{d}\tau} = -\frac{1}{1 + \frac{1}{2}C''(y)[C'(y)]^{-3/2}},$$

and therefore $-1 \leqslant \mathrm{d}y^{\mathrm{m}}/\mathrm{d}\tau < 0$. Now, from $g^{\mathrm{m}}(\tau) = \tau + \tau_u[y^{\mathrm{m}}(\tau)/(y^{\mathrm{m}}(\tau) + \tau)]^2$ we have that

$$\frac{\mathrm{d}g^{\mathrm{m}}}{\mathrm{d}\tau} = 1 + 2\tau_u \frac{y^{\mathrm{m}}}{(y^{\mathrm{m}} + \tau)^3}\left(\frac{\mathrm{d}y^{\mathrm{m}}}{\mathrm{d}\tau}\tau - y^{\mathrm{m}}\right),$$

which is positive for y^{m} close enough to 0 (and/or τ large enough). This shows that g^{m} is increasing for τ large enough and for τ close enough to $[C'(0)]^{-1/2}$ when $C'(0) > 0$. □

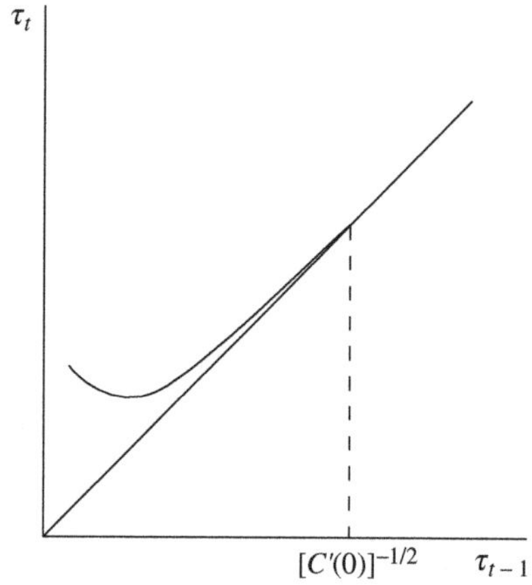

Figure 6.1. The market policy function: $g^{\mathrm{m}}(\cdot)$.

It is worth noting that the policy function need not be increasing for any τ. (See figure 6.1, in which a case where the function is quasiconvex is depicted.) For example, $\mathrm{d}g^{\mathrm{m}}(0)/\mathrm{d}\tau = 1 - 2\tau_u/y^{\mathrm{m}}(0) < 0$ for τ_u large enough. This means that starting with a larger public precision it is possible that at the following iteration we end up with a lower public precision than if we had started from a lower base. This is possible because private (τ_ε) and public (τ) precisions are strategic substitutes in the minimization of the expected period loss Λ. That is, $\partial^2\Lambda/\partial\tau_\varepsilon\partial\tau > 0$. This implies that the purchase of private information decreases with the amount of (inherited) public precision. An increase in τ reduces the incentives to purchase private information and moderates the increase in τ since the weight given to private information $a = (1 + \tau/\tau_\varepsilon)^{-1}$ is reduced. This is a manifestation of the self-correcting property of learning from others.

As an important consequence of this there are instances where more public information hurts. More precisely, aggregate the losses across generations of agents with discount factor $\delta > 0$ and let the aggregate loss be $\ell^{\mathrm{m}}(\tau) \equiv \sum_{t=0}^{\infty} \delta^t L_t$, where L_t is evaluated at the market solution for an initial public precision τ. Then $\ell^{\mathrm{m}}(\tau)$ can be increasing with τ. For instance, it can be checked that this happens if $C(y) = y$, $\tau_u = 2$, and $\delta = 0.98$ for $\tau \leqslant 0.61$. (Exercise 6.2 examines the case where the cost function C is linear.[18]) The result is akin to the remark by Smith and Sørensen (1995) that the observation of larger samples of predecessors does not necessarily improve welfare at the market solution. In a somewhat related vein, Banerjee (1993) in a model of the economics of rumors finds that speeding up the transmission of information (the rumor) has no welfare effect since then the rumor must be received sooner to be trusted (in his model, after a certain, endogenously determined time, a rumor is not trusted).

[18] However, for these parameter values it is easily seen that $\mathrm{d}g^{\mathrm{m}}/\mathrm{d}\tau < 0$ and therefore the range $\tau \leqslant 0.61$ is never "visited" after the initial period for any market sequence τ_t^{m} (see figure 6.1).

Note that even in the model of section 6.3.1 with exogenous private signals the same effect is potentially present. Indeed, when the private precision is fixed at $\tau_\varepsilon > 0$ (and $\varsigma = 0$), then we have that the policy function is $g(\tau) = \tau + \tau_u(\tau_\varepsilon/(\tau_\varepsilon + \tau))^2$, which is strictly convex, can be easily seen to be increasing for $\tau \geqslant \frac{8}{27}\tau_u$, but it may be decreasing for τ_u large. Note also that $g(\tau) > \tau$ and $g' \to 1$ as $\tau \to \infty$. With $\frac{8}{27}\tau_u > \tau_\theta > \tau'_\theta$, it may happen that $g(\tau_\theta) < g(\tau'_\theta)$ and starting from a lower base more public precision is accumulated since, because of the convexity of g, after the first period we are in the increasing portion of g.

It is remarkable that more public information may hurt even in an environment where there are no payoff externalities and only information externalities matter. Morris and Shin (2002, 2005), for example, find in a static model that more information may hurt because of a special "beauty contest" form of the payoff of agents that induces agents to have a private incentive to coordinate, which is socially wasteful (see section 1.4.3). We will confirm robustly in the next section that informational externalities alone suffice to find that more public information may hurt.

Full revelation of θ obtains with endogenous private precisions if and only if the marginal cost of acquiring information when there is no information is zero ($C'(0) = 0$). Indeed, if this marginal cost is bounded away from zero, public precision cannot accumulate without bound since then the marginal benefit of acquiring private information would tend to zero and would be strictly inferior to the marginal cost of information acquisition.

The stated facts provide a hint for a dynamic resolution of the Grossman–Stiglitz paradox (see section 4.2.2) when $C'(0) = 0$. In that case, the market is asymptotically strongly efficient in informational terms, that is, fully revealing of θ, but agents have an incentive to purchase private information throughout. The contradiction between eventual full revelation of θ and incentives to acquire information disappears.

We can see also that if $C'(0) = 0$, the speed of learning decreases as we move away from the exogenous signals situation. This can be done by considering a family of cost functions parameterized by their degree of convexity λ: $C(\tau_\varepsilon) = c\lambda^{-1}\tau_\varepsilon^\lambda$, with $\lambda \geqslant 1$, $c > 0$. For this example it is easily seen that $g^{\mathrm{m}}(\tau)$ is convex. The relative degree of convexity of C is $\tau_\varepsilon C''/C' = \lambda - 1$, and as $\lambda \to \infty$ agents are given signals of precision 1 at no cost. Then for $\lambda > 1$, it can be shown that τ_t is of order t^r with $r = (\lambda - 1)/(3\lambda + 1)$ and a_t of order $t^{-\upsilon}$ with $\upsilon = (\lambda + 1)/(3\lambda + 1)$. We have that $\upsilon > \frac{1}{3} > r > 0$ and r increases with λ. As $\lambda \to \infty$, $r \to \frac{1}{3}$, which is the order of magnitude of public precision when private signals are given exogenously (proposition 6.1). Convergence is faster the more decreasing returns to information acquisition are (the more convex is C and the closer we are to the exogenous information case as parameterized by λ). (See exercise 6.3.)

It is also worth remarking that with our natural specification of costly information acquisition, and contrary to the results of Radner and Stiglitz (1984), the value of information need not be nonpositive at zero. Indeed, the value of precision τ_ε is $\phi(\tau_\varepsilon) = -((\tau_\varepsilon + \tau)^{-1} + C(\tau_\varepsilon))$ and $\phi'(0) = \tau^{-2} - C'(0)$, which can be positive or negative. With our specification the nonconcavity in the value of information of Radner and Stiglitz does not arise.[19] Indeed, $\phi'' < 0$ for all $\tau_\varepsilon \geqslant 0$.

6.3.3 Long-Lived Agents

The model in section 6.3.1 admits an interpretation in terms of a continuum of long-lived agents interacting repeatedly in the market $t = 0, 1, \dots$. The agents are rewarded according to the proximity of their prediction to some random variable θ, unobservable to them. In any period there is an independent probability $1 - \delta$, with $1 > \delta > 0$, that θ is realized and the payoffs up to this period collected. The expected loss to agent i in period t when choosing an action/prediction q_{it} is the mean squared error: $L_{it} = E[(\theta - q_{it})^2]$. The agent has available in period t a private signal $s_i = \theta + \varepsilon_i$ (the same for every period) and a public-information vector $p^{t-1} = \{p_0, \dots, p_{t-1}\}$ as before. Agent i in period t has available the information vector $I_{it} = \{s_i, p^{t-1}\}$. Signals are conditionally independent with the same precision $\tau_\varepsilon = 1/\sigma_\varepsilon^2$, and as usual we make the convention that errors on average cancel out (so that in this case the average signal reveals θ).

Myopic behavior is optimal for an agent, solving $\mathrm{Min}_q\, E[(\theta - q)^2 \mid I_{it}]$ and setting $q_{it} = E[\theta \mid I_{it}]$. Indeed, an agent is infinitesimal and cannot affect the public statistics. Agents act simultaneously in every period and noise avoids that their average action fully reveals θ. The model is formally identical to the model in section 6.3.1 when $\varsigma = 0$. In this case public precision is given by $\tau_t = \tau_\theta + \tau_u \sum_{k=0}^{t} a_k^2$.

Amador and Weill (2007) provide a continuous-time extension of the model (for the case $\varsigma = 0$). Agent i receives the payoff $\int_0^T (\theta - q_{it})^2\, di$ at the random time T when θ is realized. T has an exponential distribution with intensity $\kappa > 0$: θ is realized at time t with probability density $\kappa e^{-\kappa t}$. This means that the expected payoff of agent i is $E(\int_0^T (\theta - q_{it})^2\, \mathrm{d}i) = E(\int_0^\infty e^{-\kappa t} (\theta - q_{it})^2\, \mathrm{d}t)$. Note that this is equivalent to our formulation according to which the probability that θ is realized at time t is δ^t by letting $\delta = e^{-\kappa}$. The nice feature of continuous time is that a closed-form solution can be provided. It is found that

$$\tau_t = (3\tau_u \tau_\varepsilon^2 t + (\tau_\varepsilon + \tau_\theta)^3)^{1/3} - \tau_\varepsilon.$$

From this result it is immediate then that τ_t is of order $t^{1/3}$ and that $t^{-1/3}\tau_t \xrightarrow[t]{} (3\tau_u \tau_\varepsilon^2)^{1/3}$. Note that now $\partial \tau_t / \partial \tau_\theta > 0$ for all t while in the discrete time version we have seen that this need not be the case in the first round.

Amador and Weill (2007) extend the model by allowing agents to receive at time zero a private exogenous signal with precision τ_ε and a public exogenous signal of precision τ_0 about the unknown θ plus a private and a public signal

[19] See section 3 in Radner and Stiglitz (1984) to see how a crucial assumption of their theorem fails in our case. See also Kihlstrom (1984) for further analysis of the potential nonconcavity of the value of information.

about the average action with, respectively, precisions τ_e and τ_u. That is, it adds to the original formulation an exogenous public signal at $t = 0$ as well as a private signal about the average action for any t. The private learning channel may arise, for example, when an agent samples from a distribution centered on the aggregate action. Now, the precision of private information evolves according to γ_t and the precision of public information according to τ_t yielding a response to private information of $\gamma_t/(\gamma_t + \tau_t)$ and a mean squared prediction error at t of $(\gamma_t + \tau_t)^{-1}$.

Amador and Weill obtain two interesting results. The first is that the path of the average prediction $q_t = \int_0^1 q_{it}\,\mathrm{d}i$ conditional on θ, $E[q_t \mid \theta] = (1 - \tau_\theta/(\gamma_t + \tau_t))\theta$ has an S-shaped diffusion pattern if private information is sufficiently dispersed initially (i.e., τ_ε is low enough). Then learning accelerates at the beginning with agents putting more weight on their private information and the public signal becoming more and more informative. Eventually, as agents learn θ the effect tapers off. Furthermore, due to learning from the private channel the dispersion of beliefs $E[(q_{it} - q_t)^2] = \gamma_t/(\gamma_t + \tau_t)^2$ can be seen to be hump-shaped. At the beginning beliefs are concentrated close to the common prior. As agents learn privately beliefs become dispersed only to converge later as θ is revealed.

The second result is that an increase in initial public precision τ_θ increases the total precision $\gamma_t + \tau_t$ in the short run but decreases it in the long run since it decreases uniformly the endogenous private precision γ_t. In fact, the same is true if the noise in the public signal is reduced (i.e., τ_u increases). These results hold provided that the private learning channel is active (i.e., provided that $\tau_e > 0$). This opens the door to an increase in total discounted expected loss $E(\int_0^\infty \mathrm{e}^{-\kappa t}(\theta - q_{it})^2\,\mathrm{d}t)$ as a result of an increase in τ_θ. Amador and Weill show that a marginal increase in public information hurts as long as the payoff is realized in a sufficiently long time (i.e., the mean of the random end T κ^{-1} is large enough) and/or the amount learned by unit of time (as measured by a common scaling factor in τ_e and τ_u) high enough. However, as expected, a sufficiently large increase in public precision would be good. As in the basic models of sections 6.3.1 and 6.3.2 welfare eventually increases with public precision starting from a high enough base.

6.3.4 Summary

We have provided in this section a central result on slow learning from others in the presence of frictions (i.e., noise). This is the outcome of the self-correcting property of learning from others. With no frictions the public statistic is sufficient for the signals of predecessors and learning is at the usual rate. However, this result is not robust to the presence of noise in the public statistic. If there is noise, the public statistic is not sufficient. If the public statistic is more informative, then agents rely less on their private information and less of this private information is incorporated into the public statistic. This slows down learning. We could say that the weight of history slows down learning. However, if the public statistic is less informative, then the opposite happens and this speeds up learning and ensures eventual full revelation. The results obtain both with short-lived and long-lived agents.

An important associated result is that public and private precision are strategic substitutes from the point of view of the decision maker. This means that increases in the initial stock of public information may discourage the use of private information and end up in a lower path of accumulation of public precision and welfare. This is particularly so when agents acquire private signals about the fundamental since then better public information discourages private-information acquisition. Furthermore, if agents have to acquire their private signals, then full revelation will be precluded if the marginal cost of acquiring information is positive at 0. Otherwise, full revelation obtains but the speed of learning decreases as we move away from the exogenous signal case.

Even more so, the potentially damaging effect of public information is more pronounced when there is an active private learning channel about aggregate activity. We therefore find that even in a world without payoff externalities and where agents are interested only in predicting the fundamentals, more public information may hurt.

6.4 Applications and Examples

This section presents several examples and applications of the basic smooth learning model of section 6.3 and a brief discussion of the relationship between the smooth herding model and dynamic rational expectations models.

6.4.1 Examples

The first two examples involve short-lived agents, the others involve long-lived agents.

Consumers learning about quality. As we have already observed the formal analysis of the model would be unchanged if agents had an *idiosyncratic* expected loss function $L_{it} = E[(\theta + \eta_{it} - q_{it})^2]$ with η_{it} being a random variable with finite variance σ_η^2 independently distributed with respect to the other random variables of the model. In this case $L_{it} = E[(\theta - q_{it})^2] + \sigma_\eta^2$.

Suppose now that in each period there are many consumers of two types: "rational" and "noise" or "random." All consumers are endowed with a utility function that is linear with respect to money. Consumers only differ in their information and live for one period. Generation t consumer i's utility when consuming q_{it} is given by

$$U_{it} = (\theta + \eta_{it})q_{it} - \tfrac{1}{2}q_{it}^2.$$

The willingness to pay of consumer i in period t is $\theta + \eta_{it}$. Consumers are uncertain about $\theta + \eta_{it}$ and only learn it after consuming the good. The parameter

θ represents the average component of the willingness to pay and will depend on the matching between product and population characteristics. Consumer i in period t receives a signal s_{it} about θ (word-of-mouth from the experience of a previous consumer or an independent test of the product). Given that the idiosyncrasy η_{it} of consumer i in period t is uncorrelated with all other random variables in the environment and that the consumer learns $\theta + \eta_{it}$ only after consuming the good we have that $E[\theta + \eta_{it} \mid I_{it}] = E[\theta \mid I_{it}]$. Assume for simplicity that firms produce at zero cost and that prices are fixed at marginal cost. Expected utility maximization plus price-taking behavior (at zero price) imply $q_{it} = E[\theta \mid I_{it}]$. If u_t denotes the purchases of the random consumers, then aggregate demand will be $p_t = \int_0^1 E[\theta \mid I_{it}]\,\mathrm{d}i + u_t$. Consumers active in period t have access to the history of past sales $p^{t-1} = \{p_0, p_1, \dots, p_{t-1}\}$. Consumer i's information set in period t is therefore $I_{it} = \{s_{it}, p^{t-1}\}$. The model is thus formally identical to the one presented in section 6.3 (under the same distributional assumptions). Indeed, the expected welfare loss with respect to the full-information first-best (where θ is known and $q_{it} = \theta$) is easily seen to be $\frac{1}{2}E[(\theta - q_{it})^2]$. The results imply that consumers will slowly learn quality from quantities consumed or market shares. Furthermore, slow learning by consumers enhances the possibilities of firms of manipulating consumer beliefs (for example, signal-jam the inferences consumers make from market shares (see Caminal and Vives 1996, 1999)).

Location decisions and information acquisition. Consider a world where an earthquake (the "big one" in California) may strike in any period with probability $1 - \delta$. The location θ is the safest from the point of view of the earthquake, the problem is that θ is unknown and it will not be known until the earthquake happens! Agents have to make (irrevocable) location decisions based on their private (costly) assessment of θ and any public information available. The latter consists of the average location decisions of past generations. These average locations contain an element of noise since for every generation there are agents who locate randomly independently of any information. The private assessment of an agent is based on geological research he conducts. The higher the effort the agent spends on this research the better estimate he obtains. This example would then correspond to the endogenous information acquisition case considered in section 6.3.2.

Macroeconomic forecasting and investment. Consider competitive firms deciding about investment in the presence of macroeconomic uncertainty, which determines profitability, represented by the random variable θ. At each period there is an independent probability $1 - \delta$ that the uncertainty is resolved. Firms invest taking into account that the profits of their accumulated investment depend on the realization of θ. The investment of a firm is directly linked to its prediction of θ. To predict θ each firm has access to a private signal as well as to public information, aggregate past investment figures compiled by a government agency. Data on aggregate investment incorporate measurement error.[20] Consequently, at each period a noisy measure of past aggregate investment of the past period is made public. The issue is whether the repeated announcement of the aggregate investment figures reveals θ, and if so how fast.

Reaching consensus and common knowledge. At a more abstract level, consider the reaching of consensus starting from disparate expectations. It has been shown that repeated public announcements of a stochastically monotone aggregate statistic of conditional expectations, which need not be common knowledge, leads to consensus (see McKelvey and Page (1986) and Nielsen et al. (1990) following up on Aumann (1976)). In the iterative process, individuals compute conditional expectations with the information they have available and the aggregate statistic is announced. Individuals then compute again their expectations on the basis of their private information plus the new public information, and the process continues. The aggregate statistic is supposed to represent the outcome of the interaction of agents in a reduced-form way. In many instances nevertheless market interaction will only provide agents with a noisy version of an aggregate statistic of individual conditional expectations due to the presence of noise in the communication channels, random traders, demand or supply shocks, etc. In the model of section 6.3.3 repeated public announcements of a linear *noisy* function of agents' conditional expectations leads to consensus but slowly. We could say, rephrasing a result in the literature (Geanakoplos and Polemarchakis 1982), that in the presence of noisy public information "we cannot disagree forever but we can disagree for a long time."

Learning by doing. Models of *learning by doing* assume that unit production costs decrease with the total accumulated production. There is empirical evidence of learning by doing on production processes which involve complex coordinated labor operations like aircraft assembly and, more recently, in computers. A typical model of learning by doing assumes that the unit cost of production with an accumulated production of t is of the form $C(t) = kt^{-\lambda}$ with λ between 0 and 1 and k a constant. A rate of cost reduction of $t^{-1/3}$ is typical for airframes and corresponds to a 20% "progress ratio" (that is, the proportionate reduction of per-unit labor input when the cumulated output doubles (see Fellner 1969)). Progress ratios oscillate in empirical studies between 20% and 30%.[21] The applied literature emphasizes the importance of group effort and "integrated adaptation effort" in the explanation of the learning curve (see, for example, Baloff 1966). Improved coordination seems to be at the root of improved productivity. The coordination problem takes a very simple (and

[20] For example, quarterly data on national accounts are subject to measurement error. See Rodríguez-Mora and Schulstald (2007) for the consequences of this measurement error on output.

[21] See Scherer and Ross (1990, pp. 98–99). The following quotation is from Arrow's seminal paper on learning by doing (1962): "It was early observed by aeronautical engineers, particularly T. P. Wright, that the number of labor-hours expected in the production of an airframe (airplane body without engines) is a decreasing function of the total number of airframes of the same type previously produced. Indeed, the relation is remarkably precise; to produce the nth airframe of a given type, counting from the inception of production, the amount of labor required is proportional to $t^{-1/3}$."

extreme) form in the model: costs are lower the closer the actions of workers are to an unknown parameter θ. The total expected cost of output in production round t is proportional to $\int_0^1 E[(\theta - q_{it})^2]\,\mathrm{d}i$, where q_{it} is the action of worker i in period t. Worker interaction reveals the statistic p_t. The model of section 6.3.3 predicts that the rate of learning, as given by the precision of public information τ_t, and consequently the period loss (expected unit cost), will be of order $t^{-1/3}$. This means that expected cost will decline at the rate $t^{-1/3}$. So we would have $\lambda = \frac{1}{3}$ in $C(t) = kt^{-\lambda}$.

6.4.2 Relation to Dynamic Rational Expectations and Preview of Results

Do the results obtained in section 6.3 extend to more complex economic situations, closer to the actual functioning of markets? In those situations payoff externalities will matter and will interact with the informational externalities examined in our prediction model. In this section we overview briefly some of the models with payoff and informational externalities that we will deal with in the following chapters. One issue of interest, as we will see in chapter 7, is whether convergence to full-information equilibria will obtain at a (relatively) fast rate in market environments. Otherwise, the Walrasian model may not be a good approximation of the behavior of agents in the economy even when repeated interaction has given the opportunity to prices to reveal information.

The smooth noisy model of learning from others of section 6.3 is close to classical dynamic rational expectations models. In the latter prices are noisy aggregators of dispersed information and agents choose from a continuum of possible actions with smooth payoffs as rewards. Nevertheless, the slow learning results cannot be applied mechanistically. Indeed, markets are more complex than the simple models of the previous sections. A general reason is that, unlike in the pure learning/prediction model, in market models the payoff of an agent depends directly on the actions of other agents. That is, there are payoff externalities. For example, the profit of a firm depends on the outputs of rivals firms.

Furthermore, learning need not always be from others, agents can also learn from the environment. An example is provided by the classical learning in the rational expectations partial equilibrium model with asymmetric information (as developed by Townsend (1978) and Feldman (1987); see sections 7.2 and 7.3). In this model long-lived firms, endowed with private information about an x_t uncertain demand parameter θ, compete repeatedly in the marketplace. Inverse demand in period t is given by $p_t = \theta + u_t - x_t$, with x_t being average output, and production costs are quadratic. The result is that learning θ and convergence to the full-information equilibrium (or shared-information equilibrium in which θ is revealed) occur at the standard rate $(1/\sqrt{t})$.[22] The reason is that public information (prices) depend directly (independently of the actions

[22] As we will see in chapter 7 (following Jun and Vives 1996), in general, learning θ and converging to a full-information equilibrium are not equivalent.

of agents) on the unknown parameter θ. Even if agents had no private information, they would learn from prices at the standard rate because, for a given output, the price observation p_t corresponds to an i.i.d. noisy signal $\theta + u_t$ of θ.

In contrast, in a variation of the classical model (see section 7.4 of the present book and Vives (1993)), where the unknown θ is a cost parameter (a pollution damage, for example) prices will be informative about θ only because they depend on the actions of firms, and the strength of the dependence will vanish as t grows large due to the self-defeating facet of learning from others. Indeed, expected profit maximization yields an optimal production which is linear in the conditional expectation of θ and in past prices, and the result is that, as in the purely statistical model of section 6.3, firms learn slowly about θ and convergence to the full-information equilibrium is also slow.

The speed at which prices reveal information is particularly important in financial markets where price or value discovery mechanisms are in place. An example is provided by the information *tâtonnement* designed to decrease the uncertainty about prices after a period without trade (overnight) in the opening batch auction of some continuous stock trading systems. At the beginning of trade there is a period where agents submit orders to the system and *theoretical* prices are quoted periodically as orders accumulate. No trade is made until the end of the *tâtonnement* and at any point agents may revise their orders. It is important that this information aggregation mechanism performs its value discovery purpose fast. A stylized version of this mechanism is considered in section 9.1.3 where it is shown that information is aggregated at a fast rate in the presence of a competitive market-making sector while without it convergence is slow. The reason why market makers (or agents using limit orders/demand schedules and supplying liquidity to the market) speed up convergence is as follows. Market makers, by expanding market depth, induce risk-averse agents not to respond less to their private information as prices become more informative about the fundamental value of the risky asset. The presence of market makers prevents the self-defeating facet of learning from others from settling in. The outcome is that price quotations converge to the underlying value of the asset at a rate of $1/\sqrt{t}$, where t is the number of periods.

In a related vein, Avery and Zemsky (1998) show how introducing a competitive market-making sector in the basic herding model (by adapting the Glosten and Milgrom (1985) model of sequential trading in financial markets, see section 9.1.1) convergence of the price to the fundamental value obtains. Indeed, the basic herding model (section 6.1) does not allow for price changes once agents buy or sell the good. Furthermore, and interestingly, Avery and Zemsky show that when traders are uncertain about the quality of information (precision) held by other traders, then "booms and crashes" based on herd behavior are possible. The reason is that a poorly informed market may not be easily distinguishable from a well-informed one from the point of view of competitive market makers. A similar explanation of market crashes has been offered by Romer (1993). (See section 8.4.1.)

In summary, in the market examples considered there is learning from others and we see how changes in the market microstructure have consequences for convergence and the speed of learning. This shows that caution must be exercised when applying herding and slow learning results to market situations. A fuller development of these models is provided in chapters 7–9.

6.5 The Information Externality and Welfare

In this section, the analysis in which follows Vives (1997) and Burguet and Vives (2000), a welfare analysis of the prediction model in section 6.3 is presented. We are particularly interested in whether agents put too little weight on their private information with respect to a well-defined welfare benchmark. The welfare analysis in herding models has been typically neglected in the literature. Here we address the issue in the smooth learning from others model developed in section 6.3.

At the root of the inefficiencies detected in models of learning from others lies an information externality. An agent when making its decision (prediction) does not take into account the benefit to other agents. Consider the basic model of section 6.3.3 (with long-lived agents). The (*ex ante* expected) loss of a representative agent in period t, $L_t = E[(\theta - E[\theta \mid I_{it}])^2] = \text{var}[\theta \mid I_{it}] = (\tau_\varepsilon + \tau_{t-1})^{-1}$, decreases with public precision τ_{t-1}. Note that L_t is independent of i since the information structure is symmetric. A larger response of agents to their private signals in period t will lead to a larger precision in period t, τ_t, and consequently a lower loss in period $t + 1$ (and in subsequent periods). This is not taken into account by an individual agent.

The analysis of the information externality leads naturally to a *welfare-based definition of herding* as an excessive reliance on public information with respect to a well-defined welfare benchmark. This, as in chapter 1, is the team solution (Radner 1962) which assigns to each agent a decision rule so as to minimize the discounted sum of period losses. The planner or team manager, however, cannot manipulate the information flows (in particular, it has no access to their private information). This solution internalizes the externality respecting the decentralized information structure of the economy. Optimal learning at the team solution then trades off short-term losses with long-run benefits. That is, it involves experimentation.

Welfare losses are discounted with discount factor δ, $1 > \delta \geqslant 0$ (consistently with the unknown θ having an independent probability of $1-\delta$ of being revealed in any period in the model with long-lived agents). The planner is restricted to using linear rules (for agent i, $q_{it}(I_{it})$, where, as before, $I_{it} = \{s_i, p^{t-1}\}$ and $p_k = \int_0^1 q_{ik}\,\mathrm{d}i + u_k$); the same family of simple rules that agents in the market use. This means that the planner only needs to convey to the agents the weight they should put on their private information. This corresponds to a low level of complexity in the instructions of the team manager to the agents.

The team manager has an incentive to depart from the myopic minimization of the short-term loss and "experiment" to increase the informativeness of public information. This is accomplished by imposing a response to private information above the market response. We look first at a two-period model, move on to the infinite-horizon model, and conclude with results when information is costly to acquire.

6.5.1 A Two-Period Example

Let us illustrate the team problem with a *two-period* example, $t = 0, 1$. The team has to choose linear decision rules $q_0(s_i)$ and $q_1(s_i, p_0)$ to minimize $L_0 + \delta L_1$, where $L_t = E[(\theta - q_t)^2]$. This is easily solved by backward recursion and a unique linear team solution is found. Posit $q_0(s_i) = a_0 s_i$ (since by assumption $\bar{\theta} = 0$). It is immediate that $L_0 = E[(\theta - q_0(s_i))^2] = (1 - a_0)^2/\tau_\theta + a_0^2/\tau_\varepsilon$ and that the precision of public information for period 1 is $\tau_0 = \tau_\theta + \tau_u a_0^2$. In period 1 for a given τ_0, the team solution is just the market (Bayesian) solution and therefore $L_1 = (\tau_\varepsilon + \tau_0)^{-1}$.

The FOC to minimize $L_0 + \delta L_1$, which turns out to be sufficient (since $L_0 + \delta L_1$ is quasiconvex in a_0), is given by

$$\frac{\partial L_0}{\partial a_0} + \delta \frac{\partial L_1}{\partial a_0} = 2\left(-\tau_\theta^{-1} + a_0(\tau_\theta^{-1} + \tau_\varepsilon^{-1}) - \delta \frac{a_0 \tau_u}{(\tau_\varepsilon + \tau_0)^2} \right) = 0.$$

This yields a unique solution a_0^{o} between the market solution $a_0^{\text{m}} = \tau_\varepsilon/(\tau_\varepsilon + \tau_\theta)$ and 1.

It is clear that $\partial L_1/\partial a_0 < 0$ and consequently $\partial L_0/\partial a_0 > 0$ at the optimum. The market solution a_0^{m} involves $\partial L_0/\partial a_0 = 0$ and therefore, given convexity, $a_0^{\text{o}} > a_0^{\text{m}}$.

Comparative static properties can be derived in the standard way obtaining $\partial a_0^{\text{o}}/\partial \delta > 0$, $\partial a_0^{\text{o}}/\partial \tau_\theta < 0$ (using the fact that $1 > a_0$) and $\partial a_0^{\text{o}}/\partial \tau_\varepsilon > 0$. Furthermore, $\operatorname{sgn}(\partial a_0^{\text{o}}/\partial \tau_u) = \operatorname{sgn}(\tau_\theta + \tau_\varepsilon - \tau_u (a_0^{\text{o}})^2)$ and $\partial a_0^{\text{o}}/\partial \tau_u$ is positive if τ_u is small ($\tau_\theta + \tau_\varepsilon > \tau_u$) and negative if τ_u is large ($\tau_\theta + \tau_\varepsilon < \tau_u(\tau_\varepsilon/(\tau_\theta + \tau_\varepsilon))^2$).

The information externality implies that there is underinvestment in public information at the market solution $a_0^{\text{o}} > a_0^{\text{m}} \equiv \tau_\varepsilon/(\tau_\theta + \tau_\varepsilon)$. The comparative statics results are intuitive: the optimal response to private information a_0^{o} increases with the discount factor (the weight given to the future) and with the precision of private information, and it decreases with the prior precision about θ. That is, it is optimal to experiment more whenever the future matters more, the quality of private information is better or the precision of prior information worse.

An increase in the noise of public information induces agents to experiment less (more) if the starting level of noise is low (high). Recall that the market solution in period 0, $\tau_\varepsilon/(\tau_\theta + \tau_\varepsilon)$, is independent of τ_u. The optimal solution does depend on τ_u. When τ_u is small there is a lot of noise in public information and reducing the noise induces more experimentation with a higher a_0^{o}; when τ_u is large there is little noise in public information and reducing the noise more induces less experimentation because it is costly and what matters is the informativeness of the public statistic.

It should be obvious also that welfare increases at the team solution with increases of either τ_θ or τ_u. An increase in τ_θ reduces L_1 and L_0 for any a_0; an increase in τ_u reduces L_1 and does not affect L_0. The situation is potentially different at the market solution since there is an indirect negative effect of an increase in τ_θ on $a_0^{\mathrm{m}} \equiv \tau_\varepsilon/(\tau_\theta + \tau_\varepsilon)$ and therefore on τ_0.

6.5.2 The Infinite-Horizon Model

Let us turn now to the infinite-horizon problem. Given decision rules $q_{it}(I_{it})$, where I_{it} is the information of agent i in period t, the average expected loss in period t is $\int_0^1 E[(\theta - q_{it}(I_{it}))^2]\,di$. Furthermore, it can be checked that there is no loss of generality in restricting our attention to symmetric rules (see exercise 6.4): $q_{it}(I_{it}) = q_t(I_{it})$ for all i. The expected loss in period t is then $L_t = E[(\theta - q_t(I_{it}))^2]$. The objective of the team is to minimize $\sum_{t=0}^{\infty} \delta^t L_t$ choosing a sequence of linear functions $\{q_t(\cdot)\}_{t=0}^{\infty}$, where q_t is a function of $I_{it} = \{s_i, p^{t-1}\}$ and $p_k = \int_0^1 q_k(s_i, p^{k-1})\,di + u_k$.

The analysis proceeds as in the market case. As before, we can write the strategy of agent i in period t as $q_k(s_i, \theta_{t-1}) = a_t s_i + c_t \theta_{t-1}$, with a_t and c_t the weights, respectively, to private and public information (with θ_{t-1} the sufficient statistic for public information). The precision of public information θ_t equals $\tau_t = \tau_\theta + \tau_u(\sum_{k=0}^{t} a_k^2)$, and therefore only the coefficients a_t matter in the accumulation of information (the coefficients c_t have no intertemporal effect). In period t, c_t is chosen, contingent on a_t, to minimize L_t. This is accomplished by setting $c_t = 1 - a_t$. It is easily seen then that $L_t = E[(\theta - q_k(s_i, \theta_{t-1}))^2] = (1 - a_t)^2/\tau_{t-1} + a_t^2/\tau_\varepsilon$, where $\tau_{t-1} = \tau_\theta + \tau_u \sum_{k=0}^{t-1} a_k^2$.

The reduced-form team minimization problem is then to choose a sequence of real numbers $\{a_t\}_{t=0}^{\infty}$ to solve

$$\mathrm{Min} \sum_{t=0}^{\infty} \delta^t L_t, \quad \text{with } L_t = \frac{(1 - a_t)^2}{\tau_{t-1}} + \frac{a_t^2}{\tau_\varepsilon},$$

where $\tau_{-1} = \tau_\theta$ and $\tau_{t-1} = \tau_\theta + \tau_u \sum_{k=0}^{t-1} a_k^2$ for $t = 1, 2, \dots$.

The team problem can be posed in a classical dynamic programming framework taking the sequence $\{\tau_t\}_{t=0}^{\infty}$ as control (noting that $\tau_t - \tau_{t-1} = \tau_u a_t^2$). It can be checked that the value function $\Lambda(\cdot)$ associated with the control problem is the solution to the functional equation

$$\Lambda(\tau) = \min_{\tau'}\{L(\tau', \tau) + \delta\Lambda(\tau')\},$$

where $L(\tau', \tau) = (1 - \sqrt{(\tau' - \tau)/\tau_u})^2/\tau + (\tau' - \tau)/\tau_u\tau_\varepsilon$.

It can be shown that $\Lambda : \mathbb{R}_+ \to \mathbb{R}$ is strictly convex, twice continuously differentiable and strictly decreasing with $\Lambda' < 0$. As $\tau \to \infty$, $\Lambda'(\tau)$ and $\Lambda(\tau)$ tend to 0. Indeed, Λ is strictly decreasing with the accumulated precision of public information τ because a higher accumulated precision today generates uniformly (strictly) lower period losses for all feasible sequences from then on. At the team solution, which takes care of the dynamic information externality, increasing the precision of public information is unambiguously good. This need not be the case at the market solution because a higher initial public precision might discourage the use of private information and subsequent accumulation of public precision.

The policy function $g^{\mathrm{o}}(\cdot)$ gives the unique solution to the team problem: the next period's public precision as a function of the current one. It can be shown (see the proof of proposition 4.4 in Vives (1997)) that g^{o} is quasiconvex, continuously differentiable, with $\mathrm{d}g^{\mathrm{o}}/\mathrm{d}\tau > 0$ for τ large enough, and $\mathrm{d}g^{\mathrm{o}}/\mathrm{d}\tau < 1$ (with $\mathrm{d}g^{\mathrm{o}}/\mathrm{d}\tau$ tending to 1 as $\tau \to \infty$). Given that $g^{\mathrm{o}}(\tau) > \tau$, it is immediate then that $\tau \to \infty$ and that a decreases over time (since $a_t^2 = (\tau_t - \tau_{t-1})/\tau_u = (g^{\mathrm{o}}(\tau_{t-1}) - \tau_{t-1})/\tau_u$).

The results for $\delta > 0$ are as follows. First of all, there is herding, in the sense that, for any given accumulated precision of public information τ, the team optimal response to private information a^{o} is strictly larger than the market solution $a^{\mathrm{m}} = \tau_\varepsilon/(\tau_\varepsilon + \tau)$ (in particular, $a_0^{\mathrm{o}} > a_0^{\mathrm{m}}$). Given the function $L(\tau', \tau)$ defined above, denote by $\partial_1 L$ the partial derivative with respect to the first argument and by $\partial_{11} L$ the second partial with respect to the first argument. The result follows from the FOC of the team problem $\partial_1 L(g^{\mathrm{o}}(\tau), \tau) + \delta\Lambda'(g^{\mathrm{o}}(\tau)) = 0$ because $\Lambda' < 0$ and therefore $\partial_1 L(g^{\mathrm{o}}(\tau), \tau) > 0$, while at the market solution τ^{m} (with $\delta = 0$) $\partial_1 L(\tau^{\mathrm{m}}, \tau) = 0$. Given that $\partial_{11} L > 0$, we conclude that $g^{\mathrm{o}}(\tau) - \tau = \tau_u(a^{\mathrm{o}})^2 > \tau_u(a^{\mathrm{m}})^2 = \tau^{\mathrm{m}} - \tau$. Second, the market underinvests in information: the team solution in any period has accumulated more public precision than the market ($\tau_t^{\mathrm{o}} > \tau_t^{\mathrm{m}}$). The second result follows from the properties of the policy function g^{o}.

For $\delta = 0$ the market solution is obtained ($a_t^{\mathrm{o}} = a_t^{\mathrm{m}}$ for all t). With $\delta > 0$ and given a certain accumulated public precision the optimal program calls for a larger response to private information because it internalizes the benefit of a larger response today in lowering future losses. Agents herd and rely too little on their private information at the market solution. However, this does not mean that the optimal program involves a uniformly larger response to private information over time because it accumulates more public precision. Simulations[23] for $\delta > 0$ show that there is a critical $\bar{t}$, increasing with δ and τ_ε, and decreasing with τ_u, after which the optimal program calls for a lower response to private information than the market to collect the benefits of the initial accumulation/experimentation phase. That is, there is a $\bar{t}$ such that $a_t^{\mathrm{o}} > a_t^{\mathrm{m}}$ for $t < \bar{t}$, and $a_t^{\mathrm{o}} < a_t^{\mathrm{m}}$ for $t > \bar{t}$. Comparative statics with the discount factor δ are as follows:

[23] Simulations have been performed for a horizon of T periods approximating the infinite horizon with the discounted loss implied by a constant public precision from period $T+1$ on at the level of public precision in period T. That is, the total present ($t = 0$) discounted loss from period $T+1$ on when the public precision in period T is τ equals $\delta^{T+1}/(1-\delta)\tau$. The range of parameter values considered is δ in $[0.75, 0.98]$, τ_u in $[0.1, 100]$, τ_ε in $[0.05, 20]$, fixing $\tau_\theta = 1$ and with T up to 50.

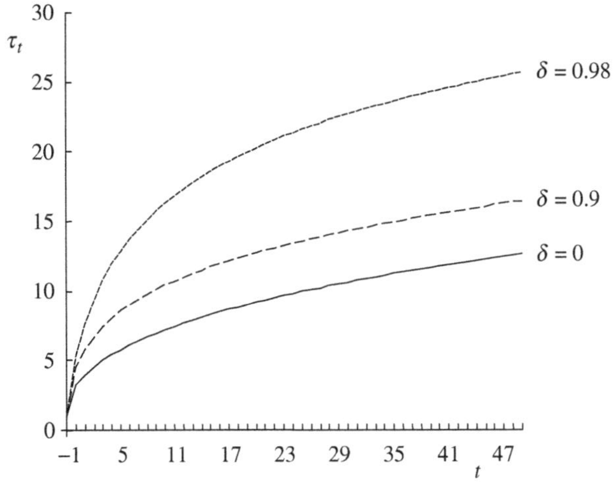

Figure 6.2. Precision of public information and discount factors: $\tau_\theta = 1$, $\tau_\varepsilon = 2$, $\tau_u = 5$.

(i) For any t, τ_t increases with δ. (See figure 6.2.)

(ii) For t large (small), L_t is decreasing (increasing) in the discount factor δ.

This is in accordance with the "investment" and "consumption" phases of the accumulation program.

Let $\ell^{\mathrm{m}} = \sum_{t=0}^{\infty} \delta^t L_t$, with L_t the period loss at the market solution and $\ell^{\mathrm{o}} = \Lambda(\tau_\theta)$ the value at the team solution. Then, the relative welfare loss of the market solution with respect to the team solution $(\ell^{\mathrm{m}} - \ell^{\mathrm{o}})/\ell^{\mathrm{m}}$ can be quite high. For example, $(\ell^{\mathrm{m}} - \ell^{\mathrm{o}})/\ell^{\mathrm{m}}$ is around 25% for $\tau_u = 5$, $\tau_\varepsilon = 0.5$, $\delta = 0.95$, and $\tau_\theta = 1$. The relative welfare loss increases with δ and nonmonotonic in τ_ε and τ_u. For extreme values of τ_ε or τ_u there is no information externality and the market and team solutions coincide. For τ_ε very large there is almost perfect information and almost no loss. For $\tau_\varepsilon = 0$ there is no private information. For τ_u very large public information is almost fully revealing and for $\tau_u = 0$ it is uninformative.

However, slow learning at the market solution is not suboptimal. The team solution has exactly the same asymptotic properties as the market. The reason is that for t large the market and the optimal program look similar because the value function of the latter is almost flat for large public precision. In both, the responsiveness to private information tends to 0 as t grows. The result follows as in the market case since at the optimal solution $a_t \tau_{t-1} \to \tau_\varepsilon$ as $t \to \infty$. This is so because at the optimal solution $\partial_1 L(\tau_t, \tau_{t-1}) + \delta \Lambda'(\tau_t) = 0$ for any t. As $t \to \infty$ so does τ_t and consequently $\Lambda'(\tau_t) \to 0$. Therefore, $\partial_1 L(\tau_t, \tau_{t-1}) = \tau_\varepsilon^{-1} - (1 - a_t)(a_t \tau_{t-1})^{-1} \to 0$ as $t \to \infty$ and $a_t \tau_{t-1} \underset{t}{\to} \tau_\varepsilon$ and $a_t \underset{t}{\to} 0$. This is the only way to enjoy the benefits of the accumulated public precision because to accumulate public precision faster would entail too large a departure from the minimization of current expected losses. In particular, to put asymptotically a constant positive weight on private information and consequently obtain an increase in precision which is linear in t is not optimal.

Proposition 6.3 summarizes the results obtained.

Proposition 6.3 (Vives 1997). *Optimal learning. Let $\delta > 0$, the team solution:*

(i) *Responds more to private information, for any given τ, than the market solution $\tau_\varepsilon/(\tau + \tau_\varepsilon)$.*

(ii) *Period by period accumulates more public precision than the market ($\tau_t^{\mathrm{o}} > \tau_t^{\mathrm{m}}$).*

(iii) *Has the same asymptotic properties as the market, in particular, the same rate of (slow) learning.*

The properties of the optimal learning program when agents are short-lived and signals potentially correlated are similar, and the same results hold. The analysis of optimal learning proceeds as before with minor variations. The presence of correlation in the signals tends to decrease the optimal weight given to private information. For example, in the two-period optimal learning problem it is easily seen that a_0^{o} decreases with ς. The reason is that with correlated error terms in the signals increasing the weight in private signals also increases the weight in the aggregate error, which now is not zero. Obviously, when $\tau_u = \infty$ there is no information externality since public information is a sufficient statistic for the information of agents (although with $\varsigma > 0$ public information is not perfectly revealing of θ) and the market solution is optimal.

In terms of the *applications* presented in section 6.4 the optimal learning results imply the following. In the learning by doing example the team problem is to coordinate workers to minimize the expected costs of production. Suppose that the team manager can impose decision rules on the workers which are measurable in the information they have. Then the theory predicts that independently of whether the team manager behaves myopically or as a long-run optimizer (taking into account the learning externality), the rate of learning as given by the precision of public information τ_t, and consequently the period loss (expected unit cost), will be of order $t^{-1/3}$. This means that expected cost will decline at the rate $t^{-1/3}$. In the consumer learning example the results imply that consumers are too cautious with respect to the welfare benchmark in responding to their private information.

6.5.3 Costly Information Acquisition

When private information is costly to acquire as in section 6.3.2 the effects of the information externality are accentuated. Consider the same model as in section 6.3.2 and a second-best welfare benchmark in which private-information purchases can be controlled, via tax-subsidy mechanisms, but otherwise agents are free to take actions (make predictions). Given a sequence of private precisions $\{\gamma_t\}$ chosen by the planner, an agent in period t will choose the action that minimizes his loss, taking τ_{t-1} and y_t as given. The agent will put a weight on his private signal equal to $a_t = y_t/(y_t + \tau_{t-1})$ inducing a period expected loss of $(y_t + \tau_{t-1})^{-1}$. The problem of the planner is to choose a sequence of nonnegative real numbers $\{y_t\}_{t=0}^{\infty}$ to solve

$$\text{Min} \sum_{t=0}^{\infty} \delta^t \left(\frac{1}{y_t + \tau_{t-1}} + C(y_t) \right),$$

where $\tau_{-1} = \tau_\theta$ and $\tau_t = \tau_{t-1} + \tau_u (y_t/(y_t + \tau_{t-1}))^2$ for $t = 1, 2, \dots$.

Burguet and Vives (2000) characterize the solution to the program. Similarly to the market solution if $C'(0) > 0$ public precision does not accumulate unboundedly. We have seen in section 6.3.2 how an increase in initial public precision may hurt welfare at the market solution. Indeed, private-information acquisition at the market solution decreases with inherited public precision and therefore the reduction of the prediction losses today may make more costly to decrease future losses. The same is true for the second-best benchmark. For instance, an increase in τ_θ increases the discounted expected losses in the range $\tau \in (0.28, 0.54)$ for $\tau_u = 2$, $C(y) = 2y$, and $\delta = 0.98$. The reason is the self-defeating aspect of learning from others. Increasing public precision today reduces the weight agents put on private information (for a given precision τ_ε) tomorrow. This means that to maintain a certain weight on private information (which is what determines the increase in the next period public precision) more effort has to be devoted to acquire private information (to raise τ_ε).

However, it can be shown that, for a large enough initial public precision τ, more public precision is always good at the second-best solution. The reason is that for τ large enough, the weight given to private information has to be small and the indirect effect of an increase in τ in discouraging private-information acquisition cannot be large while the direct effect is the same. Denote by $y^{\text{sb}}(\tau)$ the optimal purchase of private precision at the second-best solution for a given public precision τ. It follows that for large τ there is herding at the market solution, whenever $y^{\text{m}}(\tau) > 0$, in relation to the second-best. That is, less private-information purchase $y^{\text{sb}}(\tau) > y^{\text{m}}(\tau)$, and subaccumulation of public information. This subaccumulation may be very severe when $C'(0) > 0$ and the discount factor δ large.

Another relevant welfare benchmark is the *team-efficient* solution. This corresponds to the solution where the planner can assign decision rules to agents as well as control information purchases. It is a first-best solution with decentralized strategies. The team solution internalizes the dynamic information externalities.

Concentrate attention on linear and symmetric (and this is without loss of generality) decision rules. In period t the team manager has to choose parameters a_t, b_t, and y_t so that each agent will buy a private signal with precision y_t and then take a decision $q_{it} = a_t s_{it} + b_t \theta_{t-1}$, where, as before, θ_t is the summary public statistic with precision $\tau_t = \tau_\theta + \tau_u \sum_{k=0}^{t} a_k^2$. The parameter b_t has no intertemporal effect and, given the values y_t and a_t, it is set $b_t = 1 - a_t$ to minimize the one-period prediction loss. This yields a period loss of

$$L_t = \frac{a_t^2}{y_t} + \frac{(1-a_t)^2}{\tau_{t-1}} + C(y_t).$$

Notice that, given τ_{t-1} and y_t, choosing $a_t < 0$ is dominated by $|a_t| > 0$ since τ_t remains unchanged and L_t is lower. Thus, we only need to consider $a_t \geqslant 0$. Furthermore, given a_t, y_t has no intertemporal effect either, and therefore y_t is chosen to minimize the one-period loss, again. Therefore, at any interior solution y_t and given the strict convexity of L_t in y_t, the FOC to minimize L_t has to hold:

$$\left(\frac{a_t}{y_t}\right)^2 = C'(y_t).$$

If $a_t = 0$, then $y_t = 0$. We therefore have, for a given a, a unique solution $y^{\mathrm{o}}(a)$ with $y^{\mathrm{o}}(0) = 0$ and it is strictly increasing. In summary, the team problem can be written as

$$\min_{\{a_t \geqslant 0\}} \sum_{t=0}^{\infty} \delta^t L_t,$$

where

$$L_t = \begin{cases} \dfrac{a_t^2}{y^{\mathrm{o}}(a_t)} + \dfrac{(1-a_t)^2}{\tau_{t-1}} + C(y^{\mathrm{o}}(a_t)) & \text{for } a_t > 0, \\[2ex] \tau_{t-1}^{-1} & \text{for } a_t = 0, \end{cases}$$

with $\tau_t = \tau_{t-1} + \tau_u a_t^2$ and $\tau_{-1} = \tau_\theta$.

The team's problem can be written equivalently as finding a value function $\Lambda^{\mathrm{o}}(\cdot)$ such that

$$\Lambda^{\mathrm{o}}(\tau) = \inf_{a \geqslant 0}[L(a,\tau) + \delta\Lambda^{\mathrm{o}}(\tau + \tau_u a^2)],$$

where

$$L(a,\tau) = \frac{a^2}{y^{\mathrm{o}}(a)} + \frac{(1-a)^2}{\tau} + C(y^{\mathrm{o}}(a)).$$

The characterization of the solution is similar to the second-best solution but now the value function is strictly decreasing always. Indeed, this is so since $\partial L(a,\tau)/\partial\tau < 0$. Indeed, the team manager controls both y and a and therefore he does not have to worry about agents giving less weight to private information when public precision increases. A consequence is that at the team optimum it never pays to add noise to public information. More public information is always good once the dynamic information externalities are controlled for at the team solution. A consequence is that the information purchase is higher at the team solution for any τ than at the market solution. Denote by $a^{\mathrm{o}}(\tau)$ the team solution, then $y^{\mathrm{o}}(a^{\mathrm{o}}(\tau)) > y^{\mathrm{m}}(\tau)$ for any τ and the team solution accumulates more public precision. This can be heuristically checked as follows. Suppose that $\Lambda^{\mathrm{o}}(\tau)$ is differentiable and $\partial\Lambda^{\mathrm{o}}/\partial\tau < 0$. The FOC of the team control problem yields $\partial L/\partial a + 2a\tau_u\delta\partial\Lambda^{\text{o}}/\partial\tau = 0$ and therefore, since $a > 0$, at the team solution $\partial L/\partial a > 0$. At the market solution ($\delta = 0$) we have that $\partial L/\partial a = 0$ and using the envelope condition for y we obtain $\partial^2 L/(\partial a)^2 > 0$ and therefore $a^{\text{o}}(\tau) > a^{\text{m}}(\tau)$ and consequently $y^{\text{o}}(a^{\text{o}}(\tau)) > y^{\text{m}}(\tau)$.

Moreover, using the parameterized example, it can be checked that the speed of learning and asymptotic properties are the same in the market, the second-best benchmark, and the team solution.

Simulations of the model with the cost function $C(\tau_\varepsilon) = c\lambda^{-1}\tau_\varepsilon^\lambda$, with $\lambda \geqslant 1$ and $c > 0$, show the following:[24]

(a) For any t, $\tau_t^{\text{o}} > \tau_t^{\text{sb}} > \tau_t^{\text{m}}$. Typically, the second-best is much closer to the market than to the first-best. (See figure 6.3.)

(b) Underinvestment in public precision at the market solution, both with respect to the team and the second-best, increases with the distance to the exogenous signals case (as parameterized by $1/\lambda$).

(c) The relative welfare loss of the market solution, both with respect to the team and the second-best, increases with the distance to the exogenous signals case $1/\lambda$ and in the discount factor δ but is nonmonotonic in the precision of noise in the public signal τ_u. The relation between improvements in information transmission (increases in τ_u) and relative welfare losses is not monotonic. This should not be surprising since the information externality bites in an intermediate range of τ_u. If it is very low, public information is very imprecise anyway, and if it is very high, public information is almost fully revealing. The relative welfare losses can be very large (up to 35% for the first-best and up to 12% for the second-best, even for moderate values of δ and λ, such as, for example, 0.9 and 2, respectively).

(d) The team solution may display a weight for the private precision a well above 1, implying a negative weight given to public information. Furthermore, the team solution $a^{\text{o}}(\tau)$ is not always monotone in τ.

6.5.4 Summary

Learning from others involves a basic information externality that induces herding and under-accumulation of public information. A welfare benchmark that

---

[24] The simulations have been performed by using the following approximation to the infinite-horizon minimization problem:

$$\text{Min}\left(\sum_{t=0}^{T}\delta^t L_t + \delta^{T+1}((1-\delta)\tau_T)^{-1}\right),$$

with the appropriate controls in each case, and $T = 75$ for $\delta \leqslant 0.9$, $T = 100$ for $\delta = 0.95$, and $T = 150$ for $\delta = 0.98$. The range of parameter values examined has been δ in $[0.5, 0.98]$, τ_u in $[0.01, 20]$, c in $[0.01, 50]$, λ in $[1, 50]$, fixing $\tau_\theta = 0.5$.

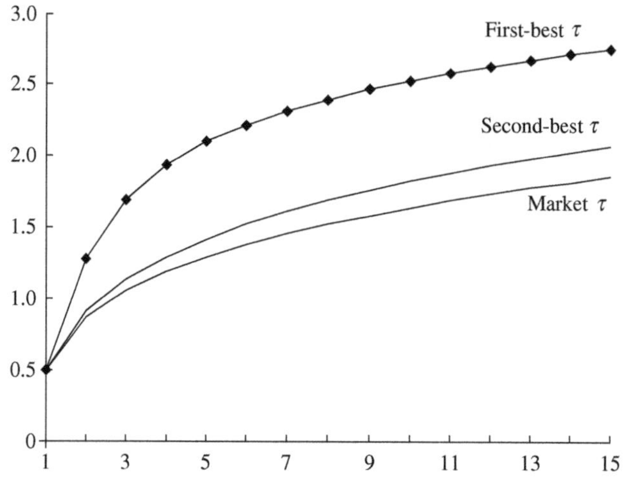

Figure 6.3. Evolution of the public precision τ_t in the three problems ($\tau_\theta = 0.5$, $\tau_u = c = 1$, $\delta = 0.9$, $\lambda = 3$).

internalizes the information externalities is needed to compare with the market solution. This is accomplished by the team-efficient solution which internalizes the information externality and provides an appropriate benchmark to compare with the market solution. The welfare loss due to the information externality may be important but the (slow) rate of learning in the market is not suboptimal. The information externality and the associated welfare loss may be substantial and are aggravated with costly information acquisition. The strategic substitutability between private and public information means that public information may hurt welfare except in the team-efficient solution.

6.6 Rational Expectations, Herding, and Information Externalities

As stated in the introduction to this chapter and in section 6.1, herding or, more generally, the insufficient reliance of agents on their private information has been put forward as an explanation for different phenomena like financial crises, fashion, and technology adoption. The herding literature has put its finger on the welfare consequences of information externalities in a very stark statistical prediction model.

We have seen in sections 6.3–6.5 how the root of inefficiency in herding models is an informational externality not taken into account by agents when making decisions. We consider here a static version of the model in section 6.3 with a rational expectations flavor. In this section agents when making predictions can condition on the current public statistic (similarly to the strategies considered in chapters 3 and 4). The rational expectations equilibrium in the prediction model can then be compared with the team-efficient solution in which the informational externality is taken into account.

We compare the team with the market solution similarly to the analysis of REE in section 3.4.[25] The analysis is basically a simplified version of sections 3.2 and 3.4, where there is an information externality but not a payoff externality.

6.6.1 A Model with a Rational Expectations Flavor

The model is a static version of the model in section 6.3, where the public-information signal is given by $p = \int_0^1 q_i \, di + u$ with q_i being the prediction of agent i and u normally distributed noise, $u \sim N(0, \sigma_u^2)$. Agent i receives a private signal s_i about θ and solves the problem

$$\operatorname*{Min}_{q} E[(\theta - q)^2 \mid I_i], \quad \text{where } I_i = \{s_i, p\}.$$

This information structure corresponds to a rational expectations solution. Indeed, think of agent i submitting a schedule contingent on the realizations of p, $q_i(s_i, \cdot)$, where p solves the equation $p = \int_0^1 q_i(s_i, p) \, di + u$. The forecast of agent i is contingent on his private signal and the (noisy) average forecast. We assume that all random variables are normally distributed with the same properties as in section 6.3. In particular, $\theta \sim N(\bar{\theta}, \sigma_\theta^2)$. The solution to the agent's problem is $q_i = E[\theta \mid I_i]$.

The minimization of the square loss function may arise from agents having quadratic utility functions. Suppose agent i has a utility function given by $U_i = (\theta + \eta_i)q_i - \frac{1}{2}q_i^2$, where η_i is an idiosyncratic random term (uncorrelated with everything else). For example, let q_i be the capacity decision of firm i, where $\theta + \eta_i$ indexes the marginal (random) value of capacity and let investment costs be quadratic. A firm decides about capacity based on its private information and the aggregate capacity choices in the industry, which includes some firms that invest for exogenous reasons, irrespective of information signals, with aggregate value u. Alternatively, competitive firms decide about investment with macroeconomic uncertainty represented by the random variable θ, which determines average profitability. Firms invest taking into account that the profits of investment will depend on the realization of θ. To predict θ each firm has access to a private signal as well as to public information, the aggregate investment figures compiled by a government agency. Data on aggregate investment incorporate measurement error. The agent could also be a consumer facing a good of random quality as in the example in section 6.4. Finally, agent i may be a retailer facing a random price $\theta + \eta_i$.

In any case the expected welfare loss with respect to the full-information first-best (where θ is known and $q_i = \theta$) is easily seen to be $\frac{1}{2}E[(\theta - q_i)^2]$.

Given the structure of the model, Bayesian equilibria will necessarily be symmetric. Let a be the coefficient of s_i in the candidate linear equilibrium strategy of agent i. Then from the normality assumption and $p = \int_0^1 q_i \, di + u$, it follows that p will be a linear transformation of $z \equiv a\theta + u$ and that $E[\theta \mid p] = E[\theta \mid z]$.

[25] This section is based on Bru and Vives (2002).

Let $\theta^* \equiv E[\theta \mid z]$. We can write the equilibrium strategy as

$$q_i(s_i, z) = E[\theta \mid s_i, z] = as_i + (1-a)\theta^*,$$

where $a = \tau_\varepsilon/(\tau + \tau_\varepsilon)$ and $\tau \equiv (\mathrm{var}[\theta \mid p])^{-1} = \tau_\theta + \tau_u a^2$.[26]

It is not difficult to check that there is a unique linear Bayesian equilibrium (the market solution). The equilibrium strategy is given by $q_i = a^{\mathrm{m}} s_i + (1 - a^{\mathrm{m}})\theta^*$, where a^{m} is the unique positive real solution to the cubic equation $a = \tau_\varepsilon/(\tau_\varepsilon + \tau_\theta + \tau_u a^2)$. We have that $0 < a^{\mathrm{m}} < \tau_\varepsilon/(\tau_\varepsilon + \tau_\theta)$ and

$$L^{\mathrm{m}} \equiv E[(\theta - E[\theta \mid s_i, z])^2] = (\tau_\varepsilon + \tau^{\mathrm{m}})^{-1} = a^{\mathrm{m}}/\tau_\varepsilon,$$

where $\tau^{\mathrm{m}} = \tau_\theta + \tau_u(a^{\mathrm{m}})^2$. Furthermore, a^{m} and L^{m} decrease with τ_θ and τ_u; a^{m} increases and L^{m} decreases with τ_ε. In this context public information does not hurt: welfare increases with either better prior information τ_θ or a less noisy transmission channel τ_u. However, the result is not trivial since there are two effects. An increase in τ_θ or τ_u has a direct positive impact on τ^{m} but an indirect negative one on a^{m}, which tends to reduce τ^{m}. The direct one prevails and public information reduces the prediction loss. The impact of an increase in private precision is positive on both accounts reducing directly the prediction loss and increasing a^{m} and τ^{m}.

6.6.2 The Team-Efficient Solution

Given decision rules $q_i(I_i)$ for the agents the average expected loss is

$$\int_0^1 E[(\theta - q_i(I_i))^2]\,\mathrm{d}i.$$

Restrict the planner to impose linear rules and let, without loss of generality, $q_i(I_i) = a_i s_i + c_i\theta^*$. Then it is optimal to set $c_i = 1 - a_i$ since public information would otherwise not be exploited efficiently (which in our context means that $\mathrm{cov}[(\theta - q_i), \theta^*] = 0$). As in section 6.5, there cannot be any gain from using asymmetric rules. With a symmetric rule $q_i(I_i) = as_i + (1-a)\theta^*$, the expected loss is given by

$$L(a) = \frac{(1-a)^2}{\tau_\theta + \tau_u a^2} + \frac{a^2}{\tau_\varepsilon}.$$

It is easily seen that $L' = -2\tau^{-1}(1 - a(\tau_\varepsilon + \tau)\tau_\varepsilon^{-1} + (1-a)^2\tau_u\tau^{-1})$ from which it follows that $L'(1) > 0$ and $L'(a^{\mathrm{m}}) < 0$ since $a^{\mathrm{m}} = \tau_\varepsilon/(\tau_\varepsilon + \tau^{\mathrm{m}})$.

Denote by a^{o} the (unique) team solution[27] and let $L^{\mathrm{o}} \equiv L(a^{\mathrm{o}})$. It follows that at the unique linear team solution $1 > a^{\mathrm{o}} > a^{\mathrm{m}}$ and a^{o} increases with τ_ε and decreases with τ_θ. This follows immediately from $\partial^2 L(a^{\mathrm{o}})/\partial a \partial\tau_\theta > 0$ and $\partial^2 L/\partial a \partial \tau_\varepsilon < 0$. However, $\mathrm{sgn}(\partial^2 L/\partial a \partial \tau_u)$ is ambiguous. L^{o} decreases with τ_ε, τ_θ, and τ_u. This follows directly from $\partial L/\partial\tau_u < 0$, $\partial L/\partial \tau_\varepsilon < 0$, and $\partial L/\partial\tau_\theta < 0$.

---

[26] It is immediate from normal theory that $E[\theta \mid s_i, z] = (\tau_\varepsilon s_i + \tau_u a z + \tau_\theta\bar{\theta})/(\tau_\varepsilon + \tau)$ and $\tau = \tau_\theta + \tau_u a^2$. Equivalently, $E[\theta \mid s_i, z] = as_i + (1-a)E[\theta \mid z]$, where $a = \tau_\varepsilon/(\tau + \tau_\varepsilon)$ because $E[\theta \mid z] = (\tau_u a z + \tau_\theta \bar{\theta})/\tau$.

[27] L is strictly quasiconvex in a.

As expected, the weight given to private information is too low and the weight given to public information is too high at the market solution. The reason is that agents at the market solution do not internalize the positive effect on others of their response to private information because of the increase in the informativeness of the public statistic p. Here public (or private) information cannot hurt because the information externality is taken care of.

The proposition summarizes the results.

Proposition 6.4 (market and team solutions (Bru and Vives 2002)).

(i) *We have that* $1 > a^{\mathrm{o}} > a^{\mathrm{m}}$.

(ii) *All coefficients increase with* τ_ε *and decrease with* τ_θ*;* a^{m} *also decreases with* τ_u.

(iii) L^{o} *and* L^{m} *decrease with* τ_θ, τ_ε, *and* τ_u.

For extreme values of the parameters τ_ε and τ_u the information externality disappears. Indeed, as $\tau_\varepsilon \to 0$ (uninformative signals), a^{o} and a^{m} tend to 0, and as $\tau_\varepsilon \to \infty$ (perfectly informative signals), a^{o} and a^{m} tend to 1. As $\tau_u \to 0$ (no public information), a^{o} and a^{m} tend to $\tau_\varepsilon/(\tau_\theta + \tau_\varepsilon)$, and as $\tau_u \to \infty$ (perfect public information), a^{o} and a^{m} tend to 0.

6.7 Summary

This chapter has presented the basic models of learning from others developing the results obtained in the social learning and herding literature and confronting the apparent contradiction between those and the ones obtained by the dynamic rational expectations literature, providing a common framework for the analysis. The chapter has also provided an appropriate welfare benchmark with incomplete information: the team-efficient solution introduced in chapter 1. The most important conclusions are the following:

- The disparate results obtained in those two strands of the literature basically reflect the underlying assumption in the herding literature that does not allow an agent to fine-tune his action to his information.
- The basic information externality problem, the fact that an agent when taking an action today does not take into account the informational benefit that other agents will derive from his action, underlies the discrepancy between market and team-efficient solutions.
    - With discrete actions spaces (and signals of bounded strength) the inefficiency may take a very stark form with agents herding on the wrong action.
    - In more regular environments learning from others ends up revealing the uncertainty, although it will do so slowly if there is observational noise or friction.

- Learning from others with noisy observation by Bayesian agents has a self-correcting property. A higher inherited precision of public information will lead a Bayesian agent to put less weight on his private signal and consequently less of his information will be transmitted by the public statistic. This slows down learning.
- However, slow learning is team-efficient; that is, it is optimal as long as attention is restricted to decentralized strategies. This does not mean that the market solution is team-efficient. Because of the information externality, the market solution under-accumulates public precision and there is herding in the sense that agents put too little weight on their private signals with respect to the team solution that internalizes the externality.
- Endogenous and costly information acquisition accentuates the effect of the information externality, slowing down learning and increasing the relative welfare loss at the market solution.
- The strategic substitutability between public and private information is behind the possibility that more public information may decrease welfare in a world without payoff externalities. This cannot happen at the team-efficient solution since then the information externality is internalized.

6.8 Appendix

Proof of (iii) in proposition 6.1: $t^{-1/3}\tau_t \xrightarrow[t]{} (3\tau_u\tau_\varepsilon^2)^{1/3}$. (This is an adaptation of the proof provided by Chamley (2004a) for the case $\varsigma = 1$.) From the analysis in section 6.3 we have that $\tau_{t+1} = \tau_t + (\varsigma\tau_\varepsilon^{-1} + (a_{t+1}^2\tau_u)^{-1})^{-1} = \tau_t + (\varsigma\tau_\varepsilon^{-1} + \tau_u^{-1}(1 + \tau_\varepsilon^{-1}\tau_t)^2)^{-1}$ since $a_{t+1} = \tau_\varepsilon/(\tau_\varepsilon + \tau_t)$. This defines the policy function $\tau_{t+1} = g(\tau_t) > 0$, $\tau_t > 0$. Let $v_t = 1/\tau_t$ and consider the function $\varphi : \mathbb{R}_+ \to \mathbb{R}$, $v_{t+1} = \varphi(v_t) \equiv 1/g(1/v_t)$. It is easily seen that

$$\varphi(v_t) = v_t - \frac{v_t^4}{v_t^3 + (\varsigma\sigma_\varepsilon^2 + \sigma_u^2)v_t^2 + 2\sigma_u^2\sigma_\varepsilon^2 v_t + \sigma_u^2\sigma_\varepsilon^4}.$$

It follows that $\varphi(0) = 0$, and, for $v > 0$, $0 < \varphi(v) < v$. Furthermore, $\varphi'(\cdot) > 0$ for v small. We know that, as $t \to \infty$, then $\tau_t \to \infty$ and $v_t \to 0$. We now obtain the convergence rate of $v_t \to 0$. Given that $v_t \to 0$ and $\tau_u\tau_\varepsilon^2 = (\sigma_u^2\sigma_\varepsilon^4)^{-1}$ we can write $v_{t+1} = v_t - v_t^4\tau_u\tau_\varepsilon^2(1 + O(v_t))$, where $O(v_t)$ is a term of order of at most v_t (see section 10.3.2).

Define the sequence $\{b_t\}$ by $b_t = t^{1/3}v_t$. We obtain

$$\frac{b_{t+1}}{(t+1)^{1/3}} = \frac{1}{t^{1/3}}\left(b_t - \frac{b_t^4}{t}\tau_u\tau_\varepsilon^2\left(1 + O\left(\frac{b_t}{t^{1/3}}\right)\right)\right)$$

or

$$b_{t+1}\left(\frac{t+1}{t}\right)^{-1/3} = b_t - \frac{b_t^4}{t}\tau_u\tau_\varepsilon^2\left(1 + O\left(\frac{b_t}{t^{1/3}}\right)\right).$$

Therefore,

$$b_{t+1}\left(1-\frac{1}{3t}+O\left(\frac{1}{t^2}\right)\right)=b_t-\frac{b_t^4}{t}\tau_u\tau_\varepsilon^2\left(1+O\left(\frac{b_t}{t^{1/3}}\right)\right).$$

From the latter equation it can be checked that the sequence $\{b_t\}$ must be bounded. We show now that it converges to $(3\tau_u\tau_\varepsilon^2)^{-1/3}$. Extract first a subsequence of $\{b_t\}$ which converges to some limit $\bar{b}$. Extract then from this subsequence another subsequence such that b_{t+1} converges to a limit $\hat{b}$. It must then hold that

$$\hat{b}\left(1-\frac{1}{3t}+O\left(\frac{1}{t^2}\right)\right)=\bar{b}-\frac{\bar{b}^4}{t}\tau_u\tau_\varepsilon^2\left(1+O\left(\frac{b_t}{t^{1/3}}\right)\right).$$

Taking the limit as t goes to ∞ we obtain that $\bar{b}=\hat{b}=b$. Equating the terms of the order $1/t$ and disregarding those of smaller order we obtain

$$\tfrac{1}{3}b=b^4\tau_u\tau_\varepsilon^2$$

and therefore

$$b=(3\tau_u\tau_\varepsilon^2)^{-1/3}.$$

□

6.9 Exercises

6.1 (*the* $2\times 2\times 2$ *herding model*). Consider the $2\times 2\times 2$ herding model of section 6.1 and assume that an agent does not adopt when the net value of adoption is 0. Let the public belief be $\theta_i=\mathrm{P}(\theta=1\mid x^i)$. Use Bayes's rule to show that $\mathrm{P}(\theta=1\mid x^i,s_\mathrm{L})<\theta_i<\mathrm{P}(\theta=1\mid x^i,s_\mathrm{H})$. Show that:

(i) If $\theta_i\leqslant 1-\ell$, agent i rejects no matter the value of his signal.

(ii) If $\theta_i>\ell$, agent i adopts no matter the value of his signal.

(iii) If $1-\ell<\theta_i\leqslant\ell$, then agent i adopts if and only if his signal is high ($s=s_\mathrm{H}$).

(iv) Provide an argument to show that the probability that an informational cascade has not started when it is the turn of i to move converges to zero exponentially as i increases.

Solution. (i), (ii), and (iii) are immediate. *Hint for (iv).* A necessary condition to avoid a cascade is that signals alternate between high and low values.

6.2 (*endogenous private information with linear acquisition costs*). Let $C(y)=cy$ with $c>0$. Show that for a given precision of the inherited public information, τ, agents buy signals with precision

$$y=\begin{cases}c^{-1/2}-\tau & \text{if } c^{-1/2}>\tau,\\ 0 & \text{otherwise,}\end{cases}$$

and therefore

$$g^{\mathrm{m}}(\tau) = \begin{cases} \tau + \tau_u(1 - c^{1/2}\tau)^2 & \text{if } c^{-1/2} > \tau, \\ \tau & \text{otherwise.} \end{cases}$$

Show that if $\tau_\theta \leqslant (\tau_u c^{1/2} - 1)/\tau_u c$, then $y = 0$ and $\tau = \tau_\theta + \tau_u(1 - c^{1/2}\tau_\theta)^2 \geqslant c^{-1/2}$ for all $t \geqslant 1$. Otherwise, $y_t > 0$ and $\tau_t < c^{-1/2}$ for all t, whereas $\tau_t \underset{t}{\rightarrow} c^{-1/2}$. Interpret the results.

Solution. Follow the steps in section 6.3.2 for the general case. If τ_θ is low enough and $c^{1/2} > 1/\tau_u$, only the first generation buys private signals, whereas, later on, agents simply rely on past, public information when taking their decisions. This means that the precision of the information on which these decisions are taken will remain constant over time. Otherwise, first-generation agents buy less precise signals, and they continue buying private precision at every point in time, although at a decreasing rate. The result is an increasing precision of the public information, which will converge to $c^{-1/2}$.

6.3 (*the rate of learning when information is endogenous*). Consider the model in section 6.3.2 and let $C(y) = c\lambda^{-1}y^\lambda$ with $\lambda > 1$. Show that $\tau_t \approx t^r$ with $r = (\lambda - 1)/(3\lambda + 1)$ and $a_t \approx t^{-\upsilon}$ with $\upsilon = (\lambda + 1)/(3\lambda + 1)$. Note that $\upsilon > \frac{1}{3} > r > 0$ and that r increases with λ.

Solution. From the FOC $y - [C'(y)]^{-1/2} = -\tau$ it is immediate that $1/c = \tau_{t-1}^{1+\lambda} a_t^{\lambda-1}/(1 - a_t)^{1+\lambda}$ and therefore $\tau_{t-1}^{1+\lambda} a_t^{\lambda-1} \to 1/c$ as $t \to \infty$ since then $a_t \to 0$. Let $a_t \approx t^{-\upsilon}$ for some $\upsilon > 0$, then $\tau_t \approx \sum_{k=0}^{t} a_k^2 \approx \sum_{k=0}^{t} k^{-2\upsilon} \approx t^{1-2\upsilon}$. Therefore, $t^{(1-2\upsilon)(1+\lambda)} t^{-\upsilon(\lambda-1)}$ is of the order of a constant and consequently

$$(1 - 2\upsilon)(1 + \lambda) - \upsilon(\lambda - 1) = 0.$$

It follows that $\upsilon = (1 + \lambda)/(3\lambda + 1)$ and $r = 1 - 2\upsilon = (\lambda - 1)/(3\lambda + 1)$.

6.4 (*optimal learning with asymmetric rules*). Show that asymmetric rules cannot improve upon symmetric ones in the optimal learning program of section 6.5.2.

Solution. First of all, using asymmetric weights a_{it} for the signals of different agents s_i it is still optimal to set the weights to public information so that $c_{it} = 1 - a_{it}$ (the reason is as before that the coefficients c_{it} do not have any intertemporal effect). This means that

$$L_{it} = E[(\theta - q_{it}(I_{it}))^2] = \frac{(1 - a_{it})^2}{\tau_{t-1}} + \frac{a_{it}^2}{\tau_\varepsilon}.$$

Let $L(a) = a^2/\tau_\varepsilon + (1 - a)^2/\tau$. Given that $L(a)$ is convex in a, $\int_0^1 L(a_i)\,di \geqslant L(\int_0^1 a_i\,di)$ and therefore there cannot be any static gain from asymmetric rules. Furthermore, there cannot be any dynamic gain either since if in period t different weights a_{it} were given to the signals of different agents, the signal-to-noise ratio in the new information of the public statistic p_t would depend only on $\int_0^1 a_i\,di$.

6.5 (*the market solution is incentive compatible*). Show that the market solution in section 6.6, $q_i = E[\theta \mid s_i, \theta^*]$, makes privately efficient use of private information (i.e., $E[\theta - q_i] = 0$ and $E[(\theta - q_i)s_i] = 0$) and efficient use of public information (i.e., $E[(\theta - q_i)\theta^*] = 0$). In contrast the team optimum is bound only by the second restriction. Depict the team and the market solutions in the space of weights to private (a) and public (c) information.

Solution. (i) From $E[\theta - q_i \mid s_i, \theta^*] = 0$ for all s_i and θ^*, and using the projection theorem for normal random variables (according to which $\text{cov}[(\theta - q_i) - E[\theta - q_i \mid s_i, \theta^*], E[\theta - q_i \mid s_i, \theta^*]] = 0$), we obtain $\text{cov}[\theta - q_i, s_i] = \text{cov}[\theta - q_i, \theta^*] = 0$ (equivalently, $E[(\theta - q_i)s_i] = E[(\theta - q_i)\theta^*] = 0$). (See Bru and Vives (2002).)

6.6 (*"business as usual" and "wisdom after the fact"*). Consider the model of section 6.3.1, where both the state of the world $\theta \in \{0, 1\}$ and actions $x_{it} \in \{0, 1\}$ are discrete. The payoff to take the action $x = 1$ (investing) is $\theta - c$ for some small $c > 0$ and the payoff of not investing ($x = 0$) is 0. The rest is as in section 6.3.1. Aggregate investment in period t is thus $\int_0^1 x_{it}\, di$ and the public statistic is $p^{t-1} = \{p_0, \dots, p_{t-1}\}$.

(i) Show that an agent will choose to invest if and only if his private signal is larger than $\frac{1}{2} - \sigma_\varepsilon^2 \lambda_t$, where λ_t is the likelihood ratio between states $\theta = 1$ and $\theta = 0$ based on public information p^{t-1}. We then have that $p_t = 1 - \Phi((\frac{1}{2} - \sigma_\varepsilon^2 \lambda_t - \theta)/\sigma_\varepsilon) + u_t$, where Φ is the cumulative distribution of the standard normal.

(ii) Argue that when the likelihood ratio λ_t is large or small (in algebraic terms), then the public statistic does not provide a very accurate signal of θ. This means that when an extremal amount of agents invest (i.e., most of them or very few) the informativeness of p_t is low.

(iii) Argue how (ii) can explain that, after a period of "business as usual" (say, with many agents investing), a crash occurs (as agents learn that the true state is bad), and then this belief seems evident ("wisdom after the fact").

Solution. The exercise is a streamlined version of Caplin and Leahy (1994). For (i) and (ii) see section 10.1 if you have trouble with likelihood ratios; for (iii) imagine what would happen if the true state is bad but that due to some realizations of noise in the past the public belief is positive about the state of the world.

6.7 (*overconfidence*). Consider the learning model in section 6.3.1. How would you model the case in which agents are overconfident with respect to the precision of their information? What are the implications of overconfidence for aggregation of information?

Hint. See Nöth and Weber (2003) for inspiration and experimental results.

References

Amador, M., and P.-O. Weill. 2007. Learning from private and public observations of others' actions. Mimeo.

Anderson, L., and C. Holt. 1997. Information cascades in the laboratory. *American Economic Review* 87:847–62.

Arrow, K. J. 1962. The economic implications of learning by doing. *Review of Economic Studies* 29:155–73.

Aumann, R. 1976. Agreeing to disagree. *Annals of Statistics* 4:1236–39.

Avery, C., and J. Chevalier. 1999. Herding over the career. *Economics Letters* 63:327–33.

Avery, C., and P. Zemsky. 1998. Multi-dimensional uncertainty and herd behavior in financial markets. *American Economic Review* 88:724–48.

Baloff, N. 1966. The learning curve. Some controversial issues. *Journal of Industrial Economics* 14:275–83.

Banerjee, A. 1992. A simple model of herd behavior. *Quarterly Journal of Economics* 107:797–817.

——. 1993. The economics of rumors. *Review of Economic Studies* 60:309–27.

Banerjee, A., and D. Fudenberg. 2004. Word-of-mouth learning. *Games and Economic Behavior* 46:1–22.

Bernhardt, D., M. Campbell, and E. Kutsoati. 2006. Who herds? *Journal of Financial Economics* 80:657–75.

Bikhchandani, S., D. Hirshleifer, and I. Welch. 1992. A theory of fads, fashion, custom, and cultural change as informational cascades. *Journal of Political Economy* 100:992–1026.

——. 1998. Learning form the behavior of others. *Journal of Economic Perspectives* 12:151–70.

Bru, L., and X. Vives. 2002. Informational externalities, herding, and incentives. *Journal of Institutional and Theoretical Economics* 158:91–105.

Burguet, R., and X. Vives. 2000. Social learning and costly information acquisition. *Economic Theory* 15:185–205.

Callander, S., and J. Hörner. 2006. The wisdom of the minority. Working Paper, Northwestern University.

Caminal, R., and X. Vives. 1996. Why market share matters: an information-based theory. *RAND Journal of Economics* 27:221–39.

——. 1999. Price dynamics and consumer learning. *Journal of Economics and Management Strategy* 8:95–131.

Caplin, A., and J. Leahy. 1994. Business as usual, market crashes, and wisdom after the fact. *American Economic Review* 84:548–65.

Çelen, B., and S. Kariv. 2004a. Distinguishing informational cascades from herd behavior in the laboratory. *American Economic Review* 94:484–98.

——. 2004b. Observational learning under imperfect information. *Games and Economic Behavior* 47:72–86.

Chamley, C. 2003. Cascades and slow social learning. Working Paper, Boston University.

——. 2004a. *Rational Herds*. Cambridge University Press.

——. 2004b. Delays and equilibria with large and small information in social learning. *European Economic Review* 48:477–501.

Chamley, C., and D. Gale. 1994. Information revelation and strategic delay in a model of investment. *Econometrica* 62:1065–85.

Chen, Q., and W. Jiang. 2006. Analysts' weighting of private and public information. *Review of Financial Studies* 19:319–55.

Chevalier, J., and G. Ellison. 1999. Career concerns of mutual fund managers. *Quarterly Journal of Economics* 114:389–432.

Cipriani, M., D. Gale, and A. Guarino. 2005. Estimating herd behavior in financial markets: a structural approach. Mimeo.

Crawford, V., and J. Sobel. 1982. Strategic information transmission. *Econometrica* 50:1431–51.

De Long, J. B., A. Shleifer, L. H. Summers, and R. J. Waldmann. 1990. Noise trader risk in financial markets. *Journal of Political Economy* 98:703–38.

Effinger, M., and M. Polborn. 2001. Herding and anti-herding: a model of reputational differentiation. *European Economic Review* 45:385–403.

Ellison, G., and D. Fudenberg. 1993. Rules of thumb for social learning. *Journal of Political Economy* 101:612–43.

——. 1995. Word-of-mouth communication and social learning. *Quarterly Journal of Economics* 110:93–125.

Feldman, M. 1987. An example of convergence to rational expectations with heterogeneous beliefs. *International Economic Review* 28:635–50.

Fellner, W. 1969. Specific interpretations of learning by doing. *Journal of Economic Theory* 1:119–40.

Foster, A., and M. Rosenzweig. 1995. Learning by doing and learning from others: human capital and technical change in agriculture. *Journal of Political Economy* 103:1176–209.

Fudenberg, D., and J. Tirole. 1991. *Game Theory*. Cambridge, MA: MIT Press.

Gale, D. 1996. What have we learned from social learning? *European Economic Review* 40:617–28.

Gale, D., and S. Kariv. 2003. Bayesian learning in social networks. *Games and Economic Behavior* 45:329–46.

Geanakoplos, J., and H. Polemarchakis. 1982. We can't disagree forever. *Journal of Economic Theory* 28:192–200.

Glosten, L., and P. R. Milgrom. 1985. Bid, ask and transaction prices in a specialist market with heterogeneously informed traders. *Journal of Financial Economics* 17:71–100.

Goeree, J., T. Palfrey, B. Rogers, and R. McKelvey. 2007. Self-correcting information cascades. *Review of Economic Studies* 74:733–62.

Graham, J. 1999. Herding among investment newsletters: theory and evidence. *Journal of Finance* 54:237–68.

Grinblatt, M., S. Titman, and R. Wermers. 1995. Momentum investment strategies, portfolio performance, and herding: a study of mutual fund behavior. *American Economic Review* 85:1088–105.

Guarino, A., H. Harmgart, and S. Huck. 2007. When half the truth is better than the truth: theory and experiments on aggregate information cascades. Working Paper, UCL.

Gul, F., and R. Lundholm. 1995. Endogenous timing and the clustering of agents' decisions. *Journal of Political Economy* 103:1039–66.

Hendricks, D., J. Patel, and R. Zeckhauser. 1993. Hot hands in mutual funds: short-run persistence of performance. *Journal of Finance* 48:93–130.

Hong, H., J. Kubik, and A. Solomon. 2000. Security analysts' career concerns and herding of earnings forecasts. *RAND Journal of Economics* 31:121–44.

Huck, S., and J. Oechssler. 2000. Informational cascades in the laboratory: do they occur for the right reasons? *Journal of Economic Psychology* 21:661–71.

Hung, A., and C. R. Plott. 2001. Information cascades: replication and an extension to majority rule and conformity-rewarding institutions. *American Economic Review* 91:1508–20.

Jun, B., and X. Vives. 1996. Learning and convergence to a full-information equilibrium are not equivalent. *Review of Economic Studies* 63:653–74.

Kihlstrom, R. 1984. A simple example of the Radner–Stiglitz nonconcavity in the value of information. In *Bayesian Models in Economic Theory*, pp. 53–61. *Studies in Bayesian Econometrics*, volume 5. North-Holland.

Kübler, D., and G. Weizsäcker. 2004. Limited depth of reasoning and failure of cascade formation in the laboratory. *Review of Economic Studies* 71:425–41.

Lamont, O. 2002. Macroeconomic forecasts and microeconomic forecasters. *Journal of Economic Behavior and Organization* 48:265–80.

Larson, N. 2006. In with the new or out with the old? Bottlenecks in social learning. Working Paper, University of Virginia.

Lee, I. 1993. On the convergence of informational cascades. *Journal of Economic Theory* 61:395–411.

McKelvey, R. D., and T. Page. 1986. Common knowledge, consensus, and aggregate information. *Econometrica* 54:109–27.

Morris, S. 2001. Political correctness. *Journal of Political Economy* 109:231–65.

Morris, S., and H. Shin. 2002. The social value of public information. *American Economic Review* 92:1521–34.

——. 2005. Central bank transparency and the signal value of prices. *Brookings Papers on Economic Activity* 2:1–66.

Nielsen, L., A. Branderburger, J. Geanakoplos, R. D. McKelvey, and T. Page. 1990. Common knowledge of an aggregate of expectations. *Econometrica* 58:1235–39.

Nöth, M., and M. Weber. 2003. Information aggregation with random ordering: cascades and overconfidence. *Economic Journal* 113:166–89.

Ottaviani, M., and P. Sørensen. 2000. Herd behavior and investment: comment. *American Economic Review* 90:695–704.

Prendergast, C., and L. Stole. 1996. Impetuous youngsters and jaded old-timers: acquiring a reputation for learning. *Journal of Political Economy* 104:1105–34.

Radner, R. 1962. Team decision problems. *Annals of Mathematical Statistics* 33:857–81.

Radner, R., and J. E. Stiglitz. 1984. A nonconcavity in the value of information. In *Bayesian Models in Economic Theory*, pp. 33–52. *Studies in Bayesian Econometrics*, volume 5. North-Holland.

Rodríguez-Mora, J. V., and P. Schulstald. 2007. The effect of GNP announcements on fluctuations of GNP growth. *European Economic Review*. 51:1922–40.

Romer, D. 1993. Rational asset-price movements without news. *American Economic Review* 83:1112–30.

Scharfstein, D., and J. Stein. 1990. Herd behavior and investment. *American Economic Review* 83:465–79.

Scherer, F., and D. Ross. 1990. *Industrial Market Structure and Economic Performance*, pp. 98–99. Boston, MA: Houghton-Mifflin.

Shiller, J. 1981. Do stock prices move too much to be justified by subsequent changes in dividends? *American Economic Review* 71:421–36.

Shiller, J. 1984. Stock prices and social dynamics. *Brookings Papers of Economic Activity* 2:457–98.

——. 1989. *Market Volatility*. Cambridge, MA: MIT Press.

Smallwood, D., and J. Conlisk. 1979. Product quality in markets where consumers are imperfectly informed. *Quarterly Journal of Economics* 93:1–23.

Smith, L., and P. Sørensen. 1995. Rational social learning by random sampling. Mimeo.

——. 2000. Pathological outcomes of observational learning. *Econometrica* 68:371–98.

Townsend, R. M. 1978. Market anticipations, rational expectations, and Bayesian analysis. *International Economic Review* 19:481–94.

Trueman, B. 1994. Analyst forecasts and herding behavior. *Review of Financial Studies* 7:97–124.

Vives, X. 1993. How fast do rational agents learn? *Review of Economic Studies* 60:329–47.

——. 1997. Learning from others: a welfare analysis. *Games and Economic Behavior* 20:177–200.

——. 1999. *Oligopoly Pricing: Old Ideas and New Tools*. Cambridge, MA: MIT Press.

——. 2005. Complementarities and games: new developments. *Journal of Economic Literature* 2005:437–79.

Welch, I. 2000. Herding among security analysts. *Journal of Financial Economics* 58:369–96.

Wermers, R. 1999. Mutual fund herding and the impact on stock prices. *Journal of Finance* 2:581–622.

Zhang, J. 1997. Strategic delay and the onset of investment cascades. *RAND Journal of Economics* 28:188–205.

Zitzewitz, E. 2001. Measuring herding and exaggeration by equity analysts and other opinion sellers. Stanford GSB Working Paper 1802.

Zwiebel, J. 1995. Corporate conservatism and relative compensation. *Journal of Political Economy* 103:1–25.

7
Dynamic Information Aggregation

In chapters 1–5 we considered static models. However, information revelation has important dynamic implications as we saw in chapter 6 when considering social learning. In chapter 6 we considered models of pure informational externalities. A first issue is whether the results obtained are robust when considering models with payoff externalities, as most market models. A second issue to explore is whether there is dynamic information aggregation when in a corresponding static market there would not be. We saw in chapter 1 that simple market mechanisms, like Cournot, need not aggregate information. However, repeated market interaction may make the economy settle in a full- (or shared-) information equilibrium. In this case we may be interested in knowing how fast this convergence occurs and how learning and equilibrium behavior interact.

This chapter studies these issues in the context of dynamic markets which are repeated interaction extensions of the basic Cournot static model with a continuum of firms of chapter 1. Section 7.1 introduces the topic by putting the problems and literature in perspective. Section 7.2 presents a basic model with demand uncertainty and uninformed firms. Section 7.3 explores market dynamics with asymmetric information. Section 7.4 considers a variation of the model with cost uncertainty that displays slow learning and convergence to full-information equilibria. It provides an important link with social learning models as developed in chapter 6. Many proofs, given their technical nature, are gathered in the appendix to the chapter.

7.1 Rational Expectations, Full-Information Equilibria, and Learning

Simple (static) market mechanisms, like Cournot, need not aggregate information (chapter 1). Fully revealing rational expectations equilibria (FRREE) replicate the outcome of a competitive economy with (shared) full information (chapter 3). In the latter case the question is how agents form rational expectations. In some situations there is a game (typically in complex strategies like demand or supply functions) that implements the FRREE. More often, the FRREE is not implementable.

The issue then is whether FRREE are dynamically implementable with simple market mechanisms or how to attain a full-information equilibrium (FIE) with competitive dynamics. Repeated interaction in the market place provides an answer to both the lack of information aggregation with simple market mechanisms and the formation of (fully revealing) rational expectations. Agents process repeated observations of public market data and learn about the relevant uncertainty (adjusting their beliefs in response to observations).

The study of convergence to a full-information equilibrium with repeated interaction is important since it provides a foundation to competitive equilibria under private information. Indeed, the competitive model with full information will be approximately right even in private-information environments if repeated interaction in the market place resolves the uncertainty.

We consider in turn the following issues: The distinction between learning about an equilibrium, or how to form equilibrium expectations, and learning within an equilibrium, where expectations are equilibrium expectations always; the distinction between learning about an unknown parameter and convergence to a full-information equilibrium; and finally the characterization of the speed of learning and the rate of convergence to a full-information equilibrium.

7.1.1 Learning in Equilibrium and Learning about an Equilibrium

A distinction has to be made between learning *within* an (or *in*) equilibrium and learning *about* an equilibrium; in other words, between learning in rational expectations and learning about rational expectations. Furthermore, the learning procedure can be Bayesian or of another type. When learning in equilibrium, agents make the most efficient use of their information and therefore the procedure must be Bayesian. Expectations are "correct" all along, in the sense that they are based in a consistent and correct model of the economy, and the important issue is the revelation of information through time. When learning about an equilibrium the issue at stake is how agents come to have the beliefs associated with the equilibrium when at the start initial beliefs do not correspond to what the model predicts will occur. In this case agents may learn about an equilibrium in a Bayesian way or using other methods like least squares, for example.

To fix ideas consider an economy with an unknown parameter θ and agents with private information about θ. If the joint information reveals θ, then the shared-information equilibrium (SIE) is just the full-information equilibrium (FIE). In models of learning *in* rational expectations, agents have a correctly specified model of the economy and of the learning process, update their beliefs, and take actions accordingly. The issue studied is then information revelation (learning about θ) through prices and convergence to an SIE or an FIE. This limit equilibrium is sometimes called the (stationary) REE although expectations are rational all along. In order to prevent any misunderstanding the limit equilibrium will be refereed to as SIE or FIE.

Equilibrium learning tends to yield at least convergence of beliefs in the presence of i.i.d. shocks. Bayesian posterior beliefs converge with probability 1 (this follows from the martingale convergence theorem because posterior beliefs have the martingale property and are bounded). Convergence to the truth obtains under some regularity conditions as we will see below. (See section 10.3.3 for more details.) In economic models with equilibrium learning this fact is then used to show that the unknown parameter (or agents' types) are learned and that convergence to a limit equilibrium also obtains (see Townsend 1978; Frydman 1982; Blume and Easley 1984, 1998; Feldman 1987; Bray and Kreps 1988). However, "learning" does not imply that "prediction" is possible. That is, that the prediction of the future path of the process given its history up to date t converges to the correct conditional distribution as t grows. This is what matters for convergence to a limit equilibrium in a dynamic model. A distinction must therefore be made between learning the unknown parameter, or the types of the other agents, and the sequence of equilibria converging to a limit equilibrium (SIE or FIE). Blume and Easley (1998) point out that the learning of types is not sufficient to yield convergence to a limit equilibrium but they do not provide an example in an economic setting. We will study in sections 7.2 and 7.3 the relationship between learning θ and converging to an FIE in the context of equilibrium learning. We will see that learning θ is neither necessary nor sufficient to converge to an FIE.

In models of learning *about* a rational expectations equilibrium, agents maintain incorrect hypotheses in the face of the evolution of the economy and either are Bayesians or use "reasonable" behavioral updating procedures, like adaptive rules or least squares estimation, for example. It has been found that in this case convergence to REE is not guaranteed although positive results are available by assuming a certain degree of coordination of the forecasting strategies of agents (Blume and Easley 1982; Bray 1982; Frydman 1982; Jordan 1985; Bray and Savin 1986; Fourgeaud et al. 1986; Marcet and Sargent 1988, 1989; Woodford 1990; Evans and Honkapohja 2001). In Brock and Hommes (1997) global complicated dynamics arise in a model where agents adapt their beliefs by choosing among a limited set of predictors. What if agents who use behavioral rules and simple heuristics to form beliefs coexist with Bayesian agents in the market? A traditional argument has been that agents that do not predict as accurately as others will be driven out of the market (Alchian 1950; Friedman 1953). The reason is that the behavioral agents will end up losing money and dissipating their wealth. Several authors have questioned this idea pointing out that agents maximize expected utility and not wealth accumulation, and the result may be that agents with incorrect beliefs drive agents with correct beliefs out of the market (see, for example, De Long et al. (1989, 1990) for behavioral traders and Kyle and Wang (1997) and Hirshleifer and Luo (2001) for the effects of overconfidence). However, Sandroni (2000) has shown that this cannot happen in a dynamic general equilibrium model. The basic intuition is that agents allocate more wealth to events they think are more likely to occur and only agents with correct beliefs end up on average being right. Sandroni (2005) goes further and compares Bayesian with behavioral belief-updating agents in an environment where agents try to learn the structure of the economy. The economy is given by a standard dynamic asset pricing model (a Lucas tree (Lucas 1978)). In the end prices reflect the empirical models used by agents with predictive properties conducive to wealth accumulation. Sandroni distinguishes between a structure of the economy which is learnable from another which is not. If the structure is learnable (e.g., when the relevant data set is unlimited), then only Bayesian agents or agents who forecast very closely to them survive (the intuition is as before: only agents with Bayesian prediction end up allocating wealth to events that actually occur). If the structure is not learnable (e.g., when there are recurrent regime switches which make past data obsolete), Sandroni finds in fact that only Bayesian agents survive (that is, Bayesian agents drive other agents out of the market according to the probability distribution generated by the data). The conclusion is that asset prices are determined under the Bayesian paradigm even in the presence of non-Bayesian agents.

In the Bayesian setting agents have priors over possible sequences of market prices and update at each date. If the prior does not coincide with the objective distribution on price sequences generated by the behavior of agents, then there is learning about REE. In general, a crucial element to obtain convergence to a limit equilibrium with correct beliefs with respect to the underlying true economy is the a priori assumed coordination of expectations of agents. Indeed, Bayesian learning does not have a lot of content per se, all depends on the assumptions about the priors of the agents. Convergence to the truth requires that prior beliefs be consistent with the true model. A Bayesian agent will never learn the truth if he puts zero weight on the true value of the parameter or model to start with. In a Bayesian statistical setting a *sufficient* condition for conditional beliefs about the future given the past to converge to correct conditional beliefs is that the true process given any parameter be absolutely continuous with respect to the prior predicted distribution on observations (sample paths). This condition basically means that if the prior assigns probability zero to an event, then the true model must also assign probability zero to the event (see Blackwell and Dubins 1962; Blume and Easley 1998). The condition is very strong since it requires a countable parameter space. It is at the base, for example, of the convergence results to Nash equilibrium in games of Kalai and Lehrer (1993) and Nyarko (1997, 1998). Agents need not have the correct model but their priors (on the entire space of paths) need to have a "grain of truth" (the absolute continuity condition) for convergence to Nash equilibrium behavior to obtain.[1] Nyarko (1997) analyzes the model of Townsend (1978) and Feldman (1987), with which we deal in section 7.3, when players form a Bayesian hierarchy of beliefs about the behavior of other players and concludes that, apart from the mutual absolute continuity condition on the beliefs of the players, a contraction property of the best response maps is needed to obtain convergence to the Nash equilibrium of the model corresponding to the true fundamentals.

There is still another approach to building foundations for an REE which is sometimes called "eductive stability." For an equilibrium to be eductively stable it must be the outcome only of the rationality of agents and common knowledge

[1] See also the discussion at the end of section 10.3.3.

about payoffs. That is, the equilibrium itself need not be common knowledge. This is an insight provided by the rationalizability literature in games (see section 10.4.1). The question then is how the agents coordinate expectations in the equilibrium. Eductive stability basically means that the equilibrium must be the outcome of the iterated elimination of dominated strategies. If this process has a unique outcome, the game is then called dominance solvable (see section 10.4.1). This approach builds on introspection, equilibrium expectations being pinned down in a thought process in the minds of agents in virtual time. Not all REE are eductively stable. Indeed, a contraction condition on best-reply maps is also typically needed to show dominance solvability or eductive stability. (See Guesnerie (2006) for a collection of papers on the issue and section 8.4.2 for an example of a coordination game where conditions are found for the game to be dominance solvable.)

7.1.2 Speed of Learning and Rate of Convergence to Limit Equilibria

Taking for granted that a learning process converges to a limit (fully revealing/shared-information) equilibrium it is of the utmost importance to know how fast and what factors affect the speed of convergence. It is not of much use for practical purposes to show convergence if it is not known whether this will happen quickly or take a long time, when the underlying conditions of the economy will have changed and the parameters learned may well be irrelevant by then. In this sense "slow" convergence may mean in practice no convergence. We would also like to know how structural market conditions—like the nature of uncertainty and its relation to market observables (namely, prices), the potential persistence of shocks (autocorrelation), the degree of asymmetric information, and the precision of private signals—affect the speed of convergence and in what direction.

A relevant distinction is whether the situation is one of "learning from others," as in chapter 6, or whether the relevant uncertainty impacts directly the public statistics that agents observe. The first situation may arise, for example, with cost uncertainty while the second with demand uncertainty. We have already seen in chapter 6 a robust result of slow learning from others. A question is how the robust result of slow learning from others may be modified in a market environment with payoff externalities.

It is also worth exploring the role of persistence of shocks since it may be presumed that some forms of autocorrelation may slow the speed of learning. This is the case for the generalized least squares (GLS) estimator, for example, in classical econometric analysis when disturbances are positively autocorrelated according to a stationary AR(1) process. Obviously, even in the context of a linear model where GLS is optimal, a dynamic market will have feedback effects which may drive us away from the classical analysis and results. Will the presence of autocorrelation impair the capacity of agents to "learn" θ and predict market prices, and to agree on price estimates so that a (fully revealing or shared-information) equilibrium obtains?

Rate-of-convergence results are usually difficult to obtain. Work by Jordan (1992a) on a class of Bayesian myopic learning processes (without noise) establishes an exponential rate of convergence to Nash equilibria for finite normal form games. In models of learning about an equilibrium partial results, relying sometimes on simulations, have been obtained by Bray and Savin (1986), Fourgeaud et al. (1986), Jordan (1992b), and Marcet and Sargent (1992). We will provide in the rest of the chapter results on the speed of learning and rate of convergence to FIE in different scenarios in the context of equilibrium learning.

In this chapter, as in the rest of the book, we will concentrate attention on equilibrium learning. We start by considering the case where θ is the unknown demand intercept in a Cournot market similar to the one presented in chapter 1. Section 7.2 deals with learning and convergence to FIE when firms are uninformed and section 7.3 when there is asymmetric information about θ. Both sections are based on Jun and Vives (1996). Section 7.4 will consider the implications of uncertainty about costs and is based on Vives (1993). In all cases the speed of learning and the rate of convergence to full-information equilibria are characterized.[2]

7.2 Learning and Convergence to a Full-Information Equilibrium with Uninformed Firms

We consider here the classical linear partial equilibrium model first studied by Muth (1961) in his seminal work about rational expectations. This is an infinitely repeated version of the continuum-of-firms Cournot model of chapter 1 with a random demand intercept subject to potentially persistent shocks and uninformed firms. Asymmetric information is introduced in the next section.

Consider an infinite-horizon market, $t = 1, 2, \dots$, with a continuum of firms, indexed by $i \in [0, 1]$, endowed with the Lebesgue measure, and producing a homogeneous product. Firms are risk neutral and have identical quadratic cost functions: $C(x_i) = \frac{1}{2}\lambda x_i^2$, with $\lambda > 0$. The inverse demand for the product in period t is random and is given by

$$p_t = \theta + u_t - \beta x_t,$$

where θ is the unknown intercept of demand, u_t is a period-specific shock, $\beta > 0$, and x_t is the average (per capita) supply in period t, $x_t = \int_0^1 x_{it}\,\mathrm{d}i$.

The temporary shocks $\{u_t\}_{t=1}^{\infty}$ are potentially persistent and generated by an AR(1) process: $u_t = \varsigma u_{t-1} + \eta_t$, with $\{\eta_t\}_{t=1}^{\infty}$ a white noise normal process.[3] When $\varsigma = 1$ the process is a random walk. We do not impose stationarity of

[2] See Bisin et al. (2006) for the study of rational expectations equilibria in dynamic economies with local interactions (in such environments the interaction capacity of an individual depends on his position on the established network of relationships).

[3] Subject to the initial condition $u_t = 0$ for $t \leqslant 0$. The results that we will derive hold for a general AR(∞) process (Jun and Vives 1996).

any sort. When $|\varsigma| < 1$ the AR(1) process is asymptotically independent and asymptotically stationary (but not stationary). Whenever the stochastic process $\{u_t\}$ is asymptotically stationary the initial conditions will not affect the asymptotic results in our model. When $|\varsigma| \geqslant 1$, the process is neither asymptotically stationary nor asymptotically independent.[4]

Firms are uninformed about θ but have a common prior which is normally distributed: $\theta \sim N(\bar{\theta}, \sigma_\theta^2)$. The distributional assumptions, including the parameters of the distributions, as well as the parameters λ and β, are common knowledge among the agents in the economy.

Firms set output levels in every period to maximize expected discounted profits by taking into account the information that past prices carry about θ. Given the structure of the economy, the market equilibrium is just a competitive equilibrium and myopic behavior is optimal. Firms have no scope for collusion because they are negligible and only prices are observable. Discounting has no influence on the equilibrium. If firms were to maximize the long-run average of profits, then whatever would happen in a finite number of periods would be irrelevant. Profit maximization leads any firm in period t to choose the output level according to

$$x_t = \lambda^{-1} E[p_t \mid I_t],$$

where $I_t = \{p^{t-1}\}$, $p^{t-1} = \{p_1, \dots, p_{t-1}\}$, is the information the firm has in period t (past prices).

Given that firms have common expectations, and consequently all firms produce the same output x_t, the information content of the price p_t is equivalent to $p_t + \beta x_t = \theta + u_t$. Let $z_t = \theta + u_t$. The problem of a firm in period t is to predict the market price $p_t = \theta + u_t - \beta x_t$, or $z_t = \theta + u_t$, with the information z^{t-1}, $z^{t-1} = \{z_1, \dots, z_{t-1}\}$. The equilibrium output

$$x_t = (\lambda + \beta)^{-1} E[z_t \mid z^{t-1}]$$

follows from the profit maximization condition $x_t = \lambda^{-1} E[p_t \mid I_t]$.

Denote by θ_t the public belief or expectation of θ conditional on public information. That is, $\theta_t = E[\theta \mid z^t]$. Given normality, the random variable θ_t is a sufficient statistic of the information in prices about the unknown θ. Let $\Delta z_t = z_t - \varsigma z_{t-1}$ with $z_0 = 0$ for $t \geqslant 1$. The random variable Δz_t equals $(1 - \varsigma)\theta + \eta_t$ and represents the new information about θ in the current price p_t. It is then clear that $\theta_t = E[\theta \mid z^t] = E[\theta \mid \Delta z^t]$, where $\Delta z^t = \{\Delta z_1, \dots, \Delta z_t\}$. Given that $z_t = \Delta z_t + \varsigma z_{t-1}$ it follows that

$$x_t = (\lambda + \beta)^{-1} E[z_t \mid z^{t-1}] = (\lambda + \beta)^{-1}((1 - \varsigma)\theta_{t-1} + \varsigma z_{t-1}).$$

The equilibrium is unique.[5]

---

[4] In our context we say that the process $\{u_t\}$ is *asymptotically independent* if $\operatorname{cov}[u_t, u_{t+h}] \to 0$ as $h \to \infty$. The process is *asymptotically stationary* if $\operatorname{cov}[u_t, u_{t+h}]$ does not depend on t in the limit as $t \to \infty$ (see Spanos 1986, chapter 8, p. 153). Under our assumptions, $\operatorname{cov}[u_t, u_{t+h}] = t\sigma_\eta^2$ if $|\varsigma| = 1$, and $\operatorname{cov}[u_t, u_{t+h}] = \sigma_\eta^2 \varsigma^h (1 - \varsigma^{2t})/(1 - \varsigma^2)$ otherwise, $h \geqslant 0$.

[5] It is worth noting that if agents are risk averse in the Muth model we may have potential nonexistence, unique or multiple linear equilibria (see McCafferty and Driskill 1980). In section 9.1.3.1 we consider a related model with risk-averse agents where there may be three linear equilibria.

If firms were to know θ, then in period t they would have access to past demand disturbances u^{t-1} because they observe past prices p^{t-1}, or equivalently z^{t-1} with $z_t = \theta + u_t$. Furthermore, $E[z_t \mid \theta, u^{t-1}] = \theta + E[u_t \mid u^{t-1}] = \theta + \varsigma u_{t-1}$. It follows that the full-information equilibrium output (denoted by "f") is

$$x_t^{\mathrm{f}} = (\lambda + \beta)^{-1}(\theta + \varsigma u_{t-1}).$$

When $\varsigma = 0$ the FIE can be thought of as the REE of a static market. Indeed, in the market with inverse demand $p = \theta - \beta x$, with θ random, the competitive equilibrium $x^{\mathrm{f}} = (\lambda + \beta)^{-1}\theta$ and $p^{\mathrm{f}} = (\lambda + \beta)^{-1}\lambda\theta$ is an FRREE which is implementable in supply functions (just the competitive supplies, $X(p) = p/\lambda$, see chapter 3).

The difference of the FIE with the market equilibrium output x_t (noting that $z_{t-1} = \theta + u_{t-1}$) is easily seen to be

$$x_t - x_t^{\mathrm{f}} = (\lambda + \beta)^{-1}(1 - \varsigma)(\theta_{t-1} - \theta) \quad \text{for } t \geqslant 2.$$

We want to examine the asymptotic behavior of $x_t - x_t^{\mathrm{f}}$, that is, *convergence* of the market equilibrium to the FIE, and of $\theta_t - \theta$ or the difference between public information θ_t about the unknown parameter θ and the true value of θ, that is, *learning* by firms about the unknown θ.

We will see that although it may difficult, or impossible, to estimate the only unknown parameter θ in the economy, yet convergence to an FIE obtains. Learning θ and convergence to an FIE are thus not equivalent in the presence of persistent shocks.

Before stating our convergence results (the first in proposition 7.1) we will recall again some measures of speed of convergence. We will say that the sequence (of real numbers) $\{b_t\}$ is of the *order* t^{υ}, with υ a real number, whenever $t^{-\upsilon}b_t \underset{t}{\rightarrow} k$ for some nonzero constant k. Denote by $\xrightarrow{\mathrm{L}}$ convergence in law (distribution). We say that the sequence of random variables $\{x_t\}$ converges to x at the rate $t^{-\kappa}$, for $\kappa > 0$, if $x_t \underset{t}{\rightarrow} x$ (a.s. or in mean square) and $t^{\kappa}(x_t - x) \xrightarrow{\mathrm{L}} N(0, \mathrm{AV})$ for some positive constant AV. The asymptotic variance AV represents a refined measure of speed for a given convergence rate. A lower AV means faster convergence.[6]

Proposition 7.1 (Jun and Vives 1996).

(i) *If $\varsigma \neq 1$, then θ_t converges to θ (a.s. and in mean square) at the rate $1/\sqrt{t}$ with asymptotic variance $\sigma_\eta^2/(1 - \varsigma)^2$, and $x_t - x_t^{\mathrm{f}} \rightarrow 0$ at the rate $1/\sqrt{t}$ with asymptotic variance $\sigma_\eta^2/(\lambda + \beta)^2$.*

(ii) *If $\varsigma = 1$, except for the first period, no information about θ can be inferred from prices (with the precision of θ_t constant at $\tau_\theta + \tau_\eta$) but the market equilibrium coincides with the FIE ($x_t - x_t^{\mathrm{f}} = 0$ for $t \geqslant 2$).*

[6] See sections 10.3.1 and 10.3.2 for a fuller development of the definitions and relationships between convergence concepts.

Proof. (i) Let $\Delta z_t = z_t - \varsigma z_{t-1}$ for $t \geqslant 1$ as before. Then $\Delta z_t = (1-\varsigma)\theta + \eta_t$ and $\theta_t = E[\theta \mid z^t] = E[\theta \mid \Delta z^t]$, where $\Delta z^t = \{\Delta z_1, \dots, \Delta z_t\}$. It follows from normal theory (see section 10.2.1) that $E[\theta \mid \Delta z^t] = (\tau_\theta \bar{\theta} + \tau_\eta z_1 + \tau_\eta (1-\varsigma)\sum_{k=2}^{t} \Delta z_k)/\tau_t$, where $\tau_t = \tau_\theta + \tau_\eta(1 + (1-\varsigma)^2(t-1))$ is the informativeness (precision) of the public statistic θ_t in the estimation of θ ($\tau_t = (\text{var}[\theta \mid \theta_t])^{-1}$). The public precision τ_t is of the order of t since $\varsigma \neq 1$ and consequently tends to ∞ with t. It follows that $\theta_t \to \theta$ (a.s. and in mean square). Furthermore, $\sqrt{t}(\theta_t - \theta) \xrightarrow{L} N(0, \sigma_\eta^2/(1-\varsigma)^2)$ because $\text{var}[\theta - \theta_t] = \text{var}[\theta \mid \theta_t] = \tau_t^{-1}$ and $t^{-1}\tau_t \to \tau_\eta(1-\varsigma)^2 = (\sigma_\eta^2/(1-\varsigma)^2)^{-1}$. (This also shows that $\theta_t \to \theta$ in mean square.) The result for $x_t - x_t^{\mathrm{f}}$ follows from $x_t - x_t^{\mathrm{f}} = (\lambda + \beta)^{-1}(1-\varsigma)(\theta_{t-1} - \theta)$ for $t \geqslant 2$.

(ii) When $\varsigma = 1$, $\Delta z_t = \eta_t$ for $t \geqslant 2$ and prices contain no information about θ. For $t = 1$, $\Delta z_1 = \theta + \eta_1$ and $\tau_1 = \tau_\theta + \tau_\eta$. Furthermore, for $t \geqslant 2$, $x_t - x_t^{\mathrm{f}} = (\lambda + \beta)^{-1}(1-\varsigma)(\theta_{t-1} - \theta) = 0$ when $\varsigma = 1$. □

Learning θ and converging to an FIE are different phenomena. While learning θ may be very slow (because ς is close to 1, or even impossible if $\varsigma = 1$), convergence to the FIE is unaffected. Indeed, the rate of convergence to the FIE is independent of ς if $\varsigma \neq 1$. If $\varsigma = 1$, then convergence is immediate. This highlights in a very stark form the fact that learning θ is not necessary for convergence to an FIE. It is worth noting that with i.i.d. shocks ($\varsigma = 0$), $x_t - x_t^{\mathrm{f}} = (\lambda + \beta)^{-1}(\theta_{t-1} - \theta)$, and learning θ is equivalent to converging to the FIE.

When $\varsigma \neq 1$ the new information in p_t about θ is $\Delta z_t = (1-\varsigma)\theta + \eta_t$ and firms face a classical ordinary least squares (OLS) estimation problem of θ. However, the asymptotic variance of the public belief $\theta_t \to \infty$ as ς tends to 1. Indeed, when $\varsigma = 1$, θ cannot be estimated since prices give no information on θ (the price innovation is pure noise, $\Delta z_t = \eta_t$ for $t \geqslant 2$). Nevertheless, firms are not interested in estimating θ but the market price p_t, or, equivalently, the statistic $z_t = \theta + u_t$. When $\varsigma = 1$, $\{z_t\}$ follows a martingale and the estimation of θ is irrelevant to the prediction of z_t: $E[z_t \mid z^{t-1}] = z_{t-1}$. Therefore, the market and the FIE outcomes coincide. When $\varsigma \neq 1$, the market equilibrium will converge to the FIE if (and only if) the expectations $E[z_t \mid z^{t-1}] - E[z_t \mid \theta, u^{t-1}]$ merge as t grows. This will happen if firms learn θ. As ς approaches 1 it becomes more and more difficult to estimate θ (the asymptotic variance of $\theta_t - \theta$ grows) but it is also less and less important to do so to predict the current price (since $E[z_t \mid z^{t-1}] = (1-\varsigma)\theta_{t-1} + \varsigma z_{t-1}$). This is why the asymptotic variance of $x_t - x_t^{\mathrm{f}}$ is independent of ς.

It is worth remarking that the asymptotic variance of $x_t - x_t^{\mathrm{f}}$ increases with σ_η^2 and decreases with λ and β. We have that the smaller the slopes of marginal cost or inverse demand, the larger the response of agents to public information and the slower the convergence rate. This means that convergence in a market with uniformly lower marginal costs (λ lower) or of larger size (β lower) will be slower.

In summary, we have characterized the speed of learning and convergence to FIE in the classical Muth rational expectations model. Convergence to the FIE happens fast (at the rate of $1/\sqrt{t}$) independently of whether learning the unknown parameter is slow or fast. We have seen in this model with uninformed agents that learning the unknown parameter and converging to a full-information equilibrium are not equivalent. We will see in section 7.3 that provided there is no positive mass of perfectly informed agents the results obtained so far will go through. That is, private information will have no asymptotic effect in the limit although equilibrium behavior will have a real feedback in learning. When there is a positive mass of perfectly informed agents, private information will have an asymptotic effect and results may change. In particular, learning the unknown parameter θ may not be *sufficient* for convergence to the FIE to obtain.

7.3 Market Dynamics with Asymmetric Information

Townsend (1978) and Feldman (1987) studied convergence to FIE in a classical linear partial equilibrium model with asymmetric information and i.i.d. shocks to demand. Their analysis is extended here to persistent shocks.[7]

We consider the same model as in section 7.2 but with firms asymmetrically informed about θ. Firm i, $i \in [0,1]$, is endowed with a private signal about θ, $s_i = \theta + \varepsilon_i$, where ε_i is an error term. We assume that θ, $\{\varepsilon_i\}$, and $\{\eta_t\}$ are independently (across agents and across time) normally distributed random variables: $\theta \sim N(\bar{\theta}, \sigma_\theta^2)$, $\eta_t \sim N(0, \sigma_\eta^2)$, and $\varepsilon_i \sim N(\bar{\theta}, \sigma_{\varepsilon_i}^2)$. The precision of the signals is given by a (measurable) function $T_\varepsilon : [0,1] \to \mathbb{R}_+ \cup \{\infty\}$, where $T_\varepsilon(i) = \sigma_{\varepsilon_i}^{-2} (\equiv \tau_{\varepsilon_i})$ is the value of this function for $i \in [0,1]$. Let $\mu \geqslant 0$ be the mass of agents with perfectly informative signals (that is, signals of infinite precision).

As in the previous chapters we adopt the "strong law of large numbers" convention about the average of a continuum of independent random variables. In particular, we write $\int_0^1 s_i \, di = \int_0^1 (\theta + \varepsilon_i) \, di = \theta + \int_0^1 \varepsilon_i \, di = \theta$ (a.s.) when signals have uniformly bounded variances.[8] If there is a positive mass of firms with signals with precisions uniformly bounded away from zero, θ is revealed by forming an average of the signals of agents with precision bounded away from zero and ignoring the signals of other agents. In this case the shared-information equilibrium coincides with the full-information equilibrium.[9] Firms know all the parameters of the model, including the parameters of the distributions, except for θ.

---

[7] See Nyarko (1997) for an analysis of the model and the conditions for convergence to an FIE to obtain when Bayesian firms are free to form beliefs about the behavior of others.

[8] See section 10.3.1 for a justification of the convention.

[9] As before, when $\varsigma = 0$ the FIE can be thought as the FRREE of a static market with inverse demand $p = \theta - \beta x$ with θ random. This FRREE is implementable in supply functions with the competitive supplies, $X(p, s_i) = p/\lambda$ for any s_i.

The dynamic game is as in section 7.2 but now firms start with their private estimates of the uncertain intercept of demand. With this information each firm sets an output level, and a market-clearing price obtains. Upon observing the first-period price, firms set the period 2 output and so on. The equilibrium of the market is just the (perfect) Bayesian equilibrium (PBE) of the dynamic game.[10] Given that agents are negligible and that the action of a single firm does not affect public information (the market price) the equilibrium has a very simple structure. It just involves a sequence of one-shot Bayes–Nash equilibria with evolving information structures according to the refinement of public information.

Profit maximization leads firm i in period t to choose the output level $x_{it} = \lambda^{-1}E[p_t \mid I_{it}]$, where $I_{it} = \{s_i, p^{t-1}\}$ is the information set of the firm. In order to estimate the market price $p_t = \theta + u_t - \beta x_t$, a firm in period t needs to estimate $\theta + u_t$ and x_t. Under private information a firm does not know the average market output x_t since it depends on the aggregate private information received by all the firms (which in our model with a continuum of firms is θ).

It is possible to show, by following a standard procedure (detailed in the appendix to this chapter, see proposition 7.6), that there is a unique linear equilibrium in the dynamic game (in fact, the equilibrium is unique in the class of strategies with bounded means and uniformly bounded variances across firms; see exercise 7.3 for a closely related result). In equilibrium

$$p_t = z_t - \beta c_t \theta_{t-1} - \beta(\lambda + \beta)^{-1} \varsigma z_{t-1},$$

with $z_t = \hat{a}_t \theta + u_t$, $\hat{a}_t = 1 - \beta a_t$, where a_t (c_t) is the average responsiveness of firms to private (public) information. The equilibrium parameters are determined in a recursive way.

It is clear that p^t is observationally equivalent to z^t. Let $\Delta z_t = z_t - \varsigma z_{t-1}$ and $\theta_t = E[\theta \mid \Delta z^t]$, where $\Delta z^t = \{\Delta z_1, \dots, \Delta z_t\}$. The random variable Δz_t represents the *new information* about θ in the price p_t. Its informativeness depends on the coefficient $\Delta \hat{a}_t = \hat{a}_t - \varsigma \hat{a}_{t-1}$. We have that $\Delta z_t = \Delta \hat{a}_t \theta + \eta_t$, where, by definition, $z_0 = 0$ and $\hat{a}_0 = 0$.

The discrepancy between the FIE output $x_t^{\mathrm{f}} = (\lambda + \beta)^{-1}(\theta + \varsigma u_{t-1})$ (see section 7.2) and the average output with private information $x_t = a_t \theta + c_t \theta_{t-1} + (\lambda + \beta)^{-1} \varsigma z_{t-1}$ is easily seen to be equal to the difference between the public predictor of θ_{t-1} and θ, weighted by the aggregate responsiveness of agents to public information:

$$x_t - x_t^{\mathrm{f}} = c_t(\theta_{t-1} - \theta).$$

This difference corresponds to the difference between average market expectations about the price, $\int_0^1 E[p_t \mid I_{it}]\,\mathrm{d}i$, and full-information expectations $E[p_t \mid I_t^{\mathrm{f}}]$, $I_t^{\mathrm{f}} = \{\theta, u^{t-1}\}$. Indeed, $\int_0^1 E[p_t \mid I_{it}]\,\mathrm{d}i - E[p_t \mid I_t^{\mathrm{f}}] = \lambda(x_t - x_t^{\mathrm{f}})$.

We now examine whether, and if so how fast, the market equilibrium with private information converges to the FIE benchmark. We show that if there is

[10] See section 10.4.4 for a short introduction to PBE.

no positive mass of *perfectly* informed firms (i.e., $\mu = 0$), then the presence of private information does not affect the convergence results obtained with uninformed firms (proposition 7.1(i) holds and (ii) also holds in a modified way). Private information has no asymptotic effect in the limit although equilibrium behavior will have a real feedback in learning. When $\mu > 0$, private information has an asymptotic effect, although convergence results and rates of convergence are not affected if the process of the shocks is not too explosive ($|\varsigma| < 1 + \lambda/\beta\mu$).

Proposition 7.2 states the result. We will say that the sequence of random variables $\{y_t\}$ converges to 0 *exponentially* if there is a constant $\kappa > 1$ such that $\kappa^t y_t \to 0$ (a.s.).[11] Obviously, this implies that $y_t \to 0$ a.s.

Proposition 7.2 (Jun and Vives 1996). *Let* $|\varsigma| < 1 + \lambda/\beta\mu$*, then as t grows:*

(i) *If* $\varsigma \neq 1$*,* θ_t *converges to* θ *at the rate* $1/\sqrt{t}$ *with asymptotic variance* $((1-\varsigma)^{-1} + \beta\mu\lambda^{-1})^2\sigma_\eta^2$*, and* $x_t - x_t^{\mathrm{f}} \to 0$ *at the rate* $1/\sqrt{t}$ *with asymptotic variance* $(1-\mu)^2\sigma_\eta^* / (\lambda + \beta)^2$.

(ii) *If* $\varsigma = 1$*,* $\theta_t - \theta$ *converges to a nondegenerate normal distribution with precision no larger than* $\tau_\theta + \tau_\eta$*, and* $x_t - x_t^{\mathrm{f}} \to 0$ *exponentially.*

Proof. See the appendix (section 7.6). □

When $\mu = 0$ and $\varsigma \neq 1$ private information does not matter asymptotically. We then obtain the same results as with uninformed firms (for $\mu = 0$, the upper bound on $|\varsigma|$, $1 + \lambda/\beta\mu$, is infinite). With $\varsigma \neq 1$ prices end up revealing θ and therefore the weight imperfectly informed firms put on their private information about θ, a_t, vanishes over time.[12] Consequently, average output is eventually known by the firms and need not be estimated. Therefore, asymptotically (and approximately) to predict p_t only $\theta + u_t$ needs to be estimated, as in the benchmark case with no private information.

As in section 7.2 the degree of serial correlation ς neither affects the rate nor the asymptotic variance of convergence to the FIE. Changes in autocorrelation are asymptotically neutral since they produce two effects that exactly offset each other. An increase in ς toward 1 makes the price statistic θ_t less informative about θ but it also makes it (via an equilibrium mechanism) less important for agents to estimate θ (and consequently firms put less weight on θ_t, a lower c_t, when choosing their production).

The asymptotic variance of $\theta_t - \theta$ is increasing with μ and with β. It is decreasing with λ. The fact that uninformed agents find prices less precise as an estimator of θ for larger μ may seem surprising. Nevertheless, perfectly informed firms by reacting to their information make the price less sensitive to θ (and the less sensitive to θ, the larger is β and the smaller is λ). The asymptotic variance of $x_t - x_t^{\mathrm{f}}$ decreases with μ. When μ approaches 1 the asymptotic variance of the discrepancy between market output and the FIE tends to 0.

---

[11] Note that this implies that convergence is at least at an exponential rate.

[12] Whenever $\mu = 0$ or $\varsigma = 1$, $a_t \to (1-\varsigma)\mu/[\lambda + (1-\varsigma)\beta\mu] = 0$.

When $\varsigma = 1$ with uninformed firms prices cannot reveal any information about θ but $x_t - x_t^{\mathrm{f}} = 0$ after the second period. With private information, prices reveal information over time (but less in the aggregate than in the first period with uninformed firms) and there is some discrepancy between x_t and x_t^{f} that vanishes fast. Now, for any $\mu \geqslant 0$ the weight a firm puts on its private information vanishes over time. When $\varsigma = 1$ agents put less and less weight on their private information (and on the price statistic) very fast. The consequence is that the new information about θ in the current price, $\Delta z_t = \Delta\hat{a}_t\theta + \eta_t$, looks like noise (since $\Delta\hat{a}_t \to 0$ very fast) and θ cannot be learned. Nevertheless, this also implies (since $\hat{a}_t \to 1$) that to predict the price in period t very quickly firms need only predict $\theta + u_t$ (that is, θ no longer matters in the estimation of $z_t = \hat{a}_t\theta + u_t$, only $\theta + u_t$) and firms therefore rely on the new information of the last-period price, z_{t-1}. Even though θ is not revealed by prices there is consensus on price expectations given the information of firms. More precisely, $\int_0^1 E[p_t \mid I_{it}]\,\mathrm{d}i - E[p_t \mid I_{it}] \to 0$ (a.s.) and $x_t - x_t^{\mathrm{f}} \to 0$ (a.s.) at an exponential rate.

We now see that when the process of shocks is sufficiently explosive, we then have fast learning and no convergence to the FIE!

Proposition 7.3 (Jun and Vives 1996). *If $\varsigma > 1 + \lambda/\beta\mu$, then as $t \to \infty$:*

(i) *$\theta_t - \theta$ tends exponentially to 0, and*

(ii) *$x_t - x_t^{\mathrm{f}}$ tends to a nondegenerate normal random variable with variance $\sigma_\eta^2(\lambda+\beta)^{-2}(1-\mu)^2(\hat{\varsigma}^2 - 1)$, where $\hat{\varsigma} = \varsigma(1 + \lambda/\beta\mu)^{-1}$.*

Proof. See the appendix (section 7.6). □

When $\varsigma > 1 + \lambda/\beta\mu$ prices reveal θ very fast (at an exponential rate) but the uninformed firms' reaction to the public information contained in prices (c_t) is so strong and increasing (also growing exponentially) that the discrepancy with the FIE, $c_t(\theta_{t-1} - \theta)$, does not disappear as $t \to \infty$. Even though public information reveals θ very fast, price expectations do not converge to the full-information level because the sensitivity of prices to public information is also growing very fast.

The combination of $\mu > 0$ with a sufficiently explosive $\{u_t\}$ process yields the nonconvergence outcome. Suppose for simplicity that a mass $1 - \mu$ of agents is uninformed. We have that $\Delta\hat{a}_t$ (and a_t, c_t) tend exponentially to $-\infty$ and $\hat{a}_t$ tends exponentially to ∞. This explosive equilibrium is sustained as follows. The price process depends more and more on θ since $\hat{a}_t$ tends exponentially to ∞ (and, in consequence, $\Delta\hat{a}_t$ tends exponentially to $-\infty$). Informed firms put an increasing negative weight on θ ($a_t \to -\infty$) since the prediction of the price innovation z_t depends more and more on θ: $E[z_t \mid \theta, z^{t-1}] = \Delta\hat{a}_t\theta + \varsigma z_{t-1}$. This makes it more and more important for uninformed firms to predict θ in order to predict the market price and consequently they put an increasing negative weight on public information θ_t: $E[z_t \mid z^{t-1}] = \Delta\hat{a}_t\theta_{t-1} + \varsigma z_{t-1}$.[13]

In summary, agents may not learn θ but converge to the FIE, and agents may learn θ but not converge to the FIE. That is, learning the unknown parameter θ is neither a necessary nor a sufficient condition for convergence to the FIE.

It must be pointed out that the phenomena mentioned above happen when usual stability assumptions imposed on the AR process are violated (although, as we have emphasized, the distinction between learning θ and converging to the FIE remains under the stability assumptions). Indeed, when $|\varsigma| \geqslant 1$ the AR(1) process is not even asymptotically stationary and the variance of u_t is unbounded.[14]

The normality assumption implies in general that prices and quantities, as well as θ, may take negative values. Nevertheless, choosing appropriately the mean and variance of θ the probability of such events can be made small provided $|\varsigma| < 1$. A problem with the variance of $\{u_t\}$ exploding is that the same happens with the variance of prices and quantities, and therefore prices and quantities become negative with increasing probability as time grows. Nevertheless it is possible to show, at least for the case $\mu = 0$, that the results in this section hold for an isoelastic-lognormal model in which prices and quantities are always positive. (See exercise 7.2.)

7.4 Slow Learning and Convergence

Consider a variation of the model in section 7.3 with no autocorrelation in demand ($\varsigma = 0$) where firms know the mean demand parameter α,

$$p_t = \alpha + u_t - \beta x_t,$$

but are uncertain about the intercept θ of their linear marginal cost function. Firm i has costs[15]

$$C(x_i) = \theta x_{it} + \tfrac{1}{2}\lambda x_{it}^2.$$

As in section 7.3 firm i is endowed with a private signal s_i about the unknown θ and the joint distribution of the random variables, and the values of the parameters β, α, and λ are common knowledge with $\alpha > \bar{\theta} > 0$ and $\lambda > 0$.

Consider the following scenario. Suppose that the firms' output pollutes or is toxic but that the level of toxicity or long-term pollution of a unit of output produced is unknown (the product is a new chemical, for example). Let θ be

---

[13] Now as t grows it does not become easier to predict the next-period price. The price prediction error, $\text{var}[z_t - E[z_t \mid z^{t-1}]] = (\Delta\hat{a}_t)^2\,\text{var}[\theta - \theta_{t-1}] + \sigma_\eta^2$, is bounded away from the full-information irreducible error σ_η^2. Indeed, as $t \to \infty$, $\text{var}[z_t - E[z_t \mid z^{t-1}]] \to (1 + \hat{\varsigma}^2) = \sigma_\eta^2$. This means that uninformed firms can never catch up with informed firms and predict prices as accurately as them.

[14] $\text{var}[u_t]$ grows linearly with t for $|\varsigma| = 1$ and exponentially (at the rate ς^{2t}) for $|\varsigma| > 1$. When $|\varsigma| < 1$, then $\sigma_\eta^2/(1 - \varsigma^2)$ provides an upper bound for $\text{var}[u_t]$.

[15] The model is inspired by an example provided by McKelvey and Page (1986). This section is based on Vives (1993).

the assessed toxicity or pollution damage of a unit of output produced. Firms have private assessments of θ and are allowed to produce but they will have to pay the corresponding damages in proportion to total production once the value of θ is realized. At each period there is an independent (small) probability $1 - \delta > 0$ that θ is realized (that is, that the tests on the toxicity of the product are definitive). In this case the probability of θ not being realized in period t, δ^t, tends to 0 as $t \to \infty$. When θ is realized the firm has to pay the damage of the accumulated production. In any period a firm, given θ, expects a damage cost per unit of production[16] of exactly θ, and the firm maximizes the (expected) discounted profits with discount factor δ.

In period t firm i produces x_{it} obtaining a net revenue $p_t x_{it} - \frac{1}{2}\lambda x_{it}^2$. If θ is realized after t periods of production, the firm has to pay $\theta(\sum_{k=1}^{t} x_{ik})$. Profits of firm i corresponding to period t are

$$\pi_{it} = (p_t - \theta)x_{it} - \tfrac{1}{2}\lambda x_{it}^2,$$

although only the net revenue $p_t x_{it} - \frac{1}{2}\lambda x_{it}^2$ is observable in period t. Firm i tries to maximize the (expectation of the) discounted sum of period profits $\sum_{k=1}^{t} \delta^k \pi_{ik}$.

The model could also be restated in terms of competition among buyers of an asset of unknown *ex post* return θ. Consider, for example, firms purchasing labor of unknown productivity θ because of technological uncertainty, and facing a random inverse linear labor supply and adjustment costs in the labor stock. Firm i would buy x_{it} in period t. The monetary return to the final labor stock $\sum_{k=1}^{t} x_{ik}$ would then be $\theta(\sum_{k=1}^{t} x_{ik})$. Buyer i would face a quadratic cost of adjustment of his position in period t, x_{it}, equal to $\frac{1}{2}\lambda x_{it}^2$, $\lambda > 0$. Inverse supply in period t would be given by $p_t = u_t + \beta x_t$, with x_t the average (per capita) quantity demanded in period t. Buyer i would obtain benefit $\theta x_{it} - \frac{1}{2}\lambda x_{it}^2$ (with profits $\pi_{it} = (\theta - p_t)x_{it} - \frac{1}{2}\lambda x_{it}^2$) from the quantity x_{it} demanded in period t.[17]

In the exposition we will keep the convention that agents are sellers. In order to save on notation set $\beta = 1$.

Firm i in period t has to decide how much to produce by estimating the period price p_t on the basis of the information it has available: the private signal s_i plus the (public) information contained in past prices $p^{t-1} = \{p_1, \dots, p_{t-1}\}$. That is, in period t the information set of firm i is $\{s_i, p^{t-1}\}$. The distributional assumptions are as in section 7.3. It is assumed that there is a positive measure set of firms who receive signals of precision bounded away from zero.

It is worth remarking that the present model is one of learning from others. That is, what agents can learn about θ is given by their joint information. This is so because prices depend on θ only through the average market action. Indeed, if agents were to receive perfectly correlated signals, then they would have the same information and there would be nothing to learn. The assumption

---

[16] That is, $(1 - \delta + \delta(1 - \delta) + \delta^2(1 - \delta) + \cdots)\theta = (1 - \delta)(1 - \delta)^{-1}\theta = \theta$.

[17] See section 9.1.2 for a financial market example.

of (conditionally) independent signals, plus the fact that a positive measure of agents receive signals of precision bounded away from zero, together with our convention on the "strong law of large numbers" for i.i.d. processes, ensures that if agents were to share information they would obtain θ, and agents can therefore, at least potentially, learn θ.

The perfect Bayesian equilibria of the dynamic game will be investigated. As in section 7.3 the equilibria will necessarily involve a sequence of Bayesian equilibria of the one-shot game. Otherwise, there would be a (positive measure) subset of agents that at some stage could, individually, improve their expected payoffs by reacting optimally to the average market action.

As in section 7.3 after t periods of trading with linear strategies the information contained in the price sequence $\{p_t\}$ will be summarized by a public belief statistic $\theta_t = E[\theta \mid z^t]$, where $z^t = \{z_1, \dots, z_t\}$ and $z_t = a_t\theta + u_t$, with a_t the average responsiveness of firms to their private signals. As before the random variable z_t represents the new information about θ in the price p_t. Profit maximization leads firm i in period t to choose the output level

$$x_{it} = \lambda^{-1}E[p_t - \theta \mid s_i, \theta_{t-1}].$$

It can be shown that there is a unique linear equilibrium (again unique in the class of strategies with bounded means and uniformly bounded variances across firms). Proposition 7.7 in the appendix provides the characterization of the equilibrium.

The strategy of a firm is a linear function of s_i and θ_{t-1} and in equilibrium

$$p_t = z_t + c_t\theta_{t-1} + \alpha\lambda(\lambda + 1)^{-1},$$

where as before c_t is the average responsiveness of firms to public information. The parameters are determined in a recursive way.

The informativeness of prices $\tau_t = \tau_\theta + \tau_u \sum_{k=1}^{t} a_k^2$ always increases and tends to ∞ and the price statistic θ_t eventually becomes fully revealing. Indeed, the only possibility for τ_t to be bounded above is for a_t to converge to zero (and fast) but this is self-contradictory: if τ_t does not tend to ∞, a_t will not tend to zero since agents will keep putting some weight on their private information. Consequently, the average responsiveness to private information a_t will (weakly) decrease with t. In fact, the average weight given to private information in $E[\theta \mid s_i, \theta_{t-1}]$, $\xi_{t-1} = \int_0^1 (\tau_{\varepsilon_i}/(\tau_{\varepsilon_i} + \tau_{t-1}))\,di$, converges to the proportion of perfectly informed agents μ, and the average weight given to public information converges to $1 - \mu$. Since $a_t = \xi_{t-1}(\lambda + \xi_{t-1})^{-1}$ we have that $a_t \underset{t}{\to} \mu(\lambda + \mu)^{-1}$.

If the informativeness of the price statistic θ_t, τ_t, is of the order t^v, define the *asymptotic precision* as $A\tau_\infty = \lim_{t\to\infty} t^{-v}\tau_t$.

If there is a positive mass of perfectly informed agents $\mu > 0$, then a_t will be bounded away from zero, $a_t \to a_\infty > 0$, because these agents put constant weight on their private perfect information since they have nothing to learn from prices. The order of magnitude of τ_t depends on the information content of current prices (the new information) for t large. This is given by the random variable $z_t = a_t\theta + u_t$ and asymptotically z_t looks like $a_\infty\theta + u_t$. This means that the information content of z_t is asymptotically constant and the order of magnitude of τ_t is t, as in the standard linear regression model or i.i.d. noisy observations of θ. For t large τ_t can be approximated by a linear function of t with slope equal to $A\tau_\infty = \tau_u(\mu/(\lambda+\mu))^2$, $\tau_t \approx \tau_\theta + A\tau_\infty t$. The asymptotic precision of τ_t (the "slope" of convergence) is larger the larger is the proportion of perfectly informed agents μ and smaller the larger is the slope of the adjustment cost λ.

If there is no positive mass of perfectly informed agents, $\mu = 0$, then $a_t \to 0$ as the number of trading periods increases and prices become more informative, and asymptotically the new information is pure noise: z_t looks like u_t for t large. This will not preclude convergence but it will slow it down. This is so since agents then put less and less weight on their private signal and more and more on the price statistic, which becomes more informative and eventually fully revealing. The consequence is that τ_t will tend to ∞ more slowly. Indeed, agents, by reacting on average less to their private information, will incorporate less of it in the current price, slowing down the convergence of the price statistic to θ. This self-correcting property of learning from others has been explored in section 6.3, where a heuristic explanation of the slow learning result was given.

When the average precision of private information in the market τ_ε is finite, the order of τ_t is $t^{-1/3}$. For t large τ_t is approximated by a strictly concave function of t: $\tau_t \approx A\tau_\infty t^{1/3}$, where $A\tau_\infty = (3\tau_u(\tau_\varepsilon/\lambda)^2)^{1/3}$. The results follow from the fact that $a_t\tau_t$ converges to τ_ε/λ as $t \to \infty$. The asymptotic precision $A\tau_\infty$ is increasing with τ_u and with τ_ε, and decreasing with the slope of the adjustment cost λ. In all cases an increase in the adjustment cost λ decreases the asymptotic precision $A\tau_\infty$. An increase in λ has a direct effect of restricting the response of agents to information, for a given price precision, and a countervailing indirect effect of decreasing the price precision, inducing agents to put more weight on their signals. The direct effect dominates eventually and the asymptotic price precision diminishes.

The following lemma summarizes the results thus far.

Lemma 7.1. *In equilibrium, as* $t \to \infty$*:*

(i) $\tau_t \to \infty$, $a_t \to \mu(\lambda+\mu)^{-1}$ *and* $c_t \to \lambda(1-\mu)(\lambda+\mu)^{-1}(\lambda+1)^{-1}$.

(ii) *The informativeness of the price statistic* θ_t, τ_t, *is of order* t^{υ}, *and* a_t *is of order* $t^{-\kappa}$, *where* $2\kappa + \upsilon = 1$, $\upsilon \in [\frac{1}{3}, 1]$, $\kappa \geqslant 0$. *Furthermore:*

(iia) *If* $\tau_\varepsilon \equiv \int_0^1 \tau_{\varepsilon_i}\,\mathrm{d}i < \infty$, *then* $\upsilon = \frac{1}{3}$ *and* $A\tau_\infty = (3\tau_u(\tau_\varepsilon/\lambda)^2)^{1/3}$.

(iib) *Otherwise, if* $\mu > 0$, *then* $\upsilon = 1$ *and* $A\tau_\infty = \tau_u(\mu/(\lambda+\mu))^2$; *if* $\mu = 0$, *then* $1 > \upsilon > \frac{1}{3} > \kappa > 0$.

Proof. See the appendix (section 7.6). □

This result generalizes the slow learning result of the prediction model of section 6.3 to a market context. More precisely, the model is closely related to the model of learning from others with long-lived agents of section 6.3.3. The difference is that here there is a payoff externality and that we allow for agents to receive signals of different precisions. The payoff externality does not change the slow learning result and the differences in the precisions of the signals of the agents do not change the result as long as the average precision τ_ε is finite. If it is infinite but $\mu = 0$, then the precision of public information τ_t still grows more slowly than the benchmark rate of t but faster than $t^{1/3}$. If there is a positive mass of informed agents ($\mu > 0$), then learning is at the benchmark rate. (Exercise 7.4 states the results for the general prediction model.)

If agents were to know θ (i.e., $\mu = 1$), the equilibrium action would be $x^{\mathrm{f}} = (\alpha - \theta)/(1 + \lambda)$ in any period. This corresponds to an FRREE of a static market with inverse demand $p = \alpha - x$. Note, however, that this FRREE is not implementable in supply functions (see section 3.2).

Once the order of magnitude and asymptotic value of the precision of the price statistic θ_t is known its asymptotic distribution follows immediately. The following propositions establish the asymptotic results for learning θ and convergence to FIE. Learning follows from τ_t tending to ∞ with t. Convergence to equilibrium then follows from lemma 7.1(i) and the fact that $x_t - x^{\mathrm{f}} = c_t(\theta_{t-1} - \theta)$. The speed of learning and the rates of convergence follow from lemma 7.1(iii) immediately.

Proposition 7.4 (learning (Vives 1993)). *As $t \to \infty$:*

(i) *The public belief θ_t converges (almost surely and in mean square) to θ.*

(ii) *If τ_ε is finite, $\sqrt{t^{1/3}}(\theta_t - \theta) \xrightarrow{\text{L}} N(0, (3\tau_u(\lambda/\tau_\varepsilon)^2)^{-1/3})$;*
if $\mu > 0$, $\sqrt{t}(\theta_t - \theta) \xrightarrow{\text{L}} N(0, (\mu/(\lambda + \mu))^{-2}\tau_u^{-1})$; and
if $\mu = 0$ and τ_ε is infinite, $\sqrt{t^{\upsilon}}(\theta_t - \theta) \xrightarrow{\text{L}} N(0, (A\tau_\infty)^{-1})$,
for some $\upsilon \in (\frac{1}{3}, 1)$ and appropriate positive constant $A\tau_\infty$.

Proposition 7.5 (convergence to FIE (Vives 1993)). *As $t \to \infty$:*

(i) *$x_t - x^{\mathrm{f}}$ converges (almost surely and in mean square) to zero.*

(ii) *If τ_ε is finite, $\sqrt{t^{1/3}}(x_t - x^{\mathrm{f}}) \xrightarrow{\text{L}} N(0, (1 + \lambda)^{-2}(3\tau_u(\tau_\varepsilon/\lambda)^2)^{-1/3})$;*
if $\mu > 0$, $\sqrt{t}(x_t - x^{\mathrm{f}}) \xrightarrow{\text{L}} N(0, (\lambda/(\lambda + 1))^2\tau_u^{-1})$; and
if $\mu = 0$ and τ_ε is infinite, $\sqrt{t^{\upsilon}}(x_t - x^{\mathrm{f}}) \xrightarrow{\text{L}} N(0, (1 + \lambda)^{-2}(A\tau_\infty)^{-1})$,
for some $\upsilon \in (\frac{1}{3}, 1)$ and appropriate positive constant $A\tau_\infty$.

Agents eventually learn the unknown parameter θ since the price statistic θ_t is a (strongly) consistent estimator of θ. Nevertheless the speed of learning depends crucially on the distribution of private information in the market. If a positive mass of agents is perfectly informed, then convergence is at the standard rate $1/\sqrt{t}$. Otherwise, convergence is at a lower rate, reaching the lower bound $1/\sqrt{t^{1/3}}$ when the average precision of private information is finite.

The asymptotic variance (AV) of the departure from the FIE is larger the larger the asymptotic variance of τ_t and the response of agents to public information. If τ_ε is finite, an increase in λ may increase or decrease AV according to whether

λ is small or large. An increase in λ increases $(A\tau_\infty)^{-1}$ but decreases c_∞ and the overall effect depends on the size of λ. If μ is positive, then AV always increases in λ, and if all agents are perfectly informed, obviously, AV equals zero.

7.5 Summary

This chapter has introduced rational learning dynamics in versions of the static Cournot market of chapter 1 with an unknown payoff relevant parameter θ. Each period firms face a demand with a period-specific shock, receive a private signal about θ in period 0, and learn from past prices. The aim has been to see how and when repeated interaction makes the economy settle in a full-information equilibrium (interpretable as a fully revealing rational expectations equilibrium) and what determines the rate of convergence to this outcome. The most important results are:

- When the unknown parameter affects directly the public statistic (θ is a parameter of the demand function):
    - If period-specific shocks are stationary, then learning θ and convergence to the FIE happen at the same rate $1/\sqrt{t}$, where t is the number of periods.
    - If period-specific shocks are nonstationary, then learning θ is neither necessary nor sufficient for convergence to the FIE:
        - When shocks follow a random walk, θ is never fully learned but convergence to the FIE obtains very fast (exponentially).
        - When the process of shocks is sufficiently explosive learning is very fast but there is no convergence.
- When the unknown parameter affects indirectly the public statistic (θ is a parameter of the cost function), the model is one of learning from others—since firms, by observing prices, at most can hope to learn the pooled information of all agents in the market—and shocks are i.i.d.:
    - If there is no positive mass of agents perfectly informed, learning θ and converging to the FIE is slow, typically of order $1/\sqrt{t^{1/3}}$.

Thus we see that when agents learn in equilibrium, learning and convergence to an FIE obtains under standard assumptions (i.e., stationary shocks) as the number of market interactions increases. However, learning and convergence may be very slow when learning is from others. The reason is that Bayesian learning from others has a self-correcting property that does not preclude convergence but slows it down in the presence of noisy observation. The slow learning result generalizes the results obtained in the prediction model of section 6.3 to a general distribution of precisions of private signals and a market environment with payoff externalities.

7.6 Appendix

7.6.1 Proofs

Section 7.3

Derivation of the linear equilibrium. Posit the following form for the candidate equilibrium price function: $p_t = z_t + L(p^{t-1})$, with L a linear function. It follows that in a linear equilibrium p^t is observationally equivalent to z^t. Firm i in period t is interested in predicting the current price p_t with the information $I_{it} = \{s_i, p^{t-1}\}$. In equilibrium $p_t = z_t - \beta c_t \theta_{t-1} - \beta(\lambda + \beta)^{-1} \varsigma z_{t-1}$, with $z_t = \hat{a}_t \theta + u_t$, $\hat{a}_t = 1 - \beta a_t$, where a_t (c_t) is the average responsiveness of firms to private (public) information. The best predictor of the current price is $E[p_t \mid I_{it}]$. This is equivalent to predicting z_t with the information $\{s_i, z^{t-1}\}$: $E[z_t \mid s_i, z^{t-1}]$. Firm i is Bayesian and will compute $E[z_t \mid s_i, z^{t-1}]$ with its knowledge of the structure of the model and the (equilibrium) knowledge of the coefficients $\hat{a}_t$. In general, to predict z_t (compute $E[z_t \mid I_{it}]$) it will be necessary to predict θ (compute $E[\theta \mid I_{it}]$).

Recall the definitions: $\Delta z_t = z_t - \varsigma z_{t-1}$ and $\Delta \hat{a}_t = \hat{a}_t - \varsigma \hat{a}_{t-1}$. Then $\Delta z_t = \Delta \hat{a}_t \theta + \eta_t$ (where, by definition, $z_0 = 0$ and $\hat{a}_0 = 0$) and $\theta_t = E[\theta \mid \Delta z^t]$. Also let $\theta_0 \equiv \bar{\theta}$ and $\tau_0 \equiv \tau_\theta$. Bayesian prediction of $z_t = \Delta z_t + \varsigma z_{t-1}$ with information $\{s_i, z^{t-1}\}$ follows from normal theory:

$$E[z_t \mid s_i, z^{t-1}] = \Delta \hat{a}_t E[\theta \mid s_i, \Delta z^{t-1}] + \varsigma z_{t-1},$$
$$E[\theta \mid s_i, \Delta z^{t-1}] = \xi_{it-1} s_i + (1 - \xi_{it-1}) \theta_{t-1},$$

where $\xi_{it} = \tau_{\varepsilon_i} / (\tau_{\varepsilon_i} + \tau_t)$ and $\tau_t = \tau_\theta + \tau_\eta \sum_{k=1}^{t} (\Delta \hat{a}_k)^2$. The estimator of θ is a convex combination of private and public information with weights according to their relative precisions. In order to predict z_t the estimation of θ matters provided $\Delta \hat{a}_t$ does not equal 0. The coefficient $\Delta \hat{a}_t = 0$ (for $t \geqslant 2$) when $\varsigma = 1$ and $\hat{a}_t = \hat{a}_{t-1}$. That is, in order to predict z_t the estimation of θ does not matter when the AR process follows a random walk *and* the sensitivity of the price to θ is stationary.

Because the triple $(s_i, \theta_{t-1}, z_{t-1})$ is sufficient in the estimation of z_t, we may restrict our attention to strategies of the type $X_{it}(s_i, \theta_{t-1}, z_{t-1})$. As usual we use notation in such a way that a parameter with subscript "i" represents the individual coefficient of the corresponding aggregate coefficient, for example, $\int_0^1 a_{it} \, di = a_t$. The following proposition provides a characterization of linear equilibria.

Proposition 7.6 (Jun and Vives 1996). *There is a unique equilibrium in which the price in period t is a linear function of θ, u_t, θ_{t-1}, and z_{t-1}:*

$$p_t = \hat{a}_t \theta + u_t - \beta c_t \theta_{t-1} - \beta(\lambda + \beta)^{-1} \varsigma z_{t-1},$$

with $\hat{a}_t = 1 - \beta a_t$, $c_t = (\lambda + \beta)^{-1} \Delta \hat{a}_t (1 - \xi_{t-1})$, and the coefficients a_t are recursively defined $a_t = (\lambda + \beta \xi_{t-1})^{-1} \xi_{t-1} (1 - \varsigma(1 - \beta a_{t-1}))$, with $a_1 = (\lambda + \beta \xi_0)^{-1} \xi_0$.

Corollary 7.1. *Firms' strategies are given by*

$$X_{it}(s_i, \theta_{t-1}, z_{t-1}) = a_{it}s_i + c_{it}\theta_{t-1} + (\lambda + \beta)^{-1}\varsigma z_{t-1},$$

with $a_{it} = \lambda^{-1}\Delta\hat{a}_t\xi_{it-1}$ *and* $c_{it} = \lambda^{-1}\Delta\hat{a}_t[(1 - \xi_{it-1}) - \beta(\lambda + \beta)^{-1}(1 - \xi_{t-1})]$.

Outline of the proof. Consider period t. Posit a linear price function as in the proposition. Profit maximization leads each firm to choose the output level according to $x_{it} = \lambda^{-1}E[p_t \mid I_{it}]$, where $I_{it} = \{s_i, p^{t-1}\}$, or, equivalently, $I_{it} = \{s_i, \theta_{t-1}, z_{t-1}\}$. Aggregate output can then be obtained by integrating the individual outputs. We now have a price function and aggregate output expressed in terms of the parameters that we want to determine. By substituting these expressions into both sides of the inverse demand and identifying coefficients, we can solve (uniquely) for these parameters. Individual and aggregate outputs follow. Firms are maximizing profit and the market clears at the expected price level. The linear structure preserves normality of distributions.

Proofs of propositions 7.2 and 7.3. Convergence of the market equilibrium x_t to the FIE x_t^{f} depends on the asymptotic behavior of the parameter c_t and the price statistic θ_t. The information contained in θ_t is determined by the sequence $\{\Delta\hat{a}_t\}$. The precision incorporated in θ_t is given by $\tau_t = \tau_\theta + \tau_\eta \sum_{k=1}^{t}(\Delta a_k)^2$. The asymptotic behavior of c_t also depends on the properties of $\{\Delta\hat{a}_t\}$ since $c_t = (\lambda + \beta)^{-1}\Delta\hat{a}_t(1 - \xi_{t-1})$. We characterize the asymptotic behavior of equilibrium parameters in lemma 7.2, and learning about θ and convergence to the FIE in propositions 7.2 and 7.3.

Lemma 7.2. *As* $t \to \infty$*:*

(i) *If* $\varsigma \neq 1$, *then* $\tau_t \to \infty$.

(ii) *If* $|\varsigma| < 1 + \lambda/\beta\mu$, *then* $\Delta\hat{a}_t \to \Delta\hat{a}_\infty$ *and* $c_t \to (\lambda + \beta)^{-1}\Delta\hat{a}_\infty$, *with* $\Delta\hat{a}_\infty = (1 - \varsigma)\lambda/[\lambda + (1 - \varsigma)\beta\mu]$.

(iii) *If* $\varsigma \neq 1$ *and* $|\varsigma| < 1 + \lambda/\beta\mu$, *then* $t^{-1}\tau_t \to (\Delta\hat{a}_\infty)^2\tau_\eta$.

Proof. (Sketch.) (i) The precision τ_t is monotone increasing. If it converges to a finite number, then $\Delta\hat{a}_t$ must converge to 0. From the definition of $\hat{a}_t$, we can obtain that $\hat{a}_t = 1 - \beta\lambda^{-1}\Delta\hat{a}_t\xi_{t-1}$. Hence, $\hat{a}_t \to 1$, but this implies $\Delta\hat{a}_t \to 1 - \varsigma \neq 0$, which is a contradiction.

(ii) An unbounded public precision means that agents who do not have perfect information asymptotically disregard private information, and therefore the aggregate weight given to private information tends to the proportion μ of perfectly informed agents ($\xi_t \to \mu$). This implies that for t large the dynamic system for a_t is approximately $a_t = (1 - \varsigma(1 - \beta a_{t-1}))(\lambda + \beta\mu)^{-1}\mu$. The system is stable, with a_t tending to $(1 - \varsigma)\mu/[\lambda + (1 - \varsigma)\beta\mu]$ as $t \to \infty$, if $|\varsigma| < 1 + \lambda/\beta\mu$. The limits for $\Delta\hat{a}_t$, c_t, and $\hat{a}_t$ ($\hat{a}_t \to \lambda/[\lambda + (1 - \varsigma)\beta\mu]$) then follow from $a_t = \lambda^{-1}\xi_{t-1}\Delta\hat{a}_t$, $\hat{a}_t = 1 - \beta a_t$, and $c_t = (\lambda + \beta)^{-1}(1 - \xi_{t-1})\Delta\hat{a}_t$. If $\varsigma = 1$ and $\tau_t \to \infty$, the same argument applies. Otherwise, $\Delta\hat{a}_t$ must converge to 0 and the result also follows.

(iii) follows from (i) and (ii) since $\tau_t = \tau_\theta + \tau_\eta \sum_{k=1}^{t} (\Delta\hat{a}_k)^2$, $\Delta\hat{a}_t \to \Delta\hat{a}_\infty$, and, therefore, $t^{-1}\tau_t \to (\Delta\hat{a}_\infty)^2\tau_\eta$. □

Proof of proposition 7.2 (see p. 259). (i) First, the result for θ_t follows as in the proof of proposition 7.1(i) by noting that now $\Delta z_t = \Delta\hat{a}_t\theta + \eta_t$, $\Delta\hat{a}_t \to \Delta\hat{a}_\infty = (1-\varsigma)\lambda/[\lambda + (1-\varsigma)\beta\mu]$. We have that $\mathrm{var}[\theta_t - \theta] = \tau_t^{-1}$ and the result follows because $t^{-1}\tau_t \to A\tau_\infty = (\Delta\hat{a}_\infty)^2\tau_\eta$. Second, we have that $x_t - x_t^{\mathrm{f}} = c_t(\theta_{t-1} - \theta) = (\lambda+\beta)^{-1}\Delta\hat{a}_t(1-\xi_{t-1})(\theta_{t-1} - \theta)$. If $\varsigma \neq 1$, then $\Delta\hat{a}_t \to \Delta\hat{a}_\infty$, $\tau_t \to \infty$, and $\xi_t \to \mu$. Hence, convergence obtains from (i). Now, $\mathrm{var}[x_t - x_t^{\mathrm{f}}] = (\lambda+\beta)^{-2}(\Delta\hat{a}_t)^2((1 - \xi_{t-1})^2 \mathrm{var}[\theta_{t-1} - \theta])$. Furthermore, from (i) $t\,\mathrm{var}[\theta_{t-1} - \theta] \to ((\Delta\hat{a}_\infty)^2\tau_\eta)^{-1}$ and therefore $t((\Delta\hat{a}_t)^2 \mathrm{var}[\theta_{t-1} - \theta]) \to \sigma_\eta^2$. The result follows since $\xi_t \to \mu$.

(ii) (Sketch.) When $\varsigma = 1$ the precision of the public statistic is bounded. Indeed, it is easily seen that $\hat{a}_t < 1$ increases with t (and therefore $\Delta\hat{a}_t = \hat{a}_t - \hat{a}_{t-1} \geqslant 0$). It then follows that

$$\sum_{k=1}^{t} (\Delta\hat{a}_k)^2 \leqslant \left(\sum_{k=1}^{t} |\Delta\hat{a}_k|\right)^2 = \left(\sum_{k=1}^{t} \Delta\hat{a}_k\right)^2 = (\hat{a}_t)^2 \leqslant 1,$$

and therefore $\tau_t = \tau_\theta + \tau_\eta \sum_{k=1}^{t} \Delta\hat{a}_k \leqslant \tau_\theta + \tau_\eta$. We conclude that $\tau_t \nrightarrow \infty$, since τ_t is increasing, with $\tau_\theta \leqslant \tau_\infty \leqslant \tau_\theta + \tau_\eta$. The increment $\Delta\hat{a}_t$ is of the same order as a_t, which converges to zero exponentially. It then follows that $x_t - x_t^{\mathrm{f}} = (\lambda+\beta)^{-1}\Delta\hat{a}_t(1-\xi_{t-1})(\theta_{t-1} - \theta)$ also converges to zero exponentially with t. □

Proof of proposition 7.3 (see p. 260). (Sketch.) (i) As in the proof of the lemma it is clear that $\tau_t \to \infty$ and that the aggregate weight given to private information tends to the proportion μ of perfectly informed agents ($\xi_t \to \mu$) as $t \to \infty$. Again this implies that for t large the dynamic system for a_t is approximately $a_t = (1 - \varsigma(1 - \beta a_{t-1}))(\lambda + \beta\mu)^{-1}\mu$ but this system is unstable with a_t tending to $-\infty$ exponentially with t if $\varsigma > 1 + \lambda/\beta\mu$. From the expressions $a_t = \lambda^{-1}\xi_{t-1}\Delta\hat{a}_t$, $\hat{a}_t = 1 - \beta a_t$, and $c_t = (\lambda+\beta)^{-1}(1 - \xi_{t-1})\Delta\hat{a}_t$ we have that $\{|\hat{a}_t|\}$ and $\{|\Delta\hat{a}_t|\}$, $\{|c_t|\}$ also tend to ∞ exponentially ($\hat{a}_t$ to ∞, $\Delta\hat{a}_t$ and c_t to $-\infty$). Given that $\tau_t = \tau_\theta + \tau_\eta \sum_{k=1}^{t} (\Delta\hat{a}_k)^2$, it is possible to show that

$$\lim_{t\to\infty} (\Delta\hat{a}_t)^{-2}\tau_t = \hat{\varsigma}^2(\hat{\varsigma}^2 - 1)^{-1}\tau_\eta.$$

(ii) This follows because τ_t grows exponentially with t.

(iii) This follows from the expression of $x_t - x_t^{\mathrm{f}} = c_t(\theta_{t-1} - \theta)$, $c_t = (\lambda+\beta)^{-1}(1 - \xi_{t-1})\Delta\hat{a}_t$, $\lim_{t\to\infty}(\Delta\hat{a}_t)^{-2}\tau_{t-1} = (\hat{\varsigma}^2 - 1)^{-1}\tau_\eta$. □

Section 7.4

Proposition 7.7 (Vives 1993). *In the model of section 7.4, there is a unique equilibrium (in the class of strategies with bounded means and uniformly—across agents—bounded variances). The equilibrium is linear and the price function is given by*

$$p_t = a_t\theta + u_t + c_t\theta_{t-1} + \lambda\alpha(1+\lambda)^{-1},$$

where $a_t = \xi_{t-1}(\lambda + \xi_{t-1})^{-1}$ *and* $c_t = (\lambda + \xi_{t-1})^{-1}(\lambda+1)^{-1}\lambda(1 - \xi_{t-1})$.

Strategies are given by

$$X_{it}(s_i, \theta_{t-1}) = \alpha(1+\lambda)^{-1} - a_{it}s_i - c_{it}\theta_{t-1},$$

where $a_{it} = \xi_{it-1}(\lambda + \xi_{t-1})^{-1}$, $c_{it} = (\lambda + \xi_{t-1})^{-1}(\lambda+1)^{-1}((\lambda+1)(1-\xi_{t-1}) - (1-\xi_{t-1}))$, *with* $\xi_{it-1} = \tau_{\varepsilon_i}/(\tau_{\varepsilon_i} + \tau_{t-1})$ *and* $\xi_{t-1} = \int_0^1 \xi_{it-1}\,\mathrm{d}i$.

Proof. Existence and characterization of a linear equilibrium are similar to the proof of proposition 7.6. Uniqueness follows from exercise 7.3. See the proofs of propositions 4.1 and 4.2 in Vives (1993). □

Proof of lemma 7.1 (see p. 264). The proof of (i) follows from proposition 7.7 and the fact that $\xi_t \to \mu$ as $t \to \infty$ (see the proof of lemma 5.1 in Vives 1993).

(ii) Let a_t be of order $t^{-\kappa}$ and τ_t be of order t^{υ}. Since $a_t \underset{t}{\to} \mu(\lambda+\mu)^{-1}$ and $\tau_t \underset{t}{\to} \infty$, necessarily $\kappa \geqslant 0$ and $\upsilon > 0$. If $\mu > 0$, then $a_\infty = \mu(\lambda+\mu)^{-1} > 0$ and therefore $\kappa = 0$ and $\upsilon = 1$. It then follows that $t^{-1}\tau_t \underset{t}{\to} \tau_\theta + \tau_u(\mu/(\lambda+\mu))^2$. If $\mu = 0$, the result follows from the two claims below. □

Claim 1. $a_t\tau_t$ converges to τ_ε/λ (τ_ε can be infinite) as $t \to \infty$.

Proof. Let $A_t \equiv \sum_{k=0}^{t} a_k^2$. Then $\tau_t = \tau_\theta + \tau_u A_t$. We show the equivalent result that $a_t\tau_{t-1}$ or a_tA_{t-1} converges to τ_ε/λ. From $a_t = \xi_{t-1}(\lambda+\xi_{t-1})^{-1}$ we have that $a_tA_{t-1} = ((A_{t-1})^{-1} + \lambda(A_{t-1}\xi_{t-1})^{-1})^{-1}$. Now,

$$A_{t-1}\xi_{t-1} = \int_0^1 A_{t-1}\xi_{it-1}\,\mathrm{d}i = \int_0^1 \tau_{\varepsilon_i}((\tau_\theta + \tau_{\varepsilon_i})(A_{t-1})^{-1} + \tau_u)^{-1}\,\mathrm{d}i.$$

Observing that $A_{t-1}\xi_{it-1}$ is a monotone increasing sequence of nonnegative measurable functions of i converging almost everywhere to $\tau_{\varepsilon_i}/\tau_u$, it is possible to conclude (Lebesgue Monotone Convergence Theorem (see Royden 1968, p. 227)) that $\int_0^1 A_{t-1}\xi_{it-1}\,\mathrm{d}i$ converges to $\tau_u^{-1}\int_0^1 \tau_{\varepsilon_i}\,\mathrm{d}i$ and the result follows (note that $A_{t-1} \to \infty$ with t). □

Claim 2. If τ_ε is finite, then $t^{-1/3}A_t \to 3^{1/3}(\tau_\varepsilon/\lambda\tau_u)^{2/3}$ as $t \to \infty$. If τ_ε is infinite (and $\mu = 0$), then $1 > \upsilon > \frac{1}{3} > \kappa > 0$.

Proof. If $\mu = 0$, then $a_t \underset{t}{\to} 0$. If τ_ε is finite, the result follows from claim 1 and lemma 7.3. If τ_ε is infinite, then $a_tA_t \underset{t}{\to} \infty$ with t. Further, $t^{-1}A_t \underset{t}{\to} 0$ (since $a_t \to 0$) and $t^{-1/3}A_t \underset{t}{\to} \infty$ (using the fact that $A_t \geqslant ta_t^2$, $(a_tA_t)^{-1} \geqslant (t^{-1/3}A_t)^{-3/2}$, from which the result follows since $a_tA_t \underset{t}{\to} \infty$). It then follows from lemma 7.3 (with $\upsilon > \kappa > 0$) that $2\kappa + \upsilon = 1$ and $1 > \upsilon > \frac{1}{3}$. Note that in all cases $2\kappa + \upsilon = 1$ and $1 \geqslant \upsilon \geqslant \frac{1}{3}$. □

Lemma 7.3. *Assume that* $a_tA_t \underset{t}{\to} k > 0$, *then* $t^{-1/3}A_t \underset{t}{\to} 3(k/3)^{2/3}$ *and* $t^{1/3}a_t \underset{t}{\to} (k/3)^{1/3}$.

Proof. See the heuristic argument in section 6.3.1 and the proof of lemma A.1 in Vives (1993). An alternative proof is provided in the appendix to chapter 6. □

Lemma 7.4. *Assume that* $t^{-\upsilon}\sum_{k=1}^{t} a_k^2 \underset{t}{\rightarrow} k$, *where* $k > 0$, *and that* a_t *is of the order* $t^{-\kappa}$, *where* $\upsilon \geqslant \kappa > 0$. *Then* $\kappa < \frac{1}{2}$ *and* $\sum_{k=1}^{t} a_k^2$ *is of the order of* $t^{1-2\kappa}/(1-2\kappa)$. *It follows that* $\upsilon + 2\kappa = 1$ *and* $1 > \upsilon \geqslant \frac{1}{3}$.

Proof. See the proof of lemma A.2 in Vives (1993). □

7.7 Exercises

7.1 (*information acquisition and fully revealing equilibria*). Consider the Cournot game in the continuum economy with increasing marginal costs of section 1.6 and add another market period. At a first stage each firm has the opportunity to purchase the precision of its signal (like in section 1.6). Firms compete in quantities contingent on the received signals at a first market period, observe the market price, and compete again in a second market period. Show that each firm purchasing "precision" ξ^* at the first stage, producing $X_i(s_i) = a(s_i - \mu) + b\mu$ at the first market period (second stage), where $a = \xi^*/(\lambda + \beta\xi^*)$ (with ξ^*, a, and b as in the two-stage game), inferring θ from the market price, and producing $x = b\theta$ at the second market period (third stage) is an equilibrium path for the three-stage game. Bearing in mind the Grossman-Stiglitz paradox (see section 4.2.2), what do you conclude about the incentives to purchase information in the presence of fully revealing equilibria?

Solution. Suppose that firms have already chosen their precision of the information, ξ_i, $i \in [0,1]$. Firm i at stage two will follow the strategy $X_i(s_i) = a_i(s_i - \bar{\theta}) + b\bar{\theta}$ as in the two-stage game (where $a_i = \xi_i/(\lambda + \beta\xi)$ and $\xi = \int_0^1 \xi_i \, di$) since in the continuum economy the firm cannot affect the market price through its quantity choice. The market price conditional on θ will then be $p = \theta - \beta\tilde{X}(\theta)$, where $\tilde{X}(\theta)$ is the average output, $\tilde{X}(\theta) = a(\theta - \bar{\theta}) + b\bar{\theta}$ with $a = \int_0^1 a_i \, di = \xi/(\lambda + \beta\xi)$. Therefore, $p = \theta(1 - \beta a) - \beta(b - a)\bar{\theta}$ and provided that $1 - \beta a \neq 0$, θ can be obtained by observing the market price: $\theta = (p + \beta(b - a)\mu)/(1 - \beta a)$ (note that $a\beta < 1$ except if $\lambda = 0$). When θ is revealed a full-information competitive equilibrium obtains at the last stage, $x = b\theta$ and $p = \lambda b\theta$. At the last stage a fully revealing rational expectations equilibrium prevails but nevertheless firms have an incentive to purchase information since this affects expected profits at the second stage before the market price is observed (see Dubey et al. (1982) for an elaboration of this idea in a strategic market game context where they show that Nash equilibria of the continuum economy are fully revealing generically).

***7.2** (*isoelastic-lognormal model*). Similarly to section 1.2.4.2, consider a market with constant elasticity inverse demand and costs. In period t inverse demand is given by $p_t = \mathrm{e}^{\theta + u_t} x_t^{-\beta}$, $\beta > 0$, where the information structure is exactly as in section 7.3 with the simplifying assumption that the signals received by agents $s_i = \theta + \varepsilon_i$ have equal (finite) precision ($\tau_{\varepsilon_i} = \sigma_\varepsilon^{-2}$ for all i). Firms have constant elasticity cost functions given by $C(x_{it}) = (1+\lambda)^{-1} x_{it}^{1+\lambda}$, $\lambda > 0$. Find an equilibrium in log-linear strategies (it looks similar to the linear model, but in log form, with the addition of a constant term which depends on the various variances). Show that the FIE output is given by

$$x_t^{\mathrm{f}} = \mathrm{e}^{(\lambda+\beta)^{-1}(\theta+\varsigma u_{t-1}+\sigma_\eta^2/2)}$$

and that convergence to the FIE is analogous to the result in the linear-normal model replacing $x_t - x_t^{\mathrm{f}}$ by $\log(x_t/x_t^{\mathrm{f}})$. (The departure from the FIE depends as before on the term $c_t(\theta_{t-1} - \theta)$ but there is an additional variance term.)

Solution (from Jun and Vives 1995). The procedure is similar to the one outlined for the proofs of propositions 7.2 and 7.6 (with $\bar{\theta} = 0$) using our convention about the average of a continuum of random variables (which implies that $\int_0^1 \mathrm{e}^{\varepsilon_i}\,\mathrm{d}i = \int_0^1 E[\mathrm{e}^{\varepsilon_i}]\,\mathrm{d}i$) and the properties of lognormal distributions (namely that if $\varepsilon_i \sim N(0, \sigma_\varepsilon^2)$, then $E[\mathrm{e}^{\varepsilon_i}] = \mathrm{e}^{\sigma_\varepsilon^2/2}$). The result is that

$$\log(X_t(s_i, \theta_{t-1}, z_{t-1})) = a_t s_i + c_t\theta_{t-1} + (\lambda + \beta)^{-1}\varsigma z_{t-1} + k_t$$

and

$$\log(p_t) = \hat{a}_t\theta + u_t - \beta c_t\theta_{t-1} - \beta(\lambda + \beta)^{-1}\varsigma z_{t-1} - \beta(k_t + \tfrac{1}{2}a_t^2\sigma_\varepsilon^2),$$

where all parameters are as in proposition 7.6 and

$$k_t = (\lambda + \beta)^{-1}[\tfrac{1}{2}\sigma_\eta^2 + \lambda^2(a_t/\xi_{t-1})^2/2\tau_{t-1} - \tfrac{1}{2}\beta a_t^2\sigma_\varepsilon^2].$$

With full information a firm at time t knows $\{\theta, u^{t-1}\}$. From the FOC of profit maximization we get

$$x_t^{\mathrm{f}} = (E[p_t \mid \theta, u^{t-1}])^{1/\lambda} = \exp\{\lambda^{-1}(\theta + \varsigma u_{t-1} + \tfrac{1}{2}\sigma_\eta^2)\}(x_t^{\mathrm{f}})^{-\beta/\lambda}.$$

The expression for x_t^{f} follows. We then have that $\ln(x_t/x_t^{\mathrm{f}}) = c_t(\theta_{t-1} - \theta) + [\lambda^2\xi_{t-1}^{-2}\tau_{t-1}^{-1} - \phi\sigma_\varepsilon^2]a_t^2/2(\alpha + \beta)$ and the asymptotic results follow with a little bit of work. As $t \to \infty$:

(i) $x_t/x_t^{\mathrm{f}} \to 1$ (a.s. and in mean square), and

(ii) if $\varsigma \neq 1$, then $\sqrt{t}\log(x_t/x_t^{\mathrm{f}}) \xrightarrow{\mathrm{L}} N(0, \sigma_\eta^2/(\alpha + \beta)^2)$.

*7.3 (*uniqueness of dynamic equilibrium*). Prove the uniqueness part of proposition 7.7.

Solution. The uniqueness argument proceeds by showing that at any stage only linear equilibria are possible. Consider a generic stage, drop the period subscript, and denote by $\hat{\theta}$ the public statistic. Assume that the information available to agent i is $\{s_i, \hat{\theta}\}$, where the triple $(\theta, s_i, \hat{\theta})$ is jointly normally distributed. Then using FOCs show that for any candidate equilibrium average output $X(\theta, \hat{\theta})$, $E[(X(\theta, \hat{\theta}) - (\alpha(1+\lambda)^{-1} - a\theta - c\hat{\theta}))^2] = 0$, where $\alpha(1+\lambda)^{-1} - a\theta - c\hat{\theta}$ is the linear equilibrium. This implies that $X(\theta, \hat{\theta}) = \alpha(1+\lambda)^{-1} - a\theta - c\hat{\theta}$ (a.s.) and therefore necessarily $X_i(s_i, \hat{\theta}) = \alpha(1+\lambda)^{-1} - a_i s_i - c_i\hat{\theta}$ (a.s.). Check finally by induction that at any stage $(\theta, s_i, \hat{\theta})$ is jointly normally distributed. (See the proof of proposition 4.2 in Vives (1993) for the details.)

** **7.4** (*slow learning in the generalized prediction model*). Consider the prediction model of section 6.3.1 with no correlation in signals of agents but where the distribution of precisions of private signals for every generation is given by a (measurable) function $T_\varepsilon : [0,1] \to \mathbb{R}_+ \cup \{\infty\}$, where $T_\varepsilon(i) = \sigma_{\varepsilon_i}^{-2} (\equiv \tau_{\varepsilon_i})$ is the value of this function for $i \in [0,1]$. Denote by $\mu \geqslant 0$ the mass of agents with perfectly informative signals. Revise proposition 6.1 and show that as $t \to \infty$:

(i) $a_t \to \mu$ and $\tau_t \to \infty$.

(ii) $\theta_t \to \theta$ almost surely and in mean square;

(iii) τ_t is of order t^{υ} and a_t is of order $t^{-\kappa}$, where $2\kappa + \upsilon = 1$, $\upsilon \in [\frac{1}{3}, 1]$, $\kappa \geqslant 0$. Let $A\tau_\infty = \lim_{t\to\infty} t^{-\upsilon}\tau_t$. If $\tau_\varepsilon \equiv \int_0^1 \tau_{\varepsilon_i}\, di < \infty$, then $\upsilon = \frac{1}{3}$ and $A\tau_\infty = (3\tau_u)^{1/3}(\tau_\varepsilon)^{2/3}$. Otherwise, if $\mu > 0$, then $\upsilon = 1$ and $A\tau_\infty = \tau_u \mu^2$; if $\mu = 0$, then $1 > \upsilon > \frac{1}{3} > \kappa > 0$.

(iv) If $\tau_\varepsilon < \infty$, $\sqrt{t^{1/3}}(\theta_t - \theta) \xrightarrow{L} N(0, (3\tau_u \tau_\varepsilon^2)^{-1/3})$;
if $\mu > 0$, $\sqrt{t}(\theta_t - \theta) \xrightarrow{L} N(0, (\tau_u \mu^2)^{-1})$; and
if $\mu = 0$ and τ_ε is infinite, $\sqrt{t^{\upsilon}}(\theta_t - \theta) \xrightarrow{L} N(0, (A\tau_\infty)^{-1})$ for some $\upsilon \in (\frac{1}{3}, 1)$ and appropriate positive constant $A\tau_\infty$.

Solution. Adapt the arguments in section 7.3 and the appendix.

References

Alchian, A. 1950. Uncertainty, evolution and economic theory. *Journal of Political Economy* 58:211–21.

Bisin, A., U. Horst, and O. Özgur. 2006. Rational expectations equilibria of economies with local interactions. *Journal of Economic Theory* 127:74–116.

Blackwell, D., and L. Dubins. 1962. Merging of opinions with increasing information. *Annals of Mathematical Statistics* 33:882–86.

Blume, L. E., and D. Easley. 1982. Learning to be rational. *Journal of Economic Theory* 26:340–51.

——. 1984. Rational expectations equilibrium: an alternative approach. *Journal of Economic Theory* 34:116–29.

——. 1998. Rational expectations and rational learning. In *Organizations with Incomplete Information: Essays in Economic Analysis: A Tribute to Roy Radner*, pp. 61–109. Cambridge University Press.

Bray, M. 1982. Learning, estimation, and the stability of rational expectations. *Journal of Economic Theory* 26:318–39.

Bray, M., and D. M. Kreps. 1988. Rational learning and rational expectations. In *Arrow and the Ascent of Modern Economic Theory* (ed. G. Feiwel), pp. 597–625. London: Macmillan.

Bray, M., and N. E. Savin. 1986. Rational expectations equilibria, learning, and model specification. *Econometrica* 54:1129–60.

Brock, W., and C. Hommes. 1997. A rational route to randomness. *Econometrica* 65: 1059–95.

De Long, J., A. Shleifer, L. Summers, and R. Waldmann. 1989. The size and incidence of the losses from noise trading. *Journal of Finance* 44:681–96.

De Long, J., A. Shleifer, L. Summers, and R. Waldmann. 1990. Noise trader risk in financial markets. *Journal of Political Economy* 98:703–38.

Dubey, P., J. Geanakoplos, and M. Shubik. 1982. Revelation of information in strategic market games: a critique of rational expectations. Cowles Foundation Discussion Papers 634R, Yale University.

Evans, D., and S. Honkapohja. 2001. *Learning and Expectations in Macroeconomics.* Princeton University Press.

Feldman, M. 1987. An example of convergence to rational expectations with heterogeneous beliefs. *International Economic Review* 28:635–50.

Fourgeaud, C., C. Gourieroux, and J. Pradel. 1986. Learning procedures and convergence to rationality. *Econometrica* 54:845–68.

Friedman, M. 1953. *Essays in Positive Economics.* University of Chicago Press.

Frydman, R. 1982. Towards an understanding of market processes: individual expectations, learning, and convergence to rational expectations equilibrium. *American Economic Review* 72:652–68.

Guesnerie, R. 2006. *Assessing Expectations*, volume 2: *Eductive Stability in Economics.* Cambridge, MA: MIT Press.

Hirshleifer, D., and G. Luo. 2001. On the survival of overconfident traders in a competitive securities market. *Journal of Financial Markets* 4:73–84.

Jordan, J. S. 1985. Learning rational expectations: the finite state case. *Journal of Economic Theory* 36:257–76.

——. 1992a. The exponential convergence of Bayesian learning in normal form games. *Games and Economic Behavior* 4:202–17.

——. 1992b. Convergence to rational expectations in a stationary linear game. *Review of Economic Studies* 59:109–23.

Jun, B., and X. Vives. 1995. Learning and convergence to REE with persistent shocks. Mimeo.

——. 1996. Learning and convergence to a full-information equilibrium are not equivalent. *Review of Economic Studies* 63:653–74.

Kalai, E., and E. Lehrer. 1993. Rational learning leads to Nash equilibrium. *Econometrica* 61:1019–45.

Kyle, A. S., and F. Wang. 1997. Speculation duopoly with agreement to disagree: can overconfidence survive the market test? *Journal of Finance* 52:2073–90.

Lucas, R. 1978. Asset prices in an exchange economy. *Econometrica* 46:1429–45.

Marcet, A., and T. J. Sargent. 1988. The fate of systems with "adaptive" expectations. *American Economic Review* 78:168–72.

——. 1989. Convergence of least squares learning mechanisms in self-referential linear stochastic models. *Journal of Economic Theory* 48:337–68.

——. 1992. The convergence of vector autoregressions to rational expectations equilibria. In *Macroeconomics: A Survey of Research Strategies* (ed. A. Vercelli and N. Dimitri), pp. 139–64. Oxford University Press.

McCafferty, S., and R. Driskill. 1980. Problems of existence and uniqueness in nonlinear rational expectations models. *Econometrica* 48:1313–17.

McKelvey, R. D., and T. Page. 1986. Common knowledge, consensus, and aggregate information. *Econometrica* 54:109–27.

Muth, J. F. 1961. Rational expectations and the theory of price movements. *Econometrica* 29:315–35.

Nyarko, Y. 1997. Convergence in economic models with Bayesian hierarchies of beliefs. *Journal of Economic Theory* 74:266–96.

——. 1998. Bayesian learning without common priors and convergence to Nash equilibrium. *Economic Theory* 11:643–56.

Royden, H. L. 1968. *Real Analysis.* New York: Macmillan.

Sandroni, A. 2000. Do markets favor agents able to make accurate predictions? *Econometrica* 68:1303–41.

——. 2005. Efficient markets and Bayes' rule. *Economic Theory* 26:741–54.

Spanos, A. 1986. *Statistical Foundations of Econometric Modeling.* Cambridge University Press.

Townsend, R. M. 1978. Market anticipations, rational expectations, and Bayesian analysis. *International Economic Review* 19:481–94.

Vives, X. 1993. How fast do rational agents learn? *Review of Economic Studies* 60:329–47.

Woodford, M. 1990. Learning to believe in sunspots. *Econometrica* 58:277–307.

8

Dynamic Rational Expectations Models in Competitive Financial Markets

In chapter 4 we studied in depth different versions of the static financial market model with asymmetric information. In chapters 6 and 7 we turned to dynamic issues by studying information revelation through time in the context of stylized prediction models (chapter 6) or of simple Cournot-type models (chapter 7). It is now time to use the tools developed in those dynamic models to study financial markets. In this chapter we will deal with competitive dynamics. The next chapter will introduce strategic traders.

The chapter deals with dynamics of pricing and market quality parameters, such as price informativeness, market depth, volatility, and volume in a variety of market microstructures. Two basic factors impinge on the performance of the market: the market microstructure and the horizon of the traders. In the market microstructure it matters in particular whether market makers, and in general traders using limit orders, are risk neutral or risk averse. It matters also whether informed traders use market or limit orders. Different combinations of market microstructure and traders' horizons go a long way toward explaining supposed anomalies in pricing and volume relationships, such as market crashes and booms, departures of prices from fundamentals and "excess" volatility, and investment in information unrelated to fundamentals. More specifically, we are interested in characterizing the dynamic trading strategies of agents with a long horizon and the effects of agents with a short horizon; the dynamic impact of risk-averse market makers on market parameters; the relationship between prices and the average expectations of investors; whether and how can technical analysis (i.e., learning from past prices) make sense; and how crashes and bubbles can be explained in competitive markets with rational traders.

In order to analyze these issues we have to overcome some technical difficulties. Indeed, the modeling of financial market dynamics with asymmetric information has proved difficult, in particular in the presence of risk-averse traders. Leading papers addressing dynamic trading assume either risk-neutral traders (Kyle 1985; Glosten and Milgrom 1985; Diamond and Verrecchia 1987; Easley and O'Hara 1987; Admati and Pfleiderer 1988) or myopic traders (Singleton 1987). A basic technical difficulty in order to characterize equilibria with dynamic trading is the simultaneous presence of far-sighted (long-term) agents who are risk averse and heterogeneously informed. Wang (1993) and Gennotte and Kyle (1992) present results in continuous-time models with nested information structures, where the information sets of the speculators can be completely ordered in term of informativeness. An example with two classes of traders would be to have traders who are informed and receive the same signal, and traders who are uninformed (like in the Grossman and Stiglitz (1980) model, see section 4.2.2). Grundy and McNichols (1989) and Brown and Jennings (1989) report some results in two-period models with risk-averse traders. In the present chapter a complete closed-form solution of a T-period dynamic model with long-term agents is displayed, the first such model to provide a closed-form solution for a nonnested information structure (Vives 1995). The analysis has to overcome a potential infinite regress expectational problem (as studied by Townsend 1983). The issue is how to cut through the process of evaluation of expectations of expectations of expectations...in the presence of nonnested asymmetric information. He and Wang (1995) and Cespa and Vives (2007) present a version of the model, allowing for risk-averse market making and residual uncertainty, and study dynamic price and volume patterns.

Sections 8.1–8.3 study competitive dynamics in markets where traders can condition their trades on current prices in the rational expectations tradition. Section 8.1 starts characterizing the properties of the price process when there is a risk-neutral market-making sector and moves on to study the trading strategies of long-term investors. Section 8.2 considers the impact of risk-averse market makers and provides a rationale for technical analysis, patterns of trade with no news, and the determinants of traded volume. Section 8.3 considers the case of traders with short horizons. Section 8.4 concludes with several models that explain market crashes and crises, including a basic coordination game of investors useful to explain currency attacks and bank runs.

8.1 Dynamic Competitive Rational Expectations

In this section we consider a dynamic extension of a version of the static rational expectations model of section 4.2. We consider informed risk-averse agents and noise traders who trade with the intermediation of risk-neutral competitive market makers. All traders (except noise traders) use demand schedules as strategies and therefore will be able to condition on current prices. The properties of the price process in such a context are developed in section 8.1.1 and section 8.1.2 deals with dynamic trading when investors have a long horizon.

8.1.1 Price Formation with a Competitive Risk-Neutral Fringe[1]

A single risky asset, with random fundamental value θ, and a riskless asset (with unitary return) are traded for T periods in a market with risk-averse informed

[1] The material in this section is based on Vives (1995).

agents and noise traders with the intermediation of risk-neutral competitive market makers. In period $T+1$ the fundamental value θ ($p_{T+1} \equiv \theta$) is realized.

Noise traders' demands follow an independently identically normally distributed process $\{u_t\}_{t=1}^{T}$, independent of all other random variables in the model with $E[u_t] = 0$ and $\text{var}[u_t] = \sigma_u^2$. These are the noise trading (or random supply) increments at each period. Noise trading demand or random supply therefore follows a random walk.

In any period there is a continuum of informed traders (indexed in the unit interval). Informed trader i in period t receives a normally distributed signal $s_{it} = \theta + \varepsilon_{it}$, where θ and ε_{it} are uncorrelated, and errors are also uncorrelated across agents and periods (and with noise trade). The precision of the signals τ_{ε_t} is the same across agents in the same period but may be different across periods. We assume that $\tau_{\varepsilon_1} > 0$.

Our formalization encompasses the cases of traders having either a long or a short horizon. In period t agent i has available the vector of private signals $s_i^t = \{s_{i1}, \dots, s_{it}\}$. This could be the case if long-lived traders have a long horizon. If traders have a short horizon, then they may be long-lived but myopic and they do not forget information.[2] Alternatively, traders are short-lived with a different generation of informed agents coming to market every period, each member of generation t inheriting the private information of a member of generation $t-1$.

It is immediate from Gaussian updating formulas that a sufficient statistic for s_i^t in the estimation of θ is the weighted signal $\tilde{s}_{it} = (\sum_{k=1}^{t} \tau_{\varepsilon_k})^{-1} \sum_{k=1}^{t} \tau_{\varepsilon_k} s_{ik}$. We restrict our attention to linear equilibria. In any linear equilibrium the strategy of agent i in period t will depend on $\tilde{s}_{it}$ and public information (since the private and public signals are independent conditionally on θ). Informed agent i in period t has a demand schedule $X_{it}(\tilde{s}_{it}, p^{t-1}, \cdot)$, indicating the position desired at every price p_t, contingent on the sufficient statistic for the private information $\tilde{s}_{it}$ and the sequence of past prices $p^{t-1} = \{p_1, \dots, p_{t-1}\}$.

In period t the competitive market-making sector observes the aggregate limit-order book $L_t(\cdot)$ consisting of the net aggregate demand of informed traders and the incremental demand of noise traders: $L_t = \int_0^1 x_{it}\,di - \int_0^1 x_{it-1}\,di + u_t$. Trader i submits in period t the (net) demand schedule $X_{it}(\tilde{s}_{it}, p^{t-1}, \cdot) - X_{it-1}(\tilde{s}_{it-1}, p^{t-2}, p_{t-1})$. Indeed, his desired position in period t when p_t is realized is given by $X_{it}(\tilde{s}_{it}, p^{t-1}, p_t)$ and he enters the period with $X_{it-1}(\tilde{s}_{it-1}, p^{t-2}, p_{t-1})$. This applies to a trader with a long horizon or one with a myopic short horizon. If there is a new generation of informed traders every period, then $\int_0^1 X_{it-1}(\tilde{s}_{it-1}, p^{t-2}, p_{t-1})\,di$ is what the old generation dumps in the market at t and the trader of the new generation submits the demand schedule $X_{it}(\tilde{s}_{it}, p^{t-1}, \cdot)$.

Consider a candidate linear equilibrium: $X_{it}(\tilde{s}_{it}, p^{t-1}, p_t) = a_{it}\tilde{s}_{it} + \varphi_{it}(p^t)$, where a_{it} is the sensitivity to private information (or trading intensity) and $\varphi_{it}(\cdot)$ is a linear function of past and current prices. The noisy limit-order

[2] Traders in foreign exchange markets are taken to display such behavior (see, for example, Lyons 2001).

book at stage t is then given by

$$L_t(p_t) = \int_0^1 X_{it}(\tilde{s}_{it}, p^{t-1}, p_t)\,\mathrm{d}i - \int_0^1 X_{it-1}(\tilde{s}_{it-1}, p^{t-2}, p_t)\,\mathrm{d}i + u_t$$
$$= z_t + \varphi_t(p^t) - \varphi_{t-1}(p^{t-1}),$$

where $z_t = \Delta a_t\theta + u_t$, $\int_0^1 a_{it}\,\mathrm{d}i = a_t$, $\Delta a_t = a_t - a_{t-1}$ (with $a_0 \equiv 0$), and $\varphi_t(p^t) = \int_0^1 \varphi_{it}(p^t)\,\mathrm{d}i$. This follows by using the convention $\int_0^1 a_{it}\tilde{s}_{it}\,\mathrm{d}i = a_t\theta + \int_0^1 a_{it}\varepsilon_{it}\,\mathrm{d}i = a_t\theta$ (a.s.) assuming that the coefficients a_{it} are uniformly bounded across agents at any date t and that the average coefficients in the linear functions $\varphi_t(\cdot)$ are well-defined.[3] We therefore restrict our attention to linear equilibria of this type.

The random variable $z_t = \Delta a_t\theta + u_t$, where Δa_t is the net trading intensity of informed agents in period t, is the new information in the current price filtered from the net aggregate action of informed agents. The variable z_t is the intercept of the net aggregate demand in period t and contains the informative part about θ of the order flow.

The competitive market-making sector sets the current price p_t conditional on past public information and the new information in the aggregate limit-order schedule $L_t(\cdot)$, z_t. Past public information is summarized in the sequence $z^{t-1} = \{z_1,\dots,z_{t-1}\}$ of informational additions from the limit-order books, which is easily seen to be observationally equivalent to the sequence of prices $p^{t-1} = \{p_1,\dots,p_{t-1}\}$.[4]

The price set by the competitive market-making sector is then $p_t = E[\theta \mid z^t]$. From standard normal theory p_t equals a linear combination of $p_{t-1} = E[\theta \mid z^{t-1}]$ and z_t with weights according to their relative precisions: $p_t = \lambda_t z_t + (1 - \lambda_t\Delta a_t)p_{t-1}$, with $\lambda_t = \tau_u\Delta a_t/\tau_t$.[5] The parameter λ_t, as in chapter 4, may be taken to be an inverse measure of the depth of the market. How much does the price in period t move with a unit change in noise trading in the period u_t? The informativeness or precision of p_t, $\tau_t \equiv (\mathrm{var}[\theta \mid p_t])^{-1} = \tau_\theta + \tau_u\sum_{k=1}^t(\Delta a_k)^2$ is determined by the intensity of net trades by informed agents. An explicit expression for the price is $p_t = E[\theta \mid z^t] = (\tau_\theta\bar{\theta} + \tau_u\sum_{k=1}^t\Delta a_k z_k)/\tau_t$. The following proposition summarizes the evolution of prices at any linear equilibrium.

Proposition 8.1. *Let $p_0 \equiv \bar{\theta}$ and $p_{T+1} \equiv \theta$. At any linear equilibrium for $t = 1,\dots,T$:*

$$p_t = E[\theta \mid z^t] = \lambda_t z_t + (1 - \lambda_t\Delta a_t)p_{t-1},$$

with $\lambda_t = \tau_u\Delta a_t/\tau_t$, $z_t = \Delta a_t\theta + u_t$, and $\tau_t = \tau_\theta + \tau_u\sum_{k=1}^t(\Delta a_k)^2$.

---

[3] See section 10.3.1 for a justification of the convention.

[4] This can be shown by induction. For $t = 1$, $p_1 = E[\theta \mid z_1]$ as in the static model (section 4.2 for the case of risk-neutral market makers), which implies that z_1 is observationally equivalent to p_1, since in equilibrium the parameters of the linear function $E[\theta \mid z_1]$ are known. Now, if z^{t-1} and p^{t-1} are observationally equivalent, then z^t and p^t are also observationally equivalent. This follows since from the limit-order-book market makers infer z_t and set $p_t = E[\theta \mid z_t, z^{t-1}]$. If $\Delta a_t = 0$, the weight put by market makers on z_t is zero and $p_t = E[\theta \mid z^{t-1}] = p_{t-1}$.

[5] Whenever $\Delta a_t \neq 0$, consider $z_t/\Delta a_t = \theta + (\Delta a_t)^{-1}u_t$ and notice that $p_t = \lambda_t\Delta a_t(z_t/\Delta a_t) + (1 - \lambda_t\Delta a_t)p_{t-1}$.

The following properties follow from the characterization of the price process:

Informed trader i's desired position in period t can be written in a (symmetric) equilibrium, and with some abuse of notation, as $X_t(\tilde{s}_{it}, p_t)$. (Given the preferences of the traders and the symmetric-information structure equilibria will be symmetric.) Because of normality $p_t = E[\theta \mid z^t]$ is a sufficient statistic for the information p^t or z^t in the estimation of θ and in consequence, $p_t = E[\theta \mid p_t]$. Since the error terms in the signals s_i^t are independent of the noise trading process u^t, in the estimation of θ with the information $\{s_i^t, p^t\}$ it is sufficient to consider $\{\tilde{s}_{it}, p_t\}$, where $\tilde{s}_{it}$ is a sufficient statistic for s_i^t and p_t is a sufficient statistic for p^t.

Market depth $\lambda_t^{-1} = \tau_t/\tau_u \Delta a_t$, for a given volume of noise trading, increases with the amount of public information τ_t, which reduces the informational advantage of informed traders over market makers, and decreases with the current net trading intensity of informed traders, which makes the order flow more likely to reflect informed trading.

Historical prices or "technical analysis" are superfluous for decision making. Traders need not know about past prices since the current price is a sufficient statistic for all public information. Let $\Delta p_t = p_t - p_{t-1}$. Note that $\Delta p_t = \lambda_t(z_t - \Delta a_t p_{t-1}) = \lambda_t(\Delta a_t(\theta - p_{t-1}) + u_t)$. Given the existence of a competitive risk-neutral market-making sector the market is (semi-strong) efficient, prices follow a martingale, $E[p_t \mid p^{t-1}] = E[p_t \mid p_{t-1}] = p_{t-1}$ and $\mathrm{cov}[\Delta p_t, \Delta p_{t-1}] = 0$, and the current price is a sufficient statistic for all public information. A consequence is that prices exhibit no drift: $E[\Delta p_t \mid \Delta p_{t-1}] = E[\Delta p_t] = 0$.

At a linear equilibrium, a sufficient statistic for $\{s_i^t, p^t\}$ or $\{s_i^t, z^t\}$ in the estimation of $p_{t+1} - p_t$ is $\tilde{s}_{it} - p_t$ since $E[\Delta p_{t+1} \mid \tilde{s}_{it}, p_t] = \lambda_{t+1}\Delta a_{t+1} E[(\theta - p_t) \mid \tilde{s}_{it}, p_t]$, which equals $\lambda_{t+1}\Delta a_{t+1}(\sum_{k=1}^t \tau_{\varepsilon_k})(\sum_{k=1}^t \tau_{\varepsilon_k} + \tau_t)^{-1}(\tilde{s}_{it} - p_t)$ given that $E[\theta \mid \tilde{s}_{it}, p_t] = ((\sum_{k=1}^t \tau_{\varepsilon_k})\tilde{s}_{it} + \tau_t p_t)/(\sum_{k=1}^t \tau_{\varepsilon_k} + \tau_t)$. Obviously, at a linear equilibrium, in the estimation of $\theta - p_t$, $\tilde{s}_{it} - p_t$ is sufficient with respect to the information $\{s_i^t, p^t\}$.

Prices are biased in the sense of regression toward the mean: $\mathrm{sgn}(E[(\theta - p_t) \mid \theta]) = \mathrm{sgn}(\theta - \bar{\theta})$. Indeed, from $p_t = (\tau_\theta \bar{\theta} + \tau_u \sum_{k=1}^t \Delta a_k z_k)/\tau_t$ and $\tau_t = \tau_\theta + \tau_u \sum_{k=1}^t (\Delta a_k)^2$ it is immediate that $E[p_t \mid \theta] = (1 - \tau_\theta/\tau_t)\theta + (\tau_\theta/\tau_t)\bar{\theta}$ and therefore

$$E[\theta - p_t \mid \theta] = \frac{\tau_\theta}{\tau_t}(\theta - \bar{\theta}).$$

The average of informed investors' expectations about the fundamental value θ in period t is a convex combination of θ and p_t. Since

$$\begin{aligned} \int_0^1 E[\theta \mid s_i^t, z^t]\,\mathrm{d}i &= \int_0^1 E[\theta \mid \tilde{s}_{it}, p_t]\,\mathrm{d}i \\ &= \left(\sum_{k=1}^t \tau_{\varepsilon_k} + \tau_t\right)^{-1} \left(\left(\sum_{k=1}^t \tau_{\varepsilon_k}\right) \int_0^1 \tilde{s}_{it}\,\mathrm{d}i + \tau_t p_t\right) \end{aligned}$$

and $\int_0^1 \tilde{s}_{it}\,\mathrm{d}i = \theta$, we have that

$$\int_0^1 E[\theta \mid \tilde{s}_{it}, p_t]\,\mathrm{d}i = \Big(\sum_{k=1}^{t} \tau_{\varepsilon_k} + \tau_t\Big)^{-1}\Big(\Big(\sum_{k=1}^{t} \tau_{\varepsilon_k}\Big)\theta + \tau_t p_t\Big).$$

This means that, in the presence of a risk-neutral market-making sector, prices are always "farther away" from fundamentals (or more biased in the estimation of θ) than average expectations among the informed. Indeed, it is easy to see, using the expression for $E[p_t \mid \theta]$, that

$$\theta - E\bigg[\int_0^1 E[\theta \mid \tilde{s}_{it}, p_t]\,\mathrm{d}i \;\bigg|\; \theta\bigg] = \frac{\tau_\theta}{\sum_{k=1}^{t} \tau_{\varepsilon_k} + \tau_t}(\theta - \bar{\theta}),$$

and therefore

$$\frac{|E[\theta - p_t \mid \theta]|}{|E[\theta - \int_0^1 E[\theta \mid \tilde{s}_{it}, p_t]\,\mathrm{d}i \mid \theta]|} = 1 + \frac{\sum_{k=1}^{t} \tau_{\varepsilon_k}}{\tau_t} > 1.$$

The discrepancy between prices and average expectations of the informed is larger the larger is the ratio between private and public precision.

In a semi-strong efficient market, trading behavior affects the distribution of volatility over time but not its total magnitude. More informative prices bring forward the resolution of uncertainty. Indeed, the martingale property of prices has immediate consequences for price volatility (similar to the public belief in section 6.3.1). It follows that the unconditional volatility of p_t is given by $\operatorname{var}[p_t] = \tau_\theta^{-1} - \tau_t^{-1}$, and is nondecreasing with t (τ_t is also nondecreasing with t). As more information is incorporated in prices *ex ante* volatility increases. The *conditional volatility* $\operatorname{var}[p_t \mid p_{t-1}]$ ($= \operatorname{var}[\Delta p_t]$) equals $\tau_{t-1}^{-1} - \tau_t^{-1}$, and *total volatility* $\sum_{t=1}^{T+1} \operatorname{var}[\Delta p_t]$ is constant, and equal to the sum of conditional volatilities $\sum_{t=1}^{T+1} \operatorname{var}[p_t \mid p_{t-1}]$:

$$\sum_{t=1}^{T+1} \operatorname{var}[\Delta p_t] = \sum_{t=1}^{T+1} \operatorname{var}[p_t \mid p_{t-1}] = \operatorname{var}\bigg[\sum_{t=1}^{T+1} \Delta p_t\bigg] = \tau_\theta^{-1}$$

since $\operatorname{cov}[\Delta p_t, \Delta p_{t-1}] = 0$ and $\sum_{t=1}^{T+1} \Delta p_t = \theta - \bar{\theta}$.[6]

The dynamics of conditional volatility $\operatorname{var}[p_t \mid p_{t-1}]$ depend on the convexity/concavity properties of $\operatorname{var}[\theta \mid p_t]$ with respect to t. Indeed, $\operatorname{var}[p_t \mid p_{t-1}]$ is increasing (decreasing) in t if and only if $\operatorname{var}[\theta \mid p_t]$ is concave (convex) in t. That is, the conditional volatility of prices is increasing (decreasing) in t if and only if information revelation accelerates (decelerates) as t increases.[7] This is so since in the semi-strong efficient market prices are volatile because they are informative. It follows that when information revelation accelerates the conditional volatility of prices also increases and, in fact, it is more difficult tomorrow to predict the next-period price than today. The argument for the result is as follows. We have that $\operatorname{var}[p_t \mid p_{t-1}] = \tau_{t-1}^{-1} - \tau_t^{-1}$ and $\tau_t = (\operatorname{var}[\theta \mid p_t])^{-1}$. Therefore, $\operatorname{var}[p_{t+1} \mid p_t] \geqslant \operatorname{var}[p_t \mid p_{t-1}]$ if and only if $\operatorname{var}[\theta \mid p_t] - \operatorname{var}[\theta \mid p_{t+1}] \geqslant$

---

[6] See section 10.3 for the properties of martingales.

[7] Note also that if $\operatorname{var}[\theta \mid p_t]$ is concave in t, then $\tau_t = (\operatorname{var}[\theta \mid p_t])^{-1}$ is convex in t.

$\text{var}[\theta \mid p_{t-1}] - \text{var}[\theta \mid p_t]$. Rearranging terms the inequality is equivalent to $\text{var}[\theta \mid p_t] - \text{var}[\theta \mid p_{t-1}] \geqslant \text{var}[\theta \mid p_{t+1}] - \text{var}[\theta \mid p_t]$ and the result follows.

8.1.2 Dynamic Trading with Long-Term Investors

Consider the market setup of the last section and suppose that all informed traders have a long horizon and maximize the expectation of the utility of final wealth. Informed trader i has a CARA utility and wants to maximize

$$E[U(W_{iT})] = -E[\mathrm{e}^{-\rho W_{iT}}],$$

with $\rho > 0$, where $W_{iT} = \sum_{k=1}^{T} \pi_{ik}$ and $\pi_{it} = (p_{t+1} - p_t)x_{it}$ denote the (short-run) profits derived by trader i in period t from acquiring a position of x_{it} units of the risky asset at price p_t and selling it next period at price p_{t+1}. The initial wealth of the traders (without loss of generality) is normalized to zero. In this chapter, and unless stated otherwise, traders will have CARA preferences.

In period t an informed agent receives a private signal s_{it} about θ. We know that at linear equilibrium the information of trader i in period t, $\{s_i^t, p^t\}$, can be summarized as $\{\tilde{s}_{it}, p_t\}$. At stage t a strategy for agent i is a function that maps $\tilde{s}_{it}$ into a demand schedule $X_{it}(\tilde{s}_{it}, \cdot)$ which gives the desired position in the risky asset. We analyze the (linear) perfect Bayesian equilibria (PBE) of the T-period dynamic game. The following proposition characterizes the equilibrium (which will be symmetric given the preferences of traders and the symmetric-information structure).

It is worth noting that the potential infinite regress expectational problem analyzed by Townsend (1983) does not arise in the present setup. An informed trader does not need to estimate the private signals of other traders because at a linear equilibrium aggregate trades depend only on public information and the average of the private signals of traders, which equals the fundamental value θ because the average error terms cancel out.[8]

Proposition 8.2 (Vives 1995). *With long-term informed traders there is a unique linear PBE. The strategy for trader i in period $t = 1, \dots, T$ is given by*

$$X_t(\tilde{s}_{it}, p_t) = a_t(\tilde{s}_{it} - p_t), \quad \text{with } a_t = \rho^{-1}\left(\sum_{k=1}^{t} \tau_{\varepsilon_k}\right).$$

Remark 8.1. The strategies at each period are as in a static model (the case $\rho_U = 0$ in the model of section 4.2.1) when the information of trader i is $\{s_i^t, p^t\}$ or, equivalently, $\{\tilde{s}_{it}, p_t\}$. The desired position of a trader in period t is the same as if the asset were to be liquidated at $t + 1$. In a multiperiod setting traders follow dynamic strategies, in principle, speculating on price changes and not only on the terminal value of the asset, as in a static setting. However, in the present context the dynamic hedging component exactly compensates the risk associated with price movements.

[8] Note also that, unlike in Townsend, in the present model the history of the economy at any date is finite dimensional.

Outline of proof. Consider a candidate linear equilibrium. Then we know that proposition 8.1 applies and that prices are normally distributed and a sufficient statistic for public information. The proof then proceeds by backward recursion from the last period, for which strategies are as in a static model. From the optimal last-period strategies the value function for period $T-1$ can be derived by taking into account the sufficient statistic for the information of a trader. The demands in the last period are of the static CARA form (as in section 4.2.1 with $\rho_U = 0$) with information $\{\tilde{s}_{iT}, p_T\}$:

$$X_T(\tilde{s}_{iT}, p_T) = a_T(\tilde{s}_{iT} - p_T), \quad a_T = \rho^{-1}\left(\sum_{k=1}^{T} \tau_{\varepsilon_k}\right).$$

A recursive form for the value is found and optimal strategies derived. Using the profits obtained in the last period we can check that trader i chooses x_{iT-1} to maximize

$$E[-e^{-\rho\phi_{iT-1}} \mid s_i^{T-1}, p^{T-1}],$$

where, letting $x_{iT} = a_T(\tilde{s}_{iT} - p_T)$,

$$\phi_{iT-1} = (p_T - p_{T-1})x_{iT-1} + \tfrac{1}{2}\rho\left(\sum_{k=1}^{T} \tau_{\varepsilon_k} + \tau_T\right)^{-1}(x_{iT})^2.$$

A sufficient statistic for $\{s_i^{T-1}, p^{T-1}\}$ in the estimation of $p_T - p_{T-1}$ and $\tilde{s}_{iT} - p_T$ is $\{\tilde{s}_{iT-1}, p_{T-1}\}$. The desired position in period $T-1$, x_{iT-1}, is then different from the usual static CARA demands and needs to consider a payoff that is a quadratic form of a bivariate normal random vector. It can be shown that the optimal x_{iT-1} consists of a term similar to a static CARA demand proportional to the expected short-run return $(E[p_t \mid \tilde{s}_{iT-1}, p_{T-1}] - p_{T-1})/\rho\kappa$, for some $\kappa > 0$, plus a term proportional to the expected position in period T: $E[x_{iT} \mid \tilde{s}_{iT-1}, p_{T-1}]$, given that expected returns change over time. The possibility to trade in the future provides a hedge against adverse price movements. In the present context this hedge *exactly* compensates for the risk of price changes, and the position of a trader is as in a static market where no price changes occur (and the only risk is due to the uncertainty about the liquidation value). Indeed, after some manipulations the position of trader i boils down to the static form $x_{iT-1} = E[x_{iT} \mid \tilde{s}_{iT-1}, p_{T-1}] = a_{T-1}(\tilde{s}_{iT-1} - p_{T-1})$, with $a_{T-1} = \rho^{-1}(\sum_{k=1}^{T-1} \tau_{\varepsilon_k})$. At the next step the form of the value function is preserved and the argument is completed by induction. (See the appendix (section 8.6) for the details of the proof.)

The net trading intensity in period t depends directly on the precision of period t signals, $\Delta a_t = \rho^{-1}\tau_{\varepsilon_t}$. The more precise they are the higher is Δa_t. As t increases and traders receive more information the price precision ($\tau_t = \tau_\theta + \tau_u \rho^{-2} \sum_{k=1}^{t} \tau_{\varepsilon_k}^2$) and *ex ante* volatility ($\text{var}[p_t]$) increase. Both increase more with lower risk aversion or noise trading, and with a higher precision of information. Market makers take the counterpart of the order flow: $-(\Delta x_t + u_t) = -d_t(p_t - p_{t-1})$ with $d_t = \lambda_t^{-1} - a_t$.

Two special cases are of interest. When agents receive every period a signal of the same precision (constant flow of information) and when agents receive private information only in the first period (concentrated information arrival).

Constant flow of information. If the precision of private signals is constant every period ($\tau_{\varepsilon_t} = \tau_{\varepsilon_1}$ for all t), then, for any t, Δa_t is also constant and equal to the static trading intensity $a = \rho^{-1}\tau_{\varepsilon_1}$. The consequence is that a constant amount of information is incorporated into the prices, $\tau_t = \tau_\theta + \tau_u t a^2$, and the price precision grows linearly with t. Market depth, $\lambda_t^{-1} = \tau_t/\tau_u \Delta a_t$, also increases linearly with t since τ_t grows linearly with t and Δa_t is constant, and the conditional volatility, $\text{var}[p_t \mid p_{t-1}] = \tau_u(\Delta a_t)^2/\tau_{t-1}\tau_t$, decreases with t.

Concentrated information arrival. If private information is received only in the first period (that is, $\tau_{\varepsilon_t} = 0$ for $t = 2, \dots, T$), then $\Delta a_t = 0$ for $t \geqslant 2$ and there is no informed trading after the first period. The equilibrium strategy for informed agents is to take a position in period 1, with a trading intensity equal to the static one, and hold to it until the end (a buy and hold strategy). We have that $a_{T-1} = a$ and $p_{T-1} = p_T$ since $\Delta a_T = 0$ and therefore $\pi_{iT-1} = 0$. At this point the maximization problem of agent i in period $T - 2$ looks exactly the same as the one in period $T - 1$ and the optimal position is $X_{iT-2}(s_{i1}, p_{T-2}) = a(s_{i1} - p_{T-2})$. By backward recursion we obtain $X_{i1}(s_{i1}, p_1) = a(s_{i1} - p_1)$ in period 1.

The market price is stationary from period 1 on. In periods $t = 2, \dots, T$, noise trading is absorbed by market makers at the period 1 price p_1. When setting prices in periods $t = 2, \dots, T$ market makers obtain no information from the limit-order book since $z_t = u_t$ therefore $p_t = E[\theta \mid z_1] = p_1$. Risk-averse informed agents do not learn anything new after the first period and therefore keep the same position until the liquidation of the risky asset. We have that

$$X_t(s_{i1}, p_t) = a(s_{i1} - p_t) \quad \text{and} \quad p_t = p_1 = \lambda_1 z_1 + (1 - \lambda_1 a)\bar{\theta},$$

with $z_1 = a\theta + u_1$, $\lambda_1 = \tau_u a/\tau_1$, and $\tau_1 = \tau_\theta + \tau_u a^2$ for $t = 2, \dots, T$. Both market makers and noise traders break even in periods $t = 2, \dots, T$ since the market is infinitely deep ($\lambda_t = 0$). Noise traders lose money in period 1 when informed agents trade.

In this case the unique (linear) equilibrium replicates the static benchmark. This provides a foundation for the static rational expectations model because adding more rounds of trade is superfluous. The fact that the static equilibrium is also a long-run equilibrium should not be surprising: long-term traders condition on prices, are risk averse, and after the first round no new private or public information is forthcoming, with market makers absorbing noise trade. In section 8.2.2 we explore a context in which there may be incentives for trade after the first period even with concentrated arrival of information.

8.1.3 Summary

- Where a competitive risk-neutral market-making sector sets prices, the market is semi-strong efficient and prices follow a martingale. There is no room for technical analysis because the current price is a sufficient statistic for public information.

   - Volatility is driven by information impacts. A more informative price implies a more volatile price. Total volatility is constant and information revelation by prices advances the resolution of uncertainty.

- A closed-form solution for a linear equilibrium is found when risk-averse investors have a long horizon and heterogeneous information. In this equilibrium the trading intensity of informed agents depends only on their risk aversion and precision of information.
   - With a constant flow of information price precision and market depth grow linearly, while conditional volatility declines, with the number of periods.
   - With concentrated information arrival informed traders use a "buy and hold" strategy and market makers accommodate liquidity traders keeping prices constant after the first period.

8.2 The Impact of Risk-Averse Market Makers

When market makers are risk averse, a rich pattern of learning from prices and traded volume emerges; technical analysis makes sense; and price dynamics with potential "excess volatility" in relation to fundamentals obtain. Market makers, in general, are traders who provide liquidity to the market posting demand or supply schedules. These may be uninformed traders as in the last section (the risk-neutral market-making sector) or informed agents that also trade for market-making reasons (as in chapter 4).

We examine in turn technical analysis, trade with no news, and the dynamics of prices and volume when noise trade increments may be correlated and there is residual uncertainty in the liquidation value of the asset.

8.2.1 Technical Analysis

In the market considered in section 8.1 there is no room for technical analysis, that is, for learning from past prices. The reason is that due to the competitive market-making sector the current price is a sufficient statistic for all past public information. Market making by risk-averse traders changes this.

Consider a version of the model of section 8.1.2 in which there is no competitive risk-neutral fringe and where risk-averse informed traders also perform a market-making activity (see Cespa and Vives (2007); the model for $T = 2$ is considered by Brown and Jennings (1989)[9] and Cespa (2002)). The following proposition characterizes the equilibrium (see the appendix (section 8.6) for a proof in the case $T = 2$).

---

[9] Brown and Jennings (1989) do not prove an existence result for linear equilibria except in the case in which second-period prices are fully revealing.

Proposition 8.3. *Suppose that there is no risk-neutral fringe. Then with long-term informed traders there is a unique linear PBE. The strategy of trader i in period $t = 1, 2, \ldots, T$ is given by*

$$X_t(\tilde{s}_{it}, p^t) = a_t(\tilde{s}_{it} - p_t) + c_t(E[\theta \mid z^t] - p_t),$$

with $a_t = \rho^{-1}(\sum_{k=1}^t \tau_{\varepsilon_k})$ and $c_t = \rho^{-1}\tau_t$.

Prices are given by $p_t = \lambda_t z_t + (1 - \lambda_t \Delta a_t)p_{t-1}$, $p_0 \equiv \bar{\theta}$ with $\lambda_t = (\rho + \tau_u \Delta a_t)(\sum_{k=1}^t \tau_{\varepsilon_k} + \tau_t)^{-1}$, $z_t = \Delta a_t \theta + u_t$, $\Delta a_t = a_t - a_{t-1}$ with $a_0 = 0$ and $\tau_t = \tau_\theta + \tau_u \sum_{k=1}^t (\Delta a_k)^2$.

An important difference from the case of a competitive risk-neutral market-making sector is that in period t for the estimation of θ with the information $\{s_i^t, p^t\}$ it is not sufficient to consider $\{\tilde{s}_{it}, p_t\}$ but $\{\tilde{s}_{it}, p^t\}$ should be considered instead. Indeed, now p_t is not a sufficient statistic for $z^t \equiv \{z_1, z_2, \ldots, z_t\}$ or $p^t \equiv \{p_1, p_2, \ldots, p_t\}$. Otherwise, in period t demands have the same form as the equilibrium demands in the static model of chapter 4 (proposition 4.1) with information $\{\tilde{s}_{it}, p^t\}$. Again, it can be shown that the dynamic strategies collapse to the static ones as the increased risk due to price changes is exactly compensated for by the hedging possibilities associated with dynamic trading. There is a component of speculation with private information $a_t(\tilde{s}_{it} - p_t)$, as in section 8.1.2, and a market-making component $c_t(E[\theta \mid z^t] - p_t)$. Trading intensities correspond, respectively, to risk-adjusted private $\rho^{-1}(\sum_{k=1}^t \tau_{\varepsilon_k})$ and public $\rho^{-1}\tau_t$ precisions.[10] Now informed traders also trade to accommodate noise traders' shocks, buying (selling) when the public estimate of θ, $E[\theta \mid z^t]$, is larger (smaller) than the price p_t. With a competitive risk-neutral (uninformed) market-making sector, informed traders do not perform a market-making function since $E[\theta \mid z^t] = p_t$.

Prices bear the same relationship to information innovations as in section 8.1 (i.e., the same linear functional form $p_t = \lambda_t z_t + (1 - \lambda_t \Delta a_t)p_{t-1}$) but now the depth of the market is a different function of market parameters. In equilibrium we have

$$\lambda_t = (\tau_u \Delta a_t)\left(\sum_{k=1}^t \tau_{\varepsilon_k} + \tau_t\right)^{-1} + \rho\left(\sum_{k=1}^t \tau_{\varepsilon_k} + \tau_t\right)^{-1}.$$

The term $(\tau_u \Delta a_t)(\sum_{k=1}^t \tau_{\varepsilon_k} + \tau_t)^{-1}$ is, as before, an adverse selection component because of the presence of informed traders; the term $\rho(\sum_{k=1}^t \tau_{\varepsilon_k} + \tau_t)^{-1}$ is a risk-bearing component equal to the inverse of the price sensitivity of trader's strategy $(a_t + c_t)^{-1}$. With a competitive risk-neutral (uninformed) market-making sector, the λ parameter then reflects only the adverse selection component and is equal to $(\tau_u \Delta a_t)(\tau_t)^{-1}$. In this case prices react only to the arrival of new information ($\Delta a_t > 0$). Without the competitive risk-neutral market makers prices move with noise trading even with no new information ($\Delta a_t = 0$). Indeed, if there is no additional private information in period t

[10] We will see how the static property of strategies is lost whenever there is residual uncertainty or correlated noise trade increments in section 8.2.3.

$(\tau_{\varepsilon_t} = 0)$, then $\Delta a_t = 0$ and p_t is just p_{t-1} plus noise: $p_t = p_{t-1} + \lambda_t u_t$, with $\lambda_t = \rho(\sum_{k=1}^{t} \tau_{\varepsilon_k} + \tau_t)^{-1}$. Even though p_t reveals u_t, this does not provide any further information on θ because u_{t-1} and u_t are uncorrelated. If $u_t = 0$, then $p_t = p_{t-1}$ and there is no trade in period t. This version of the model with $T = 2$ is considered by Grundy and McNichols (1989) and is studied in the next section.

Consider period $t = 2$ for illustrative purposes. Conditional volatility is given by $\mathrm{var}[p_2 \mid p_1] = \alpha_2^2(\tau_1^{-1} - \tau_2^{-1})$, where $\alpha_2 \equiv \lambda_2/((\tau_u \Delta a_2)\tau_2^{-1})$ if $\Delta a_2 > 0$, and $\mathrm{var}[p_2 \mid p_1] = \lambda_2^2 \tau_u^{-1}$ if $\Delta a_2 = 0$. The term $\tau_1^{-1} - \tau_2^{-1}$ reflects the arrival of new information; the factor α_2 arises because of risk aversion of traders (market makers). Conditional volatility can be larger or smaller than in a semi-strong efficient market depending on whether α_2 is larger or smaller than 1. That is, depending on whether market depth is smaller or larger than in the semi-strong efficient market.

It is easy to generate cases where the volatility of prices is larger than the volatility of fundamentals. For instance, $\mathrm{var}[p_1] = \alpha_1^2(\tau_\theta^{-1} - \tau_1^{-1})$, where $\alpha_1 \equiv \lambda_1/((\tau_u a_1)\tau_1^{-1})$ and $\lambda_1 = (\rho + \tau_u a_1)(\tau_{\varepsilon_1} + \tau_1)^{-1}$. We have that for $\tau_{\varepsilon_1} = \rho = 1$, $\tau_u = 0.1$ and $\tau_\theta < 9.9$, $\mathrm{var}[p_1] > \tau_\theta^{-1}$. This may be termed "excess volatility" but it is an equilibrium phenomenon derived from the presence of risk-averse market-making traders who decrease the depth of the market by not fully accommodating shocks.[11] This can never happen in a semi-strong efficient market, where $\mathrm{var}[p_t] < \sigma_\theta^2$ for any period.

Technical analysis is useful because p_t is not a sufficient statistic for $z^t \equiv \{z_1, z_2, \dots, z_t\}$ or $p^t \equiv \{p_1, p_2, \dots, p_t\}$. For example, consider the case $T = 2$, then $E[\theta \mid z^2] = E[\theta \mid p^2]$ depends on p_1 and p_2 because p_1 has additional information on θ even conditioning on p_2. This is so because p_1 is a linear function of θ and u_1, and p_1 provides an independent signal on θ as well as information on u_1 which is useful in extracting information on θ from p_2 (which as we will see depends on $u_1 + u_2$). Let $X_t(\theta, p^t) = \int_0^1 X_t(\tilde{s}_{it}, p^t)\,di$ denote the aggregate position demand for the risky asset for informed traders in period t. Then the market-clearing condition in the second period is given by

$$X_2(\theta, p_1, p_2) - X_1(\theta, p_1) + u_2 = X_2(\theta, p_1, p_2) + u_1 + u_2 = 0$$

since $X_1(\theta, p_1) + u_1 = 0$ from market clearing in the first period.[12] If there is no additional noise trading in period 2 ($u_2 = 0$), p_1 and p_2 perfectly reveal θ.

The fact that past prices are helpful in forecasting future prices does not mean, obviously, that specific techniques based on recognizing "head and shoulders" patterns or "support levels" for asset prices can be grounded on the model presented.

---

[11] Campbell and Kyle (1993) also explain excess volatility by the risk premium demanded by risk-averse investors for absorbing time-varying noise shocks. See Campbell and Shiller (1987) and LeRoy and Parke (1992) for evidence.

[12] A further reason for technical analysis to have value arises if u_1 and Δu_2 are correlated. Then p_1 contains information on u_1, which in turn helps estimate u_2 and improve the estimation of θ via p_2.

It is worth noting that prices in period 2, as in the static case (see section 4.2.1), are just the average expectations of investors about the fundamental value $\int_0^1 E[\theta \mid \tilde{s}_{i2}, z^2]\,di$ plus noise:

$$p_2 = \int_0^1 E[\theta \mid \tilde{s}_{i2}, z^2]\,di + \rho(\tau_{\varepsilon_1} + \tau_{\varepsilon_2} + \tau_2)^{-1}(u_1 + u_2).$$

This follows from the market-clearing condition in the second period

$$X_2(\theta, p_1, p_2) + u_1 + u_2 = 0$$

and the CARA form for demands:

$$X_2(\theta, p^2) = \int_0^1 X_2(\tilde{s}_{i2}, z^2)\,di = (\tau_{\varepsilon_1} + \tau_{\varepsilon_2} + \tau_2)\rho^{-1}\left(\int_0^1 E[\theta \mid \tilde{s}_{i2}, z^2]\,di - p_2\right).$$

Perhaps more surprisingly, prices in the first period will also equal the average expectations of investors about the fundamental value plus a noise term. This is not obvious because, in principle, prices in the first period also depend on the average expectations of investors about second-period prices. This is so because demand for trader i in the first period is a linear combination of $E[p_2 \mid s_{i1}, z_1] - p_1$ and $E[X_2(\tilde{s}_{i2}, z^2) \mid s_{i1}, z_1]$, where $E[p_2 \mid s_{i1}, z_1]$ is a convex combination of $E[\theta \mid s_{i1}, z_1]$ and p_1, and $E[X_2(\tilde{s}_{i2}, z^2) \mid s_{i1}, z_1]$ proportional to $E[\theta \mid s_{i1}, z_1] - p_1$ (see the proof of proposition 8.3 in the appendix (section 8.6)). However, from the market-clearing condition $X_1(\theta, p_1) + u_1 = 0$ and the static form $X_1(s_{i1}, p_1) = \rho^{-1}(\tau_{\varepsilon_1} + \tau_1)(E[\theta \mid s_{i1}, z_1] - p_1)$, it follows that

$$X_1(\theta, p_1) = \rho^{-1}(\tau_{\varepsilon_1} + \tau_1)\int_0^1 (E[\theta \mid s_{i1}, z_1] - p_1)\,di$$

and therefore

$$p_1 = \int_0^1 E[\theta \mid s_{i1}, z_1]\,di + \rho(\tau_{\varepsilon_1} + \tau_1)^{-1}u_1.$$

A similar expression can be derived for p_t in the T-period case. Indeed, market clearing in period t implies that $X_t(\theta, p^t) + \sum_{k=1}^t u_k = 0$ (by an extension of the recursive argument from the market-clearing conditions in the first $X_1(\theta, p_1) + u_1 = 0$ and second $X_2(\theta, p_1, p_2) + u_1 + u_2 = 0$ periods). Therefore, from $X_t(\theta, p^t) = \rho^{-1}(\sum_{k=1}^t \tau_{\varepsilon_k} + \tau_t)\int_0^1 (E[\theta \mid \tilde{s}_{it}, z^t] - p_t)\,di$, we obtain

$$p_t = \int_0^1 E[\theta \mid \tilde{s}_{it}, z^t] + \rho\left(\sum_{k=1}^t \tau_{\varepsilon_k} + \tau_t\right)^{-1} \sum_{k=1}^t u_k.$$

This is, indeed, consistent with the expression for prices $p_t = \lambda_t z_t + (1 - \lambda_t \Delta a_t)p_{t-1}$ and λ_t in proposition 8.3 since

$$\begin{aligned}
p_t &= \lambda_t z_t + (1 - \lambda_t \Delta a_t)p_{t-1} \\
&= \frac{\tau_\theta \bar{\theta} + \sum_{k=1}^t (\rho + \tau_u \Delta a_k) z_k}{\sum_{k=1}^t \tau_{\varepsilon_k} + \tau_t} \\
&= \frac{\tau_\theta \bar{\theta} + \sum_{k=1}^t \tau_u \Delta a_k z_k + \sum_{k=1}^t \tau_{\varepsilon_k}\theta}{\sum_{k=1}^t \tau_{\varepsilon_k} + \tau_t} + \rho\left(\sum_{k=1}^t \tau_{\varepsilon_k} + \tau_t\right)^{-1} \sum_{k=1}^t u_k
\end{aligned}$$

and

$$\int_0^1 E[\theta \mid \tilde{s}_{it}, z^t]\,\mathrm{d}i = \frac{\tau_\theta\bar{\theta} + \sum_{k=1}^t \tau_u \Delta a_k z_k + \sum_{k=1}^t \tau_{\varepsilon_k}\theta}{\sum_{k=1}^t \tau_{\varepsilon_k} + \tau_t}.$$

Prices will be no longer be equal to the average expectations of investors plus a noise term when strategies lose their static property.

* 8.2.2 Trade without News and the No-Trade Theorem

The possibility arises in a dynamic setting that trade occurs without either new information or additional noise trading. In short, trade may be self-generating. Grundy and McNichols (1989) show in a two-period model that equilibria in which second-period prices add information about the fundamental value may coexist with equilibria in which they are noisy measures of first-period prices as long as traders receive a signal with a common error term. Their model illustrates the value of technical analysis and the possibility of trade that self-generates.

The model has two periods as before and trader i receives a signal only in the first period, $s_i = \theta + \eta + \varepsilon_i$, where η is a common error term normally distributed with mean zero and precision τ_η. The average signal now reveals $\theta + \eta$. It is also assumed that there is no additional noise trading in the second period ($u_2 = 0$).[13] Grundy and McNichols show that there is always a no-trade outcome at the second period (as when τ_η is infinite). Traders resubmit their demand schedules to the auctioneer, the same price obtains and agents maintain their positions. However, a linear fully revealing (of $\theta + \eta$) equilibrium also exists at the second round if τ_η is large enough.[14] At the first round and for τ_η finite there are two (revealing) linear equilibria. If τ_η is infinite, then all equilibria (revealing and nonrevealing) in the first round are identical.

The results are robust to the introduction of uncorrelated additional noise trading u_2 in period 2. There then exists a nonrevealing equilibrium, in which trade in the second period just absorbs the incremental noise trading, and there may also exist a partially revealing equilibrium in which the price sequence $\{p_1, p_2\}$ provides more information about $\theta + \eta$ than p_1.

The results are interesting because prices and allocations may change even with no new information at the second round (and no additional noise trading). At first blush these may seem to contradict the no-trade theorem. According to this theorem there should be no trade in period 2 with strictly risk-averse traders if the allocation after period 1 is interim Pareto optimal and the beliefs about the price in period 2 (the only potentially new piece of information) are "concordant" before the price is realized (Milgrom and Stokey 1982). Beliefs are *concordant* if traders agree on the conditional likelihood of any given realization

[13] The authors follow in fact the static model of Diamond and Verrecchia (1981). As stated in section 4.2.2 the model is basically equivalent to the noise trader model.

[14] Note that at a linear equilibrium both p_1 and p_2 depend on $\theta + \eta$ and u_1, and $\theta + \eta$ and u_1 will be revealed if the linear functions are independent.

of the signal considered (the price in this case). Let $I_{i1} = \{s_i, p_1\}$ be the information set of trader i in period 1. The beliefs about signal z of θ are concordant if $\text{P}(z \mid \theta, I_{i1})$ is the same for all traders i, signals z, and realizations of θ.

Now, in a static model (or if investors behave myopically) the equilibrium is interim Pareto optimal (i.e., relative to the information sets I_{i1}). That is, the marginal rates of substitution for consumption across any two states (say, θ and θ') are equated for all the traders.[15] The subtlety is that if $\{p_1, p_2\}$ reveal $\theta + \eta$, then the static equilibrium is no longer Pareto optimal and the beliefs of investors about p_2 are not even essentially concordant (a weakening of the concept of concordant which is enough for the no-trade theorem to obtain when signals are public) at the end of the first round.[16] When τ_η is finite the outcome of the first-period equilibrium is not interim Pareto optimal given I_{i1}, and neither are beliefs about p_2 concordant. Indeed, $\text{P}(p_2 \mid \theta, I_{i1})$ will not be equated across traders if τ_η is finite because p_2 depends on $\theta + \eta$ and trader i receives an idiosyncratic signal $s_i = \theta + \eta + \varepsilon_i$. When τ_η is infinite, θ is revealed by p_2, the first-period outcome is Pareto optimal and beliefs about p_2 are concordant. The outcome is no trade in the risky asset in the second period.

Grundy and McNichols also explore the consequences of introducing a public signal $y = \theta + \upsilon$, where υ is the error term, before trade in the second period. They find that if a nonrevealing equilibrium exists, then there is no trade in the second round because agents have (essentially) concordant beliefs and the allocations in period 1 are Pareto optimal relative to the information sets in period 2. This equilibrium exists when $\text{cov}[\eta, \upsilon] = 0$ (the beliefs concerning y are concordant). It is worth remarking that in the same environment (i.e., when $\text{cov}[\eta, \upsilon] = 0$) revealing and nonrevealing equilibria coexist. At the nonrevealing equilibrium traders conjecture that there will be no trade at the second round (after the public signal is released), the first-round allocation is Pareto optimal and traders have concordant beliefs about p_2. At the revealing equilibrium traders conjecture that there will be trade at the second round (after the public signal is released), the first-round allocation is not Pareto optimal and traders do not have concordant beliefs about p_2.

8.2.3 Dynamic Patterns of Volume and Prices

He and Wang (1995) consider a more general version of the trading model with T periods where the liquidation value has residual uncertainty $\theta + \eta$, with η normally distributed with mean zero and precision τ_η. Traders have no information on η, which is distributed independently of the rest of random variables in the model. Each investor observes in each period on top of his private signal a

[15] Rubinstein (1974) showed that when traders have the same beliefs, and linear risk tolerance with identical coefficient of marginal risk tolerance (defining the HARA class of utility functions to which CARA utilities belong), markets are effectively complete and competitive equilibrium allocations are Pareto optimal. With normal distributions the result can be extended to encompass private signals.

[16] Beliefs will be essentially concordant if $\text{P}(p_2 \mid \theta, I_{i1})/\text{P}(p_2 \mid \theta', I_{i1})$ is equated across agents.

public signal $y_t = \theta + \upsilon_t$, and the stock of noise trade follows an autocorrelated AR(1) process:

$$\hat{u}_t = \varsigma \hat{u}_{t-1} + e_t, \quad \text{with } 0 < \varsigma < 1$$

and $\{e_t\}_{t=1}^{T}$ an i.i.d. normally distributed noise random process (independent of all other random variables in the model).[17] The random noise trade increment in period t is thus $\hat{u}_t - \hat{u}_{t-1}$. If $\varsigma = 1$, $\{\hat{u}_t\}$ follows a random walk and we are in the usual case of independent noise trade increments $\hat{u}_t - \hat{u}_{t-1} = e_t$ (e.g., Kyle 1985; Brown and Jennings 1989; Vives 1995). If $\varsigma = 0$, then the stock of noise trading is i.i.d. across periods, a plausible assumption only if the time between trading dates is very large.

As before all random variables are jointly normally distributed. The information available to trader i in period t is given by $I_{it} = \{s_i^t, y^t, p^t\}$. The state variables of the dynamic system in period t are $\{\theta, \hat{u}^t, y^t\}$. This is so because, as before, in a linear equilibrium the average error terms of the private signals cancel.

At a linear equilibrium, also as before, we can define random variables z_t so that public information can be expressed equivalently as $\{p^t, y^t\}$ or $\{z^t, y^t\}$. Using the market-clearing condition it is possible to show that p_t is a convex combination of z_t and $E[\theta \mid z^t, y^t]$, and the desired position of trader i in period t is a linear function of $E[\theta \mid I_{it}] - E[\theta \mid z^t, y^t]$ and $E[\hat{u}_t \mid I_{it}]$. The first part is linked to speculative trading and the second to accommodating the noise trade shock.

The model may have multiple equilibria. In the two-period model of section 8.2.2 there may be two equilibria when information is received only in the first period and $\varsigma = 1$ (that is, with independent supply increments $\hat{u}_t - \hat{u}_{t-1} = e_t$). However, the nonrevealing equilibrium disappears when $\varsigma < 1$.[18]

The case of homogeneous perfect information ($\tau_{\varepsilon_1} = \infty$) is taken as a benchmark. Then only η in the liquidation value remains unknown and the price equals θ plus a risk premium linear in the share position of investors $\hat{u}_t$ (and increasing with $\mathrm{var}[\eta]$). Volume is determined by the exogenous random noise trade increments $E[|\hat{u}_t - \hat{u}_{t-1}|]$ and market depth decreases as t approaches T. The reason is that with $\varsigma < 1$ supply shocks display mean reversion. This means that when there are many trading dates left, traders can now take additional positions to unwind them later when the shock reverses itself (and this will happen because of the nature of the process). With fewer trading dates left it becomes more risky to accommodate noise trade shocks and market depth decreases. As ς tends to 1, market depth becomes constant over time.

With private information, the price depends on the investors' expectations of the future payoff of the stock (a convex combination of θ and $E[\theta \mid \text{public information}]$) plus a risk premium of the type of the homogeneous information case. However, in this case, and contrary to section 8.2.1, the price at t does not

[17] He and Wang in fact assume an exogenous supply process (negative noise trading position).

[18] Note also that in the model of section 8.2.2 (Grundy and McNichols 1989) there is no residual uncertainty on θ but a common noise in the private signal of traders.

equal the average of investors' expectations at this date plus a risk premium. The average of investors' expectations is also a convex combination of θ and $E[\theta \mid \text{public information}]$ but with different weights than in the price. As we will see below this is because of the correlation in noise trading increments and the presence of residual uncertainty in the liquidation value. Without residual uncertainty in the liquidation value and noise trading following a random walk we have as in section 8.2.1 that informed traders speculate only on the fundamental value and the price in any period equals the average of investors' expectations in this period minus a risk premium. In any case, the price process is no longer a martingale (proposition 8.1 yielding $p_t = E[\theta \mid p_t]$ does not hold) because there is no risk-neutral market-making fringe, and the current price depends on past prices.

When τ_η is infinite there is a unique linear equilibrium which can be obtained in closed form (similar to proposition 4.2, which corresponds to the model in Vives (1995) without a competitive fringe and with $\varsigma = 1$). Informational trading only occurs when investors receive new information but prices still reveal information about θ later on because of the correlation of noise trade increments when $\varsigma < 1$.

He and Wang (1995) analyze the case of concentrated arrival of information $\tau_{\varepsilon_t} = 0$ for $t > 1$. They find that, as in Vives (1995), investors establish their positions at $t = 1$ when they receive information. However, trade now persists as risk-averse investors try to unwind their positions when the shock reverses itself (since $\varsigma < 1$). This may generate a peak in trading volume at an intermediate point of the trading horizon. With public signals investors take positions right before the announcement, and market depth drops, to close them immediately after, and market depth bounces back. This means that there is high volume around the announcement. It is also found that new information (private or public) generates at the same time high volume and large price changes. However, existing private information is capable of generating high volume with small price changes.

The presence of residual uncertainty and/or correlated patterns of noise trade increments together with market making by risk-averse traders can explain departures of prices from fundamentals.[19] Indeed, in the present context, averaging over noise trading, prices can be farther away from fundamentals than the average expectations of investors. This is the case in period t (similarly as in Allen et al. (2006)) when

$$|E[p_t - \theta \mid \theta]| > \left| E\left[\int_0^1 E[\theta \mid I_{it}] \, \mathrm{d}i - \theta \;\middle|\; \theta \right] \right|.$$

---

[19] Bacchetta and van Wincoop (2006) develop a dynamic rational expectations equilibrium model with heterogeneous information to address the exchange rate determination puzzle and argue that short-term departures of the exchange rate from macroeconomic fundamentals can be explained by traders' heterogeneous information.

Then the bias of prices in the estimation of θ is larger than the bias of the average expectations of investors and there is over-reliance of traders on public information taking as benchmark the optimal statistical weight on public information to estimate θ. When the inequality above is reversed prices are closer to fundamentals than the average expectations of investors and there is under-reliance of traders on public information.

Cespa and Vives (2007) characterize in a two-period model the parameter constellations $(\varsigma, \tau_\eta^{-1})$ for which such an over- or under-reliance on public information exists. In period 2 the market behaves as in a static market and we have seen that no such phenomenon can occur (since prices equal the average expectations of investors plus noise). The same is true in period 1 when noise trading follows a random walk and there is no residual uncertainty $(\varsigma, \tau_\eta^{-1}) = (1, 0)$ since then trading strategies also have the static property. When noise trading increments are correlated and there is residual uncertainty in the liquidation value, investors then speculate not only on the terminal fundamental value θ but also on the changes of prices and trading strategies lose the static property. For low (high) values of $(\varsigma, \tau_\eta^{-1})$ there is over-reliance (under-reliance) on public information in period 1. As ς and/or τ_η^{-1} decrease traders put less weight on their first-period private signals because they accommodate more noise trade shocks since noise trading is more predictable (ς lower)—and the shock will revert—and/or residual uncertainty τ_η^{-1} smaller and the hedge provided by the possibility of trade in period 2 less valuable. The outcome is a price in period 1 less anchored on the fundamentals. This defines a "Keynesian" region in space $(\varsigma, \tau_\eta^{-1})$ with heavy reliance on public information and prices relatively far from fundamentals. The opposite happens when ς and/or τ_η^{-1} are high and where a "Hayekian" region is defined with prices relatively close to fundamentals. The weight of public information on the price depends on the traders' reaction to order imbalances. Whenever traders deem the order-flow to be mostly driven by liquidity orders, they take the other side of the market, in this way partially sterilizing the effect of informed trades on the price. This reinforces the effect of public information on the price, driving the latter away from the fundamentals in relation to investors' average expectations. Whenever traders estimate the order-flow to be mostly information driven, they speculate on price momentum reinforcing the impact of informed trades on the price. This weakens the weight on public information, tying the price more firmly to the fundamentals in relation to investors' average expectations.[20] We will see in section 8.3.2.2 how when traders have short horizons there is always an equilibrium with over-reliance on public information.

8.2.4 Summary

- When market makers are risk averse:

[20] Kondor (2005b) studies mispricing in a two-period model where informed traders have market power.

- ∘ technical analysis is justified because prices do not follow a martingale and the sequence of prices up to the present does convey more information than the current price in the estimation of the fundamental value;
- ∘ price in any period equals, as in the static model and as long as noise trading follows a random walk and there is no residual uncertainty in the liquidation value, the average expectations of investors plus a risk-bearing component;
- ∘ there may be "excess volatility" in the sense that prices are more volatile than fundamentals;
- ∘ market depth has a risk-bearing component on top of the adverse selection component and market makers do not accommodate fully noise trading even when there is no new information.

- In a dynamic setting trade may be self-generating, occurring without either new information or additional noise trading. This does not contradict the no-trade theorem because trade in one period may reveal information that makes traders disagree about the meaning of prices in the subsequent period.
- Asymmetric information may explain peaks in volume around public announcements and how high volume may be generated either by new information coupled with price volatility or by extant private information with small price changes.
- Correlation in noise trade demand and the presence of residual uncertainty in the liquidation value imply that traders speculate not only on the terminal fundamental value but also on the changes of prices when trading strategies lose the static property. The levels of correlation in noise trading and in residual uncertainty explain the proximity of prices to prices from fundamental values in relation to the average expectations of investors in the market and the degree of reliance on public information.

8.3 Dynamic Trading with Short-Term Investors

Attention has recently been drawn to the effects of investors' short horizons in financial markets. This short-termism may come about, for example, because of liquidity needs of investors, because of incentive reasons related to the evaluation of the performance of money managers, or because of difficulties associated with financing long-term investment in the presence of capital market imperfections (see Holmström and Ricart i Costa 1986; Shleifer and Vishny 1990).

In this section we study trading dynamics with short-term investors. We simulate the temporal evolution of the basic market parameters, compare them with the case of long-term traders, and look specifically at the impact of short-term trading on price informativeness. We concentrate attention on markets with competitive risk-neutral market makers (section 8.3.1) and with risk-averse market makers (section 8.3.2). Section 8.3.3 discusses the incentives of short-term traders to acquire information.

8.3.1 Short-Term Traders and Risk-Neutral Market Makers

Consider the context of section 8.1.1 but now informed traders are assumed to maximize the utility of the short-run return. As before $\pi_{it} = (p_{t+1} - p_t)x_{it}$ denotes the short-run profits derived by agent i from buying x_{it} units of the risky asset at price p_t and selling it next period at price p_{t+1}. At stage t a strategy for agent i is a function that maps his private information $\tilde{s}_{it}$ into a demand schedule $X_t(\tilde{s}_{it}, \cdot)$.[21]

The market solution will be the (perfect) Bayesian equilibria of the T-period dynamic game (a sequence of Bayesian equilibria of the one-shot games with the defined short-run payoffs). Attention will be restricted to equilibria in linear strategies. The following proposition shows existence and characterizes equilibria for a fixed horizon T. Equilibria depend on the length of the horizon T and will be symmetric in our context.

Proposition 8.4 (Vives 1995). *Linear equilibria of the dynamic T-period trading game with short investment horizons exist. The equilibrium strategy of trader i is, for $t = 1, \dots, T$, given (implicitly) by*

$$X_t(\tilde{s}_{it}, p_t) = a_t(\tilde{s}_{it} - p_t), \quad \text{with } a_t = \rho^{-1}\left(\left(\sum_{k=1}^{t} \tau_{\varepsilon_k}\right)^{-1} + \tau_{t+1}^{-1}\right)^{-1},$$

where $\tau_t = \tau_\theta + \tau_u \sum_{k=1}^{t}(\Delta a_k)^2$ and $a_T = \rho^{-1}(\sum_{k=1}^{T} \tau_{\varepsilon_k})$.

Sketch of proof. The proof proceeds in three steps.

(i) From proposition 8.1 we have that at a candidate linear equilibrium, $p_{t+1} - p_t = \lambda_{t+1}(\Delta a_{t+1}(\theta - p_t) + u_{t+1})$, prices are normally distributed, and

$$\begin{aligned} E[p_{t+1} - p_t \mid \tilde{s}_{it}, p_t] &= \lambda_{t+1}\Delta a_{t+1} E[\theta - p_t \mid \tilde{s}_{it}, p_t] \\ &= \lambda_{t+1}\Delta a_{t+1}\left(\sum_{k=1}^{t} \tau_{\varepsilon_k}\right)\left(\sum_{k=1}^{t} \tau_{\varepsilon_k} + \tau_t\right)^{-1}(\tilde{s}_{it} - p_t). \end{aligned}$$

Indeed, $\tilde{s}_{it} - p_t$ is sufficient with respect to the information $\{s_i^t, p^t\}$ for $\theta - p_t$, and we obtain $E[\theta - p_t \mid \tilde{s}_{it}, p_t] = (\sum_{k=1}^{t} \tau_{\varepsilon_k})(\sum_{k=1}^{t} \tau_{\varepsilon_k} + \tau_t)^{-1}(\tilde{s}_{it} - p_t)$. Furthermore, we have that

$$\begin{aligned} \operatorname{var}[p_{t+1} - p_t \mid \tilde{s}_{it}, p_t] &= \lambda_{t+1}^2((\Delta a_{t+1})^2 \operatorname{var}[(\theta - p_t) \mid \tilde{s}_{it}, p_t] + \sigma_u^2) \\ &= \lambda_{t+1}^2\left((\Delta a_{t+1})^2\left(\sum_{k=1}^{t} \tau_{\varepsilon_k} + \tau_t\right)^{-1} + \tau_u^{-1}\right). \end{aligned}$$

[21] Recall that we can think of different interpretations of the short-term investment case formalizing the idea of risk-averse speculators with a short horizon. First of all, agents can be long-lived but myopic and they do not forget information. Second, a different generation of informed agents comes to market every period, each member of generation t inheriting the private information of a member of generation $t - 1$, taking a position, and liquidating it the next period.

(ii) Maximization of a CARA utility function by trader i yields then at stage t

$$X_t(\tilde{s}_{it}, p_t) = \frac{E[p_{t+1} - p_t \mid \tilde{s}_{it}, p_t]}{\rho \operatorname{var}[p_{t+1} - p_t \mid \tilde{s}_{it}, p_t]}.$$

This is a function of $(\tilde{s}_{it}, p_t)$ which is independent of i for every normally distributed price process, given the symmetric structure of the signals for the informed, and therefore the equilibria will be symmetric.

The equilibrium expression for a_t, $t < T$, then follows since from proposition 8.1 $\lambda_{t+1} = \tau_u \Delta a_{t+1}/\tau_{t+1}$ and $\tau_{t+1} = \tau_t + \tau_u(\Delta a_{t+1})^2$ and it is immediate from the expressions for $E[p_{t+1} - p_t \mid \tilde{s}_{it}, p_t]$ and $\operatorname{var}[p_{t+1} - p_t \mid \tilde{s}_{it}, p_t]$ that

$$a_t = \frac{(\sum_{k=1}^{t} \tau_{\varepsilon_k})\tau_{t+1}}{\rho(\sum_{k=1}^{t} \tau_{\varepsilon_k} + \tau_{t+1})}.$$

For $t = T$ it is as in proposition 8.2 and $a_T = \rho^{-1}(\sum_{k=1}^{T} \tau_{\varepsilon_k})$ (indeed, then $p_{T+1} = \theta$ and $\tau_{T+1}^{-1} = 0$).

(iii) It is checked that the equations

$$\begin{aligned} a_t &= g_t(a^{t+1}) \\ &\equiv \rho^{-1}\bigg(\bigg(\sum_{k=1}^{t} \tau_{\varepsilon_k}\bigg)^{-1} + \bigg(\tau_\theta + \tau_u \sum_{k=1}^{t+1} (\Delta a_k)^2\bigg)^{-1}\bigg)^{-1}, \quad t = 1, \dots, T-1, \end{aligned}$$

where $a^{t+1} = (a_1, \dots, a_{t+1})$, have a solution with $a_T = \rho^{-1}(\sum_{k=1}^{T} \tau_{\varepsilon_k})$. Note that each g_t is continuous and its range is in the compact interval $[\underline{a}, \bar{a}] \equiv [\rho^{-1}(\tau_{\varepsilon_1}^{-1} + \tau_\theta^{-1})^{-1}, \rho^{-1}(\sum_{k=1}^{t} \tau_{\varepsilon_k})]$. Recall that by convention $\tau_{\varepsilon_1} > 0$. Then let $G : [\underline{a}, \bar{a}]^{T-1} \to [\underline{a}, \bar{a}]^{T-1}$ be defined by the component functions in the natural way. The set $[\underline{a}, \bar{a}]^{T-1}$ is compact and G is continuous and therefore the existence of a fixed point follows from Brouwer's fixed point theorem. □

Remarks.

- With concentrated arrival of information (that is, $\tau_{\varepsilon_t} = 0$ for $t = 2, \dots, T$), $a_t = \rho^{-1}(\tau_{\varepsilon_1}^{-1} + \tau_{t+1}^{-1})^{-1}$ and $a_T = \rho^{-1}\tau_{\varepsilon_1} = a$, the static trading intensity.[22] With a constant flow of information (that is, $\tau_{\varepsilon_t} = \tau_{\varepsilon_1}$ for all t), $a_t = \rho^{-1}((t\tau_{\varepsilon_1})^{-1} + \tau_{t+1}^{-1})^{-1}$ and $a_T = T\rho^{-1}\tau_{\varepsilon_1} = Ta$.
- The *uniqueness* of the linear equilibrium is not asserted. However, for the $T = 2$ case uniqueness is easily established (at least for the case $\tau_{\varepsilon_t} = 0$ for $t \geqslant 2$) and simulations also support the uniqueness conjecture for larger T. We will see in section 8.3.2 that there are multiple equilibria if market makers are risk averse.

Several properties of the equilibrium are worth highlighting:

- The trading intensity a_t is strictly increasing with t (use backward recursion to show it). Consequently, $\Delta a_t > 0$, and τ_t and $\operatorname{var}[p_t]$ are strictly increasing with t.

[22] The trading intensity a_T equals the static level a because in the static model the trading intensity does not depend on the precision of prices $a = \rho^{-1}\tau_{\varepsilon_1}$.

- The intensity of trade of generation t of informed agents (a_t) depends positively, ceteris paribus, on the degree of risk tolerance ρ^{-1}, the total precision of signals $\sum_{k=1}^{t} \tau_{\varepsilon_k}$, and the precision of prices in period $t+1$ in the estimation of the fundamental value θ. The first two effects are as in the static model. The third effect means that the closer p_{t+1} is to θ the more intensely informed speculators want to trade. In the last period $p_{t+1} = \theta$ and then trading intensity reaches its maximum value. Short-term speculators have information about θ but cannot hold the asset until θ is realized. The return of generation t agents is $(p_{t+1} - p_t)x_{it}$. Traders can anticipate the information in p_t, and the more informative is p_{t+1} about θ the better they can predict p_{t+1} because they receive private signals about θ. As t increases so does the precision of price as estimator of θ and consequently the desired trading intensity of informed agents a_t. The expected return to informed trading $E[p_{t+1} - p_t \mid \tilde{s}_{it}, p_t]$ is increasing relative to the risk faced $\operatorname{var}[p_{t+1} \mid \tilde{s}_{it}, p_t]$ as t increases.

- If short-run traders only have access to the current signal (in period t trader i only has access to s_{it}), then the equilibrium is modified to $a_t = \rho^{-1}(\tau_{\varepsilon_t}^{-1} + \tau_{t+1}^{-1})^{-1}$.

- The long-term trading intensity is always larger than in the short-term case period by period. Indeed, $\rho^{-1}(\sum_{k=1}^{t} \tau_{\varepsilon_k}) > \rho^{-1}((\sum_{k=1}^{t} \tau_{\varepsilon_k})^{-1} + \tau_{t+1}^{-1})^{-1}$ for any $t < T$ since $\tau_{t+1}^{-1} > 0$. Short-term trading makes agents less responsive to private information since risk-averse short-run agents in period t have information about θ but care about p_{t+1}, which is a garbled signal of θ because of noise trading. Only when $t = T$, $p_{T+1} = \theta$ and the two intensities coincide: $a_T = \rho^{-1}(\sum_{k=1}^{T} \tau_{\varepsilon_k})$.

- The final trading intensity a_T is also the (across periods) aggregate net trading intensity: $\sum_{k=1}^{T} \Delta a_k = a_T$. Therefore, in terms of net trading intensities the long-term and the short-term cases differ in the temporal distribution of the same aggregate.

- Noise trading does affect the intensity of trade through the informativeness of prices. For example, with $T = 2$ (and $\tau_{\varepsilon_2} = 0$) an increase in noise trading decreases the trading intensity a_1 of the first generation in the unique equilibrium. Instead of a camouflage effect (as in Kyle 1985) an increase in noise trading increases the noise in the first-period return p_2 (with respect to θ) and the response of first-period risk-averse informed speculators is a decreased trading intensity.

In the case of concentrated information arrival, trading intensities are always less than the static one (a), which is reached in the last period. The trading intensity of informed speculation a_t is increasing with t (slowly at first and catching up close to the liquidation date) even when private signals are only received in the first period. Dow and Gorton (1994) obtain a similar result in an infinite-horizon model with a stock which yields random dividends in each period. Some traders may receive information in advance about the dividends of a certain period (the event date). Short-term informed traders are risk neutral and face transaction costs. The result is that short-term traders will not act on their information when far away from the event because short-term trading compounded with transaction costs reduce the profitability of speculation. Indeed, far away from the event date it is unlikely that the price next period will reflect the information. Furthermore, in any case, discounting makes the present value of a dividend far into the future small.

Simulations. Proposition 8.4 characterizes implicitly the equilibrium but does not give a closed-form solution. Simulations conducted for a range of parameter values for the two leading examples yield the following insights into the dynamics of the market.[23]

With concentrated arrival of information ($\tau_{\varepsilon_t} = 0$ for $t \geqslant 2$):

- The increase in Δa_t (starting from $T = 2$ since $\Delta a_1 = a_1$) at the beginning is very small and is only noticeable when close to the end of the horizon T.
- The conditional volatility of prices is increasing with t, slowly at first and faster when close to the end of the horizon (it may decrease from period T to the liquidation stage $T + 1$).
- In the first rounds of trade the precision of prices is almost flat and informed agents only vary their positions slightly from period to period. When closer to the end of the horizon the net trading intensity of informed agents increases and contiguous generations want to have increasingly different positions in the risky asset since the precision of prices is increasing.[24]
- Market depth is nonmonotonic in t. It increases first due to the reduced net trading in the second period (in the first period only the first generation trades); it flattens out (at a high level) later since net trading by informed agents is very small, and decreases close to the end of the horizon due to increased net informed trading activity.

With a constant flow of information ($\tau_{\varepsilon_t} = \tau_{\varepsilon_1}$, for all t) the emerging patterns are more complex:[25]

- The temporal evolution of trading intensities a_t is typically concave and then convex and, correspondingly, the net trading intensities Δa_t evolve

[23] Simulations have been performed systematically in the following ranges of parameter values: ρ in $[1,4]$, σ_u^2 in $[0.05, 2]$, $\sigma_{\varepsilon_1}^2$ in $[0.1, 2]$, letting $\sigma_\theta^2 = 1$. The length of the horizon has been considered up to $T = 25$. In all the simulations performed, equilibrium has turned out to be unique (i.e., starting the simulation to find a solution to the equilibrium parameter equations with different initial conditions the same equilibrium has been reached).

[24] Market makers trade according to $-d_t(p_t - p_{t-1})$ with $d_t = (\lambda_t)^{-1} - a_t$ and lean against the wind in general (d_t positive), although in some simulations at the end period d_T may be negative (market depth has decreased and trading by the last generation of informed agents is intense).

[25] Simulations have been extended for this case to cover $\rho = 0.1$ and $\rho = 40$, $\sigma_u^2 = 0.005$ and $\sigma_u^2 = 40$, and $\sigma_{\varepsilon_1}^2 = 0.05$ and $\sigma_{\varepsilon_1}^2 = 40$.

Table 8.1. Short-term and long-term trading (temporal evolution of magnitudes $t = 1, \dots, T$).

	Short-term		Long-term	
	$\tau_{\varepsilon_t} = 0$, $t \geqslant 2$	$\tau_{\varepsilon_t} = \tau_{\varepsilon_1}$ all t	$\tau_{\varepsilon_t} = 0$, $t \geqslant 2$	$\tau_{\varepsilon_t} = \tau_{\varepsilon_1}$ all t
Trading intensity, a_t	Increasing	Increasing	Constant (static level)	Increasing (linearly)
Net trading intensity, Δa_t	Increasing ($t \geqslant 2$)	U-shaped	Zero ($t \geqslant 2$)	Constant
Market depth, λ_t^{-1}	Inverted U-shaped	Nonmonotonic or increasing	Static level ($t = 1$) or ∞ ($t \geqslant 2$)	Increasing (linearly)
Volatility, $\mathrm{var}[p_t]$	Increasing	Increasing	Constant (static level)	Increasing
Conditional volatility, $\mathrm{var}[p_t \mid p_{t-1}]$	Increasing	Nonmonotonic or decreasing	Static level ($t = 1$) or zero ($t \geqslant 2$)	Decreasing
Price precision, τ_t	Increasing	Increasing	Constant (static level)	Increasing (linearly)

according to a U-shaped form, with mild decreases at the beginning and sharp increases close to the end of the horizon.

- For intermediate values of the parameters $(\rho, \sigma_{\varepsilon_1}^2, \sigma_u^2)$ the conditional volatility and market depth are nonmonotonic, with a pattern decreasing-increasing-decreasing or U-shaped for the first, and increasing-decreasing-increasing or inverted U-shaped for the second. Otherwise, that is, for low or high values of the parameters $(\rho, \sigma_{\varepsilon_1}^2, \sigma_u^2)$, the conditional volatility is decreasing and market depth increasing with t.[26]

The qualitative simulation results for $t = 1, \dots, T$, as well as the analytical results obtained, are summarized in table 8.1, which also compares the equilibrium with short-term traders with the long-term case.

Price informativeness and the horizon of traders. We compare the degree of information incorporated in prices when informed traders have short and long horizons. Price informativeness in period T is given by $\tau_T = \tau_\theta + \tau_u \sum_{k=1}^{T} (\Delta a_k)^2$ and the total net trading intensity is $\sum_{k=1}^{T} \Delta a_k = a_T$ (equal to $\rho^{-1}(\sum_{k=1}^{T} \tau_{\varepsilon_k})$) in both the long-term and the short-term cases. The precision τ_T is akin to an inequality index of the variables Δa_t (which add up to a_T).[27] Consequently, τ_T

[26] Notice that market depth ($\lambda_t^{-1} = \tau_t / (\tau_u \Delta a_t)$) must be increasing with t for low t since then Δa_t is decreasing and τ_t is increasing always in t. For larger t, Δa_t increases and may give rise to nonmonotonic patterns. Similarly, $\mathrm{var}[p_t \mid p_{t-1}] = \tau_{t-1}^{-1} - \tau_t^{-1} = \tau_u (\Delta a_t)^2 / (\tau_{t-1} \tau_t)$ (conditional volatility) must be decreasing for low t and nonmonotonic for larger t.

[27] For example, the Herfindahl concentration index of an industry is equal to the sum of the squares of the market shares of the firms. Concentration is maximal in the monopoly case and

will be smaller the more equally distributed are the increments, the minimum being reached for equal increments every period.

Consider the two leading examples. (See also exercise 8.3.)

Concentrated arrival of information. With long-term agents there is informed trading only in the first period and the equilibrium informativeness of prices τ corresponds to the static equilibrium level. Short horizons imply that informed agents will trade in every period. Independent of the length of the horizon T, the information revealed by prices with short-term traders will be bounded above away from the static (long-term) case τ. This is easy to understand since the long-term case involves the maximum inequality in the temporal distribution of the net trading intensities: informed trade is concentrated in the first period. In fact, the informativeness of prices is higher in the long-term case period by period.[28]

The simulations performed with short-term traders show indeed that price precision tends to decrease with an increase in the horizon ($\sum_{t=1}^{T}(\Delta a_t)^2$ decreases with T). Increasing the number of trading periods with short-term traders does not help information revelation through prices and, in the context of our model, does not matter with long-term traders. The implications for incentive provision to managers based on the evolution of the stock price are derived in exercise 8.5.

A comparison of the temporal evolution of market quality parameters in the long-term and short-term cases is provided in table 8.1. An interesting result is that the distribution of total volatility over time is quite different in the two cases.[29] With long horizons information is incorporated in prices in the first period and therefore prices are more volatile at the beginning and less at the end than with short horizons. Indeed, conditional volatility has a U-shaped temporal evolution (including the liquidation period T to $T+1$). With short-term traders (conditional) volatility slowly grows over time (with the only possible exception being the liquidation period (T to $T+1$) according to the simulations).

Constant flow of information. If informed traders receive signals of equal precision every period, with long-term traders net trading intensities are equal across periods to the static trading intensity (a), meanwhile with short-term traders net trading intensities differ across periods. The outcome now is that long-term trading induces a lower final price precision. In the present case the long-term solution of equal increments Δa_t minimizes the price precision.

---

diminishes with the number of firms and with more equal shares. Here net trading intensities play the role of market shares.

[28] The result holds for any period before the last since in the long-term case the price precision is constant from the first period while in the short-term case it is increasing up to its value at $t = T$.

[29] Note also that total volatility up to period T with short-term traders $\sum_{t=1}^{T}\operatorname{var}[p_t \mid p_{t+1}] = \operatorname{var}[p_T] = \tau_\theta^{-1} - \tau_T^{-1}$ is bounded above and away from the long-term case $(\tau_\theta^{-1} - \tau^{-1})$. This reflects that, up to period T, less information has been incorporated into prices with short-term traders.

Increasing the number of trading periods now helps the precision of the final price τ_T since with long-term traders τ_T increases linearly with T. Indeed as T grows without bound prices converge to the fundamental value θ. This should not be surprising given that traders receive a constant flow of information. Total volatility up to period T in the short-term case is bounded below and away from the long-term case. This reflects that, up to period T, less information has been incorporated into prices with long-run traders.

The fact that (according to the simulations) short-term net trading intensities are first below and then above the constant long-term case and the result that the long-term price precision ends up (for $t = T$) above the short-term one imply that price precisions with short-term traders are first below and then above than with long-term traders. In fact, for reasonable values of the parameters it is the case that only for the very last periods the short-term price precision is above the long-term one.

8.3.2 Short Horizons with Risk-Averse Market Makers

Risk-averse market makers introduce interesting pricing dynamics as well as multiple equilibria when a proportion of traders have short horizons.[30] The appearance of "excess volatility" and substantial divergences of asset prices from fundamental values ("bubbles") can be explained without resort to the presence of systematic misperceptions (e.g., De Long et al. 1990a,b; Scheinkman and Xiong 2003). Let us consider first the effects of introducing short-term traders when there is no risk-neutral fringe and then turn to considering patterns of departures of prices from fundamental values when investors have a short horizon.

8.3.2.1 Short-Term Traders and Multiple Equilibria

Consider a two-period version of the model of section 8.2.1, where there is no competitive risk-neutral market-making sector and the informed traders play a market-making role. Suppose that a proportion $\mu > 0$ of informed traders have a short horizon (one period), while the remaining proportion $1 - \mu$ have a long horizon (two periods).

Linear equilibria exist and display a combination of elements from the short-term and long-term traders' cases. Second-period strategies are as in the case where all traders have a long horizon (proposition 8.3). In the first period traders have an additional market-making motive on top of absorbing liquidity shocks. This is reflected in their first-period demands, both for long-term and short-term traders, which add a third component to incorporate the readiness to absorb the unloaded inventories due to different horizons that traders have. Short-term traders also modify their trading intensity in period 1 with respect to the case with competitive risk-neutral market makers (proposition 8.4) by a

---

[30] The presence of multiple "bootstrap" equilibria with different self-fulfilling expectations is also found in the model of Dennert (1992).

factor of α_2 (as defined in section 8.2.1), which is a measure of the effect of the trader's risk aversion on second-period market depth. (See exercise 8.2 and Cespa (2002).)

Moreover, for the case of concentrated arrival of information it can be checked that there are two equilibria, one with low (conditional) volatility and another with high (conditional) volatility. In the first (second) there is high (low) trading intensity and price informativeness in the first period. At the high (low) trading intensity equilibrium traders anticipate in the first period an upward- (downward-) sloping second-period aggregate excess demand function and this becomes self-fulfilling because risk-averse short-term traders escalate (cut back) their trades. Short-term trading coupled with risk-averse market making delivers multiplicity of equilibria. More precisely, there is:

(a) A high trading intensity, high price informativeness, and low (conditional) volatility ($\text{var}[p_2 \mid p_1]$) equilibrium in which short-term traders in the first period react more to their signals than long-term traders, reverse their positions in the second period ($\Delta a_2 < 0$), and the slope of the second-period aggregate excess demand function becomes negative ($\lambda_2 < 0$). In this equilibrium, adverse selection is lessened in the second period and prices underreact to the order flow (with respect to a risk-neutral market-making benchmark).

(b) A low trading intensity, low price informativeness, and high (conditional) volatility ($\text{var}[p_2 \mid p_1]$) equilibrium in which short-term traders in the first period react less to their signals than long-term traders, expand their positions in the second period ($\Delta a_2 > 0$), and the slope of the second-period aggregate excess demand function is positive ($\lambda_2 > 0$). In this equilibrium, both the adverse selection and risk-bearing factors make prices overreact to the order flow (with respect to a risk-neutral market-making benchmark).

Obviously, the comparative statics of the equilibria depend on the selected one. For example, an increase in μ will increase second-period price informativeness in the high volatility equilibrium (a) but may decrease it in the low volatility equilibrium (b).

8.3.2.2 *Short-Term Trading and Price Departures from Fundamentals*

Consider the same model as in section 8.3.1 with short-term traders but with a general pattern for noise trade correlation $\hat{u}_t = \varsigma \hat{u}_{t-1} + e_t$ with $0 < \varsigma < 1$ (as in section 8.2.3) and without the competitive risk-neutral market-making sector. Let $T = 2$ for the moment. In the second period a trader's optimal position is given by $X_2(\tilde{s}_{i2}, p^2) = (E[\theta \mid \tilde{s}_{i2}, z^2] - p_2)/(\rho \,\text{var}[\theta \mid \tilde{s}_{i2}, z^2])$ while market clearing implies that $\int_0^1 X_2(\tilde{s}_{i2}, p^2)\,di + \hat{u}_2 = 0$. Let $\text{var}_t[Y] \equiv \text{var}[Y \mid \tilde{s}_{it}, z^t]$ and $\bar{E}_t[Y] \equiv \int_0^1 E[Y \mid \tilde{s}_{it}, z^t]\,di$, then the second-period equilibrium price is given by

$$p_2 = \bar{E}_2[\theta] + \rho \,\text{var}_2[\theta]\hat{u}_2.$$

In the first period a trader's optimal position is given by $X_1(s_{i1}, p_1) = (E[p_2 \mid s_{i1}, p_1] - p_1)/(\rho \operatorname{var}[p_2 \mid s_{i1}, p_1])$ and market clearing yields $\int_0^1 X_1(s_{i1}, p_1)\, di + \hat{u}_1 = 0$ or

$$p_1 = \tilde{E}_1[p_2] + \rho \operatorname{var}_1[p_2]\hat{u}_1 = \tilde{E}_1[\tilde{E}_2[\theta] + \rho \operatorname{var}_2[\theta]\varsigma\hat{u}_1] + \rho \operatorname{var}_1[p_2]\hat{u}_1$$

since, for the second equality, $\hat{u}_2 = \varsigma\hat{u}_1 + e_2$ with e_2 independent of the remaining random variables. We thus have that in period 1 the price of the asset depends on the market average expectation of the market average expected liquidation value plus a risk term associated with holding a position in the asset (due to the presence of noise traders). This result generalizes to a T-period horizon where one can show (Cespa and Vives 2007) that, for $1 \leqslant t \leqslant T$,

$$\begin{aligned} p_t = \tilde{E}_t[\tilde{E}_{t+1}[\cdots \tilde{E}_{T-1}[\tilde{E}_T[\theta] + \rho \operatorname{var}_T[\theta]\varsigma^{T-t}\hat{u}_t] \\ + \rho \operatorname{var}_{T-1}[p_T]\varsigma^{T-(t-1)}\hat{u}_t \cdots] + \rho \operatorname{var}_{t+1}[p_{t+2}]\varsigma\hat{u}_t] + \rho \operatorname{var}_t[p_{t+1}]\hat{u}_t. \end{aligned}$$

When the stock of noise trading is independent, $\varsigma = 0$, it is immediate that

$$p_t = \tilde{E}_t[\tilde{E}_{t+1}[\cdots \tilde{E}_{T-1}[\tilde{E}_T[\theta]] \cdots]] + \rho \operatorname{var}_t[p_{t+1}]\hat{u}_t$$

and p_t is the average expectation at t of the average expectation at $t + 1$ of the average expectation at $t + 2$ of... the liquidation value in period $T + 1$, plus the corresponding period, risk-adjusted noise shock. This, as pointed out by Allen et al. (2006), is reminiscent of Keynes's vision of the stock market as a beauty contest (the situation in which judges are more concerned about the opinion of other judges than of the intrinsic merits of the participants in the contest).[31]

An interesting observation by Allen et al. (2006) is that, when averaging over the realizations of noise trading, the price at date t will not equal in general the period t average expectation of the fundamental value. The consensus value of the fundamentals $\tilde{E}_t[\theta]$ does not coincide with the mean price $E[p_t \mid \theta]$, with the exception of the last period $t = T$, which is as in a static market. The price p_t gives a higher weight to history—relies more on public information—than the consensus expectation $\tilde{E}_t[\theta]$ because of the bias toward public information when a Bayesian agent has to forecast the average market opinion knowing that it is also formed on the public information observed by other agents. This also implies that the current price will always be farther away from fundamentals than the average of investors' expectations and that it will be more sluggish to adjust.

When $\varsigma = 0$ there is a unique linear equilibrium. However, when $\varsigma \in (0, 1]$ there are two linear equilibria (Cespa and Vives 2007). In one of them prices are closer to fundamentals than the average expectations of investors (corresponding to equilibrium (a) in section 8.3.2.1) and in the other prices are farther away

[31] "Professional investment may be likened to those newspaper competitions in which the competitors have to pick out the six prettiest faces from a hundred photographs, the prize being awarded to the competitor whose choice most nearly corresponds to the average preferences of the competitors as a whole; so that each competitor has to pick, not those faces which he himself finds prettiest, but those which he thinks likeliest to catch the fancy of the other competitors, all of whom are looking at the problem from the same point of view" (Keynes 1936, p. 156).

from fundamentals than the average expectations of investors (corresponding to equilibrium (b) in section 8.3.2.1). However, only the second equilibrium is stable (in the sense of having a negative slope for the aggregate excess demand function).

We see that with short-term traders asset prices depend on expectations of higher order than the first. Higher-order expectations introduce a wedge in the pricing equation (the difference with the price that would arise if only first-order expectations were taken into account).[32] The same is true with long-term traders when there is residual uncertainty in the asset value or serial correlation in noise trade increments.

8.3.3 Endogenous Information Acquisition and Short Horizons

We have seen how short-term investors care only about the next-period price and not directly about the fundamental value of the asset. A consequence, not surprisingly, is that short-term investors will prefer short-term to long-term information. Furthermore, since short-term investors have to unwind their position early (before the fundamental value is realized) they are interested in their information being reflected in the (unwinding) price and this will happen only if other traders also have access to short-term information. This means that there may be strategic complementarities in information acquisition: short-term traders may care more about the information that other short-term traders are acquiring than about the fundamentals. Indeed, this may be seen as an instance of Keynes's beauty contest.

Froot et al. (1992) provide a formalization of the argument in a four-period model in which agents have to unwind their position in period 3 and each trader has to decide whether to acquire information on one of the two additive components of the fundamental value (which may be revealed in either period 3 or period 4). It is shown that for a low (high) probability of revelation of the fundamental value in period 3, information acquisition by short-term traders displays strategic complementarity (substitutability).

Short horizons of traders can also arise endogenously because of risk aversion when traders can acquire information. Indeed, risk-averse traders may want to unwind their positions early once their private information has been revealed. This means that those investors will care about prices in the short-term making herding on short-term information acquisition possible. In the noisy two-period competitive rational expectations model of Hirshleifer et al. (1994), risk-averse agents may get a piece of information (the same for all agents) about the liquidation value of the asset early ($t = 1$) or late ($t = 2$). Late informed agents will not trade in $t = 1$ because they do not then have better information than the competitive risk-neutral market-making sector. The

[32] Bacchetta and van Wincoop (2007) study the role of higher-order beliefs in asset prices in an infinite-horizon model showing that higher-order expectations add an additional term to the traditional asset pricing equation, the higher-order "wedge." Kondor (2005a) shows how public announcements may increase disagreement among traders and generate high trading volume.

market admits five possible equilibria and Hirshleifer et al. focus on equilibria with trade and price movements. In those equilibria early informed investors take positions at 1 and, on average, unwind them partially at $t = 2$. Indeed, at $t = 2$ the early informed have lost their informational advantage because the late informed have also obtained the information and market makers have also learned more. In this context it is possible to check that if information is noisy enough there are situations where the *ex ante* expected utility of a trader increases with the total mass of informed traders. In principle, increasing the mass of informed (both early and late) traders increases competition in the different periods but increasing the mass of late traders has an indirect benefit on early traders since it facilitates the unwinding of their positions. The result is that traders may try to acquire information on assets in which other traders are acquiring information.

Holden and Subrahmanyam (1996) consider a version of the previous model where traders can decide whether to acquire long-term or short-term information. Short-term information is publicly revealed in the second period ($t = 2$) and therefore fully incorporated in the second-period price. Short-term informed traders do not trade at $t = 2$ because they do not have any informational advantage with respect to the competitive risk-neutral market-making sector. Long-term information is only revealed after period 2. Holden and Subrahmanyam show that there are cases, when both risk aversion and residual uncertainty—after long-term information has been revealed—in the fundamental value are high, where all traders choose to collect only short-term information. This is so because in this situation to speculate at $t = 2$ is very risky, and speculating with long-term information at $t = 1$ is not advisable because of the price risk in period 2. Put another way, long-term information is not good to speculate in the short term, exploiting price differences between 1 and 2, and may be too risky in the long term.

8.3.4 Summary

Trading with a short horizon has important implications for market quality parameters.

- In the presence of a risk-neutral market-making sector:
    - Short horizons make traders less responsive to their information on the fundamental value of the asset. The reason is that they bear price risk.
    - The pattern of evolution of market depth and volatility is very rich and contrasts with the case with long-term traders.
    - Prices may be more or less informative with short-term trading depending on whether arrival of information is dispersed or concentrated.
- When market makers are risk averse:

- ◦ Multiple (high and low volatility) equilibria may arise and may make short-term traders either less or more responsive to private information than long-term traders. The relation of price informativeness and the proportion of short-term traders depends on which equilibrium obtains.
- ◦ There is always an equilibrium, which is stable, in which prices are farther away from fundamentals than the average expectations of investors and in which there is over-reliance on public information.

- Short horizons may induce strategic complementarities in information acquisition and traders may care more about the information that others traders acquire than about the fundamentals, as in Keynes's beauty contest.

8.4 Explaining Crises and Market Crashes

In this section we review some rational expectations models of market crashes and bubbles, and a basic coordination model of investors that explains crises.

8.4.1 Crashes in Rational Expectations Models

Several competitive rational expectations models have attempted to explain market crashes, e.g., the sudden and significant drop in stock prices in 1929 or 1987. In the October 1987 crash the Dow Jones index fell by 23% in a single day and there was no obvious connection with news of changed fundamentals. Three types of explanation of crashes based on these models have been advanced: small events or price changes may lead to a chain reaction that ends up in a crash (e.g., abrupt information revelation with small price movements (Romer 1993)); multiple equilibria and a discontinuous equilibrium price function (e.g., Gennotte and Leland 1990); and liquidity shortages (e.g., Grossman 1988). Further explanations are provided by herding models (see chapter 6 for an introduction) and models of bubbles. We will give an overview of these contributions in turn.

The idea in the two-period noisy rational expectations model of Romer (1993) is that some traders, on top of being uncertain about the fundamental value of the asset, do not know the precision of information of other traders. Traders can receive signals of high, intermediate, or low precision (and the signals can be ranked according to Blackwell's informativeness). This two-dimensional uncertainty implies that the first-period price cannot reveal everything. Then, in the second period, the price movement caused by a (known) supply shock may end by revealing a lot about the precision of information of traders, and imply a large change in prices. For example, if the traders who do not know the precision of information of other traders see an extreme price in period 1, they will infer that it is more likely that other investors received a very noisy signal (low precision) but they will not know for sure. Now, a small supply shock in period 2 (which in contrast to the models in this section is observable for the traders) may reveal the type of other investors and correct the misalignment of prices with respect to the joint information of traders. The analysis is done numerically because normality is lost due to the uncertainty about the precision of the signals. (See exercise 8.1.) Papers by Caplin and Leahy (1994) (see exercise 6.6), Hong and Stein (2003), Lee (1998), and Zeira (1999) also provide explanations of a crash where traders learn something about the fundamentals and then react and provoke the crisis. This revelation of information, however, is sometimes at odds with the increase in uncertainty associated with the crisis episode.

Gennotte and Leland (1990) perform a comparative statics analysis in a static model with multiple equilibria and show how a small supply shift can entail a large price drop if the market is sitting at a high equilibrium price level and this equilibrium disappears with the exogenous shock (think of an inverted-S-shaped demand curve and a vertical supply that moves to the right with the shock). The base model is a noisy rational expectations model as in example 4.2 (pp. 122–23). There are three types of traders: informed traders (who receive a private signal about the fundamental value of the stock), traders who are better informed about the noisy supply of the asset (say that they can distinguish better whether orders in the limit-order book are due to information trading or liquidity trading), and portfolio traders who buy when demand increases and sell when demand falls. Portfolio traders thus have a positively sloped exogenous demand for the asset. Now, with a nonlinear enough demand from portfolio trading and with uncertainty about its extent, the aggregate demand may have the inverted-S form and there may be multiple equilibria. Then traders may attribute a price drop to bad news about the fundamentals rather than to portfolio trading and a crash may occur. This potential underestimation of portfolio trading in an asymmetric-information context is portrayed as a possible explanation of the 1987 stock market crash.[33]

Demange (2002) shows that multiple equilibria and crashes can occur under standard assumptions when market participation (or the risk tolerance of traders) is uncertain. Barlevy and Veronesi (2003) use the model in Barlevy and Veronesi (2000)—see section 4.2.2—to obtain a similar result to Gennotte and Leland (1990) doing away with the presence of portfolio insurance. The mere presence of uninformed and informed traders may imply that the demand of the uninformed is upward sloping. Indeed, a low price may be bad news and indicate that the asset value is very low (as in section 3.2.2 the supply curve for firms may be downward sloping). The result again is that the aggregate demand curve may have the inverted-S shape: at low prices the uninformed do not purchase the risky asset and demand is downward sloping as usual; when prices are higher the uninformed have a positively sloped demand and, with a strong

[33] An alternative model, but based on a similar idea, is developed by Jacklin et al. (1992) introducing dynamic trading strategies in the sequential trading model of Glosten and Milgrom (1985).

enough effect, the aggregate demand is upward sloping; and at high prices the information effect is choked off and demand again is downward sloping for all traders. In this case a small price decline due to a shock may cause uninformed traders to withdraw from the market and cause a crash (technically, and as before, the equilibrium price is discontinuous in the shock).

Grossman (1988) builds a model in which large price movements are the consequence of a liquidity shortage due to an underestimation by market timers of the degree of dynamic hedging activity. The point of the paper is to show the nonequivalence between traded and synthetical options even when the payoff of the former can be replicated with the latter (with dynamic trading strategies). The reason is that traded and synthetical options are not informationally equivalent. Indeed, the price of the former may reveal relevant information in a market with asymmetric information about the extent of the use of dynamic hedging strategies. Market timers can stabilize the market by setting aside capital to smooth price movements caused by the dynamic trading strategies of a fraction of agents with increasing risk aversion when their wealth declines. Those agents sell when the market goes down and buy when it goes up. If market timers can infer the amount of dynamic hedging demand because there is an option market, then they can plan their interventions and set aside the needed capital. Otherwise, market timers have to estimate the extent of dynamic hedging strategies and if they underestimate them, or ignore altogether the presence of dynamic hedging, prices will be much more volatile. Once the liquidity shortage disappears the market goes back to normal.

The competitive models above provide different stories that rationalize market crashes. In the first two models the crash may be persistent because it corrects a mispricing due to asymmetric information (Romer 1993) or responds to fundamentals of demand and supply (Gennotte and Leland 1990; Demange 2002). In the third (Grossman 1988) prices bounce back after the liquidity crisis unravels.

Variants of herding models (see chapter 6 and section 9.1.1) can also explain crashes. Avery and Zemsky (1998) generate crashes in their dynamic model where traders are uncertain about the precision of information of other traders (as in Romer 1993). The auction literature offers related insights. For example, a parallel can be drawn between auctions in which agents decide when to bid or to stop bidding (ascending or descending auctions) and herding models in which agents decide when to move (see Bulow and Klemperer 1994, 1999). Veldkamp (2006) explains sporadic surges in asset prices (frenzies) and herding in a dynamic version of the Grossman–Stiglitz model (see section 4.2.2), where it is assumed that payoff volatility increases with the payoff level and there are increasing returns to information production. It is assumed that the market structure in the information provision market is such that the price for information decreases with the amount of information purchased and that, with multiple markets, there is a constraint in the number of information pieces a trader can purchase. The first assumption yields a strategic complementarity in information acquisition; the second yields a trade-off between learning about one market and another. It is found that information markets increase substantially the volatility of prices (associating media frenzies with price frenzies), and that with multiple assets media herds are associated with price dispersion (in otherwise identical markets) and excess cross-sectional volatility in relation to fundamentals. In a market subject to media attention (information production) asset prices are higher because the conditional variance of the fundamental value is lower. When returns in such a market start to fall, other markets then become more attractive and there may be a quick switch in the equilibrium causing a fall in assets prices in the first market and an increase in the ones subject to attention. The signal transmission constraint binds only with high demand for information, with low demand for information markets having no effect on each other. This fact induces positive correlation between price dispersion and news. The predictions contrast with typical information cascades/herding models where frenzies arise because of too little information provision (see the models in chapter 6 and Chari and Kehoe (2003)). Veldkamp finds evidence in equity markets and news coverage consistent with her model with movements in asset prices generating news and news raising both prices and price dispersion.

Finally, there is a well-established literature that explains *bubbles*, understood as departures of prices from fundamental values, both in symmetric and asymmetric-information contexts. The real estate and stock market bubble in Japan in the late 1980s or the "new economy" bubble in stocks in the late 1990s are good examples. Tirole (1982) provided conditions under which bubbles cannot arise (at least with a finite number of rational traders or with finite horizons). However, bubbles can exist with infinite horizons (Tirole 1985). (Santos and Woodford (1997) argue that conditions for bubbles to exist in general equilibrium models are restrictive.) Allen et al. (1993) show the possibility of bubbles with finite horizons when there is a lack of common knowledge. Allen and Gale (2000) trace the existence of bubbles in asset prices on agency problems in banks that lend to investors. Those leveraged investors find risky assets attractive because if asset values collapse investors limit their losses by defaulting on their loans. This is a classical risk-shifting problem that increases asset prices above their fundamental value. Credit expansions may fuel this excessive bidding of asset prices and lead to a crisis and defaults.

Other authors have departed from the assumption of a common prior for traders and explained bubbles in models where traders hold different initial beliefs about the liquidation value. Biais and Bossaerts (1998) rationalize trading patterns whereby traders with low private valuations may decide to buy an asset from traders with higher private valuations in the hope of reselling it later on during the trading day at an even higher price. Cao and Ou-Yang (2005) study conditions for the existence of bubbles (when the equilibrium price is higher than the highest price that would prevail if traders had homogeneous beliefs) in a model where traders' opinions about the liquidation value differ.

Here a bubble denotes a situation in which traders are willing to pay more than what the most "optimistic" trader would to acquire the asset.

Abreu and Brunnermeier (2003) present a model, with some behavioral features, where bubbles persist in a unique equilibrium despite the presence of rational arbitrageurs. The persistence of the bubble is due to a coordination problem faced by the arbitrageurs. In the next section a static version of the coordination problem of investors is studied.

8.4.2 Crises and Coordination Problems

In this section we present a basic coordination game that models crisis situations such as a currency attack, or a bank or creditors' run. Coordination games tend to have multiple equilibria since they are games of strategic complementarities. In a game of strategic complementarities the marginal return of the action of a player increases with the level of the actions of rivals. This leads to best replies being monotone increasing (see section 10.4.1). We first provide conditions under which the equilibrium is unique along with some applications. We then reexamine the model by introducing a financial market and making public information endogenous.

The basic model is a symmetric binary action game of strategic complementarities. Consider a game with a continuum of players of mass one where the action set of player i is $A_i \equiv \{0, 1\}$, with $y_i = 1$ interpreted as "acting" and $y_i = 0$ "not acting." To act may be to attack a currency (Morris and Shin 1998), refuse to roll over debt (Morris and Shin 2004; Corsetti et al. 2006; Rochet and Vives 2004), run on a bank, or not renew a certificate of deposit in the interbank market (Goldstein and Pauzner 2005; Rochet and Vives 2004), but also invest, adopt a technology, or revolt against the status quo.

Let $\pi^1 = \pi(y_i = 1, \tilde{y}; \theta)$ and $\pi^0 = \pi(y_i = 0, \tilde{y}; \theta)$, where $\tilde{y}$ is the fraction of investors acting and θ is the state of the world. The differential payoff to acting is $\pi^1 - \pi^0 = B > 0$ if $\tilde{y} \geqslant h(\theta)$, and $\pi^1 - \pi^0 = -C < 0$ if $\tilde{y} < h(\theta)$, where $h(\theta)$ is the critical fraction of investors above which it pays to act. The game is of strategic complementarities (see section 10.4.1.2) since $\pi^1 - \pi^0$ increases with $\tilde{y}$. It is assumed that $h(\cdot)$ is strictly increasing, crossing 0 at $\theta = \theta_L$ and 1 at $\theta = \theta_H$. It follows from these payoffs, if the state of the world is known, that if $\theta \leqslant \theta_L$, then it is a dominant strategy to act; if $\theta \geqslant \theta_H$, then it is a dominant strategy not to act; and for $\theta \in (\theta_L, \theta_H)$ there are multiple equilibria. Both everyone acting and no one acting are equilibria. Since the game is a game of strategic complementarities there is a largest and a smallest equilibrium. That is, there are extremal equilibria. The largest equilibrium is $y_i = 1$ for all i if $\theta \leqslant \theta_H$, and $y_i = 0$ for all i if $\theta > \theta_H$, and it is (weakly) decreasing with θ. This is a consequence of $\pi^1 - \pi^0$ being decreasing with θ.

A first example of the model is a streamlined version of the currency attacks model of Morris and Shin (1998), where θ represents the reserves of the central bank (with $\theta \leqslant 0$ meaning that reserves are depleted). Each speculator has one unit of resources to attack the currency ($y_i = 1$) at a cost C. Letting $h(\theta) = \theta$, the attack succeeds if $\tilde{y} \geqslant \theta$. The capital gain if there is a depreciation is fixed and equal to $\hat{B} = B + C$. The second example models coordination failure in the interbank market (Rochet and Vives 2004). Consider a market with three dates: $t = 0, 1, 2$. At date $t = 0$, the bank has equity E and collects uninsured certificates of deposit (CDs) in amount $D_0 \equiv 1$. These funds are used to finance risky investment I and cash reserves M. The returns θI on these assets are collected at date $t = 2$ and if the bank can meet its obligations, the CDs are repaid at their face value D, and the equityholders of the bank obtain the residual (if any). A continuum of fund managers make investment decisions in the interbank market. At $t = 1$ each fund manager, after the observation of the future realization of θ, decides whether to cancel ($y_i = 1$) or renew his CD ($y_i = 0$). If $\tilde{y} \geqslant M$, then the bank has to sell some of its assets to meet payments. A fund manager is rewarded for taking the right decision (that is, withdrawing if and only if the bank fails). Let $m \equiv M/D$ be the liquidity ratio, $\theta_{\mathrm{L}} \equiv (D - M)/I$ the solvency threshold of the bank, $\lambda > 0$ the fire sales premium of early sales of bank assets, and $\theta_{\mathrm{H}} \equiv (1 + \lambda)\theta_{\mathrm{L}}$ the "supersolvency" threshold such that a bank does not fail even if no fund manager renews his CDs. Under these conditions the bank fails if

$$\tilde{y} \geqslant h(\theta) \equiv m + \frac{1 - m}{\lambda}\left(\frac{\theta}{\theta_{\mathrm{L}}} - 1\right)$$

for $\theta \in [\theta_{\mathrm{L}}, \theta_{\mathrm{H}}]$ and $h(\theta) = m$ for $\theta \leqslant \theta_{\mathrm{L}}$. This example can be reinterpreted by replacing bank with country and CD with foreign-denominated short-term debt.

Consider now an incomplete-information version of the game where players have a normal prior on the state of the world $\theta \sim N(\bar{\theta}, \tau_{\theta}^{-1})$ and player i observes a private signal $s_i = \theta + \varepsilon_i$ with normally i.i.d. noise $\varepsilon_i \sim N(0, \tau_{\varepsilon}^{-1})$.[34]

Morris and Shin (2003) show that in the incomplete-information game there is a unique Bayesian equilibrium, and it is in threshold strategies of the type "act if and only if the signal received is below a certain threshold," provided that $\tau_{\theta}/\sqrt{\tau_{\varepsilon}}$ is small. In fact, the equilibrium is the outcome of iterated elimination of strictly dominated strategies. The result can be shown with the help of the tools of supermodular games (see Vives 2005). This allows us to see, in a transparent way, the forces driving the uniqueness result. Indeed, the game is one of strategic complementarities with a monotone information structure. In more technical terms the game is "monotone supermodular" since $\pi(y_i, \tilde{y}; \theta)$ has increasing differences in $(y_i, (\tilde{y}, -\theta))$ (i.e., the differential payoff to act $\pi^1 - \pi^0$ increases with the aggregate action and the negative of the state of the world $(\tilde{y}, -\theta)$, and signals are affiliated (see section 10.1.5 for the definition of affiliation and section 10.4.2.2 for the concept of a monotone supermodular game).

[34]This is referred to in the literature as a "global game." Those games were introduced by Carlsson and van Damme (1993) as games of incomplete information with types determined by each player observing a noisy signal of the underlying state. The goal is to select an equilibrium with a perturbation in a full-information game with multiple equilibria. The basic idea is that players entertain the "global picture" of slightly different possible games being played. Each player then has a noisy signal of the game being played.

This means that extremal equilibria exist, are symmetric (because the game is symmetric), and are in monotone (decreasing) strategies in type (Van Zandt and Vives 2007; Vives 2005). Since there are only two possible actions, the strategies must then be of the threshold form: $y_i = 1$ if and only if $s_i < \hat{s}$, where $\hat{s}$ is the threshold. It also follows that the extremal equilibrium thresholds, denoted $\bar{s}$ and $\underline{s}$, bound the set of strategies which are the outcome of iterated elimination of strictly dominated strategies. If $\bar{s} = \underline{s}$, the game is dominance solvable and the equilibrium is unique.[35]

An equilibrium will be characterized by two thresholds (s^*, θ^*) with s^* yielding the signal threshold to act and θ^* the state-of-the-world critical threshold, below which the acting mass is successful and an acting player obtains the payoff $B - C > 0$ (say, the currency falls or the bank fails).

Let Φ denote the cumulative distribution of the standard normal random variable $N(0, 1)$. In equilibrium: (1) the fraction of acting players $\tilde{y}(\theta^*, s^*) = \mathrm{P}(s \leqslant s^* \mid \theta^*) \equiv \Phi(\sqrt{\tau_\varepsilon}(s^* - \theta^*))$ must equal the critical fraction above which it pays to act, $h(\theta^*)$, and (2) at the critical signal threshold the expected payoff of acting and not acting should be the same:

$$\begin{aligned} &E[\pi(1, \tilde{y}(\theta, s); \theta) - \pi(0, \tilde{y}(\theta, s); \theta) \mid s = s^*] \\ &\qquad\qquad = \mathrm{P}(\theta \leqslant \theta^* \mid s^*)B + \mathrm{P}(\theta > \theta^* \mid s^*)(-C) = 0; \end{aligned}$$

or $\mathrm{P}(\theta \leqslant \theta^* \mid s^*) \equiv \Phi(\sqrt{\tau_\theta + \tau_\varepsilon}(\theta^* - (\tau_\theta\bar{\theta} + \tau_\varepsilon s^*)/(\tau_\theta + \tau_\varepsilon))) = \gamma$, where $\gamma \equiv C/(B + C) < 1$.

Equations (1) $\Phi(\sqrt{\tau_\varepsilon}(s^* - \theta^*)) = h(\theta^*)$ and (2) $\Phi(\sqrt{\tau_\theta + \tau_\varepsilon}(\theta^* - (\tau_\theta\bar{\theta} + \tau_\varepsilon s^*)/(\tau_\theta + \tau_\varepsilon))) = \gamma$, by substituting the value of s^* from (1) into (2), combine to give the equation

$$\varphi(\theta^*; \gamma, \bar{\theta}) = 0 \equiv \tau_\theta(\theta^* - \bar{\theta}) - \sqrt{\tau_\varepsilon}\Phi^{-1}(h(\theta^*)) - \sqrt{\tau_\theta + \tau_\varepsilon}\Phi^{-1}(\gamma) = 0,$$

which may have multiple solutions in θ^*. To simplify the exposition and notation suppose that $h(\cdot)$ is linear with slope $h' > 0$. It can then be checked that there is a unique solution in θ^* to $\varphi(\theta^*; \gamma, \bar{\theta}) = 0$ if and only if $\tau_\theta/\sqrt{\tau_\varepsilon} \leqslant \sqrt{2\pi}h'$.[36] In this case the equilibrium is unique and the game is dominance solvable because then $\bar{s} = \underline{s}$. Furthermore, it should be clear that the critical thresholds θ^* and s^* move together.

In order to gain some intuition into the structure of the game and the result, let us think in terms of the best reply of a player to the (common) signal threshold used by the other players. Let $H(s, \hat{s})$ be the conditional probability that the acting players succeed if they use a (common) threshold $\hat{s}$ when the player considered receives a signal s. That is,

$$H(s, \hat{s}) \equiv \mathrm{P}(\theta < \hat{\theta}(\hat{s}) \mid s) = \Phi\left(\sqrt{\tau_\theta + \tau_\varepsilon}\left(\hat{\theta}(\hat{s}) - \frac{\tau_\theta\bar{\theta} + \tau_\varepsilon s}{\tau_\theta + \tau_\varepsilon}\right)\right),$$

---

[35] See section 10.4.1 for the concept of iterated elimination of dominated strategies and dominance solvability in games.

[36] As γ ranges from 0 to 1, θ^* goes from θ_{H} to θ_{L}.

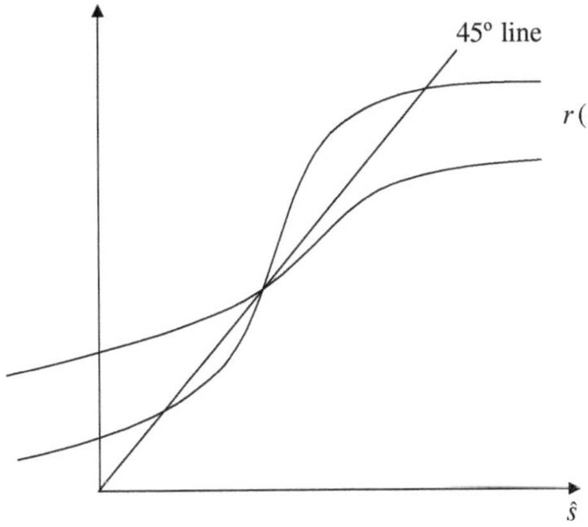

Figure 8.1. Best response of a player to the threshold strategy used by rivals (the flatter best response corresponds to the case $\tau_\theta/\sqrt{\tau_\varepsilon} \leqslant \sqrt{2\pi}h'$ while the steeper one to the case $\tau_\theta/\sqrt{\tau_\varepsilon} > \sqrt{2\pi}h'$).

where $\hat{\theta}(\hat{s})$ is the critical θ below which there is success when players use a strategy with threshold $\hat{s}$ ($\hat{\theta}(\hat{s})$ is the solution in θ of $\Phi(\sqrt{\tau_\varepsilon}(\hat{s}-\theta)) - h(\theta) = 0$, which increases with $\hat{s}$). It is immediate then that $\partial H/\partial s < 0$ and $\partial H/\partial \hat{s} \geqslant 0$. Given that other players use a strategy with threshold $\hat{s}$, the best response of a player is to use a strategy with threshold s^*, where $H(s^*, \hat{s}) = \gamma$: act if and only if $H(s, \hat{s}) > \gamma$ or, equivalently, if and only if $s < s^*$. This defines a best-response function in terms of thresholds:

$$r(\hat{s}) = \frac{\tau_\theta + \tau_\varepsilon}{\tau_\varepsilon}\hat{\theta}(\hat{s}) - \frac{\tau_\theta}{\tau_\varepsilon}\bar{\theta} - \frac{\sqrt{\tau_\theta + \tau_\varepsilon}}{\tau_\varepsilon}\Phi^{-1}(\gamma).$$

We have that $r' = -(\partial H/\partial \hat{s})/(\partial H/\partial s) \geqslant 0$ and the game is of strategic complementarities: a higher threshold $\hat{s}$ by others induces a player to also use a higher threshold. Furthermore, it is easily checked that $\hat{\theta}'(\hat{s}) \leqslant [1 + \sqrt{2\pi/\tau_\varepsilon}h']^{-1}$.[37] As a consequence, if $\tau_\theta/\sqrt{\tau_\varepsilon} \leqslant \sqrt{2\pi}h'$, then $r'(\hat{s}) = ((\tau_\theta + \tau_\varepsilon)/\tau_\varepsilon)\hat{\theta}'(\hat{s}) \leqslant 1$ (with equality only when $h(\theta) = \frac{1}{2}$). This ensures that $r(\cdot)$ crosses the 45° line only once and that the equilibrium is unique. In fact, as we have seen before, the uniqueness condition is "if and only if." In figure 8.1 the uniqueness case is illustrated with the flatter reaction curve and the one with multiple equilibria (three) with the steeper reaction curve.

The main reason why the equilibrium is unique with small noise in the signals in relation to the prior ($\tau_\theta/\sqrt{\tau_\varepsilon}$) is that decreasing the amount of noise decreases the strength of the strategic complementarity among the actions of the players. Indeed, multiple equilibria come about when the strategic complementarity is strong enough (the steeper best response in figure 8.1). With

[37] From the equation $\Phi(\sqrt{\tau_\varepsilon}(\hat{s}-\theta)) = h(\theta)$ we can solve for the inverse function and obtain $\hat{s}(\theta) = \theta + (1/\sqrt{\tau_\varepsilon})\Phi^{-1}(h(\theta))$ with derivative $\hat{s}' = 1 + (1/\sqrt{\tau_\varepsilon})h'[\phi(\Phi^{-1}(h(\theta)))]^{-1}$, where ϕ is the density of the standard normal. Since ϕ is bounded above by $1/\sqrt{2\pi}$, it follows that $\hat{s}'$ is bounded below: $\hat{s}'(\theta) \geqslant 1 + \sqrt{2\pi/\tau_\varepsilon}\,h'$. Hence, $\hat{\theta}'(\hat{s}) \leqslant [1 + \sqrt{2\pi/\tau_\varepsilon}\,h']^{-1}$ (with strict inequality, except when $h(\theta) = \frac{1}{2}$ because then $\Phi^{-1}(\frac{1}{2}) = 0$ and ϕ attains its maximum: $\phi(0) = 1/\sqrt{2\pi}$).

small noise a player faces a greater amount of uncertainty about the behavior of others and the strategic complementarity is lessened, the best response is "flattened" and $r' \leqslant 1$ (the flatter best response in figure 8.1). Consider the limit cases $\tau_\varepsilon \to +\infty$ (or, equivalently, a diffuse prior $\tau_\theta \to 0$). Then it is not hard to see that the distribution of the proportion of acting players $\tilde{y}(\theta, s^*)$ is uniformly distributed over $[0,1]$ conditional on $s_i = s^*$. This means that players face maximal strategic uncertainty.[38] In contrast, at any of the multiple equilibria with complete information when $\theta \in (\theta_L, \theta_H)$, players face no strategic uncertainty (e.g., in the equilibrium in which everyone acts, a player has a point belief that all other players will act).

In the region where the equilibrium is unique we can obtain several useful results:

Coordination failure. When $\theta < \theta^*$, the acting mass of players succeeds. In the range $[\theta^*, \theta_H)$ there is coordination failure from the point of view of players, because if all them were to act then they would succeed. For example, in the range $[\theta^*, \theta_H)$ if currency speculators were to coordinate their attack then they would succeed, but in fact the currency holds or, in the interbank example where the equilibrium failure threshold of the bank is $\theta^* \in [\theta_L, \theta_H]$, in the range $[\theta_L, \theta^*)$ the bank is solvent but illiquid. This provides a rationale for a lender of last resort intervention with the discount window.

Comparative statics. Both θ^* and s^* (and the probability that the acting mass succeeds) decrease with the relative cost of failure $\gamma \equiv C/(B+C)$ and in the expected value of the state of the world $\bar{\theta}$ (this follows immediately since the expected differential payoff to acting conditional on the private signal decreases with γ and with $\bar{\theta}$ or, equivalently, the left-hand side of $\varphi(\theta; \gamma, \bar{\theta}) = 0$ decreases with γ and with $\bar{\theta}$). Consequently, the probability of a currency crisis decreases with the relative cost of the attack $C/\hat{B}$ and with the expected value of the reserves of the central bank $\bar{\theta}$. In the interbank example the critical θ^* (and probability of failure) is a decreasing function of the liquidity ratio m and the solvency (E/I) of the bank, of the critical withdrawal probability γ, and of the expected return on the bank's assets $\bar{\theta}$; it is an increasing function of the fire-sale premium λ and of the face value of debt D.

Multiplier effect of public information. Note first that the prior mean $\bar{\theta}$ of θ can be understood as a public signal of precision τ_θ. The equilibrium threshold is determined by $r(s^*; \bar{\theta}) - s^* = 0$, from which it follows that

$$\left|\frac{\mathrm{d}s^*}{\mathrm{d}\bar{\theta}}\right| = \frac{|\partial r/\partial\bar{\theta}|}{1-r'} > \left|\frac{\partial r}{\partial\bar{\theta}}\right|$$

whenever the uniqueness condition $r' < 1$ is met and $r' > 0$ (i.e., the game is a game of strategic complementarity). Consequently, an increase in $\bar{\theta}$ will have a larger effect on the equilibrium threshold s^* than the direct impact on the best

[38] The uniqueness argument made is robust to general distributions for the uncertainty as long as the noise in the signals is small. Indeed, with very precise signals, all priors "look uniform" (Morris and Shin 2002).

response of a player $\partial r/\partial\bar{\theta} = -\tau_\theta/\tau_\varepsilon$. This multiplier effect is largest when r' is close to 1, that is, when strategic complementarities are strong and we approach the region of multiplicity of equilibria. The multiplier effect of public information is emphasized by Morris and Shin (2003) in terms of the coordinating potential of public information beyond its strict information content. Every player knows that an increase in $\bar{\theta}$ will shift downward the best replies of the rest of the players and everyone will be more cautious in acting. This happens because public information becomes common knowledge and affects the equilibrium outcome. This phenomenon may be behind the apparent overreaction of financial markets to Fed announcements or may explain why the per-viewer price of advertising in TV is higher for big sports events (Chew 1998).

In the region where there is a unique equilibrium the probability of occurrence of a "crisis" (successful mass action) $P(\theta \leqslant \theta^*)$ depends on the state of the world. In contrast, in the full-information model there are multiple self-fulfilling equilibria in the range (θ_L, θ_H). Consequently, the model builds a bridge between the self-fulfilling theory of crisis (e.g., Diamond and Dybvig 1983) and the theory that links a crisis to the fundamentals (e.g, Gorton 1985, 1988).[39]

Transparency. Releasing more public information (e.g., by the central bank in the banking example) is not necessarily good. The reason is that a public signal, which becomes common knowledge, has the capacity to destabilize expectations in the market. This means moving the interbank market from a regime with a unique equilibrium to a regime with multiple equilibria. Indeed, while without a public signal the market may be in the uniqueness region, by adding a precise enough public signal we will have three equilibria. At one extremal equilibrium the probability of crisis will increase substantially from the situation without the public signal. The analysis may therefore rationalize oblique statements by central bankers and other regulatory authorities which seem to add noise to a basic message.

It is worth noting that we can still perform comparative statics analysis even if there are multiple equilibria. This is so because the game is a monotone supermodular game. Suppose we are in the multiple equilibrium region and that $\bar{\theta}$ increases. The comparative statics result that the critical thresholds θ^* and s^* decrease still holds for extremal equilibria. Indeed, extremal equilibria of monotone supermodular games increase with the posteriors of the players (see section 10.4.2.2 and Van Zandt and Vives (2007)). A sufficient statistic for the posterior of a player under normality is the conditional expectation $E[\theta \mid s] = (\tau_\theta\bar{\theta} + \tau_\varepsilon s)/(\tau_\theta + \tau_\varepsilon)$, which increases with $\bar{\theta}$. It then follows that extremal equilibrium thresholds $(-\theta^*, -s^*)$ increase with $\bar{\theta}$. The same result holds for reasonable out-of-equilibrium dynamics that eliminate the middle "unstable" equilibrium. For example, out-of-equilibrium adjustment can take

[39] An early model with incomplete information that obtains a unique Bayesian equilibrium with a positive probability of a crisis is Postlewaite and Vives (1987). See Allen and Gale (2006) for a survey of models of financial crises.

the form of best-reply dynamics, where, at any stage after the perturbation from equilibrium, a new state of the world θ is drawn independently and a player responds to the strategy threshold used by other players at the previous stage.

The framework can be extended to include large players (see Corsetti et al. (2004) on currency attacks) and to relax the strategic complementarity condition of actions to a single-crossing condition and obtain a uniqueness result in switching strategies, assuming that signals fulfill the monotone likelihood ratio property (see Goldstein and Pauzner (2005) for a model of bank runs when the depositor's game is not one of strategic complementarities).[40] An important extension is to consider dynamic settings. See Morris and Shin (2003) and Dasgupta (2007) for a noisy social learning application, Chamley (2003) for dynamic speculative attacks (although in this model all information is public), and Frankel and Pauzner (2000), Heidhues and Melissas (2006), and Giannitsarou and Toxvaerd (2007) for uniqueness results in dynamic coordination games. Another extension to which we turn is to make public information endogenous.

Endogenous public information. Suppose now that the public signal comes from a price in a financial market with liquidation value θ (we will here follow Angeletos and Werning (2006); see also Tarashev (2007)). The financial market meets before the coordination game and is as in section 4.2.1 but without uninformed traders. There is a unit mass of CARA-informed traders ($\mu = 1$), each informed trader receiving a signal about θ of precision τ_ε, and the variance of noise trading is given by τ_u^{-1}. We know that in this market the precision of prices is given by $\tau = \tau_\theta + \tau_u a^2$, where $a = \rho^{-1}\tau_\varepsilon$ (with ρ the coefficient of absolute risk aversion of the informed traders). Suppose that in the coordination game $h(\theta) = \theta$, and note, as before, that the prior can be interpreted as a public signal. It follows that there will be multiple equilibria if and only if $\tau/\sqrt{\tau_\varepsilon} = (\tau_\theta + \tau_u\rho^{-2}\tau_\varepsilon^2)/\sqrt{\tau_\varepsilon} > \sqrt{2\pi}$ (this is the result we had before replacing τ_θ by τ). Contrary to the case where public information is exogenous, the inequality holds if τ_ε is large (and also if τ_u is large). If either τ_ε or τ_u tend to ∞, both everyone acting and no one acting are equilibria in the range $\theta \in (\theta_{\mathrm{L}}, \theta_{\mathrm{H}})$, as in the full-information case. The point is that increasing private precision τ_ε (or reducing noise in the public signal) also increases public precision $\tau = \tau_\theta + \tau_u a^2$ in such a way that we stay in the multiplicity region.

In many circumstances crises will affect the return in the asset market. For example, in a currency attack the real rate of return on (the attacked currency) peso forward contracts depends on the outcome of the crisis. This implies a new role of the price in the asset market, on top of the traditional ones as index of scarcity and conveyor of information (as in chapter 3), influencing the fundamental value by affecting the outcome of the coordination game. This

[40] However, then it cannot be guaranteed that there are no other equilibria in nonmonotone strategies.

can be incorporated in the analysis by having the asset return depend on the outcome of the coordination game. One way to do it, preserving normality in the information structure, is to let $-\Phi^{-1}(\tilde{y})$ be the liquidation value. In this case it is easy to check that the asset demand has the inverted-S form (backward bending) and therefore there is a region of values of (θ, u) for which there are three equilibria in the asset market, and this translates into multiple equilibria in the coordination game. The reason for the backward-bending demand curve for the asset is that a high price realization decreases the incentives to attack (by signaling a low θ) but a reduced attack in turn raises the return of the asset. If the second effect is strong enough demand may increase with the price. Multiple equilibria obtain again in the low noise scenarios when either τ_ε or τ_u is large. As before, as noise vanishes the common knowledge outcomes are approached. Another interesting result is that, even with no equilibrium multiplicity, price volatility may increase with a reduction in noise trading.

In the speculative-attacks model of Tarashev (2007) the information role of the interest rate allows us to explain abrupt currency attacks without resorting to sunspots and multiple equilibria. Furthermore, the analysis finds that an intervention in the foreign exchange market may reinforce a currency peg because of its influence on the precision of public information.

Hellwig et al. (2006) analyze in depth the role of interest rates in self-fulfilling currency crises. In their model multiplicity of equilibria arises in a primary market, in which interest rates have direct effects on payoffs as well as aggregate information. This is in contrast with the above model by Angeletos and Werning (2006), where information aggregation occurs through the price of a derivative asset, which has no direct effect on the payoffs of players. The root of the multiplicity is similar to the models in Gennotte and Leland (1990) and Barlevy and Veronesi (2003): the nonmonotonicity of demand and supply schedules for assets. Gennotte and Leland and Barlevy and Veronesi conclude that the results obtained in the global games literature on the uniqueness of equilibrium do not apply to models of currency markets where markets provide endogenous signals.

In Angeletos et al. (2006) public information is endogenously generated by policy interventions. To a coordination game of the type studied at the start of the section Angeletos et al. add a previous stage at which a policy maker can influence the payoff from acting (i.e., attacking the currency or running on the bank). Whenever there are different types of policy maker, and since his actions are observed by the agents before deciding whether to act, signaling is introduced in the coordination game. The consequence is that multiple equilibria are introduced as a combination of signaling and coordination. For example, by intervening the policy maker may reveal that he is in a range of intermediate types and this can be used by agents to coordinate on multiple reactions.

Angeletos et al. (2007a) extend the basic static global coordination game of regime change (the binary action game of strategic complementarities with incomplete information) to a dynamic context where each can act in many periods and can learn about the fundamentals. Here endogenous public information at any point in time comes in the form of knowledge that the regime has survived past attacks. Angeletos et al. find equilibrium multiplicity under the same conditions that guarantee uniqueness in the static benchmark. Multiplicity is generated by the combination of the endogenous public information and the arrival of new private signals. It is also found that the fundamentals may determine the eventual outcome (i.e., whether the status quo is overturned) but not the timing or the number of attacks. Furthermore, the dynamics of the economy alternate between phases of calm, where no attack is possible and agents only accumulate information, and phases of distress, where a large attack can occur triggered by a small change in information (or in the fundamentals).

Angeletos et al. (2007b) and Goldstein et al. (2007) model complementarities that arise out of information externalities. Angeletos et al. (2007b) look at a two-way feedback between investment and prices in financial markets when there is dispersed information on investment opportunities. Asset prices tend to increase with aggregate investment (the public signal) since higher investment is linked with high profitability. In turn, high asset prices induce high investment. Angeletos et al. show this endogenous complementarity makes investors react too much to noise (or correlated errors in private signals of profitability) and too little to fundamentals. This is a form of beauty-contest inefficiency in the interaction between financial and real activity (see sections 1.4.3 and 8.3.2.2 for expositions of Keynes's beauty contest metaphor).[41]

In summary, crashes can be explained in a range of competitive rational expectations models with some of the following ingredients: uncertain precision of the information of traders, multiple equilibria, or liquidity shortages. There is also a range of theories that explains bubbles in asset markets. Crises with an underlying coordination problem of investors, such as currency attacks or runs in banking markets, can be modeled as a game of strategic complementarities and we can derive comparative statics results useful for policy analysis and a multiplier effect for public information even if there are multiple equilibria. Conditions are also found so that a unique equilibrium exists. However, the consideration of the endogeneity of public signals makes the analysis more complex and will tend to restore the multiplicity of equilibria.

8.5 Summary

This chapter reviews financial dynamics with heterogeneous information in the rational expectations tradition where informed traders condition on current prices. We study Bayesian equilibria of a well-specified dynamic game in which traders make optimal use of the information they have.

---

[41] See also Subrahmanyam and Titman (2001) and Ozdenoren and Yuan (forthcoming) for other models of the feedback effect between the real sector and financial markets.

A class of markets is studied in which a competitive risk-neutral market-making sector sets prices:

- It is shown that the market is semi-strong efficient and the relation between price informativeness and volatility established.
- A closed-form solution is provided for a standard dynamic noisy rational expectations market with long-term investors and heterogeneous information. The solution cuts through a potential infinite regress expectational problem and the evolution of market parameters of interest (trading intensity, price informativeness, volatility, and volume) is studied.
- The equilibrium with long-term investors serves as a benchmark of comparison for the case of investors with a short horizon. It is found that short-term traders are less responsive to their private signals than long-term ones and that short horizons enhance or reduce accumulated price informativeness depending on the temporal pattern of private-information arrival.
    - With concentrated arrival of information, short horizons reduce final price informativeness; with diffuse arrival of information, short horizons enhance it.
    - Furthermore, short horizons may imply that traders have incentives to herd in information acquisition, either in terms of the assets researched or the type of information, or concentrate only on short-term information.

The chapter also examines markets with no risk-neutral market makers, where market making involves a risk premium, and provides explanations for technical analysis, "excess" volatility, trade with no news, general dynamic patterns of volume in the presence of private and public information, and departures of prices from fundamentals. We find, in particular that:

- Similar to the static model and as long as there is no residual uncertainty in the liquidation value and noise trade increments are uncorrelated, price in any period equals the average expectations of investors plus a risk-bearing component; otherwise, traders speculate both on the terminal value and on price changes and prices may be farther away from or closer to fundamental values than the average expectations of investors. The predictability of noise trading and lessened residual uncertainty push prices away from fundamental values in relation to average expectations.
- Market depth has a risk-bearing component on top of the adverse selection component.
- The combined presence of risk-averse market makers and traders with short horizons induces multiple equilibria (a high and a low volatility equilibrium) except if the stock of noise trading is independent across periods; there is always an equilibrium, which is stable, in which prices

are farther away from fundamental values than the average expectations of investors.

Finally, we have seen how frenzies, crashes, and crises, as well as other market anomalies, can be explained without recourse to the irrationality of market participants. Games of strategic complementarities with incomplete information prove useful in the study of crises with an underlying coordination problem and the role of policy interventions. In particular, it is possible to obtain comparative statics results even in the presence of multiple equilibria. In some circumstances the degree of strategic complementarity is lessened and a unique equilibrium is obtained. The conditions under which uniqueness holds, however, are stringent, in particular when public information is endogenously generated.

8.6 Appendix

8.6.1 Proofs

Proof of proposition 8.2 (see p. 282). At a candidate linear equilibrium, proposition 8.1 applies and prices are normally distributed. The information of trader i about θ in period T, $\{s_i^T, p^T\}$, can be summarized in $\{\tilde{s}_{iT}, p_T\}$. At stage T trader i chooses x_{iT} to maximize

$$-E\Big[\exp\Big\{-\rho\sum_{k=1}^{T}\pi_{ik}\Big\}\ \Big|\ s_i^T, p^T\Big] = -\exp\Big\{-\rho\sum_{k=1}^{T-1}\pi_{ik}\Big\}E[\mathrm{e}^{-\rho\pi_{iT}} \mid \tilde{s}_{iT}, p_T].$$

It then follows, as in the static model (as in section 4.2.1 with $\rho_{\mathrm{U}} = 0$), that $X_T(\tilde{s}_{it}, p_T) = a_T(\tilde{s}_{it} - p_T)$, $a_T = \rho^{-1}(\sum_{k=1}^{T}\tau_{\varepsilon_k})$. Substituting the optimal period-T strategy in the last-period profit π_{iT}, we obtain

$$E[\mathrm{e}^{-\rho\hat{\pi}_{iT}} \mid \tilde{s}_{iT}, p_T] = \exp\Big\{-\tfrac{1}{2}\rho^2 a_T^2\Big(\sum_{k=1}^{T}\tau_{\varepsilon_k} + \tau_T\Big)^{-1}(\tilde{s}_{iT} - p_T)^2\Big\}.$$

At stage $T-1$ agent i chooses x_{iT-1} to maximize

$$\begin{aligned}
-E\Big[\exp\Big\{-\rho\Big(\sum_{k=1}^{T-1}\pi_{ik} + \pi_{iT}\Big)\Big\}\ \Big|\ s_i^{T-1}, p^{T-1}\Big]
&= -\exp\Big\{-\rho\sum_{k=1}^{T-2}\pi_{ik}\Big\}E[\mathrm{e}^{-\rho(\pi_{iT-1}+\pi_{iT})} \mid s_i^{T-1}, p^{T-1}]\\
&= -\exp\Big\{-\rho\sum_{k=1}^{T-2}\pi_{ik}\Big\}E[E[\mathrm{e}^{-\rho\pi_{iT-1}}\mathrm{e}^{-\rho\pi_{iT}} \mid s_i^T, p^T] \mid s_i^{T-1}, p^{T-1}]
\end{aligned}$$

or (since $\pi_{iT-1} = (p_T - p_{T-1})x_{iT-1}$)

$$-\exp\Big\{-\rho\sum_{k=1}^{T-2}\pi_{ik}\Big\}E[\mathrm{e}^{-\rho\pi_{iT-1}}E[\mathrm{e}^{-\rho\pi_{iT}} \mid \tilde{s}_{iT}, p_T] \mid s_i^{T-1}, p^{T-1}].$$

This is equivalent to

$$-\exp\left\{-\rho\sum_{k=1}^{T-2}\pi_{ik}\right\}E[\mathrm{e}^{-\rho\phi_{iT-1}}\mid s_i^{T-1},p^{T-1}],$$

where $\phi_{iT-1}=(p_T-p_{T-1})x_{iT-1}+\frac{1}{2}\rho a_T^2(\sum_{k=1}^{T}\tau_{\varepsilon_k}+\tau_T)^{-1}(\tilde{s}_{iT}-p_T)^2$.

It is not difficult to see that a sufficient statistic for $\{s_i^{T-1},p^{T-1}\}$ in the estimation of p_T-p_{T-1} and $\tilde{s}_{iT}-p_T$ is $\{\tilde{s}_{iT-1},p_{T-1}\}$.

We will use the following result (see section 10.2.4). Let the n-dimensional random vector z be normally distributed with mean 0 and variance-covariance matrix Σ and $w=c+b'z+z'Az$, where $c\in\mathbb{R}$, $b\in\mathbb{R}^n$, and A is an $n\times n$ matrix. If the matrix $\Sigma^{-1}+2\rho A$ is positive definite and $\rho>0$, then

$$E[-\mathrm{e}^{-\rho w}]=-(\det(\Sigma))^{-1/2}(\det(\Sigma^{-1}+2\rho A))^{-1/2}\mathrm{e}^{-\rho[c-\rho b'(\Sigma^{-1}+2\rho A)^{-1}b/2]}.$$

Let us rewrite the term ϕ_{iT-1} in quadratic form $c+b'z+z'Az$, where z is a bivariate (column) vector $z=(\tilde{s}_{iT}-p_T-\mu_1,p_T-\mu_2)$ with $\mu_1=E[\tilde{s}_{iT}-p_T\mid\tilde{s}_{iT-1},p_{T-1}]$ and $\mu_2=E[p_T\mid\tilde{s}_{iT-1},p_{T-1}]$, and where $c=(\mu_2-p_{T-1})x_{iT-1}+\frac{1}{2}\rho a_T^2(\sum_{k=1}^{T}\tau_{\varepsilon_k}+\tau_T)^{-1}\mu_1^2$; b equals the (column) vector $(\rho a_T^2(\sum_{k=1}^{T}\tau_{\varepsilon_k}+\tau_T)^{-1}\mu_1,x_{iT-1})$; and A is a 2×2 matrix with $a_{11}=\frac{1}{2}\rho a_T^2(\sum_{k=1}^{T}\tau_{\varepsilon_k}+\tau_T)^{-1}$ and the rest zeros. Given that z is normally distributed conditional on $\{\tilde{s}_{iT-1},p_{T-1}\}$ with zero mean and nonsingular variance-covariance matrix Σ, and since $\Sigma^{-1}+2\rho A$ can be checked to be positive definite, it follows that

$$\begin{aligned}&E[\mathrm{e}^{-\rho\phi_{iT-1}}\mid\tilde{s}_{iT-1},p_{T-1}]\\&\quad=-(\det(\Sigma))^{-1/2}(\det(\Sigma^{-1}+2\rho A))^{-1/2}\mathrm{e}^{-\rho[c-\rho b'(\Sigma^{-1}+2\rho A)^{-1}b/2]}.\end{aligned}\qquad(*)$$

Denote the elements of $H=(\Sigma^{-1}+2\rho A)^{-1}$ by h_{ij}. Then the FOC to maximize $(*)$ with respect to x_{iT-1} yields

$$\mu_2-p_{T-1}-\rho(h_{22}x_{iT-1}+h_{12}b_1)=0$$

or

$$x_{iT-1}=\frac{\mu_2-p_{T-1}}{\rho h_{22}}-\frac{h_{12}}{h_{22}}\rho a_T^2\left(\sum_{k=1}^{T}\tau_{\varepsilon_k}+\tau_T\right)^{-1}\mu_1.$$

The desired position x_{iT-1} in period $T-1$ consists of a CARA-like static term $(E[p_T-p_{T-1}\mid\tilde{s}_{iT-1},p_{T-1}]/\rho h_{22})$ plus a term which is proportional to the expected position in period T $(E[a_T(\tilde{s}_{iT}-p_T)\mid\tilde{s}_{iT-1},p_{T-1}])$.

Standard (but tedious) calculations yield the following:

$$\begin{aligned}\mu_1=&\left(\tau_{T-1}\left(\sum_{k=1}^{T}\tau_{\varepsilon_k}+\tau_T\right)\left(\sum_{k=1}^{T-1}\tau_{\varepsilon_k}\right)\right)\\&\times\left(\tau_T\left(\sum_{k=1}^{T-1}\tau_{\varepsilon_k}+\tau_{T-1}\right)\left(\sum_{k=1}^{T}\tau_{\varepsilon_k}\right)\right)^{-1}(\tilde{s}_{iT-1}-p_{T-1}),\end{aligned}$$

$$\mu_2 - p_{T-1} = \Big(\Delta\tau_T\Big(\sum_{k=1}^{T-1}\tau_{\varepsilon_k}\Big)\Big)\Big(\tau_T\Big(\sum_{k=1}^{T-1}\tau_{\varepsilon_k} + \tau_{T-1}\Big)\Big)^{-1}(\tilde{s}_{iT-1} - p_{T-1}),$$

$$h_{22} = \Big(\sum_{k=1}^{T}\tau_{\varepsilon_k}\Big)^2(\tau_{\varepsilon_k})^{-1}(\det(\Sigma^{-1} + 2\rho A))^{-1},$$

$$h_{12} = -\Big(\sum_{k=1}^{T}\tau_{\varepsilon_k}\Big)\Big(\sum_{k=1}^{T-1}\tau_{\varepsilon_k}\Big)(\tau_{\varepsilon_k})^{-1}(\det(\Sigma^{-1} + 2\rho A))^{-1},$$

$$\det(\Sigma^{-1} + 2\rho A) = \Big(\sum_{k=1}^{T}\tau_{\varepsilon_k}\Big)^2\Big(\tau_T\Big(\sum_{k=1}^{T-1}\tau_{\varepsilon_k} + \tau_{T-1}\Big) - \tau_{T-1}\Big(\sum_{k=1}^{T-1}\tau_{\varepsilon_k}\Big)\Big) \times (\Delta\tau_T\tau_{\varepsilon_T})^{-1}.$$

Plugging these values into the expression for x_{iT-1}, we obtain after simplifying $x_{iT-1} = a_{T-1}(\tilde{s}_{iT-1} - p_{T-1})$, with $a_{T-1} = \rho^{-1}(\sum_{k=1}^{T-1}\tau_{\varepsilon_k})$. Substituting the optimal period $T-1$ strategy in the profit π_{iT-1} and after some (again tedious) computations, we obtain

$$E[e^{-\rho(\pi_{iT-1}+\pi_{iT})} \mid \tilde{s}_{iT-1}, p_{T-1}] = \exp\{-\tfrac{1}{2}\rho^2 a_{T-1}^2(\tau_{iT-1})^{-1}(\tilde{s}_{iT-1} - p_{T-1})^2\}.$$

At stage $T-2$ trader i chooses X_{iT-2} to maximize

$$-\exp\Big\{-\rho\sum_{k=1}^{T-3}\pi_{ik}\Big\} \text{ multiplied by }$$
$$E[E[e^{-\rho\pi_{iT-2}}e^{-\rho(\pi_{iT-1}+\pi_{iT})} \mid \tilde{s}_{iT-1}, p_{T-1}] \mid s_i^{T-2}, p^{T-2}] \quad \text{or}$$

$$-\exp\Big\{-\rho\sum_{k=1}^{T-3}\pi_{ik}\Big\} \text{ multiplied by }$$
$$E[e^{-\rho\pi_{iT-2}}E[e^{-\rho(\pi_{iT-1}+\pi_{iT})} \mid \tilde{s}_{iT-1}, p_{T-1}] \mid s_i^{T-2}, p^{T-2}],$$

which is equivalent to

$$-\exp\Big\{-\rho\sum_{k=1}^{T-3}\pi_{ik}\Big\}E[e^{-\rho\phi_{iT-2}} \mid s_i^{T-2}, p^{T-2}],$$

where $\phi_{iT-2} = (p_{T-1} - p_{T-2})x_{iT-2} + \frac{1}{2}\rho a_{T-1}^2(\sum_{k=1}^{T-1}\tau_{\varepsilon_k} + \tau_{T-1})^{-1}(\tilde{s}_{iT-1} - p_{T-1})^2$.

This is exactly of the same form as obtained in the recursion from T to $T-1$ and therefore the optimal strategy will be $x_{iT-2} = a_{T-2}(\tilde{s}_{iT-2} - p_{T-2})$, with $a_{T-2} = \rho^{-1}(\sum_{k=1}^{T-2}\tau_{\varepsilon_k})$. The result follows by induction. □

Proof of proposition 8.3 (see p. 286). At any linear equilibrium, and as in section 8.1, z^t and p^t, $t = 1, 2$, are observationally equivalent. In period $t = 2$ at a linear equilibrium a sufficient statistic for θ with the information $\{s_i^2, p^2\}$ is $\{\tilde{s}_{i2}, p^2\}$ or $\{\tilde{s}_{i2}, z^2\}$ and because of normality of random variables and CARA utility functions, we have that

$$X_2(\tilde{s}_{i2}, p^2) = (\rho\,\text{var}[\theta \mid \tilde{s}_{i2}, z^2])^{-1}(E[\theta \mid \tilde{s}_{i2}, z^2] - p_2).$$

From the expressions for

$$E[\theta \mid z^2] = \tau_2^{-1}\Big(\tau_\theta\bar{\theta} + \tau_u \sum_{t=1}^{2} \Delta a_t z_t\Big)$$

and

$$E[\theta \mid \tilde{s}_{i2}, z^2] = \Big(\tau_2 + \sum_{t=1}^{2} \tau_{\varepsilon_t}\Big)^{-1}\Big(\tau_2 E[\theta \mid z^2] + \sum_{t=1}^{2} \tau_{\varepsilon_t}\tilde{s}_{i2}\Big),$$

where $\tau_2 = \tau_\theta + \tau_u \sum_{t=1}^{2}(\Delta a_t)^2$, we obtain

$$X_2(\tilde{s}_{i2}, p^2) = \rho^{-1}\Big(\sum_{t=1}^{2} \tau_{\varepsilon_t}\Big)(\tilde{s}_{i2} - p_2) + \rho^{-1}\tau_2(E[\theta \mid z^2] - p_2).$$

Second-period market clearing implies that

$$\int_0^1 X_2(\tilde{s}_{i2}, p^2)\,\mathrm{d}i + u_1 + u_2 = a_2(\theta - p_2) + \rho^{-1}\tau_2(E[\theta \mid z^2] - p_2) + u_1 + u_2 = 0,$$

where $a_2 = \rho^{-1}(\tau_{\varepsilon_1} + \tau_{\varepsilon_2})$. Adding and subtracting $a_1\theta$ to the previous expression and some manipulation yields

$$p_2 = (1 - \lambda_2\Delta a_2)(1 - \lambda_1 a_1)\bar{\theta} + (1 - \lambda_2\Delta a_2)\lambda_1 z_1 + \lambda_2 z_2,$$

where $\lambda_2 = (1+\rho^{-1}\tau_u\Delta a_2)/(a_2+\rho^{-1}\tau_2)$ and $\lambda_1 = (1+\rho^{-1}\tau_u a_1)/(a_1+\rho^{-1}\tau_1)$. To obtain the strategies for period 1, we substitute the period-2 strategy $x_{i2} = X_2(\tilde{s}_{i2}, p^2)$ into the objective function of an informed trader, $t = 1, 2$:

$$E[-\mathrm{e}^{-\rho\pi_{i2}} \mid \tilde{s}_{i2}, z^2] = -\exp\Big\{-\tfrac{1}{2}\rho^2\Big(\tau_2 + \sum_{k=1}^{2} \tau_{\varepsilon_k}\Big)^{-1} x_{i2}^2\Big\}.$$

In period 1 trader i chooses x_{i1} to maximize

$$E\Big[-\exp\Big\{-\rho\Big((p_2 - p_1)x_{i1} + \tfrac{1}{2}\rho\Big(\tau_2 + \sum_{k=1}^{2} \tau_{\varepsilon_k}\Big)^{-1} x_{i2}^2\Big)\Big\} \;\Big|\; s_{i1}, z_1\Big].$$

Using the same technique as in the proof of proposition 8.2 we can check that the solution to the above optimization problem is given by

$$x_{i1} = \frac{E[p_2 \mid s_{i1}, z_1] - p_1}{\rho\kappa_1} + \frac{\kappa_1 - \kappa_2}{\kappa_1} E[x_{i2} \mid s_{i1}, z_1],$$

where

$$\kappa_1 = \lambda_2^2/((\tau_1 + \tau_{\varepsilon_1})\lambda_2^2 + \tau_u(1 - \lambda_2\Delta a_2)^2),$$

$$\kappa_2 = \kappa_1(\tau_u\Delta a_2\lambda_2^{-1} + \tau_{\varepsilon_2})\Big(\tau_2 + \sum_{k=1}^{2} \tau_{\varepsilon_k}\Big)^{-1},$$

$$E[p_2 \mid s_{i1}, z_1] = \lambda_2\Delta a_2 E[\theta \mid s_{i1}, z_1] + (1 - \lambda_2\Delta a_2)p_1,$$

$$E[x_{i2} \mid z_1, s_{i1}] = \rho^{-1}\Big(\tau_2 + \sum_{k=1}^{2} \tau_{\varepsilon_k}\Big)(1 - \lambda_2\Delta a_2)(E[\theta \mid s_{i1}, z_1] - p_1),$$

where $p_1 = \lambda_1 z_1 + (1 - \lambda_1 a_1)\bar{\theta}$.

Identifying parameters we have that $a_1 = \rho^{-1}\tau_{\varepsilon_1}$, and using the expression for x_{i2} we find that

$$x_{i1} = a_1 s_{i1} - \lambda_1^{-1} p_1 + \lambda_1^{-1}(1 - a_1\lambda_1)\bar{\theta} = a_1(s_{i1} - p_1) + \rho^{-1}\tau_1(E[\theta \mid z_1] - p_1).$$

□

8.7 Exercises

***8.1** (*a small supply shock can have a large price impact*). Consider the first-period market in the two-period model of section 8.2.1 but where information arrives in the form of three possible signals s^1, s^2, and s^3. Signal s^{k+1} is obtained from s^k by adding (normal) independent noise, $k = 1, 2$. There are two possible states of the world. In the first state, half the traders receive signal s^1 and the other half signal s^2. In the second state, half the traders receive signal s^2 and the other half signal s^3. Traders know the precision of the signal they receive but not the precision of the signals received by others. Therefore, only traders who receive signal s^2 are unsure about the population signal distribution. Characterize the inference problem and the trading strategies of the three types of traders. Are demand functions linear? What does a type-s^2 trader infer when he sees a price well away from his expectation? Is it plausible that the demand functions for type-s^2 traders are very responsive to price changes? Speculate now on the potential effects of a small unexpected supply shock, observable to all the traders.

Hint. See Romer (1993).

****8.2** (*multiplicity of equilibria with short-term traders and risk-averse market making*). Consider the two-period model of section 8.2.1 with concentrated information arrival where a proportion $\mu > 0$ of traders have a short horizon (one period), while the remaining proportion $1 - \mu$ of traders have a long horizon. Characterize the linear equilibria. Show that there are two equilibria. Perform a comparative statics analysis of second-period price informativeness with respect to the measure of short-term traders. Does the answer depend on the selected equilibrium?

Solution. Read the text for inspiration and propositions 3 and 8 and corollaries 2 and 3 in Cespa (2002) for the results.

8.3 (*the effect of short-term trading on price precision*). Consider the model of section 8.3 and show the following results.

(i) Let $\tau_{\varepsilon_t} = 0$ for $t = 2, \dots, T$, then the information revealed by prices with short-term traders will be bounded above away from the static (long-term) case.

(ii) Let $\tau_{\varepsilon_t} = \tau_{\varepsilon_1}$ for $t = 1, \dots, T$, then the price precision of the final price with short-term traders is bounded below and away (uniformly in T) from the long-term case.

Solution. (i) It follows from $\sum_{t=1}^{T} \Delta a_t = a$, where $\Delta a_t > 0$ for all t are the net trading intensities with short horizons and a is the static trading intensity used by long-term traders in the first period.

(ii) Fix T. The minimum of $\tau_T = \tau_\theta + \tau_u \sum_{t=1}^{T} (\Delta a_T)^2$ subject to $\sum_{t=1}^{T} \Delta a_T = a_T$ is attained by setting $\Delta a_T = a_T$, which is precisely the long-term solution. Now, let Δa_T denote the short-term solution, then $\tau_T(\text{short-term}) - \tau_T(\text{long-term}) = \tau_u(\sum_{t=1}^{T} (\Delta a_T)^2 - Ta^2) = \tau_u((a_1)^2 - a^2 + \sum_{t=2}^{T} (\Delta a_T)^2 - (T-1)a^2)$, which is bounded away from zero since $a_1 \leqslant a_1^{(2)} < a$, where $a_1^{(2)}$ is the value of a_1 when $T = 2$. The first inequality follows from the expression: $a_1 = \rho^{-1}(\tau_{\varepsilon_1}^{-1} + (\tau_2)^{-1})^{-1}$ and $\tau_2 = \tau_\theta + \tau_u((a_1)^2 + (a_2 - a_1)^2)$, noticing that a_1 increases with a_2 and a_2 reaches its maximum possible value when $T = 2$ (equal to $2a$). The second inequality is obvious.

***8.4** (*learning from volume and technical analysis*). Discuss what traders can learn from information on volume in the context of the two-period models of section 8.1.2. Consider in particular the models of Brown and Jennings (1989) and Grundy and McNichols (1989). Suppose now that traders use market orders and learn from past prices and possibly volume, but a group of traders is uncertain about the precision of the signals of another group of traders (say that this precision follows a random process). Sketch a model and conjecture results on the usefulness of technical analysis.

Hint. See Blume et al. (1994).

***8.5** (*short-term trading and managers' incentives*). Consider the model of section 8.3 with $T = 2$. Suppose that the gross liquidation value of the stock at $T + 1$ is given by $v = e + \theta$, where e is the unobservable effort exerted by the manager of the firm at $t = 0$ at cost $\frac{1}{2}e^2$. The manager has a CARA utility function over income minus the cost of effort and quits at $t = 2$ before the firm is liquidated. A manager can always earn no income with no effort. The owners of the firm give an incentive contract to the manager, linear in the stock prices of periods 1 and 2, that maximizes their wealth. Informed trader i receives a private signal $s_i = e + \theta + \varepsilon_i$ (with the usual properties) in period $t = 1$. Show that:

(i) No matter whether traders have long or short horizons, it is never optimal to base the compensation of the manager on the price in the first period.

(ii) With short-term trading the manager exerts less effort because the price in period 2 is less informative than when traders have a long horizon.

(iii) Speculate on what would be happen if there was a constant flow of private information and the gross liquidation value of the stock at $T+1$ was given by $v = e_1 + e_2 + \theta$, where e_t is the effort exerted by the manager in period t.

Solution. See Calcagno and Heider (2006) for (i) and (ii).

References

Abreu, D., and M. Brunnermeier. 2003. Bubbles and crashes. *Econometrica* 71:173–204.

Admati, A., and P. Pfleiderer. 1988. A theory of intraday patterns: volume and price variability. *Review of Financial Studies* 1:3–40.

Allen, F., and D. Gale. 2000. Bubbles and crises. *Economic Journal* 110:236–55.

——. 2006. *Understanding Financial Crises.* Oxford University Press.

Allen, F., S. Morris, and A. Postlewaite. 1993. Finite bubbles with short sale constraints and asymmetric information. *Journal of Economic Theory* 61:206–29.

Allen, F., S. Morris, and H. Shin. 2006. Beauty contests and iterated expectations in asset markets. *Review of Financial Studies* 19:719–52.

Angeletos, G., and I. Werning. 2006. Crises and prices: information aggregation, multiplicity, and volatility. *American Economic Review* 96:1720–36.

Angeletos, G., C. Hellwig, and A. Pavan. 2006. Signaling in a global game: coordination and policy traps. *Journal of Political Economy* 114:452–84.

——. 2007a. Dynamic global games of regime change: learning, multiplicity, and the timing of attacks. *Econometrica* 75:711–56.

Angeletos, G., G. Lorenzoni, and A. Pavan. 2007b. Wall Street and Silicon Valley: a delicate interaction. Mimeo, MIT and Northwestern University.

Avery, C., and P. Zemsky. 1998. Multidimensional uncertainty and herd behavior in financial markets. *American Economic Review* 88:724–48.

Bacchetta, P., and E. van Wincoop. 2006. Can information heterogeneity explain the exchange rate determination puzzle? *American Economic Review* 96:552–76.

——. 2007. Higher order expectations in asset pricing. Working Paper, FAME Research Paper Series rp110, Geneva.

Barlevy, G., and P. Veronesi. 2000. Information acquisition in financial markets. *Review of Economic Studies* 67:79–90.

——. 2003. Rational panics and stock market crashes. *Journal of Economic Theory* 110:234–63.

Biais, B., and P. Bossaerts. 1998. Asset prices and trading volume in a beauty contest. *Review of Economic Studies* 65:307–40.

Blume, L., D. Easley, and M. O'Hara. 1994. Market statistics and technical analysis: the role of volume. *Journal of Finance* 49:153–81.

Brown, D., and R. H. Jennings. 1989. On technical analysis. *Review of Financial Studies* 2:527–51.

Bulow, J., and P. Klemperer. 1994. Rational frenzies and crashes. *Journal of Political Economy* 102:1–23.

——. 1999. The generalized war of attrition. *American Economic Review* 89:175–89.

Calcagno, R., and F. Heider. 2006. Market based compensation, liquidity and short-term trading. Mimeo.

Campbell, J., and A. Kyle. 1993. Smart money, noise trading, and stock price behavior. *Review of Economic Studies* 60:1–34.

Campbell, J., and R. Shiller. 1987. Cointegration tests of present value models. *Journal of Political Economy* 95:1062–88.

Cao, H. H., and H. Ou-Yang. 2005. Bubbles and panics in a frictionless market with heterogeneous expectations. Working Paper.

Caplin, A., and J. Leahy. 1994. Business as usual, market crashes, and wisdom after the fact. *American Economic Review* 84:584–665.

Carlsson, H., and E. van Damme. 1993. Global games equilibrium selection. *Econometrica* 61:989–1018.

Cespa, G. 2002. Short-term investment and equilibrium multiplicity. *European Economic Review* 46:1645–70.

Cespa, G., and X. Vives. 2007. Dynamic trading and asset prices: Keynes vs. Hayek. Mimeo, IESE.

Chamley, C. 2003. Dynamic speculative attacks. *American Economic Review* 93:603–21.

Chari, V., and P. Kehoe. 2003. Hot money. *Journal of Political Economy* 111:1262–92.

Chew, M. 1998. Believe the hype: solving coordination problems with television advertising. Mimeo.

Corsetti, G., A. Dasgupta, S. Morris, and H. Shin. 2004. Does one Soros make a difference? A theory of currency crises with large and small traders. *Review of Economic Studies* 71:87–113.

Corsetti, G., B. Guimaraes, and N. Roubini. 2006. International lending of last resort and moral hazard: a model of IMF's catalytic finance. *Journal of Monetary Economics* 53:441–71.

Dasgupta, A. 2007. Coordination and delay in global games. *Journal of Economic Theory* 134:195–225.

De Long, J. B., A. Shleifer, L. H. Summers, and R. J. Waldmann. 1990a. Noise trader risk in financial markets. *Journal of Political Economy* 98:703–38.

——. 1990b. Positive feedback investment strategies and destabilizing rational speculation. *Journal of Finance* 45:379–95.

Demange, G. 2002. Information revelation in a security market: the impact of uncertain participation. Mimeo.

Dennert, J. 1992. Insider trading and the cost of capital in a multi-period economy. Discussion Paper 128, LSE Financial Markets Group.

Diamond, D. W., and P. Dybvig. 1983. Bank runs, deposit insurance, and liquidity. *Journal of Political Economy* 91:401–19.

Diamond, D. W., and R. E. Verrecchia. 1981. Information aggregation in a noisy rational expectations economy. *Journal of Financial Economics* 9:221–35.

——. 1987. Constraints on short-selling and asset price adjustment to private information. *Journal of Financial Economics* 19:277–311.

Dow, J., and G. Gorton. 1994. Arbitrage chains. *Journal of Finance* 49:819–49.

Easley, D., and M. O'Hara. 1987. Price, trade size, and information in securities markets. *Journal of Financial Economics* 19:69–90.

Frankel, D., and A. Pauzner. 2000. Resolving indeterminacy in dynamic settings: the role of shocks. *Quarterly Journal of Economics* 115:285–304.

Froot, K., D. Scharfstein, and J. C. Stein. 1992. Herd on the Street: informational inefficiencies in a market with short-term speculation. *Journal of Finance* 47:1461–84.

Gennotte, G., and A. Kyle. 1992. Intertemporal insider trading with a smooth order flow. Mimeo.

Gennotte, G., and H. Leland. 1990. Market liquidity, hedging, and crashes. *American Economic Review* 80:999–1021.

Giannitsarou, C., and F. Toxvaerd. 2007. Recursive global games. Working Paper.

Glosten, L., and P. R. Milgrom. 1985. Bid, ask and transaction prices in a specialist market with heterogeneously informed traders. *Journal of Financial Economics* 17:71–100.

Goldstein, I., and A. Pauzner. 2005. Demand deposit contracts and the probability of bank runs. *Journal of Finance* 60:1293–328.

Goldstein, I., E. Ozdenoren, and K. Yuan. 2007. Learning and strategic complementarities: implications for speculative. Mimeo, University of Pennsylvania and University of Michigan.

Gorton, G. 1985. Bank supervision of convertibility. *Journal of Monetary Economics* 15:177–93.

——. 1988. Banking panics and business cycles. *Oxford Economic Papers* 40:751–81.

Grossman, S. 1988. An analysis of the implications for stock and futures price volatility of program trading and dynamic hedging strategies. *Journal of Business* 61:275–98.

Grossman, S., and J. Stiglitz. 1980. On the impossibility of informationally efficient markets. *American Economic Review* 70:393–408.

Grundy, B. D., and M. McNichols. 1989. Trade and the revelation of information through prices and direct disclosure. *Review of Financial Studies* 2:495–526.

He, H., and J. Wang. 1995. Differential information and dynamic behavior of stock trading volume. *Review of Financial Studies* 8:919–72.

Heidhues, P., and N. Melissas. 2006. Equilibria in a dynamic global game: the role of cohort effects. *Economic Theory* 28:531–57.

Hellwig, C., A. Mukherji, and A. Tsyvinski. 2006. Self-fulfilling currency crises: the role of interest rates. *American Economic Review* 95:1769–87.

Hirshleifer, D., A. Subrahmanyam, and S. Titman. 1994. Security analysis and trading patterns when some invertors receive information before others. *Journal of Finance* 49:1665–98.

Holden, C. W., and A. Subrahmanyam. 1996. Risk aversion, liquidity, and endogenous short horizons. *Review of Financial Studies* 9:691–722.

Holmström, B., and J. Ricart i Costa. 1986. Managerial incentives and capital management. *Quarterly Journal of Economics* 101:835–60.

Hong, H., and J. Stein. 2003. Differences of opinion, short-sales constraints, and market crashes. *Review of Financial Studies* 16:487–525.

Jacklin, Ch. J., A. Kleidon, and P. Pfleiderer. 1992. Underestimation of portfolio insurance and the crash of October 1987. *Review of Financial Studies* 5:35–63.

Keynes, J. 1936. *The General Theory of Employment, Interest and Money.* Cambridge, MA: Macmillan Cambridge University Press.

Kondor, P. 2005a. The more we know, the less we agree: public announcements and higher-order expectations. Financial Markets Group Discussion Paper 532, London School of Economics.

——. 2005b. Rational trader risk. Financial Markets Group Discussion Paper 533, London School of Economics.

Kyle, A. S. 1985. Continuous auctions and insider trading. *Econometrica* 53:1315–35.

Lee, I. H. 1998. Market crashes and informational avalanches. *Review of Economic Studies* 65:741–59.

LeRoy, S., and W. Parke. 1992. Stock price volatility: tests based on the geometric random walk. *American Economic Review* 82:981–92.

Lyons, R. K. 2001. *The Microstructure Approach to Exchange Rates.* Cambridge, MA: MIT Press.

Milgrom, P. R., and N. Stokey. 1982. Information, trade and common knowledge. *Journal of Economic Theory* 26:17–27.

Morris, S., and H. Shin. 1998. Unique equilibrium in a model of self-fulfilling currency attacks. *American Economic Review* 88:587–97.

Morris, S., and H. Shin. 2002. The social value of public information. *American Economic Review* 92:1521–34.

——. 2003. Global games theory and application. *Advances in Economics and Econometrics: The Eighth World Congress of the Econometric Society* (ed. M. Dewatripont, L. Hansen, and S. Turnovsky). Cambridge University Press.

——. 2004. Coordination risk and the price of debt. *European Economic Review* 48:133–53.

Ozdenoren, E., and K. Yuan. Forthcoming. Feedback effects and asset prices. *Journal of Finance.*

Postlewaite, A., and X. Vives. 1987. Bank runs as an equilibrium phenomenon. *Journal of Political Economy* 95:485–91.

Rochet, J.-C., and X. Vives. 2004. Coordination failures and the lender of last resort: was Bagehot right after all? *Journal of the European Economic Association* 2:1116–47.

Romer, D. 1993. Rational asset-price movements without news. *American Economic Review* 83:1112–30.

Rubinstein, M. 1974. An aggregation theorem for securities markets. *Journal of Financial Economics* 1:225–44.

Santos, M., and M. Woodford. 1997. Rational asset pricing bubbles. *Econometrica* 65:19–57.

Scheinkman, J., and W. Xiong. 2003. Overconfidence and speculative bubbles. *Journal of Political Economy* 111:1183–219.

Shleifer, A., and R. Vishny. 1990. Equilibrium short horizons of investors and firms. *American Economic Review* 80:148–53.

Singleton, K. J. 1987. Asset prices in a time-series model with disparately informed, competitive traders. In *New Approaches to Monetary Economics* (ed. W. Barnett and K. Singleton). Cambridge, MA: Cambridge University Press.

Subrahmanyam, A., and S. Titman. 2001. Feedback from stock prices to cash flows. *Journal of Finance* 56:2389–413.

Tarashev, N. 2007. Speculative attacks and the information role of the interest rate. *Journal of the European Economic Association* 5:1–36.

Tirole, J. 1982. On the possibility of speculation under rational expectations. *Econometrica* 50:1163–82.

——. 1985. Asset bubbles and overlapping generations. *Econometrica* 53:1499–528.

Townsend, R. M. 1983. Forecasting the forecasts of others. *Journal of Political Economy* 91:546–88.

Van Zandt, T., and X. Vives. 2007. Monotone equilibria in Bayesian games of strategic complementarities. *Journal of Economic Theory* 134:339–60.

Veldkamp, L. 2006. Media frenzies in markets for financial information. *American Economic Review* 96:577–601.

Vives, X. 1995. Short-term investment and the informational efficiency of the market. *Review of Financial Studies* 8:125–60.

——. 2005. Complementarities and games: new developments. *Journal of Economic Literature* 43:437–79.

Wang, J. 1993. A model of intertemporal asset prices under asymmetric information. *Review of Economics Studies* 60:249–82.

Zeira, J. 1999. Informational overshooting, booms, and crashes. *Journal of Monetary Economics* 43:237–57.

9

Price and Information Dynamics in Financial Markets

This chapter considers dynamic markets where informed traders use market orders and introduces strategic behavior to analyze the consequences for the informational dynamics of the market and associated trading patterns. It provides the dynamic trading counterpart of the static models presented in section 4.3 and in chapter 5.

Some of the questions addressed in the chapter are:

- Can herding arise in a sequential trading market?
- Is learning from past prices (technical analysis) fast or slow?
- What is the role of market makers in the price-discovery process?
- Will an insider trade slowly, so as to control the potential information leakage out of his trades, or will he try to make a quick "killing"?
- Under what circumstances will an insider have an incentive to dissimulate his trades? When several informed traders compete, will information revelation speed up or slow down?
- In the presence of informed traders will the adverse selection problem faced by market makers improve or worsen as trade proceeds? What are the consequences for the dynamic patterns of market depth, volatility, and volume traded?
- Does it make a difference whether informed traders have long- or short-lived information on the fundamentals? What about if liquidity traders have discretion over when to trade?
- When will a large trader have incentives to manipulate the market or use contrarian strategies? Can a strategic larger trader slow down a price-discovery process?
- Do large risk-averse traders have incentives to engage in strategic hedging and if so what welfare consequences follow?

Section 9.1 addresses dynamic market-order markets and the effect of market microstructure on the informational efficiency of prices. It revisits herding and the slow learning results obtained in chapters 6 and 7 in the context of a financial market, studies the speed of information revelation in a price-discovery mechanism, and the role that market makers play. Section 9.2 considers strategic trading with long-lived information and reviews the seminal Kyle (1985) model and extensions. The main issues of interest are the determination of the trading strategy of large informed agents, with possible camouflage and dissimulation strategies, and their impact on market depth, volatility, and volume, and the effect of competition among informed traders on the speed of information revelation. Section 9.3 examines market manipulation models and the impact of strategic behavior in the price-discovery mechanism presented in section 9.1.3. The section reviews the market manipulation literature and shows how contrarian behavior by an insider may arise to manipulate the price-discovery process. Section 9.4 deals with strategic trading when information is short-lived and liquidity traders can choose when to trade. Section 9.5 studies the dynamic hedging strategies of large risk-averse traders with and without private information on the fundamentals.

9.1 Sequential Trading, Dynamic Market-Order Markets, and the Speed of Learning from Past Prices

This section studies sequential trade markets where informed traders submit market orders and highlights the role of market makers in information revelation (the speed at which prices incorporate information). We present first the benchmark model of Glosten and Milgrom (1985) and we relate it to the results on herding of section 6.1. We then present a model of learning from past prices—a variation of the Cournot-type model considered in section 7.4 (Vives 1993)—and finally a price-discovery mechanism (Vives 1995b).

9.1.1 Sequential Trading and Herding

Glosten and Milgrom (1985) present a sequential trading model in which competitive risk-neutral market makers set a bid–ask spread and earn zero expected profits every period. In their model a single investor arrives each period and trades only once. He always trades one unit and therefore the competitive market maker just sets a bid and an ask price. We present a simplified version of the model with two asset values and two signal values. The investor makes an information-based trade (having received a private binary signal about the liquidation value of the stock θ, which may in turn be high or low) with probability μ and a liquidity-based trade (say, buying, selling, or abstaining with equal probability at the set prices) with the complementary probability. The history of transactions (prices and quantities) is known in any period and the type of the trader is unknown to the market makers. The ask price is the conditional expectation of θ given a buy order and past public information, and the bid price is the conditional expectation of θ given a sell order and past public information.

Adverse selection will imply a positive, and increasing with μ, bid–ask spread. This means that an increase in μ at time t increases the spread at this time.

This does not mean that spreads will be period by period larger in a market with a higher μ since a larger proportion of insiders implies a larger initial spread but also faster information revelation (because of the impact of insiders on prices). That is, the comparison of spreads is ambiguous since more initial adverse selection in the market with a higher μ may be compensated for by more information being revealed. Market makers, as in section 8.1.1, on average lose money with informed traders and they balance the losses with the profits obtained from liquidity traders. The bid and ask prices converge to the true value as market makers accumulate information. The role of the depth parameter λ in the competitive price formation model of section 8.1.1 is played here by the bid–ask spread. Transaction prices follow a martingale. (See exercise 9.1.)

It is worth noting that even though we are in an information structure similar to Bikhchandani et al. (1992) (see section 6.1), in which the informed investor receives a noisy signal about the value of the stock, an informational cascade and herding will not occur with trading à la Glosten and Milgrom. The reason is that the price is a continuous public signal that keeps track of aggregate public information. Suppose that traders ignore their private signals, then the price cannot reveal any information, and both the bid and the ask prices must equal the probability that the value is high given public information (because of the zero expected profit condition). However, an informed trader then has an incentive to follow his signal and this contradicts the cascade assumption. This point has been emphasized by Avery and Zemsky (1998). With only two possible liquidation values there cannot be herding.[1] Still, Park and Sabourian (2006) show how herding can arise with three possible states when there is enough noise and traders believe that extreme outcomes are more likely than intermediate ones. This may happen even if signals conform to a standard monotone likelihood ratio property (see section 10.1.5).[2] Herding and crashes arise naturally when traders are uncertain about the precision of information of other traders (as in Romer (1993), see section 8.4.1). In this case market makers may update the price only a little after observing the order flow because of the uncertainty on the quality of information in the market (see Avery and Zemsky (1998) and Cipriani and Guarino (2007), who also provide experimental evidence using financial professionals as subjects).

Another way to think about the result is to realize that competitive market making induces a payoff externality on informed traders. Indeed, investors, as well as market makers, learn from past trades. The changes in the bid–ask spread due to competitive market making (implying a payoff externality) offset the incentive to herd (because of the informational externality). As market makers learn more about the fundamental value the bid–ask spread is reduced

---

[1] Drehmann et al. (2005) and Cipriani and Guarino (2005) provide experimental evidence in favor of the theoretical prediction of absence of herding by traders in the Glosten–Milgrom/Avery–Zemsky model with two states.

[2] Recall that an informational cascade implies that agents herd (i.e., agents with the same preferences choose the same action) but the converse need not hold (see section 6.1).

and this entices an informed investor to use his information. We will see that a similar phenomenon happens in dynamic market-order markets where the presence of a competitive market-making sector speeds up learning from past prices because they make the market deeper (Vives (1995b) and section 9.1.3).

Dow (2004) extends the Glosten–Milgrom model to incorporate expected-utility-maximizing liquidity traders and shows that multiple equilibria with different endogenous levels of liquidity may arise. Equilibria have the familiar bootstrap property: if a high (low) level of liquidity is anticipated, the liquidity traders increase (decrease) their trading intensity and the spread is small (large).

9.1.2 Slow Learning from Past Prices

Consider a financial market interpretation of the model in section 7.4. Informed traders are risk neutral but face a quadratic adjustment cost in their position (which can be thought of as an imperfect proxy for risk aversion). The horizon is infinite and at each period there is an independent (small) probability $1-\delta > 0$ that the *ex post* liquidation value of the risky asset θ is realized. The probability of θ not being realized in period t, δ^t, tends to 0 as $t \to \infty$.

Each agent of a continuum of long-lived traders receives a private noisy signal about θ at $t = 1$ and submits a market order to a centralized market-clearing mechanism. In period t the information set of agent i is $\{s_i, p^{t-1}\}$. The (random) demand of noise traders (which is sensitive to price) is $u_t - p_t$, where u_t is a random intercept that follows a white noise process. Denote by Δx_t the aggregate demand of the informed traders in period t. The market-clearing condition in period t is thus $u_t - p_t + \Delta x_t = 0$.

Trader i obtains profits

$$\pi_{it} = (\theta - p_t)\Delta x_{it} - \tfrac{1}{2}\lambda(\Delta x_{it})^2$$

from the quantity Δx_{it} demanded in period t.[3] Total profits associated with the final position $\sum_{k=1}^{t} \Delta x_{ir}$ are $\sum_{k=1}^{t} \pi_{ir}$. In any period an informed trader maximizes the (expected) discounted profits with discount factor δ.

This model is formally equivalent to the one developed in section 7.4 and therefore the slow learning (proposition 7.4) and convergence (proposition 7.5) results obtained apply here. Traders do learn from past prices and public information eventually reveals θ but the speed of learning is slow (at the rate $1/\sqrt{t^{1/3}}$) if there is no positive mass of perfectly informed traders. In this case the asymptotic variance of public information in relation to θ is $(3\tau_u)^{-1/3}(\lambda/\tau_\varepsilon)^{2/3}$ and it increases with the amount of noise trading, average noise in the signals, and the slope of adjustment costs. A change in the slope of adjustment costs may increase (for λ small) or decrease (for λ large) the asymptotic variance of $\Delta x_t - \Delta x_t^{\mathrm{f}}$, the difference in net trading at the market and full-information solutions.

[3] In any period a trader (given θ) expects a benefit per unit traded of θ. Note that the adjustment cost is exogenous while with CARA preferences, as in section 9.1.3, it will be endogenous and will depend, in expectation, on the degree of risk aversion times the variance of θ conditional on the information of the trader.

Technical analysis reveals information but at a slow rate. In practice this may render it ineffective. The consequence is that the market equilibrium converges to the full-information equilibrium but it does so slowly.

9.1.3 Price Discovery, Speed of Learning, and Market Microstructure

We have seen how there may be slow learning with technical analysis. We will show now in the context of a price-discovery process that the result depends on the market microstructure. We will see how market makers may accelerate the speed of learning and recover the standard $1/\sqrt{t}$ convergence rate.[4]

Consider a market with a single risky asset, with random *ex post* liquidation value θ, and a riskless asset, with unitary return. There is a continuum of risk-averse competitive informed agents and price-sensitive noise traders. The profits of agent i with position x_i in the asset at price p are given by $\pi_i = (\theta - p)x_i$. Informed agents are risk averse, have CARA utilities, $U(\pi_i) = -\mathrm{e}^{-\rho\pi_i}$, where $\rho > 0$, and their initial wealth is normalized to zero.[5] Informed agent i submits a market order contingent on the information he has. Noise traders submit in the aggregate a price-sensitive order $u - p$.

Price discovery is modeled as an information *tâtonnement* with potentially many stages. At stage t there is a probability $\gamma_t > 0$ that the market opens, the value θ is realized, and trade occurs given that there has not been trade before stage t, and with the complementary probability $1 - \gamma_t$ there is no trade and the *tâtonnement* continues. If at the beginning of stage t the market has not opened, the competitive informed agents, before knowing whether there will be trade in the period, have the opportunity to place orders and noise traders place them. These orders supersede previous orders, which are understood to be canceled if the market does not open.[6] The auctioneer or a centralized trading mechanism quote a notional price and in the next round traders can revise their orders.

Information *tâtonnement* processes are used in the preopening period of continuous, computerized trading systems in several exchanges (for example, in the Paris Bourse (now Euronext), Toronto Stock Exchange, Bolsa de Madrid, or the Arizona Stock Exchange (AZX)). The price-discovery process works as follows. Traders submit orders to the system for a certain period of time before the opening (one or one and a half hours) and theoretical market-clearing prices are quoted periodically as orders accumulate. No trade is made until the end of the *tâtonnement* and at any point agents may revise their orders. This preopening auction is designed to decrease the uncertainty about prices after a period without trade. In the Deutsche Börse with the Xetra system there is an opening

---

[4] This section follows Vives (1995b).

[5] It is worth noting that for small risk, say, when information about θ is very good, the decision of any risk-averse von Neumann–Morgentern decision maker is well approximated by the solution with a CARA function (see, for example, Pratt 1964). This provides robustness to the CARA model when public information ends up revealing θ.

[6] The model as stated may also include the case in which only the orders of noise traders are canceled if the market does not open.

auction which begins with a call phase in which traders can enter and/or modify or delete existing orders before the (short) price determination phase. The indicative auction price is displayed when orders are executable.[7] The call phase has a random end after a minimum period. In the New York Stock Exchange the specialist provides some information to floor traders but there is no organized information *tâtonnement* to set the opening price.[8]

The information *tâtonnement* serves the purpose of eliciting information about the fundamental value of the asset. Notional prices convey noisy information, because of noise trading, about θ. The described process is a crude idealization of actual preopening price-discovery processes and matches the situation with a random opening time (as in Xetra). In the former cases the real pattern of *tâtonnement* from, say, 8.30 a.m. to 10 a.m. and opening at 10 a.m. can be approximated smoothly by a sequence of probabilities $\{\gamma_t\}$ approximating a step function with no trade before 10 a.m. and opening at 10 a.m. Furthermore, the possibility of a communication breakdown at some point (with increasing probability as the opening approaches), implying that the standing order "sticks" and cannot be revised, is similar to the possibility of the market opening at any point in the process (with increasing probability as the end of the horizon approaches).[9]

The information *tâtonnement* process can be interpreted as a mechanism to elicit the aggregate information of informed agents via price quotations. It is analogous to the "dynamic information adjustment process" considered by Jordan (1982, 1985) to implement rational expectations equilibria. In both cases prices serve only as public-information signals and trades are not realized until the iterative process has stopped. Similarly, Kobayashi (1977) assumes that agents trade in any period as if it were the last.[10]

9.1.3.1 *Price Discovery with Exogenous Market Depth*

The information set of trader i is given by $\{s_i, p^{t-1}\}$, where s_i is his private signal about θ and p^{t-1} the sequence of past price quotations. The trader places

[7] Otherwise, the best limit/ask limit is displayed. See Xetra Market Model Release 3 at www.exchange.de.

[8] In some circumstances the revision of orders is allowed at the opening. In particular, this happens when the specialist plans to set an opening price which differs substantially from the previous close or when the order imbalance is large (see Stoll and Whaley 1990, section 1; Whitcomb 1985; Amihud and Mendelson 1987). Madhavan and Panchapagesan (1998) provide evidence that the specialist facilitates price discovery. Cao et al. (2000) provide evidence of price discovery in the preopening at NASDAQ.

[9] However, in the model presented the market either opens or it doesn't for everybody; meanwhile in the communication breakdown case a trader has a certain *individual* probability of being cut off from the market.

[10] Jordan and Kobayashi consider markets with a finite number of agents with no noise added in the price system. With a finite state space convergence then occurs in a finite number of steps. In the model of this section with no noise trading and with a continuum of agents the liquidation value θ would be revealed in the first round since p_1 would then be a linear function of the average signal received by agents, which, according to our convention, equals θ.

a market order $X_{it}(s_i, p^{t-1})$ and noise traders submit the aggregate price contingent order $u_t - p_t$. Taking into account that old orders are canceled, the limit-order book is thus

$$L_t(p_t) = \omega_t - p_t, \quad \text{with } \omega_t = x_t + u_t \text{ and } x_t = \int_0^1 X_{it}(s_i, p^{t-1})\,\mathrm{d}i.$$

The auctioneer quotes a price to clear the market, $p_t = u_t + x_t$. As time evolves the depth of the market is fixed (at 1) and the price elastic noise traders avoid the market breaking down.

All random variables are assumed to be normally distributed. The sequence $\{u_t\}$ is independently and identically distributed with zero mean and variance σ_u^2. Private signals are given by $s_i = \theta + \varepsilon_i$, where $\theta \sim N(\bar{\theta}, \sigma_\theta^2)$ and $\varepsilon_i \sim N(0, \sigma_\varepsilon^2)$, with $\text{cov}[\theta, u_t] = \text{cov}[\theta, \varepsilon_i] = \text{cov}[\varepsilon_i, u_t] = \text{cov}[\varepsilon_i, \varepsilon_j] = 0$, $j \neq i$ for all t.

At stage t a strategy for trader i is a function that maps his private information s_i and the observed past prices p^{t-1} into desired trades. The asset is liquidated and trade realized in the period with probability γ_t, and with probability $1 - \gamma_t$ the trader obtains the continuation (expected) utility, which, because the agent's size is negligible, is independent of his market order in period t. Consequently, the agent behaves as if the asset were to be liquidated and trade realized in the period. Myopic behavior is optimal. From the point of view of an agent the only difference between periods is in information. We restrict our attention to linear equilibria. Given the preferences of traders and symmetric-information structure, and similarly to section 8.1, equilibria will be symmetric.

Traders form a price statistic to estimate θ with their past observations of price quotations and knowledge of strategies. In period t the price sequence p^t can be summarized in a public statistic $\theta_t \equiv E[\theta \mid p^t] = E[\theta \mid z^t]$, where $z_t = a_t\theta + u_t$, with a_t the response coefficient of traders to private information. In this market the price p_t is not a sufficient statistic for the information in the sequence of prices p^t because there is no competitive risk-neutral market-making sector. Given the CARA utility function and the optimality of myopic behavior, the demand of trader i will be given by

$$X_t(s_i, \theta_{t-1}) = \frac{E[\theta - p_t \mid s_i, \theta_{t-1}]}{\rho \operatorname{var}[\theta - p_t \mid s_i, \theta_{t-1}]}.$$

Equilibrium strategies are symmetric and linear in s_i and θ_{t-1}. In equilibrium we have that $a_t = \tau_\varepsilon \tau_u (1 - a_t)/\rho((1 - a_t)^2 \tau_u + \tau_\varepsilon + \tau_{t-1})$, where $\tau_t = \tau_\theta + \tau_u \sum_{k=1}^t a_t^2$. This yields a recursive cubic equation $G_t(a) \equiv (1 - a)(\rho a \tau_\varepsilon^{-1}(1 - a) - 1)\tau_u \tau_\varepsilon + \rho a(\tau_\varepsilon + \tau_{t-1}) = 0$, with potentially three solutions in the interval $(0, 1)$.[11] (However, for t large it can be checked that the solution is unique.) We also have that the response to public information is given by $c_t = \tau_{t-1}/(a_t^{-1}\tau_\varepsilon + (\tau_\varepsilon + \tau_{t-1})(1 - a_t)^{-1})$.

[11] It is worth recalling that in the Muth (1961) rational expectations model if agents are risk averse there are potentially multiple linear equilibria (see McCafferty and Driskill 1980).

It is possible to show that for any linear equilibrium sequence, as $t \to \infty$, the weight given to private information $a_t \to 0$, and the response to public information $c_t \to (\rho\sigma_u^2 + 1)^{-1}$. The informativeness of the price statistic θ_t, $\tau_t \equiv (\text{var}[\theta \mid \theta_t])^{-1}$, is of order $t^{1/3}$ and a_t is of order $t^{1/3}$. The asymptotic precision $A\tau_\infty$ ($\equiv \lim_{t\to\infty} t^{-1/3}\tau_t$) is given by $\tau_u 3^{1/3}(\tau_\varepsilon/\rho)^{2/3}$ and the stated limit results follow from the equilibrium expression for a_t and the fact that $a_t\tau_{t-1} \xrightarrow[t]{} \tau_u(\rho\sigma_\varepsilon^2)^{-1}$ and $t^{-1/3}\tau_t \xrightarrow[t]{} 3^{1/3}\tau_u(\rho\sigma_\varepsilon^2)^{-2/3}$ (those facts follow similarly as in the proof of claims 1 and 2 in the appendix to chapter 7).

As a consequence we have that θ_t converges (almost surely and in mean square) to θ as $t \to \infty$ and $\sqrt{t^{1/3}}(\theta_t - \theta) \xrightarrow{L} N(0, ((\frac{1}{3}\rho\sigma_\varepsilon^2)^2)^{1/3}\sigma_u^2)$. Convergence to the shared-information equilibrium, where informed agents pool their information, learn θ, and trade an amount $X(\theta) = \theta(1 + \rho\sigma_u^2)^{-1}$, is at the slow rate $1/\sqrt{t^{1/3}}$.

The reason for the slow learning and convergence is as before (section 9.1.2 and section 7.4). The responsiveness to private information a_t converges to zero as t grows since Bayesian agents decrease the weight they put on their private signals as public information becomes better and better. Finally, the asymptotic variance of $1/\sqrt{t^{1/3}}(\theta_t - \theta)$ increases with the degree of risk aversion and with the noise in the signals.

9.1.3.2 Price Discovery with Endogenous Market Depth

Let us now introduce a competitive risk-neutral market-making sector in the market. Competitive market makers set p_t equal to the expectation of θ conditional on public information (including the current order flow ω_t). Current public information is given by the intercept ω_t of the order book $L_t(p_t) = \omega_t - p_t$. We thus have

$$p_t = E[\theta \mid \omega^t],$$

where $\omega^t = (\omega_1, \dots, \omega_t)$. The current price p_t is now a sufficient statistic of all past and current prices p^t and those are observationally equivalent to the history of noisy order flows or intercepts of the order books ω^t. We have $E[\theta \mid p^t] = E[\theta \mid p_t] = p_t$. Letting $\tau_t \equiv (\text{var}[\theta \mid p_t])^{-1}$ we have that $\text{var}[p_t \mid p_{t-1}] = \tau_{t-1}^{-1} - \tau_t^{-1}$.

Restricting our attention to equilibria in linear strategies it is possible to show that there is a unique linear equilibrium. The appendix (section 9.7) provides a proof of the following result.

Proposition 9.1 (Vives 1995b). *With a competitive risk-neutral market-making sector there is a unique linear equilibrium. Traders use symmetric strategies*

$$X_t(s_i, p^{t-1}) = a_t(s_i - p_{t-1}), \quad \text{where } a_t = (\rho(\sigma_\varepsilon^2 + \text{var}[p_t \mid p_{t-1}]))^{-1},$$

and prices are given by $p_t = \lambda_t\omega_t + p_{t-1}$, $\omega_t = a_t(\theta - p_{t-1}) + u_t$ *with* $\lambda_t = \tau_u a_t/\tau_t$, $\tau_t = \tau_\theta + \tau_u \sum_{k=1}^t a_k^2$, *and* $\text{var}[p_t \mid p_{t-1}] = \tau_{t-1}^{-1} - \tau_t^{-1}$.

Two properties of the equilibrium are worth highlighting:

- Trader i wants to buy or sell according to whether his private estimate of θ, s_i, is larger or smaller than the market estimate, p_{t-1}. Informed traders' response to private information, a_t, depends negatively, ceteris paribus, on ρ, σ_ε^2, and $\text{var}[p_t \mid p_{t-1}]$. The latter term affects the trading intensity because agents use market orders and face price uncertainty.
- Informed traders optimize against the linear function $p_t = \lambda_t \omega_t + p_{t-1}$ and market makers determine the price function $p_t = E[\theta \mid \omega^t] = E[\theta \mid p_t]$, making λ_t endogenous. It is easy to check that, ceteris paribus, an increase in the depth of the market induces risk-averse informed traders to respond more to their information (since $\text{var}[p_t \mid p_{t-1}]$ is lower). On the contrary, an increase in a_t, again ceteris paribus, induces market makers to put more weight on the order flow in setting p_t, decreasing market depth, as the order flow is more informative. An increase in the precision of prices τ_t, holding a_t constant, has the opposite effect.

The asymptotic properties of the linear equilibrium as $t \to \infty$ are as follows (see exercise 9.3):

- a_t converges monotonically from below to $(\rho\sigma_\varepsilon^2)^{-1}$;
- τ_t and λ_t^{-1} tend to ∞ at a rate of t;
- $\text{var}[p_t]$ converges monotonically from below to σ_θ^2;
- $\text{var}[p_t \mid p_{t-1}] \to 0$;
- the expected volume traded by informed agents $E[|x_{it}|]$ converges from above to $(2/\pi)^{1/2}(\rho\sigma_\varepsilon)^{-1}$; and
- the expected total volume traded converges from above to

$$(2\pi)^{-1/2}((\rho\sigma_\varepsilon)^{-1} + 2\sigma_u).$$

As t grows prices become more informative about θ and τ_t increases linearly. The competitive market-making sector increases the depth of the market with λ_t^{-1} also growing at the rate of t. The conditional variance of prices decreases and induces each informed trader to respond more to his information. However, the notional volume of trade of informed traders decreases since their information advantage with respect to the market makers disappears as prices become more informative. In the limit informed traders lose all information advantage.

The aggregate volume of trade of informed traders against market makers is given by $E[|x_t|] = (2/\pi)^{1/2} a_t (1/\tau_{t-1})^{1/2}$ and tends to 0 with t. From the fact that the precision of prices grows linearly with t it is immediate that

(i) p_t converges (almost surely and in mean square) to θ at a rate of $1/\sqrt{t}$, and

(ii) $\sqrt{t}(p_t - \theta)$ converges in distribution to $N(0, \sigma_u^2\rho^2\sigma_\varepsilon^4)$.

In contrast to the exogenous depth market the responsiveness to private information a_t now increases with t and converges to a positive constant. Market depth is endogenous and increasing as more *tâtonnement* rounds accumulate because of market makers. A risk-averse trader responds more to the deviations of p_{t-1} from the private signal s_i the deeper is the market. The new information in the current price p_t, $z_t = a_t\theta + u_t$, does not vanish for t large and the order of magnitude of the precision of prices τ_t is t.

With a competitive market-making sector, price quotations quickly converge to θ, at the rate $1/\sqrt{t}$, and the asymptotic precision of p_t decreases with ρ, σ_u^2, and σ_ε^2. Convergence is slower if agents are more risk averse, have less precise private information, or noise is larger. Larger ρ and σ_ε^2 make informed agents respond less to information. This same effect follows from increased noise trading if t is large. In summary, the information *tâtonnement* only needs a few rounds to get close to the value of the asset since the precision of prices τ_t grows linearly with the number of rounds t. This can be taken as an indication that the public announcement of theoretical prices proves effective in resolving the uncertainty about the value of the asset (provided that market makers, or traders using limit orders, are present)[12]. We will see in section 9.3.2 how the results are affected by the presence of large strategic traders.

9.1.4 Summary

This section has demonstrated that market microstructure matters for the information revelation properties of prices. Market makers modify the depth of the market in response to the information content of the order flow and speed up information revelation by prices. In the Glosten and Milgrom (1985) model the continuous price variable avoids informational cascades and herding. In the Vives (1993, 1995b) models, market makers avoid a slow learning outcome. Indeed, technical analysis yields slow information revelation from prices. The same lesson applies to price-discovery mechanisms.

9.2 Strategic Trading with Long-Lived Information

In this section we consider dynamic trading by a risk-neutral large informed trader ("insider") facing noise traders and risk-neutral market makers. Section 9.2.1 presents the model in Kyle (1985) and section 9.2.2 several extensions to multiple informed traders, risk aversion, the effects of compulsory disclosure of trades by the insider, as well as a connection with the Glosten–Milgrom model (section 9.1.1).

---

[12] See exercise 9.8, where it is shown that competitive informed traders using limit orders put constant weight on their private information in the *tâtonnement* and therefore ensure that convergence is fast.

9.2.1 The Kyle (1985) Model

Kyle (1985) considers a model where a large trader receives information and trades for T periods with a competitive risk-neutral market-making sector and noise traders. The model is a dynamic version of the model considered in section 5.2 (with no competitive informed traders).

Consider a market with a single risky asset, with random (*ex post*) liquidation value θ, and a riskless asset, with unitary return, traded among noise traders and a large risk-neutral informed trader (the "insider"), who observes θ, with the intermediation of competitive market makers. The informed trader acts strategically, that is, takes into account the effect his demand has on prices and faces a trade-off: taking positions early, and then increasing profits, leaks information to the market and diminishes profits later.

The horizon is finite (T periods). Consider period t. The insider's information is given by $\{\theta, p^{t-1}\}$, where $p^{t-1} = (p_1, \dots, p_{t-1})$ is the sequence of past prices. He submits a market order contingent on the information he has: $\Delta Y_t(\theta, p^{t-1})$. Noise traders submit the aggregate order u_t. The order flow is then $\omega_t = \Delta Y_t + u_t$. Competitive risk-neutral market makers set prices efficiently conditional on the observation of the order flow. That is, p_t is equal to the expectation of θ conditional on public information (including the current order flow ω_t): $p_t = E[\theta \mid \omega^t]$, where $\omega^t = (\omega_1, \dots, \omega_t)$.

All random variables are assumed to be normally distributed with the sequence $\{u_t\}$ independently and identically distributed with zero mean and variance σ_u^2. The liquidation value $\theta \sim N(\bar{\theta}, \sigma_\theta^2)$ and the sequence $\{u_t\}$ are mutually independent. Denote by π_t the profits of the insider directly attributable to his period t trade $\Delta y_t : \pi_t = (\theta - p_t)\Delta y_t$. Then the profits of the insider on trades from period t to T are $\pi_t^T = \sum_{k=t}^{T} \pi_k$. His initial wealth is normalized to zero.

Kyle (1985) solves the dynamic programming problem of the insider and shows that there is a unique linear recursive solution. This corresponds to a linear PBE of the dynamic game between the insider and the competitive market makers. The following proposition is a dynamic version of proposition 5.2 (with $\mu = 1$).

Proposition 9.2 (Kyle 1985). *There is a unique linear equilibrium and, for $t = 1, 2, \dots, T$, it is given by*

$$\Delta Y_t(\theta, p^{t-1}) = \alpha_t(\theta - p_{t-1}),$$
$$E[\pi_t^T \mid \theta, p^{t-1}] = h_{t-1}(\theta - p_{t-1})^2 + \delta_{t-1} \quad \text{and} \quad p_t = \lambda_t \omega_t + p_{t-1},$$

where $p_0 \equiv \bar{\theta}$, $\omega_t = \Delta y_t + u_t$, $\lambda_t = \tau_u \alpha_t / \tau_t$, and $\tau_t = \tau_\theta + \tau_u \sum_{k=1}^{t} \alpha_k^2$.

The constants α_t, h_t, and δ_t are the unique solution to the difference equation system

$$h_{t-1} = 1/(4\lambda_t(1 - \lambda_t h_t)),$$
$$\alpha_t = (1 - 2\lambda_t h_t)/(2\lambda_t(1 - \lambda_t h_t)),$$
$$\delta_{t-1} = \delta_t + h_t \lambda_t^2 \tau_u^{-1},$$

subject to the boundary conditions $h_T = 0$, $\delta_T = 0$, *and the second-order conditions* $\lambda_t[1 - \lambda_t h_t] > 0$ *for* $t = 1, 2, \dots, T$.

Outline of proof. The strategy of the insider and his expected profits are obtained first as a function of the market depth parameters λ_t at a linear equilibrium. Competitive market making at a linear equilibrium yields a price process of the form $p_t = \lambda_t \omega_t + p_{t-1}$ as in proposition 9.1. The boundary conditions $h_T = 0$, $\delta_T = 0$ just state that no profits are to be made after trade is completed. In the last period the trading intensity, as in the static model of proposition 5.2 (with $\mu = 1$) fulfills $\alpha_T \lambda_T = \frac{1}{2}$. The form of the strategy is also as in the static model with p_{T-1} taking the role of the prior mean $\bar{\theta}$: $\Delta Y_t(\theta, p^{T-1}) = \alpha_T(\theta - p_T)$. Indeed, from competitive market making we know that the price p_{T-1} is just the expected value of the fundamental given public information up to $t - 1$. In particular, $p_{T-1} = E[\theta \mid p^{T-1}] = E[\theta \mid p_{T-1}]$. The properties of the price process yield immediately a quadratic value function of the form

$$E[\pi_T \mid \theta, p^{T-1}] = h_{T-1}(\theta - p_{T-1})^2,$$

where $h_{T-1} = \alpha_T(1 - \alpha_T \lambda_T) = \frac{1}{4}\lambda_T$. Using an induction argument the recursive form of the value function follows as stated in the proposition. For any $t < T$ we will have that $\alpha_t \lambda_t < \frac{1}{2}$ because the insider considers the future information leakage of the impact of his trades. The insider has an incentive to trade when the market is deep (λ_t is low) and therefore if he expects depth to be high in the future he will try to trade more intensely at later dates. The second-order condition prevents the insider from destabilizing prices at auction t to make it up in excess at later auctions. When market depth is low (λ_t is high) by trading small quantities prices can be destabilized. The second-order condition puts an upper bound on λ_t that decreases with h_t, which measures the value of private information at future trading dates. The higher this value, the higher the incentives of the insider to move prices away from the fundamental value. Finally, from $\alpha_t = (1 - 2\lambda_t h_t)/(2\lambda_t(1 - \lambda_t h_t))$ and $\lambda_t = \tau_u \alpha_t / \tau_t$, we can obtain the cubic equation in λ_t

$$(1 - \lambda_t^2 \tau_t / \tau_u)(1 - h_t \lambda_t) = \tfrac{1}{2},$$

which has three real roots, the middle one satisfying the second-order condition. We can thus iterate the difference equation system backward for a given τ_T (recall that $h_T = 0$). It is easy to see then that only one terminal value τ_T is consistent with the prior τ_θ (see Kyle (1985) for the details).

As in sections 8.1.1 and 8.1.2 the risk-neutral competitive fringe makes price p_{t-1} a sufficient statistic for public information $\omega^t = (\omega_1, \dots, \omega_{t-1})$. The insider buys or sells in period t according to whether the liquidation value θ is larger or smaller than public information p_{t-1}. Information is gradually incorporated into the price, as an outcome of the trade-off faced by the insider, as price precision τ_T increases with t but remains bounded.

The question arises about whether the insider may have incentives to introduce noise in his order. The answer is no. The reason, as in the static model (see section 5.2.1), is that he is optimizing at any stage against a fixed conjecture on the behavior of market makers, that is, a fixed λ. For a given market depth it is then optimal not to introduce noise in the order since the only effect of placing a noisy order is just to distort trade from its optimal level given θ. (See exercise 9.4.) We will see below that things change if the informed trader is forced to disclose his trade at the close of the period.

Kyle also analyzes a continuous-time version of the model by letting the intervals between trades go to zero. Noise trading, as well as equilibrium prices, then follow a Brownian motion (this is due to competitive market making). A remarkable result is that market depth is constant over time and information is incorporated into prices at a constant rate with all information incorporated at the end of trading. The result is that prices converge to θ (in mean square) as the end of the horizon approaches.

Back (1992) provides an extension of the model in continuous time. Back and Pedersen (1998) consider the case in which the monopolistic insider receives a flow of private information on top of an initial stock of information. The insider also reveals the information slowly. Chau and Vayanos (forthcoming) consider a steady-state infinite-horizon model in which the insider receives information every period about the expected growth rate of asset dividends. As trading is more frequent, converging to continuous time, the insider chooses to reveal the information more and more quickly and the market approaches strong-form efficiency. The reason is that in the model the price impact is constant over time independently of whether the insider trades quickly or not. Impatience (in the form of discounting, information leakage, or obsolescence of information) then leads to a fast trading pattern. The major difference with Kyle (1985) is that there, a stock of information arrives only once.

9.2.2 Extensions

There are several other extensions available of the Kyle model, introducing competition among insiders, disclosure requirements, risk-averse traders, and building bridges with the Glosten–Milgrom model (section 9.1.1).

9.2.2.1 Competition among Insiders

Holden and Subrahmanyam (1992) introduce several insiders, all observing the fundamental value, and show that the information is incorporated into prices much more quickly. In fact, all information is incorporated immediately as the interval between auctions tends to 0. This is so because equally informed agents trade more aggressively (Holden and Subrahmanyam 1994). Moreover, if the insiders were to be risk averse they would even speed up more information revelation with a resulting increasing pattern of market depth. This may seem surprising at first glance because one could expect more cautious behavior on the part of risk-averse traders. However, risk-averse traders want to trade early to avoid future price uncertainty (and this makes market makers decrease depth to protect themselves at the beginning).

Foster and Viswanathan (1996) consider several risk-neutral informed agents each receiving a noisy signal of the fundamental value. The information structure is symmetric and error terms in the signals are potentially correlated. Therefore, both the cases of all insiders receiving the same signal and receiving (conditionally) independent signals are covered. Foster and Viswanathan focus on linear recursive Markov perfect equilibria and show that the problem of forecasting the forecast of others (infinite regress) does not arise in equilibrium, neither with one-player deviations in order to check for equilibrium, because a sufficient statistic for the past can be found. The latter is a consequence of the combination of the recursive structure of the model, normality, and competitive market making (much as in Vives (1995a), see section 8.2).

An interesting feature of the analysis, uncovered by simulations, is that prices are less revealing the lower the correlation of private signals, and that the correlation of private signals conditional on public information decreases over time and becomes negative toward the end of the horizon with enough trading rounds. The reason is that the more similar the information traders have the more they compete and the more of their information is transmitted to prices. Furthermore, the competitive market-making sector is basically learning the average of the signals of the traders (all there is to learn) and this means that the correlation between individual signals conditional on public information, when close to the average signal, must be negative. Now, an informed trader will learn faster from the order flow than the market maker and this means that by trading aggressively he will reveal more to the competitors than to the market makers. Therefore, informed traders will be cautious and play a waiting game, trying to induce the competitor to reveal information. Note the contrast with Holden and Subrahmanyam (1994), where informed traders cannot learn anything from each other because they receive the same signal.[13]

9.2.2.2 *Disclosure of Trades and Dissimulation Strategies*

Huddart et al. (2001) study a version of the Kyle model where the insider has to disclose his trade before the next round of trading. In the United States an insider of a firm (manager, officer, or large stockholder) has to report *ex post* the trades he makes on the stock of the firm in question. The report is made to the Securities and Exchange Commission (SEC) and is made public immediately.[14]

[13] See Back et al. (2000) for an analysis of the model in continuous time, obtaining closed-form solutions. They show that there is no linear equilibrium when signals are perfectly correlated, and that after some date, the market would have been more informationally efficient had there been a monopolist informed trader instead of competing informed traders.

[14] According to the Securities Exchange Act of 1934: (i) insiders have to report their trades to the SEC within ten days following the end of the month in which the trade occurs (Section 16(a)); (ii) any individual who acquires 5% or more of the stock of a firm, as well as any subsequent changes to the position, must report it within ten days (Section 13(d)).

Obviously, the equilibrium strategy of the insider in the Kyle (1985) model will no longer be optimal. Indeed, after the first round of trade it would be fully revealing of θ. This would induce the competitive market-making sector to let depth be infinite in the second period and the insider would have the opportunity to make unbounded profits. The insider has thus to dissimulate its trade by introducing noise in his order. Huddart et al. show that there is an equilibrium in which the insider adds normally distributed noise η_t to his order at every stage except the last. This noise is uncorrelated with all other random variables in the model, with mean zero and variance $\sigma^2_{\eta_t}$. The parameters of the randomization are not observable by market makers. Letting $\Delta y^t = \{\Delta y_1, \dots, \Delta y_t\}$, the linear equilibrium of the T-period market is characterized, for $t = 1, 2, \dots, T$, as follows:

$$\Delta y_t = \alpha_t(\theta - E[\theta \mid \Delta y^{t-1}]) + \eta_t, \quad \text{with } E[\theta \mid \Delta y^0] \equiv \bar{\theta},$$
$$p_t = \lambda_t \omega_t + E[\theta \mid \Delta y^{t-1}] \quad \text{and} \quad \omega_t = \Delta y_t + u_t,$$

where $\alpha_t = (2(T-t+1)\lambda_t)^{-1}$, $\lambda_t = \sqrt{\tau_u/4T\tau_\theta}$, and $\sigma^2_{\eta_t} = \sigma^2_u(T-t)/(T-t+1)$. Furthermore, $E[\theta \mid \Delta y^t] = E[\theta \mid \Delta y^{t-1}] + 2\lambda_t \Delta y_t$ and $\operatorname{var}[\theta \mid \Delta y^t] = \sigma^2_\theta \times (T-t)/T$.

The equilibrium displays several notable properties. Note first that the strategy of the insider at t is conditioned on public information $E[\theta \mid \Delta y^{t-1}]$ since p_{t-1} is a noisy version of it. The dissimulation strategy of the insider involves setting in every period the variance of added noise in his trade equal to the variance of the information-based component, that is,

$$\sigma^2_{\eta_t} = \alpha_t^2 \operatorname{var}[\theta - E[\theta \mid \Delta y^{t-1}]],$$

and the total variance of his trade equal to the variance of noise trading, that is, $\operatorname{var}[\Delta y_t] = \sigma^2_u$ (all this as evaluated by the market maker). The second part of the strategy camouflages the insider behind the noise traders and the first part makes it difficult to distinguish between information-based and random-based trades once they are disclosed. The conditional volatility of θ at the start of period t, $\operatorname{var}[\theta \mid \Delta y^{t-1}]$, is smaller than with no disclosure and its reduction over time is constant across periods. This contrasts with the slower pace of variance reduction with no disclosure. The trading intensity of the insider is increasing over time. The market depth parameter λ_t is constant over time. The latter is necessary to sustain the mixed strategy equilibrium (for reasons similar to the continuous-time version of the Kyle (1985) model). In contrast, in the Kyle (1985) discrete time model, λ_t is decreasing with t as more information is incorporated into the price. Furthermore, depth is always larger with disclosure. The reason is that with disclosure some of the trades of the insider are not information based but are randomly generated. Expected per period profits for the insider are constant over time (and equal to $\lambda_t \sigma^2_u = 1/\sqrt{4T\tau_u\tau_\theta}$), and are lower round by round than with no disclosure (where they decline over time).[15]

[15] All results are obtained with simulations and can be shown to hold analytically when $T = 2$. When $T = 2$ it is possible to show also that the trading intensity of the insider is larger period by period with disclosure.

9.2.2.3 Risk-Averse Traders

Guo and Kyle (2005) consider a continuous-time model over an infinite horizon with a risk-averse informed trader who continuously receives new information about the dividend process, noise traders, and risk-averse market makers. The informed trader and the market makers have negative exponential utility and the informed faces quadratic trading costs. They characterize linear Bayesian equilibria and use the results to explain financial anomalies. The key to explaining them, as in section 8.2, is the presence of risk-averse market makers who ask compensation for bearing risk. This explains "excess volatility." The model can also explain the momentum and reversal puzzles. Stock returns tend to show positive short-term autocorrelation (momentum) but negative long-term autocorrelation (reversal).[16] The explanation is as follows. The orders from the informed trader are positively autocorrelated in the short run because he wants to smooth his trade over time in order to minimize trading and market impact costs. This may dominate the negative autocorrelation of orders from liquidity traders. However, the informed trader is risk averse, his order is negatively related to his inventory of the stock, and private information is mean-reverting. His position will therefore be mean-reverting in the long run. Together with the mean-reverting position of liquidity traders this explains the long-run negative autocorrelation in stock returns.

The model provides an explanation of the anomalies that does not rely on the irrationality of traders. An alternative behavioral explanation is provided, for example, by Daniel et al. (1998) based on the overconfidence of investors about the precision of their information and biased self-attribution (according to which when an investor receives public information that confirms his beliefs, the confidence level increases more than it decreases when he receives disconfirming information). Other behavioral explanations of the anomalies have been provided by Barberis et al. (1998) and Hong and Stein (1999).

9.2.2.4 Kyle Meets Glosten and Milgrom

Back and Baruch (2004) extend the Glosten and Milgrom (1985) model (section 9.1.1) to consider a single informed trader who uses market orders and decides, in continuous time, the optimal trading times. Uninformed buy and sell orders arrive as a Poisson process with constant and exogenous arrival intensities. Market makers are competitive and risk neutral, post bid and ask prices and see individual trades. Back and Baruch show that if the liquidation value of the risky asset follows a Bernoulli distribution and the informed trader knows the liquidation value, there is an equilibrium in which he follows a mixed strategy between trading and waiting. This means that both informed and uninformed traders arrive stochastically from the perspective of market makers, as assumed in the Glosten and Milgrom model. Interestingly, the equilibrium in

[16] See, for example, Jegadeesh (1990), Jegadeesh and Titman (1993), Fama and French (1988), and Poterba and Summers (1986, 1988). See Daniel et al. (1998) for a literature review.

this version of the Glosten and Milgrom model is close to the equilibrium in the continuous-time version of the Kyle (1985) model when uninformed traders arrive frequently and the trade size is small. The parallel here to the gradual trade of the insider in Kyle (1985) is the probabilistic waiting to trade of the informed trader. It is also shown that the bid–ask spread is approximately twice "lambda" times the order size in the Kyle-type model. Also, it is worth noting that the informed trader, in some circumstances, may randomize over trades that go against his information. This occurs even though, in contrast to Huddart et al. (2001), trades are not disclosed *ex post*.

The results by Back and Baruch (2004) are important because they show that the more tractable Kyle (1985) model (with discrete batch auctions) is also consistent with the more common case where market makers set bid–ask prices and see individual trades. The model is generalized by Back and Baruch (forthcoming) to encompass both multiple order sizes and limit-order markets. Both the informed trader and discretionary liquidity traders submit market orders and choose between block orders or a series of small orders (i.e., use "work orders").[17] Liquidity providers are assumed to be competitive and risk neutral. The aim of the analysis is to compare floor exchanges, where a uniform price is established and an open limit-order book, where there is discriminatory pricing since each limit order executes at its limit price. With risk-neutral competitive liquidity providers, in the first case prices are the expectation of the fundamental value conditional on public information and order size; in the second case, ask (bid) prices are "upper (lower) tail" expectations of the fundamental value; i.e., expectations conditional on the size of the demand (supply) being at least (at most) the size of the order (see section 5.3.2).

The model allows for larger traders to work their orders and pool with small traders. It is shown that in a floor exchange it is never an equilibrium for all traders to use block orders. That is, any equilibrium must involve at least partial pooling. Furthermore, if traders can submit orders an instant apart, effectively with no execution difference from a block trade, then the block-order equilibrium in the limit-order market is equivalent to a fully pooling worked-order equilibrium on the floor exchange. The incentive for large traders to pool with small ones is that if they do not (i.e., in a separating equilibrium), and since small orders supposedly have a lessened adverse selection problem, prices for small orders would be more favorable. However, in a pooling equilibrium in the floor exchange, market makers cannot know whether, after an order, there will be more from the same trader in the same direction. Consequently, ask prices will also be upper-tail expectations as in the limit-order market. Back and Baruch claim that their floor-exchange model is a good representation of trade in the Chicago Board Options Exchange and that the hybrid design in the NYSE (with the proposed use of uniform pricing when a market order walks up the book) shares the features of a uniform-price market.

[17] Chordia and Subrahmanyam (2004) study order imbalances and stock returns in a competitive model where liquidity traders have an incentive to split their orders across periods.

9.2.3 Summary

The main learning points of the section are the following:

- A large informed trader (an "insider") has incentives to trade slowly so as not to reveal too much information and keep an informational advantage over uninformed traders and market makers. As the number of trading rounds increases, information is incorporated in the price at a constant rate and risk-neutral market makers keep a constant market depth.
- The insider will try to camouflage behind liquidity traders but has no incentive to introduce noise in his order to confuse market makers.
- Competition among strategic informed traders speeds up information revelation when they have symmetric information; otherwise informed traders may play a waiting game to try to induce the competitor to reveal information.
- If an insider has to disclose his trades, then he does have an incentive to dissimulate his trades by randomizing in order to optimize his camouflage behind liquidity traders and obscuring the separation of information-based from liquidity-based trades. Disclosure increases market depth and information revelation, and decreases the expected profits of the insider.
- Financial market anomalies, such as the momentum and reversal in stock returns, can be explained with rational risk-averse traders.
- Quote-driven markets (as in Glosten and Milgrom 1985) and order-driven markets (as in Kyle 1985) have a close connection when in the former uninformed traders arrive frequently and the trade size is small. This has important implications for the equivalence of trading in a floor-exchange as compared with trading in a limit-order market, and for hybrid markets as well.

9.3 Market Manipulation and Price Discovery

We have seen how an insider may have incentives to dissimulate trades if he has to disclose them before trading again. A distinct possibility is market manipulation according to which an agent takes covert actions in an attempt to change the terms of trade in his favor. First, I provide a quick survey of the literature on the topic, and then I analyze the possibilities of manipulation in the price-discovery process studied in section 9.1.3.

9.3.1 Market Manipulation in the Literature

The literature on stock-price manipulation can be classified according to whether manipulation is based on actions that change the value (or the perceived value) of the asset, or based on releasing misleading information, or purely based on trade. Examples of the first type are given in Vila (1989), of the second in Vila (1989) and Benabou and Laroque (1992), and of the third type in Hart (1977), Jarrow (1992), Allen and Gale (1992), Allen and Gorton (1992), Kumar and Seppi (1992), Fishman and Hagerty (1995), and Chakraborty and Yilmaz

(2004). Still, we can add another dimension to the classification according to whether the trader who manipulates the market is informed or uninformed. For example, Allen and Gorton (1992) explain price manipulation by an uninformed agent in the presence of asymmetries in noise trading (noise selling is more likely than noise buying) or asymmetries in whether buyers or sellers are informed (with short-sale constraints to exploit good news being easier than exploiting bad news). In Allen and Gale (1992) or Fishman and Hagerty (1995), an uninformed trader can pretend to be informed to manipulate the price and make money. In Fishman and Hagerty (1995), uninformed insiders may exploit the inability of market makers to distinguish trades of uninformed agents from those of insiders with private information. For example, the uninformed insider may buy shares, imitating an insider who has received good news, move prices up, and sell the shares after disclosure of the trade. Goldstein and Guembel (forthcoming) show how the allocation role of prices opens the possibility of market manipulation. The authors explain how an uninformed trader may want to sell a stock when the price guides the investment decisions of the firm. The informativeness of the stock price diminishes and the trader profits from the investment distortion.

Contrarian behavior, or trade against one's information, is obtained in some instances in the literature. John and Narayanan (1997) develop a variation of the model of Fishman and Hagerty (1995) in which mandatory disclosure of trades of corporate insiders gives them, under certain assumptions, incentives to manipulate the market by using a contrarian strategy. According to this strategy the insider trades in a first period against his information only to unwind his position in a second period. In their model agents are restricted to trading only one unit, the fundamental value follows a two-state distribution, and market makers fix prices before seeing the order flow. The insider manipulates either when he receives good news or when he receives bad news depending on whether the probability of receiving good news is lower or higher. Foster and Viswanathan (1994) provide an example of a duopoly where information has a common and a private component and where the better-informed agent tries to minimize the learning of the lesser-informed one. This market manipulation may lead to contrarian behavior by the better-informed trader if the private and common signals have very disparate realizations (something that happens with low probability). Chakraborty and Yilmaz (2004) find that insiders may trade in the wrong direction when there is uncertainty about their presence in the market and there are a large number of periods before information is revealed.

9.3.2 Strategic Behavior and Price Discovery

We will study here an instance of price manipulation by a strategic trader in a price-discovery mechanism used in opening auctions.[18] More specifically, we

[18] This section is based on Medrano and Vives (2001). Hillion and Suominen (2004) explain the incentives of brokers to manipulate the prices at the close to "look good" in front of customers and provide evidence of strategic behavior at the close of the Paris Bourse.

consider the price-discovery process with a random opening time for the market studied in section 9.1.3.2 but now on top of the competitive informed traders, with mass $1-\mu$, each with constant degree of risk aversion ρ, competitive risk-neutral market makers, and noise traders, there is a large risk-neutral informed trader, with mass μ, who knows the liquidation value θ. This model belongs to the third class of manipulation models with trade-based manipulation. In our case the objective of the strategic informed trader (the "insider"), who has accurate information on the liquidation value of the asset which is known to other agents, is to neutralize the informative trades that competitive informed agents make. In order to do this the insider will use a contrarian strategy. The model will make clear that introducing a random opening time, as in Xetra, limits but does not eliminate the incentives to manipulate the market.

The insider's information set at round t is given by $\{\theta, p^{t-1}\}$, where $p^{t-1} = (p_1, \dots, p_{t-1})$ is the sequence of past prices. Denote his desired position at t by y_t. The information set of competitive informed trader i is given by $\{s_i, p^{t-1}\}$, where s_i is his private signal about θ and his (symmetric) market order is of the type $X_t(s_i, p^{t-1})$. Noise traders submit the aggregate order u_t.

All random variables are assumed to be normally distributed with the same properties as in section 9.1.3.2. In particular, we use the usual convention that, given θ, the average signal of the competitive informed agents $\tilde{s} = (1-\mu)^{-1} \times \int_\mu^1 s_i \, di$ equals (a.s.) θ (i.e., errors cancel out in the aggregate, $\int_\mu^1 \varepsilon_i \, di = 0$).[19] The pooled information of informed agents reveals θ. We can interpret the insider of size μ as emerging from a coalition of small informed traders (of measure μ) who decide to form a cartel of investors and pool their information.

The order flow is then $\omega_t = \mu y_t + \int_\mu^1 X_t(s_i, p^{t-1}) \, di + u_t$. Competitive market makers set $p_t = E[\theta \mid \omega^t]$, where $\omega^t = (\omega_1, \dots, \omega_t)$. If the market opens at stage t, θ is realized, trade occurs, and this is the end of the story. Otherwise the *tâtonnement* continues. All trades are notional until the market opens. Informed traders can revise their orders before the market opens. In general they will have incentives to do so once they receive more public information since this helps them to better predict the net value $\theta - p$. Furthermore, the insider may be able to manipulate the information contained in prices and may have incentives to do so.

At stage t a strategy for the insider is a function that maps his private information θ and the observed past prices p^{t-1} into a market order $Y_t(\theta, p_{t-1})$ given that p_{t-1} is a sufficient statistic for past public information because of the presence of the risk-neutral competitive market-making sector. He knows that the asset will be liquidated and trade realized in the period with probability γ_t, obtaining in expectation $E[(\theta - p_t)\mu y_t \mid \theta, p_{t-1}]$, and with the complementary probability $1 - \gamma_t$ he will obtain the continuation expected profit $E[\pi_{t+1} \mid \theta, p_{t-1}]$, which depends on his market order in period t. Therefore, at stage t the insider will face the following expected profit conditional on his

[19] See section 10.3.1 for a justification of the convention.

information:

$$E[\pi_t \mid \theta, p_{t-1}] = \gamma_t E[(\theta - p_t)\mu y_t \mid \theta, p_{t-1}] + (1 - \gamma_t)E[\pi_{t+1} \mid \theta, p_{t-1}].$$

By restricting our attention to equilibria in linear strategies, it is possible to obtain a full characterization of equilibrium behavior. In equilibrium, competitive traders, given their preferences and symmetric-information structure, will use a symmetric strategy.

Proposition 9.3 (Medrano and Vives 2001). *Linear equilibria are characterized as follows for* $t = 1, 2, \dots, T$:

$$\begin{aligned} Y_t(\theta, p_{t-1}) &= \alpha_t(\theta - p_{t-1}), \\ X_t(s_i, p_{t-1}) &= a_t(s_i - p_{t-1}), \\ p_t &= \lambda_t \omega_t + p_{t-1}, \\ \omega_t &= A_t(\theta - p_{t-1}) + u_t, \end{aligned}$$

where $p_0 = \bar{\theta}$, $\lambda_t = \tau_u A_t / \tau_t$, $A_t = \mu\alpha_t + (1 - \mu)a_t$, *and* $\tau_t = \tau_\theta + \tau_u \sum_{k=1}^{t} A_k^2$. *At stage* t, *the insider's expected continuation profit is given by*

$$E[\pi_{t+1} \mid \theta, p_{t-1}] = \mu(h_t(\theta_{\mathrm{H}})(\theta - p_t)^2 + \delta_t).$$

The constants a_t, α_t, h_t, *and* δ_t *are the solution to the difference equation system*

$$\begin{aligned} a_t &= (\rho(\tau_\varepsilon^{-1} + \tau_{t-1}^{-1} - \tau_t^{-1}))^{-1}, \\ \alpha_t &= \frac{1 - (1 - \mu)\lambda_t a_t}{2\mu\lambda_t} \frac{\gamma_t - 2(1 - \gamma_t)\mu\lambda_t h_t}{\gamma_t - (1 - \gamma_t)\mu\lambda_t h_t}, \\ h_t &= (1 - \lambda_{t+1}A_{t+1})(\gamma_{t+1}\alpha_{t+1} + (1 - \gamma_{t+1})h_{t+1}(1 - \lambda_{t+1}A_{t+1})), \\ \delta_t &= (1 - \gamma_{t+1})(\delta_{t+1} + \lambda_t^2 h_{t+1}/\tau_u), \end{aligned}$$

subject to the boundary conditions $h_T = 0$, $\delta_T = 0$, $2\mu\alpha_T\lambda_T = 1 - (1 - \mu)\lambda_T a_T$ *and the second-order conditions* $\lambda_t\mu(\gamma_t - (1 - \gamma_t)\mu\lambda_t h_t) > 0$ *for* $t = 1, 2, \dots, T$.

Corollary 9.1. *At a linear equilibrium the following inequalities hold for any* t: $0 < a_t < \tau_\varepsilon/\rho$, $A_t > 0$, $\lambda_t > 0$, $0 < \mu\lambda_t h_t < \gamma_t/(1-\gamma_t)$, $0 < (1-(1-\mu)\lambda_t a_t) < 1$, *and* $0 < 1 - \lambda_t A_t < 1$.

The proof of the proposition is a variation of the arguments in Kyle (1985) and Vives (1995b). Note, however, that the proposition does not assert the existence of a linear equilibrium. In fact, to show existence and uniqueness of the linear equilibrium in the model is not a trivial task. This is a difference equation system with T periods and two unknowns in each period ($\{a_t, \alpha_t\}$ or $\{a_t, \lambda_t\}$). Solving the difference equation system is complicated since we cannot find a way to iterate the dynamic equation system backward, as in Kyle (1985) or Holden and Subrahmanyam (1992), nor forward, as in Vives (1995b). The reason is that the insider's responsiveness to private information at stage t (α_t) depends on all his futures trading intensities ($\alpha_{t+1}, \dots, \alpha_T$) via h_t, while the responsiveness to private information of the competitive informed agents (a_t) depends on all their past trading intensities $(a_1, \dots, a_{t-1})$ via τ_{t-1}. However, we may expect that the linear equilibrium exists and is unique for all parameter configurations because this is the case for the extreme cases $\mu = 0$ (Vives 1995b) and $\mu = 1$ (with a monopolistic informed trader), and also when $T = 2$ and γ_1 is close to zero. Furthermore, systematic simulations performed in a wide range of parameter values have always produced a unique (linear) equilibrium. When informed traders submit demand schedules, instead of market orders, the dynamics are simplified and it is possible to show that there is a unique linear equilibrium (see exercise 9.8).

We characterize now trading volume for further reference. As in section 5.2.1 we define the total volume traded at stage t, denoted by TV_t, as the sum of the absolute values of the demands coming from the different agents in the model divided by 2.[20] Its expectation is given by

$$E[\mathrm{TV}_t] = \tfrac{1}{2}((1-\mu)E[|X_t(s_i, p_{t-1})|] + \mu E[|Y_t(\theta, p_{t-1})|] + E[|\omega_t|] + E[|u_t|]).$$

The behavior of the total trading volume is driven by the behavior of the volume traded by informed (competitive and strategic) agents. As in exercise 5.7 in a linear equilibrium it is easy to check that

$$\begin{aligned}
E[|X_t(s_i, p_{t-1})|] &= (2/\pi)^{1/2} a_t (\tau_\varepsilon^{-1} + \tau_{t-1}^{-1})^{1/2},\\
E[|Y_t(\theta, p_{t-1})|] &= (2/\pi)^{1/2} (\alpha_t^2/\tau_{t-1})^{1/2},\\
E[|\omega_t|] &= (2/\pi)^{1/2} (\sigma_u^2 + A_t^2/\tau_{t-1})^{1/2},\\
E[\mathrm{TV}_t] &= (1/2\pi)^{1/2}((1-\mu)a_t(\tau_\varepsilon^{-1} + \tau_{t-1}^{-1})^{1/2} + \mu(\alpha_t^2/\tau_{t-1})^{1/2}\\
&\qquad + (\sigma_u^2 + A_t^2/\tau_{t-1})^{1/2} + \sigma_u).
\end{aligned}$$

When $\mu = 1$ and there is a monopolistic insider it is possible to show the existence of a unique linear equilibrium. Then the insider faces a starker version of the insider's trade-off in the Kyle model (section 9.2). At stage t his future profit will decrease by placing a market order if there is no trade, because of the information leaked to the market makers. By not submitting an order if trade occurs, his future profit will be zero because θ will have been revealed.[21] The optimal market order, which balances the two effects, implies a trading intensity that is lower than in the one-shot model, where there is trading with probability 1. In our monopolistic market $\lambda_t \alpha_t < \frac{1}{2}$ for all $t < T$ and $\lambda_T \alpha_T = \frac{1}{2}$ (since for $t = T$ the model becomes like the static Kyle model).

The large informed agent refrains from trading too aggressively because there is a positive probability that there is no trade. This suggests that his trading intensity α_t should be increasing with the probability γ_t (and this is confirmed by the simulations). An important result is that for the central case, where the

[20] See the explanations for trading volume in chapter 4 and in section 5.2.1.

[21] It never pays to set $\alpha_t < 0$ because it is dominated by $\alpha_t = 0$. If there is trade, with $\alpha_t < 0$ the insider makes negative profit while it makes zero with $\alpha_t = 0$; if there is no trade, with $\alpha_t = 0$ no information is revealed to the market makers while with $\alpha_t < 0$ some information is revealed. When $\gamma_t = 0$ it is optimal not to trade (set $\alpha_t = 0$).

probability is of the type $\gamma_t = \gamma^{T-t}$, and in contrast to the competitive economy (where $\mu = 0$ as in section 9.1.3.2), no matter how long the horizon is, the price precision is bounded above (and the bound depends only on the parameter γ). The monopolistic insider prevents the full revelation of θ no matter how many rounds the *tâtonnement* has.

A simulation analysis (assuming that $\gamma_t = \gamma^{T-t}$) uncovers the following properties comparing the monopolistic version of the model with the competitive version.

- *The responsiveness to private information* increases monotonically with t; in the monopolistic case at an accelerating rate and in the competitive case at a decelerating rate.
- *The informativeness of prices* τ_t increases monotonically with t; in the monopolistic case at an accelerating rate close to the opening and in the competitive case at the rate of t.
- *Market depth* $\lambda_t^{-1} \to \infty$ at a rate of t in the competitive equilibrium; in the monopolistic equilibrium, in general, it decreases during the first rounds of the *tâtonnement* and then increases as the probability that there will be trade tends to 1.
- *The unconditional volatility of prices* $\mathrm{var}[p_t]$ increases monotonically toward σ_θ^2 in both cases. However, in the competitive economy $\mathrm{var}[p_t]$ gets close to σ_θ^2 in the first few rounds of *tâtonnement* while it is close to zero in the monopolistic economy (because market depth is extremely high).
- *Expected trading volume.* In the competitive economy, the expected volume traded by informed agents is decreasing for t large, while in the monopolistic economy it increases monotonically.[22]

When the insider and the competitive informed sector coexist, the insider's responsiveness to private information α_t may be negative for t not too close to the end of the horizon. This may be interpreted as an attempt to manipulate the market because the insider goes against what his private information suggests, buying when $\theta < p_{t-1}$ and selling when $\theta > p_{t-1}$. The insider attempts to neutralize the information incorporated in prices from the demands of the competitive informed traders. The more information market makers have, the lower the speculative profits of the insider. This is how the insider can manipulate the informativeness of prices τ_t and the depth of the market λ_t^{-1}. Both $\tau_t = \tau_{t-1} + \tau_u A_t^2$ and $\lambda_t^{-1} = \tau_t/(\tau_u A_t)$ depend on the average of the trading intensities of the strategic and the competitive informed agents, $A_t = \mu\alpha_t + (1-\mu)a_t$. We have that $a_t > 0$ as long as $\tau_\varepsilon > 0$. By setting $\alpha_t < 0$ the insider can decrease A_t and he will do so if γ_t is sufficiently low. In particular, when there is no danger of the market opening ($\gamma_t = 0$) the insider trades in such a way that no information is revealed by neutralizing the response

[22] It should be clear that $E[|Y_t(\theta, p_{t-1})|] = (2/\pi)^{1/2}(\alpha_t^2/\tau_{t-1})^{1/2}$ will be increasing if the rate of increase of α_t is sufficiently high in relation to the increase in prices τ_{t-1}.

of competitive informed agents ($\alpha_t = -(1-\mu)a_t/\mu$ and $A_t = 0$).[23] At stage $t < T$, if $0 < \gamma_t < 1$, the insider must balance reducing the informativeness of prices by choosing a low (and possibly negative) trading intensity α_t, and trading intensely (choosing α_t close to the static equilibrium value) to obtain a high profit if trades are executed. If $\gamma_t = 1$, the insider behaves as in the static version of the model. At stage t we should expect that the insider's incentives to manipulate the market decrease with the probability of trading γ_t, or, equivalently, α_t increases with γ_t (and since γ_t increases with t, α_t should increase with t).

The simulations performed for the case $\gamma_t = \gamma^{T-t}$ corroborate the analysis and conjectures above:[24] α_t increases with t and in γ, τ_t is strictly convex in t; and, provided T is large enough: (i) $\alpha_t < 0$ for t low; (ii) $\text{var}[p_t \mid p_{t-1}]$ may be hump-shaped or increasing and a_t U-shaped or decreasing with t; and (iii) the total expected trading volume is U-shaped in t. Further simulations support the conjecture that for $\mu > 0$, as in the case of a monopolistic insider ($\mu = 1$), for any given γ there is an upper bound for the price precision $\bar{\tau}$, no matter what the length T of the horizon.[25] A larger size of the insider μ implies a lower limit value for the price precision and this limit is attained in fewer rounds of trade. Indeed, when μ increases the average responsiveness to information A_t tends to decrease and this impacts negatively on the informativeness of prices. A larger insider tends to decrease the price precision and the expected volume traded.

The insider manipulates the market at the beginning of the price adjustment process (result (i)). As a consequence, the informativeness of prices is very low during the first stages and increases quite fast as t gets close to T. Result (iii) is driven by the fact that the insider's expected trading volume is U-shaped. The expected volume traded by informed traders (ignoring the volume traded among competitive informed agents) equals $(\mu|\alpha_t| + (1-\mu)a_t)(\text{var}[\theta \mid p_t])^{1/2}$. For γ not too high this volume will have a U-shaped temporal pattern because $|\alpha_t|$ does and dominates. This in turn dominates the decreasing tendency of $\text{var}[\theta \mid p_t]$. (See exercise 9.7 for an explanation for result (ii).)

Finally, it is worth remarking that the general pattern of results obtained also hold in the case that the strategic and the competitive informed agents use demand schedules instead of market orders. In the presence of the insider there is market manipulation, price precision is bounded above, and volume

---

[23] However, it never pays the strategic informed trader to let $A_t < 0$ by choosing $\alpha_t < -(1-\mu)a_t/\mu$. This is worse than choosing $\alpha_t = -(1-\mu)a_t/\mu$, since in the first case the expected loss in case trade is realized would be higher and the future expected profit in case there is no trading would be lower (because then the price does reveal some information while if $\alpha_t = -(1-\mu)a_t/\mu$ it does not).

[24] We have explored the behavior of the model with $\gamma_t = \gamma^{T-t}$ in the following parameter grid: ρ in $\{1,2,4\}$, τ_u, τ_θ, and τ_ε in $\{0.5,1,2\}$, γ in $\{0.2,0.3,0.5,0.6,0.7,0.8\}$, μ in $\{0.2,0.5,0.8\}$ with T up to 30 rounds.

[25] Simulations have been performed in the range of parameters: ρ in $\{1,2,4\}$, τ_u, τ_θ, and τ_ε in $\{0.5,1,5\}$, μ between 0.01 and 1 with a step of 0.05 and γ with the same step from 0.01 until 0.5. In this range the upper bound for τ is attained in 30 rounds or fewer. For γ up to 0.7 and μ no smaller than 0.2, the upper bound for τ is attained in 40 rounds or fewer.

is U-shaped. (See exercise 9.8.) The theoretical results obtained in this section are in line with the empirical analysis of the preopening period in the Paris Bourse by Biais et al. (1999). They find that the preopening period is active, in particular close to the opening. The last fifteen minutes before the opening (say, 9.45 to 10 a.m. in the Paris Bourse) are the most active order placement period in the day (including therefore the period with real trade). Trading at the opening amounts to about 10% of the total trading of the day. About half of the preopening orders are serious orders for sure since they are actually executed and about 60% of those are executed at the opening and not later. Therefore, the preopening order flow is directly linked to the opening price. The average size of orders placed in the preopening period increases as we get closer to the opening and large traders sometimes place unaggressive orders and tend to modify their orders. The volume of trade typically has a U-shaped form dropping after the first round to increase sharply later when approaching the opening. Biais et al. do not reject the hypothesis of semi-strong efficiency for prices close to the opening. Before that the hypothesis that prices do not reflect any information cannot be discarded.[26] The speed of learning from prices is of order $t^{3/2}$ in the second part of the preopening, where t is the number of rounds in the *tâtonnement*. This means that the precision of prices grows more than linearly toward the end of the process (recall that a price precision of order t^k is associated with a speed of learning of $t^{k/2}$). This speed of learning is easy to generate in the theoretical model.[27]

The interaction between a strategic informed trader and a sector of competitive informed agents in the model presented in this section yields outcomes consistent with the empirical evidence available from the Paris Bourse. Indeed, we have seen how the presence of the insider slows down at first and later accelerates the transmission of information by prices. The price precision tends to increase sharply toward the end of the *tâtonnement*. However, the price does not fully reveal the fundamental value of the asset no matter how many rounds the *tâtonnement* has. Furthermore, trading volume displays a U-shaped pattern driven by the insider's activity.

9.3.3 Summary

Market manipulation is a distinct possibility when there are large traders in the market. In the preopening period of a price-discovery process we have seen how a strategic informed trader has incentives to use a contrarian strategy to suppress the information leakage from the price deriving from the competitive behavior of other informed traders. This manipulation is understood by everyone in the market to happen in equilibrium.

---

[26] A similar result is obtained by Sola (1999) with data from the Bolsa de Madrid.

[27] If we fit a curve of the type Kt^k to $\tau_t - \tau_\theta$, we easily find values for k close to 3 for a range of periods in which τ_t is significantly different from τ_θ.

9.4 Strategic Trading with Short-Lived Information

Up to now we have studied the impact of long-lived information on price informativeness, volatility, and volume in the presence of strategic traders and noise traders which were given no choice of when to trade. However, a strategic trader may also possess short-lived information and "noise" traders may have at least some discretion about when to trade.

It has been observed that the average intraday volume and variance of price changes in the NYSE is U-shaped. Admati and Pfleiderer (1988) try to explain this pattern by considering a T-period dynamic trading model where the information of n insiders is short-lived and where there are some liquidity traders who can choose when to trade. The basic idea is that the intraday trading patterns for volume and price volatility may be explained by the incentives of liquidity and informed traders to cluster their trades.

The liquidation value of the single risky asset is given by $\theta = \bar{\theta} + \sum_{t=1}^{T} \theta_t$, where $\bar{\theta}$ is a known parameter and $\{\theta_t\}$ are independently normally distributed random variables with mean 0 and variance σ_t^2. There are n_t informed traders in period t and they all see the same signal about the innovation next period, $s_t = \theta_{t+1} + \varepsilon_t$, where ε_t is normally distributed with mean 0 and variance $\sigma_{\varepsilon t}^2$. Error terms in signals and innovations in the fundamental value are mutually independent. The value of θ_t becomes known at the beginning of period t and therefore the information of the informed traders is short-lived. Denote by $Y_t(s_t)$ the market order of an informed trader in period t.

There are two types of liquidity traders in period t. The usual noise traders, trading according to a normal random variable u_t, and m discretionary liquidity traders, who can choose when to trade within a time interval (say, the trading day). When discretionary liquidity trader j trades he has a demand of z_j shares that cannot be split during the trading period. His demand in period t z_{jt} is z_j if he trades and 0 otherwise. All traders submit market orders and a competitive risk-neutral market-making sector sets prices upon observing the order flow and public information. Denote by y_{it} the order of informed trader i in period t. The order flow in period t is given by

$$\omega_t = \sum_{i=1}^{n_t} y_{it} + \sum_{j=1}^{m} z_{jt} + u_t.$$

It is assumed that

$$\{z_1, \dots, z_m, u_1, \dots, u_{T-1}, \theta_1, \dots, \theta_T, \varepsilon_1, \dots, \varepsilon_{T-1}\}$$

are mutually independent normally distributed random variables.

The competitive market-making sector in period t sets prices conditional on the order flow ω_t and on public information $\theta^t \equiv \{\theta_1, \dots, \theta_t\}$, $p_t = E[\theta \mid \omega_t, \theta^t]$.

Given normality this immediately yields

$$p_t = E[\theta \mid \theta^t] + \lambda_t \omega_t = \bar{\theta} + \sum_{k=1}^{t} \theta_k + \lambda_t \omega_t,$$

where $\lambda_t = \operatorname{cov}[\theta_{t+1}, \omega_t] / \operatorname{var}[\omega_t]$. The inverse of the parameter λ_t is as usual a measure of the depth of the market.

In period t the n_t informed traders compete by taking into account the price rule of the market makers and trader i demands $y_{it} = \alpha_t s_t$. In equilibrium[28]

$$\alpha_t = \sqrt{\frac{\Psi_t}{n_t \operatorname{var}[s_t]}},$$

where $\Psi_t = \operatorname{var}[\sum_{j=1}^{m} z_{jt} + u_t]$ is the variance of total liquidity trading in the period, and

$$\lambda_t = \frac{\sigma_{t+1}^2}{n_t + 1} \sqrt{\frac{n_t}{\Psi_t \operatorname{var}[s_t]}}.$$

Unsurprisingly, an increase in total liquidity demand increases the sensitivity of informed traders to their information, as they can camouflage better behind noise traders, and market depth, as the order flow becomes less informative. As the number of informed traders n_t increases, each one of them responds less to his information, since they all receive the same signal, and market depth increases, as they are not able to restrict their trade enough to control the information leakage in the order flow. With more informed traders the adverse selection problem of market makers is less severe because of competition among the informed.

A discretionary liquidity trader will choose to trade when the cost of trading is lowest, that is, when his losses are minimal. The expected losses for a liquidity trader trading z_j in period t are

$$E[(p_t - \theta) z_j \mid \omega^{t-1}, \theta^t, z_j] = \lambda_t z_j^2,$$

where $\omega^{t-1} \equiv \{\omega_1, \dots, \omega_{t-1}\}$, after substituting for the expressions for p_t and θ and using the independence assumptions made. Therefore, liquidity traders would like to trade when λ_t is lowest. This means that discretionary liquidity traders like to trade when the market is deep and this happens when there are a lot of other liquidity traders (λ_t decreases with Ψ_t). It is not difficult to see that liquidity traders face a coordination problem and that there will exist multiple equilibria. If in period t there is a lot of discretionary liquidity trading, then λ_t will be low and this will attract more liquidity traders. There is always an equilibrium where all discretionary liquidity trading happens in the same period and generically only this type of equilibrium is possible. Indeed, if for some parameters of the model there is trade in two periods, implying that the two periods must have the same market depth, a small perturbation of $\operatorname{var}[z_j]$, for

[28] The derivation is similar to the derivation of equilibrium in exercise 5.3 (but note that there the informed traders use demand schedules instead of market orders).

example, would tip the balance toward the period with a strictly deeper market. Furthermore, insiders also like to trade in a deep market to better disguise their trades (indeed, α_t increases with Ψ_t).[29]

This means that the concentration of discretionary liquidity trading in one period will induce more trading by informed traders and explains a peak in volume. In fact, this peak in volume will occur even if the rate at which information becomes public is constant (say, $\sigma_t^2 = 1$ without loss of generality), signals have the same precision, $\tau_{\varepsilon_t} = \tau_\varepsilon$, and the amount of nondiscretionary noise trading is constant, $\text{var}[u_t] = \sigma_u^2$, in any period. (See exercise 9.9.) However, the model does not explain volatility changes. Indeed, if there is the same number of informed traders in any period, $n_t = n$ (and $\tau_{\varepsilon_t} = \tau_\varepsilon$, $\sigma_t^2 = 1$) for all t, then the volatility of price changes is given by

$$\text{var}[p_t - p_{t-1}] = \frac{\tau_\varepsilon}{1+\tau_\varepsilon}\left(\tau_\varepsilon^{-1} + \frac{n}{1+n} + \frac{1}{1+n}\right) = 1.$$

And, indeed, the informativeness of prices about the dividend innovation

$$(\text{var}[\theta_{t+1} \mid p_t])^{-1} = \left(1 + \frac{n\tau_\varepsilon}{1+\tau_\varepsilon+n}\right)^{-1}$$

is also constant across time periods. All this holds irrespective of Ψ_t and therefore is true for the period in which liquidity trading is concentrated. Indeed, as in the Kyle (1985) static model (see section 5.2.1) the informativeness of prices, and therefore conditional volatility in a semi-strong efficient market, is independent of the amount of noise trading. More liquidity trading entices risk-neutral informed traders to trade more intensely and this is just sufficient to keep the order flow with the same information content. Note that with no informed trading $p_t - p_{t-1} = \theta_t$ and therefore $\text{var}[p_t - p_{t-1}] = \text{var}[\theta_t] = 1$. When there is informed trading the result is the same. To generate more interesting volatility patterns we need to have different numbers of informed traders in different periods.

Admati and Pfleiderer go on to study the incentives to acquire information and endogenize the number of insiders. Whenever the number of insiders is known in equilibrium, concentrated trading patterns are reinforced. This is because more liquidity trading incentivizes entry of informed traders and, because of enhanced competition among them, lowers trading costs for liquidity traders. This reinforces the incentive of discretionary liquidity traders to trade in the period to start with. Indeed, the expected profits of an informed trader in period t just match the (share of) expected losses of (discretionary and nondiscretionary) liquidity traders:

$$\pi(n_t, \Psi_t) = \frac{\lambda_t}{n_t}\Psi_t = \frac{1}{1+n_t}\left(\frac{\tau_\varepsilon \Psi_t}{(1+\tau_\varepsilon)n_t}\right)^{1/2},$$

[29] For other models with a coordination problem of investors concentrating trade in a single market or at certain times, see, respectively, Pagano (1989) for a model with no asymmetric information and Foster and Viswanathan (1990).

which increase with the total amount of liquidity trading in the period $\psi_t \equiv \text{var}[\sum_{j=1}^{m} z_{jt} + u_t]$. At a free-entry equilibrium where traders have to pay F to become informed, $\pi(n_t, \Psi_t) \geqslant F$ and entry by one more informed trader would induce an equilibrium with negative net expected profits. Now with more information about the dividend process concentrated when liquidity trading is high we have that volatility and volume are positively correlated.

In summary, when liquidity traders have discretion about when to trade they will tend to concentrate their trading in periods where market depth is high and this will become a self-reinforcing process where more liquidity traders and informed traders, with short-lived information, will also join in, generating volume and volatility peaks.

9.5 Strategic Hedging

The models we have considered so far display the strategic behavior of traders who are privately informed about the fundamental value of the risky asset. The motivation for trade for those large traders is to exploit their information advantage. Risk-averse large traders may also trade for insurance motives when receiving a shock to their endowments or to hedge an investment. What are the consequences of strategic behavior when large traders trade for an insurance motive?

We study the case of the endowment shock of each strategic trader being the only private information and examine the consequences for the speed of trading and welfare losses, as well as possibilities to manipulate the market. The case when the strategic trader has information about the fundamental value and wants to obtain insurance to hedge his investment has been examined in section 5.4. Chau (2002) examines the dynamic incentives of a strategic trader to exploit his private information about the fundamental value as well as controlling his inventory after an endowment shock.

We will display two patterns of trading by a large risk-averse trader who suffers an endowment shock. In the first we will see how private information about the endowment shock leads to slow trading and potentially large welfare losses. In the second we will uncover an instance of market manipulation in the presence of noise traders.

Vayanos (1999) considers a dynamic model with n CARA risk-averse infinitely long-lived strategic agents who receive an endowment shock every period and want to insure against dividend risk. Dividends follow a random walk, dividend information is public, and the endowment shock to a trader is the only private information. Traders submit (continuous) demand schedules every period to a centralized market-clearing mechanism and all random variables are normally distributed. There is no noise trading. The model may fit interdealer markets, where dealers want to share their inventory risk and participants are large. In the linear Nash equilibrium in demand functions studied in his paper, prices are fully revealing of the endowment shocks because there is no noise trading.

A first result is that agents trade slowly even when the time between trades tends to 0. This is so because making use of more trading opportunities the price impact would be very important. Indeed, a trade in one direction would indicate many more trades in the same direction. To avoid a strong price impact large agents trade slowly. The result would go away, and trade would accelerate as the interval between trades decreases, as in the Coase conjecture, if endowment shocks were to be public information. According to the Coase conjecture a durable goods monopolist sells fast and prices quickly converge to the marginal cost as the interval between trades diminishes. Private information on endowments drives the slow trading result by increasing the price impact of a trade. Indeed, in equilibrium if a trader were to sell more shares, then the other traders would incorrectly infer that he has received a larger endowment shock and would expect more sales in the future. This does not happen when endowments are public information as when in an interdealer market dealers are required to disclose the trades received from their customers. With public information on endowments there is in fact a continuum of equilibria because traders then know the market-clearing price and are indifferent to which demand function to submit for out-of-equilibrium prices (this is as in any demand function model with no uncertainty, see the introduction to section 5.1). Vayanos in this case selects an equilibrium by using a perturbation technique.

A second result is that the welfare loss due to strategic behavior increases, in contrast to the public-information case, as the time between trades shrinks. A third result is that the welfare loss is of order $1/n^2$ for a fixed length of the interval between trades (this is the same as that in a k-double auction, see section 2.5.1) but that as this time interval shrinks to zero the welfare loss is of order $1/n$. Dynamic trading with strategic behavior may imply a slower convergence to efficiency than static competition as the number of traders increases. The results may shed some light on the debate about the welfare properties of continuous versus discrete auctions in the organization of stock markets.

Vayanos (2001) studies a stationary model where one large risk-averse trader receives a privately observed endowment shock every period and submits a market order to a competitive risk-averse market-making sector in the presence of noise traders. As before, information about asset payoffs is public and the large trader trades for an insurance motive. It is shown that after receiving an endowment shock the large trader reduces his risk exposure (and shares risk with the market makers) either by selling at a decreasing rate over time or, more surprisingly, by selling first to achieve optimal risk sharing and then engaging in a round-trip transaction by selling some more shares to buy them back later. The second pattern, which happens when there is enough noise trading and the large trader is not very risk averse compared with market makers, has a manipulation flavor. Indeed, in the second pattern of trade, market makers are misled by the first sale, thinking that it has originated with the noise traders. However, the large trader knows that this is not the case and that the price will therefore fall. He then exploits the situation by selling and buying back when the price has fallen. It is also found that when the time between trades tends to 0 the information about the endowment of the large trader is reflected in the price very quickly.

In short, large risk-averse traders, when hedging endowment shocks which are private information, will trade slowly, even when trade is very frequent. A consequence is that the welfare loss due to strategic behavior may increase as trade becomes more frequent and that as the number of traders increases an efficient outcome is approached more slowly than with one-shot trading. Furthermore, large risk-averse traders, when hedging endowment shocks which are private information, may have incentives to manipulate the market by trying to mislead market makers, much as large traders with privileged information about the fundamental value of the asset will do.

9.6 Summary

This chapter has examined the dynamics of competitive market-order markets and has allowed for strategic behavior. The main insights are:

- Learning from past prices (technical analysis) may be very slow, as in the canonical model of learning from others, if market depth is fixed exogenously.
- If competitive market makers set the depth of the market, then informational cascades are not possible and learning from prices in price-discovery processes is faster.
- A large informed trader has incentives to trade slowly so as not to reveal too much information and keep an informational advantage over uninformed traders and market makers. The insider will try to camouflage behind liquidity traders but has no incentive to introduce noise in his order to confuse market makers.
- Competition among strategic informed traders speeds up information revelation when they have symmetric information; otherwise informed traders may play a waiting game by trying to induce the competitor to reveal information.
- If an insider has to disclose his trades *ex post*, then he will dissimulate by randomizing to optimize his camouflage behind liquidity traders and obscure the separation of information-based from liquidity-based trades. Disclosure increases market depth and information revelation, and decreases the expected profits of the insider.
- Market manipulation is a distinct possibility when there are large traders in the market. A strategic informed trader may have incentives to use a contrarian strategy to suppress the information leakage from the price deriving from the competitive behavior of other informed traders.

- When liquidity traders have discretion about when to trade they will tend to concentrate their trading in periods where market depth is high and this will become a self-reinforcing process where informed traders, with short-lived information, as well as more liquidity traders will also join in, generating volume and volatility peaks.
- Large risk-averse traders hedging endowment shocks which are private information will trade slowly, even when trade is very frequent, and may have incentives to manipulate the market by trying to mislead market makers.

9.7 Appendix

Proof of proposition 9.1 (see p. 337). At a linear equilibrium and given our assumptions all random variables are normally distributed. Maximization of a CARA utility function by trader i then yields at stage t

$$X_t(s_i, p^{t-1}) = \frac{E[\theta - p_t \mid s_i, p^{t-1}]}{\rho \operatorname{var}[\theta - p_t \mid s_i, p^{t-1}]},$$

where $p_t = E[\theta \mid \omega^t]$ from the competition among market makers, and where ω_t is the t-period order flow. The expression is independent of i and therefore equilibria will be symmetric.[30] As in section 8.1.1 we obtain that $p_t - p_{t-1} = \lambda_t \omega_t$, where $\lambda_t = \tau_u a_t / \tau_t$, $\omega_t = a_t(\theta - p_{t-1}) + u_t$, and a_t is the weight given to private information in the t-period strategy. (In fact, just take the expression for $p_t - p_{t-1}$ in section 8.1.1 and replace Δa_t by a_t since trade is now notional and in period t the orders from period $t-1$ are canceled.) It is immediate that

$$E[\theta \mid s_i, p_t] = (\tau_\varepsilon s_i + \tau_t p_t)/(\tau_\varepsilon + \tau_t) \quad \text{and} \quad (\operatorname{var}[\theta \mid s_i, p_t])^{-1} = \tau_\varepsilon + \tau_t.$$

Furthermore, since $p_t = \lambda_t(a_t\theta + u_t) + (1 - \lambda_t a_t)p_{t-1}$, we have that $\theta - p_t = (1 - \lambda_t a_t)(\theta - p_{t-1}) - \lambda_t u_t$. It follows that, in the estimation of $\theta - p_t$, $s_i - p_{t-1}$ is sufficient with respect to the information $\{s_i, p^{t-1}\}$. Furthermore,

$$E[\theta - p_t \mid s_i, p^{t-1}] = (1 - \lambda_t a_t)\tau_\varepsilon(\tau_\varepsilon + \tau_{t-1})^{-1}(s_i - p_{t-1}).$$

Now, we have that

$$\begin{aligned} X_t(s_i, p_{t-1}) &= \frac{E[\theta - p_t \mid s_i, p_{t-1}]}{\rho \operatorname{var}[\theta - p_t \mid s_i, p_{t-1}]} \\ &= \frac{(1 - \lambda_t a_t)E[\theta - p_{t-1} \mid s_i, p_{t-1}]}{\rho[(1 - \lambda_t a_t)^2 \operatorname{var}[\theta \mid s_i, p_{t-1}] + \lambda_t^2 \sigma_u^2]}. \end{aligned}$$

Using the expressions for $E[\theta - p_t \mid s_i, p_{t-1}]$ and $\operatorname{var}[\theta \mid s_i, p_{t-1}]$, we obtain

$$a_t = \rho(\sigma_\varepsilon^2 + a_t \lambda_t \operatorname{var}[\theta \mid p_{t-1}])^{-1} = \rho(\sigma_\varepsilon^2 + \operatorname{var}[p_t \mid p_{t-1}])^{-1}.$$

This yields the recursive cubic equation $F_t(a_t) \equiv (\rho \tau_\varepsilon^{-1} a_t - 1)\tau_{t-1} + \rho \lambda_t a_t^2 = 0$. We show that the equation $F_t(a) = 0$ has a unique positive root, which lies in

[30] See the related discussion on the symmetry of linear equilibria in section 8.1.

the interval $(0, (\rho\sigma_\varepsilon^2)^{-1})$. It is clear that positive roots must lie in $(0, (\rho\sigma_\varepsilon^2)^{-1})$. It can be easily checked that $F_t(0) < 0$, $F_t((\rho\sigma_\varepsilon^2)^{-1}) > 0$, and that $F_t(a) = 0$ implies $F_t'(a) > 0$. It then follows that there is a unique positive root. □

9.8 Exercises

***9.1** (*sequential trading à la Glosten and Milgrom*). Consider the model in section 9.1.1 with $\theta \in \{0, 1\}$ and private binary, conditionally independent, signals $s_i \in \{s_L, s_H\}$ with $P(s_H \mid \theta = 1) = P(s_L \mid \theta = 0) = \ell > \frac{1}{2}$. Given the public belief about the value (probability that the value is high given public information), write the zero expected profit condition for a buy and for a sale for a market maker, and find the bid and ask equilibrium prices. Check that transaction prices, but not the quoted bid and ask prices, follow a martingale. Show that in equilibrium an informed trader buys if and only if he receives a high signal; and that as trading periods accumulate, the public belief converges to the true value and the bid–ask spread converges to zero.

Solution. See Glosten and Milgrom (1985).

9.2 (*the Glosten and Milgrom model with transaction costs*). Consider the model of section 9.1.1. Suppose that traders have to pay a transaction cost if they want to buy or sell the asset. Show that in this case an informational cascade in which all informed traders abstain from trading occurs almost surely. Furthermore, show that in this case the price does not converge to the fundamental value of the asset. (*Hint.* Recall what happens in exercise 9.1.)

Solution. See Cipriani and Guarino (2006).

9.3 (*asymptotic properties of the price-discovery process* (*section 9.1.3.2*)). Check the following asymptotic properties as $t \to \infty$ of the linear equilibrium in proposition 9.1: a_t converges monotonically from below to $(\rho\sigma_\varepsilon^2)^{-1}$; τ_t and λ_t^{-1} tend to ∞ at a rate of t; $\operatorname{var}[p_t]$ converges monotonically from below to σ_θ^2; $\operatorname{var}[p_t \mid p_{t-1}] \to 0$; the expected volume traded by informed agents $E[|x_{it}|]$ converges from above to $(2/\pi)^{1/2}(\rho\sigma_\varepsilon)^{-1}$; and the expected total volume traded $E[\mathrm{TV}_t]$ converges from above to $(2\pi)^{-1/2}((\rho\sigma_\varepsilon)^{-1} + 2\sigma_u)$.

Solution. From the analysis of the recursive cubic equation, $F_t = (\rho\tau_\varepsilon^{-1}a - 1) \times \tau_{t-1} + \rho\lambda_t a_t^2$, which yields the equilibrium a_t (see the proof of proposition 9.1 in the appendix), it follows that a_t is increasing and therefore τ_t (and $\lambda_t^{-1} = \tau_t/\tau_u a_t$) tend to ∞ with t. Consequently, $\operatorname{var}[p_t \mid p_{t-1}] \to 0$ and $a_t \to (\rho\sigma_\varepsilon^2)^{-1}$. This implies that τ_t and λ_t^{-1} are of the order of t. Furthermore, $\operatorname{var}[p_t] = \sigma_\theta^2 - \operatorname{var}[\theta \mid p_t]$ tends monotonically upward to σ_θ^2 since $\operatorname{var}[\theta \mid p_t] = \tau_t^{-1}$ tends monotonically to zero. With respect to trading volume, both $E[|x_{it}|] = (2/\pi)^{1/2}a_t(1/\tau_\varepsilon + 1/\tau_{t-1})^{1/2}$ and $E[\mathrm{TV}_t] = (1/2\pi)^{1/2}(a_t(1/\tau_\varepsilon + 1/\tau_{t-1})^{1/2} + (\sigma_u^2 + a_t^2/\tau_{t-1})^{1/2} + \sigma_u)$ will be decreasing for t large (since then the term $1/\tau_{t-1}$ dominates) and the results follow.

9.4 (*a noisy strategy for the insider in the Kyle (1985) model*). Consider the model of section 9.2 and suppose that the insider in period t can add to his order normally distributed noise η_t uncorrelated with all other random variables in the model, with mean zero and variance $\sigma^2_{\eta_t}$. Market makers observe the aggregate order flow and do not observe $\sigma^2_{\eta_t}$. Show that it does not pay to set $\sigma^2_{\eta_t} > 0$ in any period.

Solution. The insider draws a realization of η_t and places the order

$$\Delta Y_t(\theta, p^{t-1}) = \alpha_t(\theta - p_{t-1}) + \eta_t.$$

The market makers do not observe $\sigma^2_{\eta_t}$ but have a conjecture (in equilibrium correct) about the insider's choice of $\sigma^2_{\eta_t}$. In the last period T, the optimal level of added noise is zero because it cannot affect market depth (derived from the fixed conjecture of market makers) and it distorts trading. The reasoning then applies to stage $T - 1$ and so on.

****9.5** (*the effect of trade disclosure in the Kyle (1985) model*). Consider a two-period version of the Kyle (1985) model presented in section 9.2. Derive a closed-form solution for the equilibrium parameters. Now consider the case where at $t = 1$ the trade of the insider is disclosed. Derive the equilibrium in this case and compare it with the equilibrium in the Kyle model.

Solution. See Huddart et al. (2001).

***9.6** (*long-lived information as a durable good*). Consider a two-period trading model where competitive informed traders coexist with competitive risk-neutral market makers and noise traders as in section 8.1.2 with $T = 2$. There is an information monopolist who has perfect knowledge of the fundamental value θ and who decides every period how much noise to add to the private signals sold to the traders in order to maximize his revenue. The analyst reveals information truthfully. (A static version of this model is given in exercise 5.10.)

(1) Find out how much a trader would be willing to pay for a private signal of precision τ_{ε_t}, $t = 1, 2$.

(2) Find the sequence of optimal precisions of the signals sold $\{\tau^*_{\varepsilon_1}, \tau^*_{\varepsilon_2}\}$ from the point of view of the analyst and show that $\tau^*_{\varepsilon_1} < \hat{\tau}_\varepsilon < \tau^*_{\varepsilon_2}$, where $\hat{\tau}_\varepsilon = \rho^{-1}\sqrt{\tau_\theta/\tau_u}$ is the optimal precision in the static problem (exercise 5.10). Draw an analogy of the long-lived information seller with a durable goods monopolist seller that reduces durability in the first period (Bulow 1986) and markets a new product in the second period that makes the first-period product obsolete (Waldman 1993).

(3) Compare the solution in (2) with a market with a single risk-neutral insider submitting a market order in each period (as in proposition 9.2 with $T = 2$). Show that at $t = 2$ the insider trades less aggressively than a competitive informed trader when sold a signal of equilibrium precision and this makes the market in this period thinner and the price less informative than when

there is an information monopolist. Draw an analogy with the durable goods monopolist producer who can rent the good instead of selling it in order to diminish intertemporal self-competition.

Solution. (1) Using the properties of CARA utilities (see section 10.2.4) the maximum prices that a trader is willing to pay for observing signals with precisions $\{\tau_{\varepsilon_1}, \tau_{\varepsilon_2}\}$ (when the other traders are observing signals of precision $\{\tau_{\varepsilon_1}, \tau_{\varepsilon_2}\}$) are given by $\phi_1 = (2\rho)^{-1}(\ln(1 + \tau_{\varepsilon_1}\tau_1^{-1}) + \ln(1 + \tau_{\varepsilon_1}\tau_2^{-1}))$ for τ_{ε_1} and $\phi_2 = (2\rho)^{-1}\ln(1 + \tau_{\varepsilon_2}(\tau_2 + \tau_{\varepsilon_1})^{-1})$, with τ_t the precision of prices at the competitive equilibrium: $\tau_t = \tau_\theta + \tau_u\rho^{-2}\sum_{k=1}^{t}\tau_{\varepsilon_k}^2$, $t = 1, 2$ (see section 8.1.2). (2) Optimize ϕ_1 and ϕ_2. (3) Use the equilibrium parameters for the $T = 2$ Kyle (1985) model derived in Huddart et al. (2001) as in exercise 9.5 (see Cespa (forthcoming)).

9.7 (*conditional volatility in the preopening market*). Consider the tatônnement model of section 9.1.3 and explain why the conditional volatility of prices $\text{var}[p_t \mid p_{t-1}]$ may be hump-shaped or increasing with t, implying that the responsiveness to information of the competitive agents a_t is U-shaped or decreasing, respectively.

Solution. Use the fact that the conditional volatility of prices is increasing (decreasing) if and only if information revelation accelerates (decelerates) as t increases. More precisely, $\text{var}[p_t \mid p_{t-1}]$ is increasing (decreasing) in n if and only if $\text{var}[\theta \mid p_t]$ is concave (convex) in t.[31] When γ is low, information revelation accelerates as the *tâtonnement* progresses ($\text{var}[\theta \mid p_t]$ is concave in t). Otherwise, for larger γ, $\text{var}[\theta \mid p_t]$ is first concave and then convex in t, implying that $\text{var}[p_t \mid p_{t-1}]$ is first increasing and then decreasing with t.

****9.8** (*equilibrium with demand schedules in the preopening market*). Consider a version of the preopening model of section 9.3 in which both the strategic and the competitive informed traders submit demand schedules instead of market orders. At stage t, informed agent i submits a demand schedule $X_t(p_t; s_i, p^{t-1})$, contingent on the private signal s_i he has and the past history of prices. Similarly, the insider's strategy at t is a demand function contingent on his private information and past prices, $Y_t(p_t; \theta, p^{t-1})$. As before, noise traders are assumed to submit at round t the order u_t and market makers quote prices efficiently on the basis of public information and the aggregate limit-order book, which is just a noisy version of the aggregate orders of informed agents. Competitive market making implies that p_t is a sufficient statistic for public information and therefore the strategies can be written as $X_t(s_i, p_t)$ and $Y_t(\theta, p_t)$. Show that there exists a unique linear equilibrium characterized, for $t = 1, \dots, T$, by

$$\begin{aligned} X_t(s_i, p_t) &= a(s_i - p_t), \\ Y_t(\theta, p_t) &= \alpha_t(\theta - p_t), \\ p_t &= \lambda_t\omega_t + p_{t-1}, \end{aligned}$$

[31] Note also that if $\text{var}[\theta \mid p_t]$ is concave in t, then $\tau_t = (\text{var}[\theta \mid p_t])^{-1}$ is convex in t.

where $a = \tau_\varepsilon/\rho$, $\omega_n = A_t(\theta - p_{t-1}) + u_t$, $\lambda_t = \tau_u A_t/\tau_t$, $A_t = \mu\alpha_t + (1-\mu)a$, and $\tau_t = \tau_\theta + \tau_u \sum_{k=1}^{t} A_k^2$.

At stage t, the strategic informed trader's expected continuation profit is given by $E[\pi_{t+1} \mid \theta, p_t] = \mu h_t(\theta - p_t)^2 + \mu\delta_t$.

The constants α_t, h_t, and δ_t are given by the solutions to the difference equation system

$$\begin{aligned}\alpha_t &= (\gamma_t - 2(1-\gamma_t)\mu\lambda_t h_t)/(2\gamma_t\mu\lambda_t),\\ h_t &= (1-\lambda_{t+1}A_{t+1})^2\gamma_{t+1}\alpha_{t+1} + (1-\gamma_{t+1})h_{t+1},\\ \delta_t &= \gamma_{t+1}\alpha_{t+1} + (1-\gamma_{t+1})h_{t+1}(\lambda_{t+1}\sigma_u)^2 + (1-\gamma_{t+1})\delta_{t+1},\end{aligned}$$

subject to the boundary conditions $h_T = 0$, $\delta_T = 0$, $2\mu\alpha_T\lambda_T = 1$, and the second-order conditions $\lambda_t > 0$ for all $t = 1, 2, \ldots, T$.

Hint. Get inspiration from the derivation of the equilibrium in the static model with demand schedules in section 5.2.3. Follow the steps of the proof of proposition 9.3 and note that the strategy of competitive informed traders is stationary, and therefore the difference equation system that characterizes the equilibrium parameters can be iterated backward as in the proof of proposition 9.2 (Kyle 1985).

9.9 (*volume peaks with discretionary liquidity traders*). Show in the model of section 9.4 that expected trading volume peaks in the period where discretionary liquidity trading is concentrated when $\sigma_t^2 = 1$, $\tau_{\varepsilon_t} = \tau_\varepsilon$, and $\text{var}[u_t] = \sigma_u^2$ for any t.

Solution. Immediate once the expression for expected trading volume is written (get inspiration from the expressions for volume in exercise 5.7).

References

Admati, A. R., and P. Pfleiderer. 1988. A theory of intraday patterns: volume and price variability. *Review of Financial Studies* 1:1, 3–40.

Allen, F., and D. Gale. 1992. Stock-price manipulation. *Review of Financial Studies* 5:503–29.

Allen, F., and G. Gorton. 1992. Stock price manipulation, market microstructure and asymmetric information. *European Economic Review* 36:624–30.

Amihud, Y., and H. Mendelson. 1987. Trading mechanisms and stock returns: an empirical investigation. *Journal of Finance* 42:533–53.

Avery, C., and P. Zemsky. 1998. Multidimensional uncertainty and herd behavior in financial markets. *American Economic Review* 88:724–48.

Back, K. 1992. Insider trading in continuous time. *Review of Financial Studies* 5:387–409.

Back, K., and S. Baruch. 2004. Information in securities markets: Kyle meets Glosten and Milgrom. *Econometrica* 72:433–65.

——. 2007. Working orders in limit order markets and floor exchanges. *Journal of Finance* 62:1589–621.

Back, K., and H. Pedersen. 1998. Long-lived information and intraday patterns. *Journal of Financial Markets* 1:385–402.

Back, K., H. Cao, and G. Willard. 2000. Imperfect competition among informed traders. *Journal of Finance* 55:2117–55.

Barberis, N., A. Schleifer, and R. Vishny. 1998. A model of investor sentiment. *Journal of Financial Economics* 49:307–44.

Benabou, R., and G. Laroque. 1992. Using privileged information to manipulate markets: insiders, gurus, and credibility. *Quarterly Journal of Economics* 107:921–58.

Biais, B., P. Hillion, and C. Spatt. 1999. Price discovery and learning in the preopening period in the Paris Bourse. *Journal of Political Economy* 107:1218–48.

Bikhchandani, S., D. Hirshleifer, and I. Welch. 1992. A theory of fads, fashion, custom, and cultural change as informational cascades. *Journal of Political Economy* 100:992–1026.

Bulow, J. I. 1986. Durable-goods monopolists. *Journal of Political Economy* 90:314–32.

Cao, C., E. Ghysels, and F. Hatheway. 2000. Price discovery without trading: evidence form the NASDAQ preopening. *Journal of Finance* 55:1339–65.

Cespa, G. Forthcoming. Information sales and insider trading with long-lived information. CEPR Discussion Paper 4667 (*Journal of Finance*).

Chakraborty, A., and B. Yilmaz. 2004. Informed manipulation. *Journal of Economic Theory* 114:132–52.

Chau, M. 2002. Dynamic trading and market-making with inventory costs and private information. Working Paper, ESSEC.

Chau, M., and D. Vayanos. Forthcoming. Strong-form efficiency with monopolistic insiders. *Review of Financial Studies.*

Chordia, T., and A. Subrahmanyam. 2004. Order imbalance and individual stock returns: theory and evidence. *Journal of Financial Economics* 72:485–518.

Cipriani, M., and A. Guarino. 2005. Herd behavior in a laboratory financial market. *American Economic Review* 95:1427–43.

——. 2006. Transaction costs and informational cascades in financial markets: theory and experimental evidence. Mimeo.

——. 2007. Herd behavior in financial markets: a field experiment with financial market professionals. Mimeo.

Daniel, K., D. Hirshleifer, and A. Subrahmanyam. 1998. Investor psychology and security market under- and over-reactions. *Journal of Finance* 53:1839–86.

Dow, J. 2004. Is liquidity self-fulfilling? *Journal of Business* 77:895–908.

Drehmann, M., J. Oechssler, and A. Roider. 2005. Herding and contrarian behavior in financial markets: an internet experiment. *American Economic Review* 95:1403–26.

Fama, E., and K. French. 1988. Permanent and temporary components of stock prices. *Journal of Political Economy* 96:246–73.

Fishman, M. J., and K. M. Hagerty. 1995. The incentive to sell financial market information. *Journal of Financial Intermediation* 4:95–115.

Foster, F., and S. Viswanathan. 1990. A theory of the intraday variations in volume, variance, and trading costs in securities markets. *Review of Financial Studies* 3:593–624.

——. 1994. Strategic trading with asymmetrically informed traders and long-lived information. *Journal of Financial and Quantitative Analysis* 29:499–518.

——. 1996. Strategic trading when agents forecast the forecasts of others. *Journal of Finance* 50:1437–78.

Glosten, L., and P. R. Milgrom. 1985. Bid, ask and transaction prices in a specialist market with heterogeneously informed traders. *Journal of Financial Economics* 17:71–100.

Goldstein, I., and A. Guembel. Forthcoming. Manipulation and the allocational role of prices. *Review of Economic Studies.*

Guo, M., and A. Kyle. 2005. Dynamic strategic informed trading with risk-averse market makers. Mimeo, Duke University.

Hart, O. 1977. On the profitability of speculation. *Quarterly Journal of Economics* 91: 579–97.

Hillion, P., and M. Suominen. 2004. The manipulation of closing prices. *Journal of Financial Markets* 7:351–75.

Holden, C., and A. Subrahmanyam. 1992. Long-lived private information and imperfect competition. *Journal of Finance* 47:247–70.

——. 1994. Risk aversion, imperfect competition, and long-lived information. *Economic Letters* 44:181–90.

Hong, H., and J. Stein. 1999. A unified theory of underreaction, momentum trading and overreaction in asset markets. *Journal of Finance* 54:2143–84.

Huddart, S., J. S. Hughes, and C. B. Levine. 2001. Public disclosure and dissimulation of insider trades. *Econometrica* 69:665–81.

Jarrow, R. A. 1992. Market manipulation, bubbles, corners, and short squeezes. *Journal of Financial and Quantitative Analysis* 27:311–36.

Jegadeesh, N. 1990. Evidence of predictable behavior of security returns. *Journal of Finance* 45:881–98.

Jegadeesh, N., and S. Titman. 1993. Returns to buying winners and selling losers: implications for stock market efficiency. *Journal of Finance* 48:65–91.

John, K., and R. Narayanan. 1997. Market manipulation and the role of insider trading regulations. *Journal of Business* 70:217–47.

Jordan, J. S. 1982. A dynamic model of expectations equilibrium. *Journal of Economic Theory* 28:235–54.

——. 1985. Learning rational expectations: the finite state case. *Journal of Economic Theory* 36:257–76.

Kobayashi, T. 1977. A convergence theorem on rational expectations equilibrium with price information. Working Paper 79, The Economics Series, Institute for Mathematical Studies in the Social Sciences, Stanford University.

Kumar, P., and D. Seppi. 1992. Futures manipulation with “cash settlement”. *Journal of Finance* 47:1485–502.

Kyle, A. S. 1985. Continuous auctions and insider trading. *Econometrica* 53:1315–35.

Madhavan, A., and V. Panchapagesan. 1998. Price discovery in auction markets: a look inside the black box. *Review of Financial Studies* 13:627–58.

McCafferty, S., and R. Driskill. 1980. Problems of existence and uniqueness in nonlinear rational expectations models. *Econometrica* 48:1313–17.

Medrano, L. A., and X. Vives. 2001. Strategic behavior and price discovery. *RAND Journal of Economics* 32:221–48.

Muth, J. 1961. Rational expectations and the theory of price movements. *Econometrica* 29:315–35.

Pagano, M. 1989. Trading volume and asset liquidity. *Quarterly Journal of Economics* 104:255–74.

Park, A., and H. Sabourian. 2006. Herd behavior in efficient financial markets. Mimeo.

Poterba, J., and L. Summers. 1986. The persistence of volatility and stock market fluctuations. *American Economic Review* 76:1142–51.

——. 1988. Mean reversion in stock prices: evidence and implications. *Journal of Financial Economics* 22:27–60.

Romer, D. 1993. Rational asset-price movements without news. *American Economic Review* 83:1112–30.

Sola, P. 1999. Eficiencia informativa de precios indicativos en el periodo de ajuste de la Bolsa de Madrid. Master's thesis, CEMFI, no. 9909.

Stoll, H., and R. E. Whaley. 1990. Stock market structure and volatility. *Review of Financial Studies* 3:37–41.

Vayanos, D. 1999. Strategic trading and welfare in a dynamic market. *Review of Economic Studies* 66:219–54.

——. 2001. Strategic trading in a dynamic noisy market. *Journal of Finance* 56:131–71.

Vila, J. L. 1989. Simple games of market manipulation. *Economic Letters* 29:21–26.

Vives, X. 1993. How fast do rational agents learn. *Review of Economic Studies* 60:329–47.

——. 1995a. Short-term investment and the informational efficiency of the market. *Review Financial Studies* 8:125–60.

——. 1995b. The speed of information revelation in a financial market mechanism. *Journal of Economic Theory* 67:178–204.

Waldman, M. 1993. A new perspective on planned obsolescence. *Quarterly Journal of Economics* 108:273–83.

Whitcomb, D. K. 1985. An international comparison of stock exchange trading structures. In *Market Making and the Changing Structure of the Securities Industry* (ed. Y. Amihud, T. S. Y. Ho, and R. A. Schwartz). Lexington, MA: Lexington Books.

10
Technical Appendix

This chapter reviews in a somewhat *informal* way some of the main tools used throughout the book. Accessible references to the material in this chapter can be found in Spanos (1993, 2000) for probability and statistics, Laffont (1989) for information structures, and Fudenberg and Tirole (1991) for games. More advanced treatments can be found in DeGroot (1970), Ash (1972), Chung (1974), and Billingsley (1979) for probability and statistics.

The workhorse model in the book is the linear-normal model and corresponding attention is devoted to it. We start by having a look at information structures and the principles of Bayesian inference in section 10.1. We dedicate section 10.2 to the study of the properties of normal distributions and the affine information structure (to which the normal case belongs and has the convenient property that conditional expectations are linear). Section 10.3 is devoted to convergence concepts of random variables and results, and properties of Bayesian learning. Finally, section 10.4 deals with Bayesian equilibrium.

10.1 Information Structures and Bayesian Inference

This section deals with some of the basics of probability (section 1.1) and signals (section 1.2), the concept of sufficient statistic (section 1.3), informativeness of information structures (section 1.4), and some useful concepts like properties of the likelihood ratio and affiliation (section 1.5). Section 1.6 presents some results with a finite number of states.

10.1.1 Preliminaries

Given an arbitrary set Ω, we consider the space of states of nature $(\Omega, \mathcal{E})$, where $\mathcal{E}$ is the set of events: a collection of subsets of Ω (i.e., $\mathcal{E} \subseteq 2^{\Omega}$). We put some restrictions on the set of events: $\mathcal{E}$ is a σ-algebra or σ-field (a family of sets such that (i) the set Ω belongs to it, (ii) if a set belongs to the family, its complement also belongs to the family, and (iii) the family is closed under countable unions of sets in the family). The space $(\Omega, \mathcal{E})$ is then a *measurable space* and an *event* is a measurable set. A set in a given class $\mathcal{E}$ is said to be $\mathcal{E}$-measurable.

A *probability measure* on $(\Omega, \mathcal{E})$ is a function $P : \mathcal{E} \to [0, 1]$ such that $P(\Omega) = 1$ and for every countable sequence of events, which are pairwise disjoint, the probability of the union equals the (infinite) sum of the probabilities (this property is called countable additivity). In the text the set of states will be a subset of Euclidean space. When $(\Omega, \mathcal{E})$ is endowed with a probability measure P, the triple $(\Omega, \mathcal{E}, P)$ is called a *probability space*.

Given $\mathcal{E}_1$ and $\mathcal{E}_2$, two σ-fields of Ω, we will say that $\mathcal{E}_1$ is smaller than $\mathcal{E}_2$ if, for any $A \in \mathcal{E}_1$, this implies $A \in \mathcal{E}_2$. The Borel σ-field is the one defined on the real line, and it is the smallest containing all the closed intervals for the Euclidean topology.

A *random variable* X on the probability space $(\Omega, \mathcal{E}, P)$ is a real-valued function $X : \Omega \to \mathbb{R}$ such that for any $x \in (-\infty, \infty)$, the set $\{\omega \in \Omega : X(\omega) \leqslant x\}$ is an event (belongs to $\mathcal{E}$). A real-valued function fulfilling this property is called *measurable* with respect to $\mathcal{E}$ or $\mathcal{E}$-measurable. A random variable induces a probability measure on the Borel subsets of the reals: $P_X(B) = P\{\omega \in \Omega : X(\omega) \in B\}$, where B is a Borel subset. A *support* for the probability measure induced by the random variable X is a Borel set of full measure. The *distribution function* of the random variable X is $F : \mathbb{R} \to [0, 1]$ such that $F(x) = P\{\omega \in \Omega : X(\omega) \leqslant x\}$.

A *random vector* is a mapping $X : \Omega \to \mathbb{R}^k$ $\mathcal{E}$-measurable. It is a k-tuple of random variables $X = (X_1, \dots, X_k)$. We have that $X(\omega) = (X_1(\omega), \dots, X_k(\omega))$ for $\omega \in \Omega$ and X is $\mathcal{E}$-measurable if and only if each X_i is. The σ-field generated by the random vector X is the smallest σ-field with respect to which it is measurable and is denoted by $\sigma(X)$ (i.e., the smallest σ-field generated by the events of the type $X_i^{-1}(B)$ with B a Borel set of the real line and $i = 1, \dots, k$). This is a sub-σ-field of $(\Omega, \mathcal{E})$.

Let A, B be events in a probability space $(\Omega, \mathcal{E}, P)$ with $P(B) > 0$. The *conditional probability* of A given B is $P(A \mid B) = P(A \cap B)/P(B)$. This is the probability that an observer assigns to $\omega \in \Omega$ to lie in A if he learns that ω lies in B. More generally, we can define the conditional probability of A given a sub-σ-field $\mathcal{G}$ of $(\Omega, \mathcal{E})$ and denote it by $P(A \mid \mathcal{G})$. The σ-field $\mathcal{G}$ may come, for example, from a partition of Ω or may be more general, and it can be identified with an observation or experiment (an observer may know for each $B \in \mathcal{G}$ whether ω lies in B or not). $P(A \mid \mathcal{G})$ is a random variable which is $\mathcal{G}$-measurable, integrable, and satisfies the functional equation $\int_B P(A \mid \mathcal{G})\,dP = P(A \cap B)$ for $B \in \mathcal{G}$. Any random variable fulfilling those properties is a *version* of the conditional probability and any two versions are equal with probability 1. The conditional probability of A given a random variable X is defined as $P(A \mid \sigma(X))$ and denoted by $P(A \mid X)$. In a similar way we can define the conditional expectation. Suppose that X is an integrable random variable on $(\Omega, \mathcal{E}, P)$ and $\mathcal{G}$ a σ-field in $\mathcal{E}$. The conditional expected value of X given $\mathcal{G}$ is the random variable $E[X \mid \mathcal{G}]$, which is $\mathcal{G}$-measurable, integrable, and which satisfies the functional equation $\int_B E[X \mid \mathcal{G}]\,dP = \int_B X\,dP$ for $B \in \mathcal{G}$. Any random variable fulfilling those properties is a *version* of the conditional expected value and any two versions are equal with probability 1. The conditional expected value of X given the σ-field generated by the random variable Y, $\sigma(Y)$, is $E[X \mid \sigma(Y)]$ and is denoted by $E[X \mid Y]$.

The following rule is the basis of updating probabilities.

The rule of Bayes. Let $A_1, A_2, \ldots$ be an infinite sequence of disjoint events with $P(A_i) > 0$ for any i and such that their union is Ω. Let B be another event such that $P(B) > 0$. Then

$$P(A_i \mid B) = \frac{P(B \mid A_i)P(A_i)}{\sum_{j=1}^{\infty} P(B \mid A_j)P(A_j)}, \quad i = 1, 2, \ldots.$$

A similar result applies to a finite sequence of disjoint events $A_1, \ldots, A_n$ (see DeGroot 1970, pp. 11-12).

Remark on notation. To simplify notation in general we will not distinguish between a random variable X and its realization x, and we use lowercase notation.

10.1.2 Information Structures

Consider the space of states of nature $(\Theta, \mathcal{I})$ and a probability space $(\Theta, \mathcal{I}, P)$. We may assume, as is typically done in the text, that the agent knows the probability distribution P. This is called the prior distribution. However, the agent may also have a subjective prior probability assessment that need not coincide with the objective prior.

The *information* available to an agent can be described by a partition of the state space Θ. Equivalently, by a (measurable) function $\phi : \Theta \to S$, where S is a space of signals. In this case the corresponding partition of Θ is given by the elements $\phi^{-1}(s)$, $s \in S$. When the agent receives a signal he learns in which element of the partition lies the state of nature. This formulation corresponds to an information structure without noise.

The signals received by the agent are typically noisy. Then for every state of the world in Θ, a nondegenerate distribution is induced on the (measurable) signal space S. A usual case is to have for each θ a conditional density $h(s \mid \theta)$ defining the *likelihood function* of the signals received by the agent. The information structure is then given by a space of signals and a likelihood function $(S, h(\cdot \mid \theta))$, which defines a random variable, "experiment," or signal s with values in S (recall that we do not distinguish notationally between a random variable and its realization). This implies, obviously, that the random variable s has a probability distribution which depends on θ.

Once the agent receives the signal s he updates his distribution on θ according to the rule of Bayes and forms a *posterior distribution* of θ given s. Suppose that the prior distribution is given by the density $f(\theta)$ and the likelihood by the conditional density $h(s \mid \theta)$. Denote the posterior density or conditional density of θ given the observation of s by $f(\theta \mid s)$. According to (the continuous distribution version of) the rule of Bayes, we have that

$$f(\theta \mid s) = \frac{h(s \mid \theta)f(\theta)}{\int h(s \mid \theta)f(\theta)\,d\theta}.$$

With discrete distributions we have an analogous result.

10.1.3 Sufficient Statistics

Any function Ψ of the observation of the random variable or vector s is called *statistic*. A statistic Ψ is called a *sufficient statistic* if, for any prior distribution of θ, its posterior distribution depends on the observed value of s only through $\Psi(s)$. In this case to obtain the posterior distribution of θ from any prior, the agent only needs the value of $\Psi(s)$. More formally, a statistic Ψ is a sufficient statistic for a family of distributions $\{h(\cdot \mid \theta),\ \theta \in \Theta\}$ if $f(\cdot \mid s') = f(\cdot \mid s'')$ for any prior $f(\cdot)$ and any two points $s' \in S$ and $s'' \in S$ such that $\Psi(s') = \Psi(s'')$.

A useful characterization of sufficiency is the *factorization criterion* (DeGroot 1970, pp. 155—56): a statistic Ψ is sufficient for a family of distributions $\{h(\cdot \mid \theta),\ \theta \in \Theta\}$ if, and only if, for any s in S and $\theta \in \Theta$; $h(s \mid \theta)$ can be factored as follows:

$$h(s \mid \theta) = u(s)v(\Psi(s), \theta),$$

where the function u is positive and does not depend on θ, and the function v is nonnegative and depends on s only through $\Psi(s)$.

For example, suppose an agent observes signals $s_1, \dots, s_n$ which are a random sample from a Gaussian normal distribution with unknown value of the mean θ and known variance $\sigma^2 > 0$. That is, the likelihood $h(\cdot \mid \theta)$ is normal with mean θ and variance $\sigma^2 > 0$. Then the conditional joint probability density function is

$$\begin{aligned} h_n(s_1, \dots, s_n \mid \theta) &= (2\pi\sigma^2)^{-n/2} \exp\left\{ -\frac{1}{2\sigma^2} \sum_{i=1}^{n} (s_i - \theta)^2 \right\} \\ &= (2\pi\sigma^2)^{-n/2} \exp\left\{ -\frac{1}{2\sigma^2} \sum_{i=1}^{n} s_i^2 - \frac{\theta}{\sigma^2} \sum_{i=1}^{n} s_i - \frac{n\theta^2}{2\sigma^2} \right\} \\ &= (2\pi\sigma^2)^{-n/2} \exp\left\{ -\frac{1}{2\sigma^2} \sum_{i=1}^{n} s_i^2 \right\} \exp\left\{ -\frac{\theta}{\sigma^2} \sum_{i=1}^{n} s_i - \frac{n\theta^2}{2\sigma^2} \right\}. \end{aligned}$$

Letting $u(s) = (2\pi\sigma^2)^{-n/2} \exp\{-(1/2\sigma^2)\sum_{i=1}^{n} s_i^2\}$, $\Psi(s) = \sum_{i=1}^{n} s_i$, $v(\Psi(s), \theta) = \exp\{-(\theta/\sigma^2)\Psi(s) - n\theta^2/2\sigma^2\}$, we have that $h_n(s_1, \dots, s_n \mid \theta)$ can be factored according to the criterion and $\Psi(s) = \sum_{i=1}^{n} s_i$ is a sufficient statistic. Note that sufficient statistics are not unique. Indeed, for example, the average signal $\tilde{s} = (\sum_{i=1}^{n} s_i)/n$ is also a sufficient statistic (use the decomposition $\sum_{i=1}^{n}(s_i - \theta)^2 = \sum_{i=1}^{n}(s_i - \tilde{s})^2 + n(\tilde{s} - \theta)^2$).

10.1.4 Informativeness of Signals

If the information structure is given in partition form of the state space, then one partition is more *informative* than another if it is finer (i.e., if each element of the latter can be obtained as the union of elements of the former). It should be clear that with a finer partition a decision maker cannot do worse because with the finer one he can always make decisions based only on the coarser one. Any decision maker, for any utility function and prior distribution on Θ, will prefer one information structure to another if and only if the former is finer than the latter. More information cannot hurt. This may not be true when there is interaction among different players. In fact, an improvement in information can then make everyone worse off.

Blackwell (1951) developed the concept of an information structure or experiment (S, h) being *sufficient* for information structure or experiment (S', h') when, intuitively, independent of the value of θ, s' can be obtained from s by adding noise. If this is the case, then an agent should never perform the experiment s' when s is available. We say that signal s is more informative than signal s' if s is sufficient (in the Blackwell sense) for signal s'.

For continuously distributed signals, we say that signal s is sufficient for signal s' if there exists a stochastic transformation from s to s', i.e., a function $g : S'xS \to \mathbb{R}_+$, where $\int_{S'} g(s', s)\,\mathrm{d}s' = 1$ for any s in S (and also assume for convenience that g is integrable, with positive value, with respect to s for any s'), such that $h'(s' \mid \theta) = \int_S g(s', s)h(s \mid \theta)\,\mathrm{d}s$ for any θ in Θ and s' in S'. Note that $g(\cdot, s)$ is a probability density function for any s in S since a realization s' can be generated by a randomization using $g(\cdot, s)$ given that $\int_{S'} g(s', s)\,\mathrm{d}s' = 1$ for any s in S (see DeGroot 1970, p. 434).

For example, consider the case where both the prior distribution and likelihood are given by the Gaussian normal distribution function: θ with mean $\bar{\theta}$ and finite variance σ_θ^2 (and we write $\theta \sim N(\bar{\theta}, \sigma_\theta^2)$) and s conditional on θ with mean θ and finite variance σ_ε^2 (and we write $s \mid \theta \sim N(\theta, \sigma_\varepsilon^2)$). That is, $s = \theta + \varepsilon$, where $\varepsilon \sim N(0, \sigma_\varepsilon^2)$ and $\mathrm{cov}[\theta, \varepsilon] = 0$. The precision of the signal (likelihood) is defined to be the inverse of the variance: $\tau_\varepsilon = (\sigma_\varepsilon^2)^{-1}$. Then it is immediate that s is more informative than s' if and only if $\tau_\varepsilon > \tau_{\varepsilon'}$ since s' can be obtained from s by adding noise.

A similar definition can be given for the case of discrete signals. If the number of possible states and signals is finite, then an information structure is characterized by the pair (S, L), where S has a finite number of elements and L is the likelihood matrix with entries of the type $P(s_k \mid \theta_j)$. Then information structure (S, L) is sufficient or more informative than (S', L') if and only if there is a conformable Markov matrix M (i.e., a matrix with nonnegative elements with columns adding up to 1) such that $L' = ML$.

Blackwell's theorem states that any decision maker, for any utility function and prior distribution on Θ, should prefer information structure (S, h) to (S', h') if and only if s is sufficient for signal s' (Blackwell 1951; see also Cremer 1982; Kihlstrom 1984). A more informative signal corresponds to a finer information partition.

10.1.5 Some Useful Concepts

Suppose that the agent has a prior density $f(\theta)$ on $\Theta \subset \mathbb{R}$ and the likelihood is given by the conditional density $h(s \mid \theta)$ and, as before, denote the posterior density by $f(\theta \mid s)$. According to the rule of Bayes we have that

$$f(\theta \mid s) = \frac{h(s \mid \theta) f(\theta)}{\int h(s \mid \theta) f(\theta)\, d\theta}.$$

From the rule of Bayes we obtain the *likelihood ratio* for any two states θ' and θ:

$$\frac{f(\theta' \mid s)}{f(\theta \mid s)} = \frac{h(s \mid \theta')}{h(s \mid \theta)} \frac{f(\theta')}{f(\theta)}.$$

The family of likelihoods $\{h(\cdot \mid \theta)\}$ has the *monotone likelihood ratio property* (MLRP) if for every $\theta' > \theta$ and $s > \hat{s}$ we have that $h(s \mid \theta')h(\hat{s} \mid \theta) - h(s \mid \theta)h(\hat{s} \mid \theta') \geqslant 0$. This means that the likelihood ratio $h(s \mid \theta')/h(s \mid \theta)$ increases with s for $\theta' > \theta$. A larger realization of s is to be interpreted as news that the likelihood is more likely to be $h(s \mid \theta')$ than $h(s \mid \theta)$. Many of the commonly used densities satisfy the MLRP. Examples are the normal distribution, the exponential distribution, and the Poisson distribution (all three with mean θ), the uniform distribution on $[0, \theta]$, and the chi-squared distribution (with noncentrality parameter θ) (see Milgrom 1981).

Affiliation. If the real-valued function $f : \mathbb{R}^k \to \mathbb{R}$ is twice continuously differentiable, we say it is *log-supermodular* if and only if $\partial^2 \log f / \partial x_i \partial x_j \geqslant 0$ for all $i \neq j$.[1] Suppose that the (real-valued) random variables $x_1, \dots, x_k$ have a joint density $f(\cdot)$. The random variables are *affiliated* if their joint density is log-supermodular (almost everywhere). Milgrom and Webber (1982) provide a general definition of affiliation.

For convenience suppose that the support of the family of densities $\{h(\cdot \mid \theta)\}$ is independent of θ. An equivalent way to express the MLRP is to say that $\partial \log h(s \mid \theta)/\partial\theta$ increases with s (or $\partial^2 \log h(s \mid \theta)/\partial\theta\partial s \geqslant 0$ if $h(\cdot \mid \cdot)$ is twice continuously differentiable). (We can think of $\log h(s \mid \theta)$ as the likelihood function of the model where s is the estimator for the parameter θ.) The condition is the equivalent to log-supermodularity of $h(s \mid \theta)$. In turn, this would be equivalent to log-supermodularity of the joint density $f(s, \theta) = h(s \mid \theta) f(\theta)$. We then say that the random variables s and θ are affiliated.

The MLRP implies first-order stochastic dominance. If the family of likelihoods $\{h(\cdot \mid \theta)\}$ has the MLRP, then for any nondegenerate prior distribution F for θ the posterior distribution $F(\cdot \mid s)$ first-order stochastically dominates $F(\cdot \mid s')$ for $s > s'$ (see Milgrom 1981). We say that the distribution $F(\theta; y)$ is ordered by the parameter y according to first-order stochastic dominance if $F(\theta; y)$ decreases with y.

10.1.6 Finite Number of States

Two-point support information structure. A simple example of a discrete information structure is the two-state space, $\Theta = \{\theta_L, \theta_H\}$, with respective prior

[1] In section 4.1 we provide a more general definition of supermodularity and log-supermodularity.

probabilities $P(\theta_L)$ and $P(\theta_H)$, and two-point support signals, $S = \{s_L, s_H\}$, model. The agent may receive a low (s_L) or a high (s_H) signal about θ with likelihood $P(s_H \mid \theta_H) = P(s_L \mid \theta_L) = q$, where $\frac{1}{2} \leqslant q \leqslant 1$. With this setup we have a symmetric binary model. If $q = \frac{1}{2}$, the signal is uninformative; if $q = 1$, it is perfectly informative. It is easily checked that s is more informative than s' if and only if $q > q'$. Indeed, the likelihood matrix associated with s',

$$L' = \begin{bmatrix} q' & 1-q' \\ 1-q' & q' \end{bmatrix},$$

can be obtained with a stochastic transformation of the likelihood matrix associated with s,

$$L = \begin{bmatrix} q & 1-q \\ 1-q & q \end{bmatrix}$$

since $L' = ML$, where

$$M = \frac{1}{q-(1-q)} \begin{bmatrix} q'-(1-q) & q-q' \\ q-q' & q'-(1-q) \end{bmatrix}$$

is a Markov matrix.

The *logarithm of the likelihood ratio* (LLR) of the two states

$$\lambda = \log(P(\theta_H)/P(\theta_L))$$

updates in an additive way with new information. (This generalizes to any two states out of a finite number.) After observing signal s (be it from a discrete or a continuous likelihood), it is immediate from the rule of Bayes that the updated LLR is

$$\log(P(\theta_H \mid s)/P(\theta_L \mid s)) = \lambda + \lambda(s), \quad \text{where } \lambda(s) = \log(P(s \mid \theta_H)/P(s \mid \theta_L)).$$

One possible way to define signals of *bounded strength* is to look at the LLR. A signal will be of bounded strength if the support of the distribution of the LLR is bounded. This is clearly the case with the two-point support information structure. It would not be the case if the likelihood is normally distributed $s \mid \theta \sim N(\theta, \tau_\varepsilon^{-1})$. That is, $s = \theta + \varepsilon$, where $\varepsilon \sim N(0, \tau_\varepsilon^{-1})$ with $\operatorname{cov}[\theta, \varepsilon] = 0$. Letting $P(\theta_H) = P(\theta_L) = \frac{1}{2}$, we have, since $P(s \mid \theta) = \exp\{-\frac{1}{2}\tau_\varepsilon(s-\theta)^2\}$, that $\lambda(s) = \tau_\varepsilon(\theta_H - \theta_L)(s - \frac{1}{2}(\theta_H + \theta_L))$. Then the support of $\lambda(s)$ is unbounded since s is normally distributed (see Chamley (2003) and Smith and Sorensen (2000) for applications).

10.2 Normal Distributions and Affine Information Structure

Gaussian distributions have the convenient property, among others as we shall see, that conditional expectations are linear (affine to be precise but we will often use the term "linear" instead of "affine"). This proves crucial in obtaining linear equilibria in games with quadratic payoffs or negative exponential utility. However, there are other pairs of prior and likelihood functions that also yield conditional linear expectations.

10.2.1 The Gaussian Distribution

A random variable x has a normal distribution with mean $\mu = E[x]$ and variance $\sigma^2 = \text{var}[x] > 0$ if it is continuously distributed with density at any point $-\infty < x < \infty$ given by

$$f(x) = \frac{1}{\sqrt{2\pi}\sigma} \exp\left\{ -\frac{1}{2}\left(\frac{x-\mu}{\sigma}\right)^2 \right\}.$$

We write $x \sim N(\mu, \sigma^2)$. The normal density is completely characterized by two parameters: mean and variance. An immediate implication is the following: if $x \sim N(\mu, \sigma^2)$ and $y = \alpha + \beta x$, where α and β are constants, then we have $y \sim N(\alpha + \beta\mu, \beta^2\sigma^2)$. It follows that if $x \sim N(\mu, \sigma^2)$, then $z \equiv (x - \mu)/\sigma$ is $N(0, 1)$, which is the standard normal random variable. The following facts will prove useful:

- If $x \sim N(\mu, \sigma^2)$ and β is a constant, then $E[e^{\beta x}] = e^{\beta\mu + \beta^2\sigma^2/2}$.
- If $x \sim N(0, \sigma^2)$, then $E[|x|] = \sigma\sqrt{2/\pi}$.

We can define similarly a multivariate normal distribution. Consider an n-dimensional normal random variable $(\theta, s) \sim N(\mu, \Sigma)$, with $\mu \in \mathbb{R}^n$ and variance-covariance matrix $\Sigma \in \mathbb{R}^{n\times n}$. The mean vector and variance-covariance matrix can be partitioned as

$$\mu = \begin{bmatrix} \mu_\theta \\ \mu_s \end{bmatrix} \quad \text{and} \quad \Sigma = \begin{bmatrix} \Sigma_{\theta,\theta} & \Sigma_{\theta,s} \\ \Sigma_{s,\theta} & \Sigma_{s,s} \end{bmatrix}.$$

Then marginal distributions for $\theta \sim N(\mu_\theta, \Sigma_{\theta,\theta})$ and $s \sim N(\mu_s, \Sigma_{s,s})$ are normal. The conditional expectation is characterized uniquely by the projection theorem for normal random variables: $E[\theta \mid s]$ is the unique linear function of (θ, s) such that

$$E[E[\theta \mid s]] = E[\theta]$$

and

$$\text{cov}[\theta - E[\theta \mid s], s] = 0.$$

The first property is just the law of iterated expectations. The second has a geometric interpretation. Say that $\mu_\theta = \mu_s = 0$, then $E[\theta \mid s]$ is the projection of θ onto the subspace generated by the components of s (where random variables are seen as elements of a functional space: the Hilbert space of square integrable functions (see Loeve 1955)).

It then follows (see Anderson 1958; DeGroot 1970, chapter 5, section 4) that the conditional density of θ given s is normal with conditional mean $\mu_\theta + \Sigma_{\theta,s}\Sigma_{s,s}^{-1}(s - \mu_s)$ and variance-covariance matrix $\Sigma_{\theta,\theta} - \Sigma_{\theta,s}\Sigma_{s,s}^{-1}\Sigma_{s,\theta}$, provided $\Sigma_{s,s}$ is nonsingular (i.e., $(\theta \mid s) \sim N(\mu_\theta + \Sigma_{\theta,s}\Sigma_{s,s}^{-1}(s - \mu_s), \Sigma_{\theta,\theta} - \Sigma_{\theta,s}\Sigma_{s,s}^{-1}\Sigma_{s,\theta})$).

It is worth noting that the conditional variance-covariance matrix does not depend on the signal realization s. This is a special feature of the normal distribution which simplifies computations. Linear combinations of normal random variables are also normal and, if x and y are bivariate normal and $\text{cov}[x, y] = 0$, then x and y are independent.

The projection characterization has a very important consequence: the conditional expectation $E[\theta \mid s]$ is a sufficient statistic for the information s. In order to update beliefs about θ knowing $E[\theta \mid s]$ provides the same information as knowing s. The following claim illustrates the result.

Claim. Suppose (θ, s) are jointly normally distributed and let

$$\eta = \theta - E[\theta \mid s],$$

then η and $E[\theta \mid s]$ are independent random variables. The conditional distribution of θ given s is the same as the conditional distribution of θ given $\varphi(s) \equiv E[\theta \mid s]$: both distributions are normal, with mean

$$E[\theta \mid s] = E[\theta \mid \varphi(s)]$$

and variance

$$\operatorname{var}[\theta \mid s] = \operatorname{var}[\theta \mid \varphi(s)] = \operatorname{var}[\eta].$$

Proof. We know that $E[\theta \mid s]$ is a linear function of s and therefore (since linear functions of normal random variables are normal) both $E[\theta \mid s]$ and $\eta = \theta - E[\theta \mid s]$ are normal. We have that $E[\eta] = E[\theta] - E[E[\theta \mid s]] = 0$. From the projection characterization $\operatorname{cov}[\eta, s] = \operatorname{cov}[\theta - E[\theta \mid s], s] = 0$ and therefore

$$\operatorname{var}[\theta] = \operatorname{var}[E[\theta \mid s] + \eta] = \operatorname{var}[E[\theta \mid s]] + \operatorname{var}[\eta].$$

We have that the conditional distribution of $\theta = E[\theta \mid s] + \eta$ given s is normal (since both $\varphi(s) \equiv E[\theta \mid s]$ and η are normal) with mean $E[\theta \mid s] = E[\theta \mid \varphi(s)]$ and $\operatorname{var}[\theta \mid s] = \operatorname{var}[\eta \mid s] = \operatorname{var}[\eta] = \operatorname{var}[\theta \mid \varphi(s)]$, and normal random variables are fully characterized by mean and variance. □

Example. If both θ and s are one dimensional, we then have that

$$(\theta \mid s) \sim N\left(\mu_\theta + \varsigma \frac{\sigma_\theta}{\sigma_s}(s - \mu_s), \sigma_\theta^2(1 - \varsigma^2)\right),$$

where letting $\sigma_{\theta,s} = \operatorname{cov}[\theta, s]$, $\varsigma = \sigma_{\theta,s}/\sigma_\theta\sigma_s$ is the correlation coefficient between θ and s and $\varsigma\sigma_\theta/\sigma_s = \operatorname{cov}[\theta, s]/\operatorname{var}[s]$. Provided that the signal is unbiased (i.e., $E[s \mid \theta] = \theta$), the signal can be interpreted as being the sum of the true θ plus (orthogonal) noise: $s = \theta + \varepsilon$, with $\varepsilon \sim N(0, \sigma_\varepsilon^2)$ and $\operatorname{cov}[\theta, \varepsilon] = 0$. (According to the projection characterization, $\operatorname{cov}[s - E[s \mid \theta], \theta] = 0$, and therefore for an unbiased signal, $\operatorname{cov}[s - \theta, \theta] = 0$). Denote by $\tau_x \equiv 1/\sigma_x^2$ the precision of the random variable x. In terms of the posterior distribution, we have that the precision of the signal is given by $\tau_\theta + \tau_\varepsilon$ (i.e., $\operatorname{var}[\theta \mid s] = (\tau_\theta + \tau_\varepsilon)^{-1}$). The (posterior) precision of the signal is given by the sum of the precision of the prior τ_θ and the precision of the signal τ_ε. The signal can be thought of as coming from a sample of (conditionally) independent observations from $N(\theta, \sigma^2)$. A sufficient statistic for θ is the sample mean. Therefore, for a k-sample we have that $\sigma_\varepsilon^2 = \sigma^2/k$. The precision of the signal s (the sample mean) is therefore proportional to the size of the sample.

The posterior mean can also be written as

$$E[\theta \mid s] = \xi s + (1-\xi)\mu_\theta, \quad \text{where } \xi = \frac{\operatorname{cov}[\theta, s]}{\operatorname{var}[s]} = \varsigma\frac{\sigma_\theta}{\sigma_s} = \varsigma^2 = \frac{\tau_\varepsilon}{\tau_\theta + \tau_\varepsilon}.$$

The coefficient ξ is the typical regression coefficient of θ on s ($\operatorname{cov}[\theta, s]/\operatorname{var}[s]$) and the square of the correlation coefficient between θ and s. We thus have that $E[\theta \mid s]$ is a weighted average of the signal and the prior mean with weights according to the relative precisions. When the signal is perfect ($\sigma_\varepsilon^2 = 0$), $\xi = 1$, and when the signal is useless ($\sigma_\varepsilon^2 = \infty$), $\xi = 0$. Another useful property is that the precision of conditionally independent signals is additive. This is illustrated in the next example.

Example. Suppose we have n signals $s_i = \theta + \varepsilon_i$, $i = 1, \dots, n$, where the noise terms ε_i have mean zero and are independent of θ and of each other. Then the conditional mean and variance of θ are given by

$$E[\theta \mid s_1, \dots, s_n] = \mu_\theta + \frac{1}{\tau_\theta + \sum_{i=1}^n \tau_{\varepsilon_i}} \sum_{i=1}^n \tau_{\varepsilon_i}(s_i - \mu_\theta),$$

$$\operatorname{var}[\theta \mid s_1, \dots, s_n] = \frac{1}{\tau_\theta + \sum_{i=1}^n \tau_{\varepsilon_i}}.$$

The conditional precision is

$$\tau_{\theta \mid s_1, \dots, s_n} = \tau_\theta + \sum_{i=1}^n \tau_{\varepsilon_i}.$$

It follows that the precision-weighted signal average

$$\tilde{s}_n = \left(\tau_\theta + \sum_{i=1}^n \tau_{\varepsilon_i}\right)^{-1} \sum_{i=1}^n \tau_{\varepsilon_i} s_i$$

is a sufficient statistic for the signals $s_1, \dots, s_n$. If all ε_i are identically distributed with common precision τ_ε, then

$$E[\theta \mid s_1, \dots, s_n] = \mu_\theta + \frac{1}{\tau_\theta + n\tau_\varepsilon} n\tau_\varepsilon \left(\frac{1}{n}\sum_{i=1}^n s_i - \mu_\theta\right).$$

Normal distributions have very convenient and intuitive properties. Linear combinations of normal random variables are normal, and conditional expectations are also linear in signals. A Bayesian agent in a normal world will put more weight on a signal which is more precise. The rules to update the precision of information are additive for conditionally independent signals and do not depend on the realization of information. A new signal increases total precision according to its precision. This has the consequence that new information adds precision independently of the realization of the new signal. Finally, as we will see, normal distributions fit very nicely with models where agents end up optimizing a quadratic function.

Some of the convenient properties of normal distributions are robust in other scenarios. Suppose that an unknown parameter θ with finite variance is to be estimated from the observations $z^n = \{z_1, \dots, z_n\}$, where $z_t = \theta a_t + u_t$, where a_t are known constants, $t = 1, \dots, n$, and $\{u_t\}$ are i.i.d. random variables with zero mean and finite variance σ_u^2. We know that, under general distributions, $E[\theta \mid z^n]$ is the unique best predictor of θ in the sense of minimizing the mean squared error (under normality $E[\theta \mid z^n]$ is linear and depends only on first and second moments). With finite second moments $(\sigma_\theta^2, \sigma_u^2)$ the unique best (mean squared error) *linear* predictor of θ based on z^n (that is, the linear function $\delta(z^n) = \alpha_0 + \sum_{k=1}^n \alpha_k z_k$, which minimizes $E[(\theta - \delta(z^n))^2]$ over the α coefficients) is given by the same expression as under normality:

$$E[\theta \mid z^n] = \frac{1}{\tau_n}\left(\tau_\theta \bar{\theta} + \tau_u \sum_{k=1}^{n} a_k z_k\right),$$

where $\tau_n = \tau_\theta + \tau_u \sum_{k=1}^n a_k^2$.

This implies that if agents have limited forecasting ability and use *linear prediction* to estimate θ, the same result as under normality will be obtained (since the best linear predictor of θ based on z^n is precisely $E[\theta \mid z^n]$). We will see in the next section other information structures which preserve the linearity of conditional expectations.

10.2.2 Affine Information Structure

Some of the convenient properties of normal distributions are also enjoyed for other pairs of prior and likelihood functions. Indeed, the pair normal–normal is only one example of the class for which conditional expectations are linear (affine). For example, the pairs of prior and likelihood beta-binomial and gamma-Poisson functions have the affine conditional expectation property. In this case, as in the normal–normal case, the sample mean is a sufficient statistic for θ. Other cases are when the observations are conditionally independent negative binomial, gamma, or exponential when assigned natural conjugate priors (see DeGroot 1970; Ericson 1969; Li et al. 1987).

When the precision of a signal s about θ $(\mathrm{var}[s \mid \theta])^{-1}$ is not independent of the state, we consider the inverse of the expected conditional variance $r = (E[\mathrm{var}[s \mid \theta]])^{-1}$. In terms of the posterior distribution the precision of the signal s about θ is then $(E[\mathrm{var}[\theta \mid s]])^{-1}$. If the signal is unbiased ($E[s \mid \theta] = \theta$), letting $\varepsilon = s - \theta$ we also have that $\mathrm{cov}[\varepsilon, \theta] = 0$ and $\mathrm{var}[\varepsilon] = E[\mathrm{var}[s \mid \theta]]$. Indeed, $\mathrm{cov}[s - \theta, \theta] = E[s\theta] - E[\theta^2]$, and by the law of iterated expectations $E[s\theta] = E[E(s\theta \mid \theta)] = E[\theta E[s \mid \theta]] = E[\theta^2]$ if $E[s \mid \theta] = \theta$. We then have $\mathrm{var}[s] = \mathrm{var}[\theta] + \mathrm{var}[\varepsilon] = \mathrm{var}[E[s \mid \theta]] + E[\mathrm{var}[s \mid \theta]]$ since $E[s \mid \theta] = \theta$ and therefore $\mathrm{var}[\varepsilon] = E[\mathrm{var}[s \mid \theta]]$. The precision of the signal is denoted as usual by τ_ε. A more precise signal implies a smaller mean squared prediction error $E[(\theta - E[\theta \mid s])^2]$.

If the prior distribution is beta with parameters (α, β) on the interval $(0, 1)$ (where $\alpha > 0$ and $\beta > 0$) and the signal is the average of n independent Bernoulli trials with parameter θ, then the likelihood of the signal is $1/n$ binomial (n, θ) with $r = \tau_\theta n/(\alpha+\beta)$ and the posterior distribution is beta$(\alpha+ns, \beta+n(1-s))$ since $\text{var}[s \mid \theta] = \theta(1-\theta)/n$ and $r^{-1} = E[\text{var}[s \mid \theta]] = (E[\theta] - E[\theta^2])/n = ((\alpha+\beta)\,\text{var}[\theta])/n$ since $E[\theta] = \alpha(\alpha+\beta)^{-1}$ and $\text{var}[\theta] = \alpha\beta(\alpha+\beta)^{-2}(\alpha+\beta+1)^{-1}$. If the prior distribution is gamma $\Gamma(\alpha, \beta)$ and the likelihood Poisson $\mathcal{P}(n\theta)/n$, then it can be checked that $r = \beta n/\alpha$ and the posterior distribution is $\Gamma(\alpha+ns, \beta+n)$.

The accuracy of the signal r is proportional to the size of the sample. In these examples, as well as in the normal case, s is more accurate than s' if and only if s is more informative than s' in the Blackwell sense (indeed, a more precise signal means a larger sample). The examples provided are relevant when the unbounded support assumption of the normal distribution is not reasonable. For example, if θ is the demand intercept, then we want to exclude negative intercepts and the gamma-Poisson model is appropriate. If θ is a cost parameter, for example, the support may need to be bounded and then the beta-binomial model is suitable.

The following result generalizes the characterization of conditional expectations in the normal case to the affine information structure.

Claim (see Ericson 1969; Li 1985). Consider an information structure with n unbiased conditionally independent signals $(s_1, \dots, s_n)$ about θ, with $r_i = (E[\text{var}[s_i \mid \theta]])^{-1}$ the accuracy of signal s_i. Suppose that the posterior expectation of θ is linear in the signals. Let $\bar{\theta} = E[\theta]$, then it is easily seen that

$$E[\theta \mid s_i] = E[s_j \mid s_i] = \frac{r_i}{r_i + \tau_\theta} s_i + \frac{\tau_\theta}{r_i + \tau_\theta} \bar{\theta}, \quad j \neq i,$$

and $\tilde{s}_n = \sum_{i=1}^n (r_i / \sum_{j=1}^n r_j) s_i$ is sufficient for the signals in the estimation of θ. The assumption that the signals are conditionally independent can be replaced by the assumption that, for each i and $j \neq i$, $E[s_j \mid s_i]$ is linear in s_i.

A related result is the following (see Li 1985). Suppose that θ is a random n-dimensional vector, each component with mean $\bar{\theta}_i$ and finite variance $\text{var}[\theta_i] = \sigma_i^2$ for $i = 1, \dots, n$; with linear conditional expectations $E[\theta_i \mid \theta_{-i}]$ and positive correlation $\partial E[\theta_i \mid \theta_{-i}]/\partial \theta_j \geqslant 0$, $j \neq i$. Then we have that $E[\theta_i \mid \{\theta_j\}_{j \in K \subset N}]$, $N = \{1, 2, \dots, n\}$, is linear in θ_j and $E[\theta_i \mid \theta_j] = \bar{\theta}_i + \varsigma_{ij}(\sigma_i/\sigma_j)(\theta_j - \bar{\theta}_j)$, where ς_{ij} is the correlation coefficient between θ_i and θ_j. With a symmetric joint distribution for the random vector θ, then

$$E[\theta_i \mid \{\theta_j\}_{j \in K \subset N}] = \bar{\theta} + \frac{\varsigma}{1 + (k-1)\varsigma} \sum_{j \in K} (\theta_j - \bar{\theta}),$$

where θ is the common mean, ς the correlation coefficient, and k the cardinality of K.

10.2.3 Common- and Private-Values Models

In the interaction models we consider in the text there is a set of agents which is finite, countable, or a continuum (see section 10.3, which deals with Nash equilibrium). All agents have the same prior distribution over the uncertain parameters (the state of the world) and in most instances this prior coincides with nature's distribution. Agent i receives private information about the state of the world and, since he knows how the private information has been generated, can update in a Bayesian way. Agent i also knows how the private information of other agents is generated but not the realization of the signals of others, neither of the state of the world. The information structure is supposed to be *common knowledge*, that is, everyone knows the structure, knows that everyone knows the structure, and so on ad infinitum.

The workhorse model for the analysis in the book is the normal model (or the generalized affine information structure). We now present a general framework of information structure for interacting agents encompassing common- and private-value uncertainty cases.

Assume the vector of random variables $(\theta_1, \dots, \theta_n)$ is jointly normally distributed with $E[\theta_i] = \bar{\theta}$, $\mathrm{var}[\theta_i] = \sigma_\theta^2$, and $\mathrm{cov}[\theta_i, \theta_j] = \varsigma\sigma_\theta^2$, $j \neq i, 0 \leqslant \varsigma \leqslant 1$. Agent i receives a signal $s_i = \theta_i + \varepsilon_i$, where $\varepsilon_i \sim N(0, \sigma_{\varepsilon_i}^2)$ and $\mathrm{cov}[\varepsilon_i, \varepsilon_j] = 0$. Signals can range from perfect ($\sigma_{\varepsilon_i}^2 = 0$ or ∞ precision) to pure noise ($\sigma_{\varepsilon_i}^2 = \infty$ or 0 precision). The precision of signal s_i is given by $\tau_{\varepsilon_i} = (\sigma_{\varepsilon_i}^2)^{-1}$. It follows that the average parameter $\tilde{\theta}_n \equiv (\sum_{i=1}^n \theta_i)/n$ is normally distributed with mean $\bar{\theta}$, $\mathrm{var}[\tilde{\theta}_n] = [1 + (n-1)\varsigma]\sigma_\theta^2/n$, and $\mathrm{cov}[\tilde{\theta}_n, \theta_i] = \mathrm{var}[\tilde{\theta}_n]$.

This information structure encompasses the cases of "common value" and of "private values." For $\varsigma = 1$ the parameters are perfectly correlated and we are in a *common-values* model. When signals are perfect, $\sigma_{\varepsilon_i}^2 = 0$ for all i, and $0 \leqslant \varsigma < 1$, we will say we are in a *private-values* model. Agents receive idiosyncratic shocks, which are imperfectly correlated, and each agent observes its shock with no measurement error. When $\varsigma = 0$, the parameters are independent, and we are in an *independent-values* model.

As we have seen, under the normality assumption (as well as with the generalized affine information structure) conditional expectations are linear. Considering the symmetric case $\tau_{\varepsilon_i} = \tau_\varepsilon$, and letting $\xi = \tau_\varepsilon/(\tau_\theta + \tau_\varepsilon)$, we have that

$$E[\theta_i \mid s_i] = \xi s_i + (1 - \xi)\bar{\theta},$$

and from the projection characterization and given that the variance–covariance matrix of (s_i, s_j) is

$$\tau_\theta^{-1}\begin{pmatrix} \xi^{-1} & \varsigma \\ \varsigma & \xi^{-1} \end{pmatrix},$$

we obtain

$$E[s_j \mid s_i] = E[\theta_j \mid s_i] = \xi\varsigma s_i + (1 - \xi\varsigma)\bar{\theta}.$$

When signals are perfect, $\xi = 1$ and $E[\theta_i \mid s_i] = s_i$, and $E[\theta_j \mid s_i] = \varsigma s_i + (1-\varsigma)\bar{\theta}$. When they are not informative, $\xi = 0$ and $E[\theta_i \mid s_i] = E[\theta_j \mid s_i] = \bar{\theta}$.

Suppose now that we have a continuum of agents of mass one. We posit that the average parameter $\tilde{\theta} = \int_0^1 \theta_j \, \mathrm{d}j$ is normally distributed with mean $\bar{\theta}$

and $\operatorname{cov}[\tilde{\theta}, \theta_i] = \operatorname{var}[\tilde{\theta}] = \varsigma\sigma_\theta^2$. This can be justified as the continuum analogue of the n-firm market. Then, under the assumptions, the average parameter $\tilde{\theta}_n$ is normally distributed with mean $\bar{\theta}$, $\operatorname{var}[\tilde{\theta}_n] = [1 + (n-1)\varsigma]\sigma_\theta^2/n$, and $\operatorname{cov}[\tilde{\theta}_n, \theta_i] = \operatorname{var}[\tilde{\theta}_n]$. The result is obtained by letting n tend to ∞. The vector $(\theta_i, \tilde{\theta}, s_i)$ is normally distributed with $E[\theta_i] = E[\tilde{\theta}] = E[s_i] = \bar{\theta}$ and variance–covariance matrix

$$\sigma_\theta^2 \begin{pmatrix} 1 & \varsigma & 1 \\ \varsigma & \varsigma & \varsigma \\ 1 & \varsigma & \xi^{-1} \end{pmatrix}$$

with $\xi = \tau_\varepsilon/(\tau_\theta + \tau_\varepsilon)$. As before, we have

$$E[\theta_i \mid s_i] = \xi s_i + (1-\xi)\bar{\theta} \quad \text{and} \quad E[s_j \mid s_i] = E[\theta_j \mid s_i] = \xi\varsigma s_i + (1 - \xi\varsigma)\bar{\theta}.$$

We can also derive the relationship between θ_i, s_i, and the average parameter $\tilde{\theta} = \int_0^1 \theta_j \, \mathrm{d}j$. Indeed, $E[\theta_i \mid \tilde{\theta}] = \tilde{\theta}$, $E[\tilde{\theta} \mid \theta_i] = E[\theta_j \mid \theta_i] = \varsigma\theta_i + (1-\varsigma)\bar{\theta}$, $E[\tilde{\theta} \mid s_i] = E[\theta_j \mid s_i]$, and

$$E[\theta_i \mid \tilde{\theta}, s_i] = (1-d)\tilde{\theta} + d s_i,$$

where $d = [\sigma_\theta^2(1-\varsigma)]/[\sigma_\theta^2(1-\varsigma) + \sigma_\varepsilon^2]$. If signals are perfect, then $d = 1$ and $E[\theta_i \mid \tilde{\theta}, s_i] = s_i$. If signals are useless or correlation perfect ($\varsigma = 1$), then $d = 0$ and $E[\theta_i \mid \tilde{\theta}, s_i] = \tilde{\theta}$. If both signals and correlation are perfect, then $E[\theta_i \mid \tilde{\theta}, s_i] = \tilde{\theta} = s_i$ (a.s.).

10.2.4 Some Useful Facts for Normal Random Variables and CARA Utilities

The utility function $U : \mathbb{R} \to \mathbb{R}$ displays constant absolute risk aversion (CARA) if it is of the negative exponential type: $U(w) = -\mathrm{e}^{-\rho w}$, where $\rho > 0$ is the coefficient of absolute risk aversion ($-U''/U'$). If $w \sim N(\mu, \sigma^2)$, then $E[-\mathrm{e}^{-\rho w}] = -\mathrm{e}^{-\rho(\mu - \rho\sigma^2/2)}$. More generally, we have the following result. (See Danthine and Moresi (1993) for a proof.)

Result. Let the n-dimensional random vector z be normally distributed with mean 0 and variance–covariance matrix Σ and $w = c + b'z + z'Az$, where $c \in \mathbb{R}$, $b \in \mathbb{R}^n$, and A is an $n \times n$ matrix. If the matrix $\Sigma^{-1} + 2\rho A$ is positive definite and $\rho > 0$, then

$$E[-\mathrm{e}^{-\rho w}] = -(\det \Sigma)^{-1/2}(\det(\Sigma^{-1} + 2\rho A))^{-1/2}\mathrm{e}^{-\rho[c - \rho b'(\Sigma^{-1} + 2\rho A)^{-1}b/2]}.$$

A corollary of the result (see Demange and Laroque (1995) for a direct proof) is the following. If $x \sim N(\bar{x}, \sigma_x^2)$, $y \sim N(\bar{y}, \sigma_y^2)$, and $\operatorname{cov}[x, y] = \sigma_{xy}$, then

$$E[\mathrm{e}^{x - y^2}] = \frac{1}{\sqrt{1 + 2\sigma_y^2}} \exp\left\{\bar{x} + \frac{\sigma_x^2}{2} - \frac{(\bar{y} + \sigma_{xy})^2}{1 + 2\sigma_y^2}\right\}.$$

This follows by letting

$$c = -\bar{x} + \bar{y}^2, \quad b = \begin{pmatrix} -1 \\ 2\bar{y} \end{pmatrix}, \quad A = \begin{pmatrix} 0 & 0 \\ 0 & 1 \end{pmatrix}, \quad \rho = 1, \quad \text{and} \quad z = \begin{pmatrix} x - \bar{x} \\ y - \bar{y} \end{pmatrix}.$$

We then have that $\Sigma^{-1} + 2\rho A$ is positive definite since $1 + 2\sigma_y^2 > 0$:

$$[\Sigma^{-1} + 2A]^{-1} = (1 + 2\sigma_y^2)^{-1} \begin{bmatrix} \sigma_x^2 + 2\det(\Sigma) & \sigma_{xy} \\ \sigma_{xy} & \sigma_y^2 \end{bmatrix}$$

and

$$\det(\Sigma^{-1} + 2A) = \frac{1 + 2\sigma_y^2}{\det(\Sigma)}.$$

Furthermore, if $\bar{x} = \bar{y} = 0$, then, for any $\rho \geqslant 0$ and if $\rho\sigma_x\sigma_y < 1 + \rho\sigma_{xy}$, we have that

$$E[\mathrm{e}^{-\rho xy}] = [(1 + \rho\sigma_{xy})^2 - \rho^2\sigma_x^2\sigma_y^2]^{-1/2}.$$

This follows by letting

$$A = \begin{pmatrix} 0 & \frac{1}{2} \\ \frac{1}{2} & 0 \end{pmatrix}, \quad b = \begin{pmatrix} 0 \\ 0 \end{pmatrix}, \quad \text{and} \quad c = 0.$$

Then $\Sigma^{-1} + 2\rho A$ is positive definite if $\rho\sigma_x\sigma_y < 1 + \rho\sigma_{xy}$. We have that $(\det(\Sigma))^{-1/2} = (\sigma_x^2\sigma_y^2 - \sigma_{xy}^2)^{-1/2}$ and

$$\begin{aligned}
[\det(\Sigma^{-1} + 2\rho A)]^{-1/2} &= \left[\frac{\sigma_x^2\sigma_y^2 - (\sigma_{xy} - \rho\det\Sigma)^2}{[\det(\Sigma)]^2}\right]^{-1/2} \\
&= \left[\frac{1 + 2\sigma_{xy}\rho - \rho^2\det(\Sigma)}{\det(\Sigma)}\right]^{-1/2} \\
&= \left[\frac{(1 + \rho\sigma_{xy})^2 - \rho^2\sigma_x^2\sigma_y^2}{\det(\Sigma)}\right]^{-1/2}.
\end{aligned}$$

Therefore,

$$\begin{aligned}
E[\mathrm{e}^{-\rho xy}] &= [\det(\Sigma)]^{-1/2}[\sigma_x^2\sigma_y^2 - (\sigma_{xy} - \rho\det(\Sigma))^2]^{-1/2} \\
&= [(1 + \rho\sigma_{xy})^2 - \rho^2\sigma_x^2\sigma_y^2]^{-1/2}.
\end{aligned}$$

10.3 Convergence Concepts and Results

In this section we state definitions and main results on convergence of random variables (10.3.1), rates of convergence (10.3.2), and martingales and Bayesian learning (10.3.3). General references for this section are Spanos (1993, 2000), DeGroot (1970), Ash (1972), Chung (1974), Billingsley (1979), Grimmet and Stirzaker (2001), and Jacod and Protter (2003).

10.3.1 Convergence of Random Variables

There are several convergence modes for random variables (see, for example, Spanos 1993, chapter 10).

Definition 10.1. Let $x, x_1, x_2, x_3, \dots$ be random variables on the probability space $(\Omega, \mathcal{E}, P)$. We say that

(i) $\{x_n\}$ converges to x almost surely (a.s.) and write $x_n \xrightarrow{\text{a.s.}} x$ if

$$P\Big(\omega \in \Omega : \lim_{n\to\infty} x_n(\omega) \to x(\omega)\Big) = 1;$$

(ii) $\{x_n\}$ converges to x in probability and write $x_n \xrightarrow{\text{P}} x$ if, for every fixed $\varepsilon > 0$,

$$\lim_{n\to\infty} P(|x_n - x| > \varepsilon) = 0;$$

(iii) $\{x_n\}$ converges to x in rth mean (or in L_r), $r \geqslant 1$, and write $x_n \xrightarrow{r} x$, if $E[|x_n|^r] < \infty$ for all n and

$$\lim_{n\to\infty} E[|x_n - x|^r] = 0;$$

(iv) $\{x_n\}$ with (cumulative) distribution functions $\{F_n\}$ converges to x with (cumulative) distribution function F in distribution (or in law) and write $x_n \xrightarrow{\text{L}} x$ if, for each continuity point y of F,

$$\lim_{n\to\infty} F_n(y) = F(y).$$

For our purposes it is usually sufficient to consider convergence in the second moment or mean square. The conditions for convergence in mean square are easy to verify. The following relationships can be shown to hold:

(i) If $x_n \xrightarrow{\text{a.s.}} x$, then $x_n \xrightarrow{\text{P}} x$.

(ii) If $x_n \xrightarrow{r} x$, then $x_n \xrightarrow{\text{P}} x$.

(iii) If $x_n \xrightarrow{\text{P}} x$, then $x_n \xrightarrow{\text{L}} x$.

(iv) If $r \geqslant q$, then $x_n \xrightarrow{r} x$ implies that $x_n \xrightarrow{q} x$.

Two very useful results on the convergence of sums of random variables are the law of large numbers and the central limit theorem.

Strong law of large numbers (SLLN). Let $\{x_n\}$ be a sequence of independent random variables with finite mean $E[x_i] < \infty$ and variance $\operatorname{var}[x_i] < \infty$ for all i. If $\sum_{k=1}^{\infty} k^{-2} \operatorname{var}[x_k] < \infty$, then $(1/n)\sum_{i=1}^{n}(x_i - E[x_i]) \xrightarrow{\text{a.s.}} 0$. For the case of identically distributed random variables there is a stronger result which only requires finite first moments (Khinchine's version of the SLLN). Let $\{x_n\}$ be a sequence of i.i.d. random variables with common finite mean $\mu < \infty$, then $(1/n)\sum_{i=1}^{n} x_i \xrightarrow{\text{a.s.}} \mu$.

In the text we often work with a continuum of agents and we want to invoke the SLLN. A well-known potential technical difficulty is that, given a process $(q_i)_{i\in[0,1]}$ of independent random variables, the realizations of the process need not be measurable and therefore the Lebesgue integral $\int_0^1 q_i \, di$ is not well-defined (see Judd (1985) for the measure-theoretical issues involved). Note, however, that if $E[q_i] = 0$ and $\operatorname{var}[q_i]$ are uniformly bounded, then for every sequence $\{i_k\}$ of different indices extracted from $[0,1]$, the SLLN applied to $\{q_{i_k}\}$ yields $(1/n)\sum_{k=1}^{n} q_{i_k} \xrightarrow{\text{a.s.}} 0$ (note that, if $\operatorname{var}[q_{i_k}] \leqslant M < \infty$, then

$\sum_{k=1}^{\infty} k^{-2} \operatorname{var}[q_{i_k}] \leqslant M \sum_{k=1}^{\infty} k^{-2} < \infty$). However, as pointed out by Allen (1982) and Feldman and Gilles (1985), with a continuum of agents there are countable families of sets for which a law of large numbers cannot hold.

In the text when we work with a continuum of agents, we make the *convention* that the SLLN holds for a continuum of independent random variables with uniformly bounded variances. Suppose thus that $(q_i)_{i\in[0,1]}$ is a process of independent random variables with mean $E[q_i] = 0$ and uniformly bounded variances $\operatorname{var}[q_i]$. Then we let $\int_0^1 q_i \, di = 0$ almost surely (a.s.). This convention will be used, taking as given the usual linearity property of the integral (see Admati 1985). For example, assume a continuum of agents indexed in the unit interval $[0,1]$ and endowed with the Lebesgue measure. Each agent i receives a signal $s_i = \theta + \varepsilon_i$, where $E[\varepsilon] = 0$ and θ is randomly distributed with finite variance. If signals have uniformly bounded variance, we will write

$$\int_0^1 s_i \, di = \int_0^1 (\theta + \varepsilon_i) \, di = \theta + \int_0^1 \varepsilon_i \, di = \theta \quad \text{(a.s.)},$$

using the linearity of the integral and our convention.

The case of different means can also be dealt with. Suppose that $(q_i)_{i\in[0,1]}$ is a process of independent random variables with means $E[q_i]$ and uniformly bounded variances $\operatorname{var}[q_i]$. Then we let

$$\int_0^1 q_i \, di = \int_0^1 (q_i - E[q_i]) \, di + \int_0^1 E[q_i] \, di = \int_0^1 E[q_i] \, di \quad \text{(a.s.)}$$

according to our preceding claim since $\int_0^1 (q_i - E[q_i]) \, di = E[q_i - E[q_i]] = 0$ (a.s.).

One resolution of the technical issue is to check that the solution obtained by using the continuum convention in the continuum economy is the outcome of the limit of economies with a finite number of agents as they grow large (and apply the SLLN). This is done in the text on several occasions (e.g., in chapters 2 and 5, as well in some exercises in other chapters).

Another proposed solution is to consider economies with a countably infinite set of agents. Assume that the set of agents is the natural numbers $N = \{1, 2, \dots\}$. Then we can define a charge space $(N, \Xi(N), \mu)$, where $\Xi(N)$ is the collection of all subsets of N and μ is a finitely additive signed measure such that the measure of a set A in $\Xi(N)$ is the limit of the proportion of the first n agents who are in the set A: $\lim_{n\to\infty} n^{-1}(\#(A \cap \{1, 2, \dots, n\}))$, the notation $\#(B)$ means the cardinality of the set B, whenever this limit exists. Note that $\mu(N) = 1$. We then define the "integral" of the random variables $(q_i)_{i\in N}$ in relation to the additive measure: $\int q_i \, di = \lim_{n\to\infty} n^{-1} \sum_{i=1}^{n} q_i$ (see Feldman and Gilles (1985) and He and Wang (1995) for an application of the approach). However, the use of finitely additive measures in continuum economies is not without problems, as pointed out by Aumann (1964) and analyzed by Sun (2006), who proposes a solution of the problem via a Fubini extension.

We have so far concentrated attention on the convergence of a sequence of random variables. The Central Limit Theorem provides information on the rate of convergence, a topic to which we turn our attention in the next section.

The Central Limit Theorem (CLT). Let $\{x_n\}$ be a sequence of i.i.d. random variables with finite mean $E[x_i] = \mu < \infty$ and variance $\text{var}[x_i] = \sigma^2 < \infty$. Let $y_n = (\sum_{i=1}^n x_i - n\mu)/(\sigma\sqrt{n})$, then y_n converges in distribution to y, $y_n \xrightarrow{\text{L}} y$, where $y \sim N(0,1)$.

The CLT implies that $\sqrt{n}((1/n)\sum_{i=1}^n x_i - \mu)$ converges in distribution to $N(0, \sigma^2)$ and we can identify $1/\sqrt{n}$ as the rate at which $(1/n)\sum_{i=1}^n x_i - \mu$ converges to 0 (a.s. according to the SLLN).

10.3.2 Rates of Convergence

We say that the sequence of real numbers $\{b_n\}$ is *at most of order* $\phi(n)$, for some function $\phi(\cdot)$ with integer domain, and we write $O(\phi(n))$, if there is a nonzero constant k_2 such that $b_n \leqslant k_2\phi(n)$ for $n \geqslant n_o$ for some appropriate n_o. We say that the sequence of real numbers $\{b_n\}$ is of the *order* $\phi(n)$, for some function $\phi(\cdot)$ with integer domain, if there are nonzero constants k_1, k_2 such that $k_1\phi(n) \leqslant b_n \leqslant k_2\phi(n)$ for $n \geqslant n_o$ for some appropriate n_o. A somewhat more restrictive definition, good enough for our purposes, is to say that $\{b_n\}$ is of the *order* $\phi(n)$ whenever $b_n/\phi(n) \xrightarrow[n]{} k$ as $n \to \infty$ for some nonzero constant k. Suppose that $b_n \xrightarrow[n]{} 0$ and $\{b_n\}$ is of the *order* $\phi(n)$, then we also say that $\{b_n\}$ converges to 0 at the *rate* $\phi(n)$. We will often use $\phi(n) = n^{\upsilon}$, with υ a real number. Other examples are the logarithmic $\phi(n) = \log(n)$ or the exponential $\phi(n) = \kappa^n$ with $\kappa > 1$.

For sequences of random variables things are a little more complex and we have to work with the appropriate convergence concepts by analogy. For example, we will say that the sequence of random variables $\{y_t\}$ converges to 0 almost surely (at least) at an exponential rate if there is a constant $\kappa > 1$ such that $\kappa^n y_n \xrightarrow[n]{} 0$ (almost surely).

With rth mean convergence we can apply the rate of convergence definition for real numbers easily. We will say that the sequence of random variables $\{y_n\}$ converges in *mean square* to zero at the rate $1/\sqrt{n^r}$ (or that y_n is of the order $1/\sqrt{n^r}$) if $E[y_n^2]$ converges to zero at the rate $1/n^r$ (i.e., $E[y_n^2]$ is of the order $1/n^r$).

Given that $E[y_n^2] = (E[y_n])^2 + \text{var}[y_n]$, a sequence $\{y_n\}$ such that $E[y_n] = 0$ and $\text{var}[y_n]$ is of order $1/n$, converges to zero at the rate $1/\sqrt{n}$. This is the typical convergence rate for the sample mean to converge to the population mean associated with the law of large numbers. For example, if the random variables $\{x_n\}$ are i.i.d. with finite mean $E[x_i] = \mu < \infty$ and variance $\text{var}[x_i] = \sigma^2 < \infty$, then $y_n = n^{-1}\sum_{i=1}^n x_i - \mu \xrightarrow{r=2} 0$ (i.e., in mean square) at the rate $1/\sqrt{n}$ because $E[n^{-1}\sum_{i=1}^n x_i - \mu] = 0$ and $\text{var}[n^{-1}\sum_{i=1}^n x_i] = \sigma^2/n$.

A more refined measure of convergence speed for a given convergence rate is provided by the *asymptotic variance*. Suppose that $\{y_n\}$ is such that $E[y_n] = 0$ and $E[y_n^2] = \text{var}[y_n]$ converges to 0 at the rate $1/n^r$ for some $r > 0$. Then, the asymptotic variance is given by the constant $\text{AV} = \lim_{n\to\infty} n^r \text{var}[y_n]$. A higher asymptotic variance means that the speed of convergence is slower. It is worth noting that $\sqrt{n^r}(y_n)$ converges in distribution to $N(0, \text{AV})$. Indeed, a normal random variable is characterized by mean and variance and we have that $\text{var}[\sqrt{n^r}(y_n)] = n^r \text{var}[y_n]$ tends to AV as $n \to \infty$.

Often normality is not needed for the result. Indeed, from the CLT we have that, if the random variables $\{x_n\}$ are i.i.d. with finite mean $E[x_i] = \mu < \infty$ and variance $\text{var}[x_i] = \sigma^2 < \infty$, then $\sqrt{n}(y_n)$, where $y_n = n^{-1}\sum_{i=1}^n x_i - \mu$, converges in distribution to $N(0, \sigma^2)$. From the SLLN we also have that $y_n \xrightarrow{\text{a.s.}} 0$.

All this suggests that we can say, alternatively, that $\{y_n\}$ converges to zero almost surely at the rate $1/\sqrt{n^r}$ if $y_n \xrightarrow{\text{a.s.}} 0$ and $\sqrt{n^r}(y_n) \xrightarrow{\text{L}} N(0, \text{AV})$ for some positive constant AV. In this book we will say that the sequence of random variables $\{y_n\}$ converges to 0 at the rate $n^{-\upsilon}$, with $\upsilon > 0$, if $y_n \xrightarrow[n]{} 0$ (a.s. or in mean square) and $n^{\upsilon} y_n \xrightarrow[n]{\text{L}} N(0, \text{AV})$ for some positive constant AV.

As an example with general distributions and linear prediction consider the following statistical estimation problem. An unknown parameter θ with finite variance is to be estimated from the observations $z^n = \{z_1, \dots, z_n\}$, where $z_t = \theta a_t + u_t$, with a_t known constants, $t = 1, \dots, n$, and $\{u_t\}$ are i.i.d. random variables with zero mean and finite variance σ_u^2. We know (see the last paragraph in section 2.1) that with finite second moments $(\sigma_\theta^2, \sigma_u^2)$ the unique best (mean squared error) linear predictor of θ based on z^n is given by the same expression as under normality:

$$E[\theta \mid z^n] = \frac{1}{\tau_n}\left(\tau_\theta \bar{\theta} + \tau_u \sum_{k=1}^{n} a_k z_k\right),$$

where $\tau_n = \tau_\theta + \tau_u \sum_{k=1}^n a_k^2$. Denote by y_n the OLS estimate of θ regressing z_t on a_t, that is, $y_n = A_n^{-1}\sum_{t=1}^n a_t z_t$, $A_n = \sum_{t=1}^n a_t^2$. Then $E[\theta \mid z^n] = (\tau_\theta \bar{\theta} + \tau_u A_n y_n)/\tau_n$.

The following result provides conditions under which y_n (or $E[\theta \mid z^n]$) converges to θ a.s. as $n \to \infty$ and characterizes the rate of convergence. It uses SLLN- and CLT-type arguments.

Result. Let $y_n = A_n^{-1}\sum_{t=1}^n a_t z_t$, $A_n = \sum_{t=1}^n a_t^2$ be the OLS estimator of the unknown parameter θ with finite variance based on the data $z_t = \theta a_t + u_t$, with a_t known constants, $t = 1, \dots, n$, and $\{u_t\}$ are i.i.d. random variables with zero mean and finite variance σ_u^2. Suppose $\tau_n = \tau_\theta + \tau_u \sum_{t=1}^n a_k^2$ is of the order n^{υ}, and $\{a_t\}$ is a sequence of order $t^{-\kappa}$ for some constants $\upsilon > 0$ and $\kappa \geqslant 0$ such that $\upsilon + \kappa > \frac{1}{2}$. Let $A\tau_\infty = \lim_{n\to\infty} n^{-\upsilon}\tau_n$. Then

(i) $y_n \xrightarrow{\text{a.s.}} \theta$, and

(ii) $\sqrt{n^{\upsilon}}(y_n - \theta) \xrightarrow{\text{L}} N(0, (A\tau_\infty)^{-1})$.

Proof. See the proof of lemma 3.2 in Vives (1993). □

10.3.3 Martingales and Bayesian Learning

A stochastic process is an indexed collection of random variables $\{x_t\}_{t\in T}$ defined on the same probability space $(\Omega, \mathcal{E}, P)$.

Suppose that an agent receives a sequence of signals $\{z_t\}$ about an unknown parameter θ. The agent has a prior on θ and he knows the likelihood distribution of the signals for any given value of θ. We would like to know properties of the (Bayesian) posterior probability assessment of the agent as more signals accumulate. Given a sequence of random variables $\{z_t\}_{t\geqslant 0}$, let $z^t = \{z_0, z_1, \dots, z_t\}$ denote the history of the process up to t. Information accumulation is represented by a *filtration* (an increasing sequence of sub-σ-fields of $\mathcal{E}$). This is the increasing sequence of σ-fields $\sigma(z^{t-1})$ generated by the random variables $z^{t-1} = \{z_0, z_1, \dots, z_{t-1}\}$, $t = 1, 2, \dots$. The agent does not forget once he has learned.

Consider a sequence of random variables $\{x_t\}_{t\geqslant 0}$. Recall that when we write $E[x_t \mid z^{t-1}]$ we mean the conditional expectation of x_t given the σ-field generated by the random variables $z^{t-1} = \{z_0, z_1, \dots, z_{t-1}\}$: $E[x_t \mid \sigma(z^{t-1})]$. This conditional expectation is a random variable that is $\sigma(z^{t-1})$-measurable (see Spanos 2000, section 7.3; Ash 1972, section 6.2).

Consider the sequence of random variables $\{x_t\}_{t\geqslant 0}$ on the probability space $(\Omega, \mathcal{E}, P)$ and let $\{\mathcal{E}_t\}_{t\geqslant 0}$ be an increasing sequence of σ-fields in $\mathcal{E}$ (i.e., $\mathcal{E}_t \subset \mathcal{E}_{t+1}$). The sequence $\{x_t\}_{t\geqslant 0}$ is a *martingale* relative to the σ-fields $\{\mathcal{E}_t\}_{t\geqslant 0}$ if x_t is $\mathcal{E}_t$-measurable, $E[|x_t|] < \infty$, and $E[x_t \mid \mathcal{E}_{t-1}] = x_{t-1}$ with probability 1 (a.s.).

We say that the sequence of random variables $\{x_t\}_{t\geqslant 0}$ is a martingale relative to the history z^t if, for all t, $E[|x_t|] < \infty$ and $E[x_t \mid z^{t-1}] = x_{t-1}$ (a.s.).

We will also say that the stochastic process or sequence of random variables $\{x_t\}_{t\geqslant 0}$ is a martingale if, for all t, $E[|x_t|] < \infty$ and $E[x_t \mid x^{t-1}] = x_{t-1}$ (a.s.) (i.e., $\{x_t\}_{t\geqslant 0}$ is martingale relative to the increasing σ-fields $\sigma(x^{t-1})$). Note $E[x_t \mid x^{t-1}] = x_{t-1}$ implies that $E[x_t \mid x^{t-1}] = E[x_t \mid x_{t-1}] = x_{t-1}$. The martingale property means that the conditional expectation of the present x_t given the history of the process x^{t-1} is just the immediate past x_{t-1}. It also means that the conditional expectation of the future x_{t+k}, $k \geqslant 1$, given the history of the process up to the present x^t is just the present x_t: $E[x_{t+k} \mid x^t] = x_t$ (since the σ-fields $\sigma(x^t)$ are increasing). Letting $\Delta x_t = x_t - x_{t-1}$ (with $\Delta x_0 = x_0$), we then have that $E[\Delta x_t] = 0$ and $E[\Delta x_t \mid x^{t-1}] = 0$ for $t \geqslant 1$. It is worth noting that since $x_k = \sum_{t=0}^{k} \Delta x_t$ we have that $\sigma(x_0, \dots, x_t) = \sigma(\Delta x_0, \dots, \Delta x_t)$.

Some important facts about martingales are the following.

(i) Consider a random variable θ with $E[|\theta|] < \infty$ and a stochastic process $\{z_t\}_{t\geqslant 0}$ defined on the same probability space. Then the stochastic process $\{\theta_t\}$ defined by $\theta_t = E[\theta \mid z^t]$ is a martingale relative to the history z^{t-1}. The proof is immediate:

$$E[\theta_t \mid z^{t-1}] = E[E[\theta \mid z^t] \mid z^{t-1}] = E[\theta \mid z^{t-1}] = \theta_{t-1}$$

since, when conditioning, the conditioning set (σ-field) that is coarser, i.e., the one with less information, dominates (see, for example, Ash 1972, p. 260).

With normal distributions it follows that $\theta_t = E[\theta \mid \theta_t]$ since the conditional expectation is a sufficient statistic for normal random variables.

Let $\{x_t\}_{t \geqslant 0}$ be a martingale with bounded second moments: $E[x_t^2] < \infty$ for all t. Then

(ii) $\text{cov}[\Delta x_t, \Delta x_k] = 0$, where $\Delta x_t = x_t - x_{t-1}$ for $t < k$.

Indeed, note first that $E[\Delta x_t] = 0$ and $\text{cov}[\Delta x_t, \Delta x_k] = E[\Delta x_t \Delta x_k]$. For $t < k$, $E[\Delta x_t \Delta x_k \mid x^{k-1}] = \Delta x_t E[\Delta x_k \mid x^{k-1}] = \Delta x_t E[x_k - x_{k-1} \mid x^{k-1}] = 0$ since $E[x_k - x_{k-1} \mid x^{k-1}] = E[x_k \mid x^{k-1}] - x_{k-1} = 0$.

(iii) $\text{var}[x_t] - \text{var}[x_0] = \text{var}[\sum_{k=0}^{t} \Delta x_k] = \sum_{k=0}^{t} \text{var}[\Delta x_k] = \sum_{k=0}^{t} E[\text{var}[x_t \mid x^{t-1}]]$.

Note that $\sum_{k=1}^{t} \Delta x_k = x_t - x_0$, $\text{cov}[x_t, x_{t-1}] = \text{var}[x_{t-1}]$ since $E[x_t x_{t-1}] = E[(x_{t-1})^2]$ from $E[x_t x_{t-1} \mid x^{t-1}] = x_{t-1} E[x_t \mid x^{t-1}] = (x_{t-1})^2$ and $E[x_t] = E[x_{t-1}]$ for any t. Therefore,

$$\text{var}[x_t - x_{t-1}] = \text{var}[x_t] + \text{var}[x_{t-1}] - 2\,\text{cov}[x_t, x_{t-1}] = \text{var}[x_t] - \text{var}[x_{t-1}]$$

and $\text{var}[x_t] - \text{var}[x_0] = \text{var}[\sum_{k=0}^{t} \Delta x_k]$. It follows from $\text{cov}[\Delta x_t, \Delta x_k] = 0$ that $\text{var}[\sum_{k=0}^{t} \Delta x_k] = \sum_{k=0}^{t} \text{var}[\Delta x_k]$. Furthermore,

$$\text{var}[x_t] = E[\text{var}[x_t \mid x^{t-1}]] + \text{var}[E[x_t \mid x^{t-1}]] = E[\text{var}[x_t \mid x^{t-1}]] + \text{var}[x_{t-1}]$$

and therefore $\sum_{k=0}^{t} \text{var}[\Delta x_k] = \sum_{k=0}^{t} E[\text{var}[x_k \mid x^{k-1}]]$.

Under normality $\text{var}[x_t \mid x^{t-1}]$ is nonrandom and the conditional expectation $E[x_t \mid x^{t-1}] = x_{t-1}$ is a sufficient statistic for the information x^{t-1}. Therefore, $E[\text{var}[x_t \mid x^{t-1}]] = \text{var}[x_t \mid x^{t-1}] = \text{var}[x_t \mid x_{t-1}]$.

It is a general result that *posterior (Bayesian) beliefs have the martingale property*. This is immediate from fact (i). Indeed, for an event A let $\mu_t = P(\theta \in A \mid z^t)$, and I then claim that $E[\mu_t \mid z^{t-1}] = \mu_{t-1}$. The result follows by noting that $\mu_t = P(\theta \in A \mid z^t) = E[I_A(\theta) \mid z^t]$, where $I_A(\theta)$ is the indicator function for the set A: $I_A(\theta) = 1$, $\theta \in A$, and $I_A(\theta) = 0$, $\theta \notin A$.

A very important and useful result is the martingale convergence theorem. The following is a version of the theorem (it is not the most general one; see sections 7.3 and 7.4 in Ash (1972) and section 53 in Billingsley (1979)).

Theorem 10.1 (martingale convergence theorem). *Let $\{x_t\}_{t \geqslant 0}$ be a martingale such that $E[x_t^2] \leqslant M < \infty$ for all t. Then there is a random variable x_∞ such that $x_t \xrightarrow{\text{a.s.}} x_\infty$ and $x_t \xrightarrow{r=2} x_\infty$.*

This implies that posterior Bayesian beliefs have to converge because they are a bounded martingale. That is, for an event A let the posterior belief based on history z^t be $\mu_t = P(\theta \in A \mid z^t)$, then there is a random limit belief μ_∞ to which μ_t converges almost surely and in mean square. Furthermore, the limit cannot be totally wrong. That is, when event A is true in the limit the agent will not (almost surely) assess probability 0 to event A; and when A is false in the limit there is probability zero that the agent assesses probability 1 to event A (see, for example, Bray and Kreps 1988, section 3). With a finite number of states (with prior positive weight), and given a true state, this implies that if the Bayesian updating process converges to a point, it must converge to the truth.

A corollary of the result is that the sequence of (cumulative) conditional distributions based on history z^t converges in law to a limit conditional distribution.

Remark 10.1. Consider a random variable θ with $E[\theta^2] < \infty$ and a stochastic process $\{z_t\}_{t\geqslant 0}$ defined on the same probability space. Then the stochastic process $\{\theta_t\}$ defined by $\theta_t = E[\theta \mid z^t]$ is a *bounded* martingale relative to the history z^{t-1}. Indeed,

$$\text{var}[\theta] = E[\text{var}[\theta \mid z^t]] + \text{var}[E[\theta \mid z^t]] = E[\text{var}[\theta \mid z^t]] + \text{var}[\theta_t]$$

and therefore $\text{var}[\theta_t] \leqslant \text{var}[\theta] < \infty$.

We see, therefore, that Bayesian posterior beliefs converge with probability 1. Optimal exploitation of information implies that at any point in time the change of beliefs must be uncorrelated with current beliefs (i.e., the martingale property) because future changes which can be predicted must already be incorporated in the current beliefs. Beliefs are bounded (because they are probabilities) and therefore the martingale convergence theorem applies. The consequence is that future changes in beliefs must be bounded and, in consequence, vanish with time.

Even though learning cannot be totally wrong asymptotically, this does not imply that convergence to the truth follows. Limit posterior beliefs may be incorrect in the sense of not putting almost surely all the mass at the true value of θ or true event. Convergence to the truth with probability 1 or *consistency* of Bayesian learning obtains when likelihood measures on histories are mutually singular, i.e., when they have disjoint support (see Billingsley 1979, p. 374). The central reference is Doob (1949) (see Blume and Easley 1998).

In general, convergence to the truth requires that prior beliefs be consistent with the true model. A Bayesian agent will never learn the truth if he puts zero weight on the true value of the parameter to start with. With a finite number of states, if the agent attaches prior positive weight to the true state and the Bayesian updating process converges to a point, it must converge to the truth. For Bayesian learning to obtain it is not necessary that the agent knows nature's probability distribution over the unknown parameter θ. What is needed, in a world with a finite or countable number of states, is that if a parameter has positive weight in the true model (nature's model), then it should also have positive weight in the subjective prior distribution of the agent. In more technical terms, and for general distributions, the true distribution must be absolutely continuous with respect to the prior. This means that if the prior assigns probability 0 to an event, then the true model must also assign probability 0 to the event (see Blume and Easley 1998).

10.4 Games and Bayesian Equilibrium

We start by describing briefly the basics of games in normal form and Nash equilibrium, including some material on supermodular games (section 10.4.1), and move to Nash equilibrium in games of incomplete information (Bayesian equilibrium) in section 10.4.2. Section 10.4.3 introduces mechanism design and section 10.4.4 perfect Bayesian equilibrium.[2]

10.4.1 Games and Nash Equilibrium

A *game* in *normal* or *strategic form* describes the possible actions and derived payoffs of the action profiles for each of a given set of players. It consists of a triplet (X, π, N), where the set of players N can be finite, $\{1, 2, \dots, n\}$, countably infinite, $\{1, 2, \dots\}$, or a continuum, say the interval $[0, 1]$; $X = \prod_{i \in N} X_i$, where X_i is the set of possible actions (or pure strategies) of player i; and $\pi = (\pi_i)_{i \in N}$ with $\pi_i : X \to \mathbb{R}$ the payoff function of player i. All these elements are *common knowledge* to the players. That is, every player knows them and knows that other players know and knows that other players know that he knows, and so on ad infinitum (see Aumann 1976).

A game can also be represented in *extensive form* with a complete specification for each player of the order of moves, feasible choices, information available when making a choice, and payoff for each possible outcome that follows from the choices made by the players. A strategy is then a complete contingent plan of action for any possible distinguishable circumstance that the player may have to act upon. Each player tries to maximize his payoff by choosing an appropriate strategy in his strategy set knowing the structure of the game, that is, the strategy spaces and payoffs of other players. Each player must conjecture the strategies that the rivals are going to use. In a Nash equilibrium, the conjectures of the players must be correct, and no player must have an incentive to change his strategy given the choices of rivals. With a finite number of players, denote by x_{-i} the vector $(x_1, \dots, x_{i-1}, x_{i+1}, \dots, x_n)$. A *Nash equilibrium* is then a set of strategies $x^* = (x_1^*, x_2^*, \dots, x_n^*)$ such that $\pi_i(x^*) \geqslant \pi_i(x_i, x_{-i}^*)$ for all $x_i \in X_i$ and for each i.

An example with a continuum of players is the following. Let $N = [0, 1]$ (and endow it with the Lebesgue measure). The payoff to player i is given by $\pi_i(x_i, x)$, where $x = \int_0^1 x_j \,\mathrm{d}j$ denotes the average action. A Nash equilibrium is then a strategy profile $(x_j^*)_{j \in N}$ such that $\pi_i(x_i^*, x^*) \geqslant \pi_i(x_i, x^*)$ for all $x_i \in X_i$ and for each i. Note that an individual player cannot now affect the average action.

10.4.1.1 Dominated Strategies and Rationalizability

Even in a situation where there is common knowledge of payoffs and rationality of the players, Nash behavior may not be compelling. A much weaker requirement is for agents not to play strictly dominated strategies. In the game (X, π, N) a (pure) strategy x_i is *strictly dominated* by another (pure) strategy y_i if, for all x_{-i}, $\pi_i(x_i, x_{-i}) < \pi_i(y_i, x_{-i})$. (We could consider similarly domination by a mixed strategy.) A rational player will not play a strictly dominated

[2] See chapter 2 in Vives (1999) for a fuller development of sections 10.4.1 and 10.4.2.

strategy. *Serially undominated strategies* are those that survive a process of iterated elimination of strictly dominated strategies. A game is *dominance solvable* if the set remaining after iterated elimination of strictly dominated strategies is a singleton. In this case the surviving strategy profile is a Nash equilibrium. Under the maintained assumption of common knowledge of payoffs and rationality, it is possible to rule out more strategies than by iterated elimination of strictly dominated strategies. This leads to the set of rationalizable strategies. A strategy is *rationalizable* if it is a best response to some beliefs about the play of opponents. However, since the opponents are also rational, and payoffs are common knowledge, the beliefs cannot be arbitrary. Nash equilibrium strategies are, obviously, rationalizable, but in general the rationalizable set is much larger (Bernheim 1984; Pearce 1984).

10.4.1.2 Supermodular Games

A *game of strategic complementarities* (GSC) is one where the best responses of the players increase with the actions of rivals. The technical concept of a supermodular game (to be defined below) provides sufficient conditions for best responses to be increasing. Let us start with some definitions.

Consider a partial order in $\mathbb{R}^k$ (for instance, the usual componentwise ordering: $x \leqslant y$ if and only if $x_i \leqslant y_i$ for all $1 \leqslant i \leqslant k$). A function $f : X \to \mathbb{R}$, where $X \subset \mathbb{R}^k$ is a rectangle (or "box") in Euclidean space, is *supermodular* if, for all $x, y \in X$, $f(\max(x, y)) + f(\min(x, y)) \geqslant f(x) + f(y)$; f is *log-supermodular* if it is nonnegative and its logarithm is supermodular, that is, for all $x, y \in X$, $f(\max(x, y)) \cdot f(\min(x, y)) \geqslant f(x) \cdot f(y)$. For a function $f : \mathbb{R}^2 \to \mathbb{R}$, supermodularity requires that the incremental returns to increasing x, defined by $h(t) \equiv f(x_H; t) - f(x_L; t)$ with $x_H > x_L$ must be increasing with t; log-supermodularity of a positive function requires that the relative returns, $f(x_H; t)/f(x_L; t)$, increase with t.

Let X be as before and let T be a partially ordered set. The function $f : X \times T \to \mathbb{R}$ has (strictly) *increasing differences* in its two arguments (x, t) if $f(x, t) - f(x, t')$ is (strictly) increasing with x for all $t \geqslant t'$, $t \neq t'$. Decreasing differences are defined by replacing "increasing" by "decreasing." The two concepts coincide for functions defined on a product of ordered sets. If $f : \mathbb{R}^k \to \mathbb{R}$ is twice continuously differentiable, then f is supermodular if and only if $\partial^2 f / \partial x_i \partial x_j \geqslant 0$ for all x and $i \neq j$.

In Euclidean space a supermodular game is one where for each player i the strategy set X_i is a compact rectangle (or "box"), the payoff function π_i is continuous and fulfills two complementarity properties:

- Supermodularity in own strategies (π_i is *supermodular* in a_i): the marginal payoff to any strategy of player i increases with the other strategies of the player.

- Strategic complementarity in rivals' strategies (π_i has *increasing differences in* (a_i, a_{-i})): the marginal payoff to any strategy of player i increases with any strategy of any rival player.

In a more general formulation of a supermodular game, strategy spaces and the continuity requirement can be weakened. In a supermodular game very general strategy spaces can be allowed. These include indivisibilities as well as functional strategy spaces, such as those arising in dynamic or Bayesian games. Regularity conditions such as concavity and restriction to interior solutions can be dispensed with. The application of the theory can be extended by considering increasing transformations of the payoff (which does not change the equilibrium set of the game). We say that the game is *log-supermodular* if π_i is nonnegative and if $\log \pi_i$ fulfills the complementarity conditions.

In a supermodular game:

1. There always exist extremal equilibria: a largest $\bar{x}$ and a smallest element $\underline{x}$ of the equilibrium set. If the game is symmetric, the extremal equilibria are symmetric.
2. Multiple equilibria are common. If the game displays positive spillovers (i.e., the payoff to a player increases with the strategies of the other players), then the largest equilibrium point is the Pareto best equilibrium, and the smallest one the Pareto worst.
3. Simultaneous best-reply dynamics approach the "box" $[\underline{x}, \bar{x}]$ defined by the smallest and the largest equilibrium points of the game, and converge monotonically downward (upward) to an equilibrium starting at any point in the intersection of the upper (lower) contour sets of the largest (smallest) best replies of the players. The extremal equilibria $\underline{x}$ and $\bar{x}$ correspond to the largest and smallest serially undominated strategies. Therefore, if the equilibrium is unique, then the game is dominance solvable (and globally stable).
4. If $\pi_i(x_i, x_{-i}; \theta)$ has increasing differences in (x_i, θ) for each i, then with an increase in θ: (i) the largest and smallest equilibrium points increase; and (ii) starting from any equilibrium, best-reply dynamics lead to a larger equilibrium following the parameter change.

10.4.2 Nash Equilibrium with Incomplete Information[3]

In many instances a player does not know some characteristic (or "type") of the payoff or strategy space of other players. For example, a firm may have private information about demand conditions or may not know the costs of production of the rival (as in chapters 1 and 2), or an investor may receive a private signal about the fundamental value of the asset. These are games of incomplete information. Harsanyi (1967–68) provided the fundamental insight to deal with such games.

[3] See Vives (2005) for a development of the material in this section.

In a game of incomplete information the characteristics or type of each player are known to the player but not to the other players. Harsanyi introduces a move of nature at the beginning of the game by choosing the types of the players. Each player is informed about his type but not about the types of other players. The type of a player embodies all the relevant private information in order to make his decisions. Nature's probability distribution is typically assumed to be common knowledge among the players. This is the case of a common prior. (If the prior is not common, then the beliefs of players will be inconsistent.) Each player thus has imperfect information about the move of nature and by observing his type may update his prior belief on the types of others. A *Bayes-Nash equilibrium* is then just a Nash equilibrium of the imperfect-information version of the game. We will often refer to *Bayesian* equilibrium.

Suppose the set N of players is finite. Let $\mathcal{T}_i$ be the set of possible types of player i (a subset of Euclidean space), $t_i \in \mathcal{T}_i$. The types of the players are drawn from a common prior distribution F on $\mathcal{T} = \prod_{i=0}^{n} \mathcal{T}_i$, where $\mathcal{T}_0$ represents residual uncertainty not observed by any player. Let F_i be the marginal distribution on $\mathcal{T}_i$. Let the action space of player i be a compact rectangle of Euclidean space X_i and his payoff be given by the (measurable and) bounded function $\pi_i : X \times \mathcal{T} \to \mathbb{R}$. The (*ex post*) payoff to player i when the vector of actions is $x = (x_1, \dots, x_n)$ and the realized types $t = (t_1, \dots, t_n)$ is thus $\pi_i(x; t)$.

Action spaces, payoff functions, type sets, and the prior distribution are common knowledge. A (pure) strategy for player i is a (measurable) function $\varphi_i : \mathcal{T}_i \to X_i$ which assigns an action to every possible type of the player. Let Ξ_i denote the strategy space of player i and identify two strategies of player i if they are equal F_i-almost surely (a.s.). Let $\varphi = (\varphi_1, \dots, \varphi_n)$. The expected payoff to player i, when agent j uses strategy φ_j, is given by $\Pi_i(\varphi) = E[\pi_i(\varphi_1(t_1), \dots, \varphi_n(t_n); t)]$.

A Bayes–Nash (or Bayesian) equilibrium (BNE) is a Nash equilibrium of the game where the strategy space of player i is Ξ_i and his payoff function Π_i. Given the strategies $\varphi_j(\cdot)$, $j \neq i$, denote by $\varphi_{-i}(t_{-i})$ the vector $(\varphi_1(t_1), \dots, \varphi_n(t_n))$ except the ith component. The expected payoff of player i conditional on t_i when the other players use strategies φ_{-i} and player i chooses action x_i is $E[\pi_i(x_i, \varphi_{-i}(t_{-i}); t) \mid t_i]$. The profile of strategies φ is a BNE if and only if for every i the action $x_i = \varphi_i(t_i)$ maximizes over X_i the conditional payoff $E[\pi_i(x_i, \varphi_{-i}(t_{-i}); t) \mid t_i]$ (F_i-a.s. on $\mathcal{T}_i$).

The model allows for private values when $\pi_i(x; t_i)$ (e.g., each firm observes his idiosyncratic shock to costs) or a common value with $\pi_i(x; t_i) = v_i(x; \sum_j t_j)$ (e.g., each firm observes one component of a common demand shock) or $\pi_i(x; t_0)$ (e.g., each firm receives a signal—its type—about a common demand shock).

An example with a continuum of players indexed in the interval $[0, 1]$ would be the following. Let the payoff function of firm i be $\pi(x_i, \tilde{x}; \theta_i)$, where x_i is the action of the firm, $\tilde{x}$ a vector of statistics that characterizes the distribution of the firms' actions, and θ_i a parameter drawn from a prior distribution. Suppose that player i receives a signal t_i about the parameter θ_i. As before a strategy for player i is a measurable function $\varphi_i(\cdot)$ from the signal space to the action space of the firm. A set of strategies $(\varphi_i(\cdot))_{i\in[0,1]}$ form a Bayesian equilibrium if for any player (almost surely)

$$\varphi_i(t_i) \in \arg\max_{z_i \in X_i} E[\pi(z_i, \tilde{x}^*; \theta_i) \mid t_i],$$

where $\tilde{x}^*$ is the vector of statistics that characterizes the equilibrium distribution of the actions of players. In this case player i when optimizing takes as given the equilibrium statistics since his action cannot influence them.

10.4.2.1 The Linear-Normal Model

The linear-normal model, that is, linear-quadratic payoffs with normal distributions for the uncertain parameters and signals, or distributions that yield affine conditional expectations, is a workhorse model for both the cases of a finite and a continuum of players. The information structure has been developed in section 10.2.3. The usefulness of the linear-normal model is that it typically yields a unique linear Bayesian equilibrium. This equilibrium is the unique one in games (such as Cournot or Bertrand games) where the strategy space of players is a noncontingent strategy like an output or price. There are at least two routes to show uniqueness. One is a direct proof (see the proof in a version of the continuum model in exercise 7.3). The other route is to realize that in many linear-quadratic games there is a potential or team function the optimization of which yields the Bayes–Nash equilibria of the game. If this team optimization problem has a unique solution, then the equilibrium will be unique (this method is introduced in Vives (1988); see the proof of proposition 2.1 for an n-player model and section 8.1 in Vives (1999)). Characterizations of the linear equilibrium in the continuum model in Cournot or Bertrand environments are found in section 1.2.4.1 and in the proof of proposition 1.3. In models where the strategy space is functional, a supply or a demand function like in rational expectations models, then typically we can only show that there is a unique equilibrium in the linear class. Chapters 3 and 4 for the continuum and chapter 5 for n players contain characterizations of linear Bayesian equilibrium when strategy spaces are demand or supply functions. The dynamic extensions are provided in chapters 8 and 9.

Remark 10.2. The linear-normal model admits a reinterpretation in which the joint distribution of the random variables is general (and perhaps even unknown) but with finite known second moments (variance–covariance matrix). Under these conditions agents cannot update in a Bayesian optimal way but can use linear prediction techniques. We have seen in section 10.2.1 how in these circumstances the best linear predictor of an unknown parameter coincides with the Bayesian expression for the conditional expectation under the normality assumption. Therefore, the results under the linear-normal model can also be seen in the context where agents use best linear prediction under conditions of limited knowledge.

10.4.2.2 Monotone Supermodular Games

Let $\mathcal{P}(\mathcal{T}_{-i})$ be the set of probability distributions on $\mathcal{T}_{-i}$ and let player i's posteriors be given by the (measurable) function $p_i : \mathcal{T}_i \to \mathcal{P}(\mathcal{T}_{-i})$, consistent with the prior F. A monotone supermodular game is defined by the following properties:

1. Supermodularity in own actions and complementarity with the actions of rivals: π_i is supermodular in x_i, and has increasing differences in (x_i, x_{-i}) for each i.
2. Complementarity between own actions and types: π_i has increasing differences in (x_i, t) for each i.
3. Monotone posteriors: $p_i : \mathcal{T}_i \to \mathcal{P}(\mathcal{T}_{-i})$ is increasing with respect to the partial order on $\mathcal{P}(\mathcal{T}_{-i})$ of first-order stochastic dominance (a sufficient but not necessary condition is that the prior distribution F be affiliated).

The first condition is just the usual definition of a supermodular game for given types. The other two conditions are the additional ones that ensure that there are Bayesian equilibria which are monotone in type. In a monotone supermodular game there is a largest and a smallest Bayesian equilibrium (this we knew already because the game is supermodular) and each one is an equilibrium in monotone increasing strategies in type (Van Zandt and Vives 2007; see also Vives 2005). There might be other equilibria that are in nonmonotone strategies but, if so, they will be "sandwiched" between the largest and the smallest, which are monotone in type. The result cannot be extended to log-supermodular payoffs. This result is particularly useful in the analysis of global games (section 8.4.2).

10.4.3 Mechanism Design

Information exchange is subject to an incentive compatibility problem. Indeed, absent commitment devices, players in a game must be provided incentives to truthfully reveal their information. Mechanism design concerns the problem of eliciting private information from agents in order to implement an allocation or take a collective decision.

A *mechanism* is defined by a collection of strategy sets and an outcome function that assigns outcomes to strategies. We say that a mechanism *implements* an allocation rule in Bayes–Nash equilibrium (BNE) if there is a BNE of the game induced by the mechanism such that for any realization of the types of the players the outcomes of the mechanism coincide with the outcome of the allocation rule.

According to the *revelation principle* there is no loss of generality when trying to implement an allocation to restrict our attention to direct revelation mechanisms where the strategy space of an agent is just his type space (the space of private signals). A *direct* revelation mechanism is thus a mechanism such that the strategy set of player i is just his type space and the outcome function the allocation rule to be implemented.

Revelation principle. If there is a mechanism that implements an allocation rule in BNE, then this allocation rule is Bayesian incentive compatible. That is, to tell the truth is a BNE in the direct revelation mechanism associated with this allocation rule. The revelation principle is based on the idea that if in a mechanism player i finds that a certain strategy is a best response to what other players do, then when a mediator asks for his type and assigns him the same strategy the player finds that to tell the truth is optimal provided that the other players also tell the truth.

10.4.4 Perfect Bayesian Equilibrium

In dynamic games of incomplete information we need to refine the Nash equilibrium concept. For games of complete information the idea of sequential rationality is embodied in the notion of a subgame-perfect equilibrium (SPE). For example, in a two-stage game, an SPE requires that, given any decisions at the first stage, a Nash equilibrium follows at the second stage, that is, for any subgame induced by the first-stage decisions. This rules out incredible threats which may be allowed in a Nash equilibrium since the latter only requires optimizing behavior along the equilibrium path.

The concept of perfect Bayesian equilibrium (PBE) extends the idea of sequential rationality and Bayesian equilibrium to dynamic games of incomplete (or imperfect) information. The subgame-perfect equilibrium concept may not be enough to embody sequential rationality in an extensive form game with imperfect information. This happens, for example, in games in which SPE puts no constraints because there are no subgames except the whole game.[4]

The idea of PBE is to require strategies to form a Bayesian equilibrium at every continuation game once the posterior beliefs of players are specified in a consistent way. A PBE is defined by a pair formed by a strategy profile and a system of beliefs for the players. At a PBE strategies are sequentially rational given beliefs (i.e., at any information set of any player the prescribed strategy is optimal given the beliefs of the player and the strategies used by the rivals), and beliefs are Bayesian consistent with strategies (i.e., beliefs are derived from strategies using the rule of Bayes whenever this is possible). At a Nash equilibrium, strategies have to be sequentially rational given beliefs only at the information sets reached with positive probability (i.e., only on the equilibrium path). Therefore, a PBE is a refinement of Nash equilibrium. However, PBE is a relatively weak concept because it allows the players to have any beliefs at information sets not reached with positive probability. This is a source of multiplicity of equilibria, which has called for further refinements of the PBE concept by restricting beliefs derived from out-of-equilibrium actions to some "reasonable" class.[5]

---

[4] See Fudenberg and Tirole (1991) for a proper definition of a subgame and a discussion of SPE.

[5] For a summary of possible refinements and further development of PBE, see Fudenberg and Tirole (1991, chapters 8 and 11).

Signaling interactions, where a sender or leader takes an action (or sends a message) and a receiver or follower observes the action taken (or the message sent) and in turn takes an action, provide a good example of a dynamic game of incomplete information. These types of games usually have many PBE. The reason is that when Bayes's rule is not applicable, any posterior beliefs are admissible. By choosing appropriate beliefs out of the equilibrium path, different types of equilibrium can be supported. Some may be "separating" and reveal fully the type of the sender/leader, and others are "pooling" and do not reveal anything. In between we may find partially revealing or semi-pooling equilibrium.

References

Admati, A. 1985. A noisy rational expectations equilibrium for multi-asset securities markets. *Econometrica* 53:629–57.

Allen, B. 1982. The existence of rational expectations equilibria in a large economy with noisy price observations. CARESS Working Paper 82-06, University of Pennsylvania.

Anderson, T. W. 1958. *An Introduction to Multivariate Statistical Analysis.* New York: John Wiley.

Ash, R. 1972. *Real Analysis and Probability.* New York: Academic Press.

Aumann, R. 1964. Markets with a continuum of traders. *Econometrica* 32:39-50.

——. 1976. Agreeing to disagree. *Annals of Statistics* 4:1236–39.

Bernheim, D. 1984. Rationalizable strategic behavior. *Econometrica* 52:1007–28.

Billingsley, P. 1979. *Probability and Measure.* New York: John Wiley.

Blackwell, D. 1951. The comparison of experiments. In *Proceedings, Second Berkeley Symposium on Mathematical Statistics and Probability,* pp. 92–102. Berkeley, CA: University of California Press.

Blume, L. E., and D. Easley. 1998. Rational expectations and rational learning. In *Organizations with Incomplete Information: Essays in Economic Analysis: A Tribute to Roy Radner,* pp. 61–109. Cambridge University Press.

Bray, M., and D. M. Kreps. 1988. Rational learning and rational expectations. In *Arrow and the Ascent of Modern Economic Theory* (ed. G. Feiwel), pp. 597–625. London: Macmillan.

Chamley, C. 2003. Cascades and slow social learning. Working Paper, Boston University.

Chung, K. 1974. *A Course in Probability Theory.* New York: Academic Press.

Cremer, J. 1982. A simple proof of Blackwell's "comparison of experiments" theorem. *Journal of Economic Theory* 27:439–43.

Danthine, J., and S. Moresi. 1993. Volatility, information and noise trading. *European Economic Review* 37:961–82.

DeGroot, M. 1970. *Optimal Statistical Decisions.* New York: McGraw-Hill.

Demange, G., and G. Laroque. 1995. Private information and the design of securities. *Journal of Economic Theory* 65:233–57.

Doob, J. 1949. Application of the theory of martingales. In *Le Calcul des Probabilités et ses Applications,* Colloques Internationaux du Centre National de la Recherche Scientifique 13, pp. 23–27. Paris: CNRS.

Ericson, W. 1969. A note on posterior mean of a population mean. *Journal of the Royal Statistical Society* 31:332–34.

Feldman, M., and C. Gilles. 1985. An expository note on individual risk without aggregate uncertainty. *Journal of Economic Theory* 35:26–32.

Fudenberg, D., and J. Tirole. 1991. *Game Theory.* Cambridge, MA: MIT Press.

Grimmet, G., and D. Stirzaker. 2001. *Probability and Random Processes.* Oxford University Press.

Harsanyi, J. C. 1967–68. Games with incomplete information played by Bayesian players. *Management Science* 14:159–82, 320–34, 486–502.

He, H., and J. Wang. 1995. Differential information and dynamic behavior of stock trading volume. *Review of Financial Studies* 8:919–72.

Jacod, J., and P. Protter. 2003. *Probability Essentials.* Berlin: Springer.

Judd, K. 1985. The law of large numbers with a continuum of i.i.d. random variables. *Journal of Economic Theory* 35:19–25.

Kihlstrom, R. 1984. A Bayesian exposition of Blackwell's theorem on the comparison of experiments. In *Bayesian Models in Economic Theory* (ed. M. Boyer and R. Kihlstrom). New York: Elsevier Science.

Laffont, J. J. 1989. *The Economics of Uncertainty and Information.* Cambridge, MA: MIT Press.

Li, L. 1985. Cournot oligopoly with information sharing. *RAND Journal of Economics* 16:521–36.

Li, L., R. D. McKelvey, and T. Page. 1987. Optimal research for Cournot oligopolies. *Journal of Economic Theory* 42:140–66.

Loeve, M. 1955. *Probability Theory.* Princeton, NJ: Van Nostrand.

Milgrom, P. R. 1981. Good news and bad news: representation theorems and applications. *Bell Journal of Economics* 12:380–91.

Milgrom, P. R., and R. J. Webber. 1982. A theory of auctions and competitive bidding. *Econometrica* 50:1089–122.

Pearce, D. 1984. Rationalizable strategic behavior and the problem of perfection. *Econometrica* 52:1029–50.

Smith, L., and P. Sorensen. 2000. Pathological outcomes of observational learning. *Econometrica* 68:371–98.

Spanos, A. 1993. *Statistical Foundations of Econometric Modelling.* Cambridge University Press.

——. 2000. *Probability Theory and Statistical Inference. Econometric Modeling with Observational Data.* Cambridge University Press.

Sun, Y. 2006. The exact law of large numbers via Fubini extension and characterization of insurable risks. *Journal of Economic Theory* 126:31–69.

Van Zandt, T., and X. Vives. 2007. Monotone equilibria in Bayesian games of strategic complementarities. *Journal of Economic Theory* 134:339–60.

Vives, X. 1988. Aggregation of information in large Cournot markets. *Econometrica* 56:851–76.

——. 1993. How fast do rational agents learn? *Review of Economic Studies* 60:329–47.

——. 1999. *Oligopoly Pricing. Old Ideas and New Tools.* Cambridge, MA: MIT Press.

——. 2005. Complementarities and games: new developments. *Journal of Economic Literature* 43:437–79.

Index

abstain-or-disclose rules, 184, 188–89, 195
adverse selection: and market depth, 120, 286, 294, 319; and short-term trading, 302; futures markets hedging, 135, 144–45; generated by insider trading, 8, 184, 188–89, 331–32, 356; in order- and quote-driven systems, 110; market makers move first demand schedules, 179–83; market orders versus limit orders, 132
affiliated random variables, 374
affine, versus linear, 375
affine information structures, 379–80
antiherding, 209
Arizona Stock Exchange (AZX), *tâtonnement* process, 334
asterisks, on problems, 12
asymptotic variance, 57
auctions, 38–39, 67–70. *See also* double auctions

Bayes-Nash equilibrium (BNE), 393–96
Bayes, rule of, 371
Bayesian Bertrand equilibrium, 69
Bayesian equilibrium. *See* Bayes-Nash equilibrium (BNE)
Bayesian models, appropriateness, 3–4
beauty contest models: Keynes, 1, 303–4, 306, 318; Morris and Shin, 35–37, 219
behavioral finance literature, 2
BHW (Bikhchandani, Hirshleifer, and Welch) model, 202–3, 208, 210
bid-ask spread: and adverse selection, 146, 180; and discriminatory pricing, 190; and insider trading, 184; and market power, 157, 179; in Kyle model, 346; in limit-order-book market, 180–83; reflecting asymmetric information, 120; with sequential trading, 331–33
Bikhchandani, Hirshleifer, and Welch (BHW), 202–3, 208, 210
Blackwell's theorem, 373
blogosphere, 3
BNE (Bayes-Nash equilibrium), 393–96
Bolsa de Madrid, *tâtonnement* process, 334
Borel σ-field, 370
bounded strength signals, 375
bubbles, 301, 309–10

CARA (constant absolute risk aversion) utility functions, 382–83
CARA-Gaussian model, 112–23; examples, 122–23; expected traded volume, 121–22; Grossman-Stiglitz paradox, 123–29; market depth, 120; price informativeness and volatility, 120–21, 129; summary, 129–30
central bank policy transparency, desirability, 37
Central Limit Theorem (CLT), 386
chapter outlines, 9–11
Chicago Board Options Exchange, modeling, 346
CLT (Central Limit Theorem), 386
clustering of agent actions, 204–5
Coase conjecture, 359
common-knowledge example, 224
common-values models, 31, 380–82
complementarity, degree of, 35–38. *See also* strategic complementarity (substitutability), degree of
concordant beliefs, 289–90
contagion, multiasset markets, 173–74
contrarian behavior, 348
convergence of random variables, 383–86; rates of, 386–87
coordination failure, 314
countable additivity, 370
Cournot markets, large: analysis, 17–18; constant marginal cost case, 20–21; isoelastic-lognormal model example, 25–26; linear-Gaussian model example, 21–25; price-taking Bayesian equilibrium, 18–19; summary, 26; welfare loss, 19–20, 27–29
crashes, 8, 306–9
crises, 8, 310–18

deadweight loss (DWL), 64–66
dealers, 108
demand schedules: competition in, 157–58, 167–68; convergence to price-taking, 165–67; definitions, 109; free entry and large markets, 162–65; informed traders move first (demand schedule game, 175–76; market order game, 168–74; multiasset markets and contagion, 173–74; multiple or unique equilibrium, 174–75; summary, 176); market makers move first (facing adverse selection, 179–83; summary, 183; uniform versus discriminatory pricing, 177–79); REE with imperfect competition, 158–62
Deutsche Börse, *tâtonnement* process, 334–35
discriminatory pricing, 110, 177. *See also* demand schedules, market makers move first, uniform versus discriminatory pricing
dominance solvability, 392
dominated strategies, 391–92
double auctions, 100–1
drift, 121, 123, 280
DWL (deadweight loss), 64–66
dynamic competitive rational expectations: price formation with risk-neutral market-making, 277–82; risk-averse market makers, 285, 293–94; summary, 284–85, 318–20; technical analysis, 285–89; trade without news, 289–90; volume and price patterns, 290–93; with long-term investors, 282–84. *See also* short-term traders

eductive stability, 251
endogenous information acquisition: and learning from others, 216–20; constant returns to scale, 44–45, 60–61; convergence, 58–59; decreasing returns to scale, 41–44, 59–60; model, 40–41; strategic aspects, 61–62; summary, 45, 62
equilibrium degree of coordination, 35. *See also* strategic complementarity (substitutability), degree of
excess volatility, 7, 36–37, 287, 294, 301, 345
exercises: chapter 1, 48–50; chapter 2, 74–76; chapter 3, 103–5; chapter 4, 148–52; chapter 5, 190–95; chapter 6, 241–43; chapter 7, 271–73; chapter 8, 324–25; chapter 9, 362–65

FIE (full-information equilibrium), 249
filtration, 388
First Welfare Theorem, 16
floor traders, 108
FRREE (fully revealing REE), 80–81
full-information equilibrium (FIE), 249
fully revealing REE (FRREE), 80–81
futures markets: equilibrium, 137–42; production, insurance and private information, 142–45; with hedgers, 135–38

games: and Bayes-Nash equilibrium, 393–96; and Nash equilibrium, 391–93; and perfect Bayesian equilibrium, 169, 397–98; mechanism design, 396–97; of strategic complementarities, 30–31, 392. *See also* supermodular games
Gaussian distribution, 376–79
Glosten and Milgrom sequential trading model, 331–32; and Kyle model, 345–46
Grossman-Stiglitz paradox: CARA-Gaussian model, 123–29; definition, 125
GSC (games of strategic complementarities), 30–31, 392

Harberger triangle, 75
Hayek, F., 1–2, 15–16
hedgers: and noise traders, 142; in futures markets, 136–37; strategic trading, 358–60
herding: and information loss, 5–6; and sequential trading, 331–33; definitions, 200–1; evidence regarding, 209–10; on wrong choice, 202; order of moves, 204–7; reputational, 208–9; versus information aggregation, 1–3; welfare-based definition, 227
Hirshleifer effect, 83, 102, 135, 145, 147, 189
hybrid trading systems, 110

implementation, 396
incentive efficiency, 97
independent values models, 31, 381
information aggregation: modeling issues, 17; overview, 15-17, 45-46; versus herd behavior, 1-3
information structures, 371. *See also* affine information structures; two-point support information structures
information technology aggregating procedures, 2-3
informational cascades: definitions, 200-2; partial, 204
informationally efficient prices, 111
informationally efficient REE, 80
informativeness of signals, 372-73
informed traders, in futures markets, 136
informed traders move first, 130-34
insider trading: definition, 183-84; impact, 8; literature review, 184-86; regulation, 188-89; welfare analysis framework, 186-87. *See also* strategic trading, with long-lived information, informed traders and price discovery

Kyle (1985) model, 168-73, 182, 297, 331, 340-42, 345-46
Kyle (1989) model, 156-65, 175, 177

Lange, O., 1, 79
large traders, impact, 8
LBSFE (linear Bayesian supply function equilibria), 86-87
learning: in equilibrium versus about an equilibrium, 249-52; speed and rate of convergence, 252-53; with uninformed firms, 253-57
learning by doing example, 224
learning from others: and endogenous information acquisition, 216-20; and herding, 206-7; costly information acquisition, 232-35; infinite horizon model, 229-32; learning from neighbors, 207-8; long lived agents, 220-21; model with rational expectations flavor, 237-38; overview, 199-200, 210; relation to dynamic rational expectations, 225-27; slow learning with noisy public information, 211-16, 221-22; summary, 239-40; team-efficient solution, 238-39; two-period team problem example, 228-29; welfare analysis, 227-28, 235-36; welfare consequences, 5-6
limit-order book: and crashes, 307; definitions, 109-11; demand schedule game, 175; dynamic competitive rational expectations, 278-79; informed traders move first, 130-31; market makers move first, 177, 180, 183
limit orders, 108
location decisions example, 223
log-supermodular functions, 374

macroeconomic forecasting example, 223-24
market anomalies, 7
market depth: and adverse selection, 120, 286, 294, 319; and public information, 280; and volatility, 129, 132; CARA-Gaussian model, 120; price discovery with sequential trading, 335-39
market dynamics: outline, 6-7; with asymmetric information, 257-61
market information aggregation, definition, 16
market makers: and short-term traders, 295-304; in futures markets, 136-37; market power, 179, 181, 183, 190; risk-averse market makers, dynamic competitive rational expectations, 285, 293-94
market manipulation: literature, 347-48; summary, 354. *See also* strategic trading, with long-lived information, informed traders and price discovery
market microstructure: impact, 7; orders, 108-9; participants, 108; trading systems, 109-11
market orders, 108
market power: firm reactions, 99; in Cournot markets, 54, 62-67, 71; insider trading, 187; market makers, 179, 181, 183, 190; strategic traders, 157, 160, 162, 166, 167, 178; versus asymmetric information, 8

martingales, and Bayesian learning, 387–90
measurable spaces, 369
mechanism design, 396–97
MLRP (monotone likelihood ratio property), 374
monopolistically competitive markets, 29–31, 34–35
monotone supermodular games, 396

naive traders, 101
Nash equilibrium, 391–93
New York Stock Exchange (NYSE): intraday patterns, 355; modeling, 346; *tâtonnement* process, 335
news, trade without, 289–90
no-trade theorem, 83, 122, 161, 289–90
noise traders: and hedgers, 142; and volatility, 317; as insider strategy, 172–73

order-driven markets, 7
order-driven trading systems, 109
overreactions: prices, 162, 302; to Fed announcements, 315; to public information, 36–37

Paris Bourse, *tâtonnement* process, 334
PBE (perfect Bayesian equilibrium), 169, 397–98
precision, price. *See* price precision
price bias, 121, 123, 280, 293
price precision: and constant information flow, 284–85; and demand schedules, 132, 134, 159, 162, 176; and futures markets, 141; and insider trading, 188, 190; and short-term traders, 300–1; and trading intensity, 283; and volatility, 129; definition, 121; in *tâtonnement*, 352–54; informed traders move first, 171
private values models, 31, 380–82
privately revealing REE, 94
probability measures, 369–70
probability spaces, 370
propositions: 1.1, 20; 1.2, 27–28; 1.3, 32, 46–48; 1.4, 44; 1.5, 44; 2.1, 56, 71–73; 2.2, 57, 73; 2.3, 58, 73–74; 2.4, 64–66; 4.1, 117–18; 4.2, 132; 4.3, 140–41; 5.1, 163–64; 5.2, 170; 5.3, 175; 6.1, 215, 240–41; 6.2, 217; 6.3, 232; 6.4, 239; 7.1, 255–56; 7.2, 259, 268–69; 7.3, 260, 268–69; 7.4, 265; 7.5, 265; 7.6, 267; 7.7, 269–70; 8.1, 279; 8.2, 282–83, 320–22; 8.3, 286, 322–24; 8.4, 295–96; 9.1, 337, 361–62; 9.2, 340–41; 9.3, 350
public information: and herding, 5–6; and liquidity/market making intensity, 120–21, 129; and market depth, 280; and presence of competitive market-making sector, 7; and team efficiency, 96–97; confirming beliefs with risk-averse traders, 345; endogenous public information, 316–18; expected utility of informed trader conditional upon, 114, 147–48; hedging, 359; in competitive markets, 343; LBSFE agents efficient use of, 90–92; multiplier effect, 314–15; over(under)-reliance in two-period model, 293; overreactions to, 36–37; past information included in current price, 280, 341; privately revealing REE, 93–94; semi-strong informationally efficient prices reflecting, 81, 111; slow learning with noisy public information, 211–16, 221–22; strategic complementarity (substitutability) and sensitivity to, 35–36, 46; team solution, 230–35; welfare effects, 145; where more hurts, 218–19, 221–22, 236, 238, 239–40; with risk-neutral traders, 162. *See also* herding; Hirshleifer effect; transparency

quality, consumers learning about, 222–23
quote-driven markets, 7. *See also* demand schedules, market makers move first
quote-driven trading systems, 109–10

rational expectations, definitions, 78–80
rational expectations equilibrium (REE): definitions, 80–81; existence of fully revealing REE, 102–3; strategic supply function equilibria

(convergence to price-taking, 98-99); summary, 102, 145-47; welfare analysis, 81-83, 95-98. *See also* supply function competition
rational learning dynamics: in equilibrium versus about an equilibrium, 249-52; overview, 248-49; slow learning and convergence, 261-66; speed of learning and rate of convergence, 252-53; summary, 266; with asymmetric information, 257-61; with uninformed firms, 253-57
rationalizable strategies, 392
replica markets, 53
revelation principle, 397
risk-adjusted information advantage, 113
risk premium, in futures markets, 141
risk tolerance, 113

scalpers, 108
schizophrenia problem, 81, 157
screening, 110, 157, 177, 181
semi-strong informationally efficient prices, 81, 111
semi-strong informationally efficient REE, 81
sequential trading: and herding, 331-33; price discovery with endogenous market depth, 337-39; price discovery with exogenous market depth, 335-37; slow learning from past prices, 333-34; speed of learning and market microstructure, 334-39; *tâtonnement*, 334-35
serially undominated strategies, 392
short-term traders: and market anomalies, 7; and risk-averse market makers, 301-4; and risk-neutral market makers, 295-301; endogenous information acquisition, 304-5; summary, 294-95, 305-6, 319
SIE (shared-information equilibrium), 249
signaling, 110, 157, 398. *See also* bounded strength signals; informativeness of signals
signaling games: and unique equilibria, 176, 190; multiplicity of equilibria, 174
SLBE (symmetric linear Bayesian equilibria), 158
SLLN (strong law of large numbers), 384-85
slow learning, and convergence, 261-66
smooth large markets: information aggregation, 33; linear-quadratic-Gaussian model, 30-32; overview, 29-30; welfare analysis, 34-38
social learning. *See* learning from others
specialists (NYSE), 108
speed of convergence, measures of, 56-57
spread. *See* bid-ask spread
stationary REE, 249
stock price pattern analysis. *See* technical analysis
stop orders, 108-9
strategic complementarity (substitutability), degree of, 30. *See also* GSC (games of strategic complementarities)
strategic substitutability, 35-38; between private and public information, 236; in information acquisition, 121, 125. *See also* strategic complementarity (substitutability), degree of
strategic traders: in static financial markets, 189-90. *See also* demand schedules, competition in
strategic trading: hedging, 358-60; summary, 360-61; with long-lived information (competition among insiders, 342-43; informed traders and price discovery, 348-54; insider disclosure of trades, 343-44; Kyle (1985) model, 340-42; Kyle (1985) model and Glosten and Milgrom (1985) model, 345-46; risk averse traders, 345; summary, 347); with short-lived information, 355-58
strong law of large numbers (SLLN), 384-85
substitutability. *See* strategic substitutability

sufficient statistics, 372
supermodular games, 392–93. *See also* monotone supermodular games
supply function competition: characterizing linear supply function equilibrium, general case, 92–93; illustrations, 85–88; noisy demand and one-dimensional uncertainty, 89–92; nonnoisy demand and multidimensional uncertainty, 93–95; REE model, 85; summary, 95–99. *See also* rational expectations equilibrium (REE), strategic supply function equilibria, convergence to price-taking
symmetric linear Bayesian equilibria (SLBE), 158

tâtonnement, 226, 334–35, 339, 349, 352, 354
team efficiency, 5, 17, 27, 29, 36, 46, 97. *See also* learning from others, team-efficient solution
teams, 27
technical analysis, 7, 285–89. *See also* sequential trading, slow learning from past prices
themes and issues, 5–9
timing, in futures markets, 137
Toronto Stock Exchange, *tâtonnement* process, 334
trading intensity: and informed traders, 119; and insider trading, 171, 344, 351, 353; and liquidity, 333; and market depth, 280; and noise trading, 297; and price precision, 283; and risk aversion, 285, 297; Kyle (1989) model, 161–62; market orders, 338; market orders versus limit orders, 132–33; short-term traders, 301; with concentrated information arrival, 284, 302; with constant flow of information, 284, 300; with long-term informed traders, 282
trading systems. *See* market microstructure, trading systems
trading volume: CARA-Gaussian model, 121–22; characterization, 351–52; competitive versus monopolistic, 352; concentrated arrival of information, 292; increasing with noise trading, 133; informed traders move first, 172; insider trading, 353–54; market makers move first, 181–82; noise, as measure market size, 163
transparency: as not always good, 8, 315–16; in trading systems, 111; of central bank policy, 37
two-point support information structures, 374–75

uniform pricing, 110

volatility: and complementarity, 35; and crashes, 309; and insider trading, 187–88; and market depth, 129, 132; and price precision, 129; and risk-averse market makers, 132, 146, 287, 294, 306; and risk averse traders, 132–34; and risk neutral market makers, 298–99, 305, 319; and trading behavior, 281; and trading horizons, 300–1; CARA-Gaussian model and price informativeness, 120–21, 129; conditional, 281, 284–85, 287, 298–300, 344, 357; excess, 7, 36–37, 287, 294, 301, 345; of public information, 213; total, 131, 134, 146; unconditional, 281, 352; with concentrated information arrival, 298, 302; with constant flow information revelation, 284-85; with dynamic information revelation, 281–82, 285; with reduced noise trading, 317; with short-lived information, 357–58, 361
volume and price patterns, dynamic competitive rational expectations, 290–93
voting, 38–40

wikis, 2
winner's curse, 38–39
word-of-mouth learning, 207, 211
World Wide Web, 3

Xetra, *tâtonnement* process, 334–35

Milton Keynes UK
Ingram Content Group UK Ltd.
UKHW041442041124
450642UK00004B/182